DumpIT 3.1

This figure shows DumpIT, a programming utility developed for this book. DumpIT displays the contents of DOS files in both ASCII and hexadecimal in MDI windows. You will learn about how DumpIT was initially created using CASE:W in Chapter 3. Later, in Chapter 12, you will see how DumpIT was enhanced to take advantage of new Windows 3.1 features, such as drag and drop, common dialogs, TOOLHELP, and the new STRICT programming style. As you can see in this figure, by examining the source code that's included with DumpIT, you will not only learn how to use common dialogs—you will also learn how to customize them.

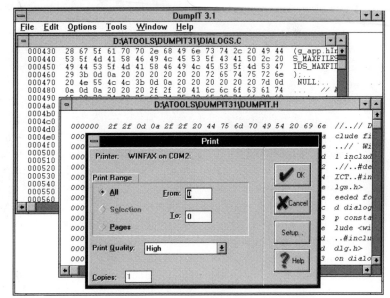

DDEML Resource Monitor

This figure shows the DDEML version of the Resource Monitor utility being used with the DDEML client utility developed by SoftBlox, Inc. Resource Monitor, another Windows development tool designed for this book, was one of the most popular utilities on the CompuServe Windows 3.1 BETA test forums, according to the Windows User Group Network (WUGNET). In Chapter 6 you will learn how Resource Monitor was constructed and how it can be used to monitor your Windows resources and help debug the Windows applications you are developing. In Chapter 11 you will learn how Resource Monitor was enhanced to be a DDE server using the new Windows 3.1 Dynamic Data Exchange Management Library (DDEML).

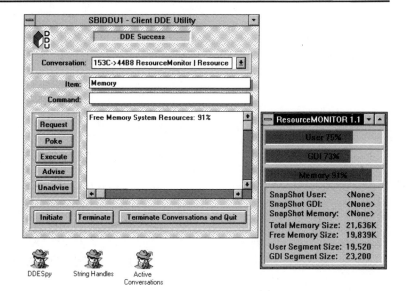

Computer users are not all alike.
Neither are SYBEX books.

We know our customers have a variety of needs. They've told us so. And because we've listened, we've developed several distinct types of books to meet the needs of each of our customers. What are you looking for in computer help?

If you're looking for the basics, try the **ABC's** series. You'll find short, uninitmidating turorials and helpful illustrations. For a more visual approach, select **Teach Yourself,** featuring screen-by-screen illustrations of how to use your latest software purchase.

Running Start books are really two books in one—a tutorial to get you off to a fast start and a reference to answer your questions when you're ready to tackle advanced tasks.

Mastering and **Understanding** titles offer you a step-by-step introduction, plus an in-depth examination of intermeditate-level features, to use as you progress.

Our **Up & Running** series is designed for computer-literate consumers who want a no-nonsense overview of new programs. Just 20 basic lessons, and you're on your way.

We also publish two types of reference books. Our **Instant References** provide quick access to each of a program's commands and functions. SYBEX **Encyclopedias** and **Desktop References** provide a *comprehensive reference* and explanation of all of the commands, features, and functions of the subject software.

Our **Programming** books are specifically written for a technically sophisticated audience and provide a no-nonsense value-added approach to each topic covered, with plenty of tips, tricks, and time-saving hints.

Sometimes a subject requires a special treatment that our standard series doesn't provide. So you'll find we have titles like **Advanced Techiques, Handbooks, Tips & Tricks,** and others that are specifically tailored to satisfy a unique need.

We carefully select our authors for their in-depth understanding of the software they're writing about, as well as their ability to write clearly and communicate effectively. Each manuscript is thoroughly reviewed by our technical staff to ensure its complete accuracy. Our production department makes sure it's easy to use. All of this adds up to the highest quality books available, consistently appearing on best-seller charts worldwide.

You'll find SYBEX publishes a variety of books on every popular software package. Looking for computer help? Help Yourself to SYBEX.

For a brochure of our best-selling publications:
SYBEX Inc. 2021 Challenger Drive, Alameda, CA 94501
Tel: (510) 523-8233/(800) 227-2346 Telex: 336311
Fax: (510) 523-2373

SYBEX

SYBEX is committed to using natural resources wisely to preserve and improve our environment. As a leader in the computer book publishing industry, we are aware that over 40% of America's solid waste is paper. This is why we have been printing the text of books like this one on recycled paper since 1982.

This year our use of recycled paper will result in the saving of more than 15,300 trees. We will lower air pollution effluents by 54,000 pounds, save 6,300,000 gallons of water, and reduce landfill by 2,700 cubic yards.

In choosing a SYBEX book you are not only making a choice for the best in skills and information, you are also choosing to enhance the quality of life for all of us.

ADVANCED TOOLS

FOR WINDOWS

DEVELOPERS

ADVANCED TOOLS
FOR WINDOWS
DEVELOPERS

Arthur V. English

SYBEX®

San Francisco ▪ Paris ▪ Düsseldorf ▪ Soest

Acquisitions Editor: David Clark
Developmental Editor: Gary Masters
Editor: Judith Bellamy
Technical Editor: Amrik Dhillon
Project Editor: Abby Azrael
Book Designer: Suzanne Albertson
Production Artist: Helen Bruno
Screen Graphics: Cuong Le
Desktop Specialist: Thomas Goudie
Proofreader/Production Assistant: Janet K. MacEachern
Indexer: Matthew Spence
Cover Designer: Ingalls + Associates
Cover Photographer: David Bishop

SYBEX is a registered trademark of SYBEX Inc.

TRADEMARKS: SYBEX has attempted throughout this book to distinguish proprietary trademarks from descriptive terms by following the capitalization style used by the manufacturer.

SYBEX is not affiliated with any manufacturer.

Every effort has been made to supply complete and accurate information. However, SYBEX assumes no responsibility for its use, nor for any infringement of the intellectual property rights of third parties which would result from such use.

Library of Congress Card Number: 92-62081
ISBN: 0-7821-1029-0

Manufactured in the United States of America
10 9 8 7 6 5 4 3 2 1

To my wife, Debby. Thank you for your encouragement and help during the long days and nights that were required to complete this book. Without your support, I could not have made it through this journey.

To Lucy, my mischievous Labrador Retriever. Thank you for your constant companionship and comic relief during the course of this project.

To my extended family: Jane and Walter Owen, and Rebekah VanArsdale and her family. You have made my world a better place to live in.

To the memory of my brother, Albert English. I wish you could be here to help celebrate the completion of my first book.

ACKNOWLEDGMENTS

Advanced Tools for Windows Developers was created through the work and contributions of many computer professionals. I want to thank the people who helped make this book possible.

Thanks to the following software experts and writers who collaborated with me on writing chapters about their areas of expertise:

Scott Suhy, a friend and Windows programmer, for helping me with writing Chapter 2 on Borland Resource Workshop, Chapter 8 on profiling Windows applications, and Chapter 10 on using Turbo Debugger for Windows. Scott also contributed the FileFind application for the book.

Harry Walden, senior programmer at Fidelity Investments in Las Colinas, Texas, for helping me with writing Chapter 11 on using DDEML.

David Jewett, an independent Windows software development consultant, for helping me fine-tune some of the Windows applications developed for the book and for serving as a source of Windows technical expertise.

A special thank-you goes to the publisher of the *WindowsWatcher* newsletter, Jesse Berst. Jesse put me in contact with his friend Dianne King at SYBEX to help get this book published. Since I met him, Jesse has usually been only a phone call away to help with this and other Microsoft Windows projects.

Thanks to everyone at Microsoft, Borland, Blue Sky Software, CASEWORKS, and the other companies that provided the Windows development tools and the technical support I needed to write about them. Greg Lobdell and Manny Vellon provided technical information at Microsoft. Carrine Greason, Erin Holland, and Wendy Slawter at Waggener Edstrom provided software coordination for Microsoft Windows development tools. Nan Borreson was always helpful at Borland. Jorgen Lien and Susan Hasbrook at Blue Sky Software helped me by providing their ideas as well as their software to write about. Terry Flaherty and Amanda West at CASEWORKS were also very supportive in helping me write about CASE:W for Windows.

ACKNOWLEDGEMENTS

Thanks to the special people at SYBEX for taking a chance with a new author and providing the helpful guidance I needed during the writing and production process. Special thanks go to Gary Masters, a fellow SYBEX book author (*DOS 5: A to Z*) and my developmental editor. Gary has helped me throughout the months of working at my computer by providing sympathy, encouragement, and advice. Thanks go to Dianne King and David Clark for helping me to formulate my ideas of what this book should be and helping me to get published by SYBEX. Also helping me greatly during the final stages of the book were Abby Azrael, Judith Bellamy, and Amrik Dhillon.

CONTENTS AT A GLANCE

TABLE OF CONTENTS

INTRODUCTION

As a Windows developer and frequent contributor of magazine articles to different publications, I have had the chance to work with many different Windows development environments and tools. When I design programs for mainframe computers (Unisys 1100/2200, to be exact) and for personal computers, I like to experiment with every development tool I can get my hands on. I'm a certified Windows programming tool addict: I collect Windows tools and use them in new ways to streamline the process of developing applications. I've even invented a few tools of my own (as you will see in this book) when I couldn't find one that I needed.

When I first became a Windows programmer, I was struck by the number and variety of tools—in addition to the C programming language and the Windows application program interface (API)—that it takes to build Windows applications. You have to master icon editors, font editors, dialog box editors, heapwalkers, spies, and debuggers.

My response to this profusion of necessary tools was to write a Windows programming book different from all others. This is an advanced book for C/C++ Windows programmers who already know how to build a Windows application. I designed it with the following goals in mind:

- To provide comprehensive information about the best Windows development tools on the market and explain in depth, through a series of practical, hands-on development projects, how to use them most effectively to create Windows applications.

- To limit the discussion to (a) the development tools included with the primary C-language Windows development systems (Borland C++, Turbo C++ for Windows, Microsoft QuickC for Windows, and Microsoft C/C++); (b) exceptional third-party Windows development tools—for example, CASE:W Corporate Edition and RoboHELP; and (c) tools developed for this book, such as DumpIT and Resource Monitor.

In other words, instead of making this an all-inclusive book about how to write a Windows program, I've focused on all the major tools that we Windows programmers must use. I hope you'll find that every chapter gives you useful information that will help you build your Windows programs more quickly, more easily, and more creatively.

What's in This Book?

Advanced Tools for Windows Developers is divided into five parts that reflect different aspects of Microsoft Windows software development. A set of two disks containing projects and programs with all their code accompanies the book, and portions of the program code for these projects and programs are printed in the book. Following is a brief description of each of these features:

- In *Part I*, Chapter 1, "An Overview of Windows Development Environments and Tools," serves as an introductory survey of the history of Windows development, covering all the major advances that led to Windows 3.1 and the tools now available.

- *Part II*, "Automating Windows Development," discusses tools that automate the process of building Windows applications. You use the tools discussed in this part of the book to build applications quickly. We'll also discuss using tools to build additional tools. For example, Chapter 3 describes how I used CASE:W Corporate Edition to create DumpIT, a Multiple Document Interface hex dump program. The program and its source files are included on the disk set that comes with this book.

- *Part III*, "Auditing Windows Development," discusses the tools that help you to evaluate how your Windows application works, so you can fix program problems and improve your application's performance. You use the tools discussed in this part of the book to test your application's uses of Windows memory and system resources, and to profile its execution.

- *Part IV*, "Debugging Windows Applications," is a tutorial as well as a discussion of how Windows debuggers work. In addition to covering each of the standard debuggers included with several Windows development systems, this section discusses the Windows-hosted debugger MultiScope for Windows.

- *Part V,* "New Windows 3.1 Development Tools," discusses some of the new tools from Microsoft that are included in the Windows software development kit (SDK). In this part of the book, you will learn how to use these new tools to implement Dynamic Data Exchange (DDE) using the new DDE Management Library (DDEML). You will also learn how to build more bug-free applications using tools such as WINDOWSX.H and the new debugging version of Windows.

- *The program code.* Many examples of program code appear throughout the book. Whether they are offset from the text or incorporated in it, they are printed in a different typeface, which looks like this:

  ```
  This is an example of what program code looks like in the book.
  ```

- *The disk set.* This book comes with two 5¼-inch high-density disks which contain (1) the projects and their source code that are incorporated in the various chapters, and (2) the programs for the tools developed specially for this book. To install the disks, execute the program SETUP.EXE *from Windows* (not from DOS), and the rest of the installation procedure will be self-prompting.

Although this book focuses on development tools, it is spiced with tips about Windows programming and with strategies for creating Windows applications. In addition, the chapters on managing memory and debugging applications include advanced tutorials, so that all readers will be at the same level for the discussion of the new Windows development tools that follows.

As a Windows programmer, you will find that every chapter of this book contains valuable information about using Windows development tools. You will learn tips for using tools you already own, and you may see how they compare with similar tools from other vendors. If you don't own a tool that is covered in this book, you will find out how that tool works, to help you decide whether to add it to your toolbox.

In this "Windows development workshop" I'll show you how you can use CASE:W Corporate Edition to construct Windows applications. I'll also give you a few tips for keeping your CASE:W development project organized and for avoiding potential problems. If you use Borland's Resource Workshop, I'll show you how to organize your resource project to create fancy dialog boxes that appear three-dimensional, with custom bitmaps on top of the push buttons—without writing a single line of C code. You won't find out how to do this by reading the Resource Workshop User's Guide, but you'll learn how to in Chapter 2 of this book.

For more information about the Windows development tool marketplace, I suggest you look at the Appendix, which contains a catalog with brief descriptions of most of the Windows development tools that were available when this book was written.

After reading this book you should have answers to questions such as the following:

- What kind of Windows development tools are available?
- I have heard of Computer Aided Software Engineering (CASE) tools and application generators for Windows, but do they really work? How much can they do?
- When and why should I use HEAPWALK?
- What are Windows system resources? How can I track down where my program fails to return system resources to Windows?
- How do I debug a Windows program? What is the best debugger to use? What are the setup options for using my debugger?
- Does DDEML really make implementing DDE easier?

Now that we know where we are going, let's see where Windows has been. We'll review the history of Windows development environments and tools to see how far they have progressed.

PART I

Overview of Windows Development Tools

Part I will introduce you to the tools that are available for developing Windows applications and to the methods we will use to explore them in this book. We'll start by looking back and reviewing the history of Windows and the Windows development tools provided by Microsoft and Borland.

Then we'll look at the development tools that Microsoft and Borland include in their Windows development systems. We'll look at each tool in Microsoft's and Borland's respective toolkits so you will know what you are getting (as well as what's left out) when you purchase one of these development systems.

Finally we'll preview the third-party Windows development tools this book will examine, as well as the Windows development tools that were developed for this book and have been included on the book disk set.

CHAPTER
ONE

An Overview of Windows Development Environments and Tools

- **A short history of Windows development tools**

- **An overview of Windows development systems**

- **The Windows development tools covered in this book**

- **The Windows development tools created for this book**

In addition to programming and writing, I also build furniture. In many ways, I consider the art of building furniture analogous to the art of building software. A cabinetmaker's toolbox easily contains hundreds of tools, including hammers, saws and saw blades, drills and drill bits, clamps, screw drivers, chisels, levels, rulers, and pencils. Many tools come as part of a kit. Sometimes I buy an entire tool kit because it is more economical than purchasing the tools individually. I purchase other sets of tools because they are designed to work together, even though some tools in the set may also work with other tools.

As a cabinetmaker, I keep my tools organized by category. For example, the toolbox in my workshop has separate drawers for screw drivers, hammers, and drill bits. In other cases, I group tools together because they work together.

As a Windows developer, I try to work in the same way. I have separate program groups set up for each C development system I work with (QuickC for Windows, Microsoft C/C++, and Borland C++). In each program group, I order the icons according to how each tool is used. If I use a tool with more than one development system, I keep it in one place on my hard disk and then create an icon that references it from each program group in which I use that tool. For example, the Borland Resource Workshop icon is in all of my Windows development groups, because I use it with every development system on my PC.

The tools we'll examine in this book are organized into categories that facilitate comparisons. Some tools, such as Borland Resource Workshop, WindowsMAKER Professional, CASE:W Corporate Edition, and DialogCoder, work with all development systems. Other tools work only with certain development systems. For example, Turbo Debugger 3.0 works only with Borland development systems, such as Borland C++, Turbo C++, and Turbo Pascal (unlike version 2.0, which worked on all Microsoft C programs as well). In discussing each tool in a category, I will note its limitations in working with other development systems.

A Short History of Windows and Its Development Tools

No matter what Apple Computer alleges, all graphical user interface (GUI) systems trace their roots back to the work done at Xerox's Palo Alto Research Center (PARC) in 1970. Xerox created a new way for users to interact with information. The development of GUI interfaces, the mouse pointing device, object-oriented programming, and the development of laser printing can all be credited to Xerox.

Early GUI Environments

The first GUI workstation developed by Xerox was called "Alto." A development system that was used internally to test how GUI systems should work, the Alto led to the first commercial GUI system, the Star 8010 workstation. The Star, introduced in April 1981, included a mouse and a bitmapped graphic display that had icons, windows, proportionally spaced typefaces, and text.

Steven Jobs, cofounder of Apple Computer along with Steve Wozniak, discovered what a "GUI" was on a tour of Xerox PARC in the late 1970s. He was so taken with the idea, he pioneered the development of Apple's first GUI workstation, the Lisa, based on the Motorola 68000 microprocessor. The Apple Lisa was introduced in 1983 but cost almost $10,000. Few companies or individuals could afford a Lisa system, and it quickly faded into oblivion.

When the Lisa was introduced, I was developing software on an Apple II system at home for fun and on a Sperry 1100 mainframe at work to earn a living. I first met the Lisa at an Apple Users Group meeting in Minneapolis. Everyone at the standing-room-only demonstration was very impressed, but we all wondered when the Lisa would become affordable.

Apple introduced its next GUI system, the Macintosh, in a television advertisement extravaganza during the 1984 Super Bowl game. In a tribute to George Orwell's novel *1984*, the Macintosh was portrayed in a series of commercials as the computer that would save the world from the nightmare of Big Brother, played by IBM. As we all know, Apple's Macintosh went on to be the first commercially successful GUI system.

In August 1981 IBM introduced the IBM PC, based on the Intel 8088 microprocessor and featuring a new operating system developed by Microsoft called DOS. Prior to developing MS-DOS, Bill Gates and Microsoft had developed a BASIC interpreter for the MITS Altair that was later developed for the CP/M operating system. One of my favorite PC toys at the time was a Microsoft board that let my Apple II run CP/M. It let me write programs in Microsoft COBOL for CP/M and develop database applications with dBASE II.

The IBM PC with its MS-DOS operating system was an instant success, and it made Microsoft a success—but it was not a GUI environment. Users and developers had to wait for Windows 1.0 to have their first GUI environment from Microsoft.

Windows 1

In February 1984 I went to the SOFTCON conference in New Orleans to see what the Macintosh was all about. I got to meet Steve Jobs, and I walked away with a Macintosh to experiment with. Also at the conference, I saw the first public demonstration of Windows, which Microsoft had started developing in 1983. It was ugly and primitive compared with the Macintosh; it used tiled windows instead of overlapped ones, and even when teamed with an EGA display system (which was very expensive at the time), Windows still could not match the Macintosh's graphical look and feel.

Although I preferred the Macintosh to Windows (I mean, the Macintosh worked—Windows didn't), my company's management emphasized PC-compatible computers, not Macintoshes. Eventually, at management's request, I gave up working on the Macintosh and started using Windows to create MAPPER View, a microcomputer front-end product I was in charge of developing. MAPPER View was part of MAPPER, Sperry's popular all-in-one, multi-user computer software system that runs on Sperry (now Unisys) mainframes, on minicomputers, and even on PCs.

The Windows 1.0 BETA that Microsoft had given us didn't work well enough, so we ended up developing MAPPER View using a character-based windowing scheme that simulated the look and feel of the Macintosh and Windows. Later, Windows matured and became more interesting. Its user interface improved with each new version, and it slowly evolved into being an operating system instead of being just a DOS add-on.

Version 1.0 of Windows started shipping in November 1985. Although this version used tiled windows for managing Windows applications, it did support overlapped windows inside a Windows application, the primary type being the dialog box. Windows 1.0 was built to run on a CGA PC-compatible system with two floppy drives (no hard disk required) with 256K of RAM. Micrografx In*A*Vision (which later evolved into Micrografx Designer) was the first Windows application that appeared. In*A*Vision was actually released with a runtime version of Windows before Windows was released, to Microsoft's consternation, as the story goes.

Windows 1 SDK

The Microsoft Windows 1.0 SDK included Icon Editor for creating cursors and icons, Dialog Editor for creating dialog boxes, HEAPWALK for analyzing memory, and a debugging version of Windows, WDEB (a limited version of SYMDEB and precursor of CodeView for Windows) for tracking down errors.

Windows 2

The next major revision of Windows was version 2.0, released in September 1987. As a result of feedback that Microsoft had received from users who did not appreciate working with tiled windows, version 2.0 featured overlapped windows and an improved user interface. The change to overlapped windows was also part of the design to make Windows look like the other GUI system that Microsoft and IBM were developing together, OS/2 Presentation Manager.

The new user interface standard derived from a larger strategy developed by Microsoft and IBM to help users move easily from one GUI system to another. This strategy is called Systems Application Architecture (SAA) Common User Access (CUA) (or both together now: SAA/CUA). An IBM document, *Systems Application Architecture, Common User Access Advanced Interface Design Guide,* was shipped with every OS/2 Presentation Manager (and later with the Windows 3.0 SDK) to show developers how to build consistent SAA applications.

In addition to an updated user interface, Windows 2 used expanded memory that conformed to the Expanded Memory Specification (EMS). Windows 2 with EMS let more Windows programs reside in memory at the same time, but it didn't completely solve the problem of multitasking Windows applications. Windows 2 ran only in Real mode. Shortly after releasing Windows 2, Microsoft released a special version of it, named Windows/386, for owners of 80386-based PCs. Windows/386 Version 2 let users run Windows and DOS applications more agreeably together on an 80386-based PC, but it did nothing to improve the performance of multiple Windows applications that ran at the same time.

Windows 2 SDK

The Windows 2 SDK came with a revised set of development tools. HEAPWALK, Icon Editor, and Dialog Editor were improved. Two new tools were introduced: Spy, for monitoring messages, and Shaker, for testing how well an application works when memory is being juggled around. Programmers were still forced to use WDEB for program debugging, since CodeView for Windows didn't come along until after Windows 2 was released (but before Windows 3 was ready).

Windows 3

Windows 3 was introduced on May 22, 1990, and Microsoft threw parties all over the world to celebrate. Within six weeks, Microsoft had shipped 500,000 copies. Within six months, the number had grown to almost 4 million copies. Windows 3 finally made Windows a success. Corporations and individuals now considered Windows to be a real GUI system that, although it had limits, had finally become usable.

With version 3, the appearance of Windows improved. It now featured a proportional system font to make text easier to read. Three-dimensional shadowing and icons in color enhanced the program's look. The MS-DOS Executive, still included with Windows 3 but hidden away, was replaced by the new Program Manager and File Manager. Both of these programs were prettier than the MS-DOS Executive, but they still needed improving. Program Manager looked more like the Macintosh because it used icons instead of MS-DOS file names to represent programs, but program groups could not be nested and File Manager was needed to navigate the MS-DOS file system. File Manager was a visual improvement, and it provided more functionality than MS-DOS Executive; but it was still just a shell on top of an inadequate MS-DOS file system that limited file names to eight characters plus a three-character extension.

Windows 3 was more colorful than previous versions, which had been limited to 8 colors. With Windows 3, you could take your pick: 16 colors, 256 colors, or 16 million colors. With the right display adapter and device driver, Windows 3 supported them all.

Even though its better looks were impressive, it was the new memory management capabilities of Windows 3 that took center stage. Windows now used 80286/80386 16-bit Protected mode addressing to run multiple Windows applications simultaneously. In Enhanced mode, virtual memory could equal up to four times the installed physical memory. However, the improved memory utilization caused new problems: disappearing system resources and Unrecoverable Application Errors (UAE).

Windows 3 SDK

The Windows 3 SDK provided developers with more tools and capabilities. SDK Paint, which replaced Icon Editor, let you create 16-color icons instead of only monochrome ones. Dialog Editor was improved again. Support for owner-draw menus, list boxes, and buttons gave programmers the ability to improvise and to make Windows applications more attractive to users. With cascading and tear-off menus added to make the user interface more flexible, programmers gained the freedom to put menus anywhere on the display that they pleased.

One of my favorite Windows 3 SDK features is Windows Help. It frees programmers from having to build Help features from scratch into their programs. Now you just build a Windows Help file document with Microsoft Word for Windows (admittedly, using a bizarre framework of footnotes and annotations), compile the Rich Text Format (RTF) document you export from Word along with a Help make file with the extension .HPJ, and then put into your Windows application the function calls that access the Windows Help Viewer. Although this is still a lot of work, it's much quicker and simpler than coding for Help features yourself. Check out Chapter 5 for an even easier way to create Help files, called RoboHELP.

New Development Tools

Until February 1991 you had to buy the Microsoft Windows SDK if you wanted to develop Windows applications. In 1991, however, the number of Windows development systems and tools increased dramatically, when Microsoft, Borland, and Zortech (now owned by Symantec) released "one-box" Windows development systems that were an alternative to using the SDK. The following two sections discuss how the Borland Windows development system has evolved since 1991 and the release that year of Microsoft's SDK alternative, QuickC for Windows.

Borland Development Systems

Borland C++ 2.0, issued in February 1991, was the first alternative to the Windows development system that freed programmers from needing the Microsoft Windows SDK. The DOS-based Borland C++ 2.0 Integrated Development Environment (IDE) was faster and easier to use than the Microsoft C Programmer's Workbench, but it was not compliant with the DOS Protected Mode Interface (DPMI) and could be run only from Windows running in Standard mode. Borland C++ 2.0 also lacked SDK documentation and some of the important Windows development tools, such as Spy.

Borland C++ 3.0, released in November 1991, provided improved development environments, better Windows development tools, and a nifty utility comparable to Spy, called WinSight. Still DOS-based, the Borland C++ IDE is now a DPMI application that runs easily in Windows Enhanced mode, letting you compile larger programs, faster.

The most important new Borland C++ tool, first included with version 3.0, is Turbo C++ for Windows. A Windows-hosted development environment for building both C and C++ applications, Turbo C++ can be purchased separately. The complete development system includes C++ class libraries for both DOS (Application Frameworks) and Windows (Object Windows Library).

Borland C++ 3.1 is the current (as of this writing) upgrade, introduced in May 1992. It improves upon a mature Windows development system. This new version is compatible with Windows 3.1 and gives you full support for multimedia, TrueType, Pen Windows, and Object Linking and Embedding (OLE). Both Borland C++ 3.1 and Borland C++ and Application Frameworks 3.1 ship with Borland C++ for Windows, an optimizing Windows-hosted compiler that replaces Turbo C++ for Windows. This combination provides full access from Windows to the Borland globally optimizing compiler. You no longer have to recompile a Turbo C++ for Windows application using a DOS-hosted IDE to take advantage of program optimizations. Turbo C++ for Windows 3.1 is Borland's entry-level C/C++ development system for Windows and is now a completely separate product.

Microsoft QuickC for Windows

In September 1991 Microsoft released QuickC for Windows, a "one box" application development system that doesn't require the use of the Windows SDK. As the first Windows-hosted IDE based on the C language, QuickC for Windows lets you experience the benefits of working within Windows while you are developing a Windows application. The editor, compiler, and debugger are all integrated and all Windows-based; there's no need to switch to a DOS window to use the compiler or the debugger, as you must do with Microsoft C/C++ 7 and the Windows SDK. For developing C—but not C++ —I find QuickC for Windows the easiest and most productive development environment to use.

Windows 3.1

Finally we come to Windows 3.1—the focus of this book. Version 3.1 may sound like a minor Windows revision; however, if you are a Windows programmer, you know it represents a major advance. Visually, Windows 3.1 looks like an incremental improvement, but under the covers, it's Microsoft's biggest rewrite of Windows so far. It is the predecessor and bridge to Win32, the new Windows 32-bit API (Say goodbye to worrying about near, far, and huge pointers!), and Windows New Technology (NT), the Microsoft 32-bit operating system that Win32 runs best on. NT will be available on Intel 80386/80486/80586-based and RISC-based workstations.

On the surface of Windows 3.1, users find a new File Manager; a built-in scalable font technology called TrueType; OLE, which lets users build compound documents with objects linked to the applications that created them; and the ability to drag file icons from File Manager and drop them on application Windows to open the files and on the Print Manager icon to print them. Users may also notice that application dialog boxes suddenly appear more functional and consistent. The programming feature *common dialogs* is responsible, since it makes Windows application dialog boxes easier to create for common program functions such as File Open, File Save, and Choose Font.

Below the surface, developers will find more Windows features and more development tools to implement them than in version 3.0. The new Windows 3.1 SDK includes the following additions:

- Help for building "bug-free" applications that can be ported more easily to Win32. The Windows 3.1 SDK provides optional safe type-checking in the improved WINDOWS.H header file. WINDOWS.H features a new set of data type definitions for "STRICT" type-checking that let the compiler spot potential problems before they occur. If you turn on STRICT type-checking and call `CreateWindow`, the first parameter must be defined as an HWND—not a HANDLE or an HDC. The 3.1 SDK also includes a new header file, WINDOWSX.H, which contains new API macros for working with dialog boxes and handling Windows messages in a "safer" fashion. These macros will make your C Windows programs easier to code and to read. In Chapter 12 you will learn how STRICT type-checking and the new macro APIs defined in WINDOWSX.H were used to construct the Resource Monitor program that's introduced in Chapter 6.

- The new debugging version of Windows. This can be used to eliminate many of the UAE errors that plagued Windows 3 and its applications.

- Common dialogs. This feature provides dialog boxes that are not only more functional and consistent to use, but that are also easier for programmers to create. Using the common dialogs API and the COMMDLG dynamic link library, you can create a File Open dialog box using only 30 lines of code instead of 150 lines. You will learn more about how Windows 3.1 common dialogs works in Chapter 3.

- Easier DDE. Windows 3.1 improves application interprocess communication using DDE with DDEML—the Dynamic Data Exchange Management Library. DDEML is a function-based layer built on top of message-based DDE. The DDEML and its related tools are covered in Chapter 11.

- Drag and drop. An easy feature to implement, drag and drop should be in every Windows application that can take advantage of it. In Chapter 3 you will learn how drag and drop is implemented in DumpIT, the Multiple Document Interface (MDI) hex dump program created for this book.

- Windows Setup Toolkit. There is no longer a reason not to have a Windows-based installation program, because the new Windows Setup Toolkit gives you a construction set for building one.

- TOOLHELP. The new TOOLHELP API can be used to get information about the inner working of Windows and Windows applications. You will learn in Chapter 6 how some of the TOOLHELP functions are used in the Resource Monitor program to track Windows resources.

- Easier printing. Windows 3.1 now has "escapeless" printing functions to make printing easier for Windows developers. You will learn how DumpIT takes advantage of this feature for printing file hex dumps in Chapter 3.

Windows 3.1 also includes two new sets of extensions, one for multimedia and one for pen computing. All the multimedia features are now included in Windows 3.1. Previously, Microsoft had offered and supported two versions of Windows—one with only some multimedia features (released in September 1991) and another version with full implementation.

Microsoft C/C++ 7

Microsoft C/C++ 7 was released in April 1992, along with Windows 3.1. It contains a complete Windows development system. Although the Windows SDK still exists, all of its components are now included in Microsoft C/C++ 7.

As you can see, keeping on top of the latest Windows development tools and programming features is a growing challenge for Windows developers. The purpose of this book is to explore the world of Windows development tools and empower you to meet the challenge of Windows software development more effectively.

Now that we have looked at the history of Windows and Windows development tools, let's take a look at the specific development systems this book covers.

Windows Development Systems

In the beginning, there was only the Microsoft Windows SDK. Since 1991 many other Windows development systems have appeared, and there are now more than a half-dozen of them for the C and C++ programming languages.

Many of the tools discussed in this book can be used with other Windows development systems. For example, CASE:W Corporate Edition is an excellent application generator that can be used with any Windows development system. The Borland Resource Workshop is the best tool available for creating and managing the development of Windows resources. It can also be used with any Windows development system.

Let's now begin to look at the leading systems—the Windows SDK, Microsoft QuickC for Windows, Microsoft C/C++, Borland's Turbo C++ for Windows, and Borland C++ —and explore the tools that come with them, as well as some third-party tools that can make Windows programming more productive and easier.

Microsoft Windows SDK

The Windows SDK was the first Windows development system, and it's still available from Microsoft. It does not include a C compiler, but its tools can be used with any Windows development system. Microsoft C/C++ 7 contains the complete

Windows SDK in addition to a C compiler and associated tools. Microsoft QuickC for Windows contains some of the Windows SDK tools, but not all of them. Microsoft offers a supplemental SDK toolkit for QuickC that includes the missing tools. The complete Windows 3.1 SDK includes the following:

- Sets of libraries and header files for building Windows applications that replace and augment those provided with the C compiler. These libraries also include the functionality for using Microsoft's Multimedia and Pen Windows extensions.

- Dialog Editor, for creating dialog boxes.

- Image Editor, for creating icons, cursors, and bitmaps.

- Font Editor, for creating bitmapped fonts for the screen.

- Zoom Utility, to edit and capture screen images.

- On-line SDK Reference, in Windows Help format. Help is also included for Multimedia, Media Control Interface (MCI), programming tips for Windows 3.1, and a guide to the sample applications included with the SDK.

- Spy, for monitoring Windows messages.

- DDE Spy, for monitoring DDE conversations.

- Shaker, to test the effect of Windows memory movement on your application.

- Stress Application, to test how well your program performs under low memory and low system resources situations.

- Swap, to analyze procedure calls across segment boundaries.

- Heap Walker (also called HEAPWALK), for examining Windows memory.

- SYMDEB, CodeView, and 386DEB debuggers for Windows.

- Hotspot Editor, for defining a cursor's hot spot.

- DBWIN, a tool for redirecting debug output from Windows into a window. This tool will be discussed in Chapter 9.

- The debugging version of Windows, to provide enhanced error checking and diagnostic messages.

- Help compiler, for creating Windows Help files for your application.

- CodeView for Windows 3.07 debugger. This debugger can be used with Microsoft C 6.0 and QuickC for Windows. For Microsoft C/C++ 7 you should use the new CodeView for Windows 4.0 debugger included with the compiler.

- Windows Setup Toolkit, providing you with the tools you need to create custom Windows-hosted installation and setup systems for your applications.

Figure 1.1 shows the default Program Manager screen with the icons for the Windows-hosted tools displayed, to give you a visual idea of the SDK's contents.

Microsoft QuickC for Windows

QuickC for Windows is a "one-box" C application development system that does not require the use of the Windows SDK. All of QuickC's tools—even the debugger—run from within its integrated Windows-hosted environment. This means that you use the Windows environment while developing Windows-based applications, making the development process much easier.

FIGURE 1.1:

The Windows 3.1 SDK contents

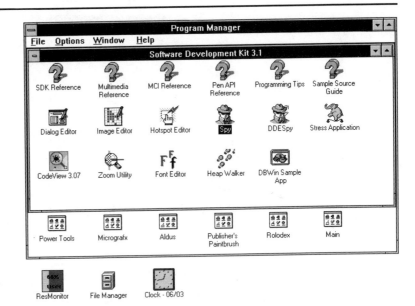

QuickC incorporates a toolbar similar to that found in the Microsoft Word for Windows word processing program and the Microsoft Excel spreadsheet. Figure 1.2 shows the QuickC for Windows graphical development environment while a Windows program is being edited. You can access the tools that come with QuickC from its Program Manager group on the desktop or from its Tools menu.

QuickC includes some of the same tools that are in the Windows SDK. The following Windows development tools come with QuickC for Windows:

- Sets of libraries and header files for building Windows applications. Unlike the Windows SDK, however, QuickC does not include Multimedia and Pen Windows extensions.
- QuickC graphical development environment which includes
  - the C compiler,
  - a program editor, and
  - an integrated debugger.

FIGURE 1.2:
Editing a program using QuickC for Windows

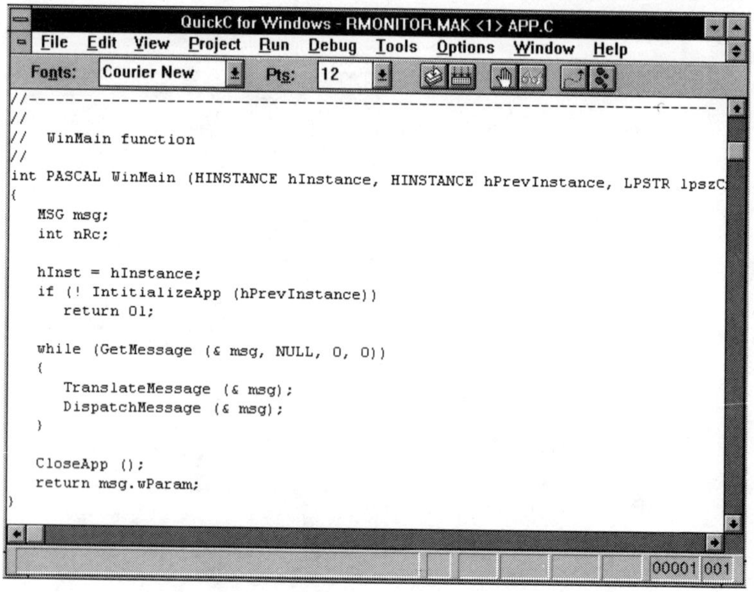
QuickC for Windows - RMONITOR.MAK <1> APP.C
File Edit View Project Run Debug Tools Options Window Help
Fonts: Courier New Pts: 12
//
// WinMain function
//
int PASCAL WinMain (HINSTANCE hInstance, HINSTANCE hPrevInstance, LPSTR lpszC
{
MSG msg;
int nRc;
hInst = hInstance;
if (! IntitializeApp (hPrevInstance))
return 0l;
while (GetMessage (& msg, NULL, 0, 0))
{
TranslateMessage (& msg);
DispatchMessage (& msg);
}
CloseApp ();
return msg.wParam;
}
00001 001

- QuickCase:W, a GUI builder, for creating the C source code for a Windows application.

- Dialog Editor, for creating dialog boxes.

- Image Editor, for creating icons, cursors, and bitmaps.

- On-line Reference in Windows Help format, for help in using QuickC for Windows, using the C programming language, and writing a Windows application in C.

- QuickWin library, for converting DOS C programs to Windows.

Microsoft C/C++ 7

Microsoft C/C++ 7 is a complete Windows development environment. It contains an ANSI standard 2.1 C++ compiler that comes with all of the tools that are included in the Windows SDK. The C/C++ compiler still uses a DOS-based environment called Programmer's Workbench (PWB), but PWB is now much more intimately linked to the Windows environment. You can easily run PWB from Windows to edit and build applications. Using the new WX Server Windows application, you can even run Windows applications from the PWB. The Microsoft PWB running inside a window in the Windows 3.1 environment is shown in Figure 1.3.

The most important Microsoft C/C++ feature to many Windows developers is its support of AT&T C++ 2.1, but it also offers features such as a DPMI-hosted development environment and support of DPMI program development for DOS applications. (Windows applications don't need to be aware of DPMI, since Windows 3 already is.) The Microsoft Foundation Class library included with Microsoft C/C++ 7 is a complete C++ implementation that encapsulates all of the Windows API, including OLE.

In addition to the class libraries, the PWB development environment, the Windows SDK, and the compiler, Microsoft C/C++ 7 includes the following tools:

- Sets of general-purpose libraries and header files for building Windows applications.

- Programmer's Workbench, which includes

  - a C/C++ optimizing compiler,

  - a program editor, and

- an object browser that lets you visualize and use complex C++ class hierarchies. The PWB browser is not graphical or nearly as elegant as the Borland C++ ObjectBrowser, but it is packed with functionality. You can easily use it to find function and variable definitions in your project, as well as browse C++ class libraries.

- Microsoft Foundation Class (MFC) C++ library for Windows. With more than 60 classes, MFC abstracts the functionality of the entire Windows API. These class libraries are the first in a family with an extensible and scalable class architecture known as "AFX" (for Application Framework Extensions). The AFX architecture is designed to dovetail with the long-term Windows operating system architecture, including Win32 and the Windows NT operating system.

- WX Server, which automatically runs Windows-based tools and applications from within PWB.

- 386MAX by Qualitas, which provides advanced memory management and acts as a DPMI server to run PWB from the DOS prompt when you don't want to run it from Windows.

FIGURE 1.3:

The Microsoft C/C++ 7 PWB

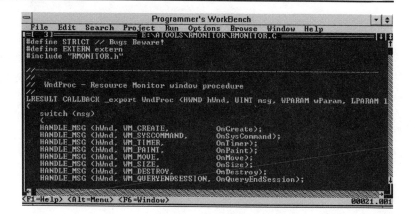

- CodeView for Windows 4.0 debugger. As you can see from the next two items on this list, Microsoft has beefed up its C/C++ debugging system with more tools. CodeView for Windows is also improved and can now do remote debugging across any RS232 serial link. CV/1 from Nu-Mega Technologies is built into the CodeView debugger so you can run CodeView on one monitor without swapping screens. If you build C/C++ applications with Microsoft C/C++ 7, you must use Codeview for Windows 4.0—not version 3.07 that comes with the SDK.

- Source Profiler, a tool to measure the performance of your program by quantifying code paths. It lets you add only debug information (as with CodeView) to your code, and it lets you use the release version of Windows. The Microsoft Source Profiler for Windows is an excellent tool to use when you need to perform active analysis. It is very good at obtaining timing, coverage, and counting information about an application. You will learn how to analyze and fine-tune Windows applications using the Source Profiler in Chapter 8.

Turbo C++ for Windows

Turbo C++ is a Windows-hosted development environment for building both C and C++ applications. It can be purchased separately or as part of Borland C++. (If you want to get every Borland C/C++ development tool available, you should consider Borland C++ with Applications Frameworks.) Turbo C++ for Windows 3.1 includes the following Windows development tools:

- Sets of libraries and header files for building applications.

- A Windows-hosted graphical IDE which includes

  - the C/C++ compiler,
  - a program editor, and
  - ObjectBrowser, for keeping track of C/C++ functions and variables as well as C++ classes.

- Turbo Debugger for Windows, a DOS-based debugger that is much more powerful than Microsoft's CodeView.

- The ObjectWindows Library application framework for Windows. Nick-named OWL, ObjectWindows is a powerful class library that makes creating C++ applications much easier.

- Resource Workshop, the most powerful tool available for creating Windows resources for your application.

- Help Compiler, for building Windows Helps systems.

- WinSight, to help you gain a greater understanding of the Windows environment and to help you debug Windows applications by tracking the messages being passed in your Windows environment. WinSight shows all the registered window classes and the hierarchical relationships among them. It also provides full details on all the windows and window classes in your Windows environment. (WinSight is discussed in detail in Chapter 7, "Monitoring Windows and Window Messages.")

- EasyWin library, for porting DOS programs to Windows.

- On-line Reference in Windows Help format, for help in using Turbo C++ for Windows, using the C/C++ programming language, and writing a Windows application in C/C++. The on-line Help reference that comes with Turbo C++ is the most comprehensive Windows Help system available. At four and one-half megabytes, it's almost twice as large as the Help file included with QuickC for Windows.

I found ObjectBrowser to be especially helpful—even for developing C programs. For example, to find where a variable inside a C program was defined:

1. Click on the variable's name, using the right mouse button to display the ObjectBrowser window.

2. Click on the SpeedBar button to go to the source code for the selected object.

3. ObjectBrowser puts you back in the program editor with the cursor on the variable name in the source code file it is defined in.

I found Turbo C++ for Windows to be an impressive development system. Its user interface is intuitive and easy to use. I had no trouble using Turbo C++ to build sample applications and to rebuild some of my own Windows applications that I had created using Microsoft C—without even referring to a manual.

Turbo C++ includes many sample C++ applications that utilize the OWL libraries, including games. OWL contains the full source code for an expert-level checkers game. (Maybe it wasn't expert-level, but it could defeat me every time!) There is also Bonk, which lets you take out your hostilities on bugs by smashing them with a hammer. While the games show off some of the sophisticated programming you can do with C++, there are also simple applications that help novice C++ programmers. For example, the sample program BTNTEST.CPP is only 91 lines of C++ code and illustrates how to use push buttons, radio buttons, and check boxes in C++.

Borland C++

Borland C++ is a comprehensive C/C++ development system for creating both Windows and DOS applications. As mentioned before, version 3.1 is DPMI-compliant, so it can be run from Windows in both Standard and Enhanced modes. Borland C++ comes in two flavors: Borland C++ and Borland C++ with Application Frameworks.

Borland C++, by itself, includes the Borland C++ DOS-based compiler and Borland C++ for Windows. Borland C++ 3.1 for Windows includes an enhanced version of Turbo C++ for Windows that matches the features found in Borland's DOS-based IDE—including access to all optimizations. Note, however, that Borland C++ does not contain the Object Windows Library when it's purchased without Application Frameworks. Borland C++ with Application Frameworks is Borland's ultimate C++ development system and includes the following components:

- Sets of libraries and header files for building applications.
- A Windows-hosted graphical IDE, called Borland C++ for Windows, which includes
    - the C/C++ compiler,
    - a program editor, and
    - ObjectBrowser, for keeping track of C/C++ functions and variables, as well as C++ classes.
- Help Compiler, for building Windows Help systems.
- Turbo Debugger for Windows, a DOS-based debugger that is much more powerful than Microsoft's CodeView for Windows.

- The ObjectWindows Library application framework for Windows. Nick-named OWL, ObjectWindows is a powerful class library that makes creating C++ applications much easier.

- Resource Workshop, the most powerful tool available for creating Windows resources for your application.

- WinSight, to help you gain a greater understanding of the Windows environment and to help you debug Windows applications by tracking the messages being passed in your Windows environment.

- EasyWin library, for porting DOS programs to Windows.

- On-line Reference in Windows Help format, for help in using Borland C++ for Windows, using the C/C++ programming language, and writing a Windows application in C/C++.

- Borland C++, a DOS-based development environment.

- Application Frameworks, a C++ class library for developing windowed DOS applications.

- WinSpector, to help you analyze fatal program errors. WinSpector is Borland's alternative to Microsoft's Dr. Watson. It understands Borland's debug information and does not require that you have a map file prepared in order to provide a detailed stack trace.

- Turbo Profiler, an interactive profiler for both DOS and Windows applications, which can monitor your program while it is running to pinpoint where you need to speed up the program.

- Turbo Assembler, for writing assembly language programs for DOS and Windows.

   Figure 1.4 shows the the Borland C++ for Windows 3.1 IDE.

Other Windows Development Tools

Now that we have discussed the Windows development systems and the tools included with them, let's take a quick peek at the other Windows development tools we will examine and use during the course of this book. Each of these tools is sold

FIGURE 1.4:

The Borland C++ for
Windows 3.1 IDE

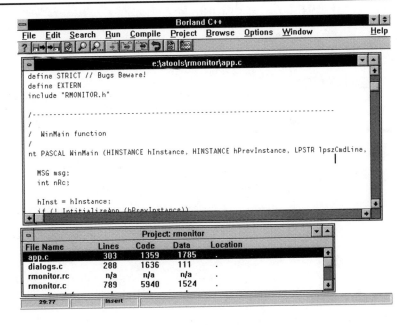

separately. Some of them, such as the Borland Resource Workshop, are also included as part of a development system. We'll discuss these tools in the order they appear in the book.

Borland Resource Workshop

The Resource Workshop, explored in Chapter 2, provides an integrated set of tools in an MDI Windows program for creating and editing Windows resources. The Resource Workshop not only gives you the most powerful set of resource editors available; it also brings order to the process of creating your application's resources by integrating the tools into one program, instead of giving you separate tools as in the Windows SDK.

The Resource Workshop treats your resource script file as a project file for your application resources, similar to the way a make or a project file is used for building your application. This means that the resource script file is created for you automatically when you save your resource project. So instead of having to code your program resources, you can create them visually and the Resource Workshop will generate the code (the resource script) for you.

CASE:W and WindowsMAKER Professional

CASE:W and WindowsMAKER Professional are the two leading Windows application generators. We will develop a Windows program using CASE:W in Chapter 3, and we will discuss WindowsMAKER Professional in Chapter 4.

Both CASE:W and WindowsMAKER Professional are point-and-click application generators. Both create C source code programs using any of the Windows development systems covered in this book. Both programs assist you in creating your Windows application by

- creating menus

- creating windows (main, MDI, and child)

- defining window attributes (color, frame style, scroll bars, and caption)

- linking icons and cursors to windows

- linking menus to program objects (dialog boxes, MDI windows, secondary windows, and user-defined functions)

- using dialog boxes as templates for putting control windows in the client area of a window

- letting you test your application without compiling it

- defining the messages to be processed by your Windows application and building the case statement to process them

- configuring compile and link options such as memory model

- making your application from inside the application generator

- running other Windows development tools from the application generator workbench.

Magic Fields

Magic Fields is a custom control library that lets you put a much more powerful edit control in your dialog boxes than the one that is built into Windows. After you put one of these powerful new edit controls (called a Magic Field) into your dialog box, you can give your entire dialog box a 3-D appearance and gain access to a powerful set of functions for converting data to and from a Magic Field. All of this is implemented in the Magic Fields dynamic link library, MFEDIT.DLL. Magic Fields is discussed in Chapter 5.

RoboHELP

RoboHELP is a powerful assistant that works inside Word for Windows to create a Help file. You design the structure of your Help file using topics, hypertext links, hot buttons, and graphics. RoboHELP is always there to assist you in the process. I found that RoboHELP made creating a Help file much less painful and—yes—even fun. RoboHELP makes creating Help files so easy, you may even find yourself looking for an excuse to create one. For instance, you may want to make a README.HLP for your application instead of a README.TXT. In Chapter 5, you will learn what RoboHELP does and see how it can be used to construct a Windows Help system.

DialogCoder

DialogCoder is almost an application generator. However, it does only two things: it is a dialog box editor and it generates the code for dialog box functions. DialogCoder excels at generating the C code for dialog box procedures, and it is especially proficient at establishing relationships between controls. Tackling the time-consuming job of coding complex relationships between control windows inside a dialog box, it leaves you free to concentrate on the core functionality of the dialog box function code.

For example, you can set up a dialog box that has three controls: a push button, an edit control, and a list box. Using DialogCoder, you can have the currently selected line in the list box moved or copied to the edit control when the push button is clicked on. DialogCoder will generate all the C code to do this. All you have to do is link the controls using tools in DialogCoder's toolbar. In Chapter 5, you will see how to construct and integrate into a Windows application a dialog box function created with DialogCoder.

MultiScope Debugger for Windows

MultiScope for Windows is a Windows-hosted debugger. This book has two chapters that explain the ins and outs of debugging a Windows application and that cover each of the Windows debuggers in the development systems the book examines: QuickC for Windows Debugger, CodeView for Windows, and Turbo Debugger for Windows. In Chapter 10 we'll explore what makes MultiScope for Windows different from the other debuggers.

Windows Development Tools Included with This Book

In the course of writing this book, I developed several programming projects and tools. The projects are included on the enclosed disk set, so you can try each of them as you go through the book; this is the best way to learn how each programming tool works.

The Windows development tools that I designed for this book are valuable because they give you some extra widgets to add to your programming toolbox. They allow you to add floating toolbars to programs, control the position of windows on the desktop, locate missing files, examine a file's contents, and monitor your Windows system resources. Look at the ATOOLS.HLP Help file for a description of the contents of all the files included on the disk set.

Programming Projects

The following programming projects are included in this book. They illustrate how certain Windows development tools are used and point out Windows programming tips along the way. The projects can also be found in the \ATOOLS directory after you have installed the disk set on your PC.

Corporate Information Menu System

Corporate Information Menu System (CIMS) is a project that shows you how to use the WindowsMAKER Professional application generator. CIMS is built in Chapter 3, and the source files may be found in the \ATOOLS\CIMS subdirectory.

Magic

Magic is a project that shows you how to use the Magic Fields control library. Magic is built in Chapter 5, and the source code may be found in the \ATOOLS\MAGIC subdirectory.

Party Plan

Party Plan is a project that shows you how to use DialogCoder to add functionality to a dialog box. Party Plan is built in Chapter 5, and the source code may be found in the \ATOOLS\PARTYPLN subdirectory.

WinDraw

WinDraw illustrates how to debug a Windows application in Chapters 9 and 10. The source files for WinDraw may be found in the \ATOOLS\DEBUG subdirectory.

Tools Developed for This Book

The following tool programs included in this book illustrate how a Windows development tool can be used to create more Windows development tools. These programs can be found in the \ATOOLS directory after you have installed the disk set on your PC.

Some of the tools, such as Topper, are discussed in only one chapter. Other tools are used for projects in multiple chapters. For example, Resource Monitor gets created in Chapter 6, when we discuss Windows memory. Later, in Chapter 8, we'll use it as a project to show how to profile a Windows application. Then we'll add DDE-server capabilities to it in Chapter 11. And finally, in Chapter 12, we'll use it to show how to write a STRICT Windows application that uses the new Windows 3.1 "message cracker" macros.

FileFind

FileFind is a programming utility that you can use to locate files on your hard disk and copy them to your project directory. The 3-D dialog box that FileFind uses was built using the Borland Resource Workshop, as described in Chapter 2. The application code for FileFind was created using WindowsMAKER Professional and DialogCoder. You will find FileFind in the \ATOOLS\FILEFIND directory after you have installed the disk set on your PC.

DumpIT

DumpIT is an MDI hex dump program that was built using CASE:W and QuickC for Windows. All the details about how DumpIT was created are in Chapter 3. You will also learn about implementing Windows 3.1 common dialogs in Chapter 3, as well as how drag and drop was added to DumpIT to make it work with File Manager. You will find another version of DumpIT in the \ATOOLS\DUMPIT31 subdirectory. This version of DumpIT was derived from DumpIT 2.0 and has more features. DumpIT 3.1 is discussed in Chapter 12.

Resource Monitor

Resource Monitor tracks and monitors your Windows resources. You can use it to keep track continuously of Windows resources instead of choosing the About command in Program Manager's Help menu. You can also use its advanced capabilities to help debug your Windows application to discover "leaking" resources. You will find a DDE-server version of Resource Monitor in \ATOOLS\DDE\RMONITOR. This version is discussed in Chapter 11.

Topper

Topper lets you select any application window and put it on top of all the other windows running, then lock it or unlock it in the top position. Topper is very handy for making sure that the Help window containing the Windows SDK reference is always on top so you can reference it while you are working on your program in a text editor or a Windows-based debugger. You will find another version of Topper in \ATOOLS\TOPPER2. Instead of using push buttons in windows, this enhanced version uses graphical buttons created using the Windows GDI. Both versions of Topper are discussed in Chapter 7.

ToolPAL

ToolPAL is a floating tool palette for QuickC for Windows and the Borland C++ IDE, which you will find adds more point-and-click functionality. You can use the source code for ToolPAL as a starting point for building a tool palette that will work with any Windows application. ToolPAL is located in \ATOOLS\TOOLPAL on the disk set.

ATOOLS.DLL

ATOOLS.DLL is a library of utility functions included on the disk set. In this library, you will find functions that will help you debug your program, display messages, manipulate strings, and do data conversions. ToolPAL is located in the \ATOOLS.DLL directory.

Harnessing Windows Development Tools

The best way to learn about the tools we'll discuss in the following sections is to use them right away to see how they work. All the projects we describe are included on the accompanying disks, along with their source code. Even if you don't have the development tool we are discussing, examine the source code. Try out each of the Windows application projects and tools to see how it works. In the case of application generators, read through the source code they generate to see what they are capable of producing.

Once you've worked through this book, you should feel prepared to use the full power of the tools we've covered to design even more creative Windows applications and development tools.

Well, it's time to get started. Let's go on to Part II, "Automating Windows Development."

P A R T II

Automating
Windows Development

In Part II we'll investigate a number of programs that are especially useful in automating the development of Windows applications. The tools we'll cover in the following four chapters will allow you to build applications quickly and to construct yet more tools. In addition, you will see how some of the tools developed for this book were built using the tools discussed here. Be sure to use the disk set that comes with this book as we go along, so you can take full advantage of the information by trying it out yourself.

In Chapter 2 we'll explore in detail the Borland Resource Workshop development environment for automating the creation of Windows applications.

In Chapter 3 we'll use my application DumpIT to examine and work with the Graphical User Interface (GUI) builder CASE:W Corporate Edition as it works in the Microsoft QuickC for Windows development environment.

In Chapter 4 we'll look at another popular GUI builder, WindowsMAKER Professional, using the Corporate Information Menu System (CIMS) application as an sample project.

In Chapter 5 we'll examine three specialized tools, Magic Fields, DialogCoder, and RoboHELP, for adding functionality to your applications.

#### TWO

Using the Borland Resource Workshop

- Borland Resource Workshop fundamentals

- Creating bitmaps, icons, and cursors using the Borland Resource Workshop

- Creating dialog boxes using the Borland Resource Workshop

- Creating dialog box controls using the Borland Custom Control Library

- Adding custom bitmap push buttons to dialog boxes

Atypical Microsoft Windows program contains many different resources, including bitmaps, accelerators, cursors, dialog boxes, menus, icons, and strings. Resources are data that's included in a program's executable file but that don't reside in the program's data segment.

When Windows loads a program into memory for execution, it usually leaves the program's resources on the disk, thereby reducing memory demands. Resources are loaded only when they are needed, and they occupy separate data segments in memory that's managed by Windows. Most resources are read-only data marked as discardable. When Windows needs more memory, resource memory segments can be easily discarded. Since resources are separate from a program's code and data in the executable file, it is easy for Windows and other programs to change resources in, and extract resources from, a program executable without accessing the source code. The ability to read resources from and to write resources to an executable file is one of the special features that you will find in the Borland Resource Workshop (BRW).

Microsoft provides many tools for creating program resources, each of which is a stand-alone program. The Windows resource development tools do an adequate job, but they are not very innovative. For creating program resources, the Windows 3.1 SDK provides Dialog Editor, for creating dialog boxes; Image Editor, for creating icons, cursors, and bitmaps; and Font Editor, for creating bitmapped screen fonts.

Using the Windows SDK, you must code by hand all text resources, such as menus, string tables, and accelerators. Normally, these resources are included in one or more resource script (.RC) files. The .RC file is an ASCII text file which contains text descriptions of text resources such as menus and dialog boxes, and which defines the whereabouts of graphic resources by including a reference to the file they are located in. Wouldn't it be nice if you had a way to create all program resources visually, instead of having to code them? Wouldn't it be nice to have all the tools necessary to create program resources in one program that would also give you a tool to manage resource organization?

As you might have guessed, there is such a tool—the Borland Resource Workshop (BRW). The BRW provides an integrated set of tools for creating program resources in a multiple document interface (MDI) Windows program. It provides the most powerful set of resource editors available for Windows development, as well as additional functions for managing and compiling program resources. BRW is easier to use than the Microsoft tools, and it eliminates the need to code the resource script file that ties all the resources together for your application.

BRW is included as part of Turbo C++ for Windows, Borland C++, Borland C++ with Borland C++ & Application Frameworks, and Turbo Pascal for Windows, versions 3.1 and above. You can also purchase BRW separately from Borland, and you can use it with Microsoft QuickC for Windows, Microsoft C/C++ 7.0, the Microsoft Windows SDK, and Zortech C++.

Now let's see how BRW provides an automated development environment for building Windows resources.

> **TIP**
>
> I recommend purchasing Turbo C++ for Windows to get the best deal on BRW. Inexpensive and heavily discounted, Turbo C++ for Windows includes BRW as well as many other Borland development tools, such as WinSight and WinSpector. You will likely find that it doesn't cost much more than purchasing BRW by itself.

The BRW Resource Development Environment

You may ask, "How does a tool provide such integration?" Well, BRW uses the resource script (.RC) file as a project file for building your Windows application's resources in a way similar to using a project file (.PRJ for Borland C++ and .MAK for Microsoft C/C++) for managing how an application is built. It's a simple concept, yet an ingenious one.

BRW's resource editors are more powerful than the SDK's, and they give you an abundance of new features. BRW offers extensive multilevel Undo and Redo, easily added custom controls, and a Paint editor that lets you create bitmap resources that are not limited to 64x64 pixels. It lets you concentrate on building your application resources (menus, dialog boxes, icons, bitmaps, cursors, string tables, and accelerators) using powerful graphic editors, and it generates the .RC file for your application automatically—so you don't have to code it.

BRW can decompile resources from existing applications and compile resources into binary formats, such as resource object files (.RES) and program executables. BRW also replaces the Microsoft resource compiler as well as the resource editors—it comes with a resource compiler built-in that is almost Microsoft compatible. The following list details the incompatibilities between the Microsoft Resource Compiler (MRC) and the Borland Resource Compiler (BRC):

- BRC does not support token pasting in preprocessor statements using `/**/`, but it does allow the ANSI-specified pair `##`. For example, the definition `#define VAR(x,y) (x ## y)` expands to `(xy)`, or the call `VAR(9,i)` expands to `(9i)`, and the definition `#define VAR(x,y) (x /**/ y)` does not work! This is an example of Borland's using an ANSI-specified standard. The `/**/` method is old and is nonportable.

- BRC's use of the `#undef` preprocessor directive is limited. If you try to use `#undef` after previously referencing a `#define` in a resource, you will get fatal compile errors. This is a limitation of the Resource Workshop.

- BRC consistently treats numeric constants that are preceded by zeros, used as part of a preprocessor directive, as octal numbers. Microsoft's resource compiler doesn't. This is an inconsistency caused by the MRC. Numbers with leading zeros in preprocessor expressions are interpreted as octal numbers, but the same numbers used as identifiers are interpreted as decimal numbers.

The Borland Resource Compiler also has a number of significant enhancements in comparison to the Microsoft Resource Compiler. The following are some of BRC's improvements:

- Support for file references in RCDATA and user-defined resources. As with all of the graphic resources, you can now store user-defined data either as part of the resource definition in a project file or as a separate file.

- Addition of the new data type hex string consisting of a number of hexadecimal digits that describe data bytes. The hex data can be space delimited or all together, but it must be surrounded by single quotes, for example, `'123456789A'` or `'1 2 3 4 5 6 7 8 9 A'`.

- Support for text descriptions of bitmapped resources. You can now add text to any resource that was created with the Paint editor.

- Correctly parses numeric expressions, such as

  `1 + 99 DIALOG FILEFIND.DLG`

  This is interpreted as a dialog resource with the ID of 100.

BRW provides you with the tools to manage the process of creating resources and of editing your resources in either text or binary format. BRW contains a Paint editor, a Font editor, a Dialog editor, a Menu editor, a String editor, and an Accelerator editor.

To learn about what BRW does and how it works, we will review its features and examine each of its resource editors. You will also learn how BRW was used to build the FileFind tool that's included on the book's disk set and to create the bitmaps and the dialog boxes for the Corporate Information Menu System (CIMS). The CIMS application in Chapter 4 is a project that will show you how to use WindowsMAKER Professional. You will find all the files that were used for these projects in the \ATOOLS\FILEFIND and the \ATOOLS\CIMS directories that were created when you installed the book's disk set on your hard drive.

BRW Fundamentals

As mentioned previously, BRW uses the application resource script file (.RC) as its project file for managing the creation of your application's resources. BRW lets you work with and view the project file in several different ways. Let's look at how an .RC file is constructed and how BRW uses it as a project file.

The Resource Script File

Windows resources come in two different flavors: ASCII text and bitmap graphics. ASCII text resources include menus, dialog boxes, string tables, and accelerators. Bitmap graphic resources include icons, cursors, and bitmaps.

A resource script file is an ASCII text file used to define an application's ASCII text resources and the location of the bitmap graphic resource files. You can define each ASCII text resource separately within the .RC file, or you can include references to the files that contain the resources, such as the .DLG files created by the Microsoft Dialog Editor.

You can use BRW to work on a project file that BRW created or on one that you coded yourself. You can use it to manage your entire project from beginning to end or have it step in at any point along the way.

To illustrate what an .RC file looks like and how BRW can work with any existing one, let's look at the .RC file for DumpIT, the hex dump program included with this book as a Windows programming tool. The resource file for DumpIT, as well as its C source code files, were generated by CASE:W. If you would like to learn more about what DumpIT does and how it works, you can skip ahead to Chapter 3 and read about it. When you come back, you'll learn how you can edit DumpIT's resources using BRW.

DumpIT is a good example for showing how BRW can be used to edit existing program resources. The following code shows what the resource script file for DumpIT looks like.

```
#include "windows.h"
#include "resource.h"
#include "dialogs.h"

DUMPIT ICON DUMPIT.ICO
DUMPWIN ICON TRASHCAN.ICO

DUMPIT MENU
 BEGIN
  POP-UP "&File"
   BEGIN
    MENUITEM "&Open File...", IDM_OPENFILE
    MENUITEM SEPARATOR
    MENUITEM "E&xit", IDM_EXIT
   END
   POP-UP "&Window"
    BEGIN
       MENUITEM   "&Tile",        IDM_TILE
       MENUITEM   "&Cascade",   IDM_CASCADE
       MENUITEM   "Arrange &Icons", IDM_ARRANGE
       MENUITEM   "Close &All",   IDM_CLOSEALL
    END
  POP-UP "&Help"
   BEGIN
     MENUITEM "&Help for help",  IDM_HELPHELP
     MENUITEM "Help &index",  IDM_INDEXHELP
     MENUITEM SEPARATOR
     MENUITEM "&About...",     IDM_ABOUTHELP
   END
 END

 DUMPWIN MENU
```

```
BEGIN
 POP-UP "&File"
  BEGIN
   MENUITEM "&Open File...", IDM_OPENFILE
   MENUITEM "File Si&zes...", IDM_FILESIZES
   MENUITEM "&Print...", IDM_PRINT
   MENUITEM "Print &Setup...", IDM_PRINTSETUP
   MENUITEM "&Close", IDM_CLOSE
   MENUITEM SEPARATOR
   MENUITEM "E&xit", IDM_EXIT
  END
 POP-UP "&Edit"
  BEGIN
   MENUITEM "&Find...", IDM_FIND
  END
 POP-UP "&Options"
  BEGIN
   MENUITEM "Choose &Font...", IDM_CHOOSEFONT
   MENUITEM SEPARATOR
   POP-UP "Text Color"
    BEGIN
     MENUITEM "&Red", IDM_TEXTRED
     MENUITEM "&Blue", IDM_TEXTBLUE
     MENUITEM "&Green", IDM_TEXTGREEN
     MENUITEM "Blac&k", IDM_TEXTBLACK, CHECKED
     MENUITEM "&White", IDM_TEXTWHITE
    END
   POP-UP "&Text Background Color"
    BEGIN
     MENUITEM "&Red", IDM_BGRED
     MENUITEM "&Blue", IDM_BGBLUE
     MENUITEM "&Green", IDM_BGGREEN
     MENUITEM "Blac&k", IDM_BGBLACK
     MENUITEM "&White", IDM_BGWHITE, CHECKED
    END
   POP-UP "&Highlight Text Color"
    BEGIN
     MENUITEM "&Red", IDM_HITEXTRED
     MENUITEM "&Blue", IDM_HITEXTBLUE
     MENUITEM "&Green", IDM_HITEXTGREEN
     MENUITEM "Blac&k", IDM_HITEXTBLACK, CHECKED
    END
   POP-UP "Highlight &Background Color"
    BEGIN
     MENUITEM "&Red", IDM_HIBGRED
```

```
      MENUITEM "&Blue", IDM_HIBGBLUE
      MENUITEM "&Green", IDM_HIBGGREEN
      MENUITEM "&Cyan", IDM_HIBGCYAN, CHECKED        MENUITEM "&Yel-
low", IDM_HIBGYELLOW
      MENUITEM "Blac&k", IDM_HIBGBLACK
    END
  END
 POP-UP "&Tools"
  BEGIN
   MENUITEM "&Notepad", IDM_NOTEPAD  MENUITEM "&Calculator",
IDM_CALCULATOR
  END
  POP-UP "&Window"
   BEGIN
      MENUITEM  "&Tile",    IDM_TILE
      MENUITEM  "&Cascade",  IDM_CASCADE
      MENUITEM  "Arrange &Icons", IDM_ARRANGE
      MENUITEM  "Close &All",  IDM_CLOSEALL
   END
POP-UP "&HELP"
 BEGIN
   MENUITEM "&HELP for HELP",    IDM_HELPHELP
   MENUITEM "Help &Index",      IDM_INDEXHELP
   MENUITEM SEPARATOR
   MENUITEM "&About...",    IDM_ABOUTHELP
 END
END

 ABOUT DIALOG -20, 15, 196, 95
 STYLE DS_MODALFRAME ¦ WS_POPUP ¦ WS_VISIBLE ¦ WS_CAPTION ¦
WS_SYSMENU
 CAPTION "About DumpIT 3.1..."
 FONT 10, "System"
 BEGIN
   CTEXT    "DumpIT is a file hex-dump program written for Win-
dows.",
     101, 6, 13, 186, 8
   CTEXT    "Copyright 1992, Arthur English and Digital Artistry",
     103, 13, 24, 172, 8
   PUSHBUTTON  "OK", IDOK, 76, 73, 40, 14
   CTEXT    "Text1", IDC_MEMTOTAL, 11, 42, 170, 8
```

```
   CTEXT    "Text2", IDC_MEMFREE, 11, 50, 170, 8
   CTEXT    "Text3", IDC_SIZELIST, 11, 58, 170, 8
END

FILESIZE DIALOG LOADONCALL MOVEABLE DISCARDABLE 37, 32, 230, 112
CAPTION "File Size"
FONT 10 "System"
STYLE DS_MODALFRAME ¦ WS_POPUP ¦ WS_VISIBLE ¦ WS_CAPTION
BEGIN
 CONTROL "OK", IDOK, "button", BS_PUSHBUTTON ¦ WS_TABSTOP, 39,88,
40,
14
 CONTROL "&Help", IDC_HELP, "button", BS_PUSHBUTTON ¦ WS_TABSTOP,
  95, 88, 40, 14
 CONTROL "&Calculator", IDC_CALCULATOR, "button", BS_PUSHBUTTON ¦
WS_TABSTOP,
  151, 88, 40, 14
 CONTROL "", IDC_SIZELIST, "listbox",
  WS_BORDER ¦ LBS_SORT ¦ WS_VSCROLL ¦ WS_TABSTOP ¦
LBS_USETABSTOPS,
  2, 24, 226, 56
 CONTROL "File Size:", -1, "static", SS_LEFT ¦ WS_GROUP, 2, 5,
32, 8
 CONTROL "Decimal", -1, "static", SS_LEFT ¦ WS_GROUP, 2, 14, 30, 8
 CONTROL "Hexadecimal", -1, "static", SS_LEFT ¦ WS_GROUP, 42, 14,
46, 8
 CONTROL "File name:", -1, "static", SS_LEFT ¦ WS_GROUP, 97, 14,
46, 8
END

FIND DIALOG 15, 18, 270, 78
CAPTION "Find"
FONT 10 "System"
STYLE DS_MODALFRAME ¦ WS_POPUP ¦ WS_VISIBLE ¦ WS_CAPTION ¦ WS_SYS-
MENU
BEGIN
RTEXT "Find what?", -1, 6, 10, 38, 8
CONTROL "", IDC_FINDWHAT, "edit", WS_TABSTOP ¦ WS_BORDER ¦
ES_AUTOHSCROLL,
 48, 8, 158, 12
CONTROL "Direction", -1, "button", BS_GROUPBOX ¦ WS_GROUP, 8, 23,
75, 29
CONTROL "Up", IDC_UP, "button", BS_AUTORADIOBUTTON ¦ WS_TABSTOP,
 16, 36, 26, 10
```

```
CONTROL "Down", IDC_DOWN, "button", BS_AUTORADIOBUTTON, 48, 36,
31, 10
CONTROL "Format", -1, "button", BS_GROUPBOX | WS_GROUP, 99, 23,
107, 29
CONTROL "ASCII", IDC_ASCII, "button", BS_AUTORADIOBUTTON |
WS_TABSTOP,
 104, 36, 33, 10
CONTROL "Hexadecimal", IDC_HEX, "button", BS_AUTORADIOBUTTON,
 143, 36, 60, 11
CONTROL "Ma&tch Case",
 IDC_MATCHCASE, "button", BS_AUTOCHECKBOX | WS_GROUP |
WS_TABSTOP,
 8, 56, 56, 10
PUSHBUTTON "&Find Next", IDC_FINDNEXT, 217, 6, 47, 14,
 WS_CHILD | WS_VISIBLE | WS_TABSTOP
PUSHBUTTON "&Close", IDCANCEL, 217, 23, 47, 14,
 WS_CHILD | WS_VISIBLE | WS_TABSTOP
PUSHBUTTON "&Help", IDC_HELP, 217, 40, 47, 14
PUSHBUTTON "C&alculator", IDC_CALCULATOR, 217, 57, 47, 14,
 WS_CHILD | WS_VISIBLE | WS_TABSTOP
END

ABORTDLG DIALOG 20, 20, 166, 64
STYLE DS_MODALFRAME | WS_VISIBLE | WS_CAPTION | WS_SYSMENU
CAPTION "Print File"
BEGIN
 DEFPUSHBUTTON "Cancel", IDCANCEL, 67, 43, 32, 14, WS_GROUP
 CTEXT    "Sending", -1, 38, 7, 90, 8
 CTEXT    "text", IDC_FILENAME, 38, 18, 90, 8
 CTEXT    "to print spooler.", -1, 38, 27, 90, 8
END
   STRING TABLE
BEGIN
 IDS_REGISTER_CLASS_ERROR  "Error registering window class"
 IDS_CREATE_DIALOG_ERROR  "Dialog creation failed!"
 IDS_APPNAME       "DumpIT 3.1"
 IDS_GDI_ERROR_CAP    "GDI Error!"
 IDS_DC_PRINTER_ERROR_MSG  "Could not get a printer device
 IDS_MAXFILES_CAP     "Too Many Files!"
 IDS_MAXFILES_MSG     "Only 8 files are allowed open at once."
 IDS_LOCALMEMORY_ERROR_CAP "Local Memory Error!"
 IDS_LOCALMEMORY_ERROR_MSG "Couldn't alloc. buffer %d bytes"
 IDS_GLOBALMEMORY_ERROR_CAP "Global Memory Error"
 IDS_GLOBALMEMORY_ERROR_MSG "Couldn't alloc. buffer size %l bytes"
 IDS_FILEERROR_CAP    "File Error!"
```

```
IDS_FILEERROR_MSG     "Bad file handle returned for File name: %s"
IDS_FILEREADERROR_MSG  "File read error. Cannot read in file."
IDS_DUMPIT_ERROR      "DumpIT Error!"
IDS_MAXFONTS        "You have exceeded the number of fonts allowed!"
IDS_PRINTERDC_ERROR   "Could not get a printer device context."
IDS_FIND_ERROR_CAP    "Find Dialog Error"
IDS_FIND_ERROR1_MSG    "Direction not set!"
IDS_FIND_ERROR2_MSG    "HEX numbers must be even number of char!"
IDS_FIND_ERROR3_MSG    "Invalid HEX value! "
IDS_FIND_ERROR4_MSG    "Could not locate value"
IDS_PRINT_ERROR_CAP    "Print Error!"
IDS_PRINT_ERROR1_MSG   "Unable to start print job!"
IDS_PRINT_ERROR2_MSG   "Cannot create print dialog box!"
END
```

NOTE Some of the string table entries have been abbreviated so the text all fits on one line. You can have string table entries of up to 255 characters, but the text string itself must fit entirely on one line. These error messages were shortened for readability. If you check out the DumpIT .RC file, you will find that the messages are longer and that they each fit on just one line.

The DumpIT .RC file includes two menus, four dialog boxes, and a string table, as well as references to external resource files (DUMPIT.ICO and TRASHCAN.ICO). In a similar fashion, you can also include bitmaps, cursors, and fonts in your program's resources. Graphic resources can be included as external binary files, or their entire source can be placed right into the .RC file. In this chapter you will see how you can use BRW to work on the resources of an existing application, such as DumpIT, as well as to create new applications such as FileFind.

Displaying Messages in DumpIT

If you examine the string table entries in DumpIT, you will notice that some of them look like `printf` format statements. As a matter of fact, that's just what they are. I have found that it's a good programming practice always to keep text strings separate from program code whenever possible. This way the text strings are easier to maintain and change. If my project is a small one, or if the text strings are unlikely to change (such as the class name for a window), I'll relax this rule. Resource script files provide an easy way to manage text strings for a Windows program.

In some cases, you will need to insert data into a text string that's displayed in a message box in order to notify the user of a file name or other information that is available only when the program is executing. That's where my `printf`-type format strings are useful. In the C source code modules for DumpIT, I use my own function `DisplayMessage` instead of the Windows API `MessageBox`. `DisplayMessage` accepts a variable number of parameters like `printf`, so you can insert data values into the text string that's displayed. For example, to display a simple error message that does not include any inserted data values, call `DisplayMessage` as follows:

```
if (nFileCount >= 8)
  {
  DisplayMessage (IDS_MAXFILES_CAP, IDS_MAXFILES_MSG);
  return NULL;
  }
```

`DisplayMesssage` doesn't work with strings—it uses string table identifiers instead. The first parameter identifies the string table entry for the `MessageBox` caption. The second parameter identifies the string table entry for the message to be displayed in the `MessageBox`. The string table entry identified by the second parameter may be text only or a `printf`-type format string. The following call to `DisplayMessage` adds an extra parameter that is inserted into the format string:

```
if (fstat (hFile, & FileStatus) != 0)
  {
  DisplayMessage (IDS_FILEERROR_CAP,
    IDS_FILEERROR_MSG, lpNewWV->szFileName);
  return NULL;
  }
```

These function calls to `DisplayMessage` can be found in the DumpIT function `Do-WmFileOpen` in the source file DIALOGS.C. The format string identified by `IDS_FILEERROR_MSG` in DUMPIT.RC is

```
"Bad file handle returned from OpenFile\nFile name: %s"
```

The function `DisplayMessage` is also in DIALOGS.C. It uses `wsprintf` to build a text string to display with the Windows `MessageBox` function. Here's the C code for `DisplayMessage`, so you can see what it does:

```
//------------------------------------------------------------
//
// DisplayMessage function - displays a MessageBox using resource
strings.
```

```
//
void DisplayMessage (UINT nCaption, UINT nFormat, ...)
{
  char szBuffer[256], szCaption[80], szFormat[256];
  LPSTR pArguments;

  LoadString (g_app.hInst, nCaption, szCaption, sizeof (sz-
Caption));
  LoadString (g_app.hInst, nFormat, szFormat, sizeof (szFormat));
  pArguments = (char *) & nFormat + sizeof nFormat;

  // Wvsprintf works like sprintf but takes a pointer to a list
  // of variables instead of the variables themselves.
  wvsprintf ((LPSTR) szBuffer, (LPSTR) szFormat, pArguments);
  MessageBox (NULL, szBuffer, szCaption, MB_OK);
}
```

After you create your application's .RC file by coding it manually or by generating it with BRW, it must be compiled and bound to your program's executable code before it can be used. If you use the Microsoft tools for creating your application's resources, you must run the SDK resource compiler to build your resource object file (.RES) and run the resource compiler again after your program has been linked in order to bind the .RES file into your program executable. In contrast, BRW writes the resource script file for you—all you have to do is design your resources visually. BRW can also compile and save your program resources in a variety of formats that include both .RES and .EXE files. If you want, you can take an .RC file and write it directly to an .EXE file and skip creating the .RES file.

Resource files can grow quite large, and it's easy to make syntax errors when you create them manually. Let's look at how BRW lets you create resources visually and generates the .RC file for your program automatically to avoid this problem.

BRW Features

BRW's powerful integrated environment includes a set of graphic editors for creating an application's resources. BRW works with you to create your program's resources by

- providing a management facility for you—the project window;
- automating the creation of the resource script file;

- providing an outline view of the application's resources, making it easier for you to see the big picture;

- providing you with the ability to test all resources before binding them to your application;

- providing you with the ability to access and edit resources in existing applications, even if you don't have access to the source code;

- allowing you to work with resources in either text or binary format. BRW contains a text editor for directly manipulating resource scripts;

- compiling your resources for you;

- undoing changes you have made to resources; and

- checking for errors such as duplicate resource IDs.

WARNING BRW can read an .RC file and write to an executable file, but not the reverse. If you want to keep your project as an .RC file, make sure to save it as one. When you save it to other formats such as .EXE and .RES, remember you always have to save it as an .RC file first—you can't save it as an .RC file after you have saved it as an .EXE or an .RES file.

Starting BRW

After starting BRW you choose the New Project command from the File menu to create a new project, or choose the Open Project command to open an existing project. Normally, you would start a new project as an .RC file. You can also choose to create a new bitmap (.BMP), cursor (.CUR), icon (.ICO), font (.FON), or resource object file (.RES). Using BRW, you can create the individual resource objects or an entire project. Let's look at how a project is created.

The Project File (.RC)

The most important aspect of BRW is the project file. The project file contains one or more resources or refers to files that contain resources. BRW makes it easy to connect other .RC, .DLG, .BMP, .ICO, .CUR, .FON and .H files to your application by providing references to these files within the project file.

The new project you start or the existing one you open is displayed in the project window. The project window shows you the resource objects that make up your project and how the project is organized. Figure 2.1 shows the project window for the DumpIT application. You may want to compare the contents of this window with the .RC file listing we just discussed. In the project window, you see the big picture with only major resource objects listed. The .RC file listing, on the other hand, is brimming with detail to guide Windows in constructing your program resources.

Project Views

BRW gives you many different ways of looking at your project. Within the View menu, you can select either By Type or By File to view your resources. By Type is the default when you start BRW. From Type or File, you have the following choices:

- *Show Identifiers* lists all the symbolic identifiers associated with your project that are defined in header files.

- *Show Resources* lists the major resource components of your project.

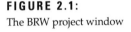

FIGURE 2.1:
The BRW project window

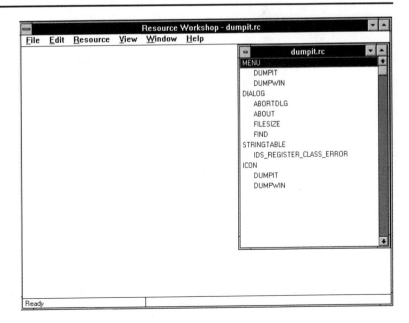

- *Show Items* provides further detail to show each item within a menu, each control within a dialog box, and each string within a string table.

For example, you can view your project by file and display only the major resource components of the project, as shown in Figure 2.2.

As you can see, all resources and file names are listed in the order they appear in the source files. If you want to see all the resources listed according to type instead of file name, simply choose the By Type command from the View menu. If you want to see project detail, choose Show Items to list the items that make up your application's resource objects, as shown in Figure 2.3.

After selecting the View By Type command—as well as Show Identifiers, Show Resources, and Show Items—you can get a complete outline of your resources in the project window. If this is not enough detail for you, you can also see an entire resource as it appears within the .RC file. All you need to do is select the resource you want to focus on within the project window and choose the Edit As Text command from the Resource menu. In Figure 2.4 you can see a menu within the .RC file as well as within the project window.

FIGURE 2.2:

Project window with By File selected in the View menu

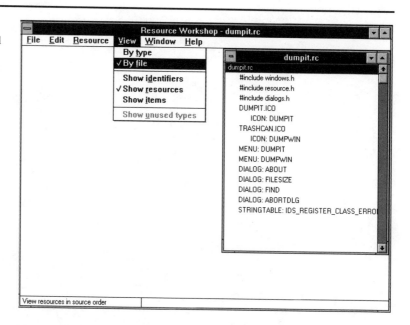

FIGURE 2.3:

Project window with Show Items selected in the View menu

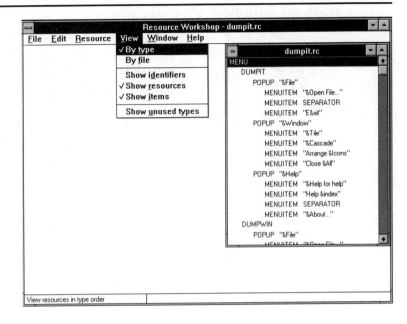

FIGURE 2.4:

The Menu resource using the internal text editor

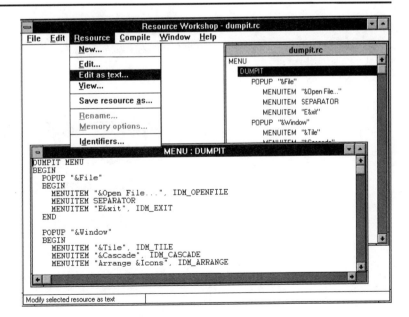

Working with Resource Objects

Working in the project window you can easily cut, copy, paste, delete, and duplicate resource objects. To delete a resource object in the project window, highlight it and press delete. You can't copy and paste a resource object in the same project, but you can duplicate it. To duplicate a resource object:

1. Highlight it in the project window.

2. Choose Duplicate from the Edit menu. The object created will be automatically assigned a name by BRW. For example, if you duplicate a menu, it will be given the name MENU_1.

3. After the new object is created, define a name and an identifier for it by choosing Rename from the Resource menu.

To add resources to your project file, choose the New command from the Resource menu. It opens up the New Resource dialog box, shown in Figure 2.5.

You can then select any of the resources within the list box and be taken to the appropriate resource editor. BRW automatically adds the resource to the project

FIGURE 2.5:

The New Resource dialog box

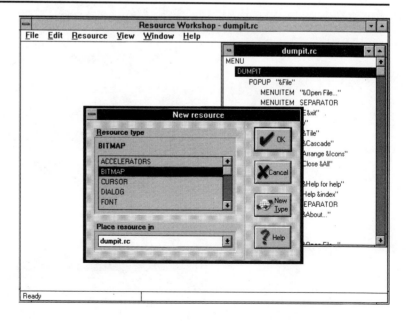

window. This makes it easy to return to the resource once it is created. All you need to do is double-click on the resource in the project window, and the correct editor for that resource type is started with the resource already loaded.

WARNING

If you add a new graphic resource to your project, BRW asks you whether you want it to be in source or in binary format—the two types of graphic resources BRW can create for your program (see Figure 2.6). Graphic resources stored in your .RC file as source code are large and difficult to read, and they are incompatible with other graphic editors, such as Image Editor. When you create a new graphic resource using BRW, you should always specify the binary format (.BMP, .ICO, .CUR, or .FON) that is compatible with the SDK resource editors.

Copying Resources

The easiest way to copy resources from one project to another is to open two copies of BRW. Open up one copy for each project and use the Windows Clipboard to copy the resource from the source project and paste it into the destination project.

FIGURE 2.6:

Deciding on the type of graphic resource

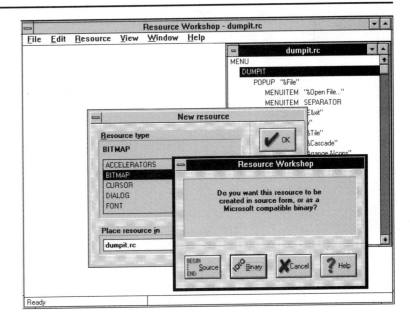

To preserve any identifiers in the resource project, the destination project must have a reference to an identifier file (BRW's term for a C header file). If there is no identifier file open, choose the Add to Project command from the File menu to open one.

Once you choose the Paste command from the Edit menu, the Paste Resource dialog box appears, as shown in Figure 2.7. There must be an identifier file listed in the Paste Identifiers Into edit box for the identifiers to be preserved.

Using Graphic Resources

Bitmaps, icons, cursors, and fonts can be time-consuming to draw using any graphic editor. If you are not the artistic type or if you're just in a hurry to produce an application, there are many places to find existing resources, such as the following:

- Microsoft Windows, which contains a number of nice bitmaps.

- Norton Desktop for Windows, which contains many different icons. Check out the file NDW.NIL.

FIGURE 2.7:

Copying resources from one project into another

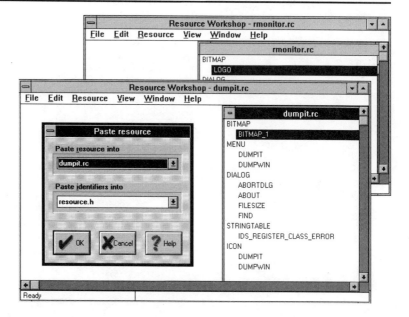

- CompuServe. There are many files within the libraries of CompuServe that provide abundant resources. Most of these files can be found in the Windows application forums WINAPA, WINAPB, WINAPC, and WINAPD. If you are new to CompuServe, it's best to start from the top and browse around using the menus after entering the Microsoft forum (GO MSOFT).

- WINLIB. Published by EMS in Olney, Maryland, and updated quarterly, WINLIB contains more than 40 high-density disks of public domain Windows resources and code. On these disks you will find thousands of icons and hundreds of bitmaps. The disks also contain a growing number of Windows programming utilities, including source code. Information about contacting EMS can be found in the Appendix.

- Visual Basic. This package comes with a vast array of resources.

- Clip art libraries that come with drawing and paint programs from Aldus (Freehand and Persuasion), Computer Support Corporation (Arts & Letters), Corel Systems (CorelDRAW), Micrografx (Designer, Charisma, and Windows Draw), and ZSoft (Publishers Paintbrush).

Using Vector-Based Clip Art

Vector-based clip art can be easily converted to a bitmap and made part of your program's resources. Many of the bitmaps included in the programs on this book's disk set were created this way. One way to convert a drawing to a bitmap is to export it from the drawing program in a bitmap format—preferably .BMP. If the drawing program does not support .BMP, .PCX is almost as good, because you can use the Paint program included with Windows to convert the bitmap to .BMP. If you can export your drawing only to a bitmap format other than .PCX or .BMP—for instance, .TIF—you can use a conversion program, such as Hijaak or DoDot, to convert the bitmap to .BMP. If the drawing cannot be exported to a bitmap format, you can display the drawing at the size, color (16 or 256), and resolution you need using your drawing program, then use Windows' built-in screen capture to make it into a bitmap following these steps:

1. Display the drawing in the color, size, and resolution in which you would like it to be displayed. You may want to consider capturing several versions of the bitmap for your program, such as VGA 16-color, VGA 256-color, 8514 16-color, and 8514 256-color.

2. Press PrintScreen to capture the screen to the Windows Clipboard.

3. Set up Windows Paintbrush correctly for your screen resolution. Choose Image Attributes from the Options menu. When the Image Attributes dialog box appears, set the correct resolution of your screen in Pels. For example, VGA is 640 horizontal by 480 vertical; 8514 is 1024 horizontal by 768 vertical.

4. Choose New from the File menu to start a new picture.

5. Choose Zoom Out from the View menu.

6. Choose Paste from the Edit menu—TWICE—to paste the clipboard into the Paint program. (You must always do this twice; the first time never works—only Microsoft knows why.)

7. At this point you can cut out the piece of the bitmap you want, using either the Pick tool to cut out a rectangular piece or the Scissors tool to cut out an irregular shape. After you have cut out the part you want, use the Copy To command in the Edit menu to save it to a .BMP format file. Using this command instead of Save in the File menu saves only the part of the bitmap you have cut out—not the entire drawing.

Using BRW's Resource Editors

To switch screen resolutions and color schemes, you need to use Windows Setup to change the screen device drivers. It's a bit of work to capture multiple bitmaps of the same image and store them in your program's resources for different display resolutions and color schemes—but your program's users will appreciate this kind of attention to detail.

You can also use BRW to obtain resources from existing Windows programs. For example, if you choose the Open Project command from BRW's File menu and change the file type to .EXE, BRW allows you to decompile the resources out of an existing Windows program. If you do this, I suggest you make a backup copy of the .EXE for safekeeping. You might say that BRW is a hacker's dream, but watch out—there are copyright restrictions on most code.

Figure 2.8 shows a bitmap resource from the decompiled WORKSHOP.EXE (the BRW executable).

You can start any of the BRW resource editors by double-clicking on a resource within the project window. If the resource is a dialog box, menu, accelerator, or

FIGURE 2.8:

A resource from the decompiled
WORKSHOP.EXE

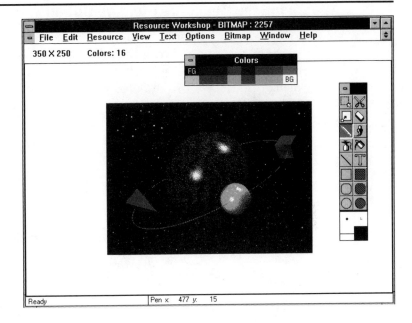

string table, the resource-specific editor opens. If the resource is a bitmap image, such as a font, an icon, or a bitmap, the Paint editor opens. BRW's resource editors are fast and convenient, because everything works within one application.

Using a Text Editor

You can edit the text for the resource script file, as well as have BRW generate it. From the project window, select the resource you want to edit, then choose the Edit as Text command from the Resource menu. BRW opens up the text editor and displays the resource script. Under some circumstances it may be faster to use the text editor. For example, if you wanted to edit a font size directly, it is probably easier to open up the text editor rather than making the same change through a drop-down menu. This is usually not the case, and most of the time you will use one of BRW's visual editors to do your work.

Specifying the Resource Memory Options

Windows resources are read-only data objects managed by Windows for your program. Every Windows data object has memory attributes (or options) to tell Windows how to treat the memory object. BRW does a good job of selecting the default memory attributes for a resource data object, but you can change these attributes if necessary. The memory options for resource data objects are defined as follows:

Load on call	The resource is loaded into memory when Windows needs it.
Movable	Windows can move the resource as needed to conserve memory.
Discardable	Windows can discard the segment from memory and reload it from the .EXE file when necessary.
Pure	This option prevents the resource segment in memory from being modified.

To add a specific memory option to a resource, select the resource in the project window, then Choose the Memory Options command from the Resource menu. The Resource Memory Option dialog box, will be displayed to let you select memory options.

The Identifier File

For applications written in C, the identifier file is generally referred to as a header file and is followed by the extension .H. This file is referenced at the top of the resource script file by the #include directive.

Since Windows requires each resource within your application to have a unique integer called a resource ID, it is common to use the C preprocessor command #define to associate the resource ID with the name you assigned the resource when it was created using BRW. BRW provides a convenient way of defining symbolic constants for resource ID numbers.

To create a header file for your program, choose the Add to Project command from the File menu. After the Add File to Project dialog box appears, you can name your header file. With most simple applications you can give the header file the same name as the application file. For example, the name of the identifier file for the FILEFIND.C application is FILEFIND.H.

Using BRW

In this section, you will learn how to use BRW by examining how it was used to create an application developed for this book—FileFind. As an example of how BRW was used to create bitmaps, we'll look at a bitmap from the CIMS (Corporate Information Menu System) project that's covered fully in Chapter 4.

The FileFind application is a program that searches your disk drive for a selected file. All the files that are used in the FileFind application can be found in the directory \ATOOLS\FILEFIND on your hard drive, created when you installed the book's disk set, so you can easily follow along with this project and examine the resources yourself.

FileFind is a simple one-window application that's shown in Figure 2.9. To find a file, all you need to do is indicate the file specification and the directory to search from. DOS wildcard characters such as * and ? may be used in the file specification.

After you have typed in the directory and the file specification, just click on Go to start your search. When the search is completed, all the files that were found are displayed in the list box at the bottom of the window. If you would like to copy, move, or delete one of these files, click on Options to expand the FileFind window, as shown in Figure 2.10.

With the FileFind window expanded, you can delete a file by highlighing it in the list box and clicking on Delete. To copy or move the file, specify a destination path in the Copy or Move To edit box and click on the appropriate push button.

In creating FileFind, BRW was used to visually design the dialog box template used for the program window and the custom controls inside it, such as chiseled steel outlines, graphic push buttons, the edit controls, and the list box. WindowsMAKER

FIGURE 2.9:

The FileFind application

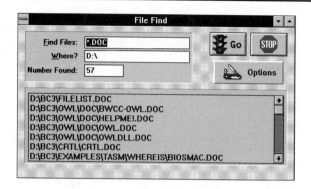

FIGURE 2.10:

The expanded FileFind window

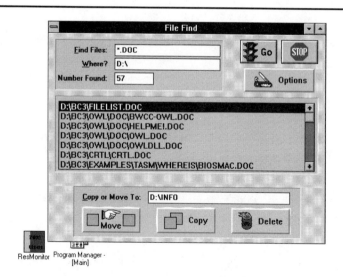

Professional was used to create the C code and other files required for a program template to build upon. In Chapter 4 you will learn how to use WindowsMAKER Professional. For now, let's see how FileFind's resources were created using BRW.

To create the FileFind application resources, I started by first opening a new project file (FILEFIND.RC) and header file (FILEFIND.H). This is the starting point for all applications. When you invoke the New Project command, make sure to choose the .RC extension in the New Project dialog box. Remember, all resources within this application should center around a project file with an .RC extension. The Add to Project command allows you to create your header (identifier) file. Choose the H C Header file type from the File Type drop-down list box in the Add File to Project dialog box. For a project of this size, it is usually a good idea to give your .RC project file and .H header file the same name.

Using the Paint Editor

Bitmaps, cursors, icons, and fonts are four separate resource types with different file extensions, but they are all graphic images. It is this graphical similarity that allows BRW to use one editor, referred to as the Paint editor, for all four resources. The Paint editor uses the same tools and similar procedures for creating each type of graphic resource. By just investigating the Paint editor's Tools palette, you can see it has many features that go beyond what's included with tools such as Image Editor. To make sure you know everything that the BRW Paint editor can do, let's quickly review some of its most important features:

- Unlimited bitmap size. Image Editor is limited to 64x64 bitmaps.

- Support for 256 colors. Image Editor supports only 16 colors.

- Split-screen viewing. This is a feature missing in both Image Editor and Windows Paint.

- Magnification. Whereas Windows Paint has only two levels of magnification, the Paint editor has a variable zoom which provides much more flexibility.

- The ability to put text inside icons, cursors, and bitmaps. This is another feature missing in Image Editor.

Now that we have reviewed the Paint editor's major features, let's discuss how to create bitmaps using the Paint editor, then cover icons, cursors, and fonts.

Creating Bitmaps

The BRW Paint editor is very versatile for creating bitmaps. As long as you have enough memory, you can create bitmaps of almost any size. Depending upon your video adapter, you can create bitmaps with up to 256 colors. To see what the Paint editor can do, let's take a look at a bitmap image created for the FileFind program. Figure 2.11 shows the Paint editor displaying the cartoon bitmap that's used in the FileFind About dialog box.

On the right-hand side of the Paint editor window you see the Tools palette. It is constant for all four types of graphic resources and can be moved or hidden if necessary. The Tools palette is the control panel for the Paint editor, and it contains the following tools:

Airbrush	Paints free-form patterns, much like a can of spray paint.
Empty frames	Draws three types of empty frames: ellipses, rectangles, and rounded rectangles.

FIGURE 2.11:

The Paint editor

Eraser	Reveals the current background or foreground color.
Filled-in frames	Draws three types of filled-in frames: ellipses, rectangles, and rounded rectangles.
Line	Paints straight lines.
Paintbrush	Paints varying-width free-form patterns.
Paint can	Fills in an entire image with a selected color.
Pick rectangle	Selects a rectangular area of your bitmap image for copying, moving, or deleting.
Pen	Paints free-form lines.
Scissors	Selects a nonrectangular area of your bitmap image for copying, moving, or deleting.
Text	Adds text to an image.
Zoom	Increases the magnification of your image, up to 1600%.
Airbrush shape	Invokes a dialog box that lets you choose the current airbrush shape.
Paintbrush shape	Invokes a dialog box that lets you choose the current paintbrush shape.
Pen style	Invokes a dialog box that lets you choose the current pen style.
Pattern	Invokes a dialog box that lets you choose the current pattern.

As you can see, BRW has a much more extensive set of tools than Microsoft's Image Editor does. BRW tools for working with bitmaps match and exceed those included with the Windows Paintbrush program.

Foreground and Background Colors

Each of the controls on the Paint editor's Tools palette can be manipulated with either the left or the right mouse button. The left mouse button selects the foreground color, and the right mouse button selects the background color. You use the foreground color to create lines and boxes on your image. You use the background color for the area behind and around the foreground color.

Paint Editor Menus

Some commands in the Paint editor menus are common among all resources. Others are particular to only one resource. For example, if you are editing an icon, the menu bar contains an icon menu, but if you are editing a bitmap, the icon menu is replaced by a bitmap menu. There are also similarities and differences within each menu, depending on which resource you're working on (for example, the View menu for a cursor versus the View menu for a bitmap). When you work on icons and cursors, the command CGA Resolution (heaven forbid that anyone still uses it!) is added to the View menu so you can see what your cursor or icon looks like in CGA resolution on an EGA or VGA monitor.

TIP   If you ever need to move an image using the Paint editor, hold down the Ctrl key and a hand will appear. You can use the hand to move your image around the editor. If you have ever used Aldus PageMaker, you will be familiar with this approach. In PageMaker the hand is referred to as the "grabber." Try it out and you will find that it's much easier to use than the scroll bars.

To create a new bitmap, choose the New command from the Resource menu. A dialog box appears and asks, "Do you want this resource to be created in source form, or as a Microsoft compatible binary?" As I mentioned previously, I recommend binary. After you choose binary as the bitmap format, another dialog box appears asking you to name the binary image. Once you've named your image, the Bitmap Attributes dialog box is displayed for you to select the bitmap size and the number of colors you want to use for it.

Viewing Your Work   The Paint editor's View menu lets you manipulate the way the bitmap image is displayed. If you want to get into the minute details of an image, you can zoom the image up to 1600%. In Figure 2.12, the bitmap is split vertically and zoomed in on. Notice in the right-hand window an outline around the part of the image that appears enlarged in the left-hand window. This makes it easy to see the changes made on the actual image while you are modifying the enlarged one.

Creating Text   The Paint editor's Text menu lets you add text to a bitmap image. This is easier than actually painting the text into the image. As Figure 2.13 shows, you can use any font available to Windows for working with text using BRW.

The screen in Figure 2.13 was taken from a Windows system that has both TrueType and Adobe Type Manager fonts installed. As shown in the figure, Helvetica Black is being selected as the font for text that will be added to one of the bitmaps in the CIMS program (discussed in Chapter 4). Figure 2.14 shows the text after it was typed in. In this picture the text was typed in twice to create a shadow effect. The first line of text was typed in using black to establish the text shadow. Then the foreground text was typed in using red.

FIGURE 2.12:

Image enlarged using the Paint editor's View menu

FIGURE 2.13:
Selecting a font in the BRW Paint editor

FIGURE 2.14:
Text created using BRW for a bitmap in the CIMS program

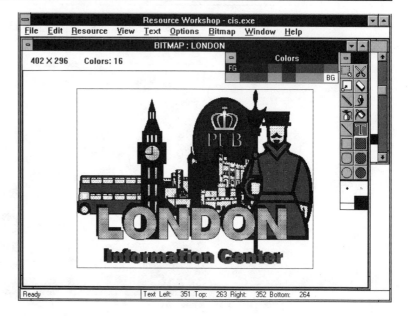

Although I am a pretty good artist when it comes to using Windows drawing programs, I am a novice when it comes to using paint programs. For the bitmap in Figure 2.14, I converted a picture from the Micrografx Designer clip art library to .BMP format. I used the procedure described earlier in the section "Using Graphic Resources." I then added the text "Information Center" using BRW.

TIP
In most paint programs, adding text to an image is a pain, because you can't change the text after it's typed in. Using BRW, this is much easier. BRW gives you a user-configurable number of Undos (the default is ten). If you are not happy with how the text you typed in looks, you can undo it. When you are creating a bitmap, feel free to experiment to get the best results. If you don't like what you did, you can always back up step-by-step using Undo. It's also a good idea to make a backup copy of the resource before you begin to add text—just in case.

The ability to work with text is a feature that BRW excels at but that is missing in Microsoft's Image Editor. You will also find the text-handling capabilities in BRW to be more robust than the features found in Windows Paint. The Paint editor's Text menu provides access to BRW's text-handling functions. Using the Text menu, you can

- align text to the left, center, or right. The text is aligned in relationship to where you initially clicked before typing it in; and

- choose the Font command to display the Select Font dialog box (shown in Figure 2.13) where you choose the typeface, size, and style of the text for any font that Windows is aware of.

Choosing Options

As you create a graphics object using the Paint editor, you need to select fill patterns, brush shapes, and pen styles. All of these functions are found in the Options menu. You can also use functions in the Options menu to align and size selected regions of your graphics object.

As the Menu Varies　Paint editor varies one menu depending upon the type of Windows resource you are editing. The BRW Bitmap menu appears in the Paint editor only when you are working on a bitmap. This menu changes to Cursor when you are working on a cursor and to Icon when you are working on a icon.

The options discussed in the following paragraphs are available on the Paint editor's Bitmap menu when you are working with a bitmap.

Creating Cursors

Cursors are a specialized form of the bitmap resource. The most common cursors in Windows are the pointer that you use when you are working and the hourglass that you watch while you are waiting for something to happen. Figure 2.15 shows one of BRW's cursors being edited. This cursor is the one used to point and click on a topic to get Help in BRW.

An important consideration when you create a cursor is where to put the cursor's active area, or hot spot. The hot spot is a single pixel in the cursor that fixes the location of an action performed when the user places the cursor and presses the left mouse button. The hot spot defines the pixel in the cursor's bitmap that defines the mouse

FIGURE 2.15:

Editing a cursor

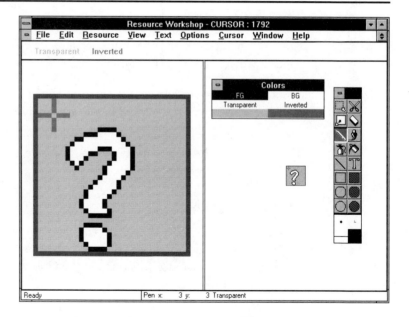

coordinates included as a part of Windows messages, such as WM_MOUSEMOVE, WM_LBUTTONUP, and WM_NCLBUTTONUP. The following steps illustrate how to set a hot spot:

1. Choose the Zoom command in the View menu to zoom in on the cursor image until it's big enough to let you precisely choose the pixel coordinates of the hot spot.

2. Display a grid on the zoomed image.

3. Select the Line tool.

4. Point to the location on the zoomed image where you want the hot spot and look at the coordinates displayed on the right-hand side of the status line. Make a note of these coordinates.

5. Choose Set Hot Spot on the Cursor menu.

6. In the Set Hot Spot dialog box, enter the hot spot's pixel coordinates, as shown in Figure 2.16.

FIGURE 2.16:

The Hot Spot dialog box

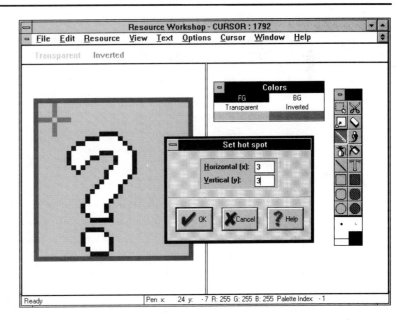

After you have specified where the cursor's hot spot should be, you can test it using the following steps:

1. Choose the Zoom command from the View menu to zoom in on the cursor image.

2. Display a grid on the zoomed image.

3. Select the Paint Can tool.

4. Choose the Test command on the Cursor menu.

5. Move the hot spot to a particular pixel on the zoomed image and click the mouse. The Test cursor disappears and is replaced by the Paint Can tool. If you correctly set the hot spot, the Paint Can tool points to the same pixel your Test cursor pointed to.

Creating Icons

Icons are the images used to represent applications when they are parked at the bottom of the screen. The most common use of an icon is to represent a minimized program. Icon images operate in a slightly different manner from fonts, bitmaps, or cursors. When an icon is selected from the project window, the Paint editor opens up another window, called the Icon window. This window lists different images of your icon, giving you the ability to create a number of different versions of the same icon. For instance, you may want to create a version for monochrome monitors as well as one for color monitors.

I am amazed at the creativity of some people who can make attractive icons using just 32x32 bits and 16 colors. Personally, it's beyond my talents. Instead, I borrow and modify icons. One of the best tools for doing this is the sample Icon Viewer application that's included with Microsoft Visual Basic. It displays all the icons in a directory on your disk and lets you point and click to choose the one you want. You can then copy the icon to the Windows Clipboard and paste it into BRW to work on and to include in your program's resources. Visual Basic comes with a large, attractive set of icons. You can also find many public domain Windows icons in the CompuServe forums, mentioned previously. In Figure 2.17, you can see the icon used in the FileFind application being created in the Paint editor. Notice how you can work on the icon in split-screen mode. One window is for working on the icon in a magnified view; the other is for seeing how the icon will actually appear.

FIGURE 2.17:

Creating an icon using the Paint editor

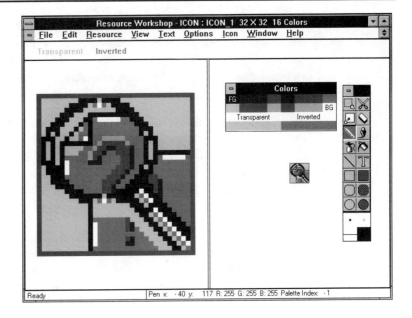

Fonts and the Paint Editor

Although BRW has a Font editor that's superior to the Microsoft Font Editor, I am going to skip discussing it because creating bitmap screen fonts for Windows is quickly becoming a relic of the past. Windows 3.1 includes TrueType vector fonts that are automatically scaled and rasterized for the screen, eliminating the need for creating bitmap screen fonts. Adobe Type Manager (ATM) also provides this feature for PostScript fonts. ATM is an inexpensive product that is included for free with many Windows applications, among them Aldus PageMaker, Aldus Freehand, Micrografx Designer, and Lotus 1-2-3 for Windows.

Dialog Boxes

A medium for presenting and gathering information within the scope of a window, dialog boxes are complicated to create. Dialog boxes are interactive, and they are usually used for obtaining additional input from the user in order to execute a task invoked from a menu.

A dialog box is a form of pop-up window containing various child-window controls. Using either the Microsoft Dialog Editor or BRW, you can specify the size and placement of these controls when you create a dialog box template. With BRW, besides putting standard Windows controls, such as static text, list boxes, edit boxes, radio buttons, and push buttons, in a dialog box, you can also put in custom controls you create yourself (or the custom controls included with BRW).

BRW can also be used to create dialog boxes with a three-dimensional appearance, as for the FileFind dialog box in Figure 2.13. Both BRW and the Turbo C++ for Windows IDE use 3-D dialog boxes. In the following section, we will explore how to create dialog boxes that have a 3-D appearance using the new set of Borland custom controls included with BRW.

The BRW Dialog Editor

The BRW Dialog editor provides a number of tools for aligning, sizing, drawing, and positioning dialog box controls. To start the Dialog editor, choose the New command from the Resource menu. When the New Resource dialog box appears, choose the Dialog item from the Resource Type list box. The Dialog editor can also be invoked from the project window, once a dialog box has been created, by double-clicking on a dialog box name in the window.

When you start the Dialog editor you will see a Tools palette, an Alignment palette, a Caption window, and an empty dialog box. The Tools palette consists of 28 icons that represent dialog box element types and features. Figure 2.18 shows all of the BRW Dialog editor features and the FileFind application dialog box created with them.

The window you will work with the most to create a dialog box is the Tools palette. The left-hand column of the Tools palette puts the Dialog editor in various modes, such as Duplicate or Undo. The two middle columns of the Tools palette contain the tools used to create dialog box controls, such as push buttons and list boxes. The right-hand column provides tools for creating the seven types of Borland custom controls. We will discuss these tools later when you learn how to create dialog boxes with a 3-D look.

The Alignment palette consists of eight icons that allow you to adjust the arrangement of controls within a dialog box. This is very handy if you have one or more push buttons and want to line them up horizontally or vertically. Using the Microsoft Dialog Editor, you need to go through menus to align controls. With BRW all you need to do is point and click.

FIGURE 2.18:

BRW being used to create the FileFind dialog box

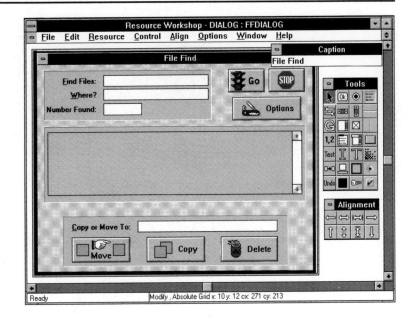

The Caption window lets you add a caption to your dialog box. This can also be done by double-clicking on the dialog box's caption bar or its frame and entering a name in the Caption edit box in the Window Style dialog box that appears, shown in Figure 2.19.

Using the Window Style dialog box, you define dialog box style attributes, such as the caption, the frame border style, the font to be used for dialog box text (here you can choose only one font style and size for all the text in the dialog box—check out the tip following this section to learn how to use multiple fonts inside the same dialog box), whether to use scroll bars, and other features. To learn what these style attributes mean, you should read the Resource Workshop User's Guide or the Windows Programming Reference that comes with your Windows development system.

FIGURE 2.19:
The Window Style dialog box

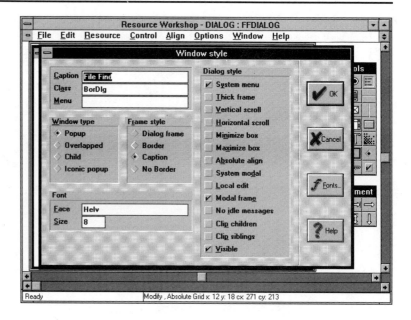

> **TIP**
>
> When you initially design a dialog box using a dialog box editor, you can use only one type and one size of font for the entire dialog box. At execution time, you can change the font and font size for any control in the dialog box. This is done by sending the Control window the WM_SETFONT message, usually when the dialog box function processes the WM_INITDIALOG message. To learn more about how this procedure works, read your Windows Programming Reference discussion of the WM_SETFONT message.

The Tools Palette   The first column in the BRW Tools palette contains the tools that help you to select dialog box controls to work on and define their respective attributes. The following tools for working on dialog boxes and dialog box controls are located in the first column of the Tools palette:

- The *Pick* tool (which is equivalent to the Modify Controls command in the Options menu) lets you choose a control or group of controls within a dialog box. To select a group of controls, you can lasso them by holding down the left mouse button and dragging the mouse to form a rectangle that touches each control. You can also select a group of controls by holding down the Shift key and clicking in turn on each control you want to select. After a group of controls is selected, it may be moved, sized, or aligned.

- The *Tab Set* tool lets you specify which controls are tab stops, so that users can use the Tab key to move to the control. Click with this tool on the controls you want to make tab stops.

- The *Set Groups* tool lets you define a group of controls. You select the controls to put into a group by clicking on them with this tool.

- The *Set Order* tool lets you rearrange the tab order of controls. As you click on each control, you assign a sequence number to it that specifies the tab order.

- The *Test* tool lets you test the controls in your dialog box—just to make sure you set up everything correctly.

- The *Duplicate* tool lets you make multiple copies of a control in an array of rows and columns that you specify.

- The *Undo* tool lets you undo any editing step you perform in the Dialog editor. BRW has a user-configurable, multiple-level Undo.

Windows dialog boxes contain the standard set of dialog box controls that are built into Windows itself. You can also add custom dialog box controls like the ones included with BRW.

The following standard dialog box controls that come with Windows are found in the second and third columns of the BRW Tools palette in the order shown below. Simply use the Pick tool to select the controls and use one of the Alignment tools to position them.

Second Column	Third Column
Push Button	Radio Button
Horizontal Scroll Bar	Vertical Scroll Bar
List Box	Check Box
Group Box	Combo Box

Second Column	Third Column
Edit Text	Static Text
Icon	Black Frame
Black Rectangle	Custom Control

The Custom Control icon (last tool in the third column) brings up the New Custom Control dialog box. Here you can put a control in your dialog box that doesn't fit into any of the predefined window types.

The fourth column in the Tools palette contains the set of Borland custom controls for putting into a "Borland-style" dialog box. We will discuss these controls later when we discuss how to create 3-D–look dialog boxes.

Dialog Box Control Styles   After you place a control within a dialog box, you can double-click on the control to display its Style dialog box. Each different type of control has a slightly different Style dialog box. Figure 2.20 shows the Button Style dialog box.

FIGURE 2.20:

The Button Style dialog box

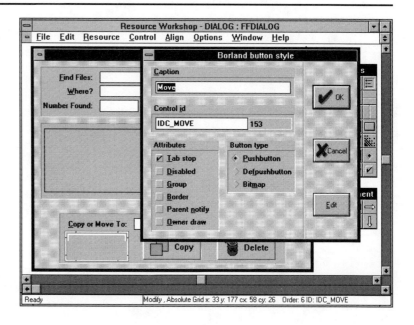

The Options Menu   Most of the commands on the Options menu can also be found on the Tools palette, such as Modify Controls, Set Tabs, Set Groups, Set Order, and Test Dialog. Others, such as Hide Tools, Alignment, and Caption, can be executed by double-clicking on the system menu box of each window. You will find this flexibility throughout BRW. It allows the user to accomplish a task a number of different ways. Some of the commands in the Options menu that you should be aware of are these:

- *Preferences*. This invokes a dialog box that lets you change the number of undo levels, the text editor to use for changing the ASCII resource script file, the include path for C header files, and the multifile save preference.

- *Install Control Library*. This is where you install a dynamic link library (.DLL) file that contains a custom control library. When the .DLL file is installed, the custom controls in that .DLL will be available, just like any standard Windows control.

- *Redraw Now*. This redraws the dialog box. No software tool is perfect—including BRW. Sometimes screen debris may appear in your dialog box, and you need to know if it's really worth worrying about. Redraw cleans up screen debris and can put your mind at ease.

The Align Menu   The Align menu lets you align, size, and rearrange the controls inside a dialog box with the following commands:

- *Align*. This command displays a dialog box that duplicates the functionality in the Alignment palette. (I personally find that the Alignment palette is quicker and easier to use.)

- *Size*. Selecting this control opens the Size Control dialog box, allowing you to resize a single control or group of controls. The easiest way to use Size is to select a group of controls first and then choose the Size command to display the Size dialog box. Then you can change the size of all selected controls to match either the largest or smallest control in the group in height, width, or both.

- *Array*. This command lets you arrange a group of controls that have already been selected into a row, a column, or multiple rows or columns. The outside boundaries of the rows and columns are defined by the outside boundaries of the selected controls.

- *Grid*. This command lets you define a grid on which to align your controls, based on dialog box measurement units inside the dialog box. You can select the desired height and width of the grid as well as use the Absolute or Relative options to control grid snap. You can also optionally display the grid to help you visually align the controls.

Installing Custom Controls

Custom controls can be added to your dialog box, but first they must be installed. They are stored in .DLL files and are available just like any standard Windows control. To add a custom control, choose the Install Control Library command from the Options dialog box. Figure 2.21 shows the dialog box that lets you install a new control library.

Once the library is installed, you can use the Custom command on the Control menu or the Custom Control tool in the Tools palette to add any of the controls to your dialog box.

FIGURE 2.21:

The Install a New Control Library dialog box

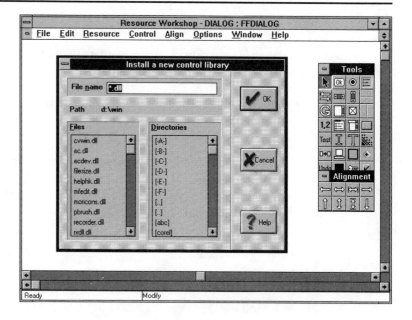

Using BWCC to Create 3-D Dialog Boxes

The FileFind dialog box shown in Figure 2.18 has a 3-D appearance with a new type of check box that comes from the Borland collection of custom controls. FileFind and CIMS use the Borland Workshop custom control (BWCC) dynamic link library (BWCC.DLL) to implement these new custom controls.

BWCC is a collection of custom controls and a custom dialog box window class that implement the look and feel of Borland-style dialog boxes, such as those in Resource Workshop. Let's examine the tools in the right-hand column of the BRW Tools palette—from top to bottom—to see what each type of tool can do.

Gray Panels   Gray panels provide areas that appear to be cut into the "chiseled steel" background. Other controls can be placed on these areas. Gray panels themselves are "static" controls, meaning that the user does not interact with them at runtime.

Dips and Bumps   Dips and bumps (derivation: speed dips and speed bumps) are thin lines that act as horizontal and vertical dividers to separate areas within a dialog box. Dips appear as incised lines, or grooves; bumps appear as raised lines. The Tool palette gives you two buttons, one with a horizontal line and one with a vertical line. Each button can be configured as either a dip or a bump by double-clicking on it to invoke its Style dialog box and selecting either "dip" or "bump" as the style. The default style for both buttons is "dip." Figure 2.21 shows how BRW uses a vertical dip in the Install a New Control Library dialog box to visually separate the push buttons from the rest of the dialog box.

Bitmapped Push Buttons   The next two tools create push buttons that use bitmaps to enhance the behavior of standard Windows push buttons. The first bitmap button can use a 32x32 bitmap as a button. The second one paints a bitmap on top of a button. They both also implement two enhancements over standard Windows buttons:

- An additional level of parent-window notification and control over keyboard focus and tab movement.

- An owner-draw style that allows a programmer to override the look of a standard Windows push button while the push button inherits all other standard behavior.

In addition to push buttons, the second tool implements a "nonpushable button" bitmap style for displaying "splash" images (such as the bitmapped image that appears when you start Resource Workshop). This style is called a "Bitmap."

Seven standard types of better-looking push buttons are included in the BWCC.DLL. They are shown in Figure 2.22.

To select a particular type of push button, specify its symbolic identifier in the control ID field of its Button Style dialog box. To display the Button Style dialog box, double-click on the push button after it has been created. You can use either the integer 1 through 7 or the symbolic identifier shown in Figure 2.22. These identifiers are defined in Borland's version of WINDOWS.H.

Better-Looking Radio Buttons   The radio button tool creates radio button controls that implement the behavior of standard Windows radio buttons and auto-radio buttons, and that provide an improved look. Like the push button tools, it implements two enhancements over standard Windows buttons:

- An additional level of parent-window notification and control over keyboard focus and tab movement.

FIGURE 2.22:

Borland-style push buttons

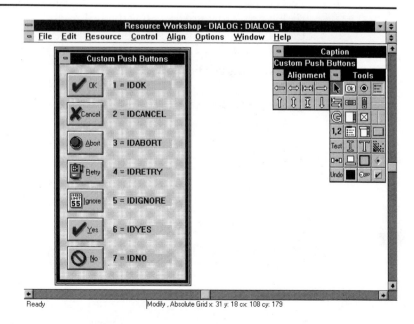

- An owner-draw style that allows a programmer to override the look of a standard Windows radio button while the radio button inherits all other standard behavior.

Better-Looking Check Boxes   These check boxes implement the behavior of standard Windows check boxes and auto-check boxes and look better. Like the push buttons, they implement two enhancements over Windows standard check boxes:

- An additional level of parent window notification and control over keyboard focus and tab movement.
- An owner-draw style which allows a programmer to override the look of a standard Windows check box while the check box inherits all other standard behavior.

Borland's Custom Dialog Box Window Class

All of these better-looking controls will not look as nice in a white-background dialog box. To get Borland's chiseled-steel dialog box, you must use Borland's custom dialog box window class, BorDlg. It does two things:

- It paints the dialog box window background with a brush appropriate to the display device—speckled (chiseled steel) for VGA and above, white for EGA and monochrome.
- It optimizes drawing of the dialog boxes by taking over from the custom controls and drawing them directly on the surface of the dialog box window. This "turbo-painting" allows Borland's dialog boxes to implement a sophisticated look without a sluggish feel.

Customizing Background Color for Standard Controls   When you create dialog boxes using the BorDlg style, almost all the controls, except edit control windows, get painted with a gray background that complements the Borland-style dialog box. If you would like to make edit controls a gray color that matches the other Borland controls, you need to use the WM_CTLCOLOR message. The WM_CTLCOLOR message is sent to the parent of a system-defined control class or a message box when the control or message box is about to be drawn. The following controls send this message:

- Combo boxes
- Edit controls

- List boxes

- Buttons

- Static controls

- Scroll bars

If an application processes the WM_CTLCOLOR message, it must return a handle to the brush that is to be used for painting the control background or it must return NULL. The WM_CTLCOLOR message is sent to the parent window for all control types except dialog boxes. To change the background color of a single-line edit control, the application must set the brush handle in both the CTLCOLOR_EDIT and the CTLCOLOR_MSGBOX message codes, and the application must call the SetBkColor function in response to the CTLCOLOR_EDIT code. For example, let's create a gray brush and pass the handle of the brush to a single-line edit control in response to a WM_CTLCOLOR message:

```
static HBRUSH hbrGray;

switch(msg) {
 case WM_INITDIALOG:
  // Create a gray brush
  hbrGray = CreateSolidBrush(RGB(192, 192, 192));
  return TRUE;
 case WM_CTLCOLOR:
  switch(HIWORD(lParam))
   {
   case CTLCOLOR_EDIT:
    // Set the background to gray
    SetBkColor((HDC) wParam, RGB(192, 192, 192));
    return (LRESULT) hbrGray;
   case CTLCOLOR_MSGBOX:
     // For single-line edit controls, this code must be
     // processed so that the background color of the format
     // rectangle will also be painted with the new color.
    return (LRESULT) hbrGray;
   }
  return (LRESULT) NULL;
}
```

Creating the 3-D FileFind Dialog Box

Creating the FileFind dialog box using BWCC is easy. Follow these steps to get everything to work:

1. Use the Resource Workshop Dialog editor to lay out your dialog boxes.

   - Double-click the dialog box caption to bring up the Windows Style dialog box, then type "bordlg" in the Class text box. Your dialog box now will display the "chiseled steel" background on displays with VGA or better resolution.

   - Use the Borland-style controls from the rightmost column of the Tools palette for your dialog box controls. If you select a Borland push button and want to make it an OK, Help, or Cancel button, double-click on the button to display the Borland Button Style dialog box, then enter IDOK, IDHELP, or IDCANCEL as the control ID.

2. Put the following code in your program to make sure the BWCC.DLL gets loaded. This code should be executed before you try to use any of the Borland-style dialog boxes.

```
{ // Programmer inserted code to load Borland Library for
//custom controls
 HANDLE hBorlandDLL;
 hBorlandDLL = LoadLibrary ("BWCC.DLL");
 if (hBorlandDLL < 32)
   MessageBox (NULL, "Error loading Borland Custom Control  }
// End programmer code
```

You should also make sure to free the .DLL, using the FreeLibrary Windows function call, when your program terminates.

3. Make the dynamic link library BWCC.DLL available for your application to use at runtime. For Windows to find it, it must be in one of the following places:

   - The same directory as your application's .EXE file
   - The Windows startup directory
   - The Windows system directory
   - A directory on your PATH

Creating Custom Push Buttons

I bet at this point you're wondering how I created the custom push buttons for Stop, Go, Options, Move, Copy, and Delete. Creating your own custom bitmap buttons is just a little more work than creating standard push buttons. BRW uses a very simple numbering scheme to map a button's control ID in a dialog box to the resource IDs of its bitmaps. For each bitmap button, there are six images—three for EGA and monochrome devices and three for VGA and higher-resolution devices. The control ID becomes the base from which BRW derives the resource IDs of the button's bitmaps, using the following formulas:

```
ControlId + 1000: Normal VGA-resolution image
ControlId + 3000: Pressed VGA-resolution image
ControlId + 5000: Focused VGA-resolution image
ControlId + 2000: Normal EGA-resolution image
ControlId + 4000: Pressed EGA-resolution image
ControlId + 6000: Focused EGA-resolution image
```

Figure 2.23 shows a bitmap I created for the Go button in FileFind that was given the control ID 1151.

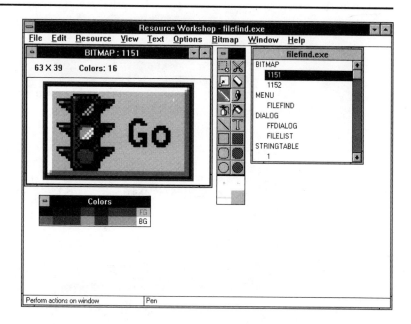

I borrowed the outline for the button by copying it from BRW itself. The traffic light came from one of the Traffic icons included with Visual Basic. I used the Visual Basic sample application Icon Viewer to copy the icon to the Windows Clipboard. I then pasted the icon bitmap into my button bitmap in BRW. I added the text for the button using BRW.

The numbering scheme is the critical issue here. In this example, the control ID for the bitmap I created is *1151*. When I created the Borland-style push button, I gave it the control ID *151*. This specifies the bitmap for the push button control as a normal VGA-resolution image.

NOTE The information presented in this section about how to create 3-D–style dialog boxes was completely omitted from the BRW User Guide. To find out more details of how all of the BWCC custom controls work, you should print out and read the file BWCCAPI.RW, found in the \DOCS directory that is in the directory where you installed your Borland development system. Not all of the documentation in this file was completely clear, and it took a lot of experimenting to find out how all this works and present this information to you. Although here I haven't gone into all the detail contained in BWCCAPI.RW, I believe you will find the preceding section more understandable than BWCCAPI.RW.

Now that we have creating dialog boxes under our belt, let's take a look at how to use BRW to create menus.

Menus

Menus provide a list of program commands that can execute actions or call submenus with additional commands. Most Windows applications have their own menus, represented by names in the menu bar at the top of the application window. In Windows you select a menu and then choose a command from that menu. The command carries out the action. BRW makes it easy to create these menus by providing you with the Menu editor.

The Menu Editor

To invoke the Menu editor, choose the New command from the Resource menu and select the Menu resource from the list box. The editor provides you with the means to create, edit, and test menu resources. It operates by constructing three panes. The Outline pane is where the menu table is constructed. When you add menu items, pop-up commands, and separators, they appear in this pane as pseudo code. In the Dialog Box pane you specify information about the currently highlighted item in the outline. The Test menu pane displays your menu and lets you test it. As you'll see in the next sections, these three panes provide you with all the flexibility you need to create extensive menu resources.

To see how menus work, let's use DumpIT as an example again. DumpIT has two menus in its .RC file. Figure 2.24 shows you what the Menu editor looks like when the DumpIT DUMPWIN menu is displayed.

The Outline Pane   The lower-right pane in the Menu editor is the Outline pane. As I mentioned previously, it displays the menu items, pop-up commands, and separators of the new menu. The first line in the pane tells you the name of the menu, followed by indented statements defining each item on the menu.

FIGURE 2.24:

The Menu editor

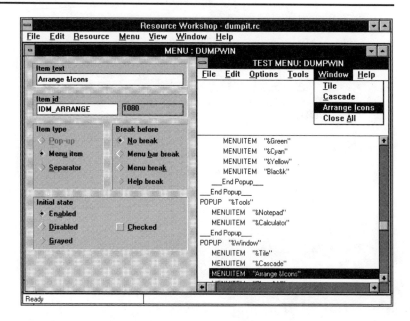

The Outline pane does not show how the exact menu resource appears in the resource script file, but it gives you a general outline of the menu structure.

When the Menu editor is invoked, the Outline pane will include one pop-up menu with one menu item. This is your starting point for a menu. You can edit these two lines and add more functionality by using the Menu menu.

The Dialog Box Pane   The Dialog Box pane, on the left-hand side of the Menu editor, gives you the ability to change a menu item's text, identifier, item type, state, and break information:

- The *Item Text* is what the user of your application sees on the display screen. If you want to add an underscore to the activation character for an item entry, add an ampersand character (&) in front of the key character.

- The *Item ID* is the integer value or the name associated with the integer value from the identifier file.

- The *Item Type* is selected automatically depending on the line selected in the Outline pane.

- The *Break Before* control lets you specify the way the menu items appear to the user. If you want to move the menu to the far right of the menu bar, use the *Help Break* control. Select this option only for top-level menu items. You may want the menu to appear horizontally across the screen; select *Menu Break* or *Menu Bar Break*, depending on whether you want line separators. I like to use the plain approach with the *No Break* control.

- The *Initial State* control enables, disables, grays, or puts a check mark next to your menu item.

The Test Pane   The Test pane is located above the Outline pane. It lets you display and test each menu as it is created. If this pane is active, it even lets you test the activation characters specified in the Dialog Box pane with the ampersand character.

Menu Editor Menus

As described previously, the BRW menus change depending on the type of resource you are editing. When you use BRW to work with menu resources, you should become familiar with both the Menu and the View menus.

The Menu Menu   When you first start the Menu editor, there is only one pop-up menu and one menu item defined. You use the Menu menu on the BRW main window menu to add more pop-up menus, menu items, and menu separators to your menus, as well as adding standard File, Edit, or Help pop-up menus to the menu resource. It also provides you with the means to test your menu for duplicate IDs. Following is an explanation of each of the items on the Menu menu:

- *New Pop-up*. This command inserts a new pop-up menu below the line that's currently highlighted in the Outline pane.

- *New Menu Item*. This command inserts a new menu item below the line that's currently highlighted in the Outline pane.

- *New Separator*. This command inserts a new separator below the line that's currently highlighted in the Outline pane.

- *New File Pop-up*. This command inserts a standard file pop-up menu below the line that's currently highlighted in the Outline pane.

- *New Edit Pop-up*. This command inserts a standard edit pop-up menu below the line that's currently highlighted in the Outline pane.

- *New Help Pop-up*. This command inserts a standard edit pop-up menu below the line that's currently highlighted in the Outline pane.

- *Check Duplicates*. This command tests your menu at any time. The test menu is updated as you make changes to your menu, so you can test changes as often as you want. If there are duplicates, the Menu editor displays a message box with the message "Duplicate command value found." When you close this box, the Menu editor highlights the statement in the Outline pane that contains the duplicate value. You can type a new value in the Item ID input box.

The View Menu   The View menu gives you the ability to display the Menu editor's panes in two different configurations, and the ability to display the Test menu either as a pop-up or on the menu bar. Following is a brief description of each command on the View menu:

- *View as Pop-up*. This command controls whether the Test menu is displayed on the menu bar or as a pop-up menu. Select this command if you are developing a menu as a separate resource, such as a floating menu.

- *First Graphic*. This command represents the default configuration of the three panes. It puts the Dialog Box pane on the left, the Test menu on the upper-right, and the Outline pane on the lower-right.

- *Second Graphic*. This command is the alternate configuration of the three panes. It puts the Test menu at the top of the window and the Dialog Box and Outline panes underneath. This is useful if you have more pop-up commands than fit into the Outline pane.

Accelerators

Accelerators are hot keys for issuing application commands. Using an accelerator is the same as choosing the command on a pop-up menu. A WM_COMMAND or WM_SYS-COMMAND message gets created either way. Since accelerators are resources, they must be stored in a format referred to as an accelerator table. Each entry in the table refers to one hot-key sequence.

The Accelerator Editor

The Accelerator editor provides a means to store accelerator key and code information in an application resource. To start the editor, simply choose the New command from the Resource menu and select Accelerator from the list box. Figure 2.25 shows how accelerators for DumpIT can be created.

The right-hand pane of the editor's screen is the Outline pane. The top line in the pane gives the name of the accelerator table, and each line following shows an accelerator table entry. There are two parts to each of these entries; the first is the actual key (virtual or ASCII) and the second is the item ID of the command the accelerator is connected to.

NOTE If the accelerator is to represent a command on a menu that is already created, use the same identifier as you used for the menu command.

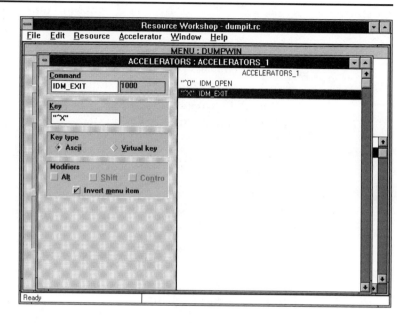

The left-hand pane of the Accelerator editor's screen is the Dialog Box pane. This shows the accelerator information about each table entry as the table entry is selected in the Outline pane. You can change the information manually or use the Key Value command on the Accelerator menu to change the value of the key.

ASCII and Virtual Keys   A virtual accelerator key typically doesn't produce a character. It is more like a function key or an arrow key. To utilize virtual keys you must use the standard Windows identifiers that represent certain keys. These identifiers are defined in WINDOWS.H. Examples of virtual keys are VK_UP, VK_DOWN, and VK_F1. Virtual keys allow the use of the Ctrl, Shift, and Alt combinations but do not provide a separate virtual key identifier for each. If you want to use these keys, turn on the appropriate Modifier check box in the Accelerator editor dialog box.

An ASCII key is a displayable key (examples: a-z, @, 6). It appears in the Key input box surrounded by quotation marks. I do not suggest that you use ASCII characters as accelerator keys unless you combine them with Alt or Ctrl.

If you use the Key Value command on the Accelerator menu, you do not need to type the Virtual Key or ASCII identifiers manually. When you press the appropriate key, either the Virtual Key identifier or the ASCII character appears, surrounded in quotes.

The Accelerator Menu   The Accelerator menu provides you with the means to add a new item to the table, change the Key Value mode, and check for duplicate keys.

String Tables

String tables contain status messages, error messages, systems messages, and window captions. Because the string table is a resource and is a separate part of the executable, strings can be edited and translated without the program's source code being affected. As with all Windows resources, it also allows the string to be loaded into memory when needed.

Because of the way Windows loads strings into memory, it is wise to group all string resources within the resource script file. Windows loads 16 string segments at a time. For example, if your application calls on string ID 3, then strings 0 through 15 are loaded into memory. For this reason, if associated strings are grouped together, Windows has to do fewer loads, which reduces memory overhead.

Some of the advantages of using string tables are the following:

- It's a good programming practice always to isolate all ASCII text outside of a program, instead of inside it. String tables make this easy and convenient.

- Putting string text in resources eliminates space from your program's stack and heap, reducing its execution-time size.

- Putting text in string tables makes it easier to have a program's text translated to a foreign language—and BRW makes it easier for a nontechnical translator to do the job.

BRW provides you with a convenient way to group and manipulate string resources. It is the String editor.

The String Table Editor

The String Table editor displays a string table in three columns. The first column is the ID Source. It can be an integer ID or an alphanumeric identifier that stands for an integer. The second column is the ID Value. This value is the integer that represents the string. If an alphanumeric identifier is listed as the ID Source, the value in the second column will always contain the integer associated with the identifier. The third column contains the string. It can be no longer than 255 characters. Figure 2.26 displays the string table resource for DumpIT.

The String Table Editor Menus Because the string table is a very simple concept, it has few options. The String Table menu consists of all the commands necessary to add, delete, and edit a string, as well as a command to undo your most recent changes. The Resource menu contains the Memory Options command, as it always does. The memory options for a string should always be set to Load On Call, Discardable, and Movable.

User-Defined Resources

What would you do if you needed a string to be more than 255 characters in length (the maximum for a string table entry)? The answer is: create a User-Defined Resource. For example, you may want a message box with a paragraph or two in it to appear when a user first invokes your program.

FIGURE 2.26:
The DumpIT string table resource

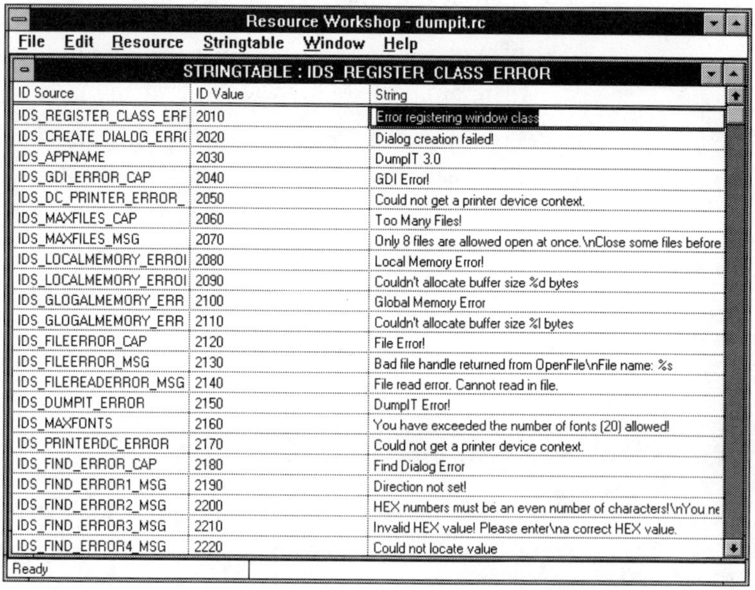
Resource Workshop - dumpit.rc
File Edit Resource Stringtable Window Help
STRINGTABLE : IDS_REGISTER_CLASS_ERROR
ID Source
ID Value
String
IDS_REGISTER_CLASS_ERF 2010 Error registering window class
IDS_CREATE_DIALOG_ERR(2020 Dialog creation failed!
IDS_APPNAME 2030 DumpIT 3.0
IDS_GDI_ERROR_CAP 2040 GDI Error!
IDS_DC_PRINTER_ERROR_ 2050 Could not get a printer device context.
IDS_MAXFILES_CAP 2060 Too Many Files!
IDS_MAXFILES_MSG 2070 Only 8 files are allowed open at once.\nClose some files before
IDS_LOCALMEMORY_ERROI 2080 Local Memory Error!
IDS_LOCALMEMORY_ERROI 2090 Couldn't allocate buffer size %d bytes
IDS_GLOGALMEMORY_ERR 2100 Global Memory Error
IDS_GLOGALMEMORY_ERR 2110 Couldn't allocate buffer size %l bytes
IDS_FILEERROR_CAP 2120 File Error!
IDS_FILEERROR_MSG 2130 Bad file handle returned from OpenFile\nFile name: %s
IDS_FILEREADERROR_MSG 2140 File read error. Cannot read in file.
IDS_DUMPIT_ERROR 2150 DumpIT Error!
IDS_MAXFONTS 2160 You have exceeded the number of fonts (20) allowed!
IDS_PRINTERDC_ERROR 2170 Could not get a printer device context.
IDS_FIND_ERROR_CAP 2180 Find Dialog Error
IDS_FIND_ERROR1_MSG 2190 Direction not set!
IDS_FIND_ERROR2_MSG 2200 HEX numbers must be an even number of characters!\nYou ne
IDS_FIND_ERROR3_MSG 2210 Invalid HEX value! Please enter\na correct HEX value.
IDS_FIND_ERROR4_MSG 2220 Could not locate value
Ready

To create a user-defined resource you must first create a type for it. To do so, follow these steps:

1. Choose the New command from the Resource menu.

2. When the New Resource dialog box appears, press the New Type push button.

3. When the New Resource Type dialog box appears, give the new resource a name.

4. When you are asked if you want to assign an identifier to the new resource, answer Yes, because this is how Windows and your program identify this new resource.

5. Choose OK in the New Resource dialog box so BRW can open up the text editor and you can begin to add the data for your resource. Figure 2.27 shows how to create a user-defined ASCII text resource.

FIGURE 2.27:

The user-defined resource

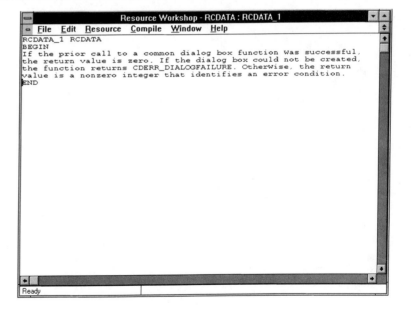

Summary

The Borland Resource Workshop provides you with the easiest and most powerful way to create and modify Windows resources. It is more than just a set of resource editor utilities. It gives you a means of gathering, maintaining, and copying resource elements as well as compiling and decompiling applications. It can also create header files, providing a link between the integer values returned by resource elements. Overall, I believe it is the best tool in its category.

This chapter discussed how to automate the process of creating a Windows application resource script file (.RC). The next chapter takes us one step further, discussing how to use CASE:W Corporate Edition to automate the process of creating the application source code (.C).

CHAPTER
THREE

Using CASE:W and QuickC for Windows

- Using QuickC for Windows with CASE:W

- Comparing QuickCase:W and Case:W Corporate Edition

- Building DumpIT using Case:W AND QuickC for Windows

- Guidelines for using CASE:W

- Evaluating the C code that CASE:W generates

In this chapter we will learn how a GUI builder, a point-and-click application generator, can make the process of building a Windows application easier. GUI builders create C source code programs that can be used with all the following development environments:

- QuickC for Windows

- Microsoft C/C++ Version 7 (which includes the Windows 3.1 SDK)

- Borland C++ (and Turbo C++)

- Other Windows development systems, such as Zortech C++

Currently, there are many different GUI builders available. Some of the most notable ones are

- QuickCase:W, developed by CASEWORKS Inc. and included with Microsoft QuickC for Windows;

- CASE:W Corporate Edition, CASEWORKS Inc.'s upgrade to QuickCase:W;

- WindowsMAKER Professional from Blue Sky Software; and

- ProtoGen and ProtoView by ProtoView Development Corp.

GUI builders can take a lot of the drudgery out of Windows programming. It is much more fun to design the user interface shell for a Windows program by drawing it on the screen with the mouse and having a GUI builder generate the C code for you than to be spending your time writing the C code for managing menus and dialog boxes. A GUI builder lets you concentrate your C coding skills on building functionality into your program—as well as putting in graphics pizzazz.

As helpful as GUI builders are, you should also be aware of their drawbacks. The GUI builders from CASEWORKS, for example, can serve as excellent training tools for novice Windows programmers, but they still require that you know every aspect of how a Windows program works. If the C code generated by a GUI builder fails, you need to be able to debug it in order to get your program running. You also need to know how to write a Windows program that will correctly attach your C code to the C code generated by the GUI builder.

GUI builders are not flexible in the way they generate your application code. For example, an application built with a GUI builder inherits the characteristics of the application generator. When you examine such a program, you can tell not only that a GUI builder was used to create it, but exactly which one was used. Furthermore, GUI builders may not write code the way you or your organization likes. For instance, the GUI builders developed by CASEWORKS still use the old slash-asterisk style comments instead of the double-slash style. I also found that CASE:W defines variables that are not used in the program.

In this chapter, we will examine and work with the GUI builder CASE:W Corporate Edition for QuickC for Windows. We will also compare CASE:W Corporate Edition with its entry level version, QuickCase:W, to detail CASE:W's additional functionality. For brevity's sake, I'll refer to CASE:W Corporate Edition from now on simply as CASE:W and to QuickC for Windows as QuickC.

Using QuickC with CASE:W

The flowchart in Figure 3.1 illustrates the process of building a one-window application using CASE:W with QuickC. The process is the same for both Quick-Case:W and CASE:W. Although it looks complicated when diagramed like this, many of its complexities are hidden from you by QuickC's development environment. This is OK when everything works the way it is supposed to. However, when things go awry, it's essential that you understand how the process works.

The figure shows the process for building a one-window application. However, CASE:W can also build multiple-window and Multiple Document Interface (MDI) Windows applications, as we will learn in our project later on in this chapter.

Setting Up a Working Directory

When you start to create a Windows application by building it from scratch or by using a GUI builder, you should set up a working directory to put all your application files in. As you create icons, cursors, bitmaps, dialog boxes, and C source code files, put them all in the same directory. Simply stated, one directory equals one Windows application. By keeping all the application files for one Windows application in the same directory, you avoid confusion and mistakes while you are developing your application.

FIGURE 3.1:

The development process using
CASE:W with QuickC

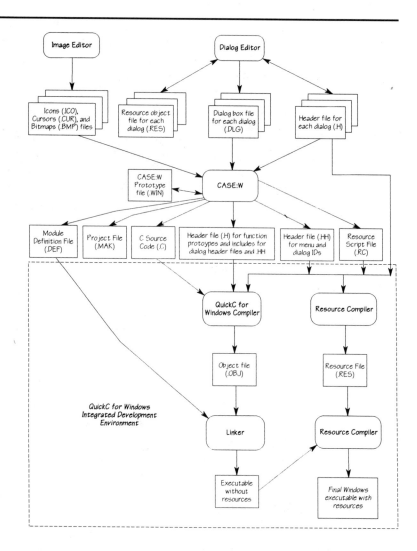

Starting Your Project

To start a project, you create your user interface using the Image Editor and the Dialog Editor included with QuickC, or the ones that come with the 3.1 SDK. The Dialog Editor includes a toolbar for editing control properties and a floating toolbox to create dialog box controls. New features also include alignment and spacing of groups of controls.

The Image Editor provides you with a grid and a floating toolbox to help you create graphic resources. While the Image Editor is easier to use than SDK Paint, included with the Windows 3.0 SDK, it does not contain as many significant new features as the new Dialog Editor. Both the Dialog Editor and the Image Editor now include context-sensitive help. As you learned in the previous chapter, Borland Resource Workshop (BRW) is more powerful than the Microsoft resource editors. For most of my projects, I use BRW instead of the Microsoft tools.

TIP

QuickC's Dialog Editor and Image Editor are upgraded versions of the tools included with the 3.0 SDK. They were upgraded again with the 3.1 SDK, so if you have a choice you should use the ones that come with the 3.1 SDK instead of those included with QuickC.

Using the Dialog Editor

When you save a new dialog box, the Microsoft Dialog Editor creates three files:

- a resource file (.RES) in binary format, which can contain multiple dialog boxes;

- a source dialog box file (.DLG) that may be processed by both CASE:W and the resource compiler. These matched files may contain multiple dialog box descriptions; and

- a header file with the constants defined for control IDs defined in the dialog box. This file is not created if you don't define any control IDs for the dialog box in the .RES file.

There are several important points to remember when using the Dialog Editor to create dialog boxes for use in CASE:W. They are:

- When you create a dialog box using the Dialog Editor, put each dialog box in separate .DLG and .RES files. To do this choose New from the File menu each time you start a new dialog box design. If you don't do this the Dialog Editor puts the source code for all your dialog boxes in the same .DLG and .RES files. CASE:W works with only one dialog box in a .DLG file.

- When you specify control IDs in the Dialog Editor, it creates a header file (.H) for your dialog box. This header file must be saved with the same file prefix as the .DLG and .RES files. For instance, if you name the .RES file SAVEAS.RES (the .DLG file gets saved for you automatically with the same name), you should name the header file: SAVEAS.H.

- No dialog box's name may match the name of the application. A name match causes a conflict in header file names used in the application.

- In CASE:W, if you want to create your own application header file (instead of using the ones created by Dialog Editor), choose Generate Options from the User Files submenu in the Options menu to display the User Defined Files dialog box. Then type in the name of your header file in the Header File edit box.

- CASE:W names each dialog box resource using the dialog box file name— regardless of the internal name specified for the dialog box when it was created using the Dialog Editor.

- The Dialog Editor can read resource files only in binary format (.RES), not source code format (.DLG). You need to keep the individual resource files for each dialog box to be able to open and modify dialog boxes with the Dialog Editor. If you accidentally delete an .RES file for a dialog box, do the following, using the Dialog Editor, to build a new .RES file:

  1. Open the .RES file for the application and save it using a new name for the .DLG file.

  2. Select each dialog box you want to delete by choosing Select Dialog in the Edit menu, and then delete it.

  3. After deleting all the dialog boxes except for the one you want, save the dialog box.

  4. Rename the .RES file with the name of the dialog box resource file you accidentally deleted. Don't use a dash (-) character when you specify the file name for resources such as icons and bitmaps. CASE:W doesn't flag this as an error, but the resource compiler doesn't accept file names with a dash in them, and it generates errors when they are encountered.

Using the Image Editor

Using the Image Editor is much easier than using the Dialog Editor. You create only one type of file for each type of graphic resource that can be processed by the Windows development tools such as Image Editor, CASE:W, and Borland's Resource Workshop. You should save all your icons, cursors, and bitmaps in the working directory so you can find them easily when you are building your program prototype using CASE:W.

Using CASE:W

CASE:W is an interactive prototyping tool for creating Windows applications. After creating the dialog boxes and graphical resources (cursors and icons) for your application, you use CASE:W to draw your program's user interface. CASE:W saves this information in a .WIN file—a CASE:W file that describes the attributes of your application.

When you start CASE:W, you see the CASE:W window with a blank application window inside it, as shown in Figure 3.2.

FIGURE 3.2:

Starting a new Windows application prototype using CASE:W

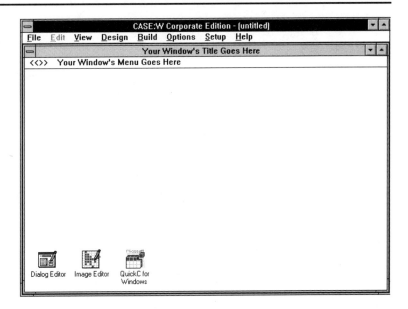

CASE:W is somewhat object-oriented. You assign a title to your application by double-clicking the mouse on the title bar and responding to the dialog box that appears asking you the title of your new application. When you click with your mouse on the symbol <<>> in your application's menu bar, a dialog box appears with which you set up the menus for your application. Using CASE:W's graphical user interface, you create user interface objects for your program, such as

- pull-down menus;

- cascading menus linked to a pull-down menu;

- multiple types of windows. CASE:W supports the Windows Multiple Document Interface (MDI). You can create as many different types of windows as your application design requires; and

- window attributes such as color, frame style, and scroll bars.

CASE:W does not include a dialog box editor to create dialog boxes or a graphics editor to create application graphic resources such as icons, bitmaps, and cursors. You'll need to use the tools included with your Windows development system to create these application objects. CASE:W is designed to work with your Windows development system either as just another programming tool or as the focal point for building your application. It lets you run other Windows programming tools from its application generator workbench. Just choose Add Tools in the CASE:W Setup menu to configure the Windows programming tools you want to use from CASE:W. As you can see in Figure 3.2, I have my CASE:W system configured to run the Dialog Editor, the Image Editor, and QuickC. All I need to do is double-click on a tool's icon to run it. I can also use the Tool command in the Build menu to run the tool of my choice.

> **NOTE**
>
> Both the Dialog Editor and the Image Editor support multiple instances. To avoid confusion and mistakes, make sure you don't have another instance of one of these tools running before you start it from either CASE:W or QuickC.

Creating Relationships between Application Objects

After you have created the user interface objects for your application, you'll want to establish relationships between the objects. CASE:W lets you create and modify relationships between application objects using its graphical point-and-click user interface. Using CASE:W you can

- link icons and cursors to windows;

- link menu items to application objects such as dialog boxes, MDI windows, secondary windows, and user-defined functions; and

- link dialog box buttons to application objects such as other dialog boxes or user-defined functions.

Using Extended Code Support

CASE:W offers Extended Code Support that generates the C code to handle dialog boxes. Although the code support is basic, it is helpful in building your application. You can use Extended Code Support to associate dialog box controls to associate with application variables and with data structures. You can also use it to specify whether or not a field is required and to perform basic input validation: numeric, alphabetic, alphanumeric, integer, floating-point numbers, dates, and currency.

Receiving and Offering Help

CASE:W offers you help in two ways: on-line help to guide you in using CASE:W, and a feature that includes help in the application you are building. CASE:W automatically builds the Help file for the Windows application you are creating when you turn the Help feature on. All you need to do is choose Help System from the Additional Support submenu in the Design menu. The Help file CASE:W generates is in Rich Text Format (RTF) with the indexing already created. All you have to do is fill in the blanks with a word processor that supports RTF, such as Microsoft Word for Windows, WordPerfect for Windows, or Ami Professional.

Creating Consistent Applications

Although you and I know how to build a Windows user interface that is consistent with other Windows applications, there are software developers who don't know how. CASE:W comes to the rescue for these developers by letting them validate their application as they are building it against IBM's System Application Architecture (SAA) Common User Access (CUA) standard. CUA validation is turned on by default. To turn it off choose CUA Validation in the Options menu. If this feature is turned on and you violate a rule, dialog boxes appear to let you know where you have gone astray. I find the SAA/CUA validation feature very helpful, because it warns me about all the user interface mistakes I make when creating applications.

Since Microsoft and IBM have parted ways, Microsoft has rewritten the CUA specification based on IBM's standard. Microsoft's version, titled *The Windows Interface: An Application Design Guide,* is different from IBM's, but not entirely. If you use CASE:W CUA validation and want to follow Microsoft's CUA standard, you should become familiar with the new version that is included with the 3.1 SDK. Ultimately, an updated version of CASE:W will support the new Microsoft CUA standard as well as IBM's.

Testing Your Application User Interface

After you have created your first application prototype, you can test your application without compiling it by choosing the Test command in the CASE:W View menu. The CASE:W simulated execution lets you test all the different aspects of your application's user interface. The ability to test user-defined functions is the only limitation of CASE:W Test mode.

Generating Your Application

When you are ready to create your program, CASE:W generates the following files for you:

- C program source files (.C).

- An application header file (.H) that includes the other header files required by the application and the function prototypes for the application.

- An additional header file (.HH) that includes the menu and control ID constants for the application menus and dialog boxes.

- A resource script file (.RC) that contains the source code for all the dialog boxes included in the application by CASE:W. The dialog box file source code generated by the Dialog Editor is incorporated in the .RC file and is not referenced by the QuickC development environment.

- A project file (also called a make file, .MAK) that tells the QuickC development environment which files make up the application and indicates their dependencies among each other for controlling the program building process.

- A module definition file (.DEF).

You should become familiar with each of these file types and their contents while you are building a Windows application using CASE:W and QuickC. It will help you isolate problems in building your application if you understand what each file type is for.

A common source of programming problems using CASE:W and QuickC is header files. Sometimes header files get overwritten during the course of development and don't contain what they were intended to. I personally recommend using your own header file—instead of the one generated by CASE:W—to avoid problems in creating your Windows application.

Additional CASE:W Features

Besides the features already mentioned, CASE:W includes two features to help you code your program for working with scroll bars and dialog boxes. Using CASE:W you can define the range for window scroll bars and automatically generate the code to handle the scroll bar messages sent to the window. Although this is simple coding, it saves you some tedious work.

CASE:W also lets you use dialog boxes as templates for putting control windows in the client area of any child or MDI window. This is a very valuable feature that can be a real time-saver in creating an application. CASE:W doesn't generate any code to handle the control windows for you after they are created, but it saves you the effort of manually calculating the location and size of control windows and writing the C code to create them.

Building a CASE:W Application Prototype with QuickC

After building and generating an application prototype using CASE:W, you open the project (.MAK file) created by CASE:W with QuickC , and compile and run the application using the QuickC development environment. At this point, your program displays only the user interface created with CASE:W—you still have to use QuickC to add functionality to the user interface code generated by CASE:W.

Besides speeding up the user interface design process, CASE:W eliminates the chore of creating a basic Windows program structure. CASE:W generates the Win-Main, window procedures, and basic routines of a Windows application. As most Windows programmers know, you seldom start a Windows program from scratch. You usually take another Windows program you have already written, strip it down to the essentials you need, and start coding to add the new functionality. With CASE:W you can start with the source code of an application that already reflects the user interface design you are heading toward.

The code that CASE:W generates is straightforward and clean. It includes function prototypes in header files besides the declarations of global variables. The resource script file contains string tables for all the program text, including error messages.

CASE:W generates comprehensive comments that are inserted in your C program source code. There are three levels of control over comments in the generated code: low, moderate, and high. *Low commenting* produces only brief comments. *Moderate commenting* produces descriptive program and function headers as well as comment prompts telling you the correct place to insert your own code. *High commenting* adds much more detail and extended comments to explain all the Windows API calls.

CASE:W's most notable features are its code clarity and the comments it produces, but it still has some flaws. It uses traditional function headers and braces, and the comment delimiters are still the traditional slash-asterisk style. I personally find the double-slash style easier to read and less prone to cause error.

Using Projects

CASE:W Corporate Edition comes in a version designed to work with the Windows SDK, as well as the version that works with QuickC. These two versions are almost identical, with the following exception.

The QuickC project file is automatically maintained for you by CASE:W and QuickC. You choose options in QuickC for your application project file, using buttons in a dialog box to specify program memory model (QuickC supports small, compact, medium, and large memory models for Windows applications), compiler warning levels, and optimizations. You choose the files to include in your application project file by selecting them from a list.

CASE:W Corporate Edition for the Windows SDK, on the other hand, lets you specify these options using CASE:W. CASE:W then generates the make file for using Microsoft C and the Windows SDK to build your application. These features were deleted from CASE:W Corporate Edition for QuickC, because they can be easily specified using dialog boxes in the QuickC development environment.

If you start a new project using QuickC (instead of using CASE:W), QuickC automatically prompts you to create a new project file. Creating a project file is fairly easy. First, you use a directory list box to change to the appropriate directory, then select the type of files you want to add to the project (*.C, *.H, and so on) from a combo box. QuickC lets you specify option settings for both debug and release versions of your program, as well as directory paths used by the linker and compiler. You no longer have to worry about setting DOS environment variables for the location of header, library, and Help files. You can either accept the default setup defined when QuickC is installed or define new settings for each project.

To set the compiler and linker options using QuickC, choose Project from the Options menu to display a dialog box from which you select the executable program type (Windows Executable or Windows Dynamic Link Library). You can also use this dialog box to invoke other dialog boxes for setting compiler and linker options. These dialog boxes let you select the memory model, compiler warning level, program optimizations, and whether debugging information is generated in your program.

QuickC project files are compatible with NMAKE, which comes with Microsoft C/C++. If you are currently using the old-style Microsoft C 5.X make file syntax for your development projects, you need to use QuickC to create a new project file or convert your old make file to the new NMAKE syntax supported by Microsoft C 6.0 and QuickC.

NOTE
Microsoft C/C++ Version 7 will build applications using the QuickC make file, but QuickC does not support all the Microsoft C/C++ 7 make file features. If you plan to use Microsoft C/C++ 7, you should create a Microsoft C/C++ 7 make file in addition to the QuickC make file.

Building Your Program

After you have opened an application project you generated in CASE:W and selected all the program options using QuickC, you build your program using the QuickC IDE. Using your project (.MAK) file to guide it in building your application, QuickC executes the integrated C source code compiler, resource compiler, and linker to build your Windows application. During application building, a dialog box is displayed to show you the status of the process and which component (compiler, resource compiler, or linker) is executing, as shown in Figure 3.3.

FIGURE 3.3:
Building a Windows application using QuickC

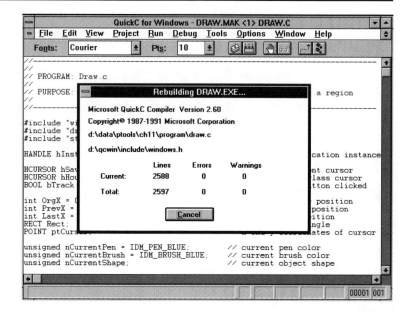

Comparing QuickCase:W and CASE:W

As mentioned earlier, QuickCase:W is included with the QuickC for Windows development environment, and CASE:W Corporate Edition for QuickC for Windows is a product upgrade that can be ordered from CASEWORKS. QuickCase:W does not handle all the nuances of a complete Windows application. You can only create applications with one window, and you cannot put custom controls in the window. You must add these features to your Windows application by creating the code to support them in C. Neither CASE:W nor QuickCase:W relieves you of having to understand how to write a Windows application—they just make some of the tedious, time-consuming work easier. Using a GUI builder is not a substitute for Windows programming knowledge.

The upgrade to CASE:W Corporate Edition is well worth having for the following additional features that QuickCase:W doesn't provide:

- The ability to prototype and generate multiple-window applications, including Multiple Document Interface (MDI) applications.

- The ability to test your program's user interface while you are creating it without generating the application source code and compiling it. With Quick-Case:W you have to generate your application and then build it using Quick C before you can see how it works.

- The ability to prototype and generate source code for linking individual control windows with application variables and user logic. Using QuickCase:W, you can attach only menu items to program objects.

- The ability to use dialog boxes as templates for putting control windows inside a program window.

- The ability to monitor the creation of the user interface to insure that your application follows the industry standard Common User Access (CUA) interface design specifications.

- Extended Code Support to create dialog box procedures for having your dialog boxes perform basic editing functions.

- The ability to generate the program hooks and RTF files to implement Windows Help for your application. (This feature alone will save you enough time-consuming work to justify the purchase price of CASE:W.)

- A message browser to customize Windows procedures to support additional Windows messages.

Now that you have learned what CASE:W can do, let's take a tour of this GUI builder by seeing how it can be used to build a Windows application.

Building a Windows Application Using CASE:W and QuickC

To understand how CASE:W works, we'll look at a project that I developed for this book—a Windows file dump application called DumpIT. This project covers the basics as well as providing tips for using CASE:W. In the project, I will show how I took a simple one-window file dump application and beefed it up with additional features by using the GUI design and C code generating facilities of CASE:W.

Before we start, let's look at the FileDump application that I used as a starting point for this project. FileDump is a basic one-window application that displays a file's contents in both hexadecimal and ASCII, as shown in Figure 3.4.

FIGURE 3.4:

The one-window FileDump application

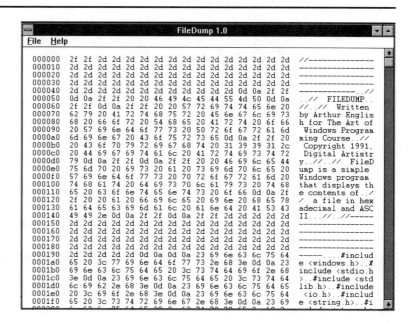

FileDump displays one file at a time in its main window. It uses the new Windows 3.1 common dialogs dynamic link library to

- get the user to supply the file name to display when the new `GetFileOpen-Name` Windows function call is used, and

- let the user change the font in which the file is displayed using the new `ChooseFont` Windows function call.

Planning the Project

As you can see, FileDump is a very simple program. Since CASE:W gives me many new application capabilities that weren't available when I first created FileDump, I decided to make a better FileDump renamed DumpIT to test how well CASE:W can be used to build useful Windows applications. I decided to add the following new features to FileDump to create DumpIT:

- Multiple Document Interface (MDI). DumpIT can display up to eight files at once in MDI child windows—as long as there is enough global memory to hold the files.

- A File Size dialog box to display the file sizes of all the files currently being displayed by DumpIT.

- A Find dialog box to search for data in a file using either an ASCII text or a hexadecimal search string. This dialog box is not fully functional in DumpIT 2.0. I left it the way it was to show how much (and how little) CASE:W Extended Code Support does for you to generate code for dialog box functions. This feature is fully functional in DumpIT Version 3.1, which will be discussed shortly.

- Easy access to the Calculator and Notepad programs included with Windows from the DumpIT menu and from push buttons in the DumpIT File Size and Find dialog boxes, so you can takes notes and do calculations about the file you are examining.

- Context-sensitive Help using the Windows Help facility. I left the Help file created by CASE:W in the state that CASE:W generated to show you exactly what CASE:W is capable of doing. For DumpIT 3.1, I completed the Help file so you would have a full-featured hex dump utility.

Figure 3.5 show the finished product, DumpIT for Windows. As you can see, DumpIT now sports a new user interface that can display multiple files at once with the option of using a unique font for each window.

You will find DumpIT on your book's disk set. All the files that were used for this project are in the directory \ATOOLS\DUMPIT2. Now that you know what DumpIT 2.0 does, let's see how DumpIT was created and how much using CASE:W helped the project.

NOTE

You will notice that there is also a directory named \ATOOLS\DUMPIT31 that was created when you installed your disk set. This directory contains an enhanced version of DumpIT, named DumpIT Version 3.1. This version was created using the source code from DumpIT Version 2, and it contains more features than are covered here in this chapter. While both versions of DumpIT include all the source code files, DumpIT Version 3.1 includes the following additional features:

DumpIT 3.1 can print the contents of the file as well as display it. DumpIT 3.1 also lets you set up the printer by choosing Setup Printer in the File menu. Both of these functions use Windows 3.1 common dialogs.

DumpIT 3.1 lets you choose the color scheme for individual child windows by selecting the color from the Options menu.

DumpIT 3.1 uses the AppendMenu Windows function to list the last four files opened in its File menu. It keeps track of these file names by storing them in an .INI file, along with other user-specified information.

DumpIT 3.1 has a new command—Go To Address—in its Edit menu.

Borland Resource Workshop was used to build DumpIT 3.1's 3-D–type dialog boxes.

The Dumpit 2.0 Help file contains only what CASE:W created, so you can see exactly what's generated. In DumpIT 3.1, I revised the Windows function calls to Windows Help and used RoboHELP to create the Windows Help file. Using the code from DumpIT 2.0, I completely reorganized and rewrote DumpIT 3.1, using the new Windows 3.1 "STRICT" coding style. I also used the new Windows 3.1 message crackers and macro APIs found in WINDOWSX.H. By rewriting DumpIT 3.1 in this fashion, I made the source code completely portable to Win32. You will learn more about the new STRICT coding style and the WINDOWSX.H macro APIs in Chapter 12, "Creating Robust Windows Applications."

FIGURE 3.5:

DumpIT for Windows

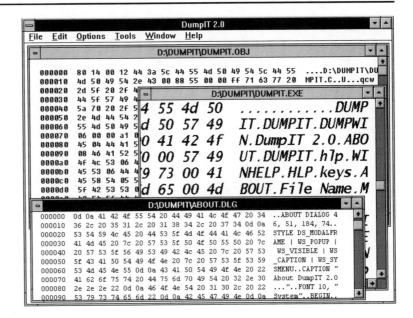

Preparing FileDump to Be Reused

CASE:W can be used to build your initial application and regenerate it without disturbing the source code you add to the application. This lets you create a Windows application and still use CASE:W to modify and add to your program's user interface after you have added your own source code. However, this feature should not be relied on too heavily, because it makes program maintenance more difficult (which code did CASE:W write and which code did the programmer develop?) and forces CASE:W to do more work when it is regenerating the application.

When you develop a Windows application using CASE:W (or any GUI builder), you should follow three strategies:

• Keep the code you develop as separate as possible from the code generated by CASE:W. Use function calls to interface the CASE:W code to your code, and put your code in separate source code files. For the DumpIT project, the CASE:W code is in DUMPIT.C and DUMPIT.H. The source code I developed is in CUSTCODE.C and CUSTCODE.H.

- Include comments along with the C source code you add to the CASE:W-generated code to identify it as source code that you developed and not CASE:W's.

- Use some kind of version control program.

To prepare FileDump for integration into the prototype I was developing with CASE:W, I removed all inline C source code from the main window procedure and put it into functions called by the window procedure. I also put this source code in a separate C source code module named CUSTCODE.C. During this process, I removed all the local variables from the window procedure and made them either local to the function they were in or global.

The following listing shows the FileDump main window procedure with all inline code replaced by calls to functions located in the CUSTCODE.C source code module.

```c
//-------------------------------------------------------------------
//
//   WndProc - This function processes the messages sent to the File Dump
//             window procedure. The program has one window and one
//             window procedure.
//
//-------------------------------------------------------------------
long FAR PASCAL WndProc (HWND hWnd, WORD Message, WORD wParam, LONG lParam)
{
    switch (Message)
    {
    case WM_COMMAND : // Process menu commands
        switch (wParam)
        {
        case IDM_OPEN :
            DoWmfileOpen (hWnd);
            break;

        case IDM_ABOUT : // Display About dialog box
            DoWmAbout (hWnd);
            break;

        case IDM_FILESIZE : // Display the size of the file in decimal and hex.
            DoWmFileSize (hWnd);
            break;

        case IDM_FONT : // Let the user choose a different font
```

```
        DoChooseFont (hWnd);
        break;

    case IDM_EXIT : // Outta here!
        PostQuitMessage (0);
        break;

    default :
        break;
    }
    break;

case WM_CREATE : // Process WM_CREATE message
    InitializeFont (hWnd);  // Initialize font metrics for window
    break;

case WM_SIZE :
    ResetScrollBars (hWnd);
    break;

case WM_VSCROLL : // Process vertical scroll bar messages
    DoWmVScroll (hWnd);
    break;

case WM_HSCROLL :    // Process horizontal scroll bar messages
    DoWmHScroll (hWnd);

case WM_PAINT : // Paint the window
    DoWmPaint (hWnd);
    break;

case WM_DESTROY :
    DoWinCleanup (hWnd);
    break;

default :
    return DefWindowProc (hWnd, Message, wParam, lParam);
}
return OL;
}
// End of WndProc
```

During this process I realized that I was rewriting FileDump the way it should have been designed in the first place. By rebuilding FileDump into a more modular and flexible program, I eliminated redundant code and variables and made the C source code more portable for reuse in other applications. Because of disk space limitations I did not include FileDump on the disk set, but I did include the source code in DumpIT versions 2.0 and 3.1.

Now that FileDump is ready to be dismembered and rebuilt as DumpIT, let's see how CASE:W built the user interface C code used as the shell in which to put the functional C code from FileDump.

Creating DumpIT Using CASE:W

In order to follow the process of creating the user interface prototype application for DumpIT, refer back to Figure 3.1, which shows how the process of building a CASE:W application works. This figure serves as a road map for developing CASE:W applications using QuickC. The process is similar for creating CASE:W applications with Microsoft C/C++ 7.0 and Borland C++. As the figure shows, the first step in building a Windows application with CASE:W is creating dialog boxes and other resources. Let's skip over how to build an icon and look at the dialog boxes that are used in DumpIT.

Dialog Boxes

DumpIT uses both dialog boxes created with the common dialogs feature introduced in Windows 3.1 and custom ones created with the Dialog Editor. Windows 3.1 provides the following functions for using common dialogs:

CommDlgExtendedError	Retrieves error data
ChooseColor	Creates a color-selection dialog box
ChooseFont function	Creates a font-selection dialog box
FindText	Creates a find-text dialog box
GetFileTitle	Retrieves a file name
GetOpenFileName	Creates an open-filename dialog box
GetSaveFileName	Creates a save-filename dialog box
PrintDlg function	Creates a print-text dialog box
ReplaceText	Creates a replace-text dialog box

Using common dialogs helps you in two ways:

- Your application is more consistent with Windows and other Windows applications. By using common dialogs, your application is easier to learn and use.

- Common dialogs require less C code to support. To build a full-featured File Open dialog box takes about 150 lines of C code. In contrast, using common dialogs you can provide more functionality with only 30 lines of C code.

DumpIT 2.0 uses two common dialog functions: GetOpenFileName and ChooseFont. For finding text in a file, I did not use the FindText common dialog function for two reasons: I wanted to use a customized Find dialog box that would let you switch between searching for ASCII or for hexadecimal search strings; and I also wanted a moderately complex dialog box to use for example purposes, to show how CASE:W extended code support works with dialog boxes.

The custom dialog boxes created for DumpIT using the QuickC Dialog Editor are About, File Size, and Find. The Find dialog box is shown being created using the Dialog Editor in Figure 3.6.

FIGURE 3.6:

Creating the Find dialog box using the QuickC Dialog Editor

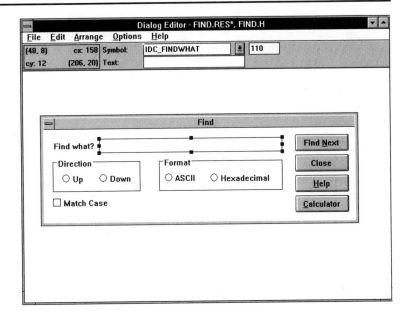

Designing the MDI Child Window

After you have created all your application resources, it's time to use CASE:W to create your Windows application. Building a multiple-window application with CASE:W is more complex but follows the same process for building a simple one-window application shown in Figure 3.1. You build one CASE:W prototype file (.WIN) for each application window. For instance, an MDI application with two different types of MDI child windows would require three different CASE:W prototype files—one for the MDI frame window and one for each different type of MDI child window. If you have not worked with MDI Windows applications before, you should read the next section, "MDI Application Structure."

MDI Application Structure

MDI is a user interface standard for displaying and managing multiple documents within a single application. An MDI application has one main window, called the *frame window,* within which the user can open and work with several documents. Each document appears in a *child window* in the frame window. Each child window has a frame, a system menu, maximize and minimize buttons, and an icon—allowing the user to work with it just as if it were an independent window. However, since the window is a child window, it cannot move outside the frame window.

The frame window of an MDI application is similar to that in most Windows applications. It differs from a normal main window, however, because its client area is filled by a special child window, called the *client window,* which is similar to a standard control such as a push button.

Because Windows maintains the MDI client window and controls the MDI interface for your program, an MDI application needs to store very little information about the user interface. Your application uses the client window but doesn't need to provide code that defines how the window appears or behaves.

To the user the client window is invisible, providing a background upon which the child windows appear. Your application defines the MDI child windows; they look like the main window, having window frames, system menus, and minimize and maximize buttons. The main difference to the user is that each child window contains a separate document; also, the child windows cannot move outside the client window. You can also have different types of MDI child windows, specified by different window classes. Refer to Figure 3.5 to see the child windows in the MDI application, DumpIT, built for this chapter.

In general, an application controls the MDI interface by passing messages up and down the hierarchy of MDI windows. The MDI client window, which Windows controls, carries out many operations on behalf of the application.

Initializing an MDI Application

An MDI application needs to be initialized differently than a normal Windows application. Although the overall process is the same, an MDI application requires that you set certain values in the window class structure. To initialize an MDI application, you first register its window classes. You then create and display any windows that will be initially visible. In DumpIT two different types of window classes are registered:

- A window class for the application's MDI frame window. The class structure for the frame window is similar to the class structure for the main window in non-MDI applications.

- A window class for the application's MDI child windows. The class structure for the MDI child windows is slightly different from the structure for child windows in non-MDI applications. An application may have more than one window class for its MDI child windows if there is more than one type of document available in the application.

NOTE The application does not register a class for the MDI client window. It is defined by Windows and therefore does not need to be registered.

The class structure for MDI child windows differs from that for normal child windows in the following ways:

- The class structure should have an icon, because the user can minimize an MDI child window as if it were a normal application window.

- The menu name should be NULL, because MDI child windows cannot have their own menus.

The class structure should reserve extra space in the window structure. This lets the application associate data, such as a file name, with a particular child window. In DumpIT the pointer to the locally allocated data structure that contains the set of variables associated with each file being displayed is stored in the window data structure maintained by Windows.

Creating the Windows

After registering its window classes, your MDI application can create its windows. It first creates its frame window using the CreateWindow function. Then it creates its client window using the CreateWindow function. MDICLIENT, a preregistered window class defined by Windows, should be specified as the client window's class name. MDICLIENT is the lParam parameter to the CreateWindow function and should point to a CLIENTCREATESTRUCT data structure.

The MDI Application Message Loop

The main message loop for an MDI application is similar to a normal message loop, except that the MDI application uses the TranslateMDISysAccel function to translate child window accelerators. The system menu accelerators for an MDI child window are similar to accelerators for a normal window's system menu. The difference is that child window accelerators respond to the Ctrl key rather than the Alt (Menu) key.

The Frame Window Procedure

The frame window function for an MDI application is similar to a normal application's main window function. However, there are a few differences:

- Instead of passing on messages that are not processed to DefWindowProc, an MDI frame window procedure passes messages to the DefFrameProc function.

- Your MDI frame window procedure should pass WM_SIZE messages to Def-FrameProc, which handles them by resizing the MDI client to fit into the new client area. The application can calculate a smaller area for the MDI client if it chooses to allow room for status or ribbon windows.

DefFrameProc will also set the focus to the client window when it sees a WM_SET-FOCUS message. The client window sets the focus to the active child window, if there is one. As illustrated in DumpIT, the WM_CREATE message causes the frame window to create its MDI client window.

DumpIT's frame window procedure is called FrameWndProc. Its handling of messages is similar to that of non-MDI applications. WM_COMMAND messages in DumpIT are handled by DumpIT's frame window procedure, which calls the DefFrameProc function for command messages DumpIT does not handle. If DumpIT did not do this, then the user would not be able to activate a child window from the Window menu, since the WM_COMMAND message sent by selecting the menu item would be lost.

The MDI Child Window Procedure

Like the frame window function, MDI child window functions use a special function for processing messages by default. All messages the child window function doesn't handle are passed to the DefMDIChildProc function rather than the DefWindowProc function. In addition, some window-management messages (such as WM_SIZE, WM_MOVE, WM_GETMINMAXINFO) must be passed to DefMDIChildProc, even if the application handles the message, in order for the MDI interface to function correctly.

Associating Data with Child Windows

Since the number of child windows varies depending on how many documents the user opens, the MDI application must be able to associate data (for example, a pointer to the current file buffer loaded into memory) with each child window. When DumpIT registered the class of the MDI child window, it reserved extra space in the window structure for a far pointer to a locally allocated data structure that contains all the program variables associated with the window. To store and retrieve data in this extra space, DumpIT uses the functions GetWindowLong and SetWindowLong.

Creating Child Windows

To create an MDI child window, the application sends a WM_MDICREATE message to the MDI client window. (The application must not use the CreateWindow function to create MDI child windows.) The lParam parameter of a WM_MDICREATE message is a far pointer to a structure called an MDICREATESTRUCT, which contains fields similar to CreateWindow function parameters.

Destroying Child Windows

To destroy an MDI child window, use the WM_MDIDESTROY message. Pass the child window's window handle in the message's wParam parameter.

> **TIP**
>
> If you use CASE:W, you might want to set the comment level to High. You can do this by choosing the Comment Level command in the Generate Options submenu in the Options menu. The Comment Level dialog box will be displayed to let you select either Low, Moderate, or High comment levels. A comment level of High will put a detailed tutorial on Windows programming into your C source code.

Making DumpIT an MDI Application

Application design done with CASE:W should be done from the bottom up. In the old days of structured software design, we always had to conceive of how things worked from the top down. Now with object-oriented systems, such as CASE:W, sometimes we have to work bottom up. This means that you should design your MDI child windows first because that is where most of the application functionality resides.

The DumpIT menu automatically changes to reflect the state of the application, so that only the menu commands that are available for a specific program state or mode are displayed. This helps the user by displaying only what the user can do, not what he or she can't. Thus, when you start DumpIT, you will notice that there is a limited menu when you start the program that provides menus only for File, Window, and Help: the only actions you can take when you start the program are to open a file or get help. After you open you first file the menu expands to include File, Edit, Options, Window, and Help. The File menu expands to include two new commands, File Sizes and Close.

The limited and the expanded menus are each associated with a window in the CASE:W design. The first menu you encounter is associated with the MDI frame window, which we will look at later. The expanded menu is associated with the MDI child window that we are about to examine in more detail.

As I discussed in the section on MDI application structure, the MDI child window is the focus of your programming activity for a Windows application. When you design this window using CASE:W, you specify its attributes and what the application menu looks like when the child window is active.

Designing DumpIT's Window

In the CASE:W Design menu you will find two submenus, Window and Additional Support. Both of these submenus are cascaded to access more commands. The Window submenu gives you access to CASE:W functions, including the following, for selecting window attributes:

- *Style* lets you select window style attributes, including options for selecting (or not) a menu bar, a system menu, minimize and maximize buttons, whether the window is redrawn when sized, and other style attributes that can be specified in the CreateWindow function call.

- *Title* lets you define the text appearing on the Windows title bar.

- *Icon* lets you define the window icon to be used when the window is minimized. If the window being designed is an MDI child window, this icon will be the one shown in the MDI frame window when the child window is minimized. If the window being designed is the frame window, the icon defined will be the one used for the application.

- *Cursor* lets you select the cursor to be used for the window.

- *Colors* lets you select a background color for the window.

- *Scroll Bars* lets you define whether or not the window uses scroll bars and what the scroll bar range is.

- *Size and Location* lets you specify the size and location of the window when it is created.

- *Message Support* lets you select the messages you expect the window to process. This way you let CASE:W add them to the window procedure switch case statement instead of writing the code yourself.

- *MDI Frame* lets you specify whether or not a window is an MDI frame window.

When I started to design the MDI child window for DumpIT, I first pulled down the Design Window submenu and went straight down the list of commands. The Style dialog box lets you choose the style bits for the window, as shown in Figure 3.7. CASE:W gave me the default style I wanted—a title bar, a system menu, minimize and maximize

FIGURE 3.7:

Selecting window styles for the MDI child window

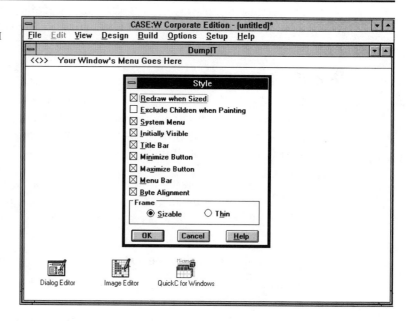

buttons, a menu bar, having the window redrawn when sized, and child clipping.

Next, I double-clicked on the application title bar in the CASE:W prototype window—a CASE:W object-oriented shortcut. This displayed a dialog box from which I selected the title bar caption, instead of using the Title command in the Window submenu. I then selected the icon for the DumpIT MDI child window by choosing the Icon command in the Window submenu to display the Window Icon dialog box, as shown in Figure 3.8. The Window Icon dialog box allowed me to browse my disk to locate an icon to attach to the child window.

WARNING

Although disk-browsing is a nice feature on the surface, I don't recommend it. Instead, you should copy all the files you need into one work directory for your application. If you do use browse and you specify another directory for an icon, CASE:W puts the full file name, including the icon's directory, in your resource script file. If you move files around and the resource compiler can no longer find your icon in the specified directory, you will get a compile error. As I stated earlier, one directory equals one Windows application.

FIGURE 3.8:

Choosing an icon for the MDI child window

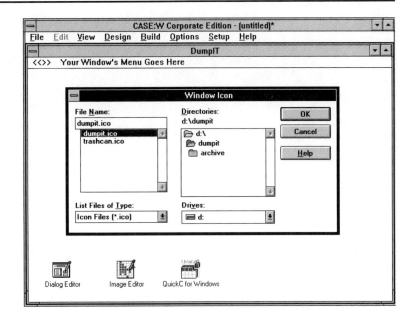

To create DumpIT, I went through the rest of the commands in the Window menu in sequence. I let the defaults apply for Cursor, Colors, and Size and Location. I made sure that the child window would have scroll bars, but I set a range of ten that I knew I would never use, because I would end up replacing the CASE:W code to manage the scroll bars with the C code I was reusing from my FileDump application.

After working my way through the Window menu in the Design menu, I turned to the Additional Support submenu. This submenu contains options that let you attach unlinked dialog boxes and unlinked secondary windows to the main window of the application. You can also select a dialog box to be used as the About box for your application. Figure 3.9 shows the Additional Support submenu during DumpIT's creation. Help has just been selected as an option for the DumpIT application.

The Additional Support submenu lets you set many different options that can have a powerful effect on the application you create. The CASE:W options in the Additional Support submenu are described in the following sections in the sequence they appear in the submenu.

FIGURE 3.9:

The Additional Support submenu

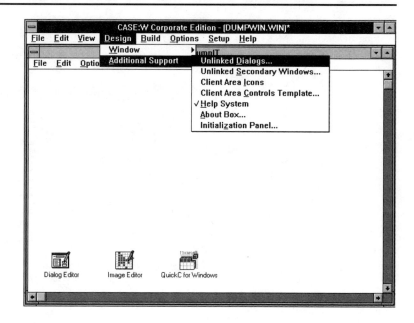

Unlinked Dialog Boxes

Unlinked dialog boxes are ones not linked to a menu command, a client area icon, or a dialog box push button. CASE:W generates all code necessary for an unlinked dialog box, except for the call to bring it up. The code to invoke the dialog box is generated within comments, so you can easily move it to the desired location in your program.

Unlinked Secondary Windows

Unlinked secondary windows are not linked to a menu command, a client area icon, or a dialog box push button. CASE:W generates all code necessary for an unlinked secondary window, except for the call to bring it up. Except for MDI child windows, the code to invoke the window is generated within comments, so it can be moved to the desired location in your program.

Client Area Icons

Client area icons can be placed anywhere in the client area of your window. These icons act like the Tools icons in the client area of the CASE:W prototype window shown in Figure 3.2.

Client area icons can be linked to the following types of application objects:

- Menu item
- Dialog box
- Secondary window (including a Windows program)
- User-defined code

Client Area Controls Template

The Client Area Controls Template dialog box allows you to choose a dialog box to be used as a template for creating control windows in the client area of the window you are creating. This option provides you with a method of placing controls directly in the client area of your main window. When you tell CASE:W to fill the client area with controls, CASE:W presents a list of .DLG files. You select a dialog box, and CASE:W extracts only the control window definitions from it. If you select Client Area Controls, CASE:W generates the code to create the control windows for you by using the CreateWindow function call to Windows.

You can also attach icons to the client area. For instance, if you had an icon representing a calculator, you could position it in the client area of the main window and tell CASE:W to invoke the Windows Calculator, CALC.EXE, when the icon is double-clicked on. Linking icons to actions is the equivalent of linking menu items to actions. I personally prefer to use owner-draw push buttons instead of icons, because they give the user the visual feedback that the object was clicked on, whereas CASE:W icons don't.

Help System

CASE:W is capable of generating a complete Help system for your application. It will generate support for the Help manager that is a part of Windows. This support includes source code in your .C and .RC files, a Help project file (.HPJ), a Help header file (.HH), a compile statement in your application make file, and the Help text source file (.RTF). The actual Help text for your application can be added to the

.RTF file with a Rich Text Format editor, such as Microsoft Word for Windows, as shown in Figure 3.10.

Help is generated by CASE:W for each of the menu bar and pull-down menu items in your application, and for any dialog boxes that have a Help push button. You can add Help push buttons to dialog boxes using the Dialog Editor, and CASE:W will generate the links automatically for them to invoke Help. CASE:W also automatically generates the Help menu that is included on your application menu bar—so you don't have to code it yourself.

In a multiple-window application such as DumpIT, a Help file is generated for each window. Each set of Help files (.RTF and .HPJ) must be compiled by the Microsoft Help compiler for the Help system to function correctly. It is up to you to fill in the blanks for each section of the RTF Help file to explain how your Windows application works. Figure 3.11 shows the Windows Help manager displaying the .HLP file for the DUMPWIN window.

FIGURE 3.10:

Editing the RTF Help file generated by CASE:W with Microsoft Word for Windows

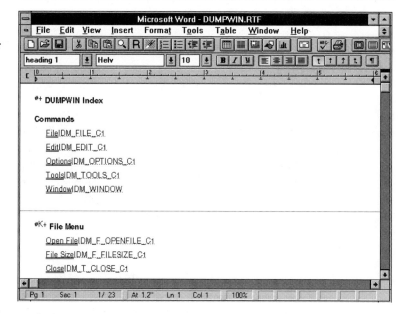

FIGURE 3.11:

Windows Help using the
DUMPWIN.HLP file generated by
CASE:W for DumpIT

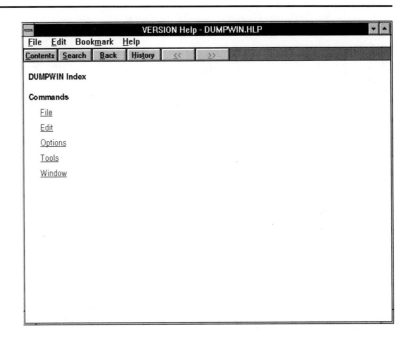

> **NOTE**
>
> QuickC for Windows does not include the Microsoft Help compiler. This programming tool can be ordered directly from Microsoft, by itself or as part of an additional toolkit available for Windows developers.
>
> Since QuickC does not include the Help compiler, CASE:W for QuickC does not generate calls to the Help compiler to build the Windows Help files (.HLP). This must be done manually. Two Help files are generated for each window in a CASE:W application. For instance, the two help files for the DumpIT MDI child window are DUMPWIN.HPJ and DUMPWIN.RTF. The .HPJ file is the project file for the help compiler. The RTF file you edit, as stated previously, using a word processor that can import RTF files, such as Microsoft Word For Windows.
>
> To compile the Help file for the DUMPWIN MDI child window,, you type in from the DOS command line HC DUMPWIN.HPJ.

Help is one of CASE:W's most significant features. By turning on this single option,, you can generate a Help system for your application that can save you hours (maybe even days) of C coding. Context-sensitive Help is automatically generated for your application. It can be invoked by the user by pressing function key F1 or by clicking on a Help button in a dialog box.

About Box

The About box is a dialog that usually displays information about your application, such as the version, the copyright, and any other application-specific or company-specific information you wish. The CASE:W menu item About Box in the Additional Support submenu in the Design menu remains disabled (grayed) unless you have selected the Help System option in the same menu. After you have selected Help System, the About Box menu item is enabled. When you select it, a dialog box is displayed for you to specify the dialog box you want to use as the About box.

Initialization Panel

An initialization panel is a dialog box that is displayed before your application displays its primary window. This dialog box usually displays your company or application logo and a copyright message. If your application requires some level of security, this is a good place to ask for a password. The Initialization Panel option is valid only for an MDI frame window or the main application window.

For the DumpIT MDI child window DUMPWIN, the only menu option I selected was Help System. When I design the MDI frame window, I will use more of the options from this menu.

Designing the Menu for the MDI Child Window

After stepping through the CASE:W Design menu, I was ready to build the menu that would be active when an MDI child window is open. Because the application menu is usually the primary way a user interacts with your program, you should make sure that its organization is logical and consistent. To build your menu, you start by clicking on the menu bar template at the top of the prototype window. The menu bar marks the insertion point for new items by displaying the symbol <<>>. Figure 3.12 show the Tools menu for DumpIT's MDI child window.

When you click on <<>> to create a new menu item, the Edit Menu Item dialog box is displayed so you can enter information about the new menu item. If you need to

FIGURE 3.12:

Creating the Tools menu for the MDI child window

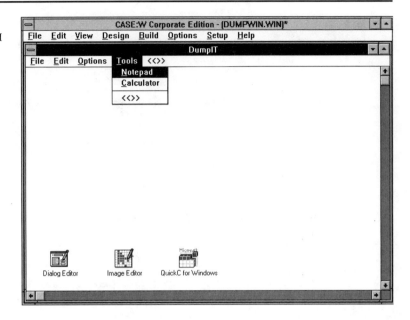

edit a menu item you have already created, you first select the menu item and then choose the Update command in the CASE:W Edit menu. This two-step process is used in CASE:W Corporate Edition, but not in QuickCase:W. Using QuickCase:W, you click on the menu item you want to edit and the Edit Menu Item dialog box appears, in which you can choose the style of a menu item. It may be a string, a separator, or a bitmap. Bitmaps cannot be put on the menu bar—they can only be put in a pull-down menu. For menu items in a pull-down menu, you can choose an accelerator key that will invoke the menu action. When the user presses the accelerator key, a WM_COMMAND message is generated by Windows, with the identifier of the menu item in the wParam message field. The Edit Menu Item dialog box also lets you specify the initial status of a menu item—normal, checked, or grayed.

NOTE It is always a good idea to save your work often when you are writing a program using a program editor, creating a complicated worksheet using Excel or Lotus 1-2-3, or creating an application prototype with CASE:W. If you do save your prototype before you have finished creating it, make sure to define at least one menu first. If you don't, CASE:W will save the prototype without a menu. If you think your application has lost its menu forever, don't worry. You can turn it back on by selecting Menu in the Style dialog box, accessed by choosing Style in the Window submenu in the Design menu.

For the DumpIT project, I created four menus using CASE:W: File, Edit, Options, and Tools. The Window and Help menus are created automatically for DumpIT, because it is an MDI application with the Help option turned on.

In the File menu, I created four menu items: Open File, File Sizes, Close, and Exit. I did not specify any file links for Open File, Print, Print Setup, Close, or Exit. I added my own code for processing these WM_COMMAND messages when the prototype was complete. Finally, I linked the File Sizes menu item to the File Sizes dialog box.

The Edit menu has only one menu item, Find. I linked the Find menu item to the Find dialog box. The Options menu also has only one menu item, Choose Font. I did not define a link for this menu item, however, because I planned to add the code for invoking the ChooseFont common dialog function when the prototype was completed.

Now that I have summarized the menus and menu items created for DumpIT, let's see how to link menu items to other application objects using CASE:W.

Linking CASE:W Application Objects

The real power in building menus using CASE:W (or other GUI builders) is the ability to link menu items to other application objects. Using CASE:W you can link a menu item to a dialog box, a secondary window (which may be an overlapped window, an MDI window, or a Windows or DOS executable program), another menu, or user-defined code. The secondary window you link to can be defined by another CASE:W window prototype (.WIN) or a dialog box you want to use as a window template.

User-defined code modules are files that contain C code that you create. They should have the .INC extension; CASE:W generates code to include these user-defined code modules in the files it generates. For instance, you may want to write custom code to do the processing for the WM_PAINT message. To do this, you place your C code in an .INC file, which could then be referenced by the CASE:W-generated files. When you link a menu item to a user-defined code file, CASE:W lets you start an editor to create or edit the custom code. CASE:W also lets you associate a user-defined code file with any available Windows message.

As I stated previously, I try to keep the amount of C code I write that's in the source code modules built by CASE:W to a minimum. Usually, I include only a function call to a subroutine that exists in a source code module that I build. For DumpIT, this source code module is called CUSTCODE.C.

If you have the CUA validation feature turned on, CASE:W will warn you when you violate any of its rules. For instance, you should always follow a menu item name that links to a dialog box with three periods (...); if you don't, CASE:W displays a dialog box that details the error and lets you back up to fix it.

Figure 3.13 shows how I linked the Find command in the Edit menu to the Find dialog box. After selecting Dialog Box as the type of link for the Find menu item, I clicked on the Configure Link push button to display the Dialog Box dialog box.

In the Dialog Box dialog box, I chose FIND from the list of available dialog boxes located in my working directory. I selected Modeless as its type, to let the user access either the MDI frame or child windows while the dialog box is displayed. Modal dialog boxes don't allow you to access any other application window until the modal dialog box is closed. Before choosing OK, I selected Center on Client Area to position the Find dialog box when it is displayed, and Extended Code Support to have CASE:W give me some help with creating the dialog box procedure for the Find dialog box.

Using Extended Code Support

When you select Extended Code Support for a dialog box, CASE:W displays the dialog box on the screen after you choose OK. You can then click the mouse on any of the control windows in the dialog box, and CASE:W lets you specify behavior for the control. Using CASE:W Extended Code Support, you can establish the

FIGURE 3.13:

Linking the Find command in the
Edit menu to the Find dialog box
created using the QuickC Dialog
Editor

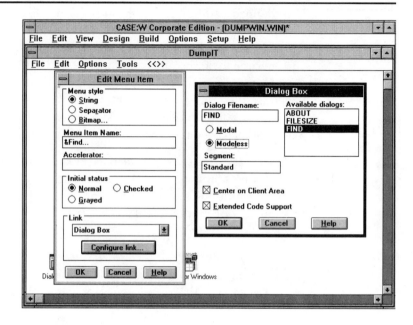

FIGURE 3.13:

Linking the Find command in the
Edit menu to the Find dialog box
created using the QuickC Dialog
Editor

following attributes for the following control types:

Buttons   For check boxes and radio buttons, you may specify the initial state of the
control and the name of a variable that records its current state. For push buttons,
you can tell CASE:W whether the button accepts or dismisses the dialog box (for
OK and Cancel push buttons), or whether it is linked to another application object,
such as a secondary window, a Windows executable, or a dialog box. In DumpIT, I
linked the Calculator push button in the Find dialog box to CALC.EXE, the Windows Calculator, as shown in Figure 3.14. If you give a push button the caption
"Help," CASE:W will automatically link the push button to the Help system it
generates for your application. All you need to do is supply the button caption
without specifying a link.

List Boxes   You can fill list boxes with a file listing, with a directory listing, or with
data from an array in your program when the dialog box procedure processes the
`WM_INITDIALOG` message. You can also specify the identifier of a control in
the dialog box that will receive information about the currently selected item. For a
list box, this identifier could point to a static text control that displays the name of
the currently selected item in the list box.

FIGURE 3.14:

Selecting the application link between the Calculator push button and a Windows executable

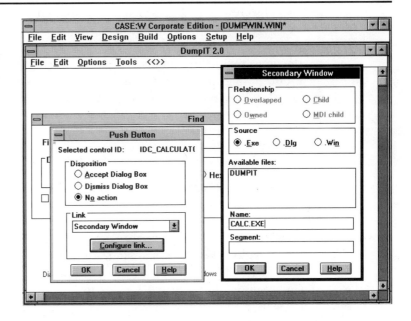

If you specify the list box as either a directory or a file list box, CASE:W generates code that refreshes the file list boxes when a new directory or file is selected. Although CASE:W can generate all the C code you need to build a File Open dialog box, you should ignore it and use the GetOpenFileName common dialog box function instead. Although this requires some C coding (about 30 lines), it has the advantage of presenting the user with a full-featured dialog box for opening a file which is consistent with Windows and other Windows applications.

Edit Controls   Edit control processing is the most extensive part of Extended Code Support. You can define the name of a character array variable to hold the contents of the edit control. The variable type associated with the control can be a character string, an integer, or a real number. Along with the variable type, you can specify the number of bytes in the edit control. For real numbers, you can specify the number of digits before and after the decimal point.

CASE:W generates the code to implement formatted data entry fields. Validation can be performed at either the character or the field level. You can specify that the edit control contains a date or a time, or you can choose a custom format for data such as telephone numbers and social security numbers.

An edit control may be defined as a required field. If it is, the user must enter data into the edit control before the dialog box is dismissed. The edit field can also be a duplicate field, where the initial contents of the edit control are filled in from the previous transaction. For instance, if the user is inputting a number of transactions for the business day, and if there's a date field in the dialog box, the user would not have to type in the date repeatedly. After it is typed once, the date should carry over to subsequent invocations of the dialog box. Figure 3.15 shows how to specify the edit control attributes for the "Find What?" search string in the DumpIT Find dialog box.

Combo Boxes   Combo boxes are combinations of edit controls and list box controls. The Extended Code Support for combo boxes is a combination of the support for list boxes and that for edit controls.

Creating DumpIT's Dialog Boxes   For the DumpIT project, I created three dialog boxes—About, File Sizes, and Find. About is a simple dialog box that didn't require any Extended Code Support. In the File Sizes dialog box, I used CASE:W Extended Code Support to define the array to be used for the list box, IDC_SIZELIST. CASE:W automatically recognized the buttons labeled OK and Help and

---

FIGURE 3.15:

Selecting the content attributes of the edit field in the Find dialog box using CASE:W Extended Code Support

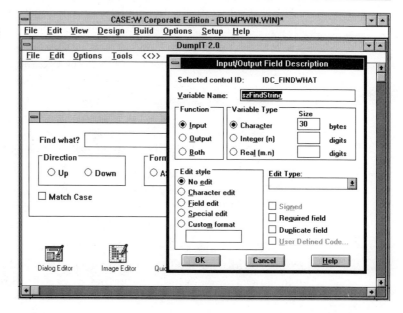

generated the correct C code to support them. For the push button labeled Calculator, I used Extended Code Support to link it to CALC.EXE. The following listing shows the code generated by CASE:W for the Find dialog box procedure:

```
/************************************************************************/
/*                                                                    */
/* Dialog Window Procedure                                            */
/*                                                                    */
/* This procedure is associated with the dialog box that is included in */
/* the function name of the procedure. It provides the service routines */
/* for the events (messages) that occur because the end user operates  */
/* one of the dialog box's buttons, entry fields, or controls.         */
/*                                                                    */
/* The SWITCH statement in the function distributes the dialog box      */
/* messages to the respective service routines, which are set apart by  */
/* the CASE clauses. Like any other Windows window, the Dialog Window    */
/* procedures must provide an appropriate service routine for their end */
/* user initiated messages as well as for general messages (like the   */
/* WM_CLOSE message).                                                 */
/* Dialog messages are processed internally by windows and passed to the*/
/* Dialog Message Procedure. IF processing is done for a Message the    */
/* Message procedure returns a TRUE, else , for messages not explicitly */
/* processed, it returns a FALSE                                       */
/*                                                                    */
/************************************************************************/

BOOL FAR PASCAL FINDMsgProc(HWND hWndDlg,
                            WORD Message,
                            WORD wParam,
                            LONG lParam)
{
 int    nRc;                         /*  Return code from Dialog boxes  */
 int    nJ ;                         /*  Counter                        */
 HANDLE hCtl;                        /*  Handle to dialog controls      */
 static char szarWorkBuf[64];        /*  Work buffer for processing     */
 static NPSTR lpszEndPtr;  /*  Temporary pointer.          */
 static int nInitVars;               /*  Used as a boolean to load      */
                                     /*  default status of radio and    */
                                     /*  check boxes only once.         */
```

```
static int nRadioGroup_Direction[BUTTONMAX]; /* Radio button group      */
static int nRadioGroup_SearchType[BUTTONMAX]; /* Radio button group      */

switch(Message)
  {
  case WM_INITDIALOG:
        CwCenter(hWndDlg, 0);
        /* initialize working variables                               */
        nRc = 0;
        hCtl = 0;
        nJ = 0;
        strcpy(szarWorkBuf, "");
        lpszEndPtr = 0;
        SendDlgItemMessage(hWndDlg, IDC_FINDWHAT, EM_LIMITTEXT, 30, OL);

        if (!nInitVars)
          {
            nInitVars = 1;
            Find_C1.Direction = IDC_DOWN;
            Find_C1.SearchType = IDC_ASCII;
            Find_C1.bMatchCase = TRUE;
          }  /* Set the default state for the controls in the Dialog  */
        /* Initialize radio button group for variable : Direction     */
          for (nJ = 0; nJ < BUTTONMAX; nJ++)
              nRadioGroup_Direction[nJ] = 0;

        /* store the radio button Ids for group variable : Direction  */
        {
            int nI = 0;
            nRadioGroup_Direction[nI++] =  IDC_UP;
            nRadioGroup_Direction[nI++] =  IDC_DOWN;
         }

        /* Read the current status of Radiobuttons from the DLG structs */
        /* and set them before display for group variable : Direction  */
        nCwCheckRadioButtons(hWndDlg, nRadioGroup_Direction,
    Find_C1.Direction);

        /* Initialize radio button group for variable : SearchType     */
          for (nJ = 0; nJ < BUTTONMAX; nJ++)
              nRadioGroup_SearchType[nJ] = 0;

        /* store the radio button Ids for group variable : SearchType  */
                        {
            int nI = 0;
```

```
            nRadioGroup_SearchType[nI++] =  IDC_ASCII;
            nRadioGroup_SearchType[nI++] =  IDC_HEX;
        }

    /* Read the current status of Radiobuttons from the DLG structs */
    /* and set them before display for group variable : SearchType */
    nCwCheckRadioButtons(hWndDlg, nRadioGroup_SearchType,
    Find_C1.SearchType);

    /* Initialize check box control: bMatchCase                   */
    SendDlgItemMessage(hWndDlg, IDC_MATCHCASE, BM_SETCHECK,
    Find_C1.bMatchCase, OL);


    break; /* End of WM_INITDLG                                   */

case WM_CLOSE:
    /* Closing the Dialog behaves the same as Cancel              */
    PostMessage(hWndDlg, WM_COMMAND, IDCANCEL, OL);
    break; /* End of WM_CLOSE                                     */

case WM_COMMAND:
    switch(wParam)
      {
        case IDC_UP: // Control text: "Up"
          {
            // Set this Radiobutton as ON and all others in the
            // group OFF.
            nCwCheckRadioButtons(hWndDlg, nRadioGroup_Direction, IDC_UP);
            break;
          }

        case IDC_DOWN: // Control text: "Down"
                      {
            // Set this Radiobutton as ON and all others in the
            // group OFF.
            nCwCheckRadioButtons(hWndDlg, nRadioGroup_Direction, IDC_DOWN);
            break;
          }

        case IDC_ASCII: // Control text: "ASCII"
          {
            // Set this Radiobutton as ON and all others in the
            // group OFF.
            nCwCheckRadioButtons(hWndDlg, nRadioGroup_SearchType,
```

```
        IDC_ASCII);
        { // Code inserted by programmer
          // to enable Match Case check box when ASCII is selected.

          HWND hCtrl;

          hCtrl = GetDlgItem (hWndDlg, IDC_MATCHCASE);
          EnableWindow (hCtrl, TRUE);
        }
      break;
    }

case IDC_HEX: // Control text: "Hexadecimal"
  {
      // Set this Radiobutton as ON and all others in the
      // group OFF.
      nCwCheckRadioButtons(hWndDlg, nRadioGroup_SearchType,
        IDC_HEX);

        { // Code inserted by programmer
          // to disable Match Case check box when Hex is selected.
          HWND hCtrl;

          SendDlgItemMessage (hWndDlg, IDC_MATCHCASE,
            BM_SETCHECK, FALSE, OL);
          hCtrl = GetDlgItem (hWndDlg, IDC_MATCHCASE);
          EnableWindow (hCtrl, FALSE);
        }
      break;
    }

case IDC_MATCHCASE: /* Checkbox text: "Match Case"   */
      {
      WORD    checked;

      /* Query check box control for current state      */
      /* on return i is set to:                         */
      /*          1 if check box is in unchecked state  */
      /*          0 if check box is in checked state    */
      checked = !IsDlgButtonChecked(hWndDlg, wParam);
      }
      break;

case IDC_FINDWHAT: /* Entry field variable: "szFindString"  */
      switch(HIWORD(lParam)) /* switch on Notification Code  */
```

```
                    {
                      case EN_SETFOCUS: /* Edit ctrl is receiving the focus */
                            break;

                      case EN_KILLFOCUS: /* Edit ctrl is losing the focus */
                            break;

                      default:              /* Default other messages        */
                            return FALSE;
                            break;
                    }
                 break;

            case IDC_FINDNEXT: /* Button text: "Find &Next"            */
                 // Call function to find search string in file buffer.
                 //
                 FindString (hWndDlg, wParam);
                 break;

            case IDCANCEL:
                 /* Ignore data values entered into the controls      */
                 /* and dismiss the dialog window returning FALSE      */
                 DestroyWindow(hWndDlg);
                 hDlgFIND = 0;
                 FreeProcInstance(lpfnFINDMsgProc);
                 break;

            case IDC_HELP: /* Button text: "&Help"                     */
                 PostMessage(hWndDlg, WM_HELPMSG, 0, 0L);
                 break;

            case IDC_CALCULATOR: /* Button text: "&Calculator"         */
                 WinExec("CALC", SW_SHOW);
                 break;

          }
        break;    /* End of WM_COMMAND                                 */

   case WM_HELPMSG:
        WinHelp(hWndDlg, szarHelpFile, HELP_CONTEXT, IDLG_FIND);
        break;

   default:
        return FALSE;
}
```

```
 return TRUE;
} /* End of FINDMsgProc                                          */
```

As I discussed previously, CASE:W generates ample comments in its source code. For DumpIT, I selected a comment level of Moderate. The C code I added to the dialog box procedure has //-style comments included with it. As you can see by examining the code, CASE:W generated almost all the code needed for managing the dialog box and for providing functionality.

Testing Your Application

As I was working on the design for the DumpIT MDI child window, I tested it using CASE:W Test mode without having to generate and build my application. To test a CASE:W prototype, you choose Test in the View menu. Test mode lets you exercise your application as you are creating it. Since CASE:W is running your application for you, you are limited in what you can test. Menu items do link to dialog boxes, but you can't test the C code you have added to your application. Radio buttons in dialog boxes may be toggled on and off, but all push buttons close the dialog box instead of linking to the application object they are connected to.

Figure 3.16 shows the DumpIT MDI child window running in CASE:W Test mode.

FIGURE 3.16:

Running the MDI child window in CASE:W Test mode

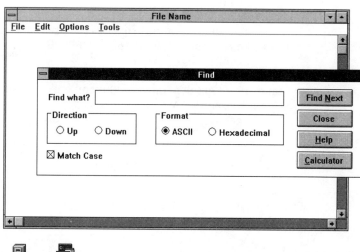

NOTE
The dialog box editor and CASE:W use a specific Windows measurement system for defining the size of dialog boxes and the predefined control windows inside the dialog box. This unit of measurement is called a *dialog box unit.* In Windows a dialog box unit is one-eighth the height of the System font and one-fourth its width. Windows will reapply this measurement to any font that you specify instead of the System font as the base for a dialog box. This causes problems internally with CASE:W in the following manner:

CASE:W uses a call to Windows named `GetDialogBaseUnits` to size control windows in Test mode. Windows uses only the System font for calculating dialog box base units when this function is called. If you use a font other than the System font when you create a dialog box, Windows will use the selected font to calculate the size in which to display the dialog box and the control windows inside it.

If you use the System font when you create a dialog box, CASE:W displays dialog boxes and their control windows properly in Test mode. If you select a font other than the System font, CASE:W will not display the dialog box and control windows sized accurately,, because Windows uses only the System font when `GetDialogBaseUnits` is called.

The default font for the QuickC dialog box editor is Helv (abbreviation for Helvetica)—not System. To have CASE:W display dialog boxes correctly, you must change the default font to System for each dialog box. To change the font, double-click on the dialog box after it is created. The Dialog Styles dialog box appears. Select System from the Font Face Name combo box to make it the default font for the dialog box. You should do this before creating any control windows, because all the sizes will change after you select a new default font.

Saving Your Work

After the DumpIT MDI child window was complete, I saved it as DUMPWIN.WIN. I did not generate it yet, because that would be done automatically for me when I generated the MDI frame window that it would be linked to. You generate a CASE:W Windows application from the main application window. Generating a child window only creates a set of useless files that clutter up your working directory.

Designing the MDI Frame Window

Once the DumpIT MDI child window was created, it did not take much more work to build the MDI frame window and generate the application. Here are the steps I went through to define the MDI frame window for DumpIT:

1. Used the default window styles that CASE:W selected.

2. Defined the window title as "DumpIT 2.0."

3. Chose DUMPIT.ICO as the application icon.

4. Skipped selecting a Cursor, Colors, Scroll Bars, Size and Location, and Message Support, and instead let the CASE:W defaults apply to the frame window.

5. Selected MDI Frame as the application type in the Window submenu—a very important step.

6. Selected Help System.

7. Selected the ABOUT dialog box as the About Dialog Box and Initialization Panel.

Designing the Menu for the MDI Frame Window

After defining the MDI Frame window attributes, I built one menu—File. The only items in it are Open File and Exit. I did not define any links for Exit because I would be adding the code later on to make the Exit command work. Open File does two things: it opens and reads a file into global memory and it opens an MDI child window in which the file's contents will be displayed (WM_PAINT processing takes care of displaying the window's contents).

The C code to open and read in the file was reused from FileDump and was added after the CASE:W prototype was developed. The code for creating and displaying an MDI child window can be created by CASE:W. Let's see how to get CASE:W to link to the MDI child window prototype created earlier, so that DumpIT will create and display this MDI child window when the user chooses Open File. Figure 3.17 shows the process of linking the CASE:W prototype window, DUMPWIN.WIN, to the File Open command.

After creating (or updating) the Open File menu item and specifying its initial attributes, choose Secondary Window for link and choose the Configure Link push button. When the Secondary Link dialog box is displayed, choose DUMPWIN from the list of Available Files and select MDI child as the Relationship. Click on OK to close the dialog box.

TIP

What if your MDI window is not linked to an application object such as a menu item or a push button? How do you get CASE:W to generate the C code for creating and displaying the MDI child window? To link an MDI child window to the frame window of a CASE:W application—when the only link to it will be user code—choose Unlinked Secondary Windows in the Additional Support submenu in the Design menu. In the Unlinked Secondary Window dialog box, you can specify the MDI child window prototype files to be linked to the application's main window. For all window types *except* MDI child, CASE:W generates the C code—as part of the comments—on how to create and display the window. Here's a trick to get CASE:W to do it for MDI child windows:

After specifying the MDI child window as an Unlinked Secondary Window, link it to a menu item you will be supplying the C code for later on—in other words, a menu item that's not being used. Then Save and Generate the application. After the C code for the application is generated, copy the code for the variable definitions and C code statements to create and display the MDI child window from the program to another C code source file for safekeeping. Then go back to your CASE:W prototype, remove the menu item link to the MDI child window, and generate (or, if you have already started adding C code to your application, choose Regenerate) your application again. Now you have the C code to create and display an MDI child window that you can use when you add your own C source code to the CASE:W application.

Linking Dialog Boxes to Dialog Boxes

Before seeing how the application is generated, let's tackle one more topic about linking application objects: linking one dialog box to another, and another, and another . . .

This is easy to do using CASE:W, but it might not be obvious. As we discussed previously, you can link a dialog box (secondary window or executable) to a push button

FIGURE 3.17:

Selecting the CASE:W MDI child window just developed (DUMPWIN.WIN) as a secondary window linked to the Open File menu item in the MDI frame window of the application

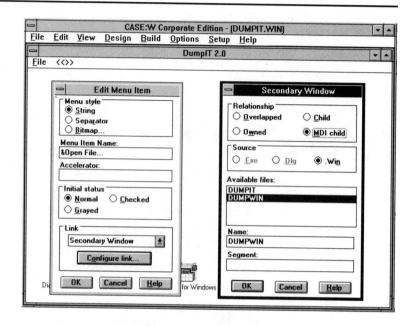

in a dialog box using Extended Code Support. But how do you get to the dialog box you are linking to define its Extended Code Support? If a dialog box is not linked to a menu and it is linked to by a push button in a dialog box (or user code), you add it to the CASE:W application by choosing Unlinked Dialogs in the Additional Support submenu. When you choose this command, the Unlinked Dialogs dialog box is displayed, as shown in Figure 3.18.

After the Unlinked Dialogs dialog box is displayed, select its Mode and Extended Code Support. When you are finished, choose Add (or Update, if you are modifying a dialog box), and Extended Code Support will be invoked so you can specify links and attributes for the controls inside the dialog box.

Generating the Application

The last step in the process is generating the application prototype. Figure 3.19 shows CASE:W generating DumpIT. Normally the Generate function runs as an icon in the CASE:W window. If you double-click on the Generate icon, it will open a Window to show you the code as it is generated. Depending upon your application size and the speed of your PC, generation may take quite a bit of time to complete—but it's still faster than writing it yourself.

FIGURE 3.18:

Choosing unlinked dialog boxes

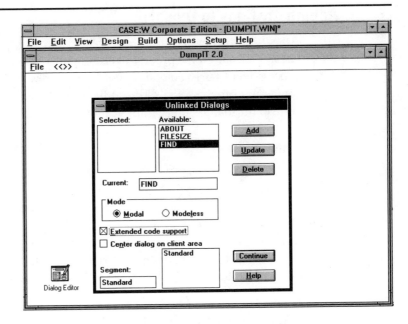

FIGURE 3.19:

Generating the DumpIT Windows application using CASE:W

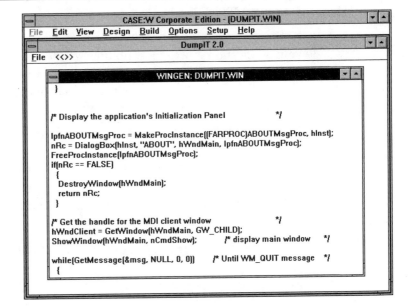

Adding My Code to DumpIT

After I had generated, built, and tested the DumpIT prototype built for me by CASE:W, I started the process of adding my own code. I found that this part of the process went fairly smoothly, with only a few bugs scattered along the way to hinder my progress. Let's look at the steps I went through to reuse my FileDump code to finish my DumpIT application.

Header Files

CASE:W creates several header files for your application, as described previously. The main header file CASE:W created for DumpIT was DUMPIT.H. DUMPIT.H has #include statements for all the other header files needed by the application. DUMPIT.H also includes all the application's global variables and function prototypes. Although CASE:W Corporate Edition for QuickC supports all the QuickC memory models, it will not build multiple C source code files for you like the version of CASE:W Corporate Edition for the Windows SDK—you must set this up for yourself.

If you look in DUMPIT.C, you will find the following C code to include the CASE:W-generated header file DUMPIT.H:

```
#define EXTERN
#include "DUMPIT.H"
```

Notice the definition of EXTERN. CASE:W is designed to use one header file for all your application source code modules. In the main C source code module, EXTERN is defined as nothing, because the variables are being defined for the first time. In all the other C source code modules, you should put the following C code at the start:

```
#define EXTERN extern
#include "DUMPIT.H"
```

This correctly references the global variables defined in a CASE:W-created header file as EXTERN. If you use the version of CASE:W Corporate Edition for the Windows SDK to create your additional C source code modules for you, it will put this reference in for you.

To include my header file, CUSTCODE.H, I added the following lines to DUMPIT.C:

```
#define MAINPROGRAM
#include "CUSTCODE.H"
```

In DUMPIT.H, I followed CASE:W's use of the EXTERN define. I also added one of my own, MAINPROGRAM. This lets me initialize global variables in the DumpIT main code module without doing it again in the other source code modules. Doing otherwise is not allowed in C and is flagged as a compiler error. In CUSTCODE.C, I used the following header file include statements:

```
#define EXTERN extern
#include "DUMPIT.H"
#include "CUSTCODE.H"
```

Notice EXTERN is defined as extern and MAINPROGRAM is undefined. The C code in my header file for defining and initializing global variables shows how EXTERN and MAINPROGRAM are referenced:

```
// Global variables
//
EXTERN LOGFONT lf;
EXTERN HFONT hFont;
EXTERN HFONT hFontResource[20];
EXTERN HWND hActiveMDIWin;

#ifdef MAINPROGRAM
EXTERN int nFontNumber = 0;
EXTERN int nFileCount = 0;
EXTERN BOOL bBufferAvailable = FALSE;
EXTERN LOCALHANDLE hWinVar = NULL;
EXTERN WINDOWVARIABLES _far *lpWinVar = NULL;
#else
EXTERN int nFontNumber;
EXTERN int nFileCount;
EXTERN BOOL bBufferAvailable;
EXTERN LOCALHANDLE hWinVar;
WINDOWVARIABLES _far *lpWinVar;
#endif
```

Setting Up Data Structures

Since FileDump was a simple one-window program, defining data variables was easy. I encapsulated as much data as was reasonable inside the scope of a function; other variables I defined as globals. DumpIT is an MDI application that requires a more sophisticated approach to dealing with the data variables associated with a window. One approach would have been to set up a table to keep track of a window's variables, but that approach is not very object-oriented. Instead, I set up the following data structure:

```c
// Very important data structure. This structure contains all the
// data associated with a file that has been read in and the MDI
// child window that displays it. A pointer to this structure is
// in the MDI child window extra bytes.
//
typedef struct
    {
    char szFileName[129];        // File Name
    LOCALHANDLE hWinVar;         // Handle to this data structure
    LONG lFileSize;              // File size and buffer size
    LONG lNumLinesInFile;        // Number of lines needed to display entire file
    float fFudgeFactor;          // Fudge factor for calc'ing scrolling position
                                 // position when lNumLinesInFile > 32,000
    LONG lAdjPosition;           // Offset for scrolling when NumLines > 32,000
    LONG lFindLine;              // Line with something found on it
    char _huge *hpFileBuffer;    // Pointer to buffer the file is in
    char _huge *hpFindPtr;       // Pointer to found data
    int nFindCnt;                // Number of bytes found
    int cxClient;                // Size of MDI child client window
    int cyClient;                // Size of MDI child client window
    int nVscrollPos;             // Vertical scroll position of MDI child window
    int nVscrollMax;             // Maximum vertical scroll of MDI child window
    int nHscrollPos;             // Horizontal scroll position of MDI child window
    int nHscrollMax;             // Maximum horizontal scroll of MDI child window
    int cxChar;                  // X size of selected font for window
    int cyChar;                  // Y size of selected font for window
    int nMaxWidth;               // Maximum width of window in characters
    HFONT hFont;                 // Handle to the display font
    }
WINDOWVARIABLES;
```

This data structure has every variable I need to keep track of the following types of information for each window DumpIT is managing:

- File name.

- Handle and pointer to the global memory buffer that holds the file contents. Notice that I used a _huge pointer instead of FAR, so I could do pointer arithmetic to work with a global memory buffer that exceeded 64K.

- Variables for keeping track of how many displayable lines are in the file (16 bytes per line) and the position being currently displayed: lNumLinesinFile and lAdjPosition, nVscrollPos, and nVscrollMax.

- A fudge factor, fFudgeFactor, that is applied when the scroll bar thumb is moved with the mouse and the number of lines in the file exceeds the maximum scroll bar range—32,767.

- Font characteristics.

- Variables needed to keep track of the window size and position: cxClient, cyClient, and nMaxWidth.

As described in the section on MDI program structure, it's a good idea to set aside extra bytes in the window's data structure to link it to the data object needed to manage the window. In versions of Windows prior to 3.1, the recommended practice was to put a handle to the locally or globally allocated data structure in the window. It was also recommended that you lock and unlock the data structure—if it was global—each time you used it. This was because Windows running in Real mode could not move program segments that were locked, as it can in Standard and Enhanced modes. (More detailed information is provided on this subject in Chapter 6, "Managing Windows Memory and Resources.")

Since Windows 3.1 doesn't support Real mode anymore, it isn't necessary to lock and unlock global (or local) data every time you use it. This lets you use pointers instead of handles for working with allocated data objects. You need a handle only to allocate the data object and to free it. Since this is the case for Windows 3.1, I stored a far pointer—not a handle— to the data object associated with my window in the window. I used SetWindowLong to put the pointer in the window data structure and GetWindowLong to retrieve it.

The data object to manage a window is allocated and initialized when the file is opened and read in the function DoWmOpenFile as follows:

```
if (! (hWinVar = LocalAlloc (LMEM_MOVEABLE, sizeof (WINDOWVARIABLES))))
{
OkMsgBox ("Local Memory Error!",
"Couldn't allocate buffer size %d bytes", sizeof (WINDOWVARIABLES));
return NULL;
}
lpNewWV = (WINDOWVARIABLES _far *) LocalLock (hWinVar);
```

After the data object is allocated and initialized, a pointer to it is in a global variable, lpWinVar. This pointer is put into the window data structure when the window procedure for the MDI child window processes the WM_CREATE message as follows:

```
SetWindowLong (hWnd, 0, (LONG) lpWinVar);
```

Any time a function wants to use a window, it must get the pointer to the window's data object. For instance, in the DoWmPaint function, the first executable statement is

```
lpWinVar = (WINDOWVARIABLES _far *) GetWindowLong (hWnd, 0);
```

Adding Functionality to the MDI Frame Window Procedure

As you can see, organizing your data for an MDI Windows application takes some planning and care. Now we can look at something more simple. In the MDI frame window procedure, I needed to add a function call to DoWmFileOpen to the section of C code that processes the WM_COMMAND message for the File Open menu command. I needed to put this function call before the WM_MDICREATE message is sent to the client window to tell it to create an MDI child window. DoWm_FileOpen is responsible for asking the user for a file name to open using the GetOpenFileName common dialog API, allocating global memory for the file, and reading the file into the global memory block. Later, the file will be displayed in the MDI child window after it's created. The C code for processing the WM_COMMAND for the File Open menu item is:

```
case IDM_F_OPENFILE: // Open a file and display it in an MDI child window
// Program code inserted by programmer to open and read a file into
// a global memory buffer. lpWinVar is the pointer to the data object to
// attach to the window data structure. Its global so it can be referenced
// by the MDI child window proc when it processes the WM_CREATE message.
lpWinVar = DoWmFileOpen (hWnd);
if (lpWinVar == NULL)
break;

// Program code generated by CASE:W to create
// a window for a file to be displayed in when it's opened.
DUMPWINChildStruct.szClass = szarDUMPWINAppName;
DUMPWINChildStruct.szTitle = "File Name";
DUMPWINChildStruct.hOwner  = hInst;

DUMPWINChildStruct.x = CW_USEDEFAULT;
DUMPWINChildStruct.y = CW_USEDEFAULT;
DUMPWINChildStruct.cx = CW_USEDEFAULT;
DUMPWINChildStruct.cy = CW_USEDEFAULT;
```

```
DUMPWINChildStruct.style = O ;
DUMPWINChildStruct.lParam = NULL;

ChildHandle = (HWND)SendMessage(hWndClient,
WM_MDICREATE, O,
(LONG)(LPMDICREATESTRUCT) &DUMPWINChildStruct);
hWndDUMPWIN = ChildHandle;
break;
```

A proportional font would look very messy for a file dump display. So I added the following statement to make sure the default font was a fixed—not a proportional—font when the MDI frame window procedure receives a WM_CREATE message.

```
hFont = GetStockObject (ANSI_FIXED_FONT);
```

To exit the program, I only needed to call a PostQuitMessage where the WM_COM-MAND message was processed by the window procedure. The processing to open the file and create an MDI child window was more complex.

Adding Functionality to the MDI Child Window Procedure

In the DumpIT MDI child window procedure, I added code to process the following messages generated by menu items:

- IDM_F_OPENFILE_C1. For the Open File menu item, I copied into a global memory buffer the code for opening and reading the file, as well as the code to build an MDI child window from the code in the frame window procedure.

- IDM_F_EXIT_C1. Added PostQuitMessage function call.

- IDM_O_CHOOSEFONT_C1. Added a function call to DoWmChooseFont in CUSTCODE.C.

All of the other WM_COMMAND message-processing was taken care of by the code generated by CASE:W. But I still needed to add code to process the following other messages:

- WM_CREATE. Added a function call to DoWmMDIChildCreate in CUSTCODE.C.

- WM_SIZE and WM_SETFOCUS. Added a function call to ResetScrollBars in CUSTCODE.C.

- WM_PAINT. Added a function call to DoWmPaint in CUSTCODE.C.

- WM_VSCROLL. Replaced the C code generated by CASE:W with a function call to DoWmVScroll in CUSTCODE.C.

- WM_HSCROLL. Replaced the C code generated by CASE:W with a function call to DoWmHScroll in CUSTCODE.C.

- WM_DESTROY. Added a function call to DoWinCleanup in CUSTCODE.C.

After finishing with DumpIT's window procedures, I moved on to the last aspect of the program I had to implement functionality in: dialog boxes. The only two dialog boxes I needed to worry about were File Sizes and Find.

The File Sizes Dialog Box   In the File Sizes dialog box I added the following statement where the WM_INITDIALOG message is processed, so that the list box used to display the file names and sizes was initialized correctly for using tab stops:

```
SendMessage (hCtl, LB_SETTABSTOPS, 2, (LONG) (LPSTR) &nTab);
```

The array that CASE:W uses to initialize the File Sizes list box is initialized in the function DoWmMDIChildCreate in CUSTCODE.C. The function is called when a WM_CREATE message is received by the MDI child window while it is being created.

The Find Dialog Box   In the Find dialog box I added code for the following message processing:

- IDC_HEX. When the Hexadecimal radio button is clicked on, the Match Case check box (IDC_MATCHCASE) is unchecked and disabled, because it becomes irrelevant.

- IDC_ASCII enables the Match Case check box (IDC_MATCHCASE).

- IDC_FINDNEXT calls the function FindString in CUSTCODE.C that searches for the contents in the IDC_FINDWHAT edit box as either a hexadecimal or an ASCII value, depending on the setting the user selected in the Find dialog box.

Taking Advantage of 3.1 Features

Now that we have discussed how I converted FileDump into DumpIT, let's look at two features that I added to DumpIT that only became available with Windows 3.1: drag and drop, and reading and writing to huge (over 64K) global data objects.

Using Drag and Drop   One of the easiest Windows 3.1 features to implement in your programs is drag and drop. Drag and drop lets users drag files from the File Manager and drop them on your program window or icon when it's minimized. To start, your program needs to register itself with Windows as a drag and drop client. When a file icon dragged from File Manager is dropped on DumpIT, it opens and displays the file in an MDI child window.

Being a drag and drop client application involves only one new message type and four new function calls. It took me less than an hour to implement drag and drop in DumpIT as an alternative to using a File Open dialog box. Let's see how.

To use the new APIs, you must include the SHELLAPI.H file in your application source code and link your application with the SHELL.LIB library. Both are included with Microsoft C/C++ 7, the Windows 3.1 SDK, and Borland C++ 3.1. Next, you need to register DumpIT to accept files dragged from File Manager. I did this by using the following Windows API call in the FrameWndProc function in DUMPIT.C when the frame window procedure processes the WM_CREATE message:

```
DragAcceptFiles (hWnd, TRUE);
```

Alternatively, I could have let Windows know that I was a drag and drop client by using the extended window style WS_EX_ACCEPTFILES. To use this style you have to create your window using the CreateWindowEx function instead of CreateWindow.

The next step was to add a case statement to handle the WM_DROPFILES message in the FrameWndProc function in DUMPIT.C. The following code shows the case statement I wrote to process the WM_DROPFILES message:

```
case WM_DROPFILES:
    {
    static char szDragFileName[129];
    int nNumFiles, nDragFileIx;

    nNumFiles = DragQueryFile (wParam, -1, (LPSTR) szDragFileName, 129);

    for (nDragFileIx = 0; nDragFileIx < nNumFiles; nDragFileIx++)
        {
        DragQueryFile (wParam, nDragFileIx, (LPSTR) szDragFileName, 129);
        //return a pointer here to attach to window
        lpWinVar = DoWmFileOpen (hWnd, szDragFileName);
```

```
if (lpWinVar == NULL)
            break;

DUMPWINChildStruct.szClass = szarDUMPWINAppName;
DUMPWINChildStruct.szTitle = "File Name";
DUMPWINChildStruct.hOwner  = hInst;
DUMPWINChildStruct.x = CW_USEDEFAULT;
DUMPWINChildStruct.y = CW_USEDEFAULT;
DUMPWINChildStruct.cx = CW_USEDEFAULT;
DUMPWINChildStruct.cy = CW_USEDEFAULT;
DUMPWINChildStruct.style = 0 ;
DUMPWINChildStruct.lParam = NULL;

ChildHandle = (HWND)SendMessage(hWndClient,
            WM_MDICREATE, 0,
            (LONG)(LPMDICREATESTRUCT) &DUMPWINChildStruct);
hWndDUMPWIN = ChildHandle;
}
DragFinish (wParam);

}
break;
```

After the WM_DROPFILES message is received, the DragQueryFile function is called to determine the number of files that have been dropped on the window. The first time it's called, I pass "-1" as the second parameter, the index of the file to query. This returns the number of files dropped on DumpIT. I then use this index in a for loop that calls DragQueryFile to get each file name and DoWmFileOpen to open and copy each file into a global memory buffer. The wParam parameter of the WM_DROP-FILES message is a handle to the block of memory that Windows puts the file and path names in. This is used in each call to DragQueryFile. By passing this parameter and an index to identify each file to DragQueryFile, I have a file and path name returned to me in szDragFileName.

After I get the file name, I call DoWmFileOpen to open the file and read it into a global memory buffer. Then I set up the parameters in an MDICREATESTRUCT and send the WM_MDICREATE message to the client window to create a new MDI child window in which to display the file.

After everything else was done, I needed to free the memory block associated with the WM_DROPFILES message. I did this with a call to the DragFinish function, passing it the handle in wParam that identifies the memory block.

Since all the code to open the file existed previously, all I needed to do was add the function calls to `DragQueryFile` and set up a `for` loop to process multiple dropped files. I also added one parameter to pass the name of the dragged file, `szDragFile-Name`, to `DoWmFileOpen`. If `szDragFileName` is a valid name, it's used to open the file. Otherwise, `DoWmGetFileOpen` calls `DoGetFileOpenName` to call the common dialog function `GetOpenFileName` to display a File Open dialog box.

Reading and Writing Huge Data Objects   When I wrote FileDump, Windows let me read (or write) data blocks up to only 64K. FileDump is designed to read an entire file into global memory, processing it in multiple chunks if the file is larger than 64K. FileDump has always used huge pointers, so it could do pointer arithmetic across segment boundaries. The following code shows how FileDump (and DumpIT) reads a file into memory using Windows versions prior to 3.1.

```
// Read file into buffer
for (lFileSz = lpNewWV->lFileSize, lBytesRead = 0;
     lFileSz > 0;
     lFileSz -= 60000, lBytesRead += 60000)
{
   if (lFileSz > 60000)
      wFileSz = 60000;
   else
      wFileSz = (WORD) lFileSz;

   if (_lread (hFile, lpNewWV->hpFileBuffer + lBytesRead, wFileSz) == -1)
   {
      OkMsgBox ("File Error!", "Couldn't read file");
      GlobalUnlock (lpNewWV->hFileBuffer);
      GlobalFree (lpNewWV->hFileBuffer);
      LocalUnlock (hWinVar);
      LocalFree (hWinVar);
      return NULL;
   }
}
```

Windows 3.1 provides new functions for reading (`_hread`) and writing (`_hwrite`) huge memory blocks. Instead of having to use a loop to read all of a file into memory, I can now read the entire file in one operation. The following code shows how DumpIT 2.0 for Windows 3.1 reads a file into global memory:

```
lResult = _hread (hFile,
    (void _huge *)lpNewWV->hpFileBuffer,
    lpNewWV->lFileSize);
```

```
if (lResult == -1)
    {
        OkMsgBox ("File Error!", "Couldn't read file");
        GlobalUnlock (lpNewWV->hFileBuffer);
        GlobalFree (lpNewWV->hFileBuffer);
        LocalUnlock (hWinVar);
        LocalFree (hWinVar);
        return NULL;
    }
```

As you can see, using _hread and _hwrite makes C code simpler and easier to maintain. Its only limitation is incompatibility with Windows versions prior to 3.1. Personally, I don't feel that this is a major limitation.

Summary

This project walked you through the process I went through to build DumpIT using CASE:W. It is meant to show you in a broad way what the capabilities and limitations of a GUI builder like CASE:W are—not to explain every project detail. CASE:W saved me a significant amount of work in building DumpIT. For many projects you will find that using a GUI builder can save you a moderate to significant amount of work.

Even though I later rewrote the CASE:W-generated code to create DumpIT 3.1, having this code as a starting point saved me development time. Using CASE:W and other GUI builders has been both a time-saver and a learning experience for me. Using these tools has also taught me new Windows programming tricks.

Now that you understand how a GUI builder works, let's take a look at CASE:W's most significant competition, WindowsMAKER Professional. WindowsMAKER Professional is easy to use, has a flashy user interface, and generates code at warp speed. In the next chapter, you'll learn how to use WindowsMAKER Professional and how it stacks up against CASE:W.

4

Create Windows Applications with WindowsMAKER Professional

- Comparing WindowsMAKER Professional and CASE:W

- Building a Windows application using WindowsMAKER Professional

- Using Animation Test mode to test-drive your application

- Using the built-in Dialog Designer to create dialog boxes and add functionality to them

- Examining the C code that WindowsMAKER Professional generates

In Chapter 3 we looked at what application generators are and how they automate some of our programming tasks. We examined CASE:W Corporate Edition 4.0 for Windows and its little brother, QuickCase:W (included with Microsoft QuickC for Windows). Now that we have learned how application generators work in general and how CASE:W works in particular, we'll look at what CASE:W's closest competitor, WindowsMAKER Professional, has to offer.

This chapter builds on the information you learned in the last chapter. It doesn't go into the detail that Chapter 3 does to explain the basics of how application generators work, so if you are not familiar with Windows application generator basics and you skipped over Chapter 3, you should read it before tackling this chapter. At a minimum, you should read Chapter 3 up to the section "Building a Windows Application Using CASE:W and QuickC."

Now, let's see how WindowsMAKER Professional 4.0 (WMP) works, and why some programmers prefer it as their Windows application generator of choice.

Evaluating WindowsMAKER Professional

The best way to learn how to use a programming tool is to see how it is used to build something—in this case, a Windows application. In this chapter, we will overview WindowsMAKER Professional's features. Then we'll learn how it can be used to create a Windows application by examining a prototype program, Corporate Information Menu System (CIMS), that acts as a front-end menu system for a worldwide information network. This application prototype was developed for a real company; only the names have been changed to protect the company's anonymity.

WindowsMAKER Professional (WMP) is quick, easy to use, and matches many of the features found in CASE:W Corporate Edition. I personally use and like both application generators, but this is the exception, not the norm. As a Windows development consultant and writer, I need to know how to use more than one tool for doing the same task. (This can be both a blessing and a curse!) In most cases, you will want to work with only one application generator—just as you work with one program editor and one C compiler.

As the writer of this book, I try to present the best features of each tool I cover and distinguish the differences between each of them. Since you already know what CASE:W can do, let's first look at the WMP features that match the features CASE:W offers. Then we will examine the features that WMP offers, but that CASE:W doesn't—and vice versa.

At the end of the next chapter, after we've looked at a few more tools, I'll summarize my evaluations of Windows programming tools that automate Windows software development and offer my personal opinion on which tools I like the best. First, let's see how WMP compares to CASE:W.

Comparing Similar Features in WMP and CASE:W

Both CASE:W and WMP generate C/C++-language Windows applications. CASE:W is a stand-alone product. WindowsMAKER Professional can be augmented with the two other Blue Sky Software development tools for generating Windows applications, Magic Fields and RoboHELP. Although they don't match up completely, Magic Fields could be compared with CASE:W's Extended Code Support for dialog boxes, and RoboHELP could be compared with the Help feature in CASE:W. However, since WMP is the Windows application generator, when I compare CASE:W to WMP, I am comparing only CASE:W and WindowsMAKER Professional. In the next chapter I will cover both Magic Fields and RoboHELP separately, as well as another product called DialogCoder.

TIP Even though Magic Fields and RoboHELP were designed to work with Windows MAKER Professional, both tools can also augment CASE:W functionality. In the process of testing these applications, I used both tools with CASE:W, as well as with WindowsMAKER Professional, and had good results. To learn more about what Magic Fields and RoboHELP do and how they work with other Windows development tools, read Chapter 5. For a product comparison of all the tools covered in this book, check the Appendix, where each development tool is summarized.

When you start either CASE:W or WMP, you see the application generator window with a blank application prototype window inside it. To assign a caption to your application window, double-click your mouse on the title bar, and a dialog box will appear asking you the title of your new application. Both WMP and CASE:W are very similar in this way. Figure 4.1 shows the WMP window with the application prototype window for a new Windows application inside it. If you want to compare CASE:W and WMP at this point, look at Figure 3.2 in Chapter 3 to see what the CASE:W application generator window looks like.

Blue Sky Software's development tools match many of the CASE:W features we discussed in Chapter 3. In addition, both CASEWORKS and Blue Sky Software are in the process of developing code generators for other programming languages and environments, such as Win32 and New Technology. Presently, both CASE:W and the Blue Sky development tools can

- Create C source code programs that can be used with Microsoft C/C++, Borland C++, and Zortech C++. Both CASE:W and WindowsMAKER Professional can generate

  - ANSI C

  - Microsoft MFC C++

  - Borland OWL C++

FIGURE 4.1:

The WMP application generator window with a new application prototype window inside it

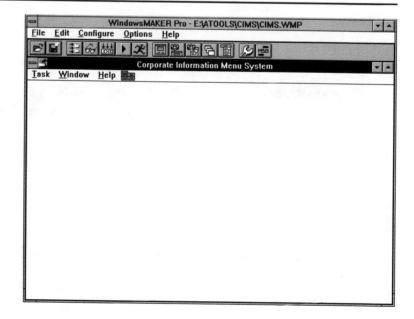

- Create windows (main, MDI, and child windows).

- Create menus and link menu items to dialog boxes, application windows (MDI and secondary), executable programs, and user-defined C code. WMP can also link menus to different menu sets. CASE:W lets you specify only one menu per window and doesn't generate code to switch menu sets automatically the way WMP does.

- Link push buttons in a dialog box to dialog boxes, application windows (MDI and secondary), executable programs, and user-defined C code. WMP can link icons and bitmaps in a dialog box—as well as push buttons—to other application objects. WMP can also link push buttons, icons, and bitmaps to different menu sets.

- Define window attributes (color, frame style, scroll bars, and caption).

- Link icons and cursors to windows.

- Use dialog boxes as templates for putting control windows in the client area of a window.

- Let you test your application without compiling it. CASE:W provides a basic test mode and WMP provides an elegant one that lets you interactively step in and out of Test mode to fine-tune program aspects.

- Define the messages to be processed by your Windows application and build the case statement to process them.

- Let you configure compile and link options such as memory model.

- Let you make your application from inside the application generator.

- Let you run other Windows programming tools from the application generator workbench.

Both CASE:W and WMP are designed to be used as the central component of your software development workbench. Now that you know what both programs can do, let's see where WMP excels and CASE:W doesn't.

- WMP has a more object-oriented interface than CASE:W. I find that the WMP user interface is easier to get used to and provides more shortcuts. For instance, to define a color for the client area of the window, you just double-click in the prototype window client area and the Color Setting dialog box appears, to let you define the window color. Using CASE:W you must choose the Colors command in the Window submenu of the Design menu. To define the window style using WMP, you double-click on the minimize or maximize buttons or the System menu box of the prototype window, and the Set Window Style dialog box appears. Using CASE:W you must choose the Style command from the Window submenu in the Design menu. CASE:W does let you double-click on the window title bar to display a dialog box to define the window caption, as WMP does.

- WindowsMAKER Professional provides a toolbar to give you fast access to program functions. As shown in Figure 4.1, the toolbar buttons (from left to right) access the following WMP functions:

  Open an existing file

  Save an application design file

  Generate source code

  View source code

  Run application in Animation Test mode

  Run the application

  Start the Dialog Box Designer

  Capture a dialog box from another application

  Capture a menu from another application

  Select application type

  Configure compiler settings

  Specify custom message processing

- CASE:W gives you minimal configuration options for setting up the compile-link process. WMP lets you configure almost every possible compile-link option.

- WMP comes with a useful dialog box editor. With it you can capture dialog boxes from other Windows applications while they are running to edit and put them in your application. Using WMP Animation Test mode, you can easily start the dialog box editor to fine-tune a dialog box and then go back to testing your application without compiling it.

- WMP includes a set of useful development utilities that add to the product's value. Here is a description of them:

  - QuickMENU attaches itself to your active window next to the system menu box in the upper left-hand corner of the window. It looks like a small button with the Blue Sky Software logo in it. When you select the window with your mouse, a menu appears listing all the Windows-MAKER utilities, all the SDK tools, all the standard Windows programs, and any program you want to configure. It is very easy to add, change, and replace the items in QuickMENU. Figure 4.2 shows QuickMENU after it's been clicked on with the mouse.

  - FileSEARCH is a basic file-find utility that, given a set of file name search criteria, fetches a list of files. Any file in the list can then be examined.

  - CodeSEARCH is similar in function to TS.EXE in the Norton Utilities or GREP in UNIX. It works like a charm and proves to be a useful utility. CodeSEARCH can change the current directory to that of the file containing the specified search string. Text can be cut from the View window to the Clipboard.

FIGURE 4.2:
The WMP QuickMENU utility

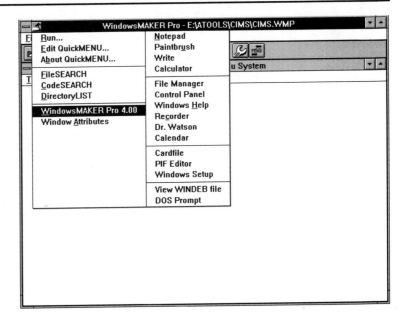

- DirectoryLIST scans the directory structure on all your hard disks and displays two views in list boxes: alphabetical and hierarchical. Directories are easily selected from either window, and the current directory can be changed.

- Windows Attributes displays information about all the active windows on the screen.

- WINDEB debugger is a debugging aid that lets you put trace statements in your source code to monitor the value of selected variables, check array boundaries, verify return codes, and check program states. The debugging code can be turned on or off using the WINDEB Debugging command in the Options menu. You can direct your debugging output to a file, a remote terminal connected to a COM port, or a secondary monochrome display adapter. Although this is a handy debugging tool, I personally rely on a good interactive debugger instead. For further information on how to use an interactive Windows debugger and for comparisons of the ones available, check out the section on Windows debuggers in this book, starting at Chapter 9.

CASE:W has significant features not included in WMP. These capabilities include the following:

- WMP can put control windows only in the client area of the main program window. CASE:W can put controls in any child or MDI window.

- WMP provides features that support building MDI applications and gives you an example MDI application to start from. CASE:W can generate a complete MDI application for you automatically—you don't have to do any coding or customization.

- CASE:W lets you define scroll bar range for a window and builds the code to handle the messages sent to the window.

- CASE:W can generate your Help files automatically for you. This feature is very easy to use, and the results are great.

- CASE:W provides a point-and-click graphic editor to define dialog box control window attributes and generate the C code for the associated dialog box function.

- CASE:W offers on-line help to guide you in using CASE:W.

- CASE:W lets you validate your program's user interface against IBM's Common User Access standard. If you turn this feature on and violate a rule, dialog boxes appear to let you know where you have gone astray.

When you get to the bottom line in comparing CASE:W and WMP, two issues are critical in the comparison: code generation and speed. WMP builds a Windows application in seconds and CASE:W takes minutes. Using a moderately complex design, CASE:W took 20 minutes to regenerate an application; WMP took 12 seconds. If you want fast turnaround in your design process, choose WMP.

CASE:W creates "classic" Windows C source code that you can add to and still use CASE:W for maintaining your application. WMP creates two source code files for each module of your program, which contain functions that call each other. You can update the WMP files that have the .C extension but not those with the .WMC extension. CASE:W C code is easier to read and to follow. CASE:W also lets you control the level of comments it includes in the source code. If you turn on a High comment level, you will get a tutorial on Windows programming written into your source code files.

TIP

In this discussion of application generators, it is easy to assume that you use only one of these programs to generate a whole application prototype. In many instances, I have used an application generator to create C code with which to augment an existing Windows application. It is much easier to use an applications generator's point-and-click user interface to write C code than to write it all by yourself. In these cases, CASE:W is much more useful than WMP because of the straightforward C code it generates. CASE:W's C code is clear, modular, and well-commented. WMP's C code is not as easy to follow and integrate into another application, because it jumps from function to function in the .C and .WMC source code modules it generates.

At this point you should have a good idea of how WMP and CASE:W compare on features. Both products work well, and you should expect to see more features added to both programs in the future. One feature I don't expect to see change in either product in the near future is the speed of both code generation and application generation. Besides all the other product bells and whistles, these are the two most important features you should consider when you are deciding which one to use for generating your Windows applications.

Now that you have learned what WMP is capable of, let's look at it in action and see how I used it to build a Windows application prototype.

Building a Windows Application Using WMP

To understand how CASE:W works, let's look at a project that I developed for this book. It's a Windows application prototype called Corporate Information Menu System—CIMS for short. I originally created CIMS for one of my customers who wanted a point-and-click menu system for its in-house software system. The CIMS project here is similar to the system developed for this customer, but I modified it specifically for this book. CIMS and all its source files are in the \ATOOLS\CIMS directory on the book's disk set. This version of CIMS was developed using WMP and Microsoft QuickC for Windows.

I created the first version of CIMS using the built-in WMP Dialog Box Designer. The .DLG file I created is named CIMS.DLG. Later, I used Borland Resource Workshop to give the CIMS dialog boxes a 3-D appearance. This new .DLG file is named CIMS_BRW. WMP 4.0 is not fully compatible with Borland Resource Workshop, so I had to use two separate .DLG files while creating the CIMS project. I used CIMS.DLG while working with WMP and CIMS_BRW.DLG for compiling my final version of CIMS. All of the figures show the BRW version of the CIMS dialog boxes. You will find both CIMS.DLG and CIMS_BRW.DLG in the CIMS directory. If you look inside the CIMS.RC file, you will see the following code that notes what is going on:

```
//  This code will get wiped out when WindowsMAKER Professional
//  generates the application.
//
//  MAKE SURE TO SAVE IT!
//
//  include one of the following .DLG files depending upon the
//  dialog style you want:
//  #include "CIMS.DLG"      // Microsoft plain style dialogs
//  #include "CIMS_BRW.DLG"  // Borland Resource Workshop 3-D
    dialogs.
    #include "CIMS_BRW.DLG"
```

WindowsMAKER Professional 5.0 supports BRW-style dialog boxes and has no incompatibilities with BRW. At the time of this writing, WMP 5.0 was available only in an ALPHA test version. WMP 5.0 should be available by the end of 1992. It will include many new features and will fully support Borland Resource Workshop.

Using CIMS

To understand CIMS, let's imagine a make-believe corporation that spans the world, with its headquarters in Boston, Massachusetts, and offices in London, England; Dallas, Texas; Dillon, Colorado; and Seattle, Washington. As the company's hot-shot Windows programmer, you have been asked to develop a working prototype to show how a point-and-click menu system could connect a Windows workstation to a host system at any one of these locations. Each location offers a different menu system that reflects the services available at that location. Figure 4.3 shows the opening screen of CIMS—the version created using BRW.

The CIMS opening screen has three push buttons to let you

- connect to one of the host systems at any corporate office location,

- go to the local menu window for using Windows applications, and

- exit the program.

There is also a menu bar to let you choose the same functions offered by the push buttons in the main program window, let you switch between the windows in the application prototype, and get help on using the application. The Window menu is

FIGURE 4.3:
The CIMS opening screen

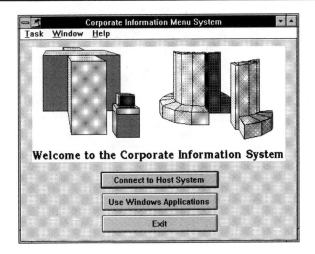

a shortcut to bypass the push buttons in the windows. This menu exists to test the program's interface, because the program is an application prototype, not a working application. Let's try clicking on Connect to Host System to see what happens.

Choosing the Connect to Host System push button displays the Select Host System dialog box, shown in Figure 4.4. As you can see, our corporate system spans the globe, offering us a wide variety of systems to connect to. Let's choose the Apple II computer system (a very appropriate computer system for most corporate headquarters), located at the corporate headquarters in Boston.

Next you see a dialog box with a colorful picture displayed in it (Figure 4.5) to confirm your host system selection. Clicking on OK takes you to a window that displays icons for the variety of services available at the corporate headquarters system.

Now we are almost at the end of the road in trying out the CIMS prototype. As you can see in Figure 4.6, we have a desktop with icons on it representing a number of system services that are available, such as Corporate Travel, Company News, and Who's Who at Corporate HQ. Since CIMS is a prototype, clicking on any of these icons displays a dialog box to let us know that the function is under construction and has not been implemented yet.

FIGURE 4.4:

Selecting a host system

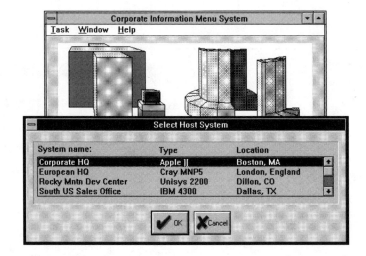

FIGURE 4.5:

The entry screen for the corporate headquarters computer system

FIGURE 4.6:

The CIMS corporate headquarters desktop window

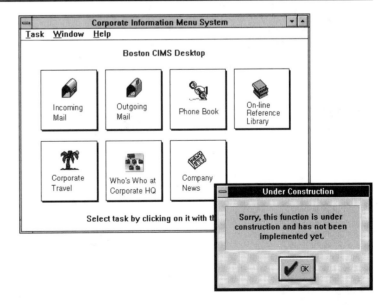

Before we complete our test drive of CIMS, let's go to the Windows Applications desktop using the Window menu. This menu lets us subvert the on-screen push buttons so we can go to any window in the prototype. Choose Windows Applications from the Window menu, as shown in Figure 4.7.

The Windows Applications desktop, shown in Figure 4.8, offers a variety of local services—and some of them even work! As shown in the figure, clicking on the Calculator executes the Windows Calculator program.

After playing with CIMS you can see it's a colorful—but limited—prototype that lets a systems designer show how the proposed system would work. A prototype is an excellent tool to use for communicating to others how you want a proposed Windows application to look and feel.

The CIMS project covers the basics of using WMP and provides tips about how to use it. As you will see when I show you how CIMS is constructed, WMP excels at building this type of application. WMP is your best choice for building C-based Windows application prototypes, if your project calls for

- flashy bitmap graphics,

- quick application generation for faster development cycles, or

- building the prototype in an interactive fashion with a built-in dialog box editor.

Now let's see how WMP was used to build CIMS.

FIGURE 4.7:
Switching windows in CIMS

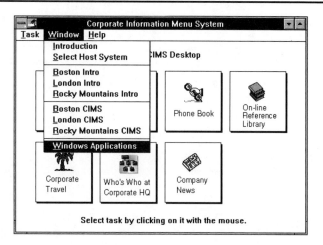

FIGURE 4.8:
The CIMS Windows Applications
desktop window

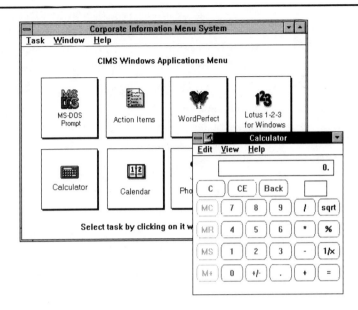

Creating CIMS using WindowsMAKER Professional

Whether you start to create a Windows application by building it from scratch or by using WMP, you should set up a working directory to hold all your application files. As I recommended in Chapter 3, one directory should equal one Windows application. As you create icons, cursors, bitmaps, dialog boxes, and C source code files, put them all in the same directory to avoid confusion and mistakes while you are developing your application.

Using WMP, first start a new project and save it immediately in your working directory. Then create your application's user interface using the built-in WMP Dialog Box Designer. To create application icons and bitmaps, you need to use the Image Editor supplied with the Microsoft Windows SDK or a comparable program. I used the Borland Resource Workshop for creating CIMS's bitmaps, icons, and cursors.

The WMP Dialog Box Designer is much easier to use than the Windows 3.1 Dialog Editor. It includes a floating edit window in which you choose edit control tools and select functions such as control alignment and spacing. The WMP Dialog Box Designer is also the means you use to access WMP functions such as linking dialog box push buttons to other application objects. You must use the WMP built-in Dialog Box Designer to take advantage of all of WMP's features.

As we discussed in Chapter 3, managing dialog boxes using CASE:W is complicated and sometimes error-prone. In contrast, you will find building and maintaining dialog boxes in WMP one of the program's more endearing features. Using the WMP Dialog Box Designer you can

- put as many dialog boxes in one dialog box (.DLG) file as you want and have as many dialog box files as you want. WMP does not limit you to one dialog box per file the way CASE:W does;

- interactively step in and out of Animation Test mode to adjust a dialog box, using the WMP Dialog Box Designer to fine-tune your application; and

- link push buttons, icons, and bitmaps inside a dialog box to other application objects.

The process for creating our WMP application is similar to the process described in Chapter 3 for generating applications using CASE:W. To build an application using WMP, you normally go through the following steps, in this order:

1. Define your main application window characteristics and save your WMP application prototype file (.WMP) in your working directory.

2. Design your application's dialog boxes. These can be used as normal dialog boxes or as ones that will be used inside a program window.

3. Create you application's menus and link application menu items to other application objects, such as dialog boxes and user-defined code.

4. Test your application using the WMP Test feature. While you are testing your program, you can interactively step in and out of Test mode to work on dialog boxes using the WMP Dialog Box Designer.

5. Add more dialog boxes and update the application's menu and window characteristics.

6. Link dialog box buttons, bitmaps, and icons to other application objects.

7. Test and fine-tune your application some more.

8. Generate your application.

9. Add your code to the application.

10. Build your application using your favorite Windows development system.

11. Test your application, go back to a previous step to make changes, and go through the process again.

Creating the Main Window

When you first choose New from the File menu to save your new application to a working directory, the New Application dialog box is displayed to let you name and save your application prototype file. If you have not created a working directory for your application yet, just choose the Create Dir push button in the New Application dialog box and WMP will create it for you.

After you have given your application a name and saved it, you can begin by specifying the following attributes of your main program window using the WMP Edit menu:

- Title Bar, to define the text appearing on the window's title bar.

- Color, to select a background color for the window.

- Cursor to be used for the window.

- Icon to be used when the window is minimized.

- Style, including options for selecting (or not) a menu bar, a system menu, minimize and maximize buttons, whether the window is redrawn when sized, and other style attributes that can be specified in the CreateWindow function call.

- Size and Location, to specify the size and location of the window when it is created.

- Application Type, to let you select the type of application you are building: Standard, MDI, or Controls in Main Window. Controls in Main Window lets you use a dialog box template to put a dialog box inside the main program window.

WMP is much more object-oriented than CASE:W is, and it lets you specify more of these program attributes by clicking on objects in the application prototype window. For instance:

- To specify the window caption, double-click on the application prototype title bar.

- To specify the window style, double-click on the application prototype system menu or minimize/maximize boxes.

- To specify the window color, double-click on the application prototype window client area.

For the CIMS application, I specified the title bar and the application icon. I let WMP use its application defaults for Color, Cursor, Style, Size and Location, and Application Type. Later on I will specify Controls in Main Window as the Application Type when I have completed the dialog boxes for the CIMS application. The Controls in Main Window feature will allow me to create the opening screen for CIMS (shown in Figure 4.3) and let me display a dialog box inside an overlayable window.

Creating Dialog Boxes Using the WMP Dialog Box Designer

After specifying the attributes for the main program window, it's time to build some dialog boxes. Some are used as dialog boxes; others are used as dialog box templates inside program windows.

To start, choose Dialog Box from the Edit menu. This command lets you view the dialog boxes for your application, edit an existing one, or create a new one. In the Edit Dialog Box dialog box that now appears, use the New button to create a new dialog box using the WMP Dialog Box Designer. You can display or edit an existing dialog box by selecting its name and choosing either the View or the Edit button. The Options button expands the dialog box to give you two more functions, Edit As Text and Include.

Use the Edit as Text button to start the text editor configured for use with WMP in order to edit the text description of the highlighted dialog box in the corresponding .DLG file. To configure a text editor, select Choose Text Editor from the Options menu. If a text editor hasn't been configured, WMP uses the Windows Notepad.

The Include button, which displays the Configure Dialog Box Files dialog box, is used to choose the dialog boxes you want to include in your application. Dialog box files can contain one or more dialog boxes. Before you can work on an existing dialog box, you must include the file (.DLG) that contains it.

Figure 4.9 shows the Edit Dialog Box dialog box with all its options visible, listing all of the dialog boxes in the CIMS application.

NOTE
If you attempt to include a dialog box file (.DLG) that contains a dialog box having the same name as one already included by another .DLG file, you will receive an error message. The names of dialog boxes must be unique. Figure 4.10 shows the Configure Dialog Box Files dialog box.

FIGURE 4.9:
The WMP Edit Dialog Box dialog box

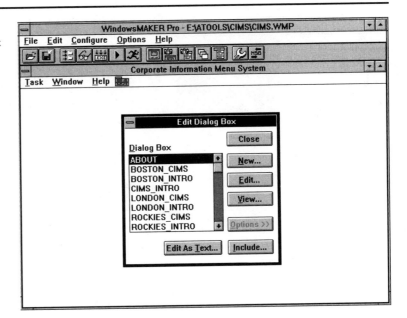

175

As you can see in the figure, the working directory contains the CIMS_BRW dialog box source file as well as the CIMS.DLG file used with WMP. The CIMS_BRW file was created from CIMS.DLG using Borland Resource Workshop.

Now let's suppose that you would like to find a dialog box file you created previously that would work as a starting point for one you have in mind for this application. We'll use WMP's FileSEARCH application to find it and then include it in our WMP project.

To start FileSEARCH from within WMP, you click on the Find push button in the Configure Dialog Box Files dialog box to display the FileSEARCH window shown in Figure 4.11. There are many file-find programs available (including the FileFind application discussed in Chapter 2 and included with this book), but FileSEARCH is already integrated nicely into WMP. All you need to do is specify the file name and the search path, then click on the Search push button. After the file has been located, click on Copy File, and FileSEARCH will copy the file to your working directory.

FIGURE 4.10:

The WMP Configure Dialog Box Files dialog box

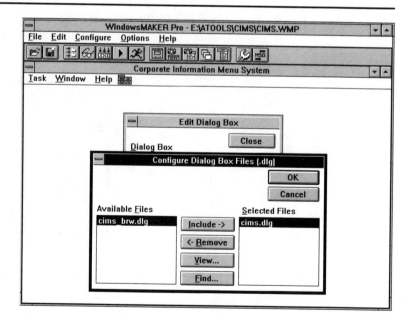

FIGURE 4.11:

The WMP FileSEARCH utility

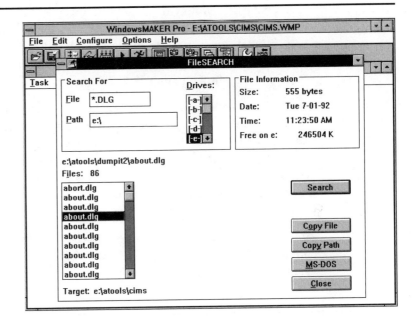

(Looking at the results of my search, I am amazed at the number of ABOUT.DLG dialog box files I have on my hard disk. I can see that when this book is finished I have to do some serious housekeeping to clean up files on my PC's hard disk!)

TIP

Before we continue our project and create dialog boxes for our application, I would like to take a moment to comment about the path we have just followed. WMP has many small, meaningful features; all you need to do is follow some of the paths through the program to find them. WMP was created with a keen sense of detail by a Windows developer for other Windows developers, and it is loaded with many interesting utilities and features. WMP is also used to maintain itself. Although we will discuss some of WMP's unique features in this book, I strongly suggest that if you purchase the program you read the User Guide thoroughly and investigate what's behind every push button in every dialog box and every item in every menu. You may find some interesting feature nuggets on your own.

If you have been following along with this book using WMP, now choose Close to exit the FileSEARCH utility and OK to close the Configure Dialog Box Files dialog box. This takes you back to the Edit Dialog Box dialog box shown in Figure 4.9. Now click on the New push button to create a new dialog box by starting the Dialog Box Designer, shown in Figure 4.12.

As you can see, the Dialog Box Designer is deceptively simple. It consists of two floating windows—one is for your dialog box prototype and the other is for the Dialog Box Designer itself. The Dialog Box Designer window includes a menu for choosing commands, a status window to give you information about the selected control, a tool palette, and the Tools list box. You can position the two windows on the screen by clicking and dragging their title bars with the mouse.

Tools for drawing dialog box controls can be selected either by clicking on a tool in the palette or by selecting its name in the list box. The most frequently used controls are in the Tools palette. The Tools list box is configurable and can contain user-installed custom controls.

FIGURE 4.12:

The WMP Dialog Box Designer

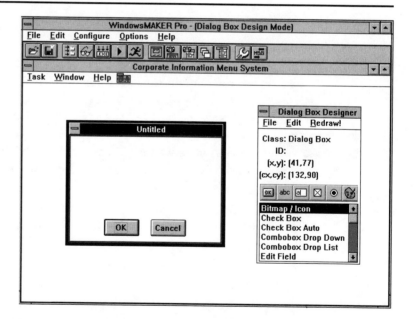

> **NOTE**
> You can add and modify predefined and custom controls in the Tools list box by editing the file WMP.INI (located in the Windows directory). Look for the section header [Controls]. This file is commented to explain how to add and modify controls in it.

By default Dialog Box Designer creates a new dialog box for you when you start it by choosing New. You can modify dialog box attributes—for instance, if you want one without a caption bar—by double-clicking inside the dialog box or by selecting it (highlighting its border) and choosing Style from the Dialog Box Designer Edit menu—not the WMP Edit menu.

The WMP Dialog Box Designer has many features that match those found in the dialog box editors that come with the Microsoft Windows SDK and Borland's Resource Workshop. Some of its key features are the following:

- The WMP Dialog Box Designer is seamlessly integrated into the WMP application generator.

- The WMP Dialog Box Designer lets you link dialog box push buttons to other application objects.

- The WMP Dialog Box Designer is easily activated from WMP Test mode to fine-tune your application's dialog boxes.

Figure 4.13 shows the CIMS London Host System dialog box being created using the WMP Dialog Box Designer. Notice that the Dialog Box Designer is "bitmap aware" and that it let me put bitmaps inside the dialog box and it displays them correctly.

To use the WMP Dialog Box Designer to create the CIMS application, I went through two phases. First, I constructed the layout of the dialog boxes—not their functionality. Second, I built the CIMS menu structures and linked the menu items in them to the dialog boxes I just built.

For the first phase, you use Dialog Box Designer—like any other dialog box editor—to create templates that specify which controls are to be used and their placement in the dialog box. For bitmap controls, you must also specify the .BMP file that is linked to the control. WMP will automatically write your application's .RC file for you and include the .BMP file in your application when it is generated.

FIGURE 4.13:

The CIMS London Host System dialog box

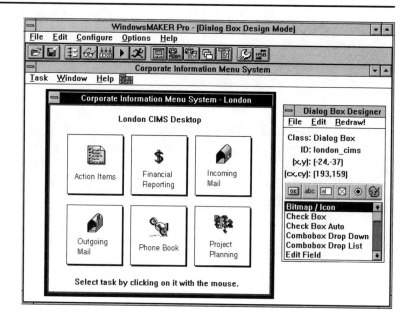

For the CIMS application, I created the following dialog boxes:

- CIMS_INTRO is used inside the main window of the program when it is first started. The bitmap in this dialog box was taken from the Micrografx Designer ClipArt Library and converted to a bitmap, using the process discussed in Chapter 2.

- SELECT_HOST includes a list box for selecting a host system to connect to. This dialog box is very straightforward and was created using only the WMP Dialog Box Designer.

- LONDON_INTRO, BOSTON_INTRO, and ROCKIES_INTRO serve as "Do you really want to Connect to Host System" types of dialog boxes. Each of these contains a bitmap image converted from the Micrografx ClipArt libraries.

- BOSTON_CIMS, LONDON_CIMS, ROCKIES_CIMS, and WINAPPS are the dialog box templates used in the main application window for the respective desktop menus at each location which you can connect to using the CIMS prototype. The icons for the desktop menu items were taken from the Visual Basic icon library. The bitmaps were created using Borland's Resource Workshop after the icons were pasted in from the Windows Clipboard.

- UNDER_CONSTRUCTION is the dialog box displayed to tell you that you can go no further because a prototype function is currently under construction.

In the next phase of working with the CIMS dialog boxes, I built the CIMS menu structures and linked the menu items in them to the dialog boxes. Then I linked the push buttons in these dialog boxes to other CIMS application objects while testing the CIMS user interface with WMP Animation Test mode.

Creating Menus

Creating menus is drudge work that WMP can make much easier. As you will see in this section, WMP creates menus very easily, but it could use some improvement—especially for multiple menu sets. In the upcoming section "Menu Sets," we will discuss in more detail how to use menu sets, as well as their limitations.

With WMP, to add an item to the menu bar, you click on the small icon of a file folder that WMP places at the insertion point on the menu bar. The New Menu dialog box appears to prompt you for the name of the menu you want to add and for the number of items in the associated pull-down menu, as shown in Figure 4.14.

FIGURE 4.14:

Creating a menu bar item using WMP

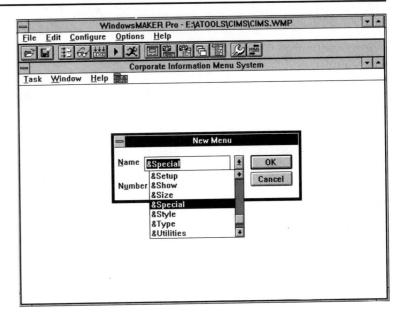

Notice that the menu Name entry field is a drop-down combo box—not just an edit field like CASE:W offers. In this case, the list box portion of the combo box contains common menu names (&File, &Save, and so on). Instead of typing a name, you can select one from the combo box list. As I mentioned earlier, handy little features like this have given WMP the reputation of being a user-friendly product.

After you have created all the menus that will appear on your menu bar, it's time to add items to each menu. To edit a menu item's parameters, you display the Modify Menu Items dialog box, shown in Figure 4.15, by choosing the item you want to modify from the pull-down menu (for a menu bar item itself, you must double-click on that item). Using this dialog box you can specify how the menu item will appear in your Windows application and the application object it will link to.

Using the Modify Menu Items dialog box you can specify the name of an item, control how an item links to another application object, rearrange or delete menu items, add a cascading submenu to an item, and define a custom identifier for a menu item. All of these functions are important, but the two you will use the most are Rename/Change and Functionality.

FIGURE 4.15:

The WMP Modify Menu Items dialog box

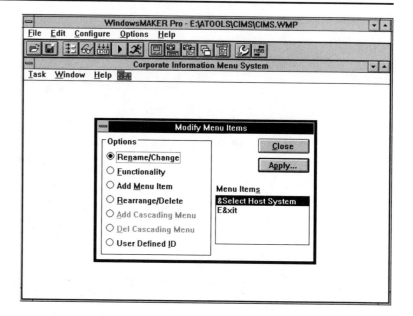

Rename/Change

Rename/Change displays the dialog box shown in Figure 4.16, which lets you do the following:

- Specify the menu item text.

- Specify whether or not a separator appears before the menu item name.

- Specify whether the menu item is initially grayed or checked.

- Specify the type of menu item, either text or bitmap. If this is a bitmap menu item, you must also specify its bitmap file. This is a small but interesting feature that is included in both CASE:W and WMP.

- Specify the accelerator key for the menu item.

Figure 4.16 shows how the Select Host System menu item in the CIMS task menu was created. In the Name combo box, you can either type in the text for your menu item or open the box to expose a list of commonly used names to choose from. Since Select Host System is the first item in the menu, the Separator check box is grayed. Notice that in this case I also specified an accelerator key for the menu item, CTRL+S.

FIGURE 4.16:

The WMP Rename/Change Menu
Item dialog box

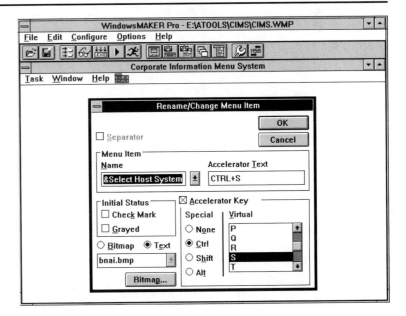

Functionality

Like CASE:W, WMP lets you link menu items to a variety of application objects, for example, a dialog box, user-defined code, or another application. In contrast to CASE:W, which allows only one menu for each window, WMP supports multiple menu sets for one window and lets you link a menu item to another menu set. Figure 4.17 shows the Select Functionality dialog box, where you specify the application object a menu item links to and how the menu item links to it. To display this dialog box, select the Functionality radio button in the Modify Menu Items dialog box (Figure 4.15) and click on the Apply push button.

TIP   You can double-click on any radio button in the Modify Menu Items dialog box to execute that button's function, instead of selecting the radio button and clicking on Apply. This is not normally a way of working with radio buttons in Windows, but it does provide a handy shortcut.

FIGURE 4.17:

The WMP Select Functionality dialog box

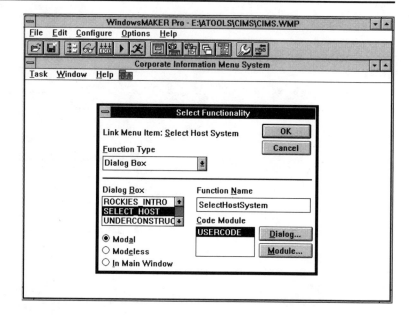

Figure 4.17 shows how the Select Host System menu item in the CIMS task menu is linked to the dialog box SELECT_HOST. The SELECT_HOST dialog box is a modal one that lists all of the different systems that can be connected to in the CIMS prototype. The dialog box function will be named `SelectHostSystem` and put into the code module USERCODE.C. The actual function name will be `BLD_SelectHostSystemDlgFunc`. WMP uses the prefix `BLD_` to identify all the functions it creates, and appends `DlgFunc` to the function name to identify it as a dialog box function. We will go into more detail about how WMP names functions later in this chapter.

NOTE

If you examine the Select Functionality dialog box in Figure 4.17 closely, you will notice the radio buttons that specify how to use the dialog box that the menu item is being linked to: Modal, Modeless, and In Main Window. The Select Functionality dialog box is used for linking all the different types of WMP application objects, including menu items, push buttons, icons, and bitmaps. These radio buttons are very important. In this case, the SELECT_HOST dialog box is being used as a modal dialog box, so I used the default Modal setting. When I created the link from the Boston CIMS menu item in the Window menu to the BOSTONS_CIMS dialog box, I specified In Main Window so the BOSTON_CIMS dialog box would be used in the main program window. It is very easy to make a mistake here and forget to set this switch according to how you want the dialog box used. If you make a mistake and select the wrong button, you need to delete the function that was created and relink the application objects. If you create a function accidentally and want to get rid of it, use the Functions command in the Configure menu to display a dialog box to delete the function. If you have already generated your application, you will need to delete the function template manually that WMP creates in USERCODE.C. See the section "Examining the C Code Generated" in this chapter for more information about the C source code modules WMP generates to learn more about how WMP manages program code modules.

The Window menu also has a Select Host System command, and it needs to be linked to the same dialog box. Since we have already let WMP create a function, SelectHostSystem, to create the SELECT_HOST dialog box, there is no need to create another function. In this case, you choose the Select Host System command in the prototype application Window menu to display the Modify Menu Items dialog box. You can then select the Functionality radio button and click on the Apply push button (or double-click on the Functionality radio button as a shortcut) to display the Select Functionality dialog box as it appears in Figure 4.18.

Instead of selecting Dialog Box as the Function Type, I selected Existing Function. I then selected SelectHostSystem from the Existing Functions list box to finish the job. Since it is better to reuse functions instead of creating new ones, you should use the following guidelines when working with WMP:

- Use meaningful function names for all the functions in your application prototype. WMP does its best to suggest a meaningful function name based on the menu item text, but sometimes it will suggest a name such as Function1. In such a case, type in a meaningful name of your own.

FIGURE 4.18:

Selecting an existing function for a menu item

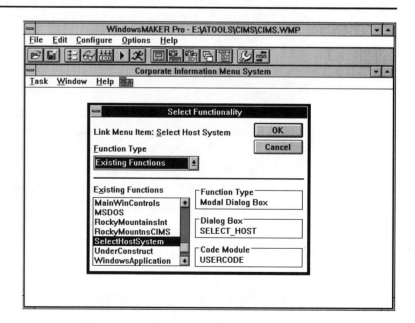

186

- Make sure to keep track of the function names you create, so they can be reused. If you create a function accidentally and want to get rid of it, use the Functions command in the Configure menu to display a dialog box to delete it. If you have already generated your application, you need to delete the function template manually that WMP creates in USERCODE.C.

- Always double-check your function names and test your application in the WMP Animation Test mode before generating it. The WMP Animation Test mode is very robust compared to CASE:W and can be used to test almost all of your user interface features. Testing before generating will save you from having to delete functions from USERCODE.C.

Menu Sets

As we already discussed, WMP gives you the capability of creating multiple menu sets to be used in your application. To work with menu sets, you choose the Menu Set command in the Edit menu to display the Edit Menu Sets dialog box, shown in Figure 4.19.

FIGURE 4.19:

Creating and specifying menu sets using WMP

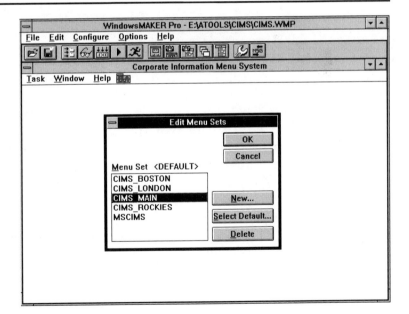

Figure 4.19 shows the different menu sets used in the CIMS application. The CIMS_MAIN menu is the default menu. It is the menu you see when the program starts. CIMS_BOSTON is the menu that's active when you have connected to the Boston Information Center and the CIMS_BOSTON dialog box is being used as the dialog box template in the main program window.

NOTE Whenever you link a menu item to a dialog box or other application object, you can specify only one action: link the menu item to this application object. The same is true for linking a push button, icon, or bitmap in a dialog box to another application object. Although this is a minor flaw in WMP, it forced me to add my own code to the generated WMP code in order to switch menus in the CIMS application. For instance, when you click on OK in the LONDON_INTRO dialog box to link to the LONDON_CIMS dialog box that is displayed in the main program window, there is no built-in WMP facility for changing the menu set too. To do this, I had to add my own code—BLDSwitchMenu(hWin,"CIMS_LONDON");—to the startup procedure (BLD_LondonCIMSClFunc) for displaying the LONDON_CIMS dialog box in the client area of a window. BLDSwitchMenu is generated for you by WMP and put into the USERCODE.C source code module to switch to a different menu set. It's located in the C source code module CIMS.WMC.

Creating application menus using WMP is easy, but it could be easier. For instance, when you have more than one menu set, as in CIMS (which has four menu sets), you expend a lot of effort to create menus . Many menu sets within the same application have duplicate menus and menu items, but there is no way to duplicate a menu set using WMP and modify the menu items you want to change. If your program has multiple menu sets, it would probably be easier to code them yourself in an .RC file, than to use WMP, because you could duplicate menu sets and make the modifications you want. Unfortunately, because WMP regenerates the .RC file completely every time you rebuild your application, you can't modify the .RC file. Therefore, if you use WMP to generate your application, you should use it to manage your menus.

Although you can't duplicate menus in WMP, you can capture menus from other applications, and even from the one you're working on. Once you've defined a menu, you save and generate your code and build an application. Then you run the application simultaneously with WMP in two separate windows, sized so you can see both of them on the screen at once. While the applications are running, select Capture Menu in WMP's Edit menu to display the Capture Menu dialog box. Double-click the mouse pointer on the menu bar of the application that contains the menu you want to capture. The New Menu Set dialog box appears, where you can type in a new name for the menu you've just captured. Click on OK and the new menu is added to the WMP application that you're working on. Now you can modify the new menu in any way. You can repeat these steps to make multiple copies of the same menu, each time giving it a different name.

Using a Dialog Box Template in the Main Window Client Area

Every window you interact with in the CIMS application prototype uses a dialog box template to put controls in the main application window. The window you interact with when CIMS starts is the CIMS_INTRO dialog box template. The first time you use a dialog box in the main window of a WMP application, you choose the Application Type command in the WMP Edit menu to display the Application Type dialog box, shown in Figure 4.20.

To specify a dialog box to use in the main program window, select the Controls in Main Window radio button and select the CIMS_INTRO dialog box in the Dialog Box list. WMP supplies the function name `MainWinControls` for the function that processes the dialog box messages. Since this default name was appropriate, I used it for the dialog box function name and clicked on OK to complete this step.

At this point all of the menus for the CIMS application have been defined, all the main window attributes have been selected, and a dialog box template has been selected for use in the main program window when CIMS starts. Now let's test the CIMS user interface using WMP Animation Test mode and add some more functionality along the way.

FIGURE 4.20:

The WMP Application Type
dialog box

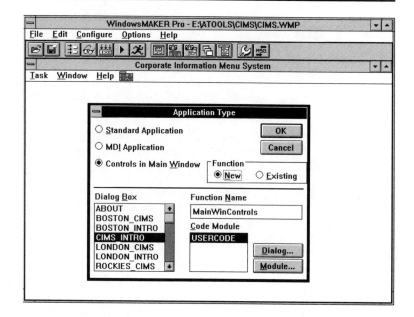

Testing and Refining the Application

After reaching this point in developing CIMS, I was very eager to see how my application would look and feel. So I decided to use the WMP Test mode, not only to test how my application would work, but also to build the links between the push buttons in my application's dialog boxes and other application objects. Let's see how this is done, and also learn a few tricks for using WMP.

To start, you choose the Animation Test mode command in the WMP Options menu. WMP then runs your program as if it were actually executing. Using WMP Animation Test mode, all the links you specify between menu items and other application objects work as designed. All the links from push buttons, icons, and bitmaps in dialog boxes to other application objects work as well. The only limitation is that WMP cannot simulate the C source code you add to your application. Figure 4.21 shows the opening screen of the CIMS application being run by WMP in Animation Test mode.

At this point you can test all the menus to see if they link to the correct application objects. If you were to test the push buttons in the main window client area, you would find that they are not linked to any application object yet.

FIGURE 4.21:

Running CIMS in WMP Animation Test mode

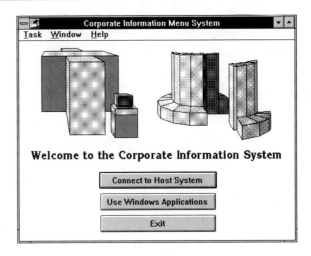

Now let's step out of Animation Test mode for a moment to link these push buttons to another application object using the built-in WMP Dialog Box Designer. To do this, you go through the following steps:

1. Double-click the mouse inside the main window client area (in an open area—not a control window) to display the WMP Dialog Box Designer, as shown in Figure 4.22.

FIGURE 4.22:

Running the WMP Dialog Box Designer from Animation Test mode

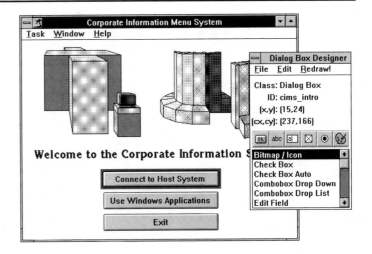

2. Double-click on the Connect to Host System push button to display its Edit Control dialog box.

3. After the Edit Control dialog box appears, click on its Functionality push button to display the Select Functionality dialog box, as shown in Figure 4.23.

4. Since a function (SelectHostSystem) has already been defined to link to the SELECT_HOST dialog box, Existing Functions is chosen for the Function Type and SelectHostSystem is selected from the list of Existing Functions.

5. After selecting the function link, choose OK to close the Select Functionality dialog box and OK again to close the Edit Control Dialog Box.

6. Now, all that's left is choosing Save in the WMP Dialog Box Designer File menu to save the modifications just made, and double-clicking on the WMP Dialog Box Designer's system menu to close it and go back to Animation Test mode.

Now when you click on the Connect to Host System push button, the Select Host dialog box appears, as shown in Figure 4.24.

FIGURE 4.23:
Selecting functionality for a push button

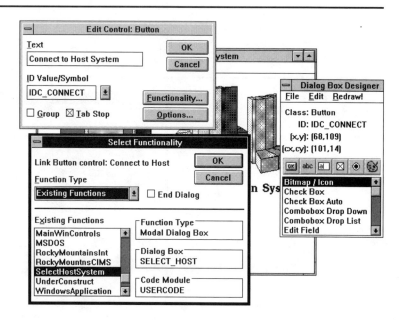

FIGURE 4.24:

Testing CIMS in Animation Test mode

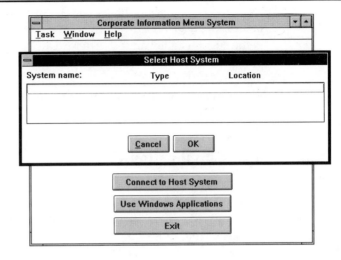

At this point in the process of creating CIMS, I completed the links for the other dialog box push buttons by stepping in and out of Animation Test mode to invoke the WMP Dialog Box Designer to link each push button to an application object. All of the steps I went though followed the same concepts just presented. I was able to build and test the CIMS application in a very interactive way, with the following exceptions:

- For the Exit push button in the opening CIMS screen and the Exit command in each menu, I linked the menu item or push button to the user-defined function ExitProgram. WMP created the ExitProgram function template for me in USERCODE.C. All I needed to add was a call to PostQuitMessage to Exit the program.

- In the Select Host dialog box, I wanted a way to link to each of the corporate location intro dialog boxes (BOSTON_INTRO, LONDON_INTRO, and ROCKIES_INTRO). To do this I created temporary push buttons in the Select Host System dialog box that linked to these dialog boxes. When I added my own code to the CIMS application to display a list of computer systems in the Select Host System dialog box, I borrowed the code WMP generated to process the messages from each of these temporary push buttons and put it in the custom code I added. After my list box was working, I deleted the temporary push buttons.

After building and testing an application prototype in WMP and taking it as far as you can go, the next step is generating the application.

Generating the Application

To generate all the files you need to compile and build a Windows application using your C compiler and Windows development system, choose Save and Generate Code in the WMP file menu. WMP generates applications quickly and easily—much faster than CASE:W does. The entire process should be completed in under a minute for a medium-sized Windows application.

Examining the C Code Created

After WMP is finished generating the CIMS Windows application, it creates the following files:

- CIMS.C is the main source code module for your program. It's all right to make additions and modifications to the C code in this file, but you should still be careful. Additions are usually OK, but I don't recommend changing any of the code generated by WMP unless you are sure of what you are doing. WMP does not overwrite the C code in this file when you subsequently regenerate your application—it only appends C code to it.

- CIMS.WMC is the main source code module that is a companion to the CIMS.C source code file. You can look inside this file to see what is going on, but you should not change a line of code. This file gets completely regenerated every time you save and generate code using WMP. Don't put any of your own code in this file.

- USERCODE.C is the file WMP sets up for you to put the majority of your own C code in. USERCODE is the default name, but you can choose any name you want when you save the application for the first time. You can also create additional code segments to put your code into by choosing Code

Modules/Segments in the Configure menu. After you have additional code modules set up, you can use any of them for specifying where to put a new function that WMP is creating for you.

- USERCODE.WMC is the companion source code file for USERCODE.C. As with CIMS.WMC, you can look inside this file to see what is going on, but you should not change a line of code. This file gets completely regenerated every time you save and generate code using WMP. Don't put any of your own code in this file.

- CIMS.WMP is the binary WMP project file.

- CIMS.RC is the resource script file generated for your application. Since this file is overwritten when you save and generate code using WMP, you should not add code to it.

- CIMS.DEF is the module definition file generated for your application. Since this file is overwritten when you save and generate code using WMP, you should not add code to it.

- CIMS.DLG is the one dialog box file containing all the CIMS application dialog boxes. This file is maintained by the WMP Dialog Box Designer.

- CIMS.H is the header file generated for your application. Since this file is overwritten when you save and generate code using WMP, you should not add code to it.

- USERCODE.H is the header file generated for your application. Since this file is overwritten when you save and generate code using WMP, you should not add code to it.

Understanding WMP Code Generation

One factor that allows WMP to generate your application so quickly is the way it organizes the C source code it generates. WMP completely regenerates the source files it is responsible for, whereas it only appends code to the source files you are responsible for working on.

When you use WMP to help you build a Windows application, you should imagine that you are working with a group of programmers on the same application. Each programmer has a personal set of source files. You would not want another programmer to modify your source code or insert lines of code in the middle of one of your files. You should treat WMP as a programmer working along with you whose files you don't want to modify. WMP initially generates all the source files. To avoid inserting source code in the middle of one of your files, WMP needs some source files for its own use. These files have the extension .WMC.

For example, in the CIMS application there are user code modules called CIMS.C and USERCODE.C. There are also two companion files called CIMS.WMC and USERCODE.WMC. The .WMC files contain the C code that WMP manages; calls to the functions in these files are placed in the .C files you are responsible for. The .WMC files are completely handled by WMP and are regenerated when you use the Save and Generate Code command in the File menu.

Your C source files are generated initially and are appended to every time you subsequently save and generate your application. After their initial generation, your user code modules are never overwritten. Functions placed in user code modules are appended to the end of the files, thus keeping all existing code in the appended module intact.

You can add new user code modules to group your code logically. Choose the Code Modules/Segments command in the Configure menu, then choose the New button. Type in the name of the new code module, then press OK. The new source code modules are created for you when you choose the Save and Generate Code command in the File menu.

When you use WMP to build and maintain your Windows application, you must be aware of what WMP is doing for you and what it isn't. Since you use WMP to create and modify program menus, there is no need for you to make changes to the resource script file. If you know that WMP is set up to process a Windows message, there is no need to subvert this process in your own code. If you need to add a new menu or rearrange menus in your program, use WMP to do it for you. This way you won't have to modify WMP source files, and you can use WMP to help maintain your application throughout its product lifetime.

How WMP Names Functions

During the design of your application you can link menu items and buttons to functionality. A call to a specified function is written into the .WMC code module. If you choose to link a menu item or a button to user-defined code, an empty function is generated in the specified user code module. An empty function has no other statements than the return statement. You fill in your own (user-defined) application-specific code here.

When linking a menu item or a button to functionality, you either specify a name for the function or let WMP suggest a name for you. For menu items, the name is based upon that of the menu item you are linking to. The complete name of a function consists of the name you specify, a prefix BLD_ to indicate it's a WMP function, and a suffix that indicates the type of function. The parameters of the function are the same as those sent to the window procedure:

hWnd	Handle to the window
message	Type of message
wParam	16-bit parameter
lParam	32-bit parameter

There are five types of functions for menu or button functionality. The suffix defines the function type:

UDCFunc	Function for user-defined code
ExeFunc	Startup of an executable file
MenuFunc	Function to switch menu set
DlgFunc	Dialog box creation
DlgProc	Dialog box message handling procedure

The DlgFunc and DlgProc functions are always generated together when a menu item is linked to a dialog box.

This discussion of how WMP generates code is just an overview, so you can have a better understanding of how WMP operates and of its benefits and pitfalls. A more thorough discussion is in the WMP User Guide. WMP can generate code very fast because of the way it splits code between the .WMC and the .C source code modules. However, while this makes code generation much faster, it also makes the generated code more complicated, linking back and forth between the two files. Whereas WMP-generated code is good for creating and maintaining Windows applications, you cannot easily reuse it in existing applications, because of the way the code path travels back and forth between the two source code modules.

Adding My Code to CIMS

The primary reason I choose WMP instead of CASE:W for this project was to avoid having to add my own C code for custom processing to the CIMS application. In most cases my plan was fulfilled. WMP allowed me easily to use bitmap images inside dialog boxes, a feature missing in CASE:W. It also let me use dialog boxes inside the main program window with ease. This would have been a bit more difficult using CASE:W, but not much. The real thrill of using WMP instead of CASE:W was the way I could step in and out of the WMP Dialog Box Designer in Animation Test mode. CASE:W can't even come close to this feature. So now that my first draft of CIMS is completed (no computer program is ever finished), I'll summarize where I added my custom code to the application.

- For the Exit push button in the opening CIMS screen and the Exit command in each menu, I linked the menu item or push button to the user-defined function `ExitProgram`. WMP created the `ExitProgram` function template for me in USERCODE.C. All I needed to add was a call to `PostQuitMessage` to Exit the program.

- In the Select Host dialog box, I wanted a way to link to each of the corporate location intro dialog boxes (BOSTON_INTRO, LONDON_INTRO, and ROCKIES_INTRO). To do this I created temporary push buttons in the Select Host System dialog box that linked to these dialog boxes. When I added my own code to the CIMS application to display a list of computer systems in the Select Host System dialog box, I borrowed the code WMP generated to process the messages from each of these temporary push buttons and put it in the custom code I added. After my list box was working, I deleted the temporary push buttons.

- The Select Host list box contains two locations I did not build dialog boxes for: Dallas and Seattle. If the user were to select Dallas or Seattle, the Windows `MessageBox` function would display a message that the office was closed for the day.

- In each of the startup functions for using a dialog box template inside the main program window, I put some C code to call `BLDSwitchMenu` to switch to the correct menu set. I did this because WMP can do only one thing when linking one application object to another. (Maybe this will be fixed in a new feature release after Blue Sky Software reads this book.)

Using Borland Resource Workshop

After completing CIMS, I decided to make a version of it that uses 3-D dialog boxes created by the Borland Resource Workshop (BRW). To do this I went through the following steps:

1. Added a `LoadLibary` call to the CIMS program initialization to make sure the BRW DLL, BWCC.DLL, is loaded while CIMS is executing. To create a function template using WMP, I chose Initialization from the Configure menu to display the Custom Initialization dialog box. I then typed in the name of the function I wanted WMP to call during program initialization, `ApplicationInit`, and clicked on OK to close the dialog box.

2. Added a `FreeLibrary` call to the CIMS program termination processing to make sure that the BWCC.DLL library was freed when the program terminated. I added this function call to the processing of the main program window's `WM_DESTROY` message. To create a function that WMP calls for processing `WM_DESTROY`, I chose Message Processing from the Configure menu to display the Custom Message Processing dialog box. In this dialog box, I selected the `WM_DESTROY` message from the Message list box and clicked on OK. Now WMP would generate a function for the `WM_DESTROY` message in USERCODE.C.

   To keep things simple, I used the WMP default file name (USERCODE.C) for my source code file throughout this chapter. For your projects, you can name this file anything you want. You can also have WMP create as many user code source files for your project as you want.

3. Opened the dialog box source file, CIMS.DLG, and modified all the dialog boxes inside it to give them a 3-D appearance. I used the same procedures discussed in Chapter 2 to do this.

4. Saved the dialog box source file in a new file, CIMS_BRW.DLG. I made sure not to change any dialog box or control window identifiers when I made appearance changes to the dialog boxes in CIMS.DLG—except for OK and Cancel push buttons, so they could use the fancier Borland custom control push buttons that use owner-draw graphics.

5. Since I changed the symbolic identifiers for the OK push buttons to the symbolic ID, IDOK, in some of the CIMS dialog boxes (BOSTON_INTRO, LONDON_INTRO, and ROCKIES_INTRO), I also needed to make some minor C

code modifications. In the code WMP generated for each of the dialog boxes, a unique symbolic identifier was used for each of the OK push buttons to link it to another dialog box that was put in the main program window.

- The BOSTON_INTRO OK push button was linked to BOSTON_CIMS.
- The LONDON_INTRO OK push button was linked to LONDON_CIMS.
- The ROCKIES_INTRO OK push button was linked to ROCKIES_CIMS.

To correct the links I had just broken, I borrowed the code generated by WMP in the USERCODE.WMC source code file to perform each link. I copied it to USERCODE.C and used it where the WM_COMMAND message for IDOK is processed for each of these dialog boxes. For example, the C code I put into the `BLD_LondonDlgProc` function in USERCODE.C was:

```
case WM_COMMAND:
          switch(wParam)
              {
          case IDOK:
              // Code duplicated from USERCODE.WMC to link to
              // LONDON.CIMS dialog
              BLD_LondonCIMSClFunc(hDlg,message,wParam,lParam);
              EndDialog(hDlg,IDC_LONDONCIMS);
              break;
```

6. With these changes made, I rebuilt my program using the QuickC for Windows compiler with the BORCIMS.RC file—not the CIMS.RC file. The dialog box source file created using BRW is compatible with Microsoft C/C++, Microsoft QuickC for Windows, and Borland-language products. It is not compatible with WMP. To continue to use WMP and BRW together, I kept two separate dialog box source files, CIMS.DLG for working with WMP and CIMS_BRW for working with BRW. This works as long an you are not making many changes to your application design using WMP that affect the application's dialog box source file. If you have to make major changes, you can always use BRW to copy dialog boxes from one resource script file to another to update it.

Summary

As you can see from the CIMS project, WMP has a fancy user interface, provides a lot of flexibility in developing applications, and generates applications quickly. The source code generated by WMP is more difficult to follow than the code generated by CASE:W, but it has advantages when compared to CASE:W's. First, there is more attention to programming detail in the WMP-generated code. If a dialog box can't be displayed, WMP includes a call to `MessageBox` to let you know what happened—CASE:W doesn't. Sometimes CASE:W regeneration doesn't work and some of your source code gets wiped out. Using WMP, your source code is always preserved if you follow its code-generation rules. I also found that WMP generated fewer Compiler Warning errors.

WMP is a fast way to generate Windows applications and it is constantly improving. During the course of writing this book, I worked with WindowsMAKER Professional 4.0. Toward the end of the project, I had the chance to begin to learn about WindowsMAKER Professional 5.0 by testing an ALPHA version of it. You can expect that Version 5 will contain many new features, such as the ability to build icon tool palettes and generate function calls to Windows Help. Version 5 will also offer an updated user interface that improves on what WindowsMAKER Professional already has.

Now that you have learned how the two leading GUI builders work, let's move on to see how we can automate creating code for dialog boxes and building Help files. In the next chapter you will see how to use Magic Fields to add powerful edit controls to your program dialog boxes, how to use DialogCoder to automate the process of coding dialog box procedures, and how to use RoboHELP to automate the process of writing Windows Help files.

Using Magic Fields, RoboHELP, and DialogCoder

5

- The basics of creating custom controls

- Using Magic Fields to augment the functionality of dialog boxes

- Using RoboHELP to build Windows Help files

- Creating dialog box functions using DialogCoder

In previous chapters we explored how to automate Windows software development using Borland Resouce Workshop to manage resource development and GUI builders to create a Windows application platform that we can build upon. In this chapter we examine three specialized tools: Magic Fields, RoboHELP, and Dialog-Coder. Magic Fields and DialogCoder work with you to build functionality for the dialog boxes you create. RoboHELP is an expert assistant for helping you build Windows Help files.

This chapter builds on the topics covered in the previous chapters on automating Windows development, but it can be read out of sequence. When a topic in this chapter can be more clearly understood by reading a topic in a previous chapter, I will provide a chapter and section reference for that topic. Now that you know what's ahead, let's go explore Magic Fields.

Making Magic Fields

Magic Fields is an application from Blue Sky Software that aids you in creating dialog boxes for your Windows applications. While Magic Fields provides functionality similar to CASE:W's Extended Code Support, it is actually quite different. With an introduction like that, I bet you are wondering, "What does Magic Fields do and how does it work?"

Magic Fields is a custom control library that lets you put a much more powerful edit control in your dialog boxes than the one that is built into Windows. Once you put one of these powerful new edit controls, called a Magic Field, into your dialog box, you get the ability to give your entire dialog box a 3-D appearance and you gain access to a powerful set of functions for converting data to and from a Magic Field. All of this is implemented in the Magic Fields dynamic link library, MFEDIT.DLL.

Although Magic Fields was developed by Blue Sky Software and can be used with WindowsMAKER Professional, it can also be used with any Windows dialog box editor that supports custom controls. For instance, you can use the Magic Fields custom control library with the Windows SDK Dialog Editor and the Borland Resource Workshop. You could even use a dialog box that has Magic Fields in it with CASE:W.

At this point I am assuming you already know what a custom control is—at least conceptually—and how a custom control works. You have already encountered custom controls once in this book when we discussed the custom control library that comes with Borland Resource Workshop in Chapter 2. If you have heard about custom controls (or even if you haven't) but are not sure how they work, I'll summarize what they do and how they work in the next section, "What Does a Custom Control Do?" If you are already familiar with custom controls, you can jump over the following section and learn more about Magic Fields.

What Does a Custom Control Do?

Control windows are application objects that a Windows program uses to interact with the user. Predefined Windows controls include scroll bars, radio buttons, check boxes, push buttons, list boxes, combo boxes, edit fields, and static text objects. You can design your own custom control windows, or you can purchase others from third-party software developers. As you already know, the Borland Resource Workshop includes a set of custom controls.

The standard controls supplied by Windows provide a foundation for a dialog box's user interface. You should not consider creating a custom control window just to add features to a standard control window for a single application. Instead, you should add the features your application needs by subclassing or superclassing the control window.

Creating a Custom Control

There are two ways to create control windows. You can use the CreateWindow function, or you can use the dialog box editor and define controls as part of a dialog box. Although the latter method is more common, let's first discuss CreateWindow.

Almost everything you interface with in the Windows environment is some kind of window. Standard dialog box controls, as you would expect, are predefined windows that can be used throughout your application. These standard control windows are similar to the windows registered and created by your own programs. However, unlike most of the windows you create, controls are more object-oriented in nature and consist of completely reentrant code. This implies that a control should not access static data or be dependent on the fact that only one thread of execution may be present. Also, in order for the control to be correctly handled by the dialog box manager, a custom control must process all keyboard or mouse input received in a consistent manner.

Although control windows may sound like a complex topic, they are actually fairly easy to create. You must first decide on a class name for each control you implement. This same class name is also used in your .RC file whenever you wish to use the control in a dialog box. Be careful not to use one of the predefined class names provided by Windows; the results can be quite spectacular if you accidentally duplicate one of these names.

Now that you know what a custom control is, let's go over the process for creating one.

1. Register the control window class, as with any other type of window. Any attempt to use the control before it has been registered will result in a serious system error, and may even prevent your application from running.

2. Define a window's style using the `dwStyle` parameter in the `CreateWindow` and `CreateWindowEx` functions. Each control window has its own style within its window class. These styles define the control window's behavior and appearance. When you create a control window, you use styles that are used for all window types that including WS_BORDER, WS_VISIBLE, and WS_CHILD. You can also use styles specific to a window class. For instance, all the window styles specific to the list box window class have the Hungarian notation prefix LBS_. When you design a control, you can define custom styles that determine behavior and appearance.

3. Define all instance variables. Instance variables are private static data associated with each instance of your control. This data must be allocated dynamically and be readily accessible to each thread of execution. Although you could develop your own scheme for instance variables, you should probably consider using local or global atoms or property lists, or perhaps defining extra bytes to be associated with every instance of the window class data structure.

4. Define your control window function. Each control must have an associated window function responsible for processing all related messages. Since your control will usually be managed by the dialog box manager, you should consider implementing both a keyboard and a mouse user interface. A window function's primary purpose is to process messages, and a control window is

no different. A control window should be able to process all standard window messages that apply, such as `WM_CREATE` and `WM_PAINT`. You can also define custom messages specific to the control window class. Just make sure to document them correctly, using program comments to explain what the message does, the values of `wParam` and `lParam`, and what the return value is for.

A control window is also responsible for sending messages to its parent window when some action takes place. The control tells the parent something happened by sending a `WM_COMMAND` message. The `wParam` parameter of the `WM_COMMAND` message contains the control window ID; the `lParam` contains the control window's notification code in the high word and its handle in the low word.

5. Export the control window function. As is the case with any other window function in your application, you must export it before use. Failure to do so is a very common problem encountered by even the most experienced Windows programmers.

Putting Custom Controls in a Dialog Box Using a Dialog Box Editor

Now that you know the basics of creating a control window inside a Windows application, you are likely wondering how a control window can be put into a common library which can be accessed using a dialog box editor and used by multiple programs at once. The answer is to put the control window into a dynamic link library (DLL). The fundamentals of creating a dynamic link library are well covered in the Microsoft Windows SDK Guide to Programming (as well as many other books on Windows programming), so I will not go into the details of creating a DLL here. Instead, let's discuss the specifics of putting a custom control window inside a DLL.

Once you have a custom control window working inside a Windows application, it is not much work to cut and paste the code for the control window inside a DLL. In many cases I hack out custom control windows inside a Windows application first, before I try to generalize it and move it into a DLL.

After you have created a custom control window, you can put it inside a dialog box by using a dialog box editor. For instance, to install a basic custom control using the Windows 3.1 SDK Dialog Editor to display a dialog box to configure custom styles, you follow these steps:

1. Choose New Custom from the Dialog Editor File menu to display the New Temporary Custom Control dialog box.

2. Type in the Class Name for the control window. This is the name you used when the control window was registered either in your own code or in a DLL.

3. Define the Control Defaults for the control window's style, height, and width. If the control has a caption, type that in as well. Normally, you can go with the defaults here—especially if the control window sizes itself when it processes the WM_CREATE message.

4. After you have completed defining your custom control as a Temporary Custom Control, use the Custom Control tool from the Dialog Editor Tools palette to put the control in your dialog box. When you place the control, the Select Custom Control dialog box appears, asking you to select the control you have just defined from the Available Controls list.

5. After the dialog box is saved, it is almost ready for using in a Windows application. If your custom control is included in your application—not in a DLL—the only thing that is left to do is to build your application. However, if the custom control is in a DLL, you must use the LoadLibrary function call to make sure that the DLL is loaded before you display the dialog box that utilizes it. You should also remember to use the FreeLibrary function call to release the library before your Windows application exits.

Making the Custom Control DLL Interact with a Dialog Box Editor

As you will see shortly, the Magic Fields custom controls pop up a dialog box when they are clicked on in a dialog box editor to define an extensive set of attributes for the Magic Fields control window. The previous discussion overviews the process for installing a simple control window, in either a Windows application or a DLL, that does not provide this functionality. To use a custom control globally and have it interact with a dialog box editor, it must be put inside a DLL. The DLL must also contain seven functions that the dialog box editor can call to retrieve information about the custom control window. These functions are:

- `LibMain`. This function is called by Windows when the DLL is loaded into memory. It must be part of every DLL—not just custom control DLLs.

- `WEP`. This function is called by Windows when the DLL is removed from memory. It must be part of every DLL—not just custom control DLLs.

- `ClassWndFn`. This is the window function for the custom control window. The `Class` part of the function name is the class name of your control window that is defined when you register it. This function must have the ordinal value of 5 defined in the module definition file (.DEF) of the DLL.

- `ClassInfo`. This function is called by a dialog box editor to inform it of the controls supported by this DLL. The function must have the ordinal value of 2 defined in the module definition file (.DEF) of the DLL.

- `ClassStyle`. This function is called by a dialog box editor when the user double-clicks on the control window in the dialog box template to change the control window's ID, text, or styles. It must have the ordinal value of 3 defined in the module definition file (.DEF) of the DLL.

- `ClassDlgFn`. This is the dialog box function for the custom control's Style dialog box that is displayed when the user double-clicks on the control window in a dialog box editor. This function must have the ordinal value of 6 defined in the module definition file (.DEF) of the DLL when it is created.

- `ClassFlags`. This function is called by a dialog box editor when the dialog box template is saved. It converts the control window's styles to a string defining the class-specific style IDs that the dialog box editor writes into the CONTROL statement in the .DLG file. This function must have the ordinal value of 4 defined in the module definition file (.DEF) of the DLL.

Control windows can be simple or complex. It just depends on how much functionality they need to include and whether or not they interact with the user within a dialog box editor. This section is meant to overview the aspects of implementing control windows, not to serve as an in-depth how-to guide. Unfortunately, there has not been a whole lot written about how to implement global custom controls in a Windows DLL—especially in the Windows SDK documentation. If you would like to learn more about how to implement custom controls in a Windows application, I suggest the following sources:

- The Windows 3.1 SDK includes three examples of creating custom control windows in the \WINDEV\GUIDE directory. These applications are RAINBOW, ROTARY, and MUSCROLL.

- Microsoft University publishes a video training course that explores every aspect of building control windows, including creating custom controls. This course is called *EXPLORING CONTROLS: Video Training for Developers Using the Microsoft Windows Environment.*

Magic Fields Features

Now that you understand custom controls, it is easier to describe what a Magic Field does and how it works. Magic Fields is a custom control library that provides the following features:

- A Magic Field is a powerful alternative to the edit control window class provided by Windows. It gives you powerful data field entry validation using dBASE-like picture templates.

- A Magic Field lets you replace your standard Windows edit controls with Magic Field controls without making any source code changes.

- The Magic Fields DLL provides you with a complete Application Programming Interface that has powerful date, time, number, and text manipulation.

- A Magic Field provides full support for international dates, times, and currencies.

- The Magic Fields DLL stores the validation setup, including the picture code, color, and font selection, in an external configuration file so that changes don't require recompiling.

- Magic Fields may be subclassed or superclassed like any other control window.

- Magic Fields provides error-handling to warn users of incorrect field contents.

- If you use a Magic Field inside a dialog box, the Magic Fields DLL can give the entire dialog box a "NeXt-like" font, border, and color settings.

- Magic Fields works with the Microsoft Windows SDK Dialog Editor, the Borland Resource Workshop, and the WindowsMAKER Professional Dialog Box Designer.

Now that you understand what Magic Fields does, let's take a look at how it works by seeing how to develop a dialog box that has some "Magic" in it.

Making a Magic Field

To understand how Magic Fields works, we'll look at a small project that I developed for this book. The Magic Fields project, named Magic Fields Example (MAGIC for short), is a simple Windows application I created using WindowsMAKER Professional (WMP) and Magic Fields. All MAGIC does is display a dialog box that has three Magic Fields in it, as shown in Figure 5.1.

The Magic Fields Example dialog box has three Magic Fields in it: one for typing in a name, one for typing in a birth date, and one for displaying the age of the person whose birth date is typed in. The person's age is calculated when you click on the

FIGURE 5.1:

A "Magical" Windows application

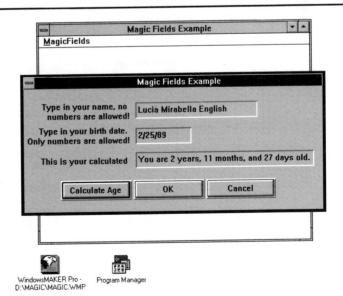

Calculate Age push button. This dialog box also has that new "NeXt look" that is the latest trend in Windows application interfaces. In this example I used the name of my constant companion who is always nearby when I am working at my PC, Lucia Mirabella English. Lucy (her nickname) is my precocious Labrador Retriever.

Now that you have seen what MAGIC does, let's learn how to create it. To start, let's run the WMP Dialog Box Designer to edit the Magic Fields Example dialog box. Remember, Magic Fields also works with the Borland Resource Workshop and the Windows SDK Dialog Editor in exactly the same was as I'll describe it working with the WMP Dialog Box Designer. Figure 5.2 shows the Magic Fields Example dialog box being edited by the WMP Dialog Box Designer.

To look more closely at how a Magic Field is constructed, all you have to do is double-click on the Magic Field control to display the Magic Fields Control Panel dialog box for the control, as shown in Figure 5.3.

FIGURE 5.2:

Editing the Magic Fields Example dialog box

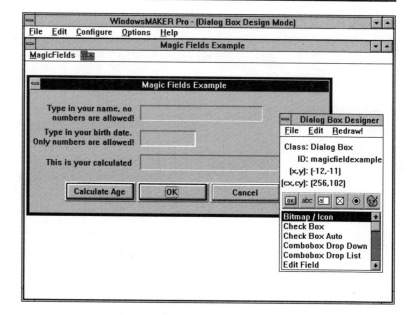

FIGURE 5.3:

The Magic Fields Control Panel

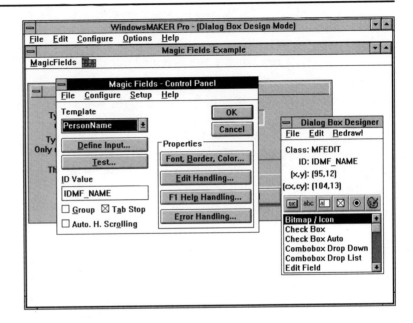

The Magic Fields Control Panel

You use the Control Panel to access all of the Magic Fields functionality. From this dialog box you can use push buttons to perform the following functions:

- *Define Input* lets you determine what kind of input validation you want the field to allow.

- *Test* lets you test the effect of the input validation criteria, edit handling, help handling, and error handling you specify for a Magic Field. If you use Magic Fields along with WMP, you can test all the Magic Fields in a dialog box in WMP Animation Test mode with the same results. This lets you test many aspects of your Magic Fields user interface without having to generate and build your program.

- *Font, Border, Color* lets you pick these attributes for each Magic Field. Using this feature, you can distinguish one Magic Field from another by its appearance—without any programming. Although this is an interesting feature, it should not be overused. In most cases, using a consistent color scheme and font in all your program dialog boxes will give your Windows application a more polished appearance.

- *Edit Handling* lets you select from a variety of field editing capabilities, including disabling field input, managing how the input focus is handled, and specifying special input effects, such as automatically filling in slash characters when a user is typing into a date field.

- *F1 Help Handling* lets you supply custom Help messages that are displayed when the user presses Ctrl+F1 when the field has the input focus.

The Magic Fields Control Panel also has an edit field where you supply the control ID for the control window and a menu for utilizing other program features. One of these features is the Look & Feel command in the Configure menu. After you have included one Magic Field in a dialog box, you can give the entire dialog box a 3-D appearance by selecting the Look & Feel command to display the dialog box shown in Figure 5.4.

Defining Dialog Box Appearance

Selecting the Next Look Painting and the Gray Background check boxes gives your dialog box a 3-D gray appearance, similar to what you can create with the Borland Resource Workshop described in Chapter 2. The Next Look Above and Below

FIGURE 5.4:
The Look & Feel dialog box

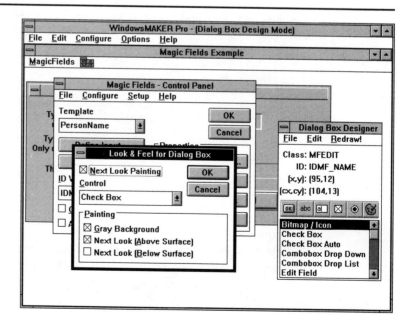

Surface check boxes will give all the standard EDIT and BUTTON class controls in your dialog box a 3-D appearance as well. With Above Surface checked, the 3-D effect appears to be chiseled above the surface of the dialog box; with Below Surface, it appears to be chiseled into the surface.

After configuring the overall dialog box appearance of my Magic Windows application, I configured the appearance of the Magic Field control window, IDMF_NAME. As shown in Figure 5.5, I selected black for the text color and light gray for the background color. I also selected Next Look (Below Surface) for the control window border. I let the font default to the System font.

After making all my selections, I saved the control window's appearance as a Scheme template, called NextLook. For all the other Magic Fields in the dialog box, all I needed to do was select the NextLook Scheme template to apply the attributes of the template to the control. Once a Scheme template is created, it can be used in other dialog boxes as well.

FIGURE 5.5:

Selecting font, color, and border for a Magic Field

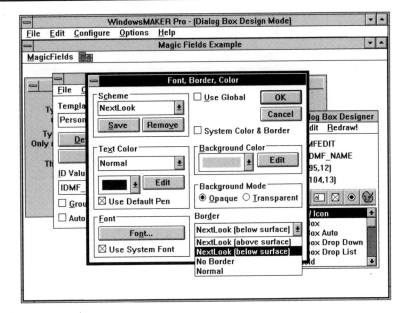

Defining Magic Field Functionality

Now that the look and feel of the dialog box and its controls have been configured, it's time to specify some functionality. To start, click on the Define Input push button back in the Magic Fields Control Panel to display the dialog box shown in Figure 5.6.

Magic Fields provides you with a variety of options for defining format validation for an edit field. Your first step in defining how a field is to be validated is selecting a Format. Formats may be selected from the Format combo box. The formats provided with Magic Fields are

- Date

- Time

- Number

- Currency

- Integer

- Custom (same as the picture format used in dBASE)

FIGURE 5.6:

Defining input validation for a Magic Field

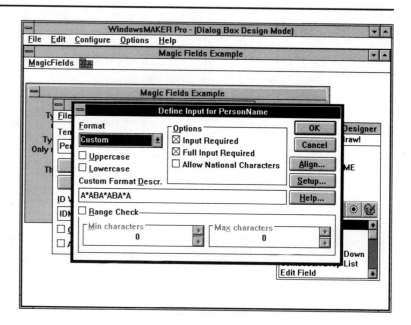

As you can see in Figure 5.6, I used a custom picture format to define the field validation for the IDMF_NAME field in the dialog box I created. The character *A* is the picture code for alphabetic characters. The character * means zero or more occurrences of the preceding character. The character *B* is the picture code for a blank or a space. In this description, I have defined a name to be one or more alphabetic characters followed by a space, followed by one or more alphabetic characters, followed by a space, followed by one or more alphabetic characters.

After I completed defining the input validation specifics for the IDMF_NAME field, I chose OK, and the Save Template As dialog box appeared for me to give my custom validation definition a name.

Magic Field Templates   Magic Field templates are a useful and powerful feature. A template lets you give a name to the validation specifics you define in the Define Input dialog box. You can then apply this name to other dialog box fields as you create them for your application.

After a template name has been defined and used for several fields in several dialog boxes, any change to the validation attributes for the template will be applied globally to all the Magic Fields that use that template. Templates are a powerful feature that promote consistency for the control windows inside all the dialog boxes for your application. However, you must use a little caution when working with a template, always remembering that any validation attribute you change for a template will be applied to all the Magic Fields in all your application's dialog boxes.

In the Magic Fields Example dialog box, I used the predefined Date template for the Birth Date field and the predefined Text template for the Calculated Age field. After defining how the input should be handled for each field in the dialog box, I defined the Edit Handling for each field.

Magic Field Edit Handling   A standard Windows edit control is a rectangle in which you can enter text from the keyboard. When you select an edit field, you give it the input focus by clicking in it or moving to it by using the Tab key. You can enter text when the field displays a flashing cursor called the caret. Like the Windows Notepad (which uses a large Windows edit control that fills up the entire client area of the window), you can use the cursor keys, the Backspace key, or the mouse to move the caret and select text in the field. You can configure additional edit handling attributes for a Magic Field by choosing the Edit Handling push button in the

Magic Fields Control Panel dialog box to display the Edit Handling dialog box shown in Figure 5.7.

Magic Fields extends the capabilities of a Windows standard edit control by offering the following features found in the Edit Handling dialog box:

- *Disable Input* initializes the field so it can't be selected and edited. This option is the same as using the WS_DISABLED Window-style flag.

- *Insert Mode* is the default behavior of an input field. The typed character is inserted at the position of the caret.

- *Overwrite Mode* replaces the next character, if any, at the position of the caret.

- *Automatic Mode* lets Magic Fields decide whether the typed character should be inserted or should replace the next character. Magic Fields will replace variable characters (such as letters) but will insert before static characters (such as / or -). When Automatic Mode is selected, Magic Fields floats the typed separators through the format string for number and currency fields to keep the format valid.

FIGURE 5.7:

Specifying edit handling for a Magic Field

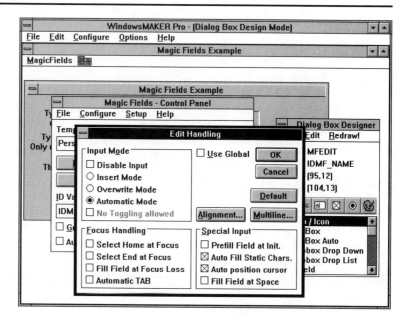

- *No Toggling Allowed.* Toggling is switching between Insert Mode and Overwrite Mode by pressing the Ins key. Selecting this option disables toggling.

- *Fill Field at Focus Loss* supports filling of system values, such as date and time, when the user presses Tab and the field loses input focus.

- *Select Home at Focus* positions the caret at the beginning of the field that gets the input focus when the user presses Tab key. If the field is selected with a mouse, the caret will be positioned where the user clicked.

- *Select End at Focus* positions the caret at the end of the field that gets the input focus when the user presses the Tab key. If the field is selected with a mouse, the caret will be positioned where the user clicked.

- *Automatic TAB* automatically moves to the next field when the current field's input is complete. This selection is for input fields using templates built on the Time, Date, and Custom formats. For example, you could use this selection to have the caret move from a date field to the next field when the date has been typed in. The user would not have to press Tab or Enter.

- *Auto Position Cursor* causes the caret to jump over all fixed characters that were defined in the format specification. For example, in a date format, when the user starts to type in the date, the caret will jump over the / / characters.

- *Auto Fill Static Chars.* automatically fills out all fixed characters as defined in the format specification while the user types. For example, for a date format, when the user starts to type in the date, the field will automatically add the / / as the user types.

- *Prefill Field at Init* prefills all fixed characters defined in the format specification when the field is displayed. For example, for a date field, the / / will already be shown in the field, before the user starts to type.

- *Fill Field at Space* fills in system values when the user types the next separator or space. This works only if the position of the caret in the field allows this action. Filling of system values is supported for Date, Time, Currency, and Number.

For the `IDMF_NAME` field, I used the default Edit Handling features. For the `IDMF_BIRTHDATE` field, I turned on the Auto Fill Static Chars. and Auto Position Cursor. In the `IDMF_AGE` field, I disabled input, since this field is only for output to display the user's calculated age.

Specifying Magic Field Help   The Help settings for a field are stored as Help topics, identified by a name and a description. Help topics for an application are stored in the Help Templates section in the application setup file. You can use the Magic Fields standard Help topics or define your own Help for a field by choosing the F1 Help Handling push button in the Magic Fields Control Panel, as shown in Figure 5.8.

Figure 5.9 shows how I specified my own Help message for the IDMF_BIRTHDATE field. The figure shows what happens when a user presses Ctrl+F1 when the IDMF_BIRTHDATE field has the input focus. When you use the Magic Fields Help feature, make sure your Help messages are brief. You are limited to approximately 90 characters.

Specifying Magic Field Error Handling   The Error Handling push button in the Magic Fields Control Panel lets you specify how field validation errors will be handled. For instance, does the field beep at you when you enter the wrong character? My PC tells me "Bummer" when this happens, because I have a SoundBlaster card installed on my system and use the .WAV files that come with Multimedia Windows to enhance my system sounds.

FIGURE 5.8:

Specifying Help for a Magic Field

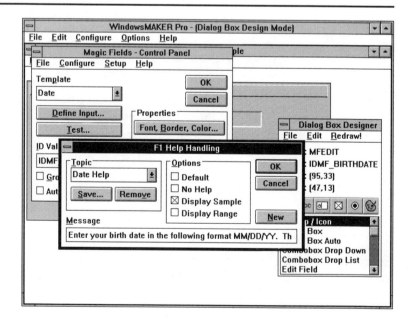

FIGURE 5.9:

Testing Magic Fields Help

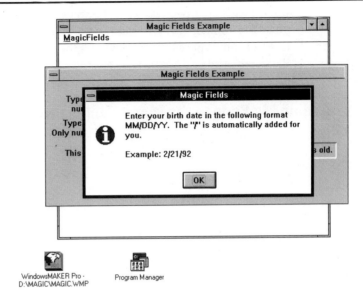

You can configure Magic Fields Error Handling to display dialog boxes when an event occurs, but you can't customize error messages. You can also specify when fields are validated. You can validate a field when it loses the input focus or when the dialog box is closed.

Setup Files

Magic Fields is designed so that more than one application can make use of Magic Fields controls at the same time. To be able to do so, however, every application needs a separate setup file. Magic Fields will try to use the setup file in the working directory when it is used from dialog box editors and in the application directory when it is used from an end-user application. If an application uses a different setup file from the one in the application directory, it can be specified by choosing Setup Files in the Setup menu.

All of the information that you define for the Magic Fields in your application is stored externally to the application in this setup file. This means that all of the Magic Field behaviors and appearances can be changed without changing the application.

Magic Fields uses two types of setup files. The Magic Fields setup file, MAGIC.INI, is needed to keep your application's global settings. The application setup file, MFEDIT.INI, is necessary for keeping the dialog box characteristics for several applications at once.

Adding My Code to the Magic Fields Project

After I finished using Magic Fields to spruce up my dialog box, I added some of my own C code to the MAGIC application to make everything work. I used WMP to generate the application and link the MAGIC application dialog box to the Magic Fields Dialog Box menu item. As you have seen, I used Magic Fields and the WMP Dialog Box Designer to build the dialog box. To make the application work as you see it, I went through the following steps:

1. Added the function call `MfInitMFEDIT` to the `BLD_ApplicationAppInit` function in USERCODE.C. When I created the MAGIC application using WMP, I specified custom processing for application initialization. I got to this dialog box in WMP by choosing Initialization in the Configure menu. When you choose custom processing, WMP generates `BLD_ApplicationAppInit` for you. The call to `MfInitMFEDIT` loads and initializes the Magic Fields DLL, MFEDIT.DLL.

2. Added the C code to calculate the age and display it in the dialog box. This code uses several Magic Fields API functions to get information from a Magic Field and do numeric conversions. The Magic Fields DLL includes 30 functions for

   - working with time: 4 functions
   - working with dates: 4 functions
   - getting information from a Magic Field: 10 functions
   - putting information into a Magic Field: 8 functions
   - initializing Magic Fields and other miscellaneous functions: 4 functions

The C source code for doing the date calculation and displaying it is in the function `BLD_CalculateAgeUDCFunc`. Wherever I used Magic Fields API functions, I marked my C code with comments. The following listing shows the C code for this function.

```
BOOL BLD_CalculateAgeUDCFunc(hWnd,message,wParam,lParam) /* User
Defined Code */
HWND hWnd;
unsigned message;
WORD wParam;
LONG lParam;
  {
  MFDATE mfdTodaysDate, mfdBirthDate;
  int iError;
  int iYears, iMonths, iDays, iSwitchMonth;
  char szMessage[60];

  // Magic Fields function to get the current date.
  MfGetCurrentDate (&mfdTodaysDate);

  // Magic Fields function to get the date out of the
  //IDMF_BIRTHDATE control window
  // the data type for mfdBirthDate is defined in MFEDIT.H
  MfGetFieldDate (hWnd, IDMF_BIRTHDATE, &mfdBirthDate, &iError);

  iYears = mfdTodaysDate.iYear - mfdBirthDate.iYear;
  if (mfdBirthDate.iMonth > mfdTodaysDate.iMonth)
    iYears--;

  if (mfdBirthDate.iMonth == mfdTodaysDate.iMonth &&
    mfdBirthDate.iDay > mfdTodaysDate.iDay)
    iYears--;

  iMonths = mfdTodaysDate.iMonth - mfdBirthDate.iMonth;
  if ((mfdTodaysDate.iMonth < mfdBirthDate.iMonth) ||
    (mfdTodaysDate.iMonth == mfdBirthDate.iMonth &&
    mfdBirthDate.iDay > mfdTodaysDate.iDay))
    iMonths += 12;

  if (mfdTodaysDate.iDay < mfdBirthDate.iDay)
    iMonths--;

  iDays = mfdTodaysDate.iDay - mfdBirthDate.iDay;
  if (mfdTodaysDate.iDay < mfdBirthDate.iDay)
    {
    if (mfdTodaysDate.iMonth == 1)
      iSwitchMonth = 12;
    else
      iSwitchMonth = mfdTodaysDate.iMonth - 1;
    switch (iSwitchMonth)
```

```
        {
        case 1:
        case 3:
        case 5:
        case 7:
        case 8:
        case 12:
          iDays += 31;
          break;

        case 2:
          iDays += 28;
          // MfIsLeapYear is a Magic Fields function to determine
          // if the current year is a leap year
          if (MfIsLeapYear (mfdTodaysDate.iYear))
            iDays++;
          break;

        default:
          iDays += 30;
        }
      }

    wsprintf (szMessage,
      "You are %d years, %d months, and %d days old.",
      iYears, iMonths, iDays);

    SetDlgItemText (hWnd, IDMF_AGE, szMessage);
    return TRUE;
```

That's all the code I added to make it work. Well, almost—I did put a call to Post-QuitMessage and a FreeLibrary call for the Magic Fields DLL in the exit processing function. Try out my MAGIC application and look at its C code to get a better idea of what Magic Fields can do. Before we move on to our next programming tool, let's compare Magic Fields to CASE:W Extended Code Support and DialogCoder.

What Magic Fields Is and Isn't

From this overview you have learned that Magic Fields is a powerful add-on for creating edit-like controls in your dialog boxes and for controlling their appearance (font, color, and border). All of the Magic Fields functionality is encapsulated in a DLL. Magic Fields does not generate C code for your application or provide functional support for any other type of control window than edit control windows.

Edit control windows are the most complicated of all the control window types, and Magic Fields adds functionality to them that exceeds the functionality for edit controls in both CASE:W Extended Code Support and DialogCoder. As an added bonus, Magic Fields lets you control the appearance of your dialog box as well.

CASE:W Extended Code Support and DialogCoder generate the C code in a Windows dialog box function to support additional functionality for dialog boxes. While neither of these tools adds the power Magic Fields does to edit controls, they support more types of dialog box controls than Magic Fields does, including list boxes, combo boxes, radio buttons, and check boxes. CASE:W Extended Code Support provides a basic level of support for all of these control types. DialogCoder provides more in-depth support for all of these control types.

So which tool should you choose? It depends. Is it OK to have the functionality encapsulated in a DLL or do you want to have your C code generated instead? Working with generated C source code lets you add to and modify C code to enhance functionality. You can also enhance Magic Fields functionality by using user-defined processing, subclassing, and superclassing. Magic Fields provides super functionality for working with edit controls, but DialogCoder supports more types of control windows.

To make this decision you should review what each of these tools does and whether or not you feel it could help you develop your Windows applications faster and easier. Remember, we still have two more Windows automation tools to cover, RoboHELP and DialogCoder, before we are done with this chapter. At the end of the chapter, I will summarize what we have covered in this part of the book and give you my personal rankings of these tools. For now, let's take a look at RoboHELP.

Using RoboHELP

RoboHELP is a software application from Blue Sky Software that works inside Word for Windows to aid you in creating Windows Help files for your application. You design the structure of your Help file using topics, hypertext links, hot buttons, and graphics. RoboHELP assists you through the entire process, including setting up a project, creating Help file objects (topics, hypertext links, pop-up windows, and graphics), saving and generating the files for the Help Compiler, and calling the

Windows Help Compiler to generate the Help files. It generates an .HH file that has symbolic identifiers in it for you to use when calling Windows Help from your application to implement context-sensitive Help. However, RoboHELP does not help you code the function calls in your program to call Windows Help, the way CASE:W does.

Although RoboHELP assists you in creating Help files, it is quite different from the CASE:W Help feature. CASE:W offers you an easy way to create Windows Help for your program by putting the Help function calls in the C source code it generates and building you a set of Help files that reflect the structure of your program. (To review how CASE:W creates a Help system for you, read Chapter 3 and the CASE:W application project, DumpIT 2.0.) RoboHELP makes creating Help files much easier, but it doesn't help you code function calls to Windows Help in your application.

Personally, I found RoboHELP a joy to use. In some projects, I have converted CASE:W-generated Help files to RoboHELP so I could have my RoboHELP assistant at my side to help me add to and organize my Help files better.

RoboHELP Components

RoboHELP is a set of Word for Windows (WinWord) macros that are inside a WinWord document template named ROBOHELP.DOT. It is so flawlessly integrated, you'll feel as if it is part of WinWord. WinWord macros are really a complete programming language, called WordBASIC, that is very similar to the BASIC programming language. The RoboHELP WordBASIC macros also call functions that exist inside a set of RoboHELP DLLs. To understand a little better how RoboHELP works, let's look at its components and where they are installed on your system by the RoboHELP installation program.

- ROBOHELP.DOT, installed in the WinWord directory, is the RoboHELP template you use to create your WinWord Help documents. All the Help systems created with RoboHELP include one WinWord document based on this template.

- ROBORTF.DOT, also installed in the WinWord directory, is a WinWord template for the additional Help files you may include in your Help system. In addition to one document based on ROBOHELP.DOT, each Help system created with RoboHELP may contain one or more documents based on ROBORTF.DOT.

- ROBOLOAD.EXE is installed in the directory where Windows is installed. It is needed to get DLLs to function correctly with WinWord 1.x.

- ROBOHELP.DLL is installed in the \WINDOWS\SYSTEM directory. It contains most of the RoboHELP functionality.

- ROBOTAPE.DLL, also installed in the \WINDOWS\SYSTEM directory, is used by ROBOHELP.DLL for the RoboHELP Tools palette.

- ROBOHELP.HLP is installed in the same directory as ROBOHELP.DLL and is the Help file for RoboHELP.

- HC.PIF is installed in the same directory as your Help compiler (HC.EXE). RoboHELP really comes with three PIF files for Help Compilers: HC30.PIF (and HC.PIF) for the Windows 3.0 Help compiler, HC31.PIF for the Windows 3.1 Help compiler, and HCC7.PIF for the Help compiler included with Microsoft C/C++ 7.0.

I should also mention that the documentation for RoboHELP was created by its developer Gen Kiyooka, who also writes many interesting and entertaining articles about Windows programming for magazines such as *Computer Language.* I enjoy Gen's sense of humor, and it comes through in the RoboHELP User Guide. If you take the time to read the User Guide, you will find it to be much better written that most, and even a bit entertaining.

RoboHELP Features

Now that you understand what RoboHELP is and what its components are, let's look at what it does to help you create a Help system. RoboHELP takes the drudgery out of creating a Help system using WinWord by providing the following features:

- RoboHELP's toolbar gives you easy access to all of the RoboHELP functions you work with on a recurring basis. The toolbar can float in a palette, be aligned vertically at the right edge of the window, or be aligned horizontally in the upper-right corner of the WinWord window.

- RoboHELP makes creating the Help objects that define the structure of your Help system a snap. These objects are topics, jumps, and pop-up windows containing glossary terms.

- Code generation creates all the files required for your Help system from the WinWord documents that you create using RoboHELP. These files include the Rich Text Format (.RTF) documents that hold the Help file information, a header file for the symbolic identifiers used in the Help system, and the Help project file (.HPJ) required by the Help compiler.

- Multiple file support lets you create large, complex Help systems by managing all the files and the links between them to build Help systems that consist of a bevy of Help files.

- A project file builder manages the Help files you create and calls the Help compiler of your choice to build your Help system.

Creating a Help File

Now that you know what RoboHELP does, let's see how it works. To show you how a Help system is built using RoboHELP, I decided to create a Help system for the WindowsMAKER Professional demonstration application, CIMS. You will find all the files that were used for this project in the \ATOOLS\CIMS directory that was created when you installed the book's disk set on your computer. Figure 5.10 shows the CIMS Help system being created and tested.

The Help topic shown in Figure 5.10 shows the Help menu icons in the Windows Application Desktop window of CIMS. As you can see, each of these bitmap icons was included in the Help system. If you put the cursor over one of the bitmaps, it becomes a hand to indicate that more information is available. If you click the left mouse button, a pop-up window appears to display more information about that Help topic.

In the background behind the Help window, you can see the Help system being created with WinWord. This was about midway through creating the CIMS Help system. I used RoboHELP frequently to save and generate the Help system and to compile it, so I could see the results of what I was creating every step of the way.

Now would be a good time for you to work with the CIMS Help system to see what it can do. When you get back, we'll begin by looking at how this project was started using WinWord and RoboHELP.

FIGURE 5.10:

Testing CIMS Help

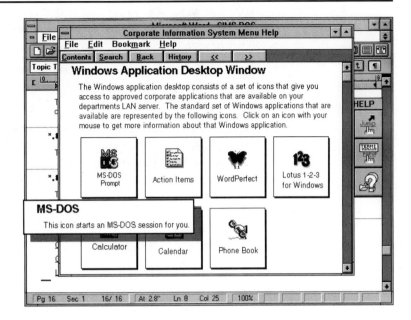

Getting Started

Before we get started creating the CIMS Help system, let's look at some of the jargon you should understand. Following are some of the terms that it's helpful to know when creating a Help system.

- *Hypertext* is a feature available in Windows Help and other hypertext-like software that lets you define links in a document so the user can travel a path through it. The reader can go through a hypertext document like a book or can travel other paths to get to the information the reader wants. Hypertext documents differ from standard documents in that they are not linear. Hypertext links to other topics are indicated in the Windows Help system by the color green and a dotted underline. Graphics can also be hypertext links to other information. If your cursor becomes a hand when it is positioned over a graphic, the graphic is a hypertext link to more information.

- A *Help topic* is a grouping of information—an information object—that is identified by a title. Help topics are the destination for all hypertext jumps.

- A *hypertext jump (or link)* happens when the reader clicks on a highlighted area in one topic and then Windows Help takes the reader to the other topic in the document.

- A *glossary term* is a pop-up window that appears when the reader clicks the left mouse button on a highlighted area in a topic. The topic appears in the pop-up window.

- *Context-sensitive Help* describes a Help system that provides help relating to what the user is doing in an application when Help is called. For instance, if the user has the File Open dialog box displayed and presses F1 for help, the user would get the Help system topic for the File Open dialog box.

All the Help systems you create with RoboHELP start with a new WinWord document. After you choose New from the WinWord File menu, the New dialog box is displayed, as shown in Figure 5.11.

FIGURE 5.11:

Starting a new Help system using WinWord and RoboHELP

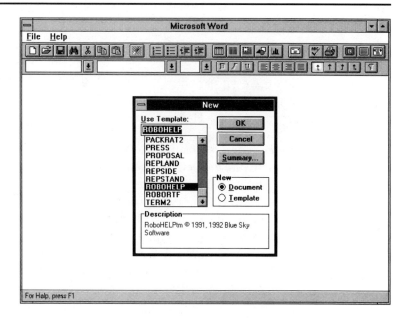

When the New dialog box is displayed, select ROBOHELP for the document template. After you click on OK to create the document, RoboHELP will display its Copyright dialog box. If you like cute things, wait while this dialog box is displayed, and you will see a small robot assemble the RoboHELP icon inside the dialog box.

After you have finished watching the robot, RoboHELP calls WinWord to display the File Save As dialog box so you can immediately save your Help project. You should save it with the same name as your program. You can use your program development working directory or a Help system working directory.

Next, RoboHELP creates the starting point for your Help system—a Help document with one topic in it for the Contents page, as shown in Figure 5.12. Notice the floating RoboHELP Tools palette for creating Help systems objects, saving and generating project files, and running the Help compiler using RoboHELP. It's now time to use the RoboHELP Tools palette to add some topics to the Help system.

FIGURE 5.12:

An initialized RoboHELP Help document

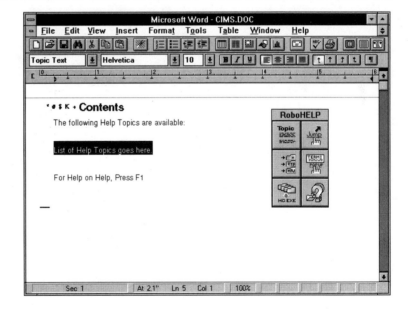

Creating Help Topics Using RoboHELP

The first Help topic I created for the CIMS Help system was named Opening Screen. In this topic, I planned to describe what the first window the user encounters with CIMS is for and where the user can go from this window by clicking on the push buttons in it.

First, I clicked on the RoboHELP Topic button in the Tools palette. The Insert New Help Topic dialog box was displayed, as shown in Figure 5.13.

I typed in my topic name and little else. RoboHELP takes care of the rest. If you are creating a regular Help topic (not a glossary entry displayed in a pop-up window), you should make sure that the Regular Help Topic radio button is highlighted. RoboHELP remembers this button's state from the last time you used the dialog box. When you click on OK, RoboHELP creates your topic on a separate page. All I needed to do was type in the information that goes with the topic.

FIGURE 5.13:

Defining a new Help topic using RoboHELP

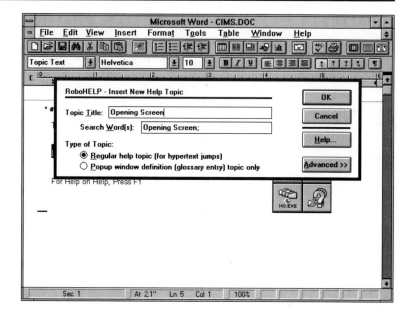

Making Jumps Using RoboHELP

After creating a topic, I needed a way to jump to it from the entry Opening Screen in the Contents topic. To do this I put the caret (the blinking text entry bar that shows where text is to be typed in using WinWord) in the Contents topic where I wanted the jump to occur. I then clicked on the RoboHELP jump tool in the Tools palette to create the jump, and RoboHELP displayed the Create New Hypertext Jump dialog box shown in Figure 5.14.

In this dialog box I typed in the Click Text that would be highlighted in the Help screen to indicate a hypertext jump, and I selected the symbolic identifier of the Help topic to jump to. Help topics can be in any Help file managed by RoboHELP. For this example I used only one Help file. Notice how RoboHELP uses Hungarian notation (IDH_) for Help topic symbolic identifiers. After providing the Click Text and the Jump To location, all I needed to do to create the jump was choose OK, and RoboHELP created the hypertext jump for me.

FIGURE 5.14:

Creating a hypertext jump using RoboHELP

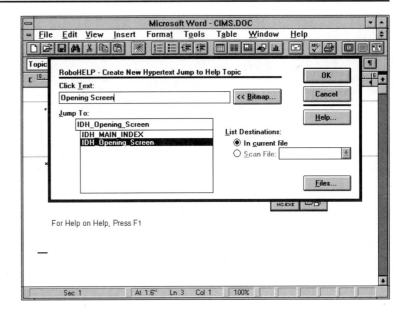

TIP

A very easy mistake to make in this dialog box is to forget to select the correct Jump To symbolic identifier. The symbolic IDs in this list appear in alphabetical order, with the first one selected when the dialog box is displayed. If you forget to select the correct jump, go back to this dialog box, write down the symbolic ID you forgot to select, and Cancel out of the dialog box. Then find the jump hypertext link that includes the wrong identifier and replace the text that has the wrong symbolic ID with the text for the correct symbolic ID.

Saving and Generating Code

After creating my first topic (Opening Screen) and a hypertext jump to it from the Contents topic, I decided it was a good time to save and generate the code for my Help system to see how I was doing. After I clicked on the Save and Generate tool in the RoboHELP Tools palette (the middle tool in the left-hand column), RoboHELP displayed a dialog box to ask me for the name I wanted to display as the title for the Help window, as shown in Figure 5.15.

FIGURE 5.15:

Defining the Windows Help window title using RoboHELP

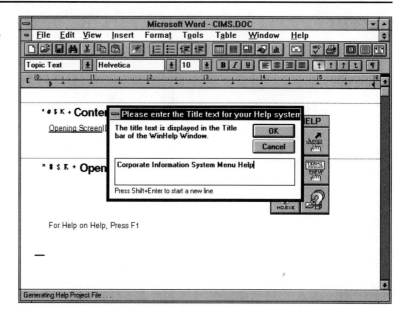

After I gave the window a name and clicked on OK, RoboHELP saved my WinWord document and generated all the files required by the Help Compiler in just a few seconds.

TIP

Before you save and generate your Help system files, make sure you have the correct Help compiler configured. RoboHELP generates some files, such as the Help project file, initially and then appends information to it later on. If you forget to choose the correct Help compiler setting, some of the code RoboHELP generates may be incorrect for the version of the Help compiler you are using. The only way you will become aware of an irregularity is through a Help compiler error message. If you have configured the incorrect Help compiler and it gives you an error message, you can start over or edit the Help project file to fix it. The syntax in the Help project file is straightforward and well-documented in your Help compiler documentation.

Building the Help System

After saving and generating my Help system files, I decided to build my Help system by clicking on the Build tool in the RoboHELP Tools palette (the tool in the lower-left corner). RoboHELP started the Help compiler, and Windows switched to a DOS screen (the Help compiler is not a Windows application) so I could monitor the progress of the Help compiler. After my Help system was compiled, I was switched back to Windows, and RoboHELP displayed the results of compiling my Help system in an inactive DOS window, as shown in Figure 5.16.

After examining the results to make sure everything had gone OK, I double-clicked on the Windows system menu to get rid of the window. Now was the time I had been waiting for—to test my Windows Help system and see if it really worked.

FIGURE 5.16:

Checking the results of compiling my Help system

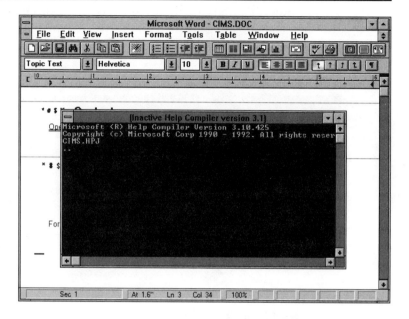

TIP

The Help compiler that's included with the first version of Microsoft C/C++ 7 and the Windows 3.1 SDK is not a DPMI client and cannot use extended memory. If you try to compile a Help file from Windows that includes graphics, you will likely run out of heap space and get a compiler error. At the time this book was written, Microsoft was supplying a DPMI-compliant Help compiler that did not have these problems. They made it available on their CompuServe Windows Developers forum, and its name was HCP.EXE. You can either download this version of the Help compiler from CompuServe or request it from Microsoft. You can find out if your Help compiler is the correct version by typing in HCP at the DOS prompt. You should see "HC 3.10.504 (extended)" to verify it's the correct version. A later version number is acceptable as long as "extended" is included in the message.

Testing the Help System

After I had closed the window that contained the Help Compiler results, I clicked on the Run Help tool in the lower-right corner of the RoboHELP Tools palette to test my Help system. RoboHELP loaded the Windows Help viewer with the Contents topic as the first screen, as shown in Figure 5.17.

When I moved the cursor over the hypertext link, Opening Screen, the cursor became a hand. When I clicked on Opening Screen, I was taken to the Opening Screen topic. Everything worked! At this point my enthusiasm was up, and I jumped into my work, creating topics, building links to them, and inserting graphics into the CIMS Help system.

Inserting Bitmaps by Reference

When I created the topic that described the Select Host dialog box for the CIMS application, I thought it would be a neat idea to put a picture of what the dialog box looked like in the CIMS Help system. You can put bitmaps in your Help system in two different ways, visually and by reference. To insert a bitmap visually, you insert the picture into your WinWord document using Insert Picture in the Insert menu. I have found this method to be error-prone, however, and I avoid it.

FIGURE 5.17:

Testing the Help system

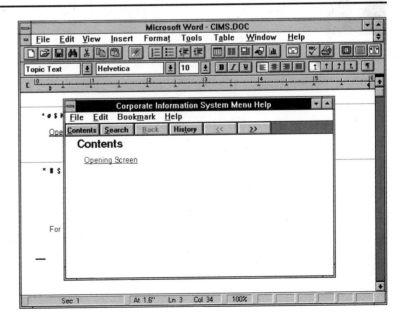

237

Instead, I put bitmap graphics in the Help system using the "by reference" method. By reference puts in your Help document a reference to the bitmap file you want included in your Help system and how it is to be aligned, but it does not put the bitmap file in your document. To reference the bitmap file SELHOST.BMP, insert it into the CIMS Help document, and align it left, the following reference should be made:

```
{bml SELHOST.BMP}
```

To create and insert a bitmap by reference using RoboHELP, I went through the following steps:

1. I ran the CIMS application and displayed the dialog box (Select Host Computer) I wanted to put into the CIMS Help system.

2. After making sure that the active window contained the dialog box I wanted a bitmap picture of, I pressed Alt+PrintScreen to copy just the bitmap of the Window to the Windows Clipboard. (PrintScreen by itself captures the entire screen to the Windows Clipboard.)

3. I set up Windows Paintbrush correctly for the screen resolution. I chose Image Attributes from the Options menu. When the Image Attributes dialog box appeared, I set the correct resolution of my screen in Pels. For example, VGA is 640 horizontal by 480 vertical; 8514 is 1024 horizontal by 768 vertical.

4. I chose New from the File menu to start a new picture.

5. I chose Zoom Out from the View menu.

6. I chose Paste from the Edit menu—TWICE—to paste the Clipboard's contents into the Paint program.

7. At this point, I cut out a rectangular piece of the bitmap that contained the dialog box, using the Pick tool Then I used the Copy To command in the Edit menu to save it to a .BMP format file in my Help system working directory.

8. I was now ready to include the picture of my dialog box in the Help system document using RoboHELP. I went back to the WinWord window and choose Bitmap by Reference in the WinWord Insert menu. This command was inserted in the WinWord menu by RoboHELP.

9. Selecting this command displayed the RoboHELP Insert Bitmap dialog box, as shown in Figure 5.18. Since there were no files listed, I clicked on the Files push button to find out where they were, and the RoboHELP Choose Project Files dialog box was displayed, as shown in Figure 5.19.

10. For a bitmap file to be included in your Help system, it must be referenced in your Help system project file (.HPJ). The Choose Project Files dialog box (Figure 5.19) gives you an easy way to include the bitmap files for your Help system in the project file managed by RoboHELP. Since I am creating the CIMS Help system in the same directory I used for building the CIMS application, all the bitmap files I used in the CIMS application are already available for using in the CIMS Help system, as shown in Figure 5.19. All I had to do was select each file I needed for the CIMS Help system in the Available Files list and click on >> to include it in the Project Files list. After I was finished I clicked on OK to go back to the RoboHELP Insert Bitmap dialog box shown in Figure 5.18.

FIGURE 5.18:

Selecting a bitmap to insert by reference

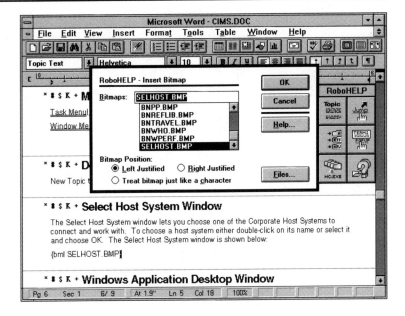

FIGURE 5.19:

Choosing project files

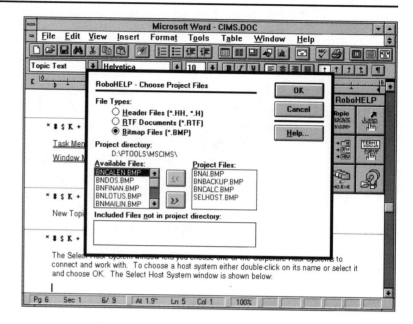

11. In the Insert Bitmap dialog box all I needed to do was select the bitmap file I wanted to include and indicate how I wanted it to be positioned. I chose Left Justified for the SELHOST.BMP that contained the picture of the CIMS Select Host System window. You can also Right Justify the bitmap or treat its position as a character. After I clicked on OK, RoboHELP put the reference to the SELHOST.BMP in the Help system document, and I was done.

NOTE In Figure 5.18 I redisplayed the Insert Bitmap dialog box after the reference to the bitmap was already created in the Help system document, so you could see what both the Insert Bitmap dialog box and the reference that was created look like. Figure 5.20 shows what the Help system window that the bitmap is in looks like after I compiled the Help system.

Popping Up Windows

After finishing the Select Host System topic, I continued my work by adding more topics, filling them with information, and creating hypertext links to them. In some

FIGURE 5.20:

The CIMS Select Host System topic

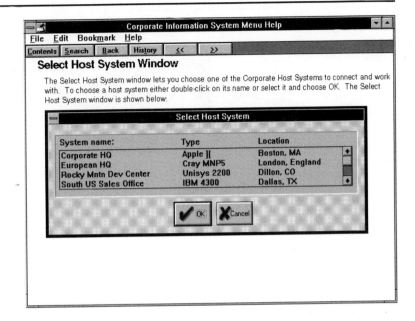

cases I created a pop-up window that had a hypertext link in the topic text. For the Windows Application Desktop Window topic, I thought it would be fun to add the button icons from the application to the CIMS Help system and make them pop-up links to a pop-up window.

First, I created topics to describe what each button does. After all of these topics were defined, I added the bitmaps to the Windows Application Desktop topic and linked each of them to the topic that described it. To do this I went through the following steps:

1. Clicked on the Pop-up icon in the RoboHELP Tools palette (the middle tool in the right-hand column) to display the Create New Help Topic Popup Window dialog box, as shown in Figure 5.21.

2. Clicked on the Bitmap button to display the Insert Bitmap in Click Text dialog box shown in Figure 5.22. I then selected the bitmap file I wanted to use (BNPHONE.BMP) and clicked on OK to go back to the previous dialog box.

3. When I returned to the Create New Help Topic Popup Window dialog box, I selected the symbolic ID of the Help topic I wanted to link to the bitmap and clicked on OK to finish the job.

FIGURE 5.21:

RoboHELP's Create New Help Topic Popup Window dialog box

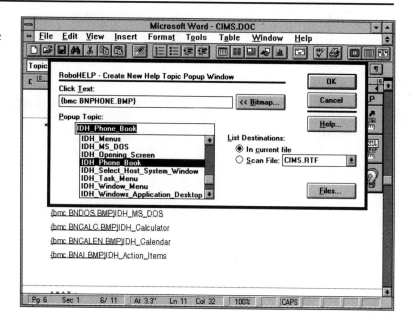

FIGURE 5.22:

Selecting a bitmap to use as a link to a pop-up window

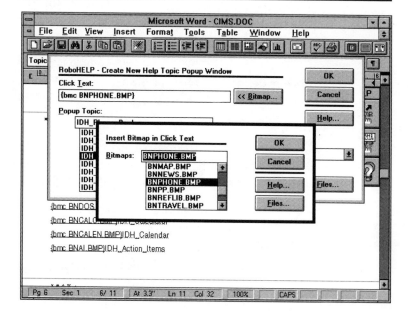

The result of my work can be seen back in Figure 5.10, which shows the Windows Application Desktop Window with its Help topics, and the MS-DOS icon selected to display the pop-up Help topic associated with it.

Summarizing RoboHELP

In the introduction to this section, I described what RoboHELP can do and compared it to the CASE:W Help feature. As you can now see, RoboHELP is a powerful assistant that works inside WinWord to help you build a Help system for a Windows application. Now that I've become familiar with using RoboHELP, I don't intend ever to try building a Help system without using it. RoboHELP is one of the best designed, and certainly one of the best documented, Windows development tools I have worked with. CASE:W gives you a good starting point to build on for creating a Windows Help system. RoboHELP works as your assistant to free you of the tedious work associated with creating a Help system, so you can concentrate on being more creative.

As good as RoboHELP is, it does have some limitations in how much it can assist you in building a Windows Help file. For instance:

- RoboHELP does not have an Undo feature. If you make a mistake, you have to know how to remove what RoboHELP creates in your .DOC and .HPJ files to correct the error.

- RoboHelp supports using .BMP graphics in a Help file to convey information and as a graphic button for a hypertext link. Although you can also use a Windows metafile (.WMF) and multiple-resolution bitmaps in a Help file, RoboHELP does not support them.

Now let's take a look at the last Windows automation tool we are going to examine, DialogCoder.

Using DialogCoder

DialogCoder is a dialog box editor and function code generator from The Software Organization. It tackles the time-consuming job of coding complex relationships between the control windows inside a dialog box, leaving you to concentrate on the core functionality of the dialog box's function code. DialogCoder is similar to, but more powerful than, CASE:W Extended Code Support.

DialogCoder is almost an application generator. It does two things only: it edits dialog boxes and it generates the code for dialog box functions. The DialogCoder dialog box editor offers features that match the Windows SDK Dialog Editor. The DialogCoder dialog box editor also lets you define the color of the dialog box and the control windows inside it. The dialog box editor comes with a set of predefined custom edit controls, called Smart Fields, for validating data such as telephone numbers, date, time, and currency. I found the DialogCoder dialog box editor flexible and easy to work with.

DialogCoder excels at generating the C code for dialog box procedures. There are other programs, such as CASE:W Extended Code Support, that do this same function, but these programs can't match DialogCoder in functionality. DialogCoder is especially proficient at establishing relationships between controls. For instance, using DialogCoder you can set up a dialog box that has three controls: a push button, an edit control, and a list box. Using DialogCoder you can have the currently selected line in the list box moved or copied to the edit control when a push button is clicked on. DialogCoder will generate all the C code to do this for you. All you have to do is describe to DialogCoder what you want to have happen when you design how you want your dialog box to work.

The DialogCoder dialog box editor is a handy new feature that has just been added, and it should not be overlooked when comparing equivalent tools. Using Dialog-Coder is much more convenient because you don't have to go to another dialog box editor to add to or modify the dialog box you are working on. However, in this section, I am going to omit talking about DialogCoder's dialog box editor and instead concentrate on its primary function: generating the C code for dialog boxes after you specify how you want them to work using DialogCoder.

In examining DialogCoder we will follow the familiar format you are becoming accustomed to. First we will compare DialogCoder with similar programs and overview its features. After you have learned what DialogCoder is capable of, you will learn more about it by seeing how it was used in a Windows programming project.

Evaluating DialogCoder

To evaluate DialogCoder, let's look at how it compares with CASE:W Extended Code support. Both DialogCoder and CASE:W Extended Code Support generate dialog box functions. As you learned in Chapter 3, CASE:W Extended Code Support is embedded in the CASE:W application generator. It is not a stand-alone feature. DialogCoder *is* a stand-alone program. It works with and extends the functionality of both CASE:W and WindowsMAKER Professional to help you generate dialog box functions that provide more features with less coding.

Now, let's see how DialogCoder compares with both CASE:W Extended Code Support and Magic Fields for validating data, capturing data, and defining relationships between controls.

Validating Data

CASE:W Extended Code Support lets you specify fixed validation schemes for edit control formats such as telephone numbers, dates, times, and currencies. CASE:W also lets you select a "validation mask" where you can specify custom validation. For instance, an "A" would have to be entered as an alphabetic character, a "9" is numeric, and "X" is alphanumeric. The validation mask for a Social Security Number would be "999-99-9999." When you include characters such as a dash or parentheses in a mask, they are inserted automatically for you.

DialogCoder also lets you validate edit controls using predefined validation schemes and masks. In addition to fixed validation schemes, it lets you specify custom masks for specifying how an edit control can be validated. Overall, DialogCoder and CASE:W Extended Code Support have equivalent edit control validation capabilities. Magic Fields extends the Windows edit control window class and provides much more functionality than either DialogCoder or CASE:W does for working with and validating dialog box edit controls.

Capturing Data

Both DialogCoder and CASE:W capture the data the user enters into the dialog box and put it into program variables for you. CASE:W Extended Code Support declares all the variables as part of a data structure that is given the dialog box name in the program header file it generates. The data structure is declared globally. If you want the data structure to be set up as an automatic variable, you must cut and paste the C code yourself.

To get the data from a Magic Fields edit control, you need to use the Magic Fields API. You must call a Magic Fields function to get and put the data in a Magic Fields edit control window.

DialogCoder lets you specify how you want your program variables to be declared: globally, locally, or externally. DialogCoder lets you choose the names of the program variables used to initialize dialog box controls, but it does not let you choose the variable names that receive the data from those controls.

NOTE The version of DialogCoder I evaluated while writing this book was a BETA and did not always remember all the program variables that should be declared. This was an easy problem to fix, after my compiler pointed out where the errors were. In most cases I skipped over letting DialogCoder declare the variables and wrote the C code myself. I chose this path because DialogCoder does not initialize variables automatically, and I wanted to use my own variable names that receive data—not the names that DialogCoder generates.

Defining Relationships

Both CASE:W and DialogCoder let you work with list boxes for files and directories. This feature is geared to help you make one of the most common Windows programming tasks easier—building File Open and File Save dialog boxes. Windows 3.1 includes a new API for building File Open and File Save dialog boxes, called common dialogs.

Although both CASE:W Extended Code Support and DialogCoder make building File Open and File Save dialog boxes easier, you should use common dialogs instead. Using common dialogs is almost as easy as setting up these dialog boxes using DialogCoder, and the application is more consistent with Windows and other Windows applications. Common dialogs also require less C code to support.

CASE:W Extended Code Support lets you define an edit or static control window that receives a line from a dialog box list box when it is clicked on. You can also link a dialog box push button to another program window, dialog box, or executable program.

DialogCoder matches the CASE:W Extended Code Support functionality and provides much more. You can link a list box to an edit control and an edit control to a list box. You can define push buttons as triggers for actions to occur in the dialog box, such as

- resizing the dialog box

- hiding and unhiding control windows

- enabling and disabling control windows

- moving or copying data from one control to another

- linking to another dialog box or executable program

As you can see, DialogCoder lets you set up many more control relationships than CASE:W Extended Code Support does. Now that we have overviewed DialogCoder's comparable features, let's see what DialogCoder does that CASE:W Extended Code Support doesn't.

Unique DialogCoder Features

After DialogCoder has read in the dialog box definition from a resource script (.RC), a dialog file (.DLG), or a compiled resource file (.RES), it lets you specify how to initialize and establish relationships between the control windows in a dialog box. Some of DialogCoder's unique functions are the following the following:

- Hiding and unhiding control windows when an event occurs that was activated by a DialogCoder-defined Trigger. A Trigger is usually a button, but it can be a list box or an edit control.

- Setting the initial focus to a particular control.

- Specifying a Trigger for an event to occur.

- Managing overlapped controls.

- Folding and unfolding a dialog box.

- Modifying the color of a control.

- Associating a bitmap with a static frame control.

- Populating a list box, a combo box, or an edit control from a program's resources, an ASCII text file, a directory list, a file list, or an array of strings.

- Saving the contents of a list box, a combo box, or an edit control to an ASCII text file.

Summarizing DialogCoder's Features

As you can see, DialogCoder handles most of the actions in generic dialog box processing. It lets you specify the actions a control window should take when another control window is clicked on. You do this by selecting a control to work as a Trigger. Then you link other controls to the Trigger. DialogCoder generates the C code to perform all these functions. You can integrate DialogCoder-generated C code into your program. You can also read and learn from DialogCoder-generated C code. Many of the things the DialogCoder-generated C code does are simple, but the C code DialogCoder generates may contain something you haven't tried before. DialogCoder creates C program code for you as a starting point for building upon. You can then take this C code and customize it to your needs and extend it to build in more functionality.

Now that you have learned what DialogCoder can do, let's see how it does it, using a project that takes advantage of some of DialogCoder's features.

Let's Have a Party!

DialogCoder's written tutorial comes with some sample dialog boxes to help you learn how DialogCoder works. One of these dialog boxes is a planner to help you set up the arrangements for having a party. I decided to use this dialog box as a starting point for showing what DialogCoder can do. I modified it and added to it to create the Party Planner application you will find in the directory \ATOOLS\PARTPLN. This directory was built for you when you installed the book's disk set.

The Party Planner application is not fully functional, because the purpose of this project is to show how far DialogCoder can take you without having to add very much C code yourself. As with any application generator, you must complete the Windows application by adding your own C code to make it fully functional. Let's see what Party Planner can do.

Examining Party Planner

Party Planner was created using CASE:W. It has one menu with three menu items:

- *CASE:W Dialog Box* displays the Party Planner dialog box that was set up using CASE:W Extended Code Support.

- *DialogCoder Dialog Box* displays the Party Planner dialog box that was set up using DialogCoder.

- *Exit* exits the program.

The CASE:W Extended Code Support Party Planner dialog box doesn't do much. It validates some of the data fields, such as Party Date. Choosing OK captures the data the user entered in the dialog box to the variables you specified using CASE:W Extended Code Support. The CASE:W Extended Code Support Party Planner dialog box is shown in Figure 5.23.

The DialogCoder Party Planner dialog box is shown in Figure 5.24, and it looks quite a bit different. First, it's smaller in width. The Party Place combo box has a name displayed in it. If you clicked on the down arrow associated with the Place combo box, you would see a list of five places to choose from. The date field is not initialized with / characters, but they appear automatically as you type in the date.

FIGURE 5.23:

The Party Planner dialog box that was built using CASE:W Extended Code Support

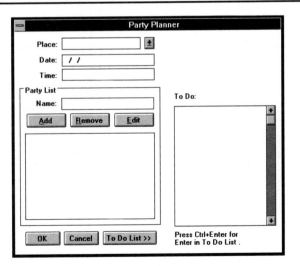

The Time edit control prompts you for the time format. The Name edit control is in-itialized to the string "Type in new name here." The names of people already on the Party List are shown in the list box. The list box was initialized automatically from the ASCII file PLIST.TXT.

If you click on the Add push button, the name in the Name edit control will be added to the Party List. If you click on the Remove push button, the selected name will be deleted from the Party List. If you click on the Edit push button, the selected name in the Party List will move from the Part List to the Name edit control. If you click on the To Do List push button, the dialog box will unfold to display a multiline edit control for typing in the things you need to prepare for the party, as shown in Figure 5.25.

Clicking on the To Do List push button toggles between folding and unfolding the dialog box. The unfolded view of the dialog box displays a colorful bitmap that is composed of party icons I borrowed from the Visual Basic icon library. A note below the To Do edit control warns you to press Ctrl+Enter when you need to type in a new line in the edit control. The Enter key, by itself, chooses OK and closes the dialog box.

FIGURE 5.24:

The Party Planner dialog box that was built using DialogCoder

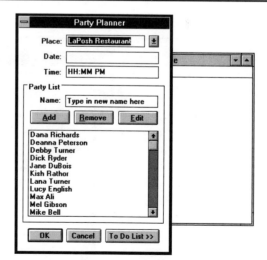

FIGURE 5.25:

The Party Planner dialog box after it is unfolded

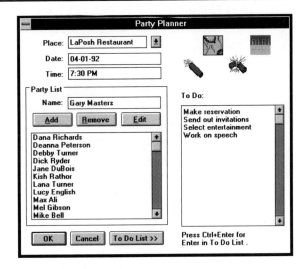

If you close the dialog box and then redisplay it, you will notice that the Party List and To Do list contents retain what you added, removed, or modified. Every time the dialog box is closed by choosing OK, the contents of the Party List are saved to the file PLIST.TXT and the contents of the To Do list are saved to the file PNOTES.TXT.

In this DialogCoder example, what you see is what you get. I added some C code to link this dialog box into the application that I constructed using CASE:W and to correct a few DialogCoder mistakes, such as undeclared variables. All of the dialog box functionality you see was created by the DialogCoder code generator. Let's take a peek and see how this dialog box is constructed.

Constructing the Party Planner Dialog Box Function Using DialogCoder

To start, I constructed the dialog box template using the Microsoft Windows 3.1 SDK Dialog Editor. As I discussed previously, I built the Party Planner application using CASE:W and linked the dialog box to the CASE:W Dialog Box menu item. I then generated and tested the Party Planner application to make sure everything worked. You can examine the C code for managing the CASE:W dialog box in the file PARTYPLN.C. The CASE:W-generated dialog box function is PPLANMsgProc.

After I had generated the Party Planner application using CASE:W, it was time to build a new dialog box function using DialogCoder to show off what DialogCoder is capable of doing. Figure 5.26 shows the Party Planner dialog box, right after it has been opened using DialogCoder.

As you can see, DialogCoder displays the dialog box for you to work on in front of the DialogCoder window. Notice the floating DialogCoder Tools palette for working with the dialog box. You use the Tools palette to specify the actions you want a control to perform. Let's start by specifying where the bitmap picture is to be displayed in the dialog box. You cannot see it, but there is a white static frame rectangle just above the To Do listbox. I started by clicking on the Bitmap tool. Once it is selected, the Bitmap tool button stays depressed, and the cursor changes to the Bitmap Select tool. I then selected the white static frame control, and the DialogCoder displayed the Display Bitmap dialog box shown in Figure 5.27.

Next, I typed in the name of the bitmap as it appears in the application resource script file. The line in the resource script file that defines and links the bitmap name to the bitmap file in my working directory is PARTYPICTURE BITMAP PARTYPIC.BMP.

FIGURE 5.26:

Working on the Party Planner dialog box using DialogCoder

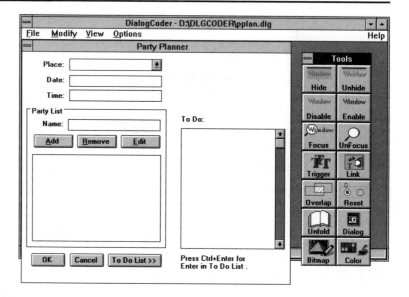

FIGURE 5.27:

Specifying a bitmap picture to display in the dialog box

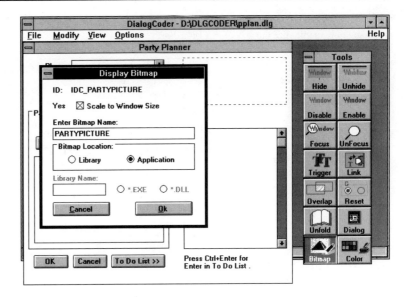

After I specified the bitmap name, I clicked on OK to close the dialog box and clicked on the Bitmap tool again to deselect it. Then it was time to go through all the controls in the dialog box that were associated with data and specify how they were going to behave. I started with the Place combo box control by clicking on it to display the Setup ComboBox dialog box, as show in Figure 5.28.

The first thing I specified in the Setup ComboBox dialog box was the Type. Type specifies whether the combo box should be treated as a Directory List, a File List, or Other. Since this dialog box is not intended to be a File Open or a File Save dialog box, I chose Other. I was then presented a choice of where the combo box was to be initialized, and I chose Resource File. In the resource file, PPLAN.RC, I set up a string table that is used to initialize this control. The associated header file is PPLAN.H. The contents of the resource file are:

```
STRINGTABLE
BEGIN
IDS_PLACE1,  "Home"
IDS_PLACE2,  "Office"
IDS_PLACE3,  "Country Club"
IDS_PLACE4,  "LaPosh Restaurant"
IDS_PLACE5,  "Charlie's Diner"
END
```

FIGURE 5.28:

Specifying how to initialize the contents of the Party Place combo box from the application's string table resources

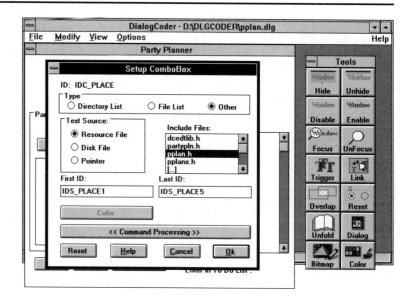

All I needed to do with DialogCoder was to make sure the symbolic IDs for the string table entries were consecutive and bounded by the first and last symbolic ID in the range. The symbolic IDs were defined in the header file PPLAN.H as follows:

```
#define IDS_PLACE1 201
#define IDS_PLACE2 202
#define IDS_PLACE3 203
#define IDS_PLACE4 204
#define IDS_PLACE5 205
```

With my resources set up the way DialogCoder wants them, all I needed to do was specify IDS_PLACE1 as the First ID and IDS_PLACE5 as the last ID. The Command Processing push button unfolds the dialog box to let you specify where the contents of the combo box will be written to when it's closed. Since I did not need to have the contents written to a file, I skipped over this and chose OK to close the dialog box.

Next, I needed to specify how I wanted the dialog box function to handle the Party Date edit control. After I clicked on the Party Date edit control, DialogCoder displayed the Setup Edit Control dialog box, as shown in Figure 5.29.

FIGURE 5.29:

Specifying how the Party Date edit control should be validated

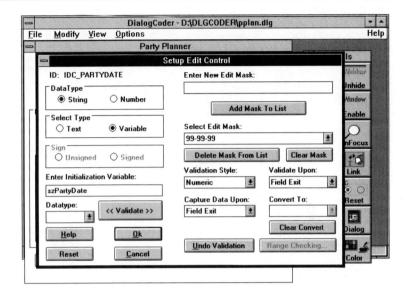

I selected the Data Type and Select Type as shown. If Select Type is a variable, you specify the variable you want the edit control to be initialized from. For this project, it's szPartyDate. If Select Type is Text, you type in a text string to be used to initialize the edit control. Clicking on the Validate push button unfolds the dialog box to let you specify how the edit control is to be validated when data is entered.

I selected the "99-99-99" date field mask from the predefined masks listed in the Select Edit Mask combo box. I also selected Field Exit from the Validate Upon combo box. DialogCoder selected the rest based upon my previous selections. After all my selections were completed as shown, I chose OK to continue on to the next dialog box control, the Party List list box, as shown in Figure 5.30.

Clicking on the Party List list box displayed the Setup ListBox dialog box to specify how the dialog box control should behave. I chose Other as the list box Type and Disk File as its Text Source for initialization. I selected the file PLIST.TXT from the Files list box to specify which text file to initialize the list box from. After specifying how the list box was to be initialized, I chose the Command Processing push button to unfold the Setup ListBox dialog box in order to choose how the Party List list box contents would be saved when the user clicked on OK. The unfolded Setup ListBox dialog box is shown in Figure 5.31.

FIGURE 5.30:
Specifying how the Party List list box should be initialized from a text file named PLIST.TXT

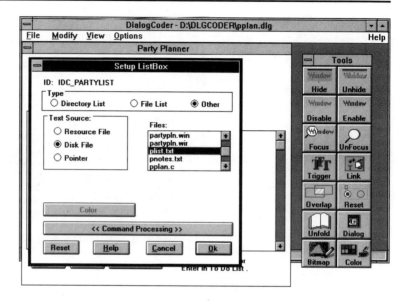

FIGURE 5.31:
Specifying where the contents of the Party List list box will be saved when the dialog box is closed

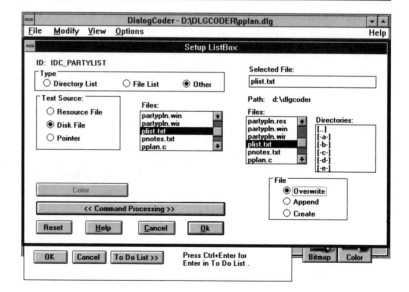

At this point all I needed to do was select from the Files list box the file name to save the list box contents to. I selected the Overwrite option for how the file was to be written. As you can see in the dialog box, I also had the options of creating a file or appending to an existing file.

Now that I had specified how the Party List list box would behave, there was one more control I needed to specify behavior for—the To Do edit control. After choosing OK to close the Setup ListBox dialog box, I clicked on the To Do edit control to display the Setup Multiline Control dialog box, as shown in Figure 5.32.

I completed the Setup Multiline Control dialog box as shown in the figure. I selected File as the String Source and PNOTES.TXT as the file to initialize the editor control from. I then clicked on the Command Processing push button to unfold the dialog box so I could specify where the file was to be saved when the user clicked on OK. For this action I used the same file name that the control was initialized from, PNOTES.TXT. I chose the Overwrite option for writing the contents of the control to a file and clicked on OK.

After the individual behavior for each control had been specified, I specified the relationships between controls. To specify relationships using DialogCoder, you work with the Trigger and Link tools.

FIGURE 5.32:

Specifying the initialization and processing of the Party Planner Notes edit control

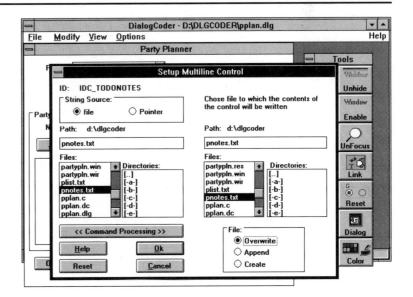

The first action I programmed was having the Add push button copy the contents of the Party Name edit control to the Party List list box. To start I specified the Add push button as a Trigger by choosing the Trigger tool from the DialogCoder Tools palette and clicking on the Add push button to select it. When the Add push button is selected, a dotted-line red rectangle appears around it. Next I chose the Link tool from the DialogCoder Tools palette and clicked on the Party Name edit control to display the Specify Edit Response dialog box, as shown in Figure 5.33.

In the Specify Edit Response dialog box, I selected Copy from the Responses to Trigger combo box. I selected IDC_PARTYLIST as the control to copy the edit control (IDC_PARTYNAME) contents to. I finished by clicking on OK. Now the Add push button copies the contents of the Party Name edit control to the Party List list box when it's clicked on.

Next I worked on Remove. To start I again clicked on the Trigger tool in the Dialog-Coder Tools palette. I then clicked on the Remove push button to specify it as the next Trigger. Next I clicked on the Link tool in the Tools palette to select the control to link the Trigger to. Then I clicked on the Party List list box to display the Specify ListBox Response dialog box, as shown in Figure 5.34.

FIGURE 5.33:

Specifying a response from the Party Name edit control for the Add push button

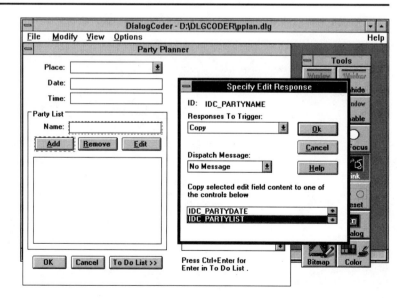

FIGURE 5.34:

Specifying a response from the Party List list box for the Remove push button

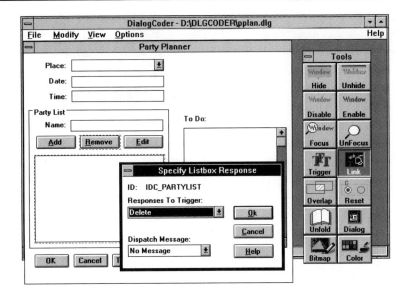

When the Specify ListBox Response dialog box was displayed, I selected Delete from the Responses To Trigger combo box and clicked on OK. As you can imagine, I went through a similar procedure to specify the Edit push button as a Trigger for copying the selected line from the Party List list box to the Party Name edit control.

The last action I programmed for the dialog box was folding and unfolding the dialog box. To accomplish this I clicked on the Unfold tool in the Tools palette and then moved the cursor inside the dialog box. After I pressed the left mouse button, the cursor changed into a hand and I was able to visually size the dialog box horizontally. After I had the dialog box sized the way I wanted it to be initially displayed, I released the left mouse button, and the dialog box titled Select Control that Unfolds the Dialog Box appeared, as shown in Figure 5.35.

In this dialog box I chose the push button identified by the IDC_TODO symbolic identifier to unfold and fold the dialog box, and clicked on OK.

At any point while you are programming a dialog box using DialogCoder, you can click on controls to review the specifications you set up. You can also choose the Specification Map command in the DialogCoder View menu, as shown in Figure 5.36, to display how the dialog box controls are programmed.

FIGURE 5.35:

Selecting the control to fold and
unfold the dialog box

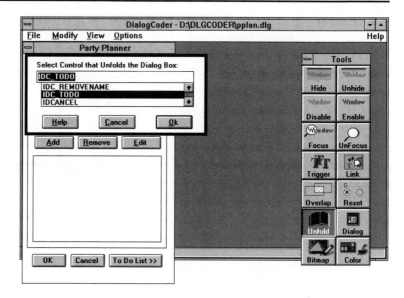

FIGURE 5.36:

Examining the DialogCoder
Specification Map

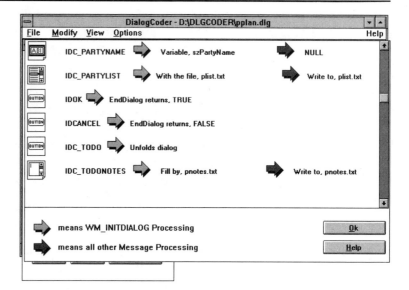

As you can see, the Specification Map graphically shows each control in the dialog box and the behaviors and relationships that were programmed for it. There are two arrows with different colors, cyan and blue, that show what happens to a dialog box control. The cyan arrow indicates processing that is executed when the WM_INIT-DIALOG message is processed by the dialog box function. The blue arrow shows what happens for all other message types.

Now that the dialog box has been programmed, it's time to generate some code. To create the dialog box function with its associated C source code, I chose the Generate Code command in the File menu, and DialogCoder displayed the File Output Parameters dialog box, as shown in Figure 5.37.

In this dialog box I typed in PartyPlan for the dialog box function name and selected Your Own as the Application Type. The options in the Application Type combo box are Your Own, CASE:W, and WindowsMAKER Professional. Your Own generates generic C code that can be used in any Windows application. CASE:W generates code that is designed to be linked to a CASE:W-generated application. DialogCoder recommends that you put this code into a dynamic link library that DialogCoder generates for you automatically. DialogCoder also generates the .INC file that CASE:W expects when you create your application using CASE:W.

FIGURE 5.37:

Specifying how to generate the C code for the dialog box function

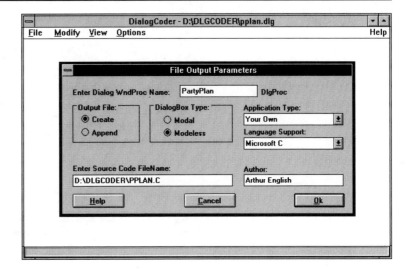

For this project I chose Your Own because I wanted generic code that I could put into the CASE:W application myself. Since I was using Microsoft QuickC for Windows to build the application, I chose Microsoft C from the Language Support combo box. My other choice was Borland C. I let the source code module default to PPLAN.C and typed my name in as the program author. When I completed my selections, I clicked on OK to generate the C code for the dialog box function. Figure 5.38 shows the C code that was generated.

After DialogCoder generates the C code for your application, it displays the code in an edit window for you to view and edit. As you can see in the File menu, you can choose Add Custom Code to put a "code fence" into the generated code so you can regenerate your dialog box function using DialogCoder without disturbing the code you add. For instance, in the Party Planner Windows application, I left the code DialogCoder generated in the PPLANC.C source code module instead of moving it to PARTYPLN.C. As you may remember from Chapter 3 where we explored CASE:W, all the additional C source code modules you include in a CASE:W application require a #define to declare the constant EXTERN as extern. For more information, review the section "Adding My Code to DumpIT" in Chapter 3. To

FIGURE 5.38:

Examining and saving the generated code

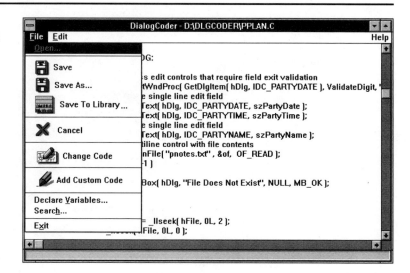

add this `#define` statement to the PPLAN.C source code module, I chose Add Custom Code from the File menu to put a code fence in the C source code and put my `#define` statement inside the code fence as follows:

```
/* -------- DC_CUSTOMCODE_BEGIN -------- */
#define EXTERN extern
/* -------- DC_CUSTOMCODE_END ---------- */
```

Completing Party Planner

Now that my dialog box function was generated, I exited DialogCoder to integrate the code DialogCoder generated into the Party Planner Windows application. To do this I used the QuickC for Windows development environment and went through the following steps:

1. Added the following code to display the Party Planner dialog box as a modeless dialog box when the `WM_COMMAND` message was processed for the Dialog-Coder Dialog Box menu item:

```
case IDM_P_DIALOGCODERDIALOGBOX:
    // Programmer inserted code
    lpfnPartyPlanDlgProc = MakeProcInstance((FARPROC)PartyPlanDlgProc, hInst);
    if(!IsWindow(hDlgPartyPlan))
     hDlgPartyPlan = CreateDialog(hInst, "PPLAN", hWnd, lpfnPartyPlanDlgProc);
    else
     SetFocus(hDlgPartyPlan);
```

2. Defined the variables `lpfnPartyPlanDlgProc` and `hDlgPartyPlan` as global variables in PPLAN.H:

```
EXTERN HWND hDlgPartyPlan;
EXTERN FARPROC lpfnPartyPlanDlgProc;
```

3. Added the code required for a modeless dialog box in the application's message loop in WinMain:

```
// Programmer inserted code
if(hDlgPartyPlan && IsDialogMessage(hDlgPartyPlan, &msg))
  continue;
// End code
```

4. Specified the additional files required for the make file using the QuickC for Windows point-and-click project editor that is called by choosing Edit from the QuickC Project menu. The additional files that I needed to specify were PPLAN.C, PPLAN.H, DCEDTLIB.H, and DCEDTLIB.LIB. The DCEDTLIB files are used by the DialogCoder-generated code to access the DCEDTLIB.DLL to perform data validation functions.

5. Built and tested the application. As you can guess, my application did not work perfectly the first time, but eventually it worked using these steps.

You can examine the C source code module generated by DialogCoder to manage the Party Planner dialog box. It's in the file PPLAN.C in the \ATOOLS\PARTYPLN directory. Each C programmer has a style of his or her own, so I will let you judge how well you think DialogCoder did at generating the dialog box function.

Summarizing DialogCoder

DialogCoder was easy to use and did an acceptable job at generating a dialog box function that handles generic dialog boxes. DialogCoder is a bit rough around the edges compared to the other programming tools I evaluated for this book. The documentation bordered on being unacceptable, and I had to correct small program bugs DialogCoder created.

DialogCoder taught me some cute but simple dialog box programming tricks that I had not tried before, such as folding and unfolding a dialog box. DialogCoder generates the C code to fold and unfold a dialog box only horizontally—not vertically. But it did show me how easy it was to do, and I was able to take what I learned and apply it to the FileFind application that we started as a project in Chapter 2. In that application I enhanced the DialogCoder folding feature to fold and unfold my dialog box vertically instead of horizontally, as shown in Figures 5.39 and 5.40.

I also used some other code generated by DialogCoder in the FileFind application. Instead of just displaying the list of files that FileFind locates, I wrote the list to a text file and used DialogCoder-generated code in the FileFind application to display the File contents in the Files list box.

DialogCoder is not perfect, but it's OK. I'm glad it's found a place on my PC's hard disk so it's there when I need it.

FIGURE 5.39:

The FileFind dialog box folded up

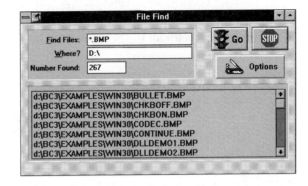

FIGURE 5.40:

The FileFind dialog box unfolded

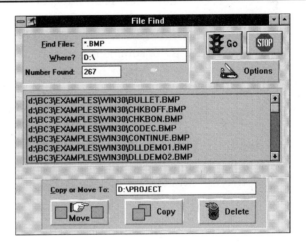

Analyzing Automation Tools

Before we move on to Part II, "Auditing Windows Development," I promised you a summary of the automation tools we have covered and how I rank them.

Each of these tools was selected for this book because it is one of the best—if not *the* best—Windows programming tool in its respective category. I did not have the space and time to cover every Windows programming tool, so I restricted the book to the basics and only covered third-party tools that deserved to be covered. Each of the tools is worth considering for your Windows programming toolkit.

Borland Resource Workshop is the best Windows programming tool available for creating Windows resources. It wins hands down. The Borland Resource Workshop is included with all the Borland Windows development systems and may be purchased separately as well.

Application generators are a difficult choice. WindowsMAKER Professional has a great user interface, it's fast, and it has an attention to detail that's woefully lacking in many development tools. I have found it tough to generate a Windows application using WindowsMAKER Professional that doesn't work. CASE:W, in contrast, is rough around the edges. It doesn't always generate applications that work, and you have to figure out why. It's not fast and its user interface could stand polishing. CASE:W beats WindowsMAKER Professional on some important features, however, such as automatic Help file generation, Extended Code Support, and easily constructed MDI applications. CASE:W also generates code that looks as if it came out of the best Windows programming books. CASE:W C code is easy to read and follow, with lots of comments inserted. You can also configure the number of comments you want CASE:W to include in your source code.

Both of these GUI builders are excellent choices. For the majority of my development projects that fit with using a GUI builder, I use WindowsMAKER Professional because of its speed and flexibility. When I turn to using a GUI builder, time is usually a critical factor, and WindowsMAKER Professional is the best choice for projects that need to be done fast. Basing my decision on my choice for real-world projects, I would have to give the edge to WindowsMAKER Professional as my overall choice of a GUI builder.

If you want to validate and work with edit controls, Magic Fields is great. You can tell it's a Blue Sky Software product by its flawless look and feel. Although the product is limited to working only with edit controls, consider it—especially if you are going to use WindowsMAKER Professional.

RoboHELP is one neat product. After experiencing RoboHELP, I will never write another text README file. From now on, it's a README.HLP file.

DialogCoder, as we just discussed, helps you create dialog box functions for your Windows applications. It's more rough around the edges than I prefer, but it works, and it can save you valuable development time after you have mastered it.

Well, that wraps up automation tools. Let's go audit some Windows applications and see what turns up.

PART III

Auditing Windows Development

Now that you have had a chance to experience Windows programming tools that help automate the process of building Windows applications, we are shifting our focus to look at Windows programming tools that help you audit your Windows applications.

In Chapter 6 we will examine Windows programming tools that let you test your programs to see how well they share Windows resources such as Memory and System resources. In Chapter 7 we will look at tools that help you understand and take advantage of how Windows uses a window as its fundamental building block. You will see how to use tools that show you how to examine other Windows programs and learn how they are constructed and how to monitor the messages being sent to them. You will even learn how you can control another Windows application by sending it messages or subclassing and superclassing its window procedures. Finally, in Chapter 8 you will learn how to profile a Windows application to improve its performance using the Microsoft and the Borland Profilers.

To start, let's look at development tools that help you audit how well your application uses Windows memory and system resources.

Managing Windows Memory and Resources

6

- Understanding Windows memory management

- Allocating local and global memory

- Tracking down lost resources

- Using HEAPWALK

- Using DBWIN with the debugging version of Windows

- Using the Resource Monitor tool developed for this book

- Tips on using memory wisely

Understanding how Windows manages memory is important for both users and programmers. Knowing how to manage memory helps users learn how to get the best performance from Windows. Understanding Windows' approach to memory helps programmers make their applications run faster and share system resources more efficiently.

Memory management is one of the most remarkable aspects of Windows. Windows' sophisticated memory management design gives you the ability to load, run, and multitask applications. Windows memory management is clearly one of its most important features.

In this chapter we will look at Windows memory management and the Windows programming tools that help you to analyze the Windows memory management process. You will learn how to use the Microsoft Windows Heap Walker (HEAP-WALK) for examining both the global heap (the system memory that Windows uses) and local heaps used by the active applications in your Windows system. HEAPWALK is useful for analyzing how your application allocates global memory and resources from Windows. You will also see how to keep track of Windows resources using Resource Monitor—a Windows application I developed for this book. Resource Monitor uses the new TOOLHELP dynamic link library included with the Windows 3.1 SDK to monitor the heap size of the User and the GDI (graphics device interface) Windows modules.

Memory Basics

As you may already know, Windows 3.1 has two modes of operation—Standard and Enhanced. Windows 3.0 supported a third memory mode that is discontinued in Windows 3.1—Real mode. Each of these modes represents a different approach to memory management. The different schemes allow Windows to function in a wide range of IBM-compatible computers. Let's look at how Windows manages memory in each of these modes.

- On a PC based on the Intel 8088 processor, Windows 3.0 runs in Real mode. This is the initial mode Windows 3.1 uses during the Windows installation process. After Windows 3.1 is installed, this mode is no longer available. Windows 3.1 requires at least an Intel 80286 microprocessor, 640K of real memory, and 256K of extended memory to function. Microsoft recommends at least 1024K of extended memory for 80286 microprocessors and 2048K of extended memory for 80386 microprocessors. I personally recommend the fastest PC you can afford with 8MB of memory and a 200MB hard disk for developing Windows applications. A minimum development system should be an 80386 microprocessor, 4MB of memory, and a 100MB hard disk.

- On a PC based on the Intel 80286 processor with at least 1MB of memory (or an 80386 processor with less than 2MB of memory), Windows 3.1 runs in Standard mode. This is 286-compatible Protected mode. Windows can use up to 16MB of conventional memory and extended memory combined.

- On a PC based on the Intel 80386 processor with at least 2MB of memory, Windows 3 runs in 386 Enhanced mode. This is essentially the same as Standard mode with two additional features:

  - Windows uses the paging registers of the 386 processor to implement virtual memory. The 386 pages are 4K in length. Windows can swap pages to disk and reload them when necessary.

  - Windows uses the Virtual-86 mode of the 386 processor to support multiple virtual DOS machines.

Standard Mode

Standard and Enhanced modes look identical to your Windows application. Standard mode runs faster than Enhanced as long as you're not using DOS applications. That's because Standard mode uses less of your computer memory to do its thing. In a sense, it has less "overhead." As shown in Figure 6.1, a DOS extender (DOSX.EXE) handles switching between Real and Protected modes. DOSX does not provide multitasking for DOS applications, and it does not create virtual machines. DOSX is compatible with both 80286-based and 80386-based PCs. The Protected mode provided by DOSX expands the Windows memory address space to 512MB using Windows 3.1 and HIMEM.SYS Version 3.07 or higher.

FIGURE 6.1:

Windows Standard mode memory
architecture

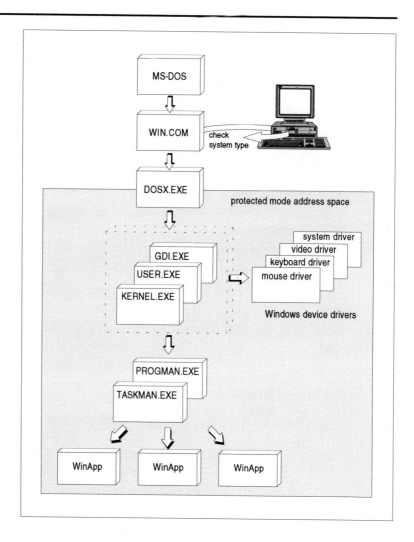

386 Enhanced Mode

Enhanced mode is slower than Standard mode, but it lets you

- run more than one DOS application,

- run each DOS application in a window, and

- use a permanent swap file to give you up to four times more virtual paged memory.

Instead of using the DOS extender DOSX.EXE, Enhanced mode uses a Virtual Machine Manager (WIN386.EXE). As its name implies, the Virtual Machine Manager creates one virtual 8086-based machine for each DOS application you run, as shown in Figure 6.2. Each of these virtual machines requires 1MB of memory.

The Virtual Machine Manager was developed from the Windows/386 Version 2.0 memory manager and goes beyond its capabilities. In particular, Windows 3.1 virtual machines allow a Protected mode environment for each virtual machine. This lets the DOS application operate in Protected mode if it is compatible with the Microsoft DOS extender. The first virtual machine created—the System VM—runs Windows and Windows applications. Other virtual machines run in either Standard DOS or Protected mode. To run in Protected mode, the DOS application needs to be compatible with the DPMI DOS extender standard.

FIGURE 6.2:

Windows Enhanced mode memory architecture

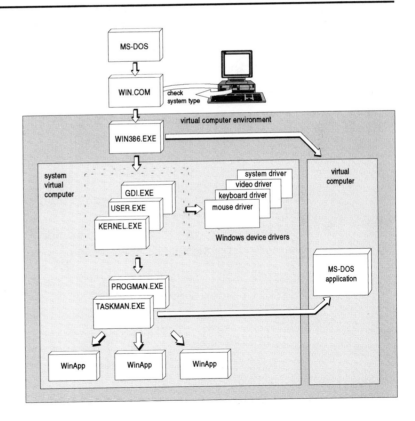

A Walk Down Memory Lane

When PCs were first introduced, applications were much less sophisticated than they are now and required much less memory. The Intel 8088 microprocessor, which the IBM PC was based on, could address 1MB of memory. When Microsoft designed DOS, it divided that 1MB address space into a 640K portion and a remaining 384K portion. The first 640K area is used by the DOS operating system, device drivers, and application programs. Of the remaining 384K, 320K of address space is reserved for physical devices connected to the microprocessor CPU, such as the video board, hard disk controllers, local area network interface boards, and any other add-in cards with ROM or RAM memory on them. The last 64K of address space is reserved for the system ROM that starts up and operates the computer.

At the time the IBM PC was introduced, few personal computers had more than 16K of memory, and 640K of memory appeared to be more than sufficient. By now, of course, times have changed. Most popular application programs can survive using 640K of memory but prefer additional memory.

Intel microprocessors designed after the 8088 don't have the 1MB memory address constraint. The Intel 80286 can address 16MB of memory, and the 80386 and 80486 microprocessors have the physical capacity to address 4 gigabytes (GB) of memory. Unfortunately, these microprocessors must emulate the 8088 (known as running in Real mode) when running DOS, because DOS was designed for the 8088. The 286 and 386 microprocessors are able to address memory beyond 1MB only when operating in Protected mode. The only way a DOS program can access this memory is to use expanded memory or extended memory using a DOS extender.

All of this can be very confusing. If you're running a program that uses a DOS extender, you want extended memory; if you're running a program that uses expanded memory, you want expanded memory. The situation is not helped by the terms extended and expanded, which sound too much alike to be informative.

Expanded memory is a bank-switched memory scheme that allows specially designed DOS programs to access more than 640K of memory. Windows requires extended memory to run in Protected and Enhanced modes. Extended memory is memory that can be recognized by the 80286 and 80386 microprocessors while they are running in Protected mode. Expanded memory can't be recognized by a microprocessor when it is running in Protected mode. Windows uses a built-in DOS extender to switch a microprocessor from Real to Protected mode when it runs in Protected or Enhanced modes. Let's look more closely at how expanded memory works.

In Windows 3.0 Real mode, Windows supports version 4.0 of the Lotus-Intel-Microsoft (LIM) Expanded Memory Specification (EMS). Version 4.0 of the LIM EMS makes more memory available for applications than DOS can physically address. This additional expanded memory is accessed by mapping 16K of memory (called a page) from a non-DOS–addressable area (above 1MB) into a specific memory location in conventional memory. By combining a series of four pages, a 64K window is created through which up to 32MB of expanded memory can be accessed. This dynamic window is referred to as the EMS page frame and is typically located in the address region between 768K and 960K—above the 640K address limit for normal DOS applications, but below the 1MB limit that DOS can access.

Extending DOS

The finest feature of Windows 3.0 and 3.1 is its Protected-mode memory manager, which enables programs running in Protected mode on 80286- and 80386-based PCs to access all installed memory. Windows applications have been pretending to run in Protected mode since Windows 1.0, because Windows has used the same memory management scheme since the product's introduction. This scheme consists of simulating in Real mode the addressing capabilities associated with a Protected-mode operating system.

Windows 1.0 could move program code and data segments in memory, allow multiple instances of a program to share code, allow programs to share code and data located in dynamic link libraries, discard program code segments from memory when not being used, and later reload them from .EXE files when needed. The only limit to Windows 1.0 was the 1MB address space. Windows 3.0 increased the address space by including a built-in DOS extender, named HIMEM.SYS, that let Windows run in Protected mode and access up to 16MB of memory.

The memory limits in Windows 3.1 have been stated by Microsoft as 512MB using the new HIMEM.SYS Version 3.07. This limit is technically correct but needs qualification. The 512MB limit applies only to 80386 and 80486 microprocessors running Standard mode Windows. The limit for 386 Enhanced mode is 256MB. This number is the sum of both physical and virtual (the Windows SWAPFILE) memory. You can also achieve this larger memory address space using either Quarterdeck Office Systems' QEMM-386 6.0 Memory Manager or Qualitas Inc.'s 386Max 6.0.

Windows 3.1 is more robust than Windows 3.0, but even imagining a 256MB address space is frivolous except for a limited number of applications that might require access to really huge blocks of global memory. I am currently using an 80486 PC that runs at 33 MHz with 16MB of memory and no SWAPFILE. Running a standard suite of Windows applications, I have never run out of memory—but I have run out of system resources. As you will learn later in the section on "Application Housekeeping," system resources are much more of a concern to most Windows programmers and users than running out of memory. As for memory limits, here are some real-world memory limits for Windows 3.1:

- 4MB is the minimum recommended amount of memory for Windows 3.1.

- 8MB of memory makes Windows 3.1 very usable.

- 8MB+ is even better. You can stop worrying about a SWAPFILE. If you turn this option off, you will even gain a little performance for your system.

- 16MB of memory was required for developing Win32 NT applications using the BETA SDK at the time this book was written. Microsoft hopes to reduce this minimum to 8MB of memory for NT users, but not for developers. Remember, this is a Microsoft goal—it may not become reality.

TIP

If you are going to purchase a new PC for developing Windows 3.1 applications and want to consider developing Win32 NT applications in the future, you should purchase a PC with at least 16MB of memory. Most PCs sold today can accommodate 8 memory SIMMs (Single In-line Memory Modules). You can purchase either 1MB or 4MB SIMMs. In most PCs, 1MB and 4MB SIMMs cannot be mixed. If you purchase 1MB SIMMs, the maximum memory capacity of your PC will be 8MB. To add more memory you will need to replace the 1MB SIMMs with 4MB SIMMs, which can bring your PC's memory capacity up to 32MB. So if you are planning to move to NT, you should seriously consider using 4MB SIMMs. Since most PCs require that you put four SIMMs in at a time, using this approach gives you a minimum memory configuration of 16MB. These recommendations are only guidelines; you should check with your prospective PC vendor on the details about how you can configure memory on specific PCs.

The Windows DOS extender has two major elements: an initialization portion that runs in Real mode, and a control program that runs (most of the time) in Protected mode. The initialization portion is the only part of the .EXE file recognized by the DOS program loader. During initialization, the DOS extender allocates conventional memory (below the 640K boundary) for the data area it needs. It also determines how much extended memory (above the 1MB boundary) is available, taking into account the amount already in use by disk caches, RAM disks, and the like.

After switching into Protected mode, Windows and Windows applications run in a "flat" address space whose size is limited only by the amount of installed extended memory and by the disk space available for swapping. Extended memory is not "banked" like expanded memory; instead, all extended memory is simultaneously accessible. When Windows or a Windows application wants to read or write to a disk (as well as some other operations), Windows switches back into Real mode to perform the operation using DOS. For example, when Windows processes an application's request to read a record from a disk file, it must go through the following steps:

1. Copy the data from the application's data area in extended memory to a Windows data area in conventional memory (below the 640K address limit).

2. Switch the microprocessor to Real mode.

3. Issue the Write function call to DOS using the data address in conventional memory.

4. Switch back to Protected mode and notify the application that the write operation was successful or what the error code is (if it wasn't successful).

Windows 3.1 FastDisk

Windows 3.1 includes a new 32-bit disk access feature that lets Windows read and write to your hard disk without leaving Protected mode. This new feature is known as "FastDisk." FastDisk is a system of Windows components that allows Windows to talk directly to your hard drive controller, bypassing the BIOS.

FastDisk replaces the disk BIOS. It watches for INT 13H calls and handles them directly or passes them on to the BIOS. FastDisk access must exactly match the hard drive controller. Windows 3.1 supports the standard introduced by Western Digital for 1003 controllers. This standard supports all types of hard drive controllers except ESDI and SCSI. As you can imagine, FastDisk can speed up your disk access dramatically, but it can also cause major problems. Your hard disk controller must be fully compatible with the Western Digital standard, and it cannot be the type of hard disk in portable computers that powers down automatically to conserve battery power. If you want to try FastDisk, I strongly recommend you check with the manufacturer of your hard disk controller first to see if it's OK. Then make sure to back up your hard drive before you turn it on.

To turn on FastDisk, start the Windows Control Panel and choose the 386 Enhanced option. After the 386 Enhanced dialog box is displayed, click on the Virtual Memory option and click on the Change push button to unfold the dialog box. At the bottom of the dialog box you will find the check box for turning on 32-bit access. You will need to restart Windows after you have selected this option for FastDisk to take effect.

Intel Segmented Addressing

All IBM-compatible personal computers are members of the Intel 8086 family of microprocessors. This microprocessor architecture uses segmented memory addressing to manage memory. Windows organizes memory in segments. This Intel family of microprocessors includes the 8088 found in the PC and PC/XT, the 8086 and the 8186 found in some compatibles, the 80286, the 80386, 80486, and the 80586.

The Intel microprocessor family uses a two-part logical address that consists of a segment identifier and an offset address.

- The *segment identifier* specifies the segment of memory that the microprocessor is working with.

- The *offset address* indicates the number of bytes into the segment identified by the segment identifier that the microprocessor is working with.

When a program addresses memory in Protected mode, Windows relies on special tables, called *descriptor tables*, that are created and maintained by Windows. There are two types of descriptor tables: the Global Descriptor Table (GDT) and the Logical Descriptor Table (LDT). The segment identifier is referred to as a segment selector in this arrangement. A *segment selector* is an index into the array of descriptors in a descriptor table. The segment selector identifies the segment descriptor that contains the address in memory of the memory segment.

When a program references a memory location, the microprocessor loads the segment descriptor into special registers for use in determining the physical address of the segment. The offset is added to this base address to access the desired bytes of memory. This process is illustrated in Figure 6.3.

When Windows runs in Protected mode, the segment descriptor does not refer to a physical memory address. Instead, the segment is an offset into the descriptor table that provides a 24-bit address in physical memory. The offset address is added to the segment address in the segment descriptor to generate a 24-bit physical address that can access up to 16MB of memory for an 80286 microprocessor. The 80386 microprocessor uses a 32-bit address that can access up to 4GB.

Four internal registers of the microprocessor hold segment identifiers. These segment registers are called:

- *CS* (code segment)
- *DS* (data segment)

FIGURE 6.3:

Protected mode addressing scheme

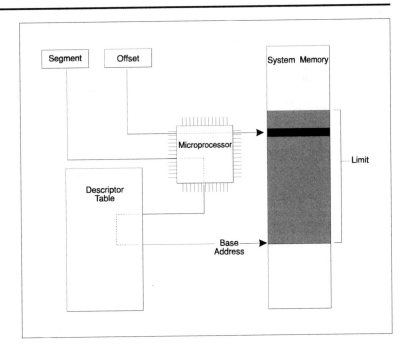

- *SS* (stack segment)

- *ES* (extra segment)

The 80386 and 80486 also have two additional segment registers that we will ignore—FS and GS.

At any given instant, four segments of memory may be immediately accessible to an executing program. The segment registers CS, DS, SS, and ES are used to identify these four current segments. Each of these registers specifies a particular kind of segment, as characterized by the associated mnemonics ("code," "data," or "stack"). Each register uniquely determines one particular segment, from among the segments that make up the program, that is to be immediately accessible at highest speed.

The segment containing the currently executing sequence of instructions is known as the current code segment; it is specified by means of the CS register. The microprocessor fetches all instructions from this code segment, using as an offset the contents of the instruction pointer.

Subroutine calls, parameters, and procedure activation records usually require that a region of memory be allocated for a stack. All stack operations use the SS register to locate the stack. Unlike CS, the SS register can be loaded explicitly, thereby permitting programmers to define stacks dynamically.

The DS and ES registers allow the specification of two data segments, each addressable by the currently executing program. The DS register should always point to a data segment containing the local heap of the currently executing task in Windows.

The microprocessor associates a base address with each segment selected by a segment register. To address an element within a segment, the offset address is added to the segment's base address. Once a segment is selected (by loading the segment selector into a segment register), a data manipulation instruction only needs to specify the offset.

The block of memory that is pointed to is called (appropriately enough) a segment. People used to think of segments as 64K blocks of memory, but this definition is becoming less common. The 80386 processor introduces 32-bit registers that parallel the 16-bit registers of older members of the 8086 family. These registers make it possible for the first time to access memory in segments larger than 64K. In fact, the maximum segment size is potentially so large (2^{32} bytes), that a flat memory model utilizing a single segment is now feasible.

This way of working with memory is available in Microsoft's 32-bit version of Windows called Win32. Win32 is currently under development by Microsoft and should be available by 1993. In this model an application's code and/or data could occupy a single segment. In Win32, applications can manipulate the 32-bit offset portion of the memory as though it were a simple pointer. The application can increment and decrement the pointer/offset throughout the address space without having to deal with multiple segment boundaries.

The use of segments is central to Windows' memory organization. The entire memory space controlled by Windows is divided into segments of various lengths. Some of these segments contain code, and others contain data. For instance, the reason why the 512MB limit for Windows 3.1 Standard mode is not practical can be explained by looking at how this number was derived. As you have just seen, the LDT is used to control the addressing of all Windows memory. This table has space for 8096 descriptors. Each of these descriptors in turn can address up to 64K of memory. The 512MB value is determined by multiplying the number of possible descriptors by each descriptor's maximum size:

8096 * 64K = 512MB

The reason this is not practical is that in order to reach 512MB, every descriptor in the LDT must point to a 64K segment—the maximum size. In the average Windows system, the segment size is nowhere near that big. A more reasonable estimate is 256MB, which allows for an average segment size of 32K.

Windows Memory Organization

The entire memory area that Windows controls is called *global memory* or the *global heap*. This area begins at the location where MS-DOS first loads Windows into memory and ends at the top of available memory, which usually is the top of physical memory. Each block of memory allocated from the global heap is a segment. Global memory not currently allocated is called *free memory*.

A Windows program can have one or more code segments and one or more data segments. When Windows loads a program into memory, it allocates at least one segment from the global heap for code and one segment for data. When the program starts to execute, the microprocessor's CS register is set to the segment address of the code segment that contains the entry point of the program. The DS and SS registers are set to the segment address of the program's automatic, or default, data segment, which is the data segment that contains the stack.

- DS is used to reference data declared as static.

- SS is used to reference data on the stack, which includes local nonstatic data and arguments passed to functions.

When loading a program, Windows allocates segments from the global heap. You can see these segments using the HEAPWALK utility, as shown in Figure 6.4.

If your program has only one code segment, then any calls it makes to functions within the program are compiled as near calls. The CS code segment register remains the same. When your program calls a Windows function, the Windows function is in a different code segment. This situation requires that the program generate a far call, which is the reason that all Windows functions (and all functions within your program that are called by Windows) must be declared as far.

FIGURE 6.4:

Memory segments listed using HEAPWALK

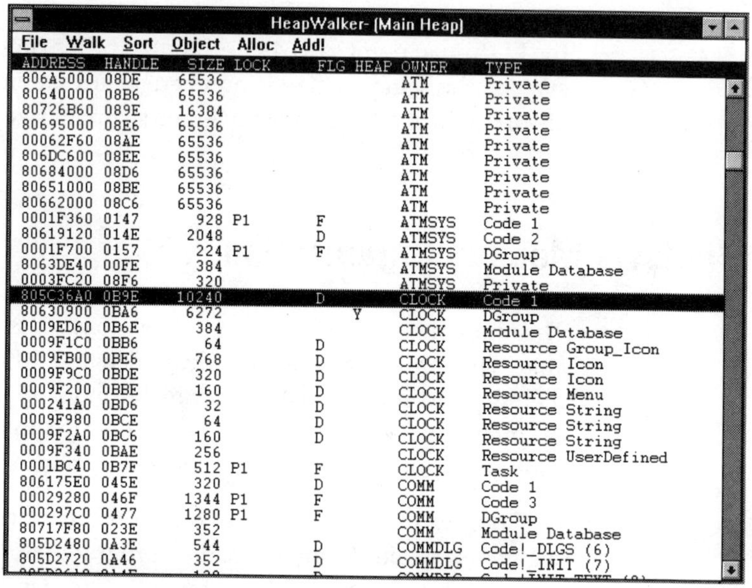

ADDRESS	HANDLE	SIZE	LOCK	FLG	HEAP	OWNER	TYPE
806A5000	08DE	65536				ATM	Private
80640000	08B6	65536				ATM	Private
80726B60	089E	16384				ATM	Private
80695000	08E6	65536				ATM	Private
00062F60	08AE	65536				ATM	Private
806DC600	08EE	65536				ATM	Private
80684000	08D6	65536				ATM	Private
80651000	08BE	65536				ATM	Private
80662000	08C6	65536				ATM	Private
0001F360	0147	928	P1	F		ATMSYS	Code 1
80619120	014E	2048		D		ATMSYS	Code 2
0001F700	0157	224	P1	F		ATMSYS	DGroup
8063DE40	00FE	384				ATMSYS	Module Database
0003FC20	08F6	320				ATMSYS	Private
805C36A0	0B9E	10240		D		CLOCK	Code 1
80630900	0BA6	6272			Y	CLOCK	DGroup
0009ED60	0B6E	384				CLOCK	Module Database
0009F1C0	0BB6	64		D		CLOCK	Resource Group_Icon
0009FB00	0BE6	768		D		CLOCK	Resource Icon
0009F9C0	0BDE	320		D		CLOCK	Resource Icon
0009F200	0BBE	160		D		CLOCK	Resource Menu
000241A0	0BD6	32		D		CLOCK	Resource String
0009F980	0BCE	64		D		CLOCK	Resource String
0009F2A0	0BC6	160		D		CLOCK	Resource String
0009F340	0BAE	256				CLOCK	Resource UserDefined
0001BC40	0B7F	512	P1	F		CLOCK	Task
806175E0	045E	320		D		COMM	Code 1
00029280	046F	1344	P1	F		COMM	Code 3
000297C0	0477	1280	P1	F		COMM	DGroup
80717F80	023E	352				COMM	Module Database
805D2480	0A3E	544		D		COMMDLG	Code!_DLGS (6)
805D2720	0A46	352		D		COMMDLG	Code!_INIT (7)

A Windows program that has one data segment can use near pointers to access memory within that data segment. However, when a Windows program passes a pointer to a Windows function, the pointer must be a far pointer; otherwise, the code that contains the Windows function will use its own data segment. The far pointer is required for the Windows function to access the data within your program's data segment.

NOTE A Windows dynamic link library uses near pointers to access its local heap that is pointed to by the DS register, but must use far pointers for automatic variables pointed to by the SS register. This is because a DLL is reentrant, and its automatic variables are always put on the stack of the calling program. Subsequently, the SS register points to the stack of the calling program.

Segment Attributes

Every segment in Windows' total memory space is marked with certain attributes that tell Windows how to manage the segment. The names Windows uses for defining segment attributes in the module definition (.DEF) file and when a program dynamically allocates memory either locally or globally are shown in Table 6.1.

Movable Segments

Windows can move movable segments in memory if necessary to make room for other memory allocations. When Windows moves a segment in memory, all existing near pointers to that segment continue to be valid, because near pointers reference an offset from the beginning of a segment. In Windows 3.0 Real mode, far

TABLE 6.1: Segment Attributes

.DEF File	LocalAlloc	GlobalAlloc
MOVEABLE	LMEM_MOVEABLE	GMEM_MOVEABLE
FIXED	LMEM_FIXED	GMEM_FIXED
DISCARDABLE	LMEM_DISCARDABLE	GMEM_DISCARDABLE

pointers became invalid when the segment they referenced was moved. Since Windows 3.1 doesn't support Real mode anymore, you don't need to worry about this happening.

Fixed Segments

A fixed segment cannot be moved in memory. Segments must be marked as fixed if Windows is incapable of modifying an existing far pointer to the segment.

All non-Windows MS-DOS programs are assigned fixed segments when they run under Windows. Windows cannot determine how these programs reference memory, so it has no choice but to make them fixed. However, you should try very hard to ensure that the code and data segments of your Windows programs are movable segments. Fixed segments stand like brick walls in memory space and clog up Windows' memory management.

Discardable Segments

Movable segments can also be marked as discardable. This means that when Windows needs additional memory space, it can free up the area occupied by the segment. Windows uses a *least recently used* (LRU) algorithm to determine which segments to discard when attempting to free up memory.

Use the discardable attribute for segments that do not change after they are loaded. Code segments of Windows programs should be discardable because programs do not modify their code segments.

Discardable segments must also be movable segments, because discardable segments can be reloaded in a different area of memory than the area they occupied earlier. However, movable segments are not always discardable segments. This is usually the case with data segments. Windows cannot discard a program's automatic data segment, because the segment always contains read-write data and the stack.

Windows Memory Layout

At the bottom of global memory (the area with the lowest memory address), Windows allocates fixed segments. Fixed segments are allocated from the bottom up. At the top of global memory, Windows allocates discardable segments. Discardable segments are allocated from the top down. Between fixed segments and discardable segments, Windows allocates movable segments and nondiscardable data segments. The largest block of free memory is usually located below the discardable segments.

> **WARNING**
>
> Windows can run out of memory space when a program attempts to allocate global memory or to load a resource. For example, your program may need a text string or icon not currently in memory to display an error message. If your program needs to report that it is low on memory, you can use a message box. Windows keeps in memory all the code necessary to create a message box. You'll want to use the MB_SYSTEMMODAL flag to prevent the user from switching to another application. MB_ICONHAND (which is supposed to accompany messages about severe problems) is also always in memory. The text message in the message box should either be in your default data segment or be a string resource that has previously been copied into your data segment.

Your Windows Application's Memory

Every Windows program has at least one data segment called the default, or automatic, data segment. A program's DS and SS segment registers both point to this segment. In contrast to Windows global memory, this data segment is called your program's *local memory*. Within Windows' global memory organization, your program's automatic data segment is usually a movable but nondiscardable segment. The segment is called *DGroup*. The memory within DGroup is organized into four areas: initialized static data, uninitialized static data, the stack, and the local heap.

- *Initialized Static Data* contains initialized variables defined outside of functions, initialized static variables within functions, and explicit strings and floating-point numbers.

- *Uninitialized Static Data* has uninitialized variables that are defined outside of functions and uninitialized variables defined as static within functions. In accordance with C standards, all uninitialized static variables are initialized to zero when the data segment is created in memory.

- The *stack* is used for automatic variables defined within functions—variables not defined as static—for data passed to functions, and for return addresses during function calls.

- The *local heap* is for free memory available for dynamic allocation by the program.

Dynamically Allocating Local Memory

In a DOS C program, you allocate memory from the local heap using the `malloc` and `calloc` functions. In a Windows programs, you allocate memory from the local heap using the Windows memory allocation functions. Windows can dynamically expand the local heap if you attempt to allocate more local memory than is specified in your module definition file. Windows can even move your data segment, if that is necessary, to expand the local heap.

Local Memory Functions

When a program allocates memory, Windows has to give the program a pointer so that the program can access the memory. The memory allocation functions do not directly return pointers that the program may use. Instead, these functions return handles. WINDOWS.H defines two data types, called LOCALHANDLE and GLOBALHANDLE. Before your program can use an allocated memory block, it must pass that handle back to Windows in another function that locks the memory block and returns a pointer.

If Windows cannot find enough memory in the local heap to allocate the block, it will attempt to expand the local heap by enlarging the size of the entire data segment. The local heap is always at the top of the automatic data segment. Windows may even move the data segment to another location in memory if that will provide the space it needs to expand the local heap. When `LocalAlloc` returns, your data segment may have been moved.

If Windows still cannot find enough memory in the local heap to allocate the memory block, the handle returned from `LocalAlloc` will be NULL. If you use local memory allocation only for small, short-lived memory blocks, you may not need to check the handle for a NULL value—but it's always a good idea.

Dynamically Allocating Memory

When your program needs to allocate blocks of memory dynamically for internal use, you use Windows functions to allocate both local and global memory. Windows includes two sets of memory allocation functions, one set for using the local heap and one for the global heap.

- *Local memory allocations* are faster and require less overhead, but the memory in the local heap is limited to 64K less the combined size of the program's initialized static variables, the program's uninitialized static variables, and the stack.

- *Global memory allocations* are not limited to 64K, either in the size of single blocks or in the total memory you can allocate. Pointers to global memory blocks are far pointers, which create more overhead than near pointers.

Working with Large Blocks of Memory

The DumpIT program developed in Chapter 3 is a good example of how to use large global memory blocks. DumpIT can display a hex dump for a file of any size, as long as it will fit into memory. Since DumpIT works with huge memory blocks that can be several megabytes or more, it uses huge pointers. Far pointers can point to large data objects, but you cannot do pointer arithmetic with them for data objects that exceed 64K. The following function from DumpIT is used for copying data from a global memory segment and parsing it to be displayed for one line of the hex dump, which will be either displayed on the screen or printed.

```
//---------------------------------------------------------------------
//
// FormatLine function
//
void FormatLine (WINDOWVARIABLES _far * lpWinVar,
    char _huge *hpFileBuf, REPORTLINE * lpReportLine, long lBufIndex)
{
  int len, shift, cnt;
  char buf[7];
  LPSTR lpTo, lpToHexStr;
  char _huge *hpFrom;

  // Calculate the address within the file, stuff it into buf, right justify it
```

```
// with leading zeros, and put it into the report line: lpReportLine->sz-
Address.
  ltoa (((lBufIndex) * 16), buf, 16);
  len = strlen (buf);

  for (cnt = 6;
     cnt > len;
     cnt--)
   {
   for (shift = 6;
      shift > 0;
      shift--)
      * (buf + shift) = * (buf + shift - 1);
    * buf = '0';
    }
  for (cnt = 0;
     cnt < 7;
     cnt++)
   * (lpReportLine->szAddress + cnt) = * (buf + cnt);

  // Set lpTo the address of the ASCII text displayed on the report line
  lpTo = (LPSTR) lpReportLine->szASCIIContents;

  // Set lpFrom to the file buffer + 16 bytes increments
  hpFrom = hpFileBuf + (lBufIndex * 16);

  // Set lpToHexStr to point to the report line field that list the hex contents.
  lpToHexStr = lpReportLine->szHexContents;

  // Copy 16 bytes from file buffer to a report line
  for (cnt = 0;
     cnt < 16;
     cnt++)
  {
   unsigned char ch, cHex[3];

   // if we have got to the end of the file put a space in the report line.
   // Otherwise, copy the character from the file to ch for processing.
   if (hpFrom + cnt >= hpFileBuf + lpWinVar->lFileSize)
     ch = ' ';
   else
     ch = * (hpFrom + cnt);

   // Put ch in the ASCII contents field. If it is a nonprintable character
```

```
   // make it a period "."
   * (lpTo + cnt) = ch;
   if (* (lpTo + cnt) < ' ')
     * (lpTo + cnt) = '.';

   // Convert ch to hex. If it is only one character, move it over one, put on
   // a leading zero, and make sure the last char is a NULL.
   itoa ((int) ch, cHex, 16);
   if (cHex[1] == NULL)
   {
     cHex[1] = cHex[0];
     cHex[0] = '0';
     cHex[2] = NULL;
   } // Copy translated hex char as string to its place in the report line
   * (lpToHexStr + (cnt * 3)) = ' ';
   * (lpToHexStr + (cnt * 3) + 1) = cHex[0];
   * (lpToHexStr + (cnt * 3) + 2) = cHex[1];
  }
// Done for processing the line
}
```

Notice the huge pointers `hpFileBuf` and `hpFrom`. These pointers are used to access the global memory buffer containing the file. Far pointers are used for the smaller data objects being worked on, because they work faster. You should use huge pointers only when you have to work with data objects that exceed 64K. Windows 3.1 also includes new input and output functions for reading and writing to memory segments larger than 64K. These functions include the following:

- `_hread` reads data from the specified file. This function supports huge memory objects (that is, objects larger than 64K, allocated using the `Global-Alloc` function).

- `_hwrite` writes data to the specified file. This function supports huge memory objects larger than 64K.

- `_hmemcpy` copies bytes from a source buffer to a destination buffer. This function supports huge memory objects larger than 64K.

Global Memory Functions

In Chapter 12 we will discuss the WINDOWSX.H header file and the new macro APIs included in it that let you deal with Windows in a more reasonable way. As a preview, let's take a look at the new macro API for using global memory, Global-AllocPtr. Since you don't have to worry about unlocking global memory segments in Windows 3.1, you should try GlobalAllocPtr as an alternative to GlobalAlloc and GlobalLock. GlobalAllocPtr uses the same parameters as GlobalAlloc. It allocates a global memory segment and returns a void FAR pointer—not a handle—to the memory segment. The macro API also has macros for reallocating memory (GlobalReAllocPtr) and for freeing global memory (GlobalFreePtr). You should also note that these macros, as well as GlobalLock, now return void pointers. In Windows 3.0, GlobalLock returned an LPSTR.

More about Global Memory

In a Windows C program, you can use almost all the normal C library functions for doing I/O and string manipulations, as long as you are working with local memory. If you are working with global memory, Windows supplies a set of functions to use that work with far pointers. The I/O functions are listed in Table 6.2. The Windows string manipulation functions for working with far pointers are listed in Table 6.3.

TABLE 6.2: Windows I/O Functions for Using Global Memory

I/O Function	Description
_lclose	Closes a file.
_lcreat	Creates a new file or opens and truncates an existing file.
_llseek	Positions the pointer to a file.
_lopen	Opens an existing file.
_lread	Reads data from a file.
_lwrite	Writes data in a file.
_hread	Reads data from a file into a global memory segment larger than 64 K. (Windows 3.1 only).
_hwrite	Writes data into a file from a global memory segment larger than 64K. (Windows 3.1 only).
OpenFile	Creates, opens, reopens, or deletes the specified file.

TABLE 6.3:   Windows String Functions for Using Global Memory

String Function	Description
lstrcat	Concatenates two strings identified by long pointers.
lstrcmp	Performs a case-sensitive comparison of two strings identified by long pointers.
lstrcmpi	Performs a case-insensitive comparison of two strings identified by long pointers.
lstrlen	Determines the length of a string identified by a long pointer.
lstrcpy	Copies one string to another; both strings are identified by long pointers.
lstrchr	Searches a string for a character. *This function is part of the ATOOLS DLL library—not Windows.*
lstrncat	Concatenates a specified number of characters from one string to another. *This function is part of the ATOOLS DLL library—not Windows.*
lstrncmp	Compares a specified number of characters in two strings. *This function is part of the ATOOLS DLL library—not Windows.*
lstrncpy	Copies a specified number of characters from one string to another; both strings are identified by long pointers. If the sending string has fewer characters than the destination string, the destination string is padded with spaces. *This function is part of the ATOOLS DLL library—not Windows.*
_hmemcpy	Copies a specified number of characters from one buffer to another. Buffers can be larger than 64 K and require _huge pointers. (Windows 3.1 only).

As you may have noticed in Table 6.3, Windows does not provide LPSTR equivalents for all the string functions included with your C compiler. Many of the companies I have worked with developed equivalent functions that match these missing functions and put them into a utility library for their programmers to use. You will find these functions—as well as others—in the ATOOLS dynamic link library included on the book's disk set. In the ATOOLS DLL, you'll find utility routines for string functions, for displaying messages, and for debugging your program. Feel free to use these and add your own utility functions to this DLL. You can use it as a starting point for your own library of Windows programming utilities.

Application Housekeeping

Now that you understand how Windows manages memory, let's see how it manages its internal accounting information that keeps track of application windows, menus, and GDI resources such as pens, brushes, and device contexts. This information is kept track of in the data segments of the Windows GDI and User segments. Let's see how it works and what you as a Windows application developer need to know about it.

Windows applications must manage their own resources, destroying objects and freeing memory when the resources are no longer needed. Although you can lock global memory objects and forget about them in Windows 3.1 Protected mode, you should always remember to free memory objects when you no longer need them. If your program neglects this task, Windows resources slowly vanish. The situation can be fixed only by restarting Windows. A good indication of what is going on can be seen when you choose About Program Manager from the Help menu of Program Manager. In Windows 3.1 you will see a dialog box like the one shown in Figure 6.5.

In this dialog box, Windows tells you how much memory and system resources are available. The memory listed is your available system memory plus SWAPFILE space you may have allocated. System resources are another thing altogether.

FIGURE 6.5:

The About Program Manager dialog box

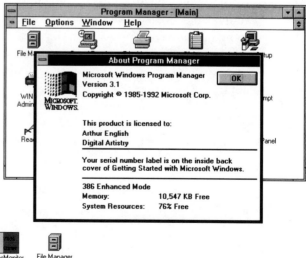

System Resources

Figures 6.1 and 6.2 show the three Windows components (Kernel, User, and GDI) that your Windows applications interact with while they are running. Each of these components is a Windows DLL. There are other Windows DLLs your program works with besides these, and the list is growing with each Windows software release. However, these three DLLs are the most important.

The GDI module manages graphic objects such as pens, brushes, and fonts. The User module manages windows, memory objects, and dialog boxes. In Windows 3.0, each of these modules is a DLL with a data segment (DGroup) limited to 64K. The available System Resources listed in the About Program Manager dialog box is the percentage of space left in the DGroup of the User or of the GDI module, depending upon which one has less memory available.

In Windows 3.1 the space allocated to keeping track of Windows resources has been increased by using an additional data segment. Both GDI and User have a 64K local heap. The User module now has an additional 64K heap for keeping track of menus. This increases the amount of overall system resources, but they are still exhaustible. Checking the size of the User and GDI local heaps is still an indicator of the state of Windows system resources, but it is not an exact indicator. By walking the local heaps of GDI and User, you will find allocated memory blocks that are marked as being free. This means that there is usually more available local heap space than the size of the User and GDI segments indicates.

A good example of how to conserve Windows resources in Windows 3.1 is the Windows Program Manager. If you used Spy or another tool that can identify Windows on the desktop, you would have found out that the Windows 3.0 Program Manager allocated a window for each icon it displayed. In Windows 3.0, Program Manager was one of the biggest system resource hogs. However, in Windows 3.1, Program Manager displays application icons without allocating a window for each one. This takes some more thoughtful programming, but it conserves system resources. In Chapter 7 you will learn more about this topic and about how to conserve system resources by not using too many windows in your application.

When you write a Windows application, you need to worry not only about Windows global memory as a whole, but also about using and not freeing resources that impact the DGroup of Kernel, User, and GDI. Of these three modules, GDI requires the most careful attention. GDI objects are intended to be shared by applications.

Although GDI knows which application allocated a particular object, it can't free the object. If it did, it would risk causing errors in other applications.

Table 6.4 lists the Windows resource objects that require the most attention. These objects *will not* be cleaned up by Windows when your program terminates. Cleanup of these resource objects is your program's responsibility.

TABLE 6.4: Windows Resource Objects that Require Deletion

Object	Allocation Function	Cleanup Function
Atoms	GlobalAddAtom	GlobalFreeAtom
Bitmap	CreateBitmap	DeleteObject
	BitmapIndirect	DeleteObject
	CreateCompatibleBitmap	DeleteObject
	CreateDIBitmap	DeleteObject
	CreateDiscardableBitmap	DeleteObject
	LoadBitmap	DeleteObject
Brush	CreateBrushIndirect	DeleteObject
	CreateDIBPatternBrush	DeleteObject
	CreateHatchBrush	DeleteObject
	CreatePatternBrush	DeleteObject
	CreateSolidBrush	DeleteObject
Clipboard	OpenClipboard	CloseClipboard
CommPort	OpenComm	CloseComm
Cursor	CreateCursor	DestroyCursor
DC	CreateDC	DeleteDC
	CreateCompatibleDC	DeleteDC
	GetDC	ReleaseDC
	GetWindowDC	ReleaseDC
	BeginPaint	EndPaint
Fonts	CreateFont	DeleteObject
	CreateFontIndirect	DeleteObject
	AddFontResource	DeleteObject
Hook	SetWindowsHook	UnhookWindowsHook

TABLE 6.4:   Windows Resource Objects that Require Deletion (continued)

Object	Allocation Function	Cleanup Function
IC	CreateIC	DeleteDC
Icon	CreateIcon	DestroyIcon
Library	LoadLibrary	FreeLibrary
Memory	AllocDStoCSAlias	FreeSelector
	AllocSelector	FreeSelector
Metafile	CreateMetaFile	DeleteMetaFile
Palette	CreatePalette	DeleteObject
Pen	CreatePen	DeleteObject
	CreatePenIndirect	DeleteObject
Regions	CreateEllipticRgn	DeleteObject
	CreateEllipticRgnIndirect	DeleteObject
	CreatePolygonRgn	DeleteObject
	CreatePolyPolygonRgn	DeleteObject
	CreateRectRgn	DeleteObject
	CreateRectRgnIndirect	DeleteObject
	CreateRoundRectRgn	DeleteObject
Sound	OpenSound	CloseSound
Caret	CreateCaret	DestroyCaret
Dialog Box	CreateDialog	DestroyWindow
	CreateDialogIndirect	DestroyWindow
	CreateDialogIndirectParam	DestroyWindow
	CreateDialogParam	DestroyWindow
File	OpenFile	_lclose

Table 6.5 lists the resource objects that Windows will automatically delete for you when your program terminates. Although Windows assures you that it will clean up after you are gone, be a good neighbor and release resources when you no longer need them.

TABLE 6.5:   Windows Resource Objects that Don't Require Deletion, but Can Be Released

Object	Allocation Function	Cleanup Function
Memory	GlobalAlloc	GlobalFree
	GlobalDOSAlloc	GlobalDOSFree
	GlobalFix	GlobalUnfix
	GlobalLock	GlobalUnlock
	GlobalPageLock	GlobalPageUnlock
	GlobalReAlloc	GlobalFree
	GlobalWire	GlobalUnwire
	LocalAlloc	LocalFree
	LocalLock	LocalUnlock
	LocalReAlloc	LocalFree
Menu	CreateMenu	DestroyMenu
	CreatePopupMenu	DestroyMenu
	LoadMenu	DestroyMenu
	LoadMenuIndirect	DestroyMenu
Resource	AllocResource	FreeResource
	LoadResource	FreeResource
	LockResource	UnlockResource
Thunk	MakeProcInstance	FreeProcInstance
Timer	SetTimer	KillTimer
Window	CreateWindow	DestroyWindow
	CreateWindowEx	DestroyWindow

Now that you know you need to clean up these resource objects in your programs—what if you forget? You can test to see if your program is not freeing the resources it allocated using HEAPWALK, the debugging version of Windows, and Resource Monitor.

HEAPWALK

HEAPWALK is one of the most useful utilities that comes with the Microsoft Windows SDK. Using HEAPWALK you can check up on what your application is doing. You can see your code segments, automatic data segments, and dynamically allocated segments. The program parts that HEAPWALK lists are the following:

- The *module database* segment contains the header portion of the program's .EXE file. This segment is used for all instances of a program, so it is allocated only for the first instance.

- The *task* segment (named Task Database in Windows versions prior to 3.1) contains information unique to each instance, such as the program's command-line string and the program's current subdirectory. When a program loads resources (such as icons, cursors, or menu templates) into memory, each resource gets its own segment in the global heap. A program may itself also allocate some memory from the global heap.

- One or more *DGroup* segments. These are your application's data segments. These segments used to be called *data* in Windows versions prior to 3.1.

- One or more *code* segments.

- One or more *resource* segments for application resources such as menus, icons, and dialog boxes loaded by Windows.

- One or more *private* segments for global memory allocated by your application. These segments used to be called *tasks* in Windows versions prior to 3.1.

If you double-click on a memory object in HEAPWALK, a pop-up window appears showing the contents of the object with a hex dump. With graphic objects such as cursors and bitmaps, HEAPWALK displays the graphic object itself. Figure 6.6 shows HEAPWALK displaying the icon for the Windows Calculator.

FIGURE 6.6:

HEAPWALK

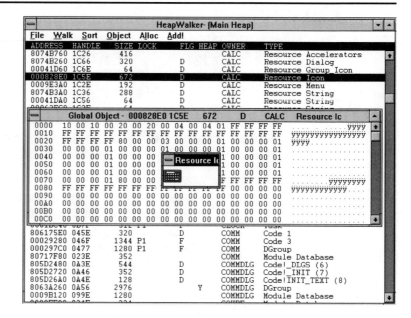

The meanings of the seven columns of information that HEAPWALK displays are as follows:

Column	Meaning
First	Segment address of object "Segment arena header"
Second	Size of object in bytes
Third	Lock count
Fourth	Discardable memory flag (such as "D")
Fifth	Name of object's owner
Sixth	Type of object (such as resource, code, data, etc.)
Seventh	Additional information, such as code segment number or type of resource

Using HEAPWALK to Track Down Lost Resources

You can use HEAPWALK to determine if your application is leaking resources and find out what kind of resources it's leaking. The following steps will determine if your application is allocating a Windows resource without freeing it.

1. Execute HEAPWALK and write down the size of the GDI's and the User's DGroup. This establishes a reference for comparing the size of the data segments later.

2. Choose the GDI LocalWalk command from the Object menu to display the GDI Heap (LocalWalk) window, which lists the different objects in the GDI data segment. Then choose the Save command from the Heap menu to copy this list to a file. The file will also contain a summary of GDI objects. You can follow the same procedure for recording information about the User segment.

3. Run your application and exercise it over a period of time, noting the changes in the size of the GDI and User data segments that HEAPWALK displays as your application runs. While your application is running, repeat step 2 a number of times to take "snapshots" of the effect your application has on the GDI and User data segments.

4. Close your application, take a final snapshot of the GDI and User data segments, and note their sizes.

5. Analyze the data that you've recorded. Look for GDI and User objects that your application creates but does not delete when they are no longer needed.

If you suspect that a certain command creates a memory object without freeing it, execute your program with a debugger and note the handle of the data object as it's created. You can also use the command OutputDebugString to send a message to your debugging monitor or to a file to record the point in your C source code where you allocated the data object along with its handles. You could also use MessageBox to record the event, but it's much more cumbersome. Once you have a log of the objects you created, compare the handles in your log to the LocalWalk of the GDI and User heaps after your program has terminated. If the handles still exist, your program is allocating memory objects without freeing them.

> **NOTE**
>
> In Windows 3.0, OutputDebugString could send messages only to a debugging monitor. In Windows 3.1, you can direct OutputDebugString messages to any device, including files and your printer. To direct this output, you need to add a Debug section to your SYSTEM.INI file with an OUTPUTTO= parameter. For example, to send OutputDebugString messages to a file named DEBUG.LOG, add a new section header [debug] to SYSTEM.INI (if it does not already exist). After the [debug] section heading, add the line outputto=debug.log.

Using the Debugging Version of Windows to Track Down Lost Resources

HEAPWALK can tell you if your Windows application is leaking resources, but there is an easier way—use the debugging version of Windows. The Windows 3.1 debugging version has been greatly enhanced beyond the previous version and includes parameter-checking for API function calls and system resource tracking.

The debugging version of Windows is included with the Windows SDK and Microsoft C/C++ 7.0. QuickC for Windows and some of the other Windows development environments don't include it. If your Windows development system doesn't include the debugging version of Windows, you can order it separately or as part of a package directly from Microsoft.

After the debugging version of Windows is installed, you can switch to it by executing the BAT file N2D from the DOS prompt. To switch back to the retail version of Windows, execute the BAT file D2N. When you execute the debugging version of Windows, it will send output messages to the device specified in the OUTPUTTO= parameter in the SYSTEM.INI file. As described earlier, you can send output to any device—even an application window.

One of the sample applications included with the Windows 3.1 SDK is DBWIN. It uses the new Windows 3.1 TOOLHELP.DLL to help you debug your Windows application. Since DBWIN is a sample application, the full source code for it is included with the Windows SDK.

If you set the OUTPUTTO= parameter to NUL and use the DBWIN application, you direct your debugging output to the DBWIN window on your Windows desktop. DBWIN has other capabilities besides just displaying the debugging messages generated by the debugging version of Windows. DBWIN allows you to control the output of various kinds of messages—whether they're displayed or whether you break to the CodeView for Windows debugger. You can save your DBWIN settings in WIN.INI so that they'll remain in effect the next time you use it to test your Windows application.

Now, instead of using HEAPWALK to test how your program allocates and frees system resources, test your program using the debugging version of Windows. When your program exits, the debugging version of Windows sends a list of all the system resources your application failed to free to the DBWIN window. Figure 6.7 shows what happened to Resource Monitor when I commented out the Delete-Object function call to free the pens used for drawing the 3-D shade lines in the Resource Monitor window.

FIGURE 6.7:
Tracking lost resources using the debugging version of Windows and DBWIN

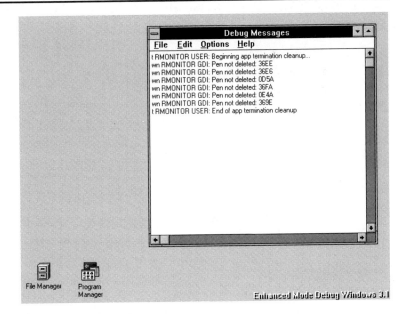

> DBWIN can be used with or without the debugging version of Windows. When used with it, DBWIN displays the most errors. If you don't have the Windows SDK, you can get a free copy of DBWIN by downloading it from the Microsoft Developer Forum on CompuServe. DBWIN and the debugging version of Windows will be discussed in more detail in Chapter 9.

If you have a secondary debugging monitor attached to your PC, you might also want to consider using OX.SYS, another free program available on the Microsoft Developer Forum on CompuServe. OX.SYS can redirect messages from the debugging version of Windows and the OutputDebugString function call to your secondary monitor instead of having to use an AUX port, file, or DBWIN.

Using the debugging version of Windows and DBWIN, you can quickly isolate application faults and make sure that when your Windows application exits, it releases all the system resources it acquired. Now that the debugging version of Windows provides more information, there is no excuse for not using it to test your Windows application before releasing it. In Chapter 9 we will discuss in more detail how to use the debugging version of Windows and DBWIN, to show you other ways you can use it to debug your Windows applications.

Other Uses for HEAPWALK

The primary reason programmers use HEAPWALK is to make sure that their program frees all its memory objects when it's supposed to. HEAPWALK can also be used to make sure your program allocated memory objects and to verify their contents. In summary, HEAPWALK lets you see a list of every object in Windows memory and look into its contents. Besides tracking down lost resources, I have found HEAPWALK useful for:

- Walking the local heap of my own application to determine the number of local memory objects allocated and how much space is left.

- Verifying the contents of a file buffer I've allocated. Using HEAPWALK you can look inside a memory buffer and step through it character by character. I found HEAPWALK very helpful in developing a parsing routine to convert a WordPerfect file to other file formats. Although I had documentation that told me what the file would look like, HEAPWALK let me see what the file contents were in my memory buffer as I was running and debugging my program.

- Debugging other applications. Sometimes you may notice that Windows slows down or just gets "weird" after executing an application—especially a BETA test version. If Windows is still up and running, you should try to execute HEAPWALK to see if the suspicious application forgot to delete memory objects; you may find that it didn't clean up after itself. If you suspect an application is causing Windows problems, it's also a good idea to test it using the debugging version of Windows. You may (or may not) be surprised at what you find.

- Checking to make sure my application doesn't leave any memory objects behind. In order for the code, data, and resources to be freed by Windows, your application must post itself a WM_QUIT message. This is usually done at the time the overlapped window for the application is destroyed. If an application doesn't process this message, its code and data will still be resident in memory after the application terminated. A good way to tell if the application has cleaned up after itself is to run HEAPWALK. Any items associated with your application will show up in the HEAPWALK list.

- Testing my program under low memory conditions. Using the HEAPWALK Alloc menu commands, you can allocate and free memory objects to test how well your program performs under low memory conditions. Using HEAP-WALK to test your program under low memory conditions is OK, but a much better tool to use is STRESS. STRESS is a new Windows 3.1 programming tool that lets you control the allocation of memory, User system resources, GDI system resources, disk space, and file handles. We will look at STRESS in detail in Chapter 12.

Resource Monitor

The Windows Resource Monitor program was developed for this book to help you keep track of three Windows resources: memory, User system resources, and GDI system resources. The Resource Monitor program files are in the \RMONITOR directory on the book's disk set. Resource Monitor's About dialog box is shown in Figure 6.8.

FIGURE 6.8:

The Resource Monitor About
dialog box

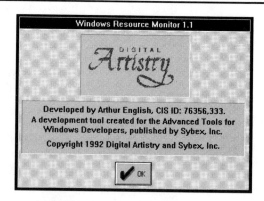

The program source files, the executable, and the Borland Resource Workshop DLL (BWCC.DLL) are included. To set up the program properly, make sure that the TOOLHELP.DLL included with Windows 3.1 is in the \SYSTEM directory of the Windows directory. You should also put BWCC.DLL in this directory.

The BWCC.DLL file contains all the functionality necessary to create the custom resources that Resource Monitor uses. Resource Monitor was created using the Borland Resource Workshop and Quick C for Windows. I have also built Resource Monitor using Borland C++ for Windows. A project file for building Resource Monitor with Borland C++ is included in the \RMONITOR directory.

The Help file (RMONITOR.HLP) contains a very detailed description of the product. The Help file for Resource Monitor was created using RoboHELP. You can refer back to Chapter 5 to see how RoboHELP automates the creation of Windows Help files.

How Resource Monitor Works

Resource Monitor keeps track of the amount of system resources available and tells you which module (GDI or User) is lower on resources and the percentage left. If you click on the Resource Monitor icon, its system menu shown in Figure 6.9 appears.

FIGURE 6.9:

The Resource Monitor system menu

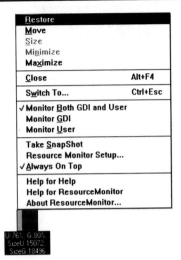

Program Manager - [Main]

File Manager

Resource Monitor lets you monitor the following Windows resources to keep track of the current Windows environment and to test Windows applications:

- Overall free system resources, including total user segment size and GDI segment size in bytes, as well as total and free memory size in kilobytes.

- Percentage and amount of free resources for the Windows User module.

- Percentage and amount of free resources for the Windows GDI module.

- Percentage and amount of free memory, including swap file memory.

NOTE You might ask where the total memory size came from and why it is not what you might have expected. If you have a 5MB SWAPFILE and 4MB of RAM, you would think that the total memory size would be 9216K. However, the amount of system memory that Resource Monitor reports will be slightly less than the memory on your system. This is because the amount of memory reported is the memory available to Windows—not the memory available on your system.

Resource Monitor is designed for both users and programmers. Users can use Resource Monitor to keep track of system resources and set alarms to warn them when

Windows system resources drop below specific levels. Programmers will find Resource Monitor much easier to use than HEAPWALK to test their program for "leaking" Windows system resources.

Resource Monitor Gauges

When you start Resource Monitor for the first time, an icon appears that is a colored bar gauge that displays the amount of critical system resources. When you double-click on the Resource Monitor icon to display its window, you will see three bar gauges. Resource Monitor uses three colors in its bar gauges to indicate the Windows resource level.

- *Green* indicates you have adequate system resources (above 60%).

- *Yellow* indicates caution (between 30% and 60%).

- *Red* indicates alert (below 30%).

You can set the colors to change at any percentage you want by modifying two constants defined in RMONITOR.H. The following two #define statements are used to determine when the bar gauge colors should change:

```
#define WARNING_LEVEL 60
#define CRITICAL_LEVEL 30
```

Resource Monitor System Menu

Resource Monitor has the following commands in its system menu:

- *Monitor Both GDI and User.* This is the default setting when you execute Resource Monitor for the first time. When this menu item is selected, Resource Monitor measures both the User and the GDI Windows modules and displays the free resources for the most critical one using the Resource Monitor icon.

- *Monitor GDI.* When this menu item is selected, the Resource Monitor icon displays information only for the GDI Windows module.

- *Monitor User.* When this menu item is selected, the Resource Monitor icon displays information only for the User Windows module.

- *Take SnapShot* records the size of free memory, User system resources, and GDI system resources. You can see the amount of change in the system resources by opening the Resource Monitor window or by adding the Snap-Shot information to the Resource Monitor window caption using the Setup dialog box.

- *Resource Monitor Setup* displays the Setup dialog box to let you configure the information displayed in the Resource Monitor window caption and to set Resource Monitor alarms.

- *Always On Top* puts the Resource Monitor icon or window on top of all other windows and locks it there so it can always be viewed.

- *Help for Help* displays help for using Windows Help.

- *Help for Resource Monitor* displays help for the Resource Monitor program.

- *About Resource Monitor* displays the About Resource Monitor dialog box.

Resource Monitor Setup Dialog Box

The Resource Monitor Setup dialog box, shown in Figure 6.10, lets you configure the Resource Monitor window caption and set Resource Monitor alarms. You also use the Setup dialog box to specify how often (the sampling rate) Resource Monitor checks the Windows resource levels.

FIGURE 6.10:

The Resource Monitor Setup dialog box

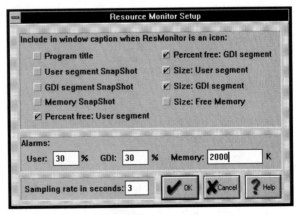

Program Manager - [Main]

File Manager

U:76%, G:78%, SizeU:15680, SizeG:18496

Resource Monitor lets you include in its window caption information about the Windows resource you want to track so it can be easily seen when Resource Monitor is an icon. For Resource Monitor to work effectively, you should choose Desktop in the Windows Control Panel and select the Wrap Title option—if you haven't already. This is the default when Windows is installed.

> **WARNING**
>
> Window captions cannot exceed approximately 60 characters, so DON'T TURN ON EVERY RESOURCE MONITOR WINDOW CAPTION OPTION. Monitor only what's needed. Unless I am debugging a program, I don't usually monitor anything in the window caption, or I monitor just the Percent Free for GDI and User. If you want to monitor as much as you can in the window caption, remember you can turn off the Program Title—this gives you additional space.

Alarms are one of Resource Monitor's handiest features. They will alert you when your system resources are critical. I set mine at 40% for both GDI and User. When an alarm goes off, Resource Monitor drops the alarm's setting by 10% to keep it from going off again in the near future. You need to reset the alarm to its previous setting after your system resources have climbed back to an acceptable level. If an alarm is set at zero, it's ignored by Resource Monitor. In other words, 0 means the alarm is OFF.

The sampling rate lets you configure how often Resource Monitor checks system resources in seconds. The acceptable range is from 1 to 600 seconds.

The Resource Monitor Window

Resource Monitor was developed to help you keep track of Windows resources on a day-by-day basis. You can use Resource Monitor to make sure Windows always has an adequate amount of resources. You can also use it to detect whether your application is leaking resources. The resource monitor icon displays a specific resource gauge, either User or GDI. You can also configure Resource Monitor using the Setup dialog box to display information about system resources in the Resource Monitor window caption. If you double-click on the Resource Monitor window, it opens to display all the Windows system resource information it monitors, as shown Figure 6.11.

FIGURE 6.11:

The Resource Monitor window

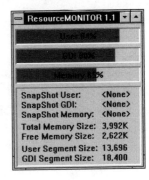

File Manager

Program
Manager

RMONITOR.INI

Resource Monitor creates a private INI file, RMONITOR.INI, in your Windows directory to remember your selections from execution to execution. You do not need to edit this file. It exists, and if you remove Resource Monitor from your hard disk, you will want to delete this file as well.

Using Resource Monitor to Test for Leaking Resources

The Resource Monitor SnapShot feature is designed to help you test your program to see if it's freeing all the Windows resources it allocates. Resource Monitor can help you determine if a problem exists, but it cannot track down individual resource objects the way the debugging version of Windows and HEAPWALK can.

Resource Monitor is helpful because it's always there at the bottom of the screen. If you think a problem exists, you can take a SnapShot instead of going through the additional work of loading HEAPWALK or the debugging version of Windows. To test your program using Resource Monitor, perform the following steps:

1. Start Resource Monitor.

2. Choose Always On Top from the Resource Monitor system menu so Resource Monitor is always visible.

3. Choose Setup Resource Monitor from the system menu to display the Resource Monitor Setup dialog box.

4. Select User segment, GDI, and Memory SnapShot information to display SnapShot information in the window caption of the Resource Monitor icon. Then choose OK.

5. Choose Take SnapShot from the system menu to capture the current state of your Windows resources.

6. Run and test your application. Make sure that you are running only your application during this test. Running other Windows applications while you are testing your application can throw test results off significantly.

7. Close your application. If the amount of SnapShot Windows resources displayed is not zero, you may have a resource leakage problem.

Looking Inside Resource Monitor

Resource Monitor is not only a handy tool to monitor system resources. It is also helpful for learning Windows programming. By studying its source code you will learn how to:

- Load a custom library for custom resources.

- Design and use .INI files.

- Use the TOOLHELP.DLL API to determine system resources.

- Make a window stay the topmost window.

- Append items to a menu.

- Implement the new Windows 3.1 STRICT coding style and macro APIs.

The Resource Monitor source code was initially generated using CASE:W Corporate Edition. CASE:W is discussed in detail in Chapter 3. After the initial application template was generated for Resource Monitor, I rewrote parts of it and added the necessary application code. I used the Borland Resource Workshop to generate the custom resources and compiled it with Borland C++ for Windows. The application source code is completely compatible with Quick C for Windows and Microsoft C/C++ Version 7.0.

After completing the functionality for Resource Monitor, I revised the source code to make it compatible with the new Windows 3.1 STRICT coding styles and the new Windows 3.1 macro APIs—including message crackers. If you have not read about how STRICT and the new macro APIs work, the C source code may look a bit strange. In Chapter 12 we will cover how STRICT and the macro APIs work in detail. For now, let's look at how some of Resource Monitor's functionality was created.

Creating Custom Resources   The Borland Resource Workshop (BRW) was used to create the About and Setup dialog boxes for Resource Monitor. I relied on the standard buttons provided by BRW and did not create custom buttons. Just using the standard BRW features, I was able to create 3-D–style dialog boxes that are more attractive than the standard ones you create using Microsoft's Dialog Editor. The only C code I needed to include in my application was a line to make sure that the Borland custom control library was loaded when Resource Monitor was initialized and freed when Resource Monitor was terminated. In the function `InitializeApp` in APP.C, you will find the code to load the Borland control library:

```
// Load up Borland's control library for fancy dialogs.
//
hLib = LoadLibrary ("bwcc.dll");
```

In the function `CloseApp` in APP.C, you will find the code to free the Borland custom control library:

```
// Free the Borland custom control library
//
FreeLibrary (hLib);
```

Using .INI Files   There isn't much in the way of documentation to be found on how to use .INI files in either the Windows SDK or other Windows programming books. It's a shame, because creating and using .INI files is easy. The function `Write-PrivateProfileString` saves the information in the .INI file, and the functions `GetPrivateProfileInt` and `GetPrivateProfileString` get information from the .INI file. These functions are used for an application .INI file. You can also use `WriteProfileString`, `GetProfileString`, and `GetProfileInt` to get and write parameters to WIN.INI. I personally prefer to use private .INI files instead of writing to the WIN.INI file to save and get configuration information. Although this creates an additional file on the user's system, it keeps the WIN.INI file less cluttered. If a user wants to delete one of my applications, all he or she has to do is delete the APP.INI file as well. The information about how to remove your Windows application should be included in your application's documentation and

Help file. Although it's not as important as how to install your application, it's still important. The C source code to save and get information in the RMONITOR.INI file is in the functions `SaveProfile` and `GetProfile` in APP.C.

```c
//-----------------------------------------------------------------
//
// GetProfile function
//
void GetProfile (void)
{
  char szBuf[24];

  Setup.bProgramTitle = GetPrivateProfileInt ("ResMonitor Setup",
    "Program Title Caption",
    1,
    "rmonitor.ini");

  nWidth = GetPrivateProfileInt ("ResMonitor Setup",
    "nWidth",
    (int) LOWORD (GetDialogBaseUnits ()) * 30,
    "rmonitor.ini");

  nHeight = GetPrivateProfileInt ("ResMonitor Setup",
    "nHeight",
    (int) HIWORD (GetDialogBaseUnits ()) * 17,
    "rmonitor.ini");

  cxWin = GetPrivateProfileInt ("ResMonitor Setup",
    "cxWin",
    nScreenWidth - nWidth - 10,
    "rmonitor.ini");

  cyWin = GetPrivateProfileInt ("ResMonitor Setup",
    "cyWin",
    nScreenHeight - nHeight - 10,
    "rmonitor.ini");

  Setup.bUserSnapShot = GetPrivateProfileInt ("ResMonitor Setup",
    "User segment SnapShot Caption",
    0,
    "rmonitor.ini");

  Setup.bGDISnapShot = GetPrivateProfileInt ("ResMonitor Setup",
    "GDI segment SnapShot Caption",
    0,
```

```
   "rmonitor.ini");

Setup.bMemSnapShot = GetPrivateProfileInt ("ResMonitor Setup",
 "Memory SnapShot Caption",
 0,
 "rmonitor.ini");

Setup.bPctFreeUser = GetPrivateProfileInt ("ResMonitor Setup",
 "User % Caption",
 0,
 "rmonitor.ini");

Setup.bPctFreeGDI = GetPrivateProfileInt ("ResMonitor Setup",
 "GDI % Caption",
 0,
 "rmonitor.ini");

Setup.bSizeUser = GetPrivateProfileInt ("ResMonitor Setup",
 "User Size Caption",
 0,
 "rmonitor.ini");

Setup.bSizeGDI = GetPrivateProfileInt ("ResMonitor Setup",
 "GDI Size Caption",
 0,
 "rmonitor.ini");

Setup.bSizeFreeMem = GetPrivateProfileInt ("ResMonitor Setup",
 "FREEMEM Size Caption",
 0,
 "rmonitor.ini");

Setup.lAlarmFreeMem = GetPrivateProfileString
 ("ResMonitor Setup",
 "Alarm for Free Memory",
 "0", szBuf, 24,
 "rmonitor.ini");
Setup.lAlarmFreeMem = atol (szBuf);

Setup.nAlarmGDI = GetPrivateProfileInt ("ResMonitor Setup",
 "Alarm for GDI",
 0,
 "rmonitor.ini");

Setup.nAlarmUser = GetPrivateProfileInt ("ResMonitor Setup",
```

```
    "Alarm for User",
    0,
    "rmonitor.ini");

  Setup.nSampleRate = GetPrivateProfileInt ("ResMonitor Setup",
    "Sampling rate in seconds",
    1,
    "rmonitor.ini");

  bAlwaysOnTop = GetPrivateProfileInt ("ResMonitor Setup",
    "Always on Top",
    0,
    "rmonitor.ini");
} // End of GetProfile
```

Calculating System Resources   The heart of Resource Monitor is in the GetSystem-Resources function. This function uses the new Windows 3.1 TOOLHELP.DLL to get information about the current state of Windows system resources. The new TOOLHELP.DLL exports 34 functions that let you find out this information and much more. Using the TOOLHELP.DLL you can find information about the entire Windows environment and create a variety of debugging tools.

TOOLHELP lets you get information about the global heap, each application's local heap, DLLs, window tasks, and registered window classes. The SDK includes two sample applications, DBWIN and TOOLHELP, to show you how to use the new TOOLHELP API. Besides teaching you how to use TOOLHELP, the DBWIN application is also a handy debugging tool that you use with the debugging version of Windows. You have already seen how DBWIN can be used to help track down lost resources.

In Resource Monitor I use the TOOLHELP API functions to report on the total system memory and free system resources. I also use the function GetFreeSpace that was available in Windows 3.0 to find out the amount of free memory. The TOOL-HELP API functions work in a fashion similar to the other new Windows 3.1 SDK functions: they initialize a data structure, pass the data structure to the Windows API function, and use the information returned by Windows in the data structure. TOOLHELP is called from the GetSystemResources function in RMONITOR.C, as shown in the following program code:

```
//-------------------------------------------------------------
//
```

```
// GetSystemResources - Uses the TOOLHELP.DLL to get the Windows
//system
// resource info.
//
void GetSystemResources (void)
{
  SYSHEAPINFO shiHeapInfo;
  static DWORD dwAllMem = 0;
  GLOBALENTRY geInfo;
  MEMMANINFO MemMan;

  shiHeapInfo.dwSize = sizeof (shiHeapInfo);
  SystemHeapInfo (& shiHeapInfo);
  wPctFreeUser = shiHeapInfo.wUserFreePercent;
  wPctFreeGDI = shiHeapInfo.wGDIFreePercent;
  wSizeUser = (WORD) GlobalSize (shiHeapInfo.hUserSegment);
  wSizeGDI = (WORD) GlobalSize (shiHeapInfo.hGDISegment);

  if (wPctFreeGDI > wPctFreeUser)
   wWhichIsMoreCritical = IDM_USER;
  else
   wWhichIsMoreCritical = IDM_GDI;

  dwGmemFree = GetFreeSpace (0);

  if (dwAllMem == 0)
  {
   MemMan.dwSize = sizeof (MEMMANINFO);
   MemManInfo (& MemMan);
   dwAllMem = (MemMan.dwTotalPages + MemMan.dwSwapFilePages)
   * MemMan.wPageSize;
   dwTotMemSize = dwAllMem;
  }

  // decide which resource value to return
  if (wMonitor == IDM_BOTH)
   wFree = (min (wPctFreeGDI, wPctFreeUser));
  if (wMonitor == IDM_USER)
   wFree = (wPctFreeUser);
  if (wMonitor == IDM_GDI)
   wFree = (wPctFreeGDI);
}
```

Putting Your Application on Top   An interesting feature of Resource Monitor is that you can make the application window or icon always be the topmost window using the new Windows 3.1 function `SetWindowPos`. Windows 3.1 supplies two z-orders that a window can be placed in. The new z-order is called the topmost z-order. Windows in the topmost z-order are on a layer above those windows that are not in the topmost z-order. When you put Resource Monitor in the topmost z-order by choosing Always On Top, it appears on top of all the windows in the lower z-order that is the Windows default. The following code that's executed when the `WM_SYSCOMMAND` message for `IDM_ALWAYSONTOP` is processed shows how this is accomplished:

```
case IDM_ALWAYSONTOP :
  if (bAlwaysOnTop)
    {
    CheckMenuItem (GetSystemMenu (hWnd, FALSE),
     IDM_ALWAYSONTOP, MF_UNCHECKED);
    SetWindowPos (hWnd, HWND_NOTOPMOST, 0, 0, 0, 0, SWP_NOMOVE |
       SWP_NOSIZE);
    bAlwaysOnTop = FALSE;
    }
  else
    {
    CheckMenuItem (GetSystemMenu (hWnd, FALSE),
     IDM_ALWAYSONTOP, MF_CHECKED);
    bAlwaysOnTop = TRUE;
    SetWindowPos (hWnd, HWND_TOPMOST, 0, 0, 0, 0, SWP_NOMOVE |
       SWP_NOSIZE);
    }
  break;
```

Dynamic Menus   Resource Monitor adds menu items to its system menu so its menu commands are always accessible—even when it's an icon. Adding items to a menu is very straightforward in Windows, using the `AppendMenu` function. The Resource Monitor system menu contains all of the Resource Monitor commands as well as the normal Restore, Move, Size, Minimize, Maximize, Close, and Switch To commands.

In the Resource Monitor C code, I used only `AppendMenu`, but there are several other Windows APIs for working with menus that you should be aware of. `DeleteMenu` deletes a command from a menu. `InsertMenu` inserts a command in a menu at any position you specify. The following C code shows how menu commands were added to the Resource Monitor system menu:

```c
//----------------------------------------------------------------
//
// OnCreate - Handle WM_CREATE message
//
BOOL OnCreate(HWND hWnd, CREATESTRUCT FAR * lpCreateStruct)
{
  HMENU hMenu;

  hMenu = GetSystemMenu (hWnd, FALSE);
  AppendMenu (hMenu, MF_SEPARATOR, 0, 0);
  AppendMenu (hMenu, MF_STRING | MF_CHECKED, IDM_BOTH,
   (LPSTR) "Monitor &Both GDI and User");
  AppendMenu (hMenu, MF_STRING, IDM_GDI,
   (LPSTR) "Monitor &GDI");
  AppendMenu (hMenu, MF_STRING, IDM_USER,
   (LPSTR) "Monitor &User");
  AppendMenu (hMenu, MF_SEPARATOR, 0, 0);
  AppendMenu (hMenu, MF_STRING, IDM_SNAPSHOT,
   (LPSTR) "Take &SnapShot");
  AppendMenu (hMenu, MF_STRING, IDM_SETUP,
   (LPSTR) "Resource Monitor Setup...");
  if (bAlwaysOnTop)
   {
   AppendMenu (hMenu, MF_STRING | MF_CHECKED, IDM_ALWAYSONTOP,
      (LPSTR) "&Always On Top");
   SetWindowPos (hWnd, HWND_TOPMOST, 0, 0, 0, 0, SWP_NOMOVE |
      SWP_NOSIZE);
   }
  else
   AppendMenu (hMenu, MF_STRING, IDM_ALWAYSONTOP,
      (LPSTR) "&Always On Top");
  AppendMenu (hMenu, MF_SEPARATOR, 0, 0);
  AppendMenu (hMenu, MF_STRING, IDM_HELP,
   (LPSTR) "Help for Help");

  AppendMenu (hMenu, MF_STRING, IDM_INDEXHELP,
   (LPSTR) "Help for ResourceMonitor");

  AppendMenu (hMenu, MF_STRING, IDM_ABOUT,
```

```
       (LPSTR) "About ResourceMonitor...");

   if (! SetTimer (hWnd, TIMER_ID, Setup.nSampleRate * 1000, NULL))
   {
   MessageBox (hWnd, "Too many timers in use!",
      "Resource Monitor    Error!",
   MB_ICONEXCLAMATION ¦ MB_OK);
   }
   OnTimer (hWnd, 0);
   return TRUE;
} // End of OnCreate
```

Using Memory Wisely

Now that you understand how Windows memory and system resources work and how to use tools such as HEAPWALK, the debugging version of Windows, and Resource Monitor to test the way your program uses Windows resources, let's take a look at the amount of memory actually consumed when you allocate Windows memory or a Windows object. This information will help you understand the overhead associated with each memory allocation your application does.

Allocating Memory Locally or Globally

The header on global memory objects is 16 bytes. In addition, each global memory object is rounded up to the next 32-byte multiple. A GlobalAlloc of 1 byte actually consumes 32 bytes from the global heap, because 1 + 16 = 17, and then the object allocated would be rounded up to 32 bytes (to make the size of the entire object an even 32-byte multiple). The header on local memory objects is 6 bytes. In addition, each local memory object is rounded up to the next 4-byte multiple. The smallest local memory object is 12 bytes. A LocalAlloc of 1 byte would consume 12 bytes (because of the minimum) and a LocalAlloc of 17 bytes would consume 24 bytes from the local heap, because 17 + 6 = 23, and then the size of the object is rounded up to 24 bytes (to make the size of the entire object an even 4-byte multiple). Knowing the overhead of these functions can help you design a more efficient memory-allocation scheme. Obviously, a linked list of 1-byte characters is not going to be very efficient memorywise.

Don't Allocate Too Many Global Memory Segments

As we discussed earlier, Windows 3.1 is limited to 8192 segment selectors in the LDT. This means that the maximum number of global memory segments available to Windows is 8192. Although this may sound like a lot, it can easily be exhausted by allocating global memory and forgetting to free it—especially inside a program loop.

If you need to allocate global memory, use a few large data objects instead of many smaller ones. If you need more global memory, consider `GlobalReAlloc` to make a global memory object larger to accommodate your data, instead of creating a new memory object. If you are keeping structures in global memory and you are using pointer arithmetic to jump from structure to structure, you should keep your global memory object under 64K. Pointer arithmetic—even using huge pointers—does not work well across segment boundaries unless you are working with only one byte at a time.

If possible, you should try to allocate global memory objects frugally and keep their size under 64K.

System Resource Impact

Windows creates and stores objects on behalf of each application in the system. Many of these objects are stored in two places, the User heap and the GDI heap.

As you have seen, a good way to see what is stored in the heaps is to use HEAP-WALK. Besides knowing you must be careful about freeing system resources when they are no longer needed, it's helpful to know exactly how much memory it costs when you allocate a Windows object. Table 6.6 lists the objects stored in the User heap and the typical sizes for these items.

The module database is used by the Kernel and contains an abbreviated version of an executable file header. The module database is used when Windows needs to load code, resources, or data from an executable file.

Items are placed in the GDI heap whenever a program creates a GDI object. While most applications create GDI objects, it is necessary to ensure that not too many objects are created at one time. Also, an object MUST be destroyed once it is no longer required by the application. Table 6.7 lists the objects stored in the GDI heap and typical sizes for these items.

TABLE 6.6: User Object Sizes

Object	Size in Bytes
Menu	20 + 20 per menu item
Window Class	40 to 50
Window	68+
Group Cursor	32
Cursor	288 (varies)
String	64 (varies)
Module Database	6560 (varies)

TABLE 6.7: GDI Heap Object Sizes

Object	Size in Bytes
Brush	32
Bitmap	28 to 32
Font	40 to 44
Pen	28
Region	28
Palette	28
Module Database	3424

Reducing Your Local Heap

It has been the rule ever since Windows 1.0 to use the medium memory model for all Windows applications. Even programs as complex as Word for Windows that contain more than one million lines of program code use the medium memory model that limits them to a 64K data segment. Now that there is more and more memory available for running Windows, I'm sure applications will drift away from using this rule. Personally, I like to develop modular programs that use memory efficiently—so I stick with using the medium memory model.

One of the questions I'm asked the most about Windows programming is how to reduce the size of a program's local heap to stay within the 64K limit imposed by the medium memory model. One way to reduce heap requirements is through the judicious use of resources. For example, static strings should be placed in a string table rather than being stored as variables. You can reduce heap requirements by using class extra bytes and window extra bytes. Although these bytes are stored on the User heap, each one is associated with a particular window or window class. This makes them a very convenient place to store a handle or a pointer to a data structure that has been allocated from global memory.

The DumpIT program developed in Chapter 3 is a good example of how to attach a window to a data structure stored in either local or global memory. For each MDI window that DumpIT displays a file in, the following data structure defined in DumpIT's header file is associated with it:

```
typedef struct
  {
  char szFileName[129];    // File Name
  LOCALHANDLE hWinVar;     // Handle to this data structure
  LONG lFileSize;          // File size and buffer size
  LONG lNumLinesInFile;    // Number of lines needed to display entire file
  float fFudgeFactor;      // Fudge factor for calc'ing scrolling position
                 // position when lNumLinesInFile > 32,000
  LONG lAdjPosition;       // Offset for scrolling when NumLines > 32,000
  LONG lFindLine;          // Line with something found on it
  char _huge *hpFileBuffer; // Pointer to buffer the file is in
  char _huge *hpFindPtr;   // Pointer to found data
  int nFindCnt;            // Number of bytes found
  int cxClient;            // Size of MDI child client window
  int cyClient;            // Size of MDI child client window
  int nVscrollPos;         // Vertical scroll position of MDI child window
  int nVscrollMax;         // Maximum vertical scroll of MDI child window
  int nHscrollPos;         // Horizontal scroll position of MDI child window
  int nHscrollMax;         // Maximum horizontal scroll of MDI child window
  int cxChar;              // X size of selected font for window
  int cyChar;              // Y size of selected font for window
  int nMaxWidth;           // Maximum width of window in characters
  HFONT hFontDisplay;      // Handle to the display font
  HFONT hFontPrinter;      // Handle to the printer font
  int nTextColor;          // Window text color
  int nBGColor;            // Window background color
  int nHiTextColor;        // Window highlighted text color
  int nHiBGColor;          // Window highlighted background color
```

```
COLORREF crText;        // Color reference for text
COLORREF crBG;          // Color reference for background color
COLORREF crHiText;       // Color reference for highlighted text color
COLORREF crHiBG;        // Color reference for highlighted background color
}
WINDOWVARIABLES;
```

A far pointer to this structure is stored in the extra bytes of the window associated with the data structure. One of the first actions a DumpIT function takes when it accesses a DumpIT window is to do a GetWindowLong function call to obtain this pointer to access the window's associated data variables. An example of this is the InitMDIChild function. It gets the pointer to the data structure and then uses it to initialize the variables in the data structure to set the defaults of how the data will be displayed in the window.

```
//-------------------------------------------------------------------------
//
// InitMDIChild function
//
void InitMDIChild (HWND hWnd)
{
  int nCnt, nStart, nTo, nFrom;

  // Make sure that the Active window variables are set correctly
  lpWinVar = (WINDOWVARIABLES _far *) GetWindowLong (hWnd, 0);

  // Set up colors for window based on last color selected
  //
  lpWinVar->nHiTextColor = g_nHiTextColor;
  lpWinVar->nBGColor     = g_nBGColor;
  lpWinVar->nTextColor   = g_nTextColor;
  lpWinVar->nHiBGColor   = g_nHiBGColor;
  SetColorRef (lpWinVar, g_nTextColor);
  SetColorRef (lpWinVar, g_nBGColor);
  SetColorRef (lpWinVar, g_nHiTextColor);
  SetColorRef (lpWinVar, g_nHiBGColor);

  for(nCnt = 0; nCnt < 8; nCnt++)
   {

   // Save info about file for displaying in the File Sizes dialog box
   //
   if(FileSizeDlgData.FileSizeList[nCnt][0] == 0x00)
     {
```

```
    ltoCommaDelimitedString (lpWinVar->lFileSize, FileSizeDlgData.FileSize-
List[nCnt], 12);
    nStart = lstrlen (FileSizeDlgData.FileSizeList[nCnt]);
    *(FileSizeDlgData.FileSizeList[nCnt] + nStart) = '\t';
    nStart++;
    ltoa (lpWinVar->lFileSize, FileSizeDlgData.FileSizeList[nCnt] + nStart,
16);
    nStart = lstrlen (FileSizeDlgData.FileSizeList[nCnt]);
    *(FileSizeDlgData.FileSizeList[nCnt] + nStart) = '\t';
    nStart++;

    for (nTo = nStart, nFrom = 0;
     nTo <= 161 && *(lpWinVar->szFileName + nFrom) != NULL;
      nTo++, nFrom++)
     FileSizeDlgData.FileSizeList[nCnt][nTo] = *(lpWinVar->szFileName + nFrom);

    FileSizeDlgData.FileSizeList_hWnd[nCnt] = hWnd;

    break;
    }
  } // for (nCnt...
  nFileCount++; // Keep track of the number of files
} // End of InitMDIChild
```

Now that you understand how to audit the way your program uses Windows memory and system resources, let's continue to the next chapter, "Monitoring Windows and Window Messages." There you will learn how to use Windows development tools such as Spy and WinSight to find out how other Windows programs are constructed and how to monitor the messages being sent to them. You will also learn how to debug your application using either Spy or WinSight to track down program bugs that are related to Windows messages.

Monitoring Windows and Window Messages

7

■ How Windows keeps track of window classes and window instances

■ Using Spy or WinSight to monitor window messages and investigate window information

■ Using Topper to lock a window on top of other windows

■ Using ToolPAL to add a floating toolbar to Borland C++ for Windows and Microsoft QuickC for Windows

■ How ToolPAL subclasses and controls another Windows application

Windows are the fundamental building blocks of Windows and Windows applications. The Windows message system provides the mechanism for window objects to communicate. The concept of working with windows and messages is the first major hurdle every programmer must overcome to become a Windows developer.

This chapter explores how windows and window messages interact within the Windows environment. It also examines some of the tools that you can use to monitor an application's windows and the messages being sent to it.

First we will overview how windows and messages work. Then we will look at Spy, a message monitoring tool from Microsoft. We will see how Spy works and learn tips for using it appropriately. After looking at Spy we will look at some more powerful tools for monitoring window messages: WinSight from Borland and Voyeur from Micro-Quill. WinSight is included with all the Borland Windows development systems. Voyeur is part of a Windows development toolkit called DeMystifiers.

While we are examining these tools you will see how they can be used to build some interesting tools that I developed for this book, ToolPAL and Topper. ToolPAL, a Windows application built using WindowsMAKER Professional, is a floating tool palette that works with either QuickC for Windows or Borland C++ for Windows. Since you have the source code for ToolPAL on your disk set, you can modify it to work with any program you want.

Topper is a tool that looks through the list of all the top-level windows that are active and displays the caption for each in a list box. After selecting a window in Topper's list box, you can click on a button to move the window to the topmost z-order so it appears on top of all the other normal windows. Topper has some interesting uses and illustrates some useful programming tricks. By exploring Topper you'll learn more about windows and messages—as well as learn how to build a graphical push button as an alternative to using control windows.

Working with Windows

Window messages are invisible to a Windows application user. Windows' message system can be compared to real-world communication systems such as the telephone. When things don't work well with a telephone system, technicians use monitoring tools to isolate the problem. As a user of a telephone, you don't care about how a telephone system works—you only want to be able to talk to the person on the other end of the line. Windows users—like telephone users—don't need to know or care about messages. Yet the developer, like the telephone technician, needs tools to monitor the message traffic

- between Windows and its applications,
- between different Windows applications, and
- within a Windows application.

Messages travel between window objects. A window object reacts to the messages it's sent and sends messages to other windows. There is a whole class of window messages dedicated for applications to communicate with each other—Windows Dynamic Data Exchange (DDE). DDE and the new Windows 3.1 Dynamic Data Exchange Management Library will be explored in detail in Chapter 11. For now, let's examine what a window is and how it's created.

Window Class

A window's class defines a window's appearance and behavior. The class must be defined before any windows derived from it can be created. Windows programs are made up of many windows that are derived from window classes. A window may contain a menu bar, a scroll bar, a border, a caption bar, a minimize box, a maximize box, a system menu, and a system menu box. Each of these components is itself a window that is based upon a window class. Another window class is the dialog box. Dialog boxes are temporary windows that also contain other windows called "controls." Examples of some of the more common controls are buttons and edit boxes.

Every window within Windows is based on a window class. The window class may be predefined by Windows, such as a push button, or it can be created within a Windows application. To create a window class you must:

- Create a function to process the messages for the window class, called a window procedure.
- Initialize a WNDCLASS structure that describes the window class attributes.
- Call RegisterClass to have Windows create the window class.

To understand how this all works, let's use Topper 1.0 as an example. Topper is a Windows application that you can use to lock any active application window as the topmost window on your desktop. Topper registers one local window class for its main window and uses system global memory classes for list box and button control windows.

I originally built Topper so I could lock a Windows Help window on top while I'm using an application. For example, in both QuickC and Borland C++ you can put the caret on any Windows API, message constant, or data type and start Help to find out the specifics about how to use that aspect of Windows programming. In QuickC, you press F1 to get Windows API help. In Borland C++ you press Ctrl+F1.

Now you have the Windows Help window right there in front of you to find out about the Windows programming information you need. But when you click or activate your program editing window—WHAM!—the Help window is covered up. Using Topper you can lock the Help window on top and leave it there as either a window or an icon. You can type in your program editing window and reference information in your Help window. Figure 7.1 shows how Topper 1.0 can be used with QuickC for Windows and Windows Help to lock the Help window on top.

FIGURE 7.1:

Using Topper 1.0 to lock the Windows SDK Reference Help window on top

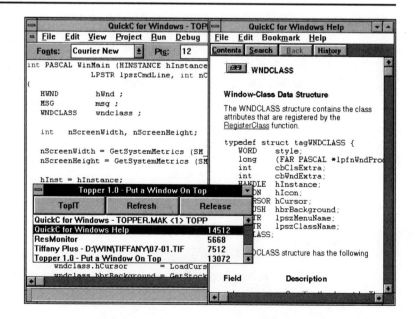

Notice the three buttons under the Topper window caption. *TopIT* locks the window selected in the list box on top. *Refresh* calls Windows to find out all the active application windows and rebuild the contents of the list box. *Release* unlocks the window highlighted in the list box from being on top.

> **NOTE**
> You may have noticed that there are two versions of Topper on the disk set. Topper Version 1.0 is a conventional Windows program that uses standard window objects, such as windows, push buttons, and a list box. Topper 2.0 uses GDI to draw its own graphical push buttons that look and feel just like standard window push buttons. For now, let's concentrate on Topper 1.0 to see how standard windows work. Later, we'll take a closer look at Topper 2.0 to see how its custom buttons work.

Some applications, such as the Resource Monitor that was created for this book, let you lock their window on top by choosing a menu command. The DBWIN application that's included with the Microsoft Windows 3.1 SDK also lets you lock its window on top using a menu command. DBWIN lets you display `OutputDebugString` messages as well as messages from the debugging version of Windows inside the DBWIN window. You will learn more about DBWIN in Chapter 9. Other Windows programming tools don't give you this option, so you can use Topper to do it instead. Some of the application windows you can lock on top with Topper are:

- Windows Help (as we have already discussed).
- Spy, the Windows message monitoring utility from Microsoft.
- WinSight, the Windows message monitoring utility from Borland.
- STRESS, the Windows environment stress-testing utility from Microsoft.
- HEAPWALK, the Microsoft utility for viewing global memory.

Now that we know what Topper does, let's look inside it to see how it registers the window class for its main window.

```
if (!hPrevInstance)
  {
  wndclass.style      = CS_HREDRAW | CS_VREDRAW ;
  wndclass.lpfnWndProc  = WndProc ;
  wndclass.cbClsExtra  = 0 ;
```

```
wndclass.cbWndExtra   = 0 ;
wndclass.hInstance    = hInstance ;
wndclass.hIcon        = LoadIcon (hInst, "TOPPER") ;
wndclass.hCursor      = LoadCursor (NULL, IDC_ARROW) ;
wndclass.hbrBackground = GetStockObject (WHITE_BRUSH) ;
wndclass.lpszMenuName = NULL ;
wndclass.lpszClassName = "TOPPER" ;

RegisterClass (&wndclass) ;
}
```

Window Class Types

There are three different flavors when it comes to window classes: system global, application global, and application local. System global classes are registered by Windows, and their window procedures are internal to Windows. This class type is available to all window applications while Windows is running. Examples of this type of window are

- buttons,

- scrollbars,

- list boxes, and

- edit boxes.

To use a system global window class, you must reference its name when you call CreateWindow, in the same way you reference the name of a window class that your application has registered. For example, if you want to create a push button window inside a window, you must call CreateWindow using the system global class button as the first parameter. When you use control windows inside a dialog box, Windows calls CreateWindow to create the child window controls based on the system global window class.

Application global classes are registered by an application or DLL, rather than by Windows, using the CS_GLOBALCLASS flag in the WNDCLASS structure. After an application global class is registered, any Windows application can create windows of that class. A custom control—such as the Borland-style buttons discussed in Chapter 2 and residing in the BWCC.DLL—is an example of an application global class window.

When your program registers a window for its private use, application local class is the default. Since applications can have a private window class, it's possible for two applications to register a window class with the same name. When an application calls CreateWindow for a new window, Windows looks for the class name to see if it's been registered. It first searches the names of local window classes, then goes to application global window classes, and finally to system global window classes to find the name.

> **WARNING**
>
> It's not a good idea to use a name for a local window class that's already being used as either an application global window class or a system global window class. For example, if you register a local window class called LISTBOX, you cannot create a Windows LISTBOX control in your program, because your application has defined a window class with that name. This also applies to control windows created for you by Windows inside a dialog box.

How Windows Keeps Track of a Window Class

When RegisterClass is called by a Windows application, Windows allocates a data structure to store information about the class. When CreateWindow is called to create an instance of a window using a window class, Windows allocates a data structure to store information about the window instance. These structures are allocated in the User DGROUP segment, as we discussed in Chapter 6. The class structure contains all the information that you provide to Windows in the WNDCLASS structure, as well as the class name and menu name for the window. You can also allocate extra bytes in the window class structure using the cbClsExtra member of the WNDCLASS structure.

If you want to find out information about a window that's already been registered, you use GetClassInfo to fill a WNDCLASS structure with information about a registered window class. You can get information about any window class, including system global window classes, window classes your application creates either globally or locally, and any other application's window class. However, GetClass-Info cannot be used to obtain information about a window class menu name, caption name, or extra bytes. You need to use GetClassWord and GetClassLong to obtain this information.

> **TIP**
>
> One of the window class styles that's easy to overlook for novice Windows programmers is CS_DBLCLKS. You must use this style in order for a window to receive mouse messages when the user double-clicks within the window. These messages are WM_LBUTTONDBLCLK, WM_MBUTTONDBLCLK, and WM_RBUTTONDBLCLK. If you put code inside a window procedure to process these messages and it doesn't work, make sure you gave the window class a CS_DBLCLKS style.

Creating Windows

There are three basic window styles you use within a Windows application:

- overlapped windows,
- pop-up windows, and
- child windows.

Typically, the main window of an application is an overlapped window. The defined control style for an overlapped window is WS_OVERLAPPED. As you soon will see, this is a value that you provide the CreateWindow function to create the main window. The pop-up windows and child windows also have defined styles; they are WS_POPUP and WS_CHILD, respectively. Pop-up windows are transient and usually support dialog boxes.

Parenting is also an important concept. Three Windows concepts about parenting that you should know are:

- Overlapped windows do not have parent windows.
- Pop-up windows may or may not have parent windows.
- Child windows always have parent windows.

Child windows are moved and destroyed when the parent is moved or destroyed, but pop-up windows may or may not exist once the parent is gone. Child windows cannot be drawn outside the border of the parent window. For example, each document window in Word for Windows is a child window. You can move a Word for Windows document window anywhere you want, but it always stays inside the border of the parent frame window.

A number of steps are required to register, create, and display a window. Most of the steps must take place before a window is ever displayed on the screen. The steps are:

1. Define a window class structure variable.

2. Fill the class structure variable with window information and the address of the window procedure that processes the messages for the window class.

3. Register the window class structure with Windows.

4. Create the window.

5. Show the window.

6. Update the window.

After class registration is complete, the window is ready to be created. The Create-Window function is one of the most important functions to a Windows programmer. You have already seen how the main window for Topper was registered. Now let's see how it's created.

```
hWnd = CreateWindow ("TOPPER",
  "Topper - Put a Window On Top",
  WS_SYSMENU ¦ WS_MINIMIZEBOX ¦ WS_VISIBLE ¦ WS_OVERLAPPED,
  nScreenWidth / 4, nScreenHeight / 3,
  nScreenWidth / 2, nScreenHeight / 3,
  NULL, NULL, hInstance, NULL) ;

ShowWindow (hWnd, nCmdShow) ;
UpdateWindow (hWnd) ;
```

As you can see, the CreateWindow function allows us to add more detailed information about the window. Topper 1.0 creates five windows. Here we create the parent window frame with the WS_OVERLAPPED window style. Next we create four more windows—three push buttons and a list box.

In the previous code segment there are two important function calls, ShowWindow and UpdateWindow. After the window is created, it is still not on the display. The ShowWindow function does this task. The UpdateWindow function causes a WM_PAINT message to be generated so the client area of the window can be painted.

The logical point at which to create windows within a window, is when the WM_CREATE message is processed by the parent window. In Topper, `Topper_On-Create` is called to process the WM_CREATE message. Topper's child windows are created in this function.

```
//
//--------------------------------------------------------------------
//
// TOPPER_OnCreate - Handle WM_CREATE message
//
BOOL TOPPER_OnCreate(HWND hWnd, CREATESTRUCT FAR * lpCreateStruct)
  {
  HDC      hDC ;
  TEXTMETRIC tm ;
  RECT rWinRect;
  HMENU hMenu;

    // Fix up System menu
    //
    hMenu = GetSystemMenu (hWnd, FALSE);
    AppendMenu (hMenu, MF_SEPARATOR, 0, 0);
    AppendMenu (hMenu, MF_STRING, IDM_PUTTOPPERONTOP,
       (LPSTR) "&Put Topper On Top");
    AppendMenu (hMenu, MF_SEPARATOR, 0, 0);
    AppendMenu (hMenu, MF_STRING, IDM_TOPPERHELP,
       (LPSTR) "&Help for Topper");
    AppendMenu (hMenu, MF_STRING, IDM_ABOUTTOPPER,
       (LPSTR) "&About Topper");
    hDC = GetDC (hWnd) ;
    GetTextMetrics (hDC, &tm) ;
    ReleaseDC (hWnd, hDC) ;

    GetWindowRect (hWnd, &rWinRect);
    MoveWindow (hWnd, rWinRect.left, rWinRect.top,
        tm.tmAveCharWidth * 54 + 2,
        tm.tmHeight * 7 + GetSystemMetrics (SM_CYCAPTION), TRUE);

    // Create a listbox control window
    //
    hWndList = CreateWindow ("LISTBOX", NULL,
     WS_CHILD | WS_VISIBLE | LBS_STANDARD | LBS_USETABSTOPS,
     0, tm.tmHeight * 2,
     tm.tmAveCharWidth * 54,
     tm.tmHeight * 5,
```

```
        hWnd, (HMENU) IDC_WINLIST,
        hInst, NULL) ;

    // Create the push button contro windows
    //
    hWndOnTop = CreateWindow ("BUTTON", "TopIT",
        WS_CHILD | WS_VISIBLE | BS_PUSHBUTTON,
        0, 0,
        tm.tmAveCharWidth * 18,
        tm.tmHeight * 2,
        hWnd, (HMENU) IDC_PUTONTOP,
        hInst, NULL) ;

    hWndOnTop = CreateWindow ("BUTTON", "Refresh",
        WS_CHILD | WS_VISIBLE | BS_PUSHBUTTON,
        tm.tmAveCharWidth * 18, 0,
        tm.tmAveCharWidth * 18,
        tm.tmHeight * 2,
        hWnd, (HMENU) IDC_REFRESH,
        hInst, NULL) ;

    hWndReleaseTop = CreateWindow ("BUTTON", "Release",
        WS_CHILD | WS_VISIBLE | BS_PUSHBUTTON,
        tm.tmAveCharWidth * 36, 0,
        tm.tmAveCharWidth * 18,
        tm.tmHeight * 2,
        hWnd, (HMENU) IDC_RELEASE,
        hInst, NULL) ;

    GetWinList (hWnd);
    return TRUE;
    }
```

The push button and list box control windows are created in the `Topper_OnCreate` function. This function also appends menu items to the Topper system menu for

- putting the Topper window on top,
- calling Help for Topper, and
- displaying the Topper About dialog box.

Topper's New Windows 3.1 Coding Style

You may have noticed that Topper's source code looks a little bit different from some of the other Windows programs you've seen. This is because it was written using the new Windows 3.1 STRICT coding style and the new Windows 3.1 macro API that's defined in the header file WINDOWSX.H.

The new STRICT option is an important feature because it provides stricter type-checking to help you find more bugs at compilation time. The idea is that you use #define STRICT before putting #include <WINDOWS.H> to turn on the STRICT option to enforce very strict type-checking in your program. For example, without STRICT defined, it's possible to pass a window handle (HWND) to a Windows API function that requires a handle to a device context (HDC) without any kind of compiler warning. With STRICT defined, this results in a compiler error.

WINDOWSX.H contains many new Windows APIs implemented as macros that call other APIs. Since the APIs implemented in WINDOWSX.H are all macros, they are backward-compatible with Windows 3.0. Using these new macro APIs in your Windows application makes your C code easier to read and write and will also save you some typing—an important consideration to some programmers. The most important aspect of using these new macros in C programs is that it makes your application much more portable to Win32.

Message crackers are one of the easiest to read—but most formidable to write—macro APIs. Message crackers are used instead of the switch case statement in a window procedure to process window messages. As an example, let's look at the Topper window procedure.

```
//-----------------------------------------------------------
//
// WndProc - Topper's window procedure
//
LRESULT CALLBACK _export WndProc(HWND hWnd, UINT Msg, WPARAM w-
Param, LPARAM lParam)
{
  switch (Msg)
    {
    HANDLE_MSG (hWnd, WM_CREATE,     TOPPER_OnCreate);
    HANDLE_MSG (hWnd, WM_SETFOCUS,   TOPPER_OnSetFocus);
    HANDLE_MSG (hWnd, WM_SYSCOMMAND, TOPPER_OnSysCommand);
    HANDLE_MSG (hWnd, WM_COMMAND,    TOPPER_OnCommand);
```

```
HANDLE_MSG (hWnd, WM_DESTROY,  TOPPER_OnDestroy);

default:
  return DefWindowProc (hWnd, Msg, wParam, lParam) ;
}
}
```

The Topper window procedure is small and serves only one purpose—to dispatch the messages it was sent from Windows to a function that handles each specific message type. The Topper window procedure doesn't have local variables, nor does it have any other purpose than being a message dispatcher. Message cracker macros are used to send a message type to the function responsible for handling it. For example, the message cracker for WM_CREATE, shown below, is responsible for passing the WM_CREATE message on to the TOPPER_OnCreate function.

```
HANDLE_MSG (hWnd, WM_CREATE,  TOPPER_OnCreate);
```

HANDLE_MSG is a macro defined in WINDOWSX.H that dispatches the WM_CREATE message to TOPPER_OnCreate. For now, all you need to understand is the basic concepts about what STRICT and message crackers are. Later, in Chapter 12, you will learn in detail about how to use STRICT and message crackers.

By examining Topper's source code you can see how both system global and application local windows are created. These windows are created by calling Create-Window or CreateWindowEx with the name of the desired window class. To create an application local window you use RegisterClass to define the window class and use CreateWindow to reference the window class name. System global window classes are already registered for you by Windows. All you need to do is use the name of the system global window class in the CreateWindow function call.

How Windows Keeps Track of a Window Instance

The CreateWindow function can only create a window based on a registered window class. After Windows finds a window class with the name specified in the CreateWindow function call, it allocates a local memory block in the User DGROUP to store information about the window instance. This information is a combination of what was in the WNDCLASS data structure that was used when the window class was registered and the information that was passed to Windows when Create-Window was called. Windows allocates extra space in the window instance structure, based on the number of bytes specified by the cbWndExtra value in the WNDCLASS data structure, and initializes these bytes to zero.

The GetWindowLong and GetWindowWord functions let you retrieve the individual members of the window instance data structure maintained by Windows. To get this information you must identify the window using its handle and supply an offset into the window instance data structure.

The SetWindowLong and SetWindowWord functions let you change members of the window instance data structure. To change information in the window instance data structure, you need to supply the window handle, an offset into the window instance data structure, and the new value.

The most common reason for changing the information (known as window extra bytes) in the window instance data structure is to associate it with a data structure in either local or global memory. This lets you associate a set of data variables with a window without having to use global variables. Associating a data structure with a window is an object-oriented approach to Windows programming that avoids many of the pitfalls of using global variables.

The DumpIT program covered in Chapter 3 shows how this approach works. Each hex dump window in the DumpIT MDI application has a pointer inside its window data structure which points to a structure in local memory that contains all the variables for the window.

Since the number of child windows varies depending on how many documents the user opens, DumpIT must be able to associate data (for example, a pointer to the current file buffer loaded into memory) with each child window. When DumpIT registers the class of the MDI child window, it reserves extra space in the window structure for a long pointer to a locally allocated data structure that contains all the program variables associated with the window. To store data in this extra space, DumpIT 2.0 uses the function SetWindowLong in the function DoWmMDIChild-Create in CUSTCODE.C.

```
void DoWmMDIChildCreate (HWND hWnd)
{
  SetWindowLong (hWnd, O, (LONG) lpWinVar);
  SetWindowText (hWnd, (LPSTR) lpWinVar->FileName);
  InitMDIChild (hWnd);
  InitializeFont (hWnd);
}
```

Whenever these variables are needed, GetWindowLong is used to get the pointer. For example, to initialize the variables in the window instance data structure that keeps track of the fonts used within a window, the InitializeFont function is called.

The first thing `InitializeFont` does is get a pointer to the window instance data structure that contains the window variables.

```
void InitializeFont (HWND hWnd)
{
  HDC hDC;
  TEXTMETRIC tm;

  lpWinVar = (WINDOWVARIABLES _far *) GetWindowLong (hWnd, 0);
  hDC = GetDC (hWnd);
  lpWinVar->hFont = hFont;
  SelectObject (hDC, lpWinVar->hFont);
  GetTextMetrics (hDC, & tm);
  lpWinVar->cxChar = tm.tmAveCharWidth;
  lpWinVar->cyChar = tm.tmHeight + tm.tmExternalLeading;
  lpWinVar->nMaxWidth = 74 * lpWinVar->cxChar;
  ReleaseDC (hWnd, hDC);
}
```

Using Window Properties

Window properties give you another way to associate data with a window. Although using properties is not as efficient as using the window extra bytes method described previously, some programmers I have met use window properties instead—without understanding why.

Properties are useful if you want to associate a data structure with a window instance for a system global window class or with any type of window class that you did not register yourself. If you didn't register the window class yourself, you don't know how many window extra bytes were specified in the WNDCLASS structure or how they were intended to be used. You can find out the number of window extra bytes using the `GetClassInfo` function call, but you may not be sure why the window extra bytes were allocated and how they are used by the window procedure for the window class.

Properties let you associate data with a window by using a string name instead of storing a global (or local) data handle or pointer in the internal window structure. You can use only 16-bit values when working with properties. Windows has four functions you can use to work with window properties:

- *SetProp* associates a property with a window.

- *RemoveProp* disassociates a property with a window.

- *GetProp* retrieves the property associated with a window.

- *EnumProps* retrieves the list of all window properties associated with a window.

To see how properties work, let's take the example we just covered on using window extra bytes and look at how to accomplish the same task using window properties. The `DoWmMDIChildCreate` function stores the handle to the local memory object as a window property. A handle must be used instead of a pointer, because only 16-bit values can be associated with a property. You can also use a near pointer if the pointer is for your local heap. In DumpIT, I used a long pointer to point to the data structure so the data structure could be allocated in either local or global memory.

```
void DoWmMDIChildCreate (HWND hWnd)
{
  SetProp (hWnd, "WINVAR", (LOCALHANDLE) hWinVar);
  SetWindowText (hWnd, (LPSTR) lpWinVar->FileName);
  InitMDIChild (hWnd);
  InitializeFont (hWnd);
}
```

To see how to use the data structure associated with the window, let's look at the `InitializeFont` function. This time it uses window properties, not extra bytes.

```
void InitializeFont (HWND hWnd)
{
  HDC hDC;
  TEXTMETRIC tm;

  // Use window properties to retrieve the handle to local memory
  // and lock it to get the pointer.
  hWinVar = GetProp (hWnd, "WINVAR");
  lpWinVar = (WINDOWVARIABLES _far *) LocalLock (hWinVar);
  hDC = GetDC (hWnd);
  lpWinVar->hFont = hFont;
  SelectObject (hDC, lpWinVar->hFont);
  GetTextMetrics (hDC, & tm);
  lpWinVar->cxChar = tm.tmAveCharWidth;
  lpWinVar->cyChar = tm.tmHeight + tm.tmExternalLeading;
  lpWinVar->nMaxWidth = 74 * lpWinVar->cxChar;
  ReleaseDC (hWnd, hDC);
```

```
   // Unlock the memory to the window variables.
   LocalUnlock (hWinVar);
}
```

When the window is destroyed, you should remove the window property, as you would any other Windows system resource. In DumpIT, I created one function that handles all the clean-up activities when an MDI child window receives a WM_DESTROY message.

```
   case WM_DESTROY:
      DoWinCleanup (hWnd);
      break; /* End of case WM_DESTROY                  */
 ~ .
 ~ .
 ~ .
void DoWinCleanup (HWND hWnd)

{
   int nCnt;
   LOCALHANDLE hActiveWV;

   // Make sure that the Active window variables are set correctly
   hWinVar = GetProp (hWnd, "WINVAR");
   lpWinVar = (WINDOWVARIABLES _far *) LocalLock (hWinVar);

   for(nCnt = 0; nCnt < 8; nCnt++)
    if (Filesize_C1.FileSizeList_hWnd[nCnt] == hWnd)
    {
      Filesize_C1.FileSizeList_hWnd[nCnt] = NULL;
      Filesize_C1.FileSizeList[nCnt][0] = 0x00;
      break;
    }
   GlobalUnlock (lpWinVar->hFileBuffer);
   GlobalFree (lpWinVar->hFileBuffer);
   hActiveWV = (lpWinVar->hWinVar);
   LocalUnlock (hActiveWV);
   LocalFree (hActiveWV);
   RemoveProp (hWnd, "WINVAR");
   nFileCount--;
}
```

Messaging

After an application creates a window on the screen, the Windows operating environment maintains and manages the window. Windows advises each window of events that affect it. An event is sent to a window in the form of a message.

Each message contains a packet of information. A message is similar to a Local Area Network in which each client workstation communicates with a server by passing packets of information (messages). Within a Windows application each window communicates with other windows and with the operating system by message packets. This all sounds logical, but what allows the application to sit and listen for messages?

Let's begin by discussing the window procedure. It is the function that is pointed to by the wc.lpfnWndProc element of the WNDCLASS structure when the window class is registered. A window procedure is nothing more than a switch statement that processes messages and directs them to other parts of the application. Notice that the window procedure is never actually called by functions in the program—it is called by Windows. Each window class has its own window procedure. The parameters passed to the window procedure are four of the six elements of the Windows message structure. The structure is defined as follows in WINDOWS.H:

```
typedef struct tagMSG
{
   HWND        hwnd;
   UINT     message;
   WPARAM      wParam;
   LPARAM      lParam;
   DWORD    time;
   POINT       pt;
} MSG;
```

The handle to the window that the message belongs to is designated by hwnd. Msg is the 16-bit unsigned integer identifying the message sent to the window. The 16-bit and 32-bit message parameters wParam and lParam provide more information about the message. The window procedure accepts messages, such as keyboard and mouse activity, from Windows and processes them by activating other parts of the Windows application. You may ask, "Who generates these messages?" They come from four places:

- hardware (keyboard, timer, and mouse),

- events (selecting menu items and sizing windows),

- other Windows programs, and

- within the same Windows program.

Messages can arrive indirectly or directly. Most messages are sent to the window procedure from the DispatchMessage function in the WinMain message loop, but some arrive directly, as a result of another API call.

Message Identifiers

The majority of window messages start with the prefix WM_. However, the button control, edit control, list box, combo box, button control notification, edit control notification, list box notification, and combo box notification messages all start with BM_ , EM_ , LB_ , CB_ , BN_ , EN_ , LBN_ and CBN_, respectively. The WM_USER message is at the very top of the standard Windows messages, at 0x400. It is available for windows to define their own messages beyond those defined in WINDOWS.H, particularly those unique to a class. For example, the following code segment from WINDOWS.H details some of the edit box messages and how they are defined with reference to WM_USER.

```
/* Edit Control Messages */
#define EM_GETSEL    (WM_USER)
#define EM_SETSEL    (WM_USER+1)
#define EM_GETRECT   (WM_USER+2)
#define EM_SETRECT   (WM_USER+3)
#define EM_SETRECTNP (WM_USER+4)
#define EM_SCROLL    (WM_USER+5)
#define EM_LINESCROLL (WM_USER+6)
```

Window message identifiers fall into four ranges. The message identifiers conform to the following standard:

.0x000-0x0400-1	Standard Windows messages with the WM_ prefix.
.0x0400-0x7fff	Class-defined messages, specific to a class of windows.
.0x800-0xbfff	Windows-reserved messages.

.0xc000-0xffff   System-defined messages
                        (RegisterWindowMessage).

Class-Defined Messages

Class-defined window messages are used for processing window messages for a specific window class. For example, let's assume that you have two windows that communicate with each other within the same application. When the user clicks on a push button in one window, the contents of the other window should change to reflect the user's choice. To use class-defined messages you define the new message types in an application header file, such as MESSAGES.H, as follows:

```
#define IDM_SHOW_ACCOUNTINFO (WM_USER + 0)
#define IDM_SHOW_BANKHISTORY (WM_USER + 1)
#define IDM_SHOW_MUTUALFUNDPOSITIONS (WM_USER + 2)
```

In the function for the window that has the push buttons inside it, you would include the following code to react when the push buttons are clicked on by posting a message to the window displaying account information:

```
case IDC_SHOW_ACCOUNTINFO:
  PostMessage (hWndAcctDisplay, IDM_SHOW_ACCOUNTINFO, NULL, NULL);
  break;
```

In the window function that displays the account information, you would include the following case statement that processes the messages sent to it by the other window:

```
case IDM_SHOW_ACCOUNTINFO:
  nDisplayAccountType = IDM_SHOW_ACCOUNTINFO;
  InvalidateRect (hWnd, NULL, TRUE);
  break;
case WM_PAINT:
  BeginPaint (hWnd, lpps);
  DisplayAcctInfo (hWnd, hDC, lpps, nDisplayAccountType);
  EndPaint (hWnd, lpps);
  break;
```

> **NOTE**
>
> Notice how the window function that receives the message changes only the static local variable that determines what's displayed in the window. The code then invalidates the window, generating a WM_PAINT message for it. The new account information is displayed in the window when the WM_PAINT message is received. This is an example of how a Windows program is designed to work. Functions such as `InvalidateRect` generate other messages such as WM_PAINT. The code to display a window's contents goes where the WM_PAINT message is processed.

System-Defined Messages

You use system-defined messages when you send a message and are unsure of the receiving window's class. When you register a system-defined message, you are telling Windows that there is a new message type that any window can recognize.

You can add a new message type by calling `RegisterWindowMessage`. This function accepts a character string and returns a numeric value in the range of 0xC000 to 0xFFFF. If another call to `RegisterWindowMessage` is made that uses the same string, Windows will return the same integer value. By using the same string, different windows (and window applications) will all be using the same integer value for the same message type.

For example, suppose you have a group of Windows applications that are designed to work together. If the user closes one application, all of the applications should close. All of these applications would call `RegisterWindowMessage` during initialization to get an integer value for the SD_CLOSEALL message they post to each other to signal it's time to exit.

Nonqueued versus Queued Messages

There are two types of messages that Windows programs deal with—nonqueued and queued. A *nonqueued message* is sent to a window immediately when Windows calls a window procedure. Calling a Windows function may result in a nonqueued message being sent back to the application. The `SendMessage` function also sends nonqueued messages.

Queued messages are placed in the message queue by Windows and are retrieved and dispatched from the message loop to the application. Most messages that an application deals with are queued messages. For example, the following messages are queued: WM_KEYDOWN, WM_MOUSEMOVE, MW_LBUTTONDOWN, WM_PAINT.

The Default Window Function

DefWindowProc is the default window function. It is responsible for processing all messages that are not processed by your application's Windows functions. You can think of the DefWindowProc function as the necessary tool to give control back to Windows. It carries out the processing of all of the nonclient area messages, such as WM_SYSCOMMAND, WM_CLOSE, or WM_ACTIVATE. If you don't pass these messages back to Windows, your application will not run properly.

TIP

One of the easiest message types to forget to pass on to DefWindowProc is WM_SYSCOMMAND. I have made this mistake myself a few times and helped other programmers correct the same problem. The symptoms are easy to recognize. Normally, you don't handle the WM_SYSCOMMAND messages in most programs until you use AppendMenu to add some menu commands to your program's system menu. The first time you try this, you may think that you can handle WM_SYSCOMMAND messages in the same way you handle WM_COMMAND messages: WM_COMMAND messages don't need to be sent on to DefWindowProc, so why should you worry about WM_SYSCOMMAND?

However, DefWindowProc needs to process the WM_SYSCOMMAND message to move your window, size it, minimize it, and maximize it. If you forget to pass along this message type to DefWinodwsProc, your application will look up on the display, and you won't be able to perform any of these functions. Fortunately, this is an easy problem to spot and fix.

If you forgot to use DefWindowProc in one of your application's window functions but do not know where, there are tools available that can help you find out where you went wrong. Let's take a look at these tools now by starting with Spy.

Spying into Windows

Spy, a Windows application included in the Microsoft Windows 3.1 SDK, is one of several available tools that let you view and monitor the messages sent to your application and to other Windows applications. It lets you record messages and verify the messages your application is receiving and that you expect it to receive. Spy also allows you to view the parameters passed with the messages. As you already know, it's important that your application receive not only the messages you expect but also the parameters you expect—wParam and lParam. As Figure 7.2 shows, there are three other values returned as well as the message: the handle of the window receiving the message, the wParam, and the lParam.

Nothing has to be added to your code to use Spy. All you have to do is specify which application it should be monitoring. Spy is a simple tool but a very important one.

Choosing a Window to Spy On

Spy allows you to monitor the messages being received by one window or by all windows on the desktop. In most cases you will monitor just one window's messages

FIGURE 7.2:

The Spy message window

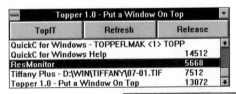

instead of all the window messages being sent. Spy is also very helpful for debugging your program when you believe you are having message-related problems.

TIP
As you will learn in the next part of the book, "Debugging Windows Applications," you can use a debugger to monitor messages and step through your code. In many ways debuggers such as CodeView for Windows and Turbo Debugger for Windows are more powerful tools than Spy for monitoring your program and the window messages being sent to it. However, these debuggers take time to set up, since you have to put breakpoints in your C source code to monitor messages. In addition, if you are using one monitor with CodeView or Turbo Debugger, you also have to put up with screen-swapping.

In contrast, Spy is a simple tool that's quick and easy to set up and execute. If you don't need to step through your program code but you do need to know more about the message being sent to a window, Spy can help you program quicker and easier than a debugger.

Being able to monitor all windows is also important. Generally, an application has more than one window. For example, Microsoft Word for Windows allows you to open a number of documents, each placed in its own window. If you maximize Word and select the All Windows command on the Spy Window menu, you can monitor the messages being received by each window. To decipher which window is receiving the listed messages, look at the window handle corresponding to the message.

You may ask, "How do I choose a window to monitor?" First choose the Window command in the Spy Window menu. A dialog box appears which displays information about the window that's currently under the cursor. When the dialog box is active and the mouse pointer is over a window, a border appears around the window, and the class information associated with that particular window is displayed in the Spy dialog box. As you move the cursor to another window, the information changes. Then click with the mouse on the window you want to spy on. Figure 7.3 shows how you can choose a window in the Microsoft Word for Windows application to spy on. Here I selected Word's Ruler window.

FIGURE 7.3:

Spying on Word for Windows

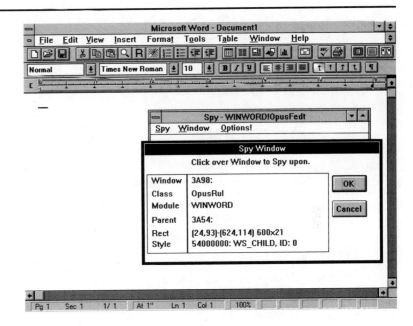

Spy not only lets you select a window to spy on; it also displays the following important information about each window that is visible on the Windows desktop:

Window	Displays the handle to the window and the window caption.
Class	Displays the window class.
Module	Displays the program that created the window.
Parent	Displays the handle to the parent window.
Rect	Displays the upper-right and lower-left screen coordinates of the window, as well as the size of the window.
Style	Displays the style bits of the window, the principal style of the window, and a window identifier (WS_CHILD only).

As you can see, Spy is useful for showing you information about an application's windows as well as for monitoring window messages. But what can you learn from peeking into an application's windows?

Peeking into Windows

You can learn a great deal about how other Windows applications are constructed using Spy. For example, if you examine the toolbars in either Microsoft Word for Windows or Excel, you will learn that the push buttons in them are not separate window controls. These pseudo buttons are managed and drawn by the window they are inside of. If you examine the Windows 3.0 Program Manager with Spy, you will notice that each application icon in a Program Manager window is a window. If you check out the Windows 3.1 Program Manager, you will find that Program Manager now draws each icon itself to conserve Windows resources.

If you examine other Windows applications such as Polaris PackRat, WindowsMAKER Professional, QuickC for Windows, and Topper 1.0, you will find that they use control windows for buttons on their toolbars—not pseudo-buttons managed and drawn by the window the buttons are located in. It isn't difficult to draw buttons yourself to conserve Windows resources. Shortly, you'll learn how to do so when we see how Topper 2.0 works.

Choosing Spy Options

After you select a window to monitor, you need to decide on the messages you want to monitor. This is where we use the Options menu. Selecting the Spy Options menu displays the dialog box shown in Figure 7.4.

Spy Options are grouped according to messages, output, and display. Spy allows you to choose the category of messages that you want to watch. You can select all categories (the default) or pick specific categories. This selection facility provides you with the ability to debug an application on a message-specific level. For example, if your application is not sizing properly, you may want to watch only Window messages—particularly WM_SIZE. Unfortunately, there is no way to watch for one particular message. Voyeur is the only tool that lets you monitor specific mes-

FIGURE 7.4:

The Spy Options dialog box

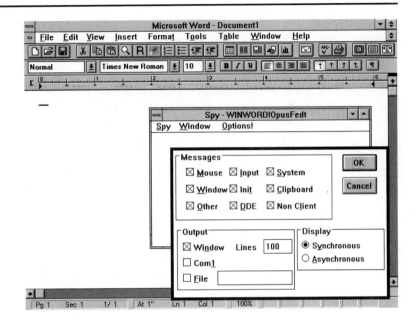

sages. You can, however, limit the selection to a message category. The following list shows each category and an example of a corresponding message:

Category	Example Message
Mouse messages	WM_MOUSEFIRST, WM_MOUSEMOVE, WM_LBUTTONDOWN
Window Manager messages	WM_SHOWWINDOW
Input messages	WM_KEYFIRST, WM_KEYDOWN, WM_KEYUP, WM_CHAR
Initialization messages	WM_INITMENU
Dynamic Data Exchange messages	WM_DDE_REQUEST
Systemwide messages	WM_TIMECHANGE
Clipboard messages	WM_CUT, WM_COPY, WM_PASTE, WM_CLEAR

| Nonclient messages | WM_NCCREATE, WM_NCDESTROY, WM_NCCALCSIZE |
| Other | Any message other than catagories listed |

After you decide on a message category to monitor, you need to decide on the destination of the output. You have three choices for your output:

- Window. All messages for the particular window selection are displayed within Spy's client area. The maximum number of saved messages Spy stores in its buffer can be changed from within the dialog box using the Lines Edit box (the default is 100). The window can be scrolled at any time.

- COM. Spy can also send the message output to the COM1 serial port, if necessary.

- File. If you are monitoring a large number of messages for an application, you may want to open a file to store the message output.

You have the ability to select one or all of the previous choices.

Spy also lets you choose how messages are displayed. You have two options:

- Synchronous. As Spy receives messages it immediately displays them to the output device. Synchronous display is the default.

- Asynchronous. As Spy receives messages it queues them for display.

A listing of application messages from Spy is usually adequate to find out about how a Windows application is constructed and about the messages that are being communicated between windows. Spy can be used to solve difficult problems. There is, however, additional window and message information that Spy does not report on. To access this information you need more advanced programs, such as WinSight and Voyeur.

Using Borland's WinSight

WinSight, as well as Spy, can be used to monitor window messages. It has more features than Spy, but it is not more difficult to use. Using Spy you can trace messages by window and by message type. WinSight also lets you trace messages by window class. It provides four windows for you to work with:

Window Tree	Displays the hierarchy of windows on the desktop (default)
Class List	Shows all registered window classes
Messages	Displays message information received by selected windows
Detail	Displays detailed information about a window class or instance

You can select which of the first three windows to display by choosing options in the WinSight View menu. The first two windows (Window Tree and Class List) let you choose the window or the class to monitor messages in. They also contain detailed information about both the window and its class. Let's see how the Class List window works.

Using the Class List Window

The WinSight Class List window lists all the currently registered window classes, as shown in Figure 7.5.

You can get the full details about a class by double-clicking on its name or by pressing Enter when it's selected. Each time a window class receives a window message, the diamond to the left of the window class name is highlighted. The information on each line in this window, from left to right, includes:

- The window class name.
- The module name in parentheses that registered the window class.
- The pointer to the window procedure for the class.
- The class styles.

FIGURE 7.5:

The WinSight Class List window

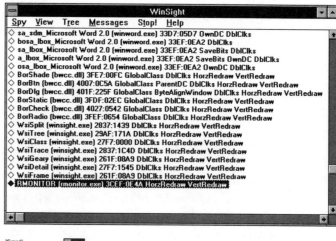

Using the WinSight Class List window, it's easy to monitor the messages being sent to a window class. Just do the following:

1. Display the Messages window by choosing it in the WinSight View menu.

2. Choose Options in the WinSight Messages menu.

3. Select the message types you want to monitor in the Message Trace Options dialog box that's displayed.

4. Choose Selected Classes in the WinSight Messages menu.

5. Select the window class you want to monitor in the WinSight Class List window.

Using the Window Tree

The WinSight Window Tree window shows an outline of the hierarchy of all existing windows. For example, you can see the hierarchical window structure of Microsoft's Word for Windows in Figure 7.6.

FIGURE 7.6:
The WinSight Window Tree window

ResMonitor

You can use this window in several different ways:

- To determine what window instances exist.
- To see the status of a window, including hidden windows.
- To see which windows are receiving messages.
- To select the windows you want to trace messages for.

As in the Class List window, each entry has a small diamond next to it. Each time a window receives a message, the diamond is highlighted. An empty diamond indicates that the window has no child windows. A plus sign (+) in the diamond indicates that the window has children, but they are hidden. A minus sign (-) in the diamond means that the window's children are currently shown. To show hidden child windows (expand the outline), click on a diamond with the plus sign. To hide child windows (collapse the outline), click on a diamond with the minus sign.

To find a window by pointing to it on the desktop, choose Find Window in the Win-Sight Spy menu. In this mode, whenever the mouse moves over a window's boundaries, a border appears around that window. You can select the window to spy on by clicking on it with the mouse or by pressing either the Enter or the Esc key.

You can easily display the messages being sent to a specific window by:

- Displaying the WinSight Messages window.

- Choosing Selected Windows in the WinSight Messages menu.

- Selecting the message types you want to monitor.

- Selecting the window in the Window Tree window or choosing Find Window in the WinSight Spy menu.

Getting the Details

You can easily find out all the details about a window or window class by double-clicking on it in the Window Tree or the Class List window. As shown in Figure 7.7, the Detail window is displayed when you double-click on either entry. This window provides all the information that Windows keeps track of to manage window classes and instances.

The WinSight program has more features than Microsoft Spy. When I just want to monitor a window's messages quickly and easily, I use Spy. Spy is good for one thing—monitoring messages. It doesn't have a lot of features, but I find it the easier of the two tools to use. WinSight is excellent when it comes to teaching others about

FIGURE 7.7:
The WinSight Detail window

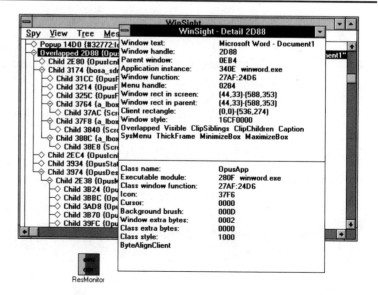

how Windows works and finding out detailed information about how a Windows application is structured.

Getting DeMystified

Another set of tools that spans the auditing category in this book is DeMystifiers. MicroQuill Inc.'s DeMystifiers set consists of five analysis utilities for Microsoft Windows that give you a comprehensive view of the Windows environment.

Most of the tools in DeMystifiers are comparable to the tools we have already discussed that are included with the Microsoft Windows SDK and Borland C++ 3.1, but in DeMystifiers they are better implemented. Following is a description of each DeMystifier tool.

- *Voyeur* is analogous to Spy in the Windows SDK and to WinSight in Borland C++. All three tools let you monitor Windows messages sent to or from a particular window, but Voyeur alone provides details on the meanings of the message parameters. Overall, I prefer WinSight to Voyeur, because of its unique Window Tree window. Voyeur is much closer in functionality to WinSight than to Spy because of its comparable set of features. Figure 7.8 shows the Voyeur window that displays information about the windows on the Windows desktop.

- *Mechanic* is a device analyzer that offers useful details about device drivers and the features they support. Mechanic also lets you examine how Windows maps display fonts to printer fonts, a capability that's not present in any other Windows programming tool.

- *Colonel* resembles Microsoft's HEAPWALK tool: it lets you view the structure of the main Windows memory list hierarchically. Colonel provides a much more logically structured and easy-to-follow view of global memory than HEAPWALK does. It presents the main blocks of tasks and allowed blocks owned by tasks to be displayed in an indented hierarchy beneath the main block. HEAPWALK, in contrast, displays the entire heap. Overall, Colonel offers more features than HEAPWALK and has a better way of displaying Windows global memory. Figure 7.9 shows Colonel displaying the global heap using its expanded hierarchical view of the Resource Monitor program that's included with this book.

FIGURE 7.8:

Using Voyeur to peer into a window

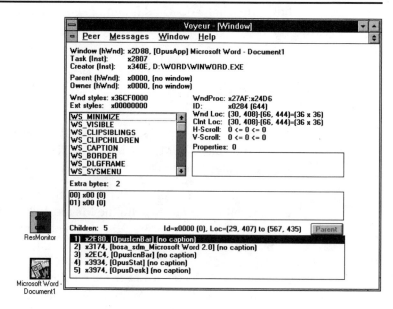

FIGURE 7.9:

Using Colonel to display the global heap

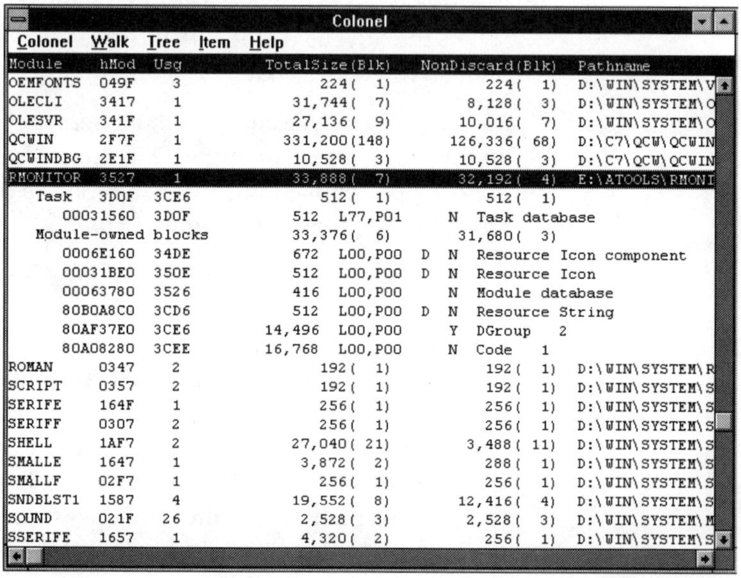

- *Ecologist* comprises three windows describing the general Windows environment. Its Global window contains many settings normally found in the Windows Control Panel; the Dynamic and Static windows describe Windows environment data.

- *BlowUp* is a tool for enlarging areas of the Windows display and viewing them in a window.

DeMystifiers is a useful set of tools, especially if you don't have both the Windows 3.1 SDK and Borland's development tools. If you are using either Borland C++ for Windows or Turbo C++ for Windows, DeMystifiers adds some useful tools to your toolbox—especially Colonel. If you are using Microsoft C/C++ and the Windows 3.1 SDK, you should first consider getting Borland's Turbo C++. It comes with both Borland Resource Workshop and WinSight. Even if you don't use the excellent Turbo C++ for Windows integrated development environment, the Resource Workshop and WinSight make the purchase worthwhile. If you still have some money left, consider getting DeMystifiers as well.

Why Spy?

Before taking a look at the two tools I developed for this chapter, let's consider the questions "Why would I use a Spy program, and when is a good time to use it?"

As we have already discussed, all of these spy tools let you find out how a Windows application is constructed. One of the best ways to learn more about Windows programming is to read the source code written by others and to examine how other programs are built.

A spy program is less obtrusive than a debugger. It's easier to set up and use, especially if you are having a program problem and know it's related to messages.

One of the easiest Windows programming blunders to make is to forget to put a `BeginPaint` and `EndPaint` in your program to process a `WM_PAINT` message. If you forget to do this in a new program that's under construction, you will effectively lock up Windows until you press Ctrl+Alt+Del (AKA the three-finger salute) to terminate your application. If you bring up Spy before you execute your program, you will immediately see what's wrong. You will see Windows bombarding your application with `WM_PAINT` messages. The only way to fix this is to add `BeginPaint` and `EndPaint` function calls to process your `WM_PAINT` messages—even if you don't do anything between this pair of functions.

A spy program is useful for tracking messages between Windows applications. When you want to monitor and test window messages being sent between two programs, a spy program is easier to use than a debugger. If you want to monitor DDE messages, you should use DDE Spy, included with the Windows 3.1 SDK. DDE Spy will be discussed in more detail in Chapter 11.

A spy program is helpful to learn what type of message Windows uses to do specific tasks. For example, let's assume that you have written a Windows application that is an accessory for another Windows application that you didn't create, such as Microsoft Excel. Part of your application's functionality should be to hide itself when Excel is minimized and show itself when Excel is maximized. You are planning to subclass Excel: which message should you use to trigger the event for hiding and showing your window? You could search through your Windows programming reference manual to find out, but you can also experiment with a spy program to determine the best message to use to trigger this event. Using Spy I found that the best message to use was `WM_SYSCOMMAND` with `wParam` values of `SC_MINIMIZE`, `SC_MAXIMIZE`, and `SC_RESTORE`.

Now that we have discussed some of the uses of a spy program, let's look at two applications that I developed for this book that illustrate some interesting windowing and messaging concepts.

Topper 2.0

As we have already discussed, Topper is a Windows application that lets you lock any window in the topmost z-order so it appears on top of all the other windows on the desktop. Topper 1.0 and Topper 2.0 have the same functionality but a different appearance. Topper 1.0 uses control windows to display its three push buttons for moving a window to the top (TopIT), refreshing the list of windows, and releasing a window from the topmost z-order, as shown in Figure 7.10.

Topper 2.0 has the same functionality as Topper 1.0, but its three push buttons are GDI RECT objects that Topper draws itself. These buttons react the same way standard control window push buttons do in Windows, but they don't use system resources. Topper 2.0 is shown in Figure 7.11.

How Topper's Buttons Work

Let's look inside Topper's source code to see how it all works. You need to perform three steps to create graphical buttons inside a window without using control windows:

- Create the RECT structure that defines the location of the button.

- Draw the buttons in their correct state, up or down, as Topper does. Optionally, you could add focused and disabled states.

- Keep track of mouse events.

FIGURE 7.10:

Topper 1.0

FIGURE 7.11:

Topper 2.0

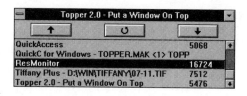

Creating RECT Structures for the Buttons

Creating the RECT structures that define the buttons' locations is the easiest of these three programming aspects to implement. In Topper 1.0 the push buttons were created in the TOPPER_OnCreate function, called when the WM_CREATE message is processed by the main window procedure. It's also a logical place to create the RECT structures that replace the push buttons, as shown in the following source code:

```
//-------------------------------------------------------------
//
// TOPPER_OnCreate - Handle WM_CREATE message
//
BOOL TOPPER_OnCreate(HWND hWnd, CREATESTRUCT FAR * lpCreateStruct)
{
    HDC       hDC ;
    TEXTMETRIC tm ;
    RECT rWinRect;
    HMENU hMenu;

    // Fix up System menu
    //
    hMenu = GetSystemMenu (hWnd, FALSE);
    AppendMenu (hMenu, MF_SEPARATOR, 0, 0);
    AppendMenu (hMenu, MF_STRING, IDM_PUTTOPPERONTOP,
        (LPSTR) "&Put Topper On Top");
    AppendMenu (hMenu, MF_SEPARATOR, 0, 0);
    AppendMenu (hMenu, MF_STRING, IDM_TOPPERHELP,
        (LPSTR) "&Help for Topper");
    AppendMenu (hMenu, MF_STRING, IDM_ABOUTTOPPER,
        (LPSTR) "&About Topper");
```

```
hDC = GetDC (hWnd) ;
GetTextMetrics (hDC, &tm) ;
ReleaseDC (hWnd, hDC) ;

GetWindowRect (hWnd, &rWinRect);
MoveWindow (hWnd, rWinRect.left, rWinRect.top,
      tm.tmAveCharWidth * 54 + 2,
      tm.tmHeight * 7 + GetSystemMetrics (SM_CYCAPTION), TRUE);

// Create a listbox control window
//
hWndList = CreateWindow ("LISTBOX", NULL,
 WS_CHILD | WS_VISIBLE | LBS_STANDARD | LBS_USETABSTOPS,
 0, (tm.tmHeight * 2),
 tm.tmAveCharWidth * 54,
 tm.tmHeight * 5,
 hWnd, (HMENU) IDC_WINLIST,
 hInst, NULL) ;

// Create RECT structures to draw graphic buttons in.
//
SetRect (& rTopit, (tm.tmAveCharWidth * 4), 5,
 (tm.tmAveCharWidth * 14),
 (tm.tmHeight * 2) - 5);

SetRect (& rRefresh,
 (tm.tmAveCharWidth * 22), 5,
 (tm.tmAveCharWidth * 32),
 (tm.tmHeight * 2) - 5);

SetRect (& rRelease,
 (tm.tmAveCharWidth * 40), 5,
 (tm.tmAveCharWidth * 50),
 (tm.tmHeight * 2) - 5);

// Build list of application windows and put it into listbox.
GetWinList (hWnd);
return TRUE;
}
```

As you can see, Topper creates three RECT structures, one for each button: rTopit, rRefresh, and rRelease. TOPPER_OnCreate also calls the function GetWinList that builds the list of active application windows and puts it into Topper's LISTBOX control window.

Drawing the Buttons

The border of each button is drawn using GDI commands. This approach allows the buttons to be drawn at any size without having to have multiple bitmaps for different display resolutions such as VGA, SuperVGA, and 8514. The interior of each button is a fixed size bitmap. The outline of the button drawn using GDI commands tells the user visually the state of the button. The function that draws the button is set up to accept two bitmap handles, one for the up state and one for the down state. The Topper buttons are drawn when the WM_PAINT message is processed by Topper's window, as shown in the following source code:

```
//---------------------------------------------------------------
//
// TOPPER_OnPaint - Process the WM_PAINT message
//
void TOPPER_OnPaint(HWND hWnd)
{
  PAINTSTRUCT ps;
  HDC hDC;

  hDC = BeginPaint (hWnd, &ps);
  // Draw GDI push buttons
  //
  DrawButton (hDC, bBDTopit, rTopit, hButtonBitmap1,
              hButtonBitmap1);
  DrawButton (hDC, bBDRefresh, rRefresh, hButtonBitmap2,
              hButtonBitmap2);
  DrawButton (hDC, bBDRelease, rRelease, hButtonBitmap3,
              hButtonBitmap3);

  EndPaint (hWnd, &ps);
}


//---------------------------------------------------------------
//
// DrawButton - Draw a graphic push button.
//
void DrawButton(HDC hDC,        // Device context
        BOOL bState,    // Button state: up or down?
        RECT rRect,     // RECT that defines where button is drawn
        HBITMAP hBMUp,  // Bitmap to be used to put on Up button
        HBITMAP hBMDown) // Bitmap to be used to put on Down Button
{
```

```
if (! bState) // Button is up!
 {
 SelectPen (hDC, hPenBlack);
 SelectBrush (hDC, hBrushLtGray);
 Rectangle (hDC, rRect.left, rRect.top,
         rRect.right, rRect.bottom);

 // Call DrawBitmap to put bitmap in center of button.
 //
 DrawBitmap(hDC, hBMUp, rRect, 3);

 MoveTo (hDC, rRect.right - 2, rRect.top + 1);
 SelectObject (hDC, hPenDarkGray);
 LineTo (hDC, rRect.right - 2, rRect.bottom - 2);
 LineTo (hDC, rRect.left + 1, rRect.bottom - 2);
 SelectObject (hDC, hPenWhite);
 LineTo (hDC, rRect.left + 1, rRect.top + 1);
 LineTo (hDC, rRect.right - 2, rRect.top + 1);

 MoveTo (hDC, rRect.right - 3, rRect.top + 2);
 SelectObject (hDC, hPenDarkGray);
 LineTo (hDC, rRect.right - 3, rRect.bottom - 3);
 LineTo (hDC, rRect.left + 2, rRect.bottom - 3);
 SelectObject (hDC, hPenWhite);
 LineTo (hDC, rRect.left + 2, rRect.top + 2);
 LineTo (hDC, rRect.right - 3, rRect.top + 2);
 }
else // Button is down!
 {
 SelectPen (hDC, hPenBlack);
 SelectBrush (hDC, hBrushLtGray);
 Rectangle (hDC, rRect.left, rRect.top,
         rRect.right, rRect.bottom);

 // Call DrawBitmap to put bitmap in center of button.
 //
 DrawBitmap(hDC, hBMDown, rRect, 3);

 MoveTo (hDC, rRect.right - 2, rRect.top + 1);
 SelectObject (hDC, hPenWhite);
 LineTo (hDC, rRect.right - 2, rRect.bottom - 2);
 LineTo (hDC, rRect.left + 1, rRect.bottom - 2);
 SelectObject (hDC, hPenDarkGray);
```

```
        LineTo (hDC, rRect.left + 1, rRect.top + 1);
        LineTo (hDC, rRect.right - 2, rRect.top + 1);

        MoveTo (hDC, rRect.right - 3, rRect.top + 2);
        SelectObject (hDC, hPenWhite);
        LineTo (hDC, rRect.right - 3, rRect.bottom - 3);
        LineTo (hDC, rRect.left + 2, rRect.bottom - 3);
        SelectObject (hDC, hPenDarkGray);
        LineTo (hDC, rRect.left + 2, rRect.top + 2);
        LineTo (hDC, rRect.right - 3, rRect.top + 2);
        }
}


//------------------------------------------------------------
//
// DrawBitmap - Draw a Draw a bitmap on top of button.
//
void DrawBitmap(HDC hDC, HBITMAP hBitmap, RECT rRect, int nBorder)
{
    BITMAP bm;
    HDC hDCMem;
    DWORD dwSize;
    POINT ptSize, ptOrg;
    int nHeight, nWidth, nBorderTop, nBorderLeft;

    hDCMem = CreateCompatibleDC (hDC);
    SelectObject (hDCMem, hBitmap);
    SetMapMode (hDCMem, GetMapMode (hDC));

    GetObject (hBitmap, sizeof (BITMAP), (void FAR *) &bm);

    ptSize.x = bm.bmWidth;
    ptSize.y = bm.bmHeight;
    DPtoLP (hDC, &ptSize, 1);

    ptOrg.x = 0;
    ptOrg.y = 0;
    DPtoLP (hDCMem, &ptOrg, 1);

    // Make calculations to center bitmap on button
    //
    nBorderTop = nBorder;
    nBorderLeft = nBorder;
    nHeight = rRect.bottom - rRect.top - (2 * nBorder);
```

```
    if (nHeight < ptSize.y)
     ptSize.y = nHeight;
    else
     nBorderTop += (nHeight - ptSize.y) / 2;

    nWidth = rRect.right - rRect.left - (2 * nBorder);

    if (nWidth < ptSize.x)
     ptSize.x = nWidth;
    else
     nBorderLeft += (nWidth - ptSize.x) / 2;


    BitBlt (hDC, rRect.left + nBorderLeft, rRect.top + nBorderTop,
        ptSize.x, ptSize.y,
        hDCMem, ptOrg.x, ptOrg.y, SRCCOPY);

    DeleteDC (hDCMem);
}
```

The function TOPPER_OnPaint is called to handle the WM_PAINT message for Topper's window procedure. TOPPER_OnPaint then calls DrawButton to draw the three graphic buttons. The parameters used to call DrawButton are

- HDC, the handle to the device context.

- bState, the state of the button. TRUE is down and FALSE is up.

- rRect, the RECT structure for the button.

- hBMUp, the handle for the bitmap to be displayed in the center of the button when it's up; and

- hBMDown, the handle for the bitmap to be displayed in the center of the button when it's down.

DrawButton is responsible for drawing the outline of the button. It calls Draw-Bitmap to display the bitmap it has passed the handle to. DrawBitmap centers the bitmap on the button and clips it if it's too large for the button.

Managing Mouse Messages

To create a pseudo push button that behaves like a standard Windows push button, you need to observe a push button's behavior. The standard Windows push button control has the following behavior:

- When you press a mouse button with the pointer on a push button, the push button becomes pressed down.

- If you move the mouse pointer outside the border of the push button without releasing the mouse button, the push button pops back up again. If you then move the mouse pointer back inside the border of the push button without releasing the mouse button, the push button becomes pressed again.

- After you press and hold down a mouse button on a push button, the push button monitors mouse activity until the mouse button is released. If the mouse button is released inside the push button border, the push button issues a WM_COMMAND message. If the mouse button is released outside the push button border, nothing happens.

Topper handles five mouse messages to duplicate these behaviors: WM_LBUTTON-DOWN, WM_LBUTTONUP, WM_NCLBUTTONUP, WM_MOUSEMOVE, and WM_NCMOUSEMOVE. The functions that handle these mouse messages include comments to describe their purpose and how they operate, as shown in the following source code:

```
//-------------------------------------------------------------
//
// TOPPER_OnLButtonDown - Process WM_LBUTTONDOWN message. If the left
// mouse button has been pressed down on a graphic button, this function
// handles it.
//
void TOPPER_OnLButtonDown(HWND hWnd, BOOL fDoubleClick,
          int x, int y, UINT keyFlags)
{
  POINT pt;

  pt.x = x;
  pt.y = y;

  // If the left mouse button is pressed on a RECT a button is in,
  // set the BOOL variable for the button to TRUE (the button is down)
```

```
    // and invalidate the RECT so the WM_PAINT message will paint it.
    //
    if (PtInRect (&rTopit, pt))
     {
     bBDTopit = TRUE;
     InvalidateRect (hWnd, &rTopit, FALSE);
     }
    if (PtInRect (&rRefresh, pt))
     {
     bBDRefresh = TRUE;
     InvalidateRect (hWnd, &rRefresh, FALSE);
     }
    if (PtInRect (&rRelease, pt))
     {
     bBDRelease = TRUE;
     InvalidateRect (hWnd, &rRelease, FALSE);
     }
    // Capture the mouse so we can tell where the user releases
    // left mouse button.
    //
    SetCapture (hWnd);
    FORWARD_WM_LBUTTONDOWN(hWnd, fDoubleClick, x, y, keyFlags, Def-
WindowProc);
}


//------------------------------------------------------------------
//
// TOPPER_OnLButtonUp - Process WM_LBUTTONUP message. This func-
tion checks to
// see if a mouse button has been released on a graphic button.
If it has
// and the left mouse button was pushed down on the button pre-
viously,
// the event is processed.
//
void TOPPER_OnLButtonUp(HWND hWnd, int x, int y, UINT keyFlags)
{
    POINT pt;

    pt.x = x;
    pt.y = y;

    ReleaseCapture ();
```

```
// Was the left mouse button pressed on the
// button it was released on? If so, send a message to
// the window to process the action and invalidate the
// RECT so a WM_PAINT message is generated for the button
// to be redrawn.
//
if (PtInRect (&rTopit, pt) && bBDTopit)
 {
 InvalidateRect (hWnd, &rTopit, FALSE);
 SendMessage (hWnd, WM_COMMAND, IDC_PUTONTOP, 0l);
 }
if (PtInRect (&rRefresh, pt) && bBDRefresh)
 {
 InvalidateRect (hWnd, &rRefresh, FALSE);
 SendMessage (hWnd, WM_COMMAND, IDC_REFRESH, OL);
 }
if (PtInRect (&rRelease, pt) && bBDRelease)
 {
 InvalidateRect (hWnd, &rRelease, FALSE);
 SendMessage (hWnd, WM_COMMAND, IDC_RELEASE, OL);
 }
// Reset BOOL variables.
//
bBDTopit = bBDRefresh = bBDRelease = FALSE;
bBUTopit = bBURefresh = bBURelease = FALSE;
FORWARD_WM_LBUTTONUP (hWnd, x, y, keyFlags, DefWindowProc);
}


//-------------------------------------------------------------
//
// TOPPER_OnNCLButtonUp - Process WM_NCLBUTTONUP message. If but-
ton was
// outside of button RECT, reset BOOL variables and release mouse
capture.
//
void TOPPER_OnNCLButtonUp(HWND hWnd, int x, int y, UINT codeHit-
Test)
{
  bBDTopit = bBDRefresh = bBDRelease = FALSE;
  bBUTopit = bBURefresh = bBURelease = FALSE;
```

```
  ReleaseCapture ();
}


//-------------------------------------------------- --------------------------------
//
// TOPPER_OnMouseMove - Process WM_MOUSEMOVE message. If the
mouse moves
// outside of button RECT, reset BOOL variables to put button
state in Up
// position (bBD... = FALSE) and set BOOL to keep record that a
button was
// pressed but not released yet (bBU... = TRUE).
//
// If the mouse moves back inside the button RECT and it has not
been released
// yet, reset BOOL variables to put button state in Down position
// (bBD... = TRUE) and set BOOL that keeps record that a button
was
// pressed but not released yet (bBU... = FALSE).
//
// Also invalidate the button RECT so a WM_PAINT message is
generated
// for the button to be redrawn in the Up state.
//
void TOPPER_OnMouseMove(HWND hWnd, int x, int y, UINT keyFlags)
{
  POINT pt;

  pt.x = x;
  pt.y = y;

  // If the button has been pressed in a button RECT and
  // it's moved out of the RECT process it accordingly.
  //
  if (bBDTopit && ! PtInRect (&rTopit, pt))
   {
   bBUTopit = TRUE;
   bBDTopit = FALSE;
   InvalidateRect (hWnd, &rTopit, TRUE);
   }
  if (bBDRefresh && ! PtInRect (&rRefresh, pt))
   {
   bBURefresh = TRUE;
   bBDRefresh = FALSE;
```

```
      InvalidateRect (hWnd, &rRefresh, TRUE);
      }
   if (bBDRelease && ! PtInRect (&rRelease, pt))
      {
      bBURelease = TRUE;
      bBDRelease = FALSE;
      InvalidateRect (hWnd, &rRelease, TRUE);
      }

   // If the button has been pressed in a button RECT,
   // it's moved out of the RECT, and now it's moved back
   // inside the RECT process it accordingly.
   //
   if (bBUTopit && PtInRect (&rTopit, pt))
      {
      bBDTopit = TRUE;
      bBUTopit = FALSE;
      InvalidateRect (hWnd, &rTopit, TRUE);
      }
   if (bBURefresh && PtInRect (&rRefresh, pt))
      {
      bBDRefresh = TRUE;
      bBURefresh = FALSE;
      InvalidateRect (hWnd, &rRefresh, TRUE);
      }
   if (bBURelease && PtInRect (&rRelease, pt))
      {
      bBDRelease = TRUE;
      bBURelease = FALSE;
      InvalidateRect (hWnd, &rRelease, TRUE);
      }
   FORWARD_WM_MOUSEMOVE (hWnd, x, y, keyFlags, DefWindowProc);
}


//---------------------------------------------------------------
//
// TOPPER_OnNCMouseMove - Mouse has moved outside the client area
// of the
// window and button is pressed but not released. Buttons were
// likely
// reset when mouse moved outside of the button in the window's
// client
// area. This just makes sure that everything works the way that
// it's
```

```
// designed.
//
void TOPPER_OnNCMouseMove(HWND hWnd, int x, int y,
                             UINT codeHitTest)
{
  if (bBDTopit)
    {
    bBUTopit = TRUE;
    bBDTopit = FALSE;
    InvalidateRect (hWnd, &rTopit, TRUE);
    }
  if (bBDRefresh)
    {
    bBURefresh = TRUE;
    bBDRefresh = FALSE;
    InvalidateRect (hWnd, &rRefresh, TRUE);
    }
  if (bBDRelease)
    {
    bBURelease = TRUE;
    bBDRelease = FALSE;
    InvalidateRect (hWnd, &rRelease, TRUE);
    }
}
```

Building Topper's List of Windows

There are two other Windows programming aspects to Topper that are worth noting: how Topper puts a window on top and how Topper builds its list of windows to display in the list box. How to put a window on top was already covered in the Resource Monitor application. To learn how this is done you can refer to Chapter 6. The C code for building Topper's list of active application windows is in the function GetWinList, shown below:

```
//------------------------------------------------------------
//
// GetWinList - Build list of windows and put it into list box
//
void GetWinList(HWND hWnd)
{
  static HWND hWndText, hCurWnd, hPrevWnd;

  hPrevWnd = hWnd;
```

```
// Using my window handle is a starting point, go through
// the Windows Managers window chain until I get to the front.
//
while (hCurWnd = (GetWindow (hPrevWnd, GW_HWNDPREV)))
 hPrevWnd = hCurWnd;

// Set the current window handle to the one before it became
//NULL
//
hCurWnd = hPrevWnd;

ListBox_ResetContent (hWndList);

// Go through the chain of window handles that are active from
// front to back.
//
while (hCurWnd)
  {
  static int nTab[1] = {150};

  ListBox_SetTabStops (hWndList, 1, nTab);

  // Convert the window handle to a string
  //
  itoa ((int) hCurWnd, szBuffer2, 10);

  // Put the string inside the listbox control window.
  //
  GetWindowText (hCurWnd, szBuffer, 80);

  if (*szBuffer != NULL)
     {
     *(szBuffer + 40) = NULL;
     *(szBuffer + lstrlen (szBuffer) + 1) = NULL;
     *(szBuffer + lstrlen (szBuffer)) = '\t';
     strcat (szBuffer, szBuffer2);
     ListBox_AddString (hWndList, szBuffer);
     }

  // Go get the next window handle in the chain.
  //
  hCurWnd = (GetWindow (hCurWnd, GW_HWNDNEXT));
  }
}
```

To build its list of windows, Topper uses the `GetWindow` function, using its `hWnd` to position itself in the linked list of active windows. Topper then walks the list to the front to find the first window. After finding the first window, the code walks to the back of the list to add every window that has a caption to the Topper list box.

When I first created Topper, my only concern was a quick and dirty program that could lock the Help window on top of QuickC and Borland C++. As Topper evolved I wanted it to be a good programming example that would show how the Windows STRICT coding style and the new Windows 3.1 macro API worked. I also wanted to create code that was reusable for drawing push buttons that don't require a window resource.

A phrase that I learned in my high school Latin class is "Mater artium necessitas." Translated into English it means "Necessity is the mother of invention." This saying comes to mind when I think about Topper and the next program I created for this chapter, ToolPAL. Neither program may be a necessity, but in both cases I perceived a need and decided to invent a solution.

ToolPAL

I invented ToolPAL because I like to use floating Windows tool palettes and was frustrated when some of the Windows applications I use didn't have a floating tool palette as a feature. I originally developed ToolPAL for the Norton Desktop for Windows Desktop Editor. I am a big fan of the Norton Desktop for Windows, and its Desktop Editor has a lot of useful features, but it doesn't have a tools palette. So I invented one.

In the \TOOLPAL directory that was created when you installed your disk set, there is an executable of ToolPAL that works with QuickC and one that works with Borland C++. If you want to alter ToolPAL's base source code and change the bitmaps it uses, you can make it work with any Windows application. Referring to Figure 7.12, let's learn how ToolPAL works by taking a look at how it can be used with QuickC.

FIGURE 7.12:

ToolPAL being used with QuickC for Windows

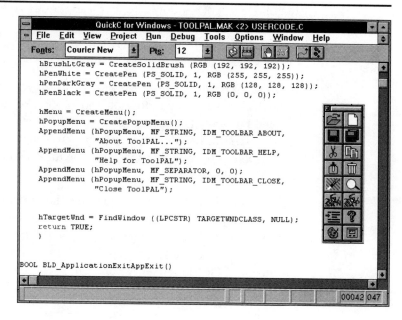

What Does ToolPAL Do?

ToolPAL's 16 buttons can be programmed to work with any Windows application to choose any command in the application's menu. They can also execute other Windows applications. Let's look at the ToolPAL window to see what it can do when it's teamed up with QuickC.

Left Column	Right Column
Open a project	Open a file
Save a file	Save all files
Cut the selected text	Copy the selected text
Paste text from the Clipboard	Delete the selected text
Undo a command	Find text
Next compile/make error	Previous compile/make error
Go to line	Execute Help for the Windows 3.1 SDK Help Reference
Execute Image Edit	Execute Dialog Edit

Now that we know what ToolPAL's functions do, let's discuss some of its behaviors. When you minimize QuickC, the ToolPAL window hides. When you restore the QuickC window, ToolPAL reappears.

I have ToolPAL configured as one of the tools in the QuickC Tools menu. Two commands get added to this menu after ToolPAL is executed:

- *Hide ToolPAL* hides the ToolPAL window and changes this menu command to Show ToolPAL. When you choose *Show ToolPAL*, the ToolPAL window reappears, and the menu command changes to Hide ToolPAL.

- *Close ToolPAL* closes the ToolPAL application.

To move ToolPAL you can grab and drag its window caption bar as you would any standard window. Unlike any standard window, however, ToolPAL doesn't really have a window caption bar—it just looks as if it does. When you click the right mouse button on the ToolPAL window caption bar, the window disappears. To make it reappear, choose Show ToolPAL in the QuickC Tools menu. If you double-click on the ToolPAL caption bar, you close ToolPAL.

ToolPAL's system menu has three commands. *About ToolPAL* displays the About ToolPAL dialog box. *Help for ToolPAL* displays help information about the application. *Close ToolPAL* closes the ToolPAL application.

Besides being a useful tool, ToolPAL illustrates several interesting Windows programming concepts:

- How to post messages to an application's window to get it to execute commands.

- How to subclass an application's window to monitor its messages.

- How to get an application's menu handle, modify its menus, and use subclassing to respond when modified menu commands are chosen.

I'm sure you have seen other programs do similar things and have wondered how they did it. By looking at ToolPAL's source code, you will learn how to do all these Windows programming tricks and learn some more about how windows and messages can interact.

How ToolPAL Works

ToolPAL was built using an ALPHA version of WindowsMAKER Professional (WMP) 5.0. In Chapter 4 you learned how WMP 4.0 could be used to generate a Windows application. The project we used to show how WMP works was the Corporate Information Menu System (CIMS) application. In many ways ToolPAL is similar to CIMS. Both applications use a dialog box mapped on top of a window to put controls such as push buttons inside a window. I was able to program the functionality of push buttons for both ToolPAL and CIMS using WMP. WMP 5.0 provides one additional feature that made building ToolPAL easier: it lets you define bitmaps to associate with owner-draw push buttons for each of the four button states—normal, pressed, disabled, and focused. In ToolPAL, I used only the normal and pressed button states.

The ToolPAL source code is in six C source code modules that were generated by WMP:

- TOOLPAL.C is the main program source code module. I didn't make any changes or additions to add ToolPAL functionality. WMP only appends code to this after it's been generated.

- TOOLPAL.WMC is the main program source code module that WMP owns. Any C code that's added or changed in a .WMC file is overwritten when the application is regenerated.

- SERVICE.C contains user-modifiable code for WMP service functions.

- SERVICE.WMC is the service function code owned by WMP.

- USERCODE.C contains all of the C code I added to create ToolPAL's functionality. This module contains all the functions called by the WMP-generated code that provide application functionality.

- USERCODE.WMC is the support code module for USERCODE.C that's owned by WMP.

Now that I've summarized how WMP was used to build a program template for ToolPAL, let's look at the source code inside USERCODE.C to see how ToolPAL works. Chapter 4 explains in much more detail how WMP works. If you skipped over Chapter 4 you may want to go back and review it before digging into the source code for ToolPAL. WMP generates source code in a unique way by building function templates for you to put your C code into to add program functionality. I sometimes refer to this method as "fill-in-the-blank Windows programming." You will be much better prepared to review the C source code in ToolPAL after you have read the information covered in Chapter 4.

Getting Information about the Target Application

Posting messages to another window is not very tricky. The key is knowing the window handle to post the messages to and the wParam value of the message to post. I used Spy to obtain this information in order to get ToolPAL to work with QuickC and Borland C++. If you look inside my program code, I refer to the application that ToolPAL works with as the target application.

Using Spy I was easily able to determine the window class of the target window to which I wanted to send a message. After finding out the window class, I executed in the target application the menu commands that I wanted to add to ToolPAL, with Spy running in the background. After executing each command, I found out its wParam value using Spy.

Keeping Track of Target Application Information

Let's look at some of the code in ToolPAL that uses the window class and the wParam value information to interact with a target application. We'll start by looking at USERCODE.H.

```
// USERCODE.H
// Header file for USERCODE.C

#include "toolpal.hh"

// These constant values are used to subclass the application the
// ToolPAL (tm) works with. Using Spy, you can obtain these values
// to build a new version of ToolPAL for any Windows application
//

// ID to identify target application
//
#define QUICKC_WINDOWS


// QuickC for Windows constant values
//
#ifdef QUICKC_WINDOWS
#define TARGETWNDCLASS      "QcQpClass"
#define TARGETAPPNAME       "QCWIN.EXE"
```

```
#define IDM_OPENPROJECT     0x0194
#define IDM_OPENFILE        0x066
#define IDM_SAVEFILE        0x069
#define IDM_SAVEALL         0x06b
#define IDM_CUT           0x0cb
#define IDM_COPY            0x0cc
#define IDM_PASTE           0x0cd
#define IDM_DELETE          0x0ce
#define IDM_UNDO            0x0c9
#define IDM_FIND          0x0cf
#define IDM_NEXTERROR       0x012F
#define IDM_PREVERROR       0x0130
#define IDM_GOTOLINE        0x012d


#define APP1 "WINHELP.EXE WIN31WH.HLP"
#define APP2 "IMAGEDIT.EXE"
#define APP3 "DLGEDIT.EXE"

// ID and number needed to indicate which menu to put
// ToolPAL menu items in.
//
#define STARTID IDC_OPENPROJECT
#define MENUBAR_POSITION_ID   IDM_OPENPROJECT
#define MENUBAR_OFFSET1_MENUITEM_ID  0
#define MENUBAR_OFFSET1     3
#define MENUBAR_OFFSET2     6

// Menu item IDs for ToolPAL menu items inserted in
// target application.
//
#define IDM_HIDETOOLPALETTE   2134
#define IDM_SHOWTOOLPALETTE   2135
#define IDM_CLOSETOOLPALETTE  2136
#define IDM_SEP1        2137
#define IDM_SEP2        2138

#endif

// Borland c++ for Windows constant values
//
#ifdef BCPP_WINDOWS
#define TARGETWNDCLASS      "BI_BCWFRAME_310"
#define TARGETAPPNAME       "BCW.EXE"
#define IDM_OPENPROJECT     0x3330
```

```
#define IDM_OPENFILE       0x32e1
#define IDM_SAVEFILE       0x32e2
#define IDM_SAVEALL        0x32e4
#define IDM_CUT            0x32f2
#define IDM_COPY           0x32f3
#define IDM_PASTE          0x32f4
#define IDM_DELETE         0x32f5
#define IDM_UNDO           0x32f0
#define IDM_FIND           0x3300
#define IDM_NEXTERROR      0x3305
#define IDM_PREVERROR      0x3304
#define IDM_GOTOLINE       0x3303


#define APP1 "WINHELP.EXE WORKHELP.HLP"
#define APP2 "WORKSHOP.EXE"
#define APP3 "WINSIGHT.EXE"

// ID and number needed to indicate which menu to put
// ToolPAL menu items in.
//
#define MENUBAR_POSITION_ID   IDM_FIND
#define MENUBAR_OFFSET1_MENUITEM_ID  0
#define MENUBAR_OFFSET1    2
#define MENUBAR_OFFSET2    7


// Menu item IDs for ToolPAL menu items inserted in
// target application.
//
#define IDM_HIDETOOLPALETTE   9134
#define IDM_SHOWTOOLPALETTE   9135
#define IDM_CLOSETOOLPALETTE  9136
#define IDM_SEP1          9137
#define IDM_SEP2          9138


#endif

// ID for starting control ID number of icons in tools palette
//
#define STARTID IDC_OPENPROJECT
// Constants that define the icon button size
//
#define XICON 33
#define YICON 27


// Menu IDs for popu menu.
```

```
//
#define IDM_TOOLBAR_ABOUT IDM_About
#define IDM_TOOLBAR_CLOSE IDM_Close
#define IDM_TOOLBAR_HELP  IDM_Help

// Global varibles
#undef EXTERN
#ifdef USERCODE
#define EXTERN
#else
#define EXTERN extern
#endif

EXTERN BOOL bButtonDown;
EXTERN FARPROC lpTargetWnd,
        lpSubclassProc;

EXTERN int   mX,
      mY,
      oX,
      oY,
      cX,
      cY,
      prevX,
      prevY,
      nCols,
      nRows,
      cyCaption,
      nBorder;

EXTERN RECT   rWnd;

EXTERN HDC   hDC;

EXTERN BOOL   bFirstTime,
      bToolbarEnable;

EXTERN HMENU hTargetMenu,
      hTargetSubMenu,
      hMenu,
      hPopupMenu;

EXTERN HWND   hTargetWnd,
```

```
        hMainDlg;

EXTERN HPEN   hPenWndOutline,
        hPenWhite,
        hPenBlack,
        hPenDarkGray;

EXTERN HBRUSH hBrushLtGray;

// Function prototypes
//
void Draw3DBox (HDC, RECT);
long FAR PASCAL SubClassProc(HWND, UINT, UINT, LONG);
```

In order to make ToolPAL work with multiple applications, I use constants in my C code for target program information, such as window class name and the wParam value of a WM_COMMAND message, that ToolPAL posts to the target application window. ToolPAL is set up to work with either QuickC or Borland C++, but you must build a separate version for each. On the disk set you will find two ToolPAL executables, TP_QC.EXE for QuickC and TP_BCPP.EXE for Borland C++. If you don't have either QuickC or Borland C++, there is another version, called TP_WRITE.EXE, on the disk set. It works with Windows Write, which is included with Windows 3.1.

Notice in USERCODE.H that there are two sets of defines, one each for QuickC and for Borland C++. You can easily build ToolPAL for either application by changing one #define statement. Currently, it's set up for QuickC:

```
// ID to identify target application
//
#define QUICKC_WINDOWS
```

To build ToolPAL for Borland C++, you need to change the define to

```
// ID to identify target application
//
#define BCPP_WINDOWS
```

In each set of #define statements the constants are the same, but the values assigned to them are different. For example, TARGETWNDCLASS is the class name of the target window, which is QcQcClass for QuickC. IDM_OPENPROJECT is the wParam value of the Open Project command in the target application.

Besides posting messages to a target application, ToolPAL can also execute Windows programs. For this version of ToolPAL, I dedicated the last three buttons for the execution of Windows applications. Notice the three `#define` statements in USERCODE.H to associate a constant with an application name.

```
#define APP1 "WINHELP.EXE WIN31WH.HLP"
#define APP2 "IMAGEDIT.EXE"
#define APP3 "DLGEDIT.EXE"
```

Now that you know how USERCODE.H is set up, let's see how the code works that uses these constants to communicate with the target application. We'll look at the initialization code first.

Initializing ToolPAL

There are two functions that handle initialization at two different points in the program: `BLD_ApplicationInitAppInit` and `BLD_CreateWindowMsg`. There is also some program initialization done in the `BLD_ToolPALClientClProc` function when `WM_INITDIALOG` is handled. `BLD_ToolPALClientClProc` is the dialog box function template that WMP builds for the dialog box that contains the ToolPAL buttons. This is the dialog box that's transparently displayed over ToolPAL's main window.

`BLD_ApplicationInitAppInit` is called before the main program window is created. In this function I initialize program variables, build ToolPAL's system menu, and allocate GDI objects. Conversely, `BLD_ApplicationExitAppExit` frees all the system resources that ToolPAL allocates. Here is the code for `BLD_ApplicationInitAppInit`.

```
BOOL BLD_ApplicationInitAppInit(hInst,hPrev,pCmdShow,lpCmd)
HANDLE hInst;
HANDLE hPrev;
int *pCmdShow;
LPSTR lpCmd;
  {
  bButtonDown = FALSE;
  nRows = 8;
  nCols = 2;
  cyCaption = GetSystemMetrics (SM_CYCAPTION) / 2;
  nBorder = GetSystemMetrics (SM_CYFRAME);
  hBrushLtGray = CreateSolidBrush (RGB (192, 192, 192));
  hPenWhite = CreatePen (PS_SOLID, 1, RGB (255, 255, 255));
  hPenDarkGray = CreatePen (PS_SOLID, 1, RGB (128, 128, 128));
```

```
hPenBlack = CreatePen (PS_SOLID, 1, RGB (0, 0, 0));

hMenu = CreateMenu();
hPopupMenu = CreatePopupMenu();
AppendMenu (hPopupMenu, MF_STRING, IDM_TOOLBAR_ABOUT,
     "About ToolPAL...");
AppendMenu (hPopupMenu, MF_STRING, IDM_TOOLBAR_HELP,
     "Help for ToolPAL");
AppendMenu (hPopupMenu, MF_SEPARATOR, 0, 0);
AppendMenu (hPopupMenu, MF_STRING, IDM_TOOLBAR_CLOSE,
     "Close ToolPAL");
return TRUE;
}
```

BLD_CreateWindowMsg is called when the WM_CREATE message is processed by the main window procedure. This function does three tasks:

- Finds the target application window. If it's not active, it starts the application and then tries again to find the target application window.

- Gets the menu handle for the target application and appends two menu items to one of its menus.

- Subclasses the target application window.

Finding the Target Application Window   To be able to post messages to a window, to subclass it, and to add menu items to its menu, we must retrieve its window handle by calling FindWindow.

```
hTargetWnd = FindWindow ((LPCSTR) TARGETWNDCLASS, NULL);
```

The first parameter is the class name of the window ToolPAL looks for. The second parameter is the caption of the window ToolPAL looks for (or NULL to match any caption). The FindWindow function is very useful for locating windows to subclass. One warning: if multiple windows exist with the same class and the same window caption, it will be difficult to identify your target window. Both QuickC and Borland C++ allow only one application instance. If the target window can't be found, ToolPAL tries to execute the program and calls FindWindow again. The code to find a window and subclass it is in BLD_CreateWindowMsg.

```
long BLD_CreateWindowMsg(hWnd,message,wParam,lParam)
HWND hWnd;
unsigned message;
```

```
WORD wParam;
LONG lParam;
  {
  hTargetWnd = FindWindow ((LPCSTR) TARGETWNDCLASS, NULL);
  if (hTargetWnd == NULL)
    {
    HCURSOR hCursor = SetCursor(LoadCursor(NULL, IDC_WAIT));
    if(WinExec((LPSTR)TARGETAPPNAME,SW_SHOWNORMAL)<32)
      {
      BLDDisplayMessage(NULL,BLD_CannotRun, TARGETAPPNAME, MB_OK |
        MB_ICONASTERISK);
      SetCursor(hCursor);
      PostMessage (MainhWnd, WM_DESTROY, NULL, NULL);
      }
    SetCursor(hCursor);
    }
  hTargetWnd = FindWindow ((LPCSTR) TARGETWNDCLASS, NULL);
  lpSubclassProc = MakeProcInstance ((FARPROC) SubClassProc,
    hInst);
  lpTargetWnd = (FARPROC) GetWindowLong (hTargetWnd, GWL_WNDPROC);
  SubclassWindow (hTargetWnd, lpSubclassProc);

  // Get the menu handle for the Tools menu
  //
  hTargetMenu = GetMenu (hTargetWnd);

  hTargetSubMenu = GetSubMenu (hTargetMenu,
  MENUBAR_OFFSET1);
  if (MENUBAR_POSITION_ID == GetMenuItemID (hTargetSubMenu,
   MENUBAR_OFFSET1_MENUITEM_ID))
    hTargetSubMenu = GetSubMenu (hTargetMenu,
    MENUBAR_OFFSET2);
  else
    hTargetSubMenu = GetSubMenu (hTargetMenu,
   MENUBAR_OFFSET2 + 1);

  AppendMenu (hTargetSubMenu, MF_SEPARATOR, IDM_SEP1, 0);
  AppendMenu (hTargetSubMenu, MF_STRING, IDM_HIDETOOLPALETTE,
        (LPSTR) "&Hide ToolPAL");
  AppendMenu (hTargetSubMenu, MF_SEPARATOR, IDM_SEP2, 0);
  AppendMenu (hTargetSubMenu, MF_STRING, IDM_CLOSETOOLPALETTE,
```

```
                (LPSTR) "&Close ToolPAL");

    SetWindowPos (hWnd, HWND_TOPMOST, 0, 0, 0, 0,
                  SWP_NOMOVE | SWP_NOSIZE);
    return DefWindowProc(hWnd, message, wParam, lParam);
    }
```

Appending Menu Items to the Target Application's Menu   The BLD_CreateWindowMsg function is also responsible for appending ToolPAL's menu items to the end of the QuickC Tools menu. This is easy once we have the window handle to QuickC. First we must make sure that none of the wParam values we use conflict with the values already in use by the target application.

I used Spy to determine the wParam values for all of QuickC's menu commands. While selecting each of the commands, I used Spy to monitor the WM_COMMAND messages and recorded all the values.

Both QuickC and Borland C++ are MDI applications. This makes appending menu items to one of their menus a little more difficult but not impossible. First we need to get the handle to the target window's menu by calling GetMenu:

```
hTargetMenu = GetMenu (hTargetWnd);
```

Next we need to get the handle to the target application submenu. If our target application is not an MDI application, we can get the handle to the submenu by calling GetSubMenu, using the position of the submenu within the menu:

```
hTargetSubMenu = GetSubMenu (hTargetMenu, SUBMENU_POSITION);
```

For example, the QuickC Tools submenu is the seventh submenu, so we would assign SUMMENU_POSITION the value of 6 in our header file, since we start counting submenus at zero. This would work just fine if we never maximized the windows with our target MDI application.

However, when an MDI child window becomes maximized, the system menu for the MDI child becomes the first pop-up menu in the application's menu bar. Because of this, the previous line of code would return the handle to the QuickC Options menu—not to the Tools menu—when an MDI child window is maximized. To work around this, I set up several constants in USERCODE.H to help ToolPAL find the correct menu:

- MENUBAR_OFFSET1 identifies the menu position number of a pop-up menu when the MDI child window is not maximized. You use the position of this pop-up menu to help ToolPAL know whether or not the MDI child window is maximized or not. The pop-up menu can be any menu in the target application for which you know the WM_COMMAND wParam value of the first item in the menu. For example, in QuickC, I used the Project menu, which has a submenu position of 3 when the MDI child window is not maximized.

- MENUBAR_OFFSET1_MENUITEM_ID is the wParam value of the first menu item in the menu identified by MENUBAR_OFFSET1.

- MENUBAR_OFFSET2 is the menu position number of the submenu you want to append ToolPAL menu items to in the target application. This menu position number identifies the pop-up menu when the MDI child window is not maximized.

Now that we have identified a pop-up menu by using the wParam value of its first menu item, we can use the following code to get the handle to the pop-up menu we want to append ToolPAL's menu items to:

```
hTargetSubMenu = GetSubMenu (hTargetMenu, MENUBAR_OFFSET1);
if (MENUBAR_POSITION_ID == GetMenuItemID (hTargetSubMenu,
    MENUBAR_OFFSET1_MENUITEM_ID))
  hTargetSubMenu = GetSubMenu (hTargetMenu, MENUBAR_OFFSET2);
else
  hTargetSubMenu = GetSubMenu (hTargetMenu, MENUBAR_OFFSET2 + 1);

AppendMenu (hTargetSubMenu, MF_SEPARATOR, IDM_SEP1, 0);
AppendMenu (hTargetSubMenu, MF_STRING, IDM_HIDETOOLPALETTE,
      (LPSTR) "&Hide ToolPAL");
AppendMenu (hTargetSubMenu, MF_SEPARATOR, IDM_SEP2, 0);
AppendMenu (hTargetSubMenu, MF_STRING, IDM_CLOSETOOLPALETTE,
      (LPSTR) "&Close ToolPAL");
```

Subclassing the Target Application Window   The code in BLD_CreateWindowMsg to subclass the target application's window is only a few lines. Instead of using Set-WindowLong, I used the new Windows 3.1 macro API defined in WINDOWSX.H to subclass the window.

```
lpSubclassProc = MakeProcInstance ((FARPROC) SubClassProc, hInst);
lpTargetWnd = (FARPROC) GetWindowLong (hTargetWnd, GWL_WNDPROC);
SubclassWindow (hTargetWnd, lpSubclassProc);
```

The subclass window function is SubClassProc. It's responsible for monitoring all of the target application window messages so ToolPAL can respond correctly when events occur, such as minimizing and restoring the target application window. The function BLD_ApplicationExitAppExit is responsible for restoring the address of the target application window procedure when ToolPAL exits so the target application can continue to function correctly without ToolPAL.

Managing ToolPAL's Dialog Box Window

The initialization when the WM_INITDIALOG message is processed in the function BLD_ToolPALClientClProc is done to size and arrange the push buttons in the ToolPAL window. This function also processes a message (WM_USER+100) that gets sent to it when the user has resized the dialog box. When the window is resized, nCols and nRows are used to determine the number of columns and rows for the push buttons inside the dialog box. The possibilities are 1C by 16R, 2C by 8R, 4C by 4R, 8C by 2R, and 16C by 1R.

```
BOOL FAR PASCAL BLD_ToolPALClientClProc(hDlg, message,
    wParam, lParam)
HWND hDlg;
unsigned message;
WORD wParam;
LONG lParam;
  {
  static HWND hCtl [16][16];
  int nRowIx, nColIx, nID;

  switch(message)
    {
  case WM_INITDIALOG:
    SetMenu (MainhWnd, hMenu);
    hMainDlg = hDlg;
    GetWindowRect (hDlg, (RECT FAR *) &rWnd);
    rWnd.right = rWnd.left + (nCols * XICON);
    rWnd.bottom = rWnd.top + (nRows * YICON);
    MoveWindow (hDlg, rWnd.left, rWnd.top,
        rWnd.right - rWnd.left,
        rWnd.bottom - rWnd.top,
        TRUE);

    nID = STARTID;
    for (nRowIx = 0; nRowIx < nRows; nRowIx++)
      {
      for (nColIx = 0; nColIx < nCols; nColIx++)
        {
        hCtl[nRowIx][nColIx] = GetDlgItem (hDlg, nID++);
```

```
         MoveWindow (hCtl[nRowIx][nColIx],
           nColIx * XICON, nRowIx * YICON,
           XICON, YICON, TRUE);
         }
        }
     bToolbarEnable = TRUE;
     return BLD_ToolPALClientDlgDefault(hDlg,message,wParam,l-
Param);
     break;

   case WM_USER + 100:
     rWnd.right = rWnd.left + (nCols * XICON);
     rWnd.bottom = rWnd.top + (nRows * YICON);
     MoveWindow (hDlg, O, cyCaption,
         rWnd.right - rWnd.left,
         rWnd.bottom - rWnd.top,
         TRUE);

     nID = STARTID;
     for (nRowIx = O; nRowIx < nRows; nRowIx++)
       {
       for (nColIx = O; nColIx < nCols; nColIx++)
        {
        hCtl[nRowIx][nColIx] = GetDlgItem (hDlg, nID++);
        MoveWindow (hCtl[nRowIx][nColIx],
          nColIx * XICON, nRowIx * YICON,
          XICON, YICON, TRUE);
        }
       }
     return BLD_ToolPALClientDlgDefault(hDlg,message,wParam,l-
Param);
     break;

   case WM_NCDESTROY:
     FreeProcInstance(ToolPALClientlpProc);
     ToolPALClienthDlg = O;
     break;

   default:
     return BLD_ToolPALClientDlgDefault(hDlg,message,wParam,l-
Param);
     break;
     }
   return TRUE;/* Did process the message */
   }
```

Handling the Target Application's Messages

ToolPAL's `SubClassProc` can monitor every message being sent to the target application's window once it has been subclassed. `SubClassProc` responds to eight different messages. A very important message is `WM_ENABLE`. It is sent to a window that is being disabled or enabled because it's displaying a modal dialog box. In my first experiment using ToolPAL, I found out that a window can receive and respond to messages even if the window has been disabled. For example, if you click on the Open File button in ToolPAL's window it will post a `WM_COMMAND` message for Open File to the target application window to display an Open File dialog box. If you click on the Open File button again, the application will display another Open File dialog box on top of the one it has just displayed.

As you can see, this causes a serious problem. ToolPAL monitors the `WM_ENABLE` message so it can disable itself from sending messages to the target application window when the window is disabled. The rest of the messages ToolPAL monitors are the following:

- `WM_DESTROY` causes the ToolPAL application to exit.

- `WM_SYSCOMMAND` with a `wParam` value of `SC_MINIMIZE` causes ToolPAL to hide its window.

- `WM_SYSCOMMAND` with a `wParam` value of `SC_MAXIMIZE` or `WM_RESTORE` causes ToolPAL to show its window if the user has not hidden it previously. ToolPAL checks the content of the target application's menu that ToolPAL created to determine whether it should show its window.

- `WM_COMMAND` with a `wParam` value of `IDM_HIDETOOLPALETTE` hides the ToolPAL window and changes the target application's menu so it contains the menu command Show ToolPAL.

- `WM_COMMAND` with a `wParam` value of `IDM_SHOWTOOLPALETTE` shows the ToolPAL window and changes the target application's menu so it contains the menu command Hide ToolPAL.

- `WM_COMMAND` with a `wParam` value of `IDM_CLOSETOOLPALETTE` causes the ToolPAL application to exit.

The following source code shows how the `SubClassProc` function works:

```
long FAR PASCAL SubClassProc(HWND hWnd, UINT msg, UINT wParam,
LONG lParam)
 {
  switch (msg)
    {
    case WM_ENABLE:
     if (wParam)
       bToolbarEnable = TRUE;
     else
       bToolbarEnable = FALSE;
     break;

    case WM_DESTROY:
     PostMessage (MainhWnd, WM_DESTROY, NULL, NULL);
     break;

    case WM_SYSCOMMAND:
     {
     switch (wParam)
       {
       case SC_MAXIMIZE:
       case SC_RESTORE:
        {
        int nIx, nMax;
        for (nIx = (GetMenuItemCount (hTargetSubMenu)) - 1;
          nIx >= 0; nIx--)
        if (IDM_HIDETOOLPALETTE ==
          GetMenuItemID (hTargetSubMenu, nIx))
          {
          ShowWindow (MainhWnd, SW_SHOW);
          break;
          }
        }
        break;

       case SC_MINIMIZE:
        ShowWindow (MainhWnd, SW_HIDE);
        break;
       }
     break;
     }

    case WM_COMMAND:
```

```
    {
    switch (wParam)
      {
      case IDM_HIDETOOLPALETTE:
       ShowWindow (MainhWnd, SW_HIDE);
       DeleteMenu (hTargetMenu, IDM_HIDETOOLPALETTE,
         MF_BYCOMMAND);
       InsertMenu (hTargetMenu, IDM_SEP2, MF_BYCOMMAND |
         MF_STRING, IDM_SHOWTOOLPALETTE,
         (LPSTR) "&Show ToolPAL");
       break;

      case IDM_SHOWTOOLPALETTE:
       ShowWindow (MainhWnd, SW_SHOW);
       DeleteMenu (hTargetMenu, IDM_SHOWTOOLPALETTE,
         MF_BYCOMMAND);
       InsertMenu (hTargetMenu, IDM_SEP2, MF_BYCOMMAND |
         MF_STRING, IDM_HIDETOOLPALETTE,
         (LPSTR) "&Hide ToolPAL");
       break;

      case IDM_CLOSETOOLPALETTE:
       PostMessage (MainhWnd, WM_DESTROY, NULL, NULL);
       break;
      }
    break;
    }

  }
  return CallWindowProc (lpTargetWnd, hWnd, msg, wParam, lParam);
}
```

Posting Messages to the Target Application Window

There isn't much to posting messages to the target application's window. If the target window is disabled, ToolPAL ignores the user's clicking on the ToolPAL push button. If the target window is enabled, ToolPAL sends a message. For example, the BLD_OpenFileUDCFunc is responsible for posting a File Open WM_COMMAND message to the target window.

```
BOOL BLD_OpenFileUDCFunc(hWnd,message,wParam,lParam)
HWND hWnd;
unsigned message;
WORD wParam;
```

```
LONG lParam;
  {
  if (bToolbarEnable)
    PostMessage (hTargetWnd, WM_COMMAND, (WPARAM) IDM_OPENFILE,
(LPARAM) 0);
  SetFocus (hTargetWnd);
  return TRUE;
  }
```

Managing the ToolPAL Window

To give ToolPAL a special look and feel, I decided to have it custom draw its system menu and caption bar. Since ToolPAL doesn't have a standard Windows caption bar, it's responsible for moving its own window. Likewise, since ToolPAL doesn't have a real system menu, it's responsible for displaying its own menu. ToolPAL also takes care of rearranging its buttons when it is sized. Let's see how it all works.

Drawing the ToolPAL Window   As we discussed previously, the ToolPAL push buttons are inside a dialog box built using WMP. To have some space to draw and manage ToolPAL's window caption bar and system menu, I had to move the dialog box created by WMP down in the window. I did this by modifying the following code in the function BLDCreateClientDlgDef in SERVICE.WMC:

```
BLDMoveWindow(ParenthWnd,rMain.left,rMain.top,
     (rMain.right-rMain.left)+dxDialog+xLeft+xRight,
     (rMain.bottom-rMain.top)+dyDialog+yTop+yBottom+cyCaption,
     TRUE);
MoveWindow(hNew,xLeft,yTop+cyCaption,
     (rDialog.right-rDialog.left),
     (rDialog.bottom-rDialog.top),
     TRUE);
```

As you know, you are not supposed to modify the code WMP generates in a WMP file. However, sometimes you have no other choice. In this case I modified the expressions generated by WMP using the variable cyCaption. This moved the dialog box mapped over the ToolPAL window down far enough for me to draw and use my custom system menu and caption bar.

> **NOTE**
> Although it's not recommended, in cases like this you sometimes need to alter the code generated by WMP in a .WMC file. When you do, you need to keep a record of what you did so you can redo the code if WMP overwrites the file when it generates the application. WMP always backs up files before they are overwritten, but you should use caution and back up your code modifications yourself as well.

The function BLD_WM_PAINTMsg is responsible for handling the WM_PAINT message and for drawing the caption bar and system menu. BLD_WM_PAINTMsg calls the function Draw3DBox to draw the system menu and caption bar. Draw3DBox is a modified version of the function I used to draw the push buttons in Topper. The height of the caption bar and system menu is one-half the height of a standard window caption bar. This value is kept in the global variable cyCaption. The following source code shows how the WM_PAINT message is handled and how ToolPAL's system menu and caption bar are drawn.

```
long BLD_WM_PAINTMsg(hWnd,message,wParam,lParam)
HWND hWnd;
unsigned message;
WORD wParam;
LONG lParam;
  {
  RECT rSysMenu,
      rButton,
      rCaptionBar;
  HDC hDC;
  int cxClient;
  PAINTSTRUCT ps;

  GetWindowRect (hWnd, &rWnd);
  cxClient = rWnd.right - rWnd.left - (2 * nBorder);
  rSysMenu.top = rSysMenu.left = 0;
  rSysMenu.right = rSysMenu.bottom = cyCaption;
  rButton.top = rButton.left = cyCaption / 4;
  rButton.right = rButton.bottom = 3 * cyCaption / 4;
  rCaptionBar.top = 0;
  rCaptionBar.left = rCaptionBar.bottom = cyCaption;
```

```
rCaptionBar.right = cxClient;

hDC = BeginPaint (hWnd, &ps);

Draw3DBox (hDC, rSysMenu);
Draw3DBox (hDC, rButton);
Draw3DBox (hDC, rCaptionBar);

EndPaint (hWnd, &ps);
return DefWindowProc(hWnd, message, wParam, lParam);
}

void Draw3DBox(HDC hDC, RECT rRect)
{
SelectPen (hDC, hPenBlack);
SelectBrush (hDC, hBrushLtGray);

Rectangle (hDC, rRect.left, rRect.top,
        rRect.right, rRect.bottom);

MoveTo (hDC, rRect.right - 2, rRect.top + 1);
SelectObject (hDC, hPenDarkGray);
LineTo (hDC, rRect.right - 2, rRect.bottom - 2);
LineTo (hDC, rRect.left + 1, rRect.bottom - 2);
SelectObject (hDC, hPenWhite);
LineTo (hDC, rRect.left + 1, rRect.top + 1);
LineTo (hDC, rRect.right - 2, rRect.top + 1);

MoveTo (hDC, rRect.right - 3, rRect.top + 2);
SelectObject (hDC, hPenDarkGray);
LineTo (hDC, rRect.right - 3, rRect.bottom - 3);
LineTo (hDC, rRect.left + 2, rRect.bottom - 3);
SelectObject (hDC, hPenWhite);
LineTo (hDC, rRect.left + 2, rRect.top + 2);
LineTo (hDC, rRect.right - 3, rRect.top + 2);
}
```

Popping Up the System Menu   If you press the left mouse button down in the RECT structure used for the system menu, ToolPAL uses TrackPopupMenu to display its menu. The menu was built in the function BLD_ApplicationInitAppInit that's called when ToolPAL is initialized.

If you press the left mouse button on the caption bar, ToolPAL captures the mouse and creates a device context for the entire display, so it can draw a rectangle to give you visual feedback when you are moving the window. All of the code for this is in the function BLD_WM_LBUTTONDOWNMsg that's called when you press the left mouse button inside the ToolPAL window, as shown in the following source code:

```
long BLD_WM_LBUTTONDOWNMsg(hWnd,message,wParam,lParam)
HWND hWnd;
unsigned message;
WORD wParam;
LONG lParam;
  {
  POINT pt;
  RECT rRect;

  pt.x = mX = LOWORD (lParam);
  pt.y = mY = HIWORD (lParam);

  rRect.top = rRect.left = 0;
  rRect.bottom = rRect.right = cyCaption;
  if (PtInRect (&rRect, pt))
    {
    ClientToScreen (hWnd, &pt);
    TrackPopupMenu (hPopupMenu, TPM_LEFTALIGN, pt.x, pt.y, 0,
        hWnd, NULL);
    return DefWindowProc(hWnd, message, wParam, lParam);
    }

  GetWindowRect (MainhWnd, &rWnd);
  cX = rWnd.right - rWnd.left;
  cY = rWnd.bottom - rWnd.top;
  oX = mX - rWnd.left;
  oY = mY - rWnd.top;
  prevX = rWnd.left;
  prevY = rWnd.top;

  bButtonDown = TRUE;
  SetCapture (MainhWnd);
  hDC = CreateDC ("DISPLAY", NULL, NULL, NULL);
  hPenWndOutline = CreatePen (PS_SOLID, 2, RGB (192, 192, 192)) ;
  return DefWindowProc(hWnd, message, wParam, lParam);
  }
```

Moving the ToolPAL Window   After you press the left mouse button on the ToolPAL caption bar, ToolPAL draws a rectangle on the screen wherever you move the mouse. The function BLD_WM_MOUSEMOVEMsg is responsible for responding to mouse move messages and for drawing the rectangle, as shown in the following source code:

```
long BLD_WM_MOUSEMOVEMsg(hWnd,message,wParam,lParam)
HWND hWnd;
unsigned message;
WORD wParam;
LONG lParam;
  {
  if (bButtonDown)
    {
    mX = LOWORD (lParam);
    mY = HIWORD (lParam);
    SelectObject (hDC, hPenWndOutline) ;
    SelectObject (hDC, GetStockObject (NULL_BRUSH));
    SetROP2 (hDC, R2_NOT);
    Rectangle (hDC, prevX + 5, prevY + 5,
        prevX + cX - 5, prevY + cY - 5);

    prevX = mX - oX;
    prevY = mY - oY;
    Rectangle (hDC, prevX + 5, prevY + 5,
        prevX + cX - 5, prevY + cY - 5);
    }
  return DefWindowProc(hWnd, message, wParam, lParam);
  }
```

NOTE   To invert the screen correctly when the rectangle is drawn on the screen and to make sure that the previous rectangle's contents are restored correctly when it is redrawn, ToolPAL calls the function SetRop2. The value R2_NOT is used for the drawn mode parameter to make sure the screen is inverted.

After the left mouse button is released, the device context and GDI objects are deleted. And should we not forget, the window is moved and mouse capture is released. The following source code shows what happens when the left mouse button is released after the user has dragged the ToolPAL window to a new location:

```
long BLD_WM_LBUTTONUPMsg(hWnd,message,wParam,lParam)
HWND hWnd;
unsigned message;
WORD wParam;
LONG lParam;
  {
  if (bButtonDown)
    {
    mX = LOWORD (lParam);
    mY = HIWORD (lParam);
    MoveWindow (MainhWnd, mX - oX, mY - oY,
     cX,
     cY, TRUE);
    DeleteDC (hDC);
    DeleteObject (hPenWndOutline);
    }
  bButtonDown = FALSE;
  ReleaseCapture();
  InvalidateRect (hWnd, NULL, hWnd);
  return DefWindowProc(hWnd, message, wParam, lParam);
  }
```

Sizing the ToolPAL Window   When the ToolPAL window is resized, Windows sends a WM_SIZE message to the ToolPAL window and the function BLD_WM_SIZEMsg processes it. BLD_WM_SIZEMsg calculates the number of rows and columns of buttons there should be, based on the proportions of the new window size. It stores these values in the global variables nRows and nCols. The following source code shows how ToolPAL processes the WM_SIZE message:

```
long BLD_WM_SIZEMsg(hWnd,message,wParam,lParam)
HWND hWnd;
unsigned message;
WORD wParam;
LONG lParam;
  {
  static HWND hCtl [16][16];
  int nRowIx, nColIx, nID, cxWnd, cyWnd, nDiff;

  GetWindowRect (hWnd, (RECT FAR *) &rWnd);
  nDiff = abs ((rWnd.right - rWnd.left) - (rWnd.bottom -
rWnd.top));
  cxWnd = (rWnd.right - rWnd.left) / XICON;
```

```
cyWnd = (rWnd.bottom - rWnd.top) / YICON;

if (nDiff < XICON)
  {
  nRows = 4;
  nCols = 4;
  cxWnd = cyWnd = 4;
  }
if (cyWnd > cxWnd)
  {
  nRows = 8;
  nCols = 2;
  }
if (cyWnd < cxWnd)
  {
  nRows = 2;
  nCols = 8;
  }
if (cxWnd < 2 && cyWnd > 2)
  {
  nRows = 16;
  nCols = 1;
  }
if (cyWnd < 2 && cxWnd > 2)
  {
  nRows = 1;
  nCols = 16;
  }
MoveWindow (hWnd, rWnd.left, rWnd.top,
      nCols * XICON + nBorder * 2,
      nRows * YICON + nBorder * 2 + cyCaption,
      TRUE);

PostMessage (hMainDlg, WM_USER + 100, NULL, NULL);
InvalidateRect (hWnd, NULL, FALSE);
return DefWindowProc(hWnd, message, wParam, lParam);
}
```

After the number of rows and columns has been calculated, BLD_WM_SIZEMsg sends a class-defined message (WM_USER+100) to the dialog box function that manages the arrangement of the push buttons. The following code in the function BLD_Tool-PALClientC1Proc processes this message when it's received:

```
case WM_USER + 100:
  rWnd.right = rWnd.left + (nCols * XICON);
```

```
  rWnd.bottom = rWnd.top + (nRows * YICON);
  MoveWindow (hDlg, 0, cyCaption,
      rWnd.right - rWnd.left,
      rWnd.bottom - rWnd.top,
      TRUE);

  nID = STARTID;
  for (nRowIx = 0; nRowIx < nRows; nRowIx++)
    {
    for (nColIx = 0; nColIx < nCols; nColIx++)
      {
      hCtl[nRowIx][nColIx] = GetDlgItem (hDlg, nID++);
      MoveWindow (hCtl[nRowIx][nColIx],
        nColIx * XICON, nRowIx * YICON,
        XICON, YICON, TRUE);
      }
    }
  return BLD_ToolPALClientDlgDefault(hDlg,message,wParam,l-
Param);
  break;
```

ToolPAL does not help you audit what your program does, as Spy and WinSight do, but it does teach many aspects of how to work with windows and window messages. Toolbars are a new aspect of the Windows user interface that is both attractive and useful. The program code in ToolPAL should help you build tool palettes in your own applications and invent independent tool palettes like ToolPAL.

Now that we have learned about windows and messages, it's time to look at how to audit windows applications further by using profilers. In the next chapter, we will finish this part of the book by learning how to use Microsoft's Source Profiler and Borland's Turbo Profiler.

Profiling Windows Applications

- How the different types of profiling work

- Choosing a profiling method

- Using the Microsoft Source Profiler

- Using Borland's Turbo Profiler

- Evaluating the results of profiling a Windows application

- Optimizing your Windows application after you have profiled it

8

In the previous chapter we examined the structure of windows and how they communicate using messages. We also examined tools (Spy, WinSight, and Voyeur) that can be used to examine window class and instance structure as well as monitor the messages that travel between window instances. Now you will learn about a Windows development tool for the postdevelopment process. After you have your application working and debugged, a profiler helps to

- eliminate dead code,

- show you where to modify program code to make your application run faster, and

- show you where your application does the most work and the least.

In this chapter we are going to discuss tools for profiling. First you will learn what profiling is and how it can help you to build faster programs. Then we will look at two profiling utilities, Microsoft's Source Profiler for Windows and Borland's Turbo Profiler for Windows. Microsoft's Source Profiler is included with Microsoft C/C++ 7.0. It works with all Microsoft-language products and can also be purchased separately. Borland's Turbo Profiler is included with all Borland-language products.

You will also learn how optimization is accomplished through using an optimizing compiler. After profiling is done, we will discuss how you can optimize your program's C code manually or by using your compiler.

How Does Profiling Work?

I'm sure you have all heard of the 80/20 rule. It can be applied in many different ways: 20 percent of the project takes 80 percent of the work; 20 percent of the program contains 80 percent of the bugs. There is also the rule that 80 percent of a program's execution time is spent executing only 20 percent of the application's code. (In many cases, this is a 90/10 rule instead of 80/20!)

Profiling is the process of analyzing your program's behavior during execution to give you a report that identifies

- the total execution time of a function,

- the total number of calls to a function,

- the number of times a line of code is executed,
- which lines of code have not been executed, and
- which files an application accesses and for how long.

You use a profiler to identify where your program spends the most time. Optimizing a program takes time, and as a developer you want to spend that time working on the parts of your program that will give you the highest payback. For example, let's say you have a program with 50 functions. Two of the functions consume 75 percent of the processing time. FunctionOne consumes 50 percent and FunctionTwo consumes 25 percent of execution time. Let's also assume that you can usually improve the speed of program code by 100 percent after it's optimized. By optimizing FunctionOne you will improve your program's speed 25 percent. If you optimize both functions you will cut your program's execution time almost in half.

Profiling Methods

A profiler offers several methods for profiling an application. The method you use is determined by the information you want from the profiling session. For example, do you want an overall picture of how your program executes, or do you need to know the specific number of times a loop iterates? There are four profiling methods: coverage, counting, passive (or sampling), and active (or timing).

Coverage

Coverage records which lines of code have been executed during a profiling session. It does not record timing or counting information, but it's very fast. Coverage is a good way of finding the code within an application that needs to be profiled in more detail. It is also a good way to find out if there is any code within an application that does not get executed (dead code).

Coverage profiling is helpful for testing programs. If you are a program tester, coverage profiling makes sure that each program component gets exercised during the test.

Counting

Counting is used to determine how often a function or line of code is executed. You use the counting technique to record how often a function is called or a line of code is executed, and how many times a loop is iterated.

Passive Profiling

Using the passive profiling, or sampling, method, your application is suspended on a regular basis by a hardware timer interrupt. When the profiler wakes up, it samples the value in the current code segment's instruction pointer register (CS:IP) and determines whether that value points to an area inside the executable being monitored by the profiler. If so, the profiler determines which function or line of source code is nearest to the CS:IP value. The profiler records the information and goes back to sleep. That information is used later to calculate how many times the function or source line was executed and how much time was spent executing it.

Passive profilers usually reprogram the timer chip and install a new interrupt service routine to handle clock ticks. The timer chip is reprogrammed to reduce the time between clock ticks. This increases the frequency of examining your program's execution. The more frequently the clock ticks, the more accurate the passive profile. This usually leads to a reduction in the program's execution speed, however, because the profiler is interrupting the application more frequently.

Speed is not the only drawback to passive profiling. What if the profiler becomes active inside a runtime library? Or, on the other hand, what if the profiler does not wake up inside an area of code that is critical to the application? This causes the results of the profile to become skewed. If you suspect this is the case, set the profile interrupt resonance frequency to another value. Resonance, meaning the frequency of sampling for a line of code or function, may not be recorded because the profiler was not called during the execution of the current function or line of code. The frequency with which the passive technique is run (at different resonance frequencies) is directly related to the accuracy of the profiling information.

Active Profiling

The active profiling, or timing, method uses the profiler much like a debugger. When you compile for debugging, you insert INT 3 at the beginning of every function or line of code to be debugged. This same strategy works for profiling. When an INT 3 is encountered, the profiler uses the debug symbol table to log the source line and function that is executing, and notes how long it takes to execute.

Two problems encountered with passive profiling are solved with active profiling. If your program is executing code from a runtime library, the profiler does not wake up because there are no breakpoints in the runtime library. The profiler wakes up on any line of code that contains an INT 3; this insures that you record all critical lines of code.

Active profiling is usually done when the profiling scope is limited to a handful of functions. This is because active profiling is slower than passive profiling, since the profiler interrupts the program execution frequently. Although passive profiling is faster than active profiling, it does not record information about your program execution as accurately as active profiling does.

Now that you have learned the theory behind profiling, you may ask, "What is the best way for me to incorporate the techniques? Should I profile my entire application line by line or function by function?"

Line Profiling versus Function Profiling

Profiling an application line by line provides you with information for finding out how small parts of code operate, such as critical loops. It is also useful when you are trying to find out how many times or for how long a routine from an external library is called (provided you do not have the source code).

In contrast, function profiling provides a general outline of an application. It records how often and for how long each function within an application is executed. This big picture helps you to isolate the function that is slowing your application down.

I find it useful to profile an application at a function level first, then profile the function that looks as if it's a problem area using line profiling.

Both line and function profiling use counting, timing, sampling, and coverage techniques. Which one you use depends on the type of information you need, as well as what level of detail you desire.

Why Profiling a Windows Application Can Be Misleading

When profiling a Windows application, most profilers report that the majority of the application's time is spent executing a window function. This is the case for profiling most Windows applications because the window function handles many events during its execution. As I mentioned before, I find it useful to profile an application at a function level first. I also include all the window procedures in my first pass. After I get a picture of where the activity is occurring, I resort to line profiling to find out how specific functions are executing. This is the recommended method for using both the Microsoft and Borland profilers, as you will see in the following sections.

Microsoft's Source Profiler for Windows

The Microsoft Source Profiler for Windows is an excellent tool to use when you need to perform active analysis. It is very good for obtaining timing, coverage, and counting information about an application. Even though the Source Profiler cannot perform passive analysis, I personally don't see this as a drawback, because of the limitations of passive analysis.

All of the Source Profiler tools are DOS programs that must be run from the command line. As you will later see, it's more difficult to set up and use the Microsoft Source Profiler than the Borland Turbo Profiler. However, even though the Source Profiler is more primitive to use than the Turbo Profiler, the results it produces are comparable.

NOTE   The Microsoft Source Profiler can be run in a more interactive way from the Microsoft Programmer's Workbench *for profiling DOS programs only.* This mode of operation is not available for profiling Windows programs using Microsoft C/C++ 7.0 and the Microsoft Source Profiler Version 1.2.

The Source Profiler comes with three programs that you use to profile a Windows application: PREP.EXE, PROFILEW.EXE, and PLIST.EXE. PROFILEW.EXE is used for profiling Windows applications. (Its counterpart, PROFILE.EXE, is used for profiling DOS applications.) These tools are used for preparing a program for profiling, for profiling a program, and for creating a report that lists the results.

To prepare a program for profiling, you must include CodeView debugging information in the executable file. With Microsoft C/C++ 7, you use the /Zi switch for compiling and the /CO switch for linking. You should also turn off all optimizations using the /Od compiler switch. When you optimize a program, it's impossible for the Source Profiler correctly to identify and report on all the lines of source code in your program.

> **NOTE** Using QuickC for Windows, you must compile the executable files and DLLs that you want to profile with CodeView 3.x information. To generate CodeView 3.x information, choose CV 3.X Format from the Customize Linker Options dialog box.

After preparing your executable by including CodeView information, it's time to use the following Source Profiler programs to profile your application:

- PREP is used for two purposes: preparing the input program for a profiling session and correlating PROFILEW's output. PREP is run twice in every profiling session. You run it first to create the .PBI file. After you have profiled the application in Windows, you run it again to correlate the .PBO file created by PROFILEW to build the .PBT file used by PLIST to produce your profile report.

- PROFILEW is run from the command line to profile your application while it's running within Windows. PROFILEW can run only in Standard and Enhanced modes. You can run PROFILEW in several different ways:

  - From the DOS command line when Windows isn't running, by typing in
    WIN PROFILEW [options] progname [arguments].

  - From Program Manager while Windows is running, by choosing Run from Program Manager's File menu and typing in the command PROFILEW [options] progname [arguments]. This is the best way to profile your program, because it minimizes Windows overhead that can affect Source Profiler timings. If you run PROFILEW from the DOS command line, the Source Profiler will attribute extra time to the code that runs in the first few seconds, because the Source Profiler starts profiling your code from the point when Windows starts—not when your program starts.

- Using the WX utility from the DOS command line while Windows is running, you can run PROFILEW by typing in `WX PROFILEW [op-tions] progname [arguments]`. The WX/WX Server Utility runs a Windows program from a DOS prompt within Windows. WX is a command-line utility that runs a Windows application from a DOS prompt, either in a full screen or in a window. WX Server is a Windows program that must be running before you can use WX. Since Windows is already running, this method has the same advantages as running PROFILEW from Program Manager.

- PLIST processes the .PBT file that PREP creates from the .PBO file that PROFILEW generates to produce a report on how your program behaved when it was profiled.

Figure 8.1 shows how PREP, PROFILEW, and PLIST interact, and names the files that they produce to profile a Windows application.

FIGURE 8.1:
The Windows profiling process

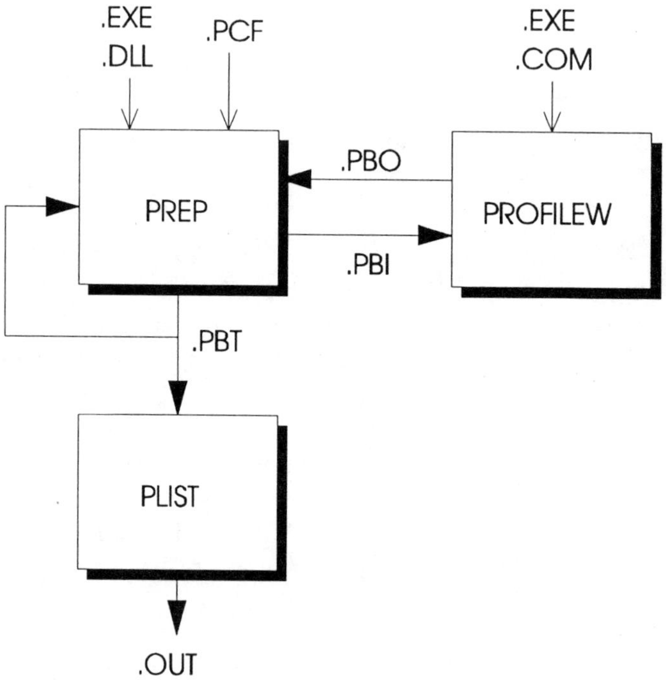

Source Profiler Program Syntax

Now that you understand how these programs are used, let's take a closer look at how to call each one to profile a Windows application.

Using PREP.EXE

PREP.EXE is used for two operations: to prepare the input module for a profiling session and to convert the output of the profile process to a format that's usable by the PLIST utility for generating reports. The syntax for the PREP command is:

```
PREP [options][input file][output file][command file]
```

The options are where we tell the profiler the type of profiling we want to accomplish. Following are some of the more common options:

Option	Description
/FC	Function Count profiling
/FT	Function Timing profiling
/FV	Function Coverage profiling
/LC	Line Count profiling
/LT	Line Timing profiling
/LV	Line Coverage profiling

The input file is the .EXE or .DLL to be read. Following are some of the more common options:

Option	Description
/P filename	Specifies the .EXE or .DLL to be read
/IT filename	Merges an existing .PBT file
/IO filename	Merges an existing .PBO file

The output file is where we tell PREP to create the .PBT file or the .PBI file. The following are the options:

Option	Description
/OT filename	Creates a .PBT file (Binary Table file). This is the file PLIST reads to create reports. It is a second-pass function.
/OI filename	Creates a .PBI file (Binary Input file). This is the file read by PROFILEW to get information about the profiling session. It is a firstpass function.

The command file is the ASCII text file containing instructions that control PREP. It gives you access to an extended control language to provide additional control of PREP. The extension of the file is .PCF (Program Command File). For more information on the commands, use the Microsoft Quick Help Advisor.

Using PROFILEW.EXE

PROFILEW.EXE is the profiler used for Windows applications. It profiles the application and generates a .PBO file (Binary Output file). The syntax of PROFILEW is as follows:

```
PROFILEW [options] [program name] [args]
```

Some of the more common options are the following:

Option	Description
/I filename	.PBI file to be read
/O filename	.PBO file to generate
/S	Sampling frequency (only if .PBI is set for sampling)
/W	Call ExitWindows to close Windows after execution

Using PLIST.EXE

PLIST.EXE creates the report after the profiling process is completed. It converts the results from the .PBT file into formatted text. The syntax is as follows:

```
PLIST [options] [input file]
```

One of the more common options is the /T option. This creates a tab-separated report that is easily imported to your favorite spreadsheet. There are also several sort options available.

Using Batch Files

As we have discussed, profiling is a four-step process: you run PREP, then PROFILEW, then PREP again, and finally PLIST. It is a somewhat tedious yet flexible system. Source Profiler comes with a set of batch files that each executes the four-step process. They make it easy to get started profiling Windows applications.

Each batch file is geared toward a particular method of profiling, and each method can be profiled by line or by function. There are six standard batch files with Source Profiler, three for line profiling and three for function profiling. The batch files used for profiling Windows applications are:

- FCOUNTW.BAT, to profile by function, using the counting method.
- LCOUNTW.BAT, to profile by line, using the counting method.
- FCOVERW.BAT, to profile by function, using the coverage method.
- LCOVERW.BAT, to profile by line, using the coverage method.
- FTIMEW.BAT, to profile by function, using the timing method.
- LTIMEW.BAT, to profile by line, using the timing method.

As you would expect, line profiling is considerably slower than function profiling. In most cases I always profile a Windows application first by function. After examining the report created by this step, I narrow my focus and use line profiling in selected functions when I profile an application further.

Profiling Resource Monitor Using Source Profiler

The best way to understand how a tool works is to see how it can be used in a "hands-on" project. In this project I am going to use Source Profiler to profile the Resource Monitor program that was introduced in Chapter 6. The Resource

Monitor program was developed for this book to help you keep track of three Windows resources: memory, User system resources, and GDI system resources. Figure 8.2 shows the Resource Monitor reporting on the current state of Windows resources. The Resource Monitor program files are in the \RMONITOR directory that was created when you installed the disk set.

Resource Monitor relies heavily on WM_TIMER messages to notify itself to check on the current state of Windows resources. As a normal Windows application, its window function should account for most of the program's activity.

In this first project we'll see how Source Profiler is used to profile Resource Monitor. Later on we'll use Borland's Turbo Profiler to profile the same application. In this way you will be able to compare how the two profilers work on the same program.

Preparing Resource Monitor

First I recompiled Resource Monitor using the Microsoft C /Zi/Od options and linked it using the /CO option. Then I used the batch files that come with the Source Profiler as a starting point to create some batch files of my own for profiling Resource Monitor.

Creating Profiler Batch Files

If you use the batch files that come with Source Profiler, you must execute Windows each time you run the batch file. Instead, I wanted to run PROFILEW.EXE from the DOS prompt with Windows already running in the background, using WX Server,

FIGURE 8.2:

The Resource Monitor in the process
of tracking Windows resources

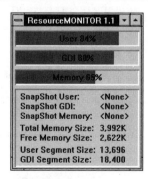

a utility included with Microsoft C/C++ 7.0. Doing this requires a two-step process, so I split the batch files that come with Source Profiler into two parts. For example, the batch file to profile a program using the function count method is FCOUNTW.BAT. To replace this file I created FCOUNTW1.BAT and FCOUNTW2.BAT. FCOUNTW1.BAT runs PREP.EXE to prepare the files to profile a Windows application and executes PROFILEW.EXE using WX Server, as shown in the following .BAT file:

```
@echo off
prep /fc /p %1.exe /ot %1.pbt /oi %1.pbi
WX profilew %1 %2 %3 %4 %5 %6 %7 %8 %9
```

FCOUNTW2.BAT calls PREP to correlate the output files and calls PLIST.EXE to create the output reports:

```
@echo off
prep /it %1.pbt /io %1.pbo /ot %1.pbt
plist /t %1.pbt > %1.tab
plist /sc %1.pbt > %1.out
del %1.pbo
del %1.pbi
```

Notice lines three and four of FCOUNTW2.BAT. I call PLIST.EXE twice. The first time it's called using the /t option to create a tabbed report for Microsoft Excel. The second time PLIST.EXE is called it creates a standard ASCII text profile report and puts it into the file PROGNAME.OUT.

Function Count Profiling

To use the first batch file, I typed in FCOUNTW1 RMONITOR at the DOS prompt. PREP.EXE then runs to prepare the input files, and PROFILEW.EXE runs and switches back to Windows. At this point I exercised Resource Monitor by choosing commands from its system menu and displaying both of its dialog boxes, About and Setup. I also ran STRESS.EXE to see how Resource Monitor performed under low system resource conditions. After I was finished profiling Resource Monitor, I exited both STRESS.EXE and Resource Monitor and went back to the DOS prompt.

After running Resource Monitor using PROFILEW.EXE, I ran the batch file to create the reports RMONITOR.OUT and RMONITOR.TAB. The following listing shows the contents of RMONITOR.OUT:

```
Microsoft PLIST Version 1.20

Profile: Function counting, sorted by counts.
```

```
Date: Mon Jul 06 10:50:20 1992

Program Statistics
------------------

 Total functions: 23
 Total hits: 3976
 Function coverage: 91.3%

Module Statistics for e:\atools\rmonitor\rmonitor.exe
-----------------------------------------------------

 Functions in module: 23
 Hits in module: 3976
 Module function coverage: 91.3%

 Hit
count % Function
--------------------
 2619 65.9 WndProc (rmonitor.c:10)
 551 13.9 SETUPMsgProc (dialogs.c:10)
 205 5.2 NumericEditProc (dialogs.c:160)
 169 4.3 About (dialogs.c:188)
 121 3.0 OnTimer (rmonitor.c:161)
 121 3.0 GetSystemResources (rmonitor.c:739)
 120 3.0 ltoCommaDelimitedString (rmonitor.c:784)
 31 0.8 OnPaint (rmonitor.c:352)
 16 0.4 OnSysCommand (rmonitor.c:83)
 6 0.2 DrawBitmap (dialogs.c:241)
 3 0.1 OnMove (rmonitor.c:675)
 3 0.1 OnSize (rmonitor.c:695)
 2 0.1 CloseApp (app.c:159)
 2 0.1 SaveProfile (app.c:281)
 1 0.0 OnCreate (rmonitor.c:33)
 1 0.0 PaintIcon (rmonitor.c:582)
 1 0.0 OnDestroy (rmonitor.c:715)
 1 0.0 WinMain (app.c:29)
 1 0.0 IntitializeApp (app.c:53)
 1 0.0 RegisterWndClass (app.c:134)
 1 0.0 GetProfile (app.c:179)
 0 0.0 OnQueryEndSession (rmonitor.c:726)
 0 0.0 DisplayMessage (rmonitor.c:828)
```

As you can see, the functions WndProc and SETUPMsgProc had most of the activity. OnTimer processed 121 WM_TIMER messages and called GetSystemResources 121 times.

In the FCOUNTW2.BAT file, PLIST was called twice: once to produce the previous report and again to produce a tabbed output that can be used in Microsoft Excel. Figure 8.3 shows the contents of RMONITOR.TAB after it has been loaded into Excel.

The Source Profiler also comes with an Excel macro that can be used to display the data in the tabbed report as an Excel chart. The macro is called PROFILER.XLM, and it's in the \PROFILER\SAMPLES\TAB directory that gets created when you install the Source Profiler. To execute the macro, I clicked on cell A1 in the RMONITOR.TAB window and chose Run in the Excel Macro menu. In the Excel Run Macro dialog box that gets displayed, I selected the CreateColumnChart macro and clicked on OK to create a chart. After the first chart was displayed, I used the buttons on the Excel Chart toolbar to choose the chart that's displayed in Figure 8.4.

As you can see, the chart produced by Excel visually depicts the results of the function count profile I ran on Resource Monitor. Next I did a function time profile to see if I would get similar results.

FIGURE 8.3:
RMONITOR.TAB being used in Microsoft Excel

	A	B	C	D	E	F	G	H	I
1	0	15	Microsoft PLIST Version 1.20						
2	1	421	Profile: Function counting, sorted by line.						
3	2	0	0	0					
4	3	3976	23	21					
5	4	0	0	0	0				
6	6	rmonitor.exe	app.c	29	1	0	0	WinMain	
7	6	rmonitor.exe	app.c	53	1	0	0	IntitializeApp	
8	6	rmonitor.exe	app.c	134	1	0	0	RegisterWndClass	
9	6	rmonitor.exe	app.c	159	2	0	0	CloseApp	
10	6	rmonitor.exe	app.c	179	1	0	0	GetProfile	
11	6	rmonitor.exe	app.c	281	2	0	0	SaveProfile	
12	6	rmonitor.exe	dialogs.c	10	551	0	0	SETUPMsgProc	
13	6	rmonitor.exe	dialogs.c	160	205	0	0	NumericEditProc	
14	6	rmonitor.exe	dialogs.c	188	169	0	0	About	
15	6	rmonitor.exe	dialogs.c	241	6	0	0	DrawBitmap	
16	6	rmonitor.exe	rmonitor.c	10	2619	0	0	WndProc	
17	6	rmonitor.exe	rmonitor.c	33	1	0	0	OnCreate	
18	6	rmonitor.exe	rmonitor.c	83	16	0	0	OnSysCommand	
19	6	rmonitor.exe	rmonitor.c	161	121	0	0	OnTimer	

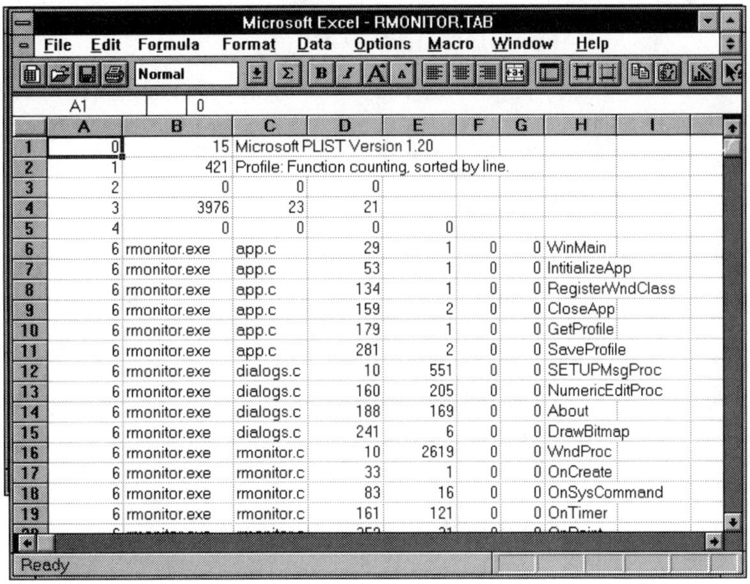

FIGURE 8.4:

The function count chart produced by Excel for Resource Monitor

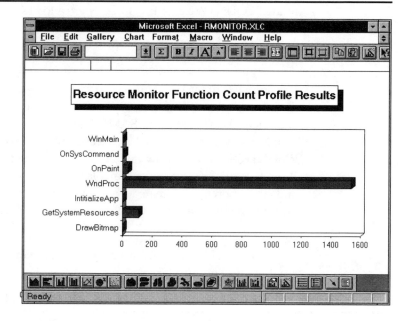

Function Time Profiling

To do a function time profile I created two more BAT files, FTIMEW1.BAT and FTIMEW2.BAT, using the same procedure already described. The contents of these .BAT files are:

```
FTIMEW1.BAT:
@echo off
prep /ft /p %1.exe /ot %1.pbt /oi %1.pbi
wx profilew %1 %2 %3 %4 %5 %6 %7 %8 %9
```

```
FTIMEW2.BAT:
@echo off
prep /it %1.pbt /io %1.pbo /ot %1.pbt
plist /t %1.pbt > %1.tab
plist /st %1.pbt > %1.out
del %1.pbo
del %1.pbi
```

While profiling Resource Monitor, I tried to duplicate the same functionality I exercised previously. The following listing shows the contents of the function time report for Resource Monitor:

```
Microsoft PLIST Version 1.20

Profile: Function timing, sorted by time.
Date: Mon Jul 06 11:31:18 1992


Program Statistics
------------------
 Total time: 268580.681 milliseconds
 Time outside of functions: 3619.416 milliseconds
 Call depth: 11
 Total functions: 23
 Total hits: 2703
 Function coverage: 91.3%

Module Statistics for e:\atools\rmonitor\rmonitor.exe
-----------------------------------------------------
 Time in module: 264961.265 milliseconds
 Percent of time in module: 100.0%
 Functions in module: 23
 Hits in module: 2703
 Module function coverage: 91.3%

  Func   Func+Child  Hit
  Time %  Time % count Function
---------------------------------------------------------
157888.355 59.6 158512.562 59.8 109 OnTimer (rmonitor.c:161)
95774.429 36.1 264961.265 100.0  1 WinMain (app.c:29)
 6102.450 2.3 7480.355 2.8 11 OnSysCommand (rmonitor.c:83)
 1756.135 0.7 2289.310 0.9 36 OnPaint (rmonitor.c:352)
 992.187 0.4 168371.059 63.5 1536 WndProc (rmonitor.c:10)
 751.720 0.3  814.207 0.3  1 IntitializeApp (app.c:53)
 624.207 0.2  624.207 0.2 109 GetSystemResources (rmonitor.c:739)
 541.215 0.2  541.215 0.2  3 DrawBitmap (dialogs.c:241)
 223.727 0.1  223.727 0.1  2 SaveProfile (app.c:281)
 112.462 0.0  114.165 0.0 246 NumericEditProc (dialogs.c:160)
  66.183 0.0   97.347 0.0 438 SETUPMsgProc (dialogs.c:10)
  47.768 0.0  611.375 0.2 70 About (dialogs.c:188)
  21.440 0.0  245.168 0.1  2 CloseApp (app.c:159)
  18.375 0.0   18.375 0.0  1 GetProfile (app.c:179)
  17.271 0.0  110.739 0.0  6 PaintIcon (rmonitor.c:582)
```

```
    17.120 0.0  17.120 0.0 120 ltoCommaDelimitedString
(rmonitor.c:784)
    3.373 0.0  203.394 0.1   1 OnDestroy (rmonitor.c:715)
    2.085 0.0    8.139 0.0   1 OnCreate (rmonitor.c:33)
    0.536 0.0    0.536 0.0   1 RegisterWndClass (app.c:134)
    0.145 0.0    0.145 0.0   5 OnMove (rmonitor.c:675)
    0.081 0.0    0.081 0.0   4 OnSize (rmonitor.c:695)
    0.000 0.0    0.000 0.0   0 OnQueryEndSession (rmonitor.c:726)
    0.000 0.0    0.000 0.0   0 DisplayMessage (rmonitor.c:828)
```

In this profile of Resource Monitor, the results show that the most time was spent in the function OnTimer, even though it had a much lower hit count than WndProc. As this report points out, the OnTimer function would be a good candidate for optimizing. I also produced a chart using Excel that visually depicts the results of the function time profiles as shown in Figure 8.5.

I skipped doing a coverage profile of Resource Monitor because the limited information it provides is included in the count profiling method. Instead, I finished my Resource Monitor profiling project by doing a line count profile to see which lines of my code were getting executed as well as how many times.

FIGURE 8.5:

The function time profile results for Resource Monitor

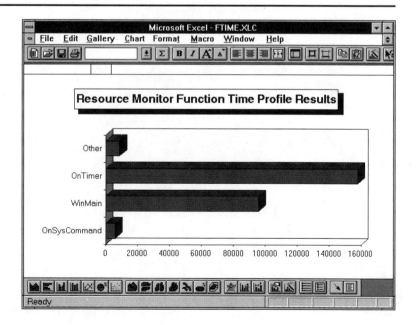

422

The first page of this report follows, showing the program statistics for the line count profile. It also gives a detailed account of the first two functions in the source code module RMONITOR.C, WndProc and OnCreate.

```
Microsoft PLIST Version 1.20

Profile: Line counting, sorted by line.
Date: Mon Jul 06 10:46:22 1992


Program Statistics
------------------
 Total lines: 659
 Total hits: 15154
 Line coverage: 74.4%


Module Statistics for e:\atools\rmonitor\rmonitor.exe
-----------------------------------------------------
 Lines in module: 659
 Hits in module: 15154
 Module line coverage: 74.4%


Source file: e:\atools\rmonitor\rmonitor.c

  Hit
Line count % Source
------------------------
 1:    #define STRICT // Bugs Beware!
 2:    #define EXTERN extern
 3:    #include "RMONITOR.h"
 4:
 5:    //-----------------------------------------------------------
 6:    //
 7:    // WndProc - Resource Monitor window procedure
 8:    //
 9:    LRESULT CALLBACK _export WndProc (HWND hWnd,
                                         UINT msg,
                                         WPARAM wParam,
                                         LPARAM lParam)
10: 1006 6.6 {
11: 1006 6.6 switch (msg)
12:    {
13: 1 0.0 HANDLE_MSG (hWnd, WM_CREATE,    OnCreate);
14:  9 0.1 HANDLE_MSG (hWnd, WM_SYSCOMMAND, OnSysCommand);
15: 91 0.6 HANDLE_MSG (hWnd, WM_TIMER,    OnTimer);
```

```
16: 20 0.1 HANDLE_MSG (hWnd, WM_PAINT,   OnPaint);
17:  3 0.0 HANDLE_MSG (hWnd, WM_MOVE,  OnMove);
18:  3 0.0 HANDLE_MSG (hWnd, WM_SIZE,  OnSize);
19:  1 0.0 HANDLE_MSG (hWnd, WM_DESTROY,  OnDestroy);
20:  0 0.0 HANDLE_MSG (hWnd, WM_QUERYENDSESSION, OnQueryEnd-
Session);
21:
22:   default:
23: 878 5.8  return DefWindowProc (hWnd, msg, wParam, lParam) ;
24:  0 0.0 }
25: 1006 6.6 }
26:
27:
28:   //----------------------------------------------------------
29:   //
30:   // OnCreate - Handle WM_CREATE message
31:   //
32:   BOOL OnCreate(HWND hWnd, CREATESTRUCT FAR * lpCreateStruct)
33:  1 0.0 {
34:   HMENU hMenu;
35:
36:  1 0.0 hMenu = GetSystemMenu (hWnd, FALSE);
37:  1 0.0 AppendMenu (hMenu, MF_SEPARATOR, 0, 0);
38:   AppendMenu (hMenu, MF_STRING | MF_CHECKED, IDM_BOTH,
39:  1 0.0  (LPSTR) "Monitor &Both GDI and User");
40:   AppendMenu (hMenu, MF_STRING, IDM_GDI,
41:  1 0.0  (LPSTR) "Monitor &GDI");
42:   AppendMenu (hMenu, MF_STRING, IDM_USER,
43:  1 0.0  (LPSTR) "Monitor &User");
44:  1 0.0 AppendMenu (hMenu, MF_SEPARATOR, 0, 0);
45:   AppendMenu (hMenu, MF_STRING, IDM_SNAPSHOT,
46:  1 0.0  (LPSTR) "Take &SnapShot");
47:   AppendMenu (hMenu, MF_STRING, IDM_SETUP,
48:  1 0.0  (LPSTR) "Resource Monitor Setup...");
49:  1 0.0 if (bAlwaysOnTop)
50:   {
51:   AppendMenu (hMenu, MF_STRING | MF_CHECKED, IDM_ALWAYSONTOP,
52:  0 0.0  (LPSTR) "&Always On Top");
53:  0 0.0  SetWindowPos (hWnd, HWND_TOPMOST, 0, 0, 0, 0,
           SWP_NOMOVE | SWP_NOSIZE);
54:   }
55:   else
56:   AppendMenu (hMenu, MF_STRING, IDM_ALWAYSONTOP,
57:  1 0.0  (LPSTR) "&Always On Top");
58:  1 0.0 AppendMenu (hMenu, MF_SEPARATOR, 0, 0);
```

```
59:    AppendMenu (hMenu, MF_STRING, IDM_HELP,
60: 1 0.0  (LPSTR) "Help for Help");
61:
62:    AppendMenu (hMenu, MF_STRING, IDM_INDEXHELP,
63: 1 0.0  (LPSTR) "Help for ResourceMonitor");
64:
65:    AppendMenu (hMenu, MF_STRING, IDM_ABOUT,
66: 1 0.0  (LPSTR) "About ResourceMonitor...");
67:
68: 1 0.0 if (! SetTimer (hWnd, TIMER_ID, Setup.nSampleRate *
1000, NULL))
69:    {
70:    MessageBox (hWnd, "Too many timers in use!", "Resource
Monitor Error!",
71: 0 0.0   MB_ICONEXCLAMATION | MB_OK);
72:    }
73: 1 0.0 OnTimer (hWnd, 0);
74: 1 0.0 return TRUE;
75: 1 0.0 } // End of OnCreate
76:
```

As the listing shows, WndProc received 1006 messages. Ninety-one messages came from WM_TIMER and were sent to the function OnTimer. Twelve WM_PAINT messages were received and sent on to the function OnPaint. A Windows program is supposed to receive only one WM_CREATE message, and that's what our profile shows. The function OnCreate was executed after it was called to process the WM_CREATE message.

The next listing shows the line count profile for the OnSysCommand function. It processed nine messages. One command message was for displaying the About dialog box. Another was for displaying the Setup dialog box. All the rest were passed on to DefWindowProc.

```
//-----------------------------------------------------------------------
79:    //
80:    // OnSysCommand - Handle WM_SYSCOMMAND message
81:    //
82:    void OnSysCommand(HWND hWnd, UINT cmd, int x, int y)
83: 9 0.1 {
84: 9 0.1 switch (cmd)
85:    {
86:    case IDM_HELP :
87: 0 0.0  WinHelp (hWnd, "WINHELP.HLP", HELP_INDEX, OL);
88: 0 0.0  break;
```

```
89:    case IDM_INDEXHELP :
90:  0 0.0  WinHelp (hWnd, "RMONITOR.HLP", HELP_INDEX, OL);
91:  0 0.0  break;
92:   case IDM_ABOUT :
93:    {
94:    DLGPROC lpProcAboutDlgProc;
95:
96:  1 0.0  lpProcAboutDlgProc = (DLGPROC) MakeProcInstance ((FARPROC) About,
hInst);
97:  1 0.0  DialogBox (hInst, "About", hWnd, lpProcAboutDlgProc);
98:  1 0.0  FreeProcInstance ((FARPROC) lpProcAboutDlgProc);
99:  1 0.0  break;
100:    }
101:
102:   case IDM_ALWAYSONTOP :
103:  0 0.0  if (bAlwaysOnTop)
104:    {
105:    CheckMenuItem (GetSystemMenu (hWnd, FALSE),
106:  0 0.0    IDM_ALWAYSONTOP, MF_UNCHECKED);
107:  0 0.0  SetWindowPos (hWnd, HWND_NOTOPMOST, 0, 0, 0, 0,
               SWP_NOMOVE | SWP_NOSIZE);
108:  0 0.0  bAlwaysOnTop = FALSE;
109:    }
110:   else
111:    {
112:    CheckMenuItem (GetSystemMenu (hWnd, FALSE),
113:  0 0.0    IDM_ALWAYSONTOP, MF_CHECKED);
114:  0 0.0  bAlwaysOnTop = TRUE;
115:  0 0.0  SetWindowPos (hWnd, HWND_TOPMOST, 0, 0, 0, 0,
               SWP_NOMOVE | SWP_NOSIZE);
116:    }
117:  0 0.0  break;
118:
119:   case IDM_SETUP :
120:    {
121:    DLGPROC lpfnSETUPMsgProc;
122:
123:  1 0.0  lpfnSETUPMsgProc = (DLGPROC) MakeProcInstance
               ((FARPROC) SETUPMsgProc, hInst);
124:  1 0.0  DialogBox (hInst, (LPSTR) "SETUP", hWnd, lpfnSETUPMsgProc);
125:  1 0.0  FreeProcInstance ((FARPROC) lpfnSETUPMsgProc);
126:    }
127:  1 0.0  break;
128:
129:   case IDM_SNAPSHOT :
```

```
130:  0 0.0  bSnapShot = TRUE;
131:  0 0.0  wSnapPctFreeUser = wPctFreeUser;
132:  0 0.0  wSnapPctFreeGDI = wPctFreeGDI;
133:  0 0.0  wSnapSizeUser = wSizeUser;
134:  0 0.0  wSnapSizeGDI = wSizeGDI;
135:  0 0.0  dwSnapSizeMem = dwGmemFree;
136:  0 0.0  wSizeGDIPrev = 0;
137:  0 0.0  break;
138:   case IDM_BOTH :
139:   case IDM_GDI :
140:   case IDM_USER :
141:  0 0.0  if (cmd == wMonitor)
142:  0 0.0  return;
143:   CheckMenuItem (GetSystemMenu (hWnd, FALSE),
144:  0 0.0  wMonitor, MF_UNCHECKED);
145:  0 0.0  wMonitor = cmd;
146:   CheckMenuItem (GetSystemMenu (hWnd, FALSE),
147:  0 0.0  wMonitor, MF_CHECKED);
148:  0 0.0  break;
149:
150:   default :
151:  7 0.0  FORWARD_WM_SYSCOMMAND (hWnd, cmd, x, y, DefWindowProc);
152:  7 0.0 }
153:  9 0.1 } // End of OnSysCommand
```

The function time profile reported that the most time was spent in the function On-Timer that processes the WM_TIMER message. One reason for this was that I let Resource Monitor run a while longer during this profile compared to the other profiles I ran. Let's take a look at the line count profile for this function to see its results.

```
  //-----------------------------------------------------------------------
157:   //
158:   // OnTimer - Handle WM_TIMER message
159:   //
160:   void OnTimer(HWND hWnd, UINT id)
161: 92 0.6 {
162: 92 0.6 GetSystemResources ();
163:
164: 92 0.6 if (Setup.nAlarmUser >= (int) wPctFreeUser)
165:    {
166:  1 0.0  KillTimer (hWnd, TIMER_ID);
167:  1 0.0  MessageBeep (0);
168:   MessageBox (hWnd, "Warning!\n"
169:   "User segment resources have dropped below alarm level!\n"
```

427

```
170:     "The alarm level has been reset 10 points below current level.",
171: 1 0.0  "ResMonitor Alarm", MB_ICONHAND | MB_SYSTEMMODAL);
172: 1 0.0  Setup.nAlarmUser = (int) wPctFreeUser - 10;
173:
174: 1 0.0  if (! SetTimer (hWnd, TIMER_ID, Setup.nSampleRate * 1000, NULL))
175:    {
176:    MessageBox (hWnd, "Too many timers in use!", "Resource Monitor Error!",
177: 0 0.0   MB_ICONEXCLAMATION | MB_OK);
178:    }
179:    }
180:
181: 92 0.6 if (Setup.nAlarmGDI >= (int) wPctFreeGDI)
182:    {
183: 1 0.0  KillTimer (hWnd, TIMER_ID);
184: 1 0.0  MessageBeep (0);
185:    MessageBox (hWnd, "Warning!\n"
186:     "GDI segment resources have dropped below alarm level!\n"
187:     "The alarm level has been reset 10 points below current level.",
188: 1 0.0  "ResMonitor Alarm", MB_ICONHAND | MB_SYSTEMMODAL);
189: 1 0.0  Setup.nAlarmGDI = (int) wPctFreeGDI - 10;
190:
191: 1 0.0  if (! SetTimer (hWnd, TIMER_ID, Setup.nSampleRate * 1000, NULL))
192:    {
193:    MessageBox (hWnd, "Too many timers in use!", "Resource Monitor Error!",
194: 0 0.0   MB_ICONEXCLAMATION | MB_OK);
195:    }
196:    }
197:
198: 92 0.6 if (Setup.lAlarmFreeMem >= (long) (dwGmemFree / 1024))
199:    {
200: 0 0.0  KillTimer (hWnd, TIMER_ID);
201: 0 0.0  MessageBeep (0);
202:    MessageBox (hWnd, "Warning! Free memory has dropped below alarm level\n"
203:     "The alarm level has been reset 256KB below current level.",
204: 0 0.0  "ResMonitor Alarm", MB_ICONHAND | MB_SYSTEMMODAL);
205: 0 0.0  Setup.lAlarmFreeMem = (long) (dwGmemFree / 1024) - 256;
206:
207: 0 0.0  if (! SetTimer (hWnd, TIMER_ID, Setup.nSampleRate * 1000, NULL))
208:    {
209:    MessageBox (hWnd, "Too many timers in use!", "Resource Monitor Error!",
210: 0 0.0   MB_ICONEXCLAMATION | MB_OK);
211:    }
212:    }
213:
```

```
214:      if ((wSizeUserPrev / 1024)!= (wSizeUser / 1024) ¦¦
215:      (wSizeGDIPrev / 1024) != (wSizeGDI / 1024)¦¦
216:      (dwSizeMemPrev / 1024) != (dwGmemFree / 1024)¦¦
217: 92 0.6  wFree != wFreePrev)
218:      {
219:      char szTemp [12];
220:
221: 16 0.1  wSizeUserPrev = wSizeUser;
222: 16 0.1  wSizeGDIPrev = wSizeGDI;
223: 16 0.1  wFreePrev = wFree;
224: 16 0.1  dwSizeMemPrev = dwGmemFree;
225:
226: 16 0.1  * szIconCaption = NULL;
227: 16 0.1  if (Setup.bProgramTitle)
228: 16 0.1    lstrcat (szIconCaption, "ResMonitor");
229:
230: 16 0.1  if (Setup.bUserSnapShot)
231:      {
232: 0 0.0    if (* szIconCaption != NULL)
233: 0 0.0     lstrcat (szIconCaption, ", SSU:");
234:      else
235: 0 0.0     lstrcat (szIconCaption, "SSU:");
236: 0 0.0    if (bSnapShot)
237:      {
238: 0 0.0     itoa (wPctFreeUser - wSnapPctFreeUser,
                   szIconCaption + lstrlen (szIconCaption), 10);
239: 0 0.0     lstrcat (szIconCaption, "%(");
240: 0 0.0     itoa (wSnapSizeUser - wSizeUser,
                   szIconCaption + lstrlen (szIconCaption), 10);
241: 0 0.0     lstrcat (szIconCaption, ")");
242:      }
243:      else
244: 0 0.0     lstrcat (szIconCaption, "None");
245:      }
246:
247: 16 0.1  if (Setup.bGDISnapShot)
248:      {
249: 0 0.0    if (* szIconCaption != NULL)
250: 0 0.0     lstrcat (szIconCaption, ", SSG:");
251:      else
252: 0 0.0     lstrcat (szIconCaption, "SSG:");
253: 0 0.0    if (bSnapShot)
254:      {
255:         itoa (wPctFreeGDI - wSnapPctFreeGDI,
256: 0 0.0      szIconCaption + lstrlen (szIconCaption), 10);
```

```
257:   0 0.0     lstrcat (szIconCaption, "%(");
258:         itoa (wSnapSizeGDI - wSizeGDI,
259:   0 0.0     szIconCaption + lstrlen (szIconCaption), 10);
260:   0 0.0     lstrcat (szIconCaption, ")");
261:       }
262:     else
263:   0 0.0     lstrcat (szIconCaption, "None");
264:     }
265:
266: 16 0.1   if (Setup.bMemSnapShot)
267:     {
268:     char buf[16];
269:   0 0.0   if (* szIconCaption != NULL)
270:   0 0.0     lstrcat (szIconCaption, ", SSM:");
271:     else
272:   0 0.0     lstrcat (szIconCaption, "SSM:");
273:   0 0.0   if (bSnapShot)
274:       {
275:       ltoCommaDelimitedString ((LONG)(dwGmemFree - dwSnapSizeMem) / 1024,
276:   0 0.0     buf, sizeof (buf));
277:   0 0.0     lstrcat (szIconCaption, buf);
278:   0 0.0     lstrcat (szIconCaption, "K");
279:       }
280:     else
281:   0 0.0     lstrcat (szIconCaption, "None");
282:     }
283:
284: 16 0.1   if (Setup.bPctFreeUser)
285:     {
286:   0 0.0     if (* szIconCaption != NULL)
287:   0 0.0       lstrcat (szIconCaption, ", U:");
288:     else
289:   0 0.0       lstrcat (szIconCaption, "U:");
290:   0 0.0     itoa (wPctFreeUser, szIconCaption + lstrlen (szIconCaption), 10);
291:   0 0.0     lstrcat (szIconCaption, "%");
292:     }
293:
294: 16 0.1   if (Setup.bPctFreeGDI)
295:     {
296:   0 0.0     if (* szIconCaption != NULL)
297:   0 0.0       lstrcat (szIconCaption, ", G:");
298:       else
299:   0 0.0       lstrcat (szIconCaption, "G:");
300:   0 0.0     itoa (wPctFreeGDI, szIconCaption + lstrlen (szIconCaption), 10);
301:   0 0.0     lstrcat (szIconCaption, "%");
```

```
302:    }
303:
304: 16 0.1  if (Setup.bSizeUser)
305:    {
306:  0 0.0   if (* szIconCaption != NULL)
307:  0 0.0    lstrcat (szIconCaption, ", SizeU:");
308:    else
309:  0 0.0    lstrcat (szIconCaption, "SizeU:");
310:  0 0.0   itoa (wSizeUser, szIconCaption + lstrlen (szIconCaption), 10);
311:    }
312:
313: 16 0.1  if (Setup.bSizeGDI)
314:    {
315:  0 0.0   if (* szIconCaption != NULL)
316:  0 0.0    lstrcat (szIconCaption, ", SizeG:");
317:    else
318:  0 0.0    lstrcat (szIconCaption, "SizeG:");
319:  0 0.0   itoa (wSizeGDI, szIconCaption + lstrlen (szIconCaption), 10);
320:    }
321:
322: 16 0.1  if (Setup.bSizeFreeMem)
323:    {
324:    char buf[16];
325:
326:  0 0.0   if (* szIconCaption != NULL)
327:  0 0.0    lstrcat (szIconCaption, ", SizeFM:");
328:     else
329:  0 0.0    lstrcat (szIconCaption, "SizeFM:");
330:  0 0.0   ltoCommaDelimitedString (dwGmemFree / 1024, buf, sizeof (buf));
331:
332:  0 0.0   lstrcat (szIconCaption, buf);
333:  0 0.0   lstrcat (szIconCaption, "K");
334:    }
335: 16 0.1  if (lstrlen (szIconCaption) > 60)
336:    MessageBox (NULL, "The window caption you created exceeds "
337:     "60 characters. Windows cannot display "
338:     "all of the window caption. I suggest you "
339:     "limit the number of your selections.",
340:  0 0.0   NULL, MB_ICONHAND);
341:
342: 16 0.1  InvalidateRect (hWnd, NULL, TRUE);
343:    }
344: 92 0.6  } // End of OnTimer
```

Looking at OnTimer's code, I can see at least one way to improve its speed. OnTimer was called once from OnCreate to initialize itself and 91 times to process a WM_TIMER message. In its first part, OnTimer checks to see if an alarm should go off for low memory, low GDI system resources, and low User system resources. After this is done, OnTimer checks to see if there has been a change in system resources before doing any more processing. If there was no change, none of the following code block is executed. In addition to other optimization, moving the alarm checks inside the program block that gets executed only when the system resources change would improve the function's speed.

As you can see from this listing, I should have spotted this problem earlier by just reading my own source code. What profiler output does is point out where source code can be rearranged and sped up by showing you exactly where your source code is executed and how many times it was executed.

Profiling Only One Function

Resource Monitor is a small program where it's easy and fast to do a full line count profile of the program. But when programs get larger, line count profiles take longer. When I did a full line count profile on DumpIT, I noticed that execution speed was slowed down considerably—and DumpIT is not a large program.

As we discussed before, you should run the following series of profiles to test your program:

- A function time profile.
- A function count profile.
- A line time profile for all or part of your program.
- A line count profile for all or part of your program.

If your program is not large, go ahead and do full line count and line time profiles. If your program is large, you may want to do function count and function time profiles to identify potential problem areas and do line count and time profiles only for specific functions.

So you can see how to set up and execute a line count profile for just one function, let's go through the steps that would need to be done to profile the OnTimer function in RMONITOR.C.

1. To profile one or more functions using the Source Profiler, you need to create a Profiler Command File (.PCF). The .PCF is a text file that you specify when PREP.EXE is called. The syntax for the .PCF commands is listed in Appendix B of Microsoft's Source Profiler User Guide. The commands needed to profile OnTimer are:

```
LPROFILE COUNT
PROGRAM RMONITOR.EXE DELETE
OBJECT RMONITOR.OBJ
FUNCTION OnTimer
```

LPROFILE specifies that this is a line count profile. PROGRAM identifies the program to be profiled. Using the DELETE option tells the profiler to include only specified functions in the profiles. By default, all functions and the lines within them are profiled. OBJECT specifies the .OBJ file. FUNCTION specifies the function to profile.

2. Use the PREP.EXE command line the first time you execute the .PCF file:

```
PREP /LC /P RMONITOR.EXE /OT RMONITOR.PBT /OI RMONITOR.OI
RMONITOR.PCF
```

3. Execute PROFILEW from the DOS command line or Program Manager. From the DOS command line, you would type in

```
WX PROFILEW RMONITOR
```

4. Use the LCOUNTW2.BAT file I created to produce the profile reports. The following listing shows the contents of this BAT file:

```
@echo off
prep /it %1.pbt /io %1.pbo /ot %1.pbt
plist /T %1.pbt > %1.tab
plist /sl %1.pbt > %1.out
del %1.pbo
del %1.pbi
```

Now that you have seen how to use the Microsoft Source Profiler, let's look at how Turbo Profiler works and how it can be used to profile Resource Monitor.

Borland's Turbo Profiler

Prior to the release of Borland C++ 3.0, the Borland C++ compiler did not offer optimizations that could compare to the Microsoft compiler. The only option Borland offered for optimizations was Turbo Profiler, an interactive profiler that works like a debugger. However, Turbo Profiler was regarded so highly that often in reviews of Borland C++ it was mentioned that the profiler offset the need for an optimizing compiler.

Both Borland C++ 3.0 and 3.1 are optimizing compilers. The optimizations Borland C++ 3.1 provides match those found in Microsoft C/C++ 7.0. Turbo Profiler 2.1 is an excellent profiler with a well-regarded reputation and is included with all Borland-language products: Borland C++, Turbo C++ for Windows, Turbo Assembler, and Turbo Pascal for Windows.

Using Turbo Profiler for Windows (TPROFW) you can profile your Windows application and access not only the typical profile information but also messages received and sent by the application, a complete list of modules loaded by Windows, and DLL profile information. TPROFW runs in Standard or 386 Enhanced mode and requires at least an 80286 with 1MB of memory.

TPROFW can run in three different configurations. Each configuration has its strong and weak points:

- Using a single-monitor configuration is the easiest way to use TPROFW. All you need to do is execute TPROFW and you are up and running. TPROFW runs in a mode similar to both Turbo Debugger for Windows and CodeView for Windows on either a dual-monitor system or in a full-screen DOS window in a Windows environment. All three of these applications are Windows programs, but they all use a DOS character-mode display that takes up the entire screen. To run TPROFW in this mode, you must put up with screen-flashing when it switches it back and forth between the DOS and Windows screens.

- Using two PCs attached by a serial cable or a NETBIOS-compatible LAN lets you run the profiler on one PC and Windows on another. This method is supposed to be the least obtrusive for testing your program, because the profiler and your application don't need to be in memory together. This configuration is tricky to set up and can be very slow to work with. When I tried using this setup, I could only run the connection at 19,200 baud. This is a slow and awkward way to profile a Windows application. I would try this method only when everything else fails.

- Using a dual-monitor system allows you to view the TPROFW screens on one monitor and your Windows application on another. However, this configuration requires extra hardware and takes some time to set up. In some cases, your current video board may not work with an extra MDA adapter in your system. If your system is an IBM PS/2, it must be configured with an 8514/a monitor as the primary monitor and a VGA as the secondary monitor—a very expensive setup. To learn how to set this configuration up, you should refer to "Setting Up CodeView for Windows" in Chapter 9. That section explains how to set up a secondary-monitor system that will work with TPROFW, Turbo Debugger for Windows, and CodeView for Windows. Although it costs more and takes more time to set up, this configuration is the preferable way to use all three programs. It's much nicer to see both your profiler (or debugger) and your Windows application at the same time. You also avoid the annoying screen-flashing you have to put up with when you use a single monitor.

Using the TPROFW Environment

If you are already familiar with Turbo Debugger for Windows, you will not have any trouble understanding TPROFW's user interface. TPROFW operates in a similar way to Turbo Debugger for Windows—it has global menus, local menus, and dialog boxes.

The dialog boxes within TPROFW are similar to the modal dialog boxes in a Microsoft Windows application. They contain buttons, check boxes, radio buttons, edit boxes, and list boxes. When you are in one of these dialog boxes, the global menus and windows of TPROFW are not accessible.

The menu bar works in a way similar to a Windows application menu bar, listing the available menus. Borland terminology refers to menu bar menus as global menus. Like most Windows applications, the TPROFW menu bar contains a File menu and a Help menu.

Whenever you work with TPROFW, you'll probably have a number of different windows open on the desktop. You can move, size, and close these windows at random with either a mouse or the keyboard in a manner similar to moving and sizing a window in Windows.

There are some differences, however, between Windows and the text-based TPROFW application. For example, TPROFW must be run full-screen. When you size a window, it must be grabbed in the lower-right corner—you can't size it using any other corner or side.

Using Local Menus

In addition to the menu bar menus (global menus), TPROFW has a convenient feature that reduces program complexity by reducing the number of menus. To understand how this works, you must realize that Borland products are context-sensitive. Besides TPROFW, Turbo Debugger for Windows, the Borland C++ IDE, and Quattro Pro work the same way.

TPROFW keeps track of which window you have open and which part of the window the mouse pointer and text caret are in. In other words, TPROFW is always aware of what object you are working with, and its local menus are tailored to that particular object. You display a local menu by clicking the right mouse button or pressing Alt+F10. Figure 8.7 shows a TPROFW local menu.

Starting TPROFW

Now that you have a feel for how the TPROFW user interface works, let's see how it can be used to profile the Resource Monitor application that we profiled with Microsoft Source Profiler in the first section of this chapter. To start TPROFW on a single-monitor system, you execute it as you would any other Windows application, by double-clicking on its icon in the Borland C++ 3.1 Program Manager group. If you have a secondary monitor set up and want to use TPROFW with it, you should alter the way TPROFW is called by adding a command line option of "-do." This is the same command line option required to run Turbo Debugger for Windows on a dual-monitor system.

TIP

You might want to consider setting up a Program Manager icon for each application you are profiling with TPROFW. To do this, copy the Program Manager icon for TPROFW by dragging it with the mouse while holding down the Ctrl key. After you have made a copy of the icon, display the Properties dialog box by choosing Properties in the File menu or by holding down the Alt key and double-clicking on the application icon in the Program Manager window. After the Properties dialog box is displayed, type in the following in the Command Line edit box: TPROFW.EXE -DO [program name]. You put the name of your program in the specified field. This command is also set up for using a dual-monitor system. Now all your options are set up and your program name is specified. All you need to do to start profiling your application is double-click on the icon. You can use this same method for debugging applications with Turbo Debugger for Windows.

After starting TPROFW you will see the two windows shown in Figure 8.6. The top one is the Module window that displays your program source code. The bottom one is the Execution Profile window. You use the Module window to specify how you want your program profiled.

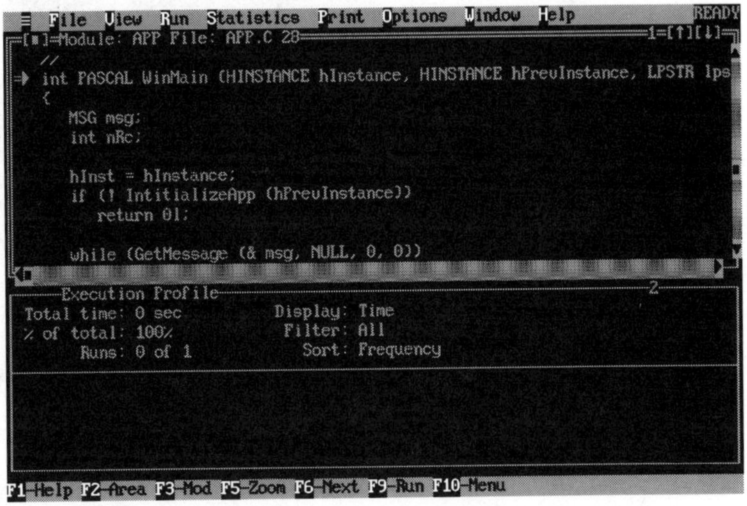

FIGURE 8.6:

The Turbo Profiler for Windows environment

Preparing Your Program for Profiling

The Module window displays the contents of the source file you are profiling. Most of your time in the profiler is spent within the Module window. You use the Module window to view your application's source code and to specify how you want your program profiled. All of the tasks you do in the Module window can be accessed through its local menu (Figure 8.7). For example:

- To move through your source code or to look for a specific function name or variable, use Line, Search, Next, or Goto.

- To specify what you want to be profiled, choose Add Areas.

- To specify what you don't want profiled, choose Remove Areas.

- To specify options for profiling your application, choose Operation.

- To specify whether or not you want TPROFW to keep track of which function calls which, choose Callers.

FIGURE 8.7:

A TPROFW local menu

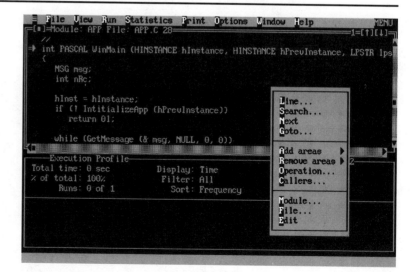

438

- To open a source code module or to specify another executable or DLL to profile, choose Module or File.

- To open a text file for editing, choose Edit.

Specifying Window Messages

After you choose Operation, the Area Options dialog box shown in Figure 8.8 is displayed.

This dialog box is your gateway to the even more important Windows Procedure Messages dialog box. You get there by selecting the Window Procedures check box in the Area Options dialog box and clicking on the Messages push button. Using the Windows Procedure Messages dialog box, you select which messages and classes you want to track for a window procedure. For Resource Monitor I selected the window classes for Mouse, Window, Input, and System. I was primarily interested in the message WM_TIMER to see how the OnTimer function performs. The Windows Procedure Messages dialog box is shown in Figure 8.9.

FIGURE 8.8:

The Area Options dialog box

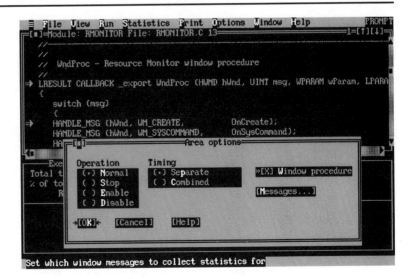

FIGURE 8.9:

The Windows Procedure Messages dialog box

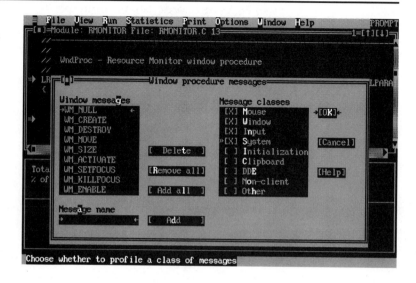

By default all message classes are selected in this dialog box. The Window Messages list box displays any or all messages that you want to follow. To add all messages, select the Add All push button. Since this adds more messages to the list box than TPROFW allows by default, you must select the Profiling Options command from the Statistics menu and change the Max Window Messages edit box to 150 or more. This causes the program to be reloaded into memory so the new area count takes effect. I suggest you do this when you first invoke TPROFW.

> **NOTE**
>
> TPROFW tracks only messages that begin with WM_. If you want to track other messages, you must use the Windows message number from the WINDOWS.H header file.

Viewing Source Code Modules

To view a source code module, choose Module from the local menu. The dialog box that's displayed shows you a list of source modules and a list of DLLs and .EXEs already loaded by Windows, as shown in Figure 8.10.

FIGURE 8.10:

The TPROFW Load Module
dialog box

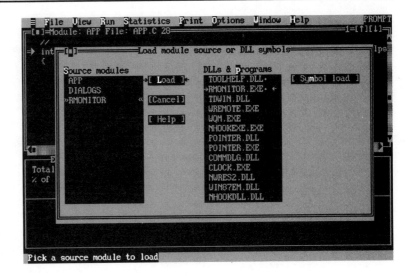

Keeping Up with Callers

Besides profiling your application, TPROFW will keep track of which function
called which function during profiling. Although this information will not help you
identify areas of your program that need optimizing, it will help you understand
how an application works. This can be particularly helpful if you are working on
an application that you didn't write. Using the Callers feature you can profile a
Windows application and create a map of how all the functions in it interact.

Adding Areas

By default, TPROFW is set up to perform an active profile of your Windows application using both timing and counting on a function level. To prevent parts of
your program from being profiled, choose Remove Areas from the local menu. To
add parts of your program to be profiled, choose Add Areas, as shown in Figure 8.11.

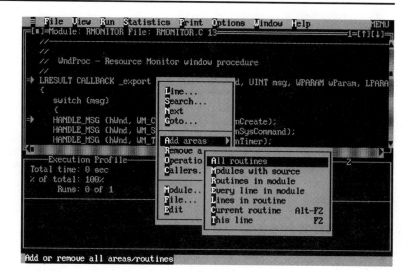

Choosing this menu command displays a cascading menu where you can choose what you want added to your program profile.

- *All Routines* (function) is the default.

- *Modules with Source* adds all the source code module functions that have debugging information included in them.

- *Routines in Module* adds all the functions in the current module displayed in the Module window.

- *Every Line in Module* adds all the lines in the current module displayed in the Module window.

- *Lines in Routine* adds all the lines in the current function displayed in the Module window.

- *Current Routine* adds the current function displayed in the Module window.

- *This Line* adds the current line displayed in the Module window.

Notice the arrows in the left margin of the module windows. These arrows mark the source code lines that will be profiled in your application. They change as you add and delete areas using the Module window local menu. Figure 8.12 shows the function OnTimer in the Module window after I specified that all lines in the routine were to be added to the profile.

Profiling Your Application

After you have specified in the Module window how you want your application to be profiled, it's time to execute the profile. Choose the Run command from the Run menu. The screen flashes and you are returned to the Windows graphical environment. After your application has started execution, it's time to exercise all the features you want to profile. After you have finished, exit your application; you are returned to TPROFW.

When TPROFW returns, you are going to see that the Execution Profile window has additional information within its lower display area, as shown in Figure 8.13.

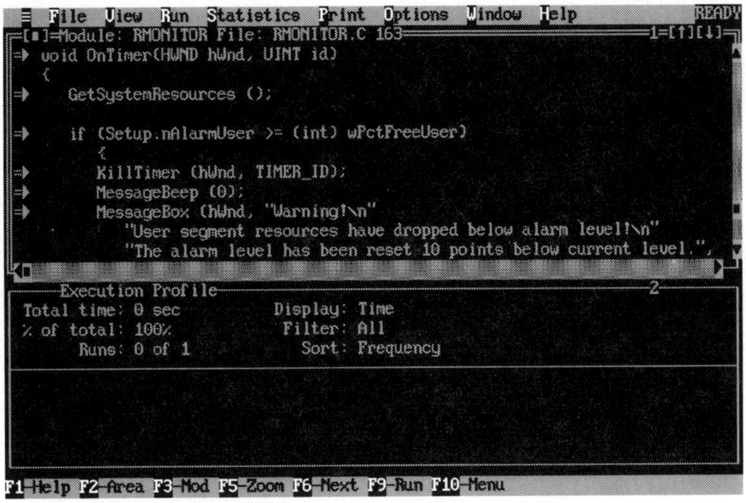

FIGURE 8.12:

The OnTimer function with arrows indicating which lines will be profiled

FIGURE 8.13:

The TPROFW Execution Profile window

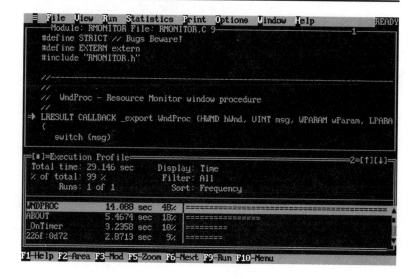

Evaluating Profile Information

The Execution Profile window displays statistical information about the application after the program has run. The window contains one pane divided into two display areas. The top display area contains the following information:

- The total time your application was executing.

- The percentage of the total time that is represented by the statistics displayed in the bottom area of the window.

- The display type: time, counts, or time and counts.

- Thee filter. You can filter what's displayed by specifying all the information that's been collected or only the information for a specific module.

- The sort order. You can sort the information displayed by frequency (high to low), name, or address.

The bottom area contains the actual statistics. Figure 8.13 shows the default timing statistics for Resource Monitor. Figure 8.14 shows the counting statistics for the profile operation in the Execution Profile window.

FIGURE 8.14:

The counting statistics for the profile of Resource Monitor

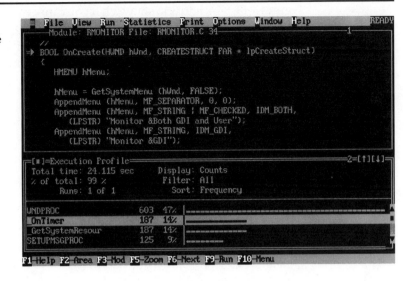

The statistics in the bottom area of the Execution Profile window pane can show the following information:

- The area's name or line number (shown in Figures 8.13 and 8.14).

- The number of times program control entered this area (shown in Figures 8.13 and 8.14).

- The percentage of the total calls for all marked areas (shown in Figure 8.13).

- The count magnitude bar (shown in Figure 8.13).

- The time spent in each marked area (shown in Figure 8.14).

- The percentage of the total execution time for all marked areas (shown in Figure 8.14).

- The time magnitude bar (shown in Figure 8.14).

To switch to the counting statistics shown in Figure 8.14, click the right mouse button in the Execution Profile window to display the local menu and choose Display to show the Display Options dialog box, as shown in Figure 8.15. This figure also shows what happens when you select Both in the Display Options dialog box to show both timing and counting statistics in the Execution Profile window.

Figures 8.13, 8.14, and 8.15 show what you can see when you run TPROFW, but they
don't show all the data that's available by scrolling the window. You can print this
information to a printer or a file by choosing Statistics from the TPROFW Print
menu. The following listing shows the information from the Timings profile of
Resource Monitor:

```
Program: E:\ATOOLS\RMONITOR\RMONITOR.EXE

Execution Profile
Total time: 436.39 sec
% of total: 0 %
  Run: 1 of 1

 Filter: All
 Show: Time
 Sort: Frequency

WNDPROC   425.30 sec 97% |*****************************************
_OnSysCommand 5.8584 sec 1% |
_OnTimer   2.3838 sec <1% |
_GetSystemResour 1.9439 sec <1% |
_PaintIcon   0.2241 sec <1% |
_OnDestroy   0.1169 sec <1% |
_OnCreate   0.0019 sec <1% |
```

FIGURE 8.15:

The Display Options dialog box with
both time and counting statistics
displayed in the Execution Profile
window

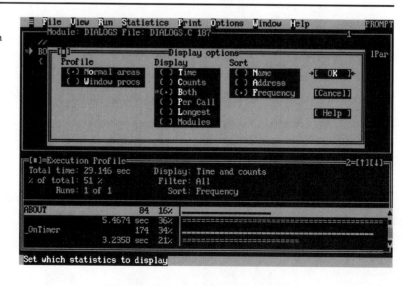

```
_ltoCommaDelimit 0.0001 sec <1% |
_OnPaint  0.0000 sec <1% |
_OnMove   0.0000 sec <1% |
_OnSize   0.0000 sec <1% |
```

Notice in the previous listing how WndProc and OnSysCommand took most of the time. OnTimer was next, but it took less that 1 percent of the processing time. The next listing shows the Count profile information from running Resource Monitor.

```
Program: E:\ATOOLS\RMONITOR\RMONITOR.EXE

Execution Profile
Total time: 436.39 sec
% of total: 0 %
  Run: 1 of 1

 Filter: All
 Show: Counts
 Sort: Frequency

WNDPROC    1027 52% |++++++++++++++++++++++++++++++++++++++++++++++++
_OnTimer    410 21% |+++++++++++++++++++
_GetSystemResour  410 21% |+++++++++++++++++++
_ltoCommaDelimit   48 2% |++
_OnPaint     18 <1% |
_OnSysCommand  13 <1% |
_PaintIcon    6 <1% |
_OnMove      5 <1% |
_OnSize      3 <1% |
_OnDestroy    1 <1% |
_OnCreate     1 <1% |
```

The Count listing shows that OnTimer had 21 percent of the Resource Monitor count hits, even though it consumed less that 1 percent of the processor time. The next listing shows both Counting and Timing profile information combined.

```
Program: E:\ATOOLS\RMONITOR\RMONITOR.EXE

Execution Profile
Total time: 436.39 sec
% of total: 0 %
  Run: 1 of 1

 Filter: All
 Show: Time and counts
```

```
Sort: Frequency  Pass count: +++ Time: ***

WNDPROC     1027 52% |+++++++++++++++++++++++++++++++++++++++++++++++++
         425.30 sec 97% |*************************************************
_OnSysCommand 13 <1% |
         5.8584 sec 1% |**********************
_OnTimer     410 21% |+++++++++++++++++
         2.3838 sec <1% |*********
_GetSystemResour 410 21% |+++++++++++++++++
         1.9439 sec <1% |*******
_PaintIcon    6 <1% |
         0.2241 sec <1% |
_OnDestroy    1 <1% |
         0.1169 sec <1% |
_OnCreate     1 <1% |
         0.0019 sec <1% |
_ltoCommaDelimit 48 2% |++
         0.0001 sec <1% |
_OnPaint     18 <1% |
         0.0000 sec <1% |
_OnMove       5 <1% |
         0.0000 sec <1% |
_OnSize       3 <1% |
         0.0000 sec <1% |
```

The Counting and Timing display is very convenient because it lets you see both types of profile information on the same display or page. You can also get this combined information using the Microsoft Source Profiler Function Time report.

The next listing shows the Statistics report when I turned on line counting for all lines in the RMONITOR.C module and did a profile of Resource Monitor. This is the same information that you would see displayed in the Execution Profile window after adding a module's lines as a profile area.

```
Program: E:\ATOOLS\RMONITOR\RMONITOR.EXE

Execution Profile
Total time: 53.340 sec
% of total: 31 %
  Run: 1 of 1

  Filter: All
```

```
Show: Time
Sort: Frequency

#RMONITOR#25   43.765 sec 82% |***********************************
#RMONITOR#151  5.6618 sec 10% |*****
#RMONITOR#23   0.7006 sec 1% |
#RMONITOR#591  0.6321 sec 1% |
WNDPROC   0.6124 sec 1% |
#RMONITOR#11   0.3897 sec <1% |
#RMONITOR#757  0.1551 sec <1% |
#RMONITOR#124  0.1011 sec <1% |
#RMONITOR#746  0.0880 sec <1% |
#RMONITOR#97   0.0778 sec <1% |
#RMONITOR#716  0.0769 sec <1% |
#RMONITOR#639  0.0623 sec <1% |
#RMONITOR#750  0.0562 sec <1% |
#RMONITOR#217  0.0560 sec <1% |
#RMONITOR#224  0.0557 sec <1% |
#RMONITOR#366  0.0557 sec <1% |
#RMONITOR#362  0.0554 sec <1% |
_PaintIcon   0.0553 sec <1% |
#RMONITOR#684  0.0553 sec <1% |
#RMONITOR#361  0.0552 sec <1% |
#RMONITOR#631  0.0072 sec <1% |
#RMONITOR#592  0.0047 sec <1% |
#RMONITOR#595  0.0043 sec <1% |
#RMONITOR#656  0.0037 sec <1% |
#RMONITOR#664  0.0032 sec <1% |
#RMONITOR#665  0.0017 sec <1% |
#RMONITOR#342  0.0010 sec <1% |
#RMONITOR#36   0.0010 sec <1% |
#RMONITOR#770  0.0010 sec <1% |
#RMONITOR#198  0.0009 sec <1% |
#RMONITOR#628  0.0008 sec <1% |
207f:1210   0.0007 sec <1% |
#RMONITOR#19   0.0006 sec <1% |
#RMONITOR#747  0.0006 sec <1% |
#RMONITOR#16   0.0006 sec <1% |
#RMONITOR#344  0.0006 sec <1% |
#RMONITOR#611  0.0005 sec <1% |
#RMONITOR#250  0.0005 sec <1% |
#RMONITOR#769  0.0005 sec <1% |
#RMONITOR#14   0.0004 sec <1% |
#RMONITOR#745  0.0004 sec <1% |
#RMONITOR#773  0.0003 sec <1% |
```

```
#RMONITOR#748 0.0003 sec <1% |
#RMONITOR#775 0.0003 sec <1% |
#RMONITOR#15  0.0003 sec <1% |
#RMONITOR#601 0.0003 sec <1% |
#RMONITOR#759 0.0002 sec <1% |
#RMONITOR#57  0.0002 sec <1% |
#RMONITOR#661 0.0001 sec <1% |
#RMONITOR#629 0.0001 sec <1% |
#RMONITOR#749 0.0001 sec <1% |
```

Although this information is helpful, it would be nicer if you could see the program lines that went with each line of statistics. You can tile the Module window and the Execution Profile window vertically to match up this information. However, an easier way to view the information is to choose Module in the Print menu and print out your source code with the profile statistics included with it, as shown in the following listing.

```
Program: E:\ATOOLS\RMONITOR\RMONITOR.EXE File E:\ATOOLS\RMONITOR\RMONITOR.C


Time Counts
    #define STRICT // Bugs Beware!
    #define EXTERN extern
    #include "RMONITOR.h"
    //-----------------------------------------------------------
    //
    // WndProc - Resource Monitor window procedure
    //
0.2796 714 LRESULT CALLBACK _export WndProc (HWND hWnd, UINT msg, WPARAM wPar
    {
0.0581 714  switch (msg)
    {
0.0000 1   HANDLE_MSG (hWnd, WM_CREATE,  OnCreate);
0.0000 9   HANDLE_MSG (hWnd, WM_SYSCOMMAND, OnSysCommand);
0.0010 82  HANDLE_MSG (hWnd, WM_TIMER,   OnTimer);
0.0552 27  HANDLE_MSG (hWnd, WM_PAINT,   OnPaint);
0.0000 2   HANDLE_MSG (hWnd, WM_MOVE,  OnMove);
0.0000 2   HANDLE_MSG (hWnd, WM_SIZE,  OnSize);
0.0000 1   HANDLE_MSG (hWnd, WM_DESTROY,  OnDestroy);
0 0   HANDLE_MSG (hWnd, WM_QUERYENDSESSION, OnQueryEndSession);

    default:
0.8839 590  return DefWindowProc (hWnd, msg, wParam, lParam) ;
    }
```

```
72.408 714 }

    //------------------------------------------------------------
    //
    // OnCreate - Handle WM_CREATE message
    //
0.0000 1 BOOL OnCreate(HWND hWnd, CREATESTRUCT FAR * lpCreateStruct)
    {
    HMENU hMenu;
0.0017 1  hMenu = GetSystemMenu (hWnd, FALSE);
0.0000 1  AppendMenu (hMenu, MF_SEPARATOR, 0, 0);
0.0000 1  AppendMenu (hMenu, MF_STRING | MF_CHECKED, IDM_BOTH,
    (LPSTR) "Monitor &Both GDI and User");
0.0000 1  AppendMenu (hMenu, MF_STRING, IDM_GDI,
    (LPSTR) "Monitor &GDI");
0.0000 1  AppendMenu (hMenu, MF_STRING, IDM_USER,
    (LPSTR) "Monitor &User");
0.0000 1  AppendMenu (hMenu, MF_SEPARATOR, 0, 0);
0.0000 1  AppendMenu (hMenu, MF_STRING, IDM_SNAPSHOT,
    (LPSTR) "Take &SnapShot");
0.0007 1  AppendMenu (hMenu, MF_STRING, IDM_SETUP,
    (LPSTR) "Resource Monitor Setup...");
0.0000 1  if (bAlwaysOnTop)
    {
0 0  AppendMenu (hMenu, MF_STRING | MF_CHECKED, IDM_ALWAYSONTOP,
    (LPSTR) "&Always On Top");
0 0  SetWindowPos (hWnd, HWND_TOPMOST, 0, 0, 0, 0, SWP_NOMOVE | S
0 0  }
    else
0.0000 1  AppendMenu (hMenu, MF_STRING, IDM_ALWAYSONTOP,
    (LPSTR) "&Always On Top");
0.0000 1  AppendMenu (hMenu, MF_SEPARATOR, 0, 0);
0.0000 1  AppendMenu (hMenu, MF_STRING, IDM_HELP,
    (LPSTR) "Help for Help");
0.0000 1  AppendMenu (hMenu, MF_STRING, IDM_INDEXHELP,
    (LPSTR) "Help for ResourceMonitor");
0.0000 1  AppendMenu (hMenu, MF_STRING, IDM_ABOUT,
    (LPSTR) "About ResourceMonitor...");
0.0000 1  if (! SetTimer (hWnd, TIMER_ID, Setup.nSampleRate * 1000, NULL)
    {
0 0  MessageBox (hWnd, "Too many timers in use!", "Resource Monit
    MB_ICONEXCLAMATION | MB_OK);
    }
0.0000 1  OnTimer (hWnd, 0);
0.0000 1  return TRUE;
```

```
0.0000 1 } // End of OnCreate


    //-------------------------------------------------------------
    //
    // OnSysCommand - Handle WM_SYSCOMMAND message
    //
0.0000 9 void OnSysCommand(HWND hWnd, UINT cmd, int x, int y)
    {
0.0000 9  switch (cmd)
    {
    case IDM_HELP :
0 0  WinHelp (hWnd, "WINHELP.HLP", HELP_INDEX, OL);
0 0  break;
    case IDM_INDEXHELP :
0 0  WinHelp (hWnd, "RMONITOR.HLP", HELP_INDEX, OL);
    break;
    case IDM_ABOUT :
    {
    DLGPROC lpProcAboutDlgProc;

0.0000 1  lpProcAboutDlgProc = (DLGPROC) MakeProcInstance ((FARPROC) A
0.0206 1  DialogBox (hInst, "About", hWnd, lpProcAboutDlgProc);
0.0000 1  FreeProcInstance ((FARPROC) lpProcAboutDlgProc);
0.0000 1  break;
    }

    case IDM_ALWAYSONTOP :
0 0  if (bAlwaysOnTop)
    {
0 0   CheckMenuItem (GetSystemMenu (hWnd, FALSE),
     IDM_ALWAYSONTOP, MF_UNCHECKED);
0 0   SetWindowPos (hWnd, HWND_NOTOPMOST, 0, 0, 0, 0, SWP_NOMOV
0 0  bAlwaysOnTop = FALSE;
0 0  }
    else
    {
0 0   CheckMenuItem (GetSystemMenu (hWnd, FALSE),
     IDM_ALWAYSONTOP, MF_CHECKED);
0 0   bAlwaysOnTop = TRUE;
0 0   SetWindowPos (hWnd, HWND_TOPMOST, 0, 0, 0, 0, SWP_NOMOVE
    }
0 0  break;
    case IDM_SETUP :
    {
```

```
      DLGPROC lpfnSETUPMsgProc;

0.0000 1   lpfnSETUPMsgProc = (DLGPROC) MakeProcInstance ((FARPROC) SET
0.0525 1   DialogBox (hInst, (LPSTR) "SETUP", hWnd, lpfnSETUPMsgProc);
0.0000 1   FreeProcInstance ((FARPROC) lpfnSETUPMsgProc);
        }
0.0000 1   break;
      case IDM_SNAPSHOT :
0 0   bSnapShot = TRUE;
0 0   wSnapPctFreeUser = wPctFreeUser;
0 0   wSnapPctFreeGDI = wPctFreeGDI;
0 0   wSnapSizeUser = wSizeUser;
0 0   wSnapSizeGDI = wSizeGDI;
0 0   dwSnapSizeMem = dwGmemFree;
0 0   wSizeGDIPrev = 0;
0 0   break;
      case IDM_BOTH :
      case IDM_GDI :
      case IDM_USER :
0 0   if (cmd == wMonitor)
0 0    return;
0 0   CheckMenuItem (GetSystemMenu (hWnd, FALSE),
      wMonitor, MF_UNCHECKED);
0 0   wMonitor = cmd;
0 0   CheckMenuItem (GetSystemMenu (hWnd, FALSE),
      wMonitor, MF_CHECKED);
0 0   break;

      default :
5.1152 7   FORWARD_WM_SYSCOMMAND (hWnd, cmd, x, y, DefWindowProc);
      }
0.0000 9  } // End of OnSysCommand

   //------------------------------------------------------------------
   //
   // OnTimer - Handle WM_TIMER message
   //
0.0000 83   void OnTimer(HWND hWnd, UINT id)
   {
0.0000 83   GetSystemResources ();
0.0000 83   if (Setup.nAlarmUser >= (int) wPctFreeUser)
   {
0.0000 1   KillTimer (hWnd, TIMER_ID);
0.1027 1   MessageBeep (0);
1.3160 1   MessageBox (hWnd, "Warning!\n"
```

```
              "User segment resources have dropped below alarm level!\n
              "The alarm level has been reset 10 points below current l
              "ResMonitor Alarm", MB_ICONHAND ¦ MB_SYSTEMMODAL);
0.0000 1   Setup.nAlarmUser = (int) wPctFreeUser - 10;
0.0000 1   if (! SetTimer (hWnd, TIMER_ID, Setup.nSampleRate * 1000, NU
           {
0 0   MessageBox (hWnd, "Too many timers in use!", "Resource Mo
           MB_ICONEXCLAMATION ¦ MB_OK);
           }
           }
0.0016 83  if (Setup.nAlarmGDI >= (int) wPctFreeGDI)
           {
0.0000 1   KillTimer (hWnd, TIMER_ID);
0.0781 1   MessageBeep (0);
1.4209 1   MessageBox (hWnd, "Warning!\n"
              "GDI segment resources have dropped below alarm level
              "The alarm level has been reset 10 points below current l
              "ResMonitor Alarm", MB_ICONHAND ¦ MB_SYSTEMMODAL);
0.0000 1   Setup.nAlarmGDI = (int) wPctFreeGDI - 10;
0.0000 1   if (! SetTimer (hWnd, TIMER_ID, Setup.nSampleRate * 1000, NU
           {
0 0   MessageBox (hWnd, "Too many timers in use!", "Resource Mo
           MB_ICONEXCLAMATION ¦ MB_OK);
           }
           }
0.0008 83  if (Setup.lAlarmFreeMem >= (long) (dwGmemFree / 1024))
           {
0 0   KillTimer (hWnd, TIMER_ID);
0 0   MessageBeep (0);
0 0   MessageBox (hWnd, "Warning! Free memory has dropped below al
              "The alarm level has been reset 256KB below current level
              "ResMonitor Alarm", MB_ICONHAND ¦ MB_SYSTEMMODAL);
0 0   Setup.lAlarmFreeMem = (long) (dwGmemFree / 1024) - 256;
0 0   if (! SetTimer (hWnd, TIMER_ID, Setup.nSampleRate * 1000, NU
           {
0 0   MessageBox (hWnd, "Too many timers in use!", "Resource Mo
           MB_ICONEXCLAMATION ¦ MB_OK);
           }
           }
0.0013 83  if ((wSizeUserPrev / 1024)!= (wSizeUser / 1024) ¦¦
           (wSizeGDIPrev / 1024) != (wSizeGDI / 1024)¦¦
           (dwSizeMemPrev / 1024) != (dwGmemFree / 1024)¦¦
           wFree != wFreePrev)
           {
           char szTemp [12];
```

```
0.0011 25    wSizeUserPrev = wSizeUser;
0.0000 25    wSizeGDIPrev = wSizeGDI;
0.0561 25    wFreePrev = wFree;
0.0553 25    dwSizeMemPrev = dwGmemFree;
0.0000 25    * szIconCaption = NULL;
0.0000 25    if (Setup.bProgramTitle)
0.0001 25    lstrcat (szIconCaption, "ResMonitor");
0.0004 25    if (Setup.bUserSnapShot)
        {
0 0      if (* szIconCaption != NULL)
0 0      lstrcat (szIconCaption, ", SSU:");
        else
0 0      lstrcat (szIconCaption, "SSU:");
0 0      if (bSnapShot)
        {
0 0        itoa (wPctFreeUser - wSnapPctFreeUser, szIconCapti
0 0        lstrcat (szIconCaption, "%(");
0 0        itoa (wSnapSizeUser - wSizeUser, szIconCaption + l
0 0        lstrcat (szIconCaption, ")");
        }
        else
0 0      lstrcat (szIconCaption, "None");
        }

0.0005 25    if (Setup.bGDISnapShot)
        {
0 0      if (* szIconCaption != NULL)
0 0      lstrcat (szIconCaption, ", SSG:");
        else
0 0      lstrcat (szIconCaption, "SSG:");
0 0      if (bSnapShot)
        {
0 0        itoa (wPctFreeGDI - wSnapPctFreeGDI,
        szIconCaption + lstrlen (szIconCaption), 10);
0 0        lstrcat (szIconCaption, "%(");
0 0        itoa (wSnapSizeGDI - wSizeGDI,
        szIconCaption + lstrlen (szIconCaption), 10);
0 0        lstrcat (szIconCaption, ")");
        }
        else
0 0      lstrcat (szIconCaption, "None");
        }
0.0000 25    if (Setup.bMemSnapShot)
        {
        char buf[16];
```

455

```
0 0    if (* szIconCaption != NULL)
0 0     lstrcat (szIconCaption, ", SSM:");
       else
0 0     lstrcat (szIconCaption, "SSM:");
0 0    if (bSnapShot)
       {
0 0    ltoCommaDelimitedString ((LONG)(dwGmemFree - dwSnapSiz
       buf, sizeof (buf));
0 0    lstrcat (szIconCaption, buf);
0 0     lstrcat (szIconCaption, "K");
       }
       else
0 0     lstrcat (szIconCaption, "None");
       }
0.0000 25   if (Setup.bPctFreeUser)
       {
0 0    if (* szIconCaption != NULL)
0 0     lstrcat (szIconCaption, ", U:");
       else
0 0     lstrcat (szIconCaption, "U:");
0 0     itoa (wPctFreeUser, szIconCaption + lstrlen (szIconCa
0 0     lstrcat (szIconCaption, "%");
       }
0.0006 25   if (Setup.bPctFreeGDI)
       {
0 0    if (* szIconCaption != NULL)
0 0     lstrcat (szIconCaption, ", G:");
       else
0 0     lstrcat (szIconCaption, "G:");
0 0     itoa (wPctFreeGDI, szIconCaption + lstrlen (szIconCap
0 0     lstrcat (szIconCaption, "%");
       }
0.0553 25   if (Setup.bSizeUser)
       {
0 0    if (* szIconCaption != NULL)
0 0     lstrcat (szIconCaption, ", SizeU:");
       else
0 0     lstrcat (szIconCaption, "SizeU:");
0 0     itoa (wSizeUser, szIconCaption + lstrlen (szIconCapti
       }
0.0000 25   if (Setup.bSizeGDI)
       {
0 0    if (* szIconCaption != NULL)
0 0     lstrcat (szIconCaption, ", SizeG:");
       else
```

456

```
0 0    lstrcat (szIconCaption, "SizeG:");
0 0    itoa (wSizeGDI, szIconCaption + lstrlen (szIconCaptio
      }
0.0000 25   if (Setup.bSizeFreeMem)
      {
      char buf[16];
0 0    if (* szIconCaption != NULL)
0 0    lstrcat (szIconCaption, ", SizeFM:");
      else
0 0    lstrcat (szIconCaption, "SizeFM:");
0 0   ltoCommaDelimitedString (dwGmemFree / 1024, buf, sizeof (
0 0    lstrcat (szIconCaption, buf);
0 0    lstrcat (szIconCaption, "K");
      }
0.0000 25   if (lstrlen (szIconCaption) > 60)
0 0   MessageBox (NULL, "The window caption you created exceeds
      "60 characters. Windows cannot display "
      "all of the window caption. I suggest you "
      "limit the number of your selections.",
      NULL, MB_ICONHAND);
0.0048 25   InvalidateRect (hWnd, NULL, TRUE);
      }
0.0567 83   } // End of OnTimer
```

This listing is very similar to the Line Time profile report that can be produced using Microsoft's Source Profiler. It gives you both timing and count information along with the contents of your source code file. By examining this listing, we can obtain the same information that we got when we used the Microsoft Source Profiler on Resource Monitor:

- We can see how many messages were processed by WndProc.

- We can see how many times WM_SYSCOMMAND was processed by OnSysCommand.

- We can see how the code in the OnTimer function could be made faster by moving the alarm checks inside the program block that gets executed only when the system resources change.

Besides the information provided by TPROFW in the Execution Profile window and these reports, three additional windows can provide useful information about your program after you have profiled it: the Callers window, the Areas window, and the Coverage window. Each of these windows can be displayed by choosing it in the View menu.

Callers

The Callers window displays information about how often a routine is called and which routines call it. For example, you can display a list of all the functions that were called to execute a particular function. This feature comes in handy when you are trying to restructure code. To open the Callers window, choose the Callers command from the View menu. This function is not turned on by default. You must select the Callers command from the Module window's local menu and turn the feature on before you profile your application.

The Callers window contains two panes. The left pane lists all the marked functions. When you highlight one of these functions, the right pane displays the hierarchy of calling functions.

Areas

The Areas window displays detailed information about data collection activities at the places marked in your source code. Each marked profile area within the Module window corresponds to a line in the Areas window. If the function is marked, then the name of the function is used as the Area name. Otherwise, the line number corresponding to the appropriate module is displayed. Other pertinent information is also displayed, such as whether or not the function is a Windows procedure. The Areas window is an easy way to get a big picture of all areas of an application you have marked to profile. You can also add, remove, and inspect areas from the local menu.

Coverage

The Coverage window displays a list of code blocks that have not been executed. It provides you with an excellent means of knowing what code within an application has yet to be profiled. This is very important for unit-testing your application's code.

The Coverage window is opened by selecting the Profiling Options command from the Statistics menu and choosing the Coverage radio button. The left pane of the two-pane window shows a list of selected modules, while the right pane shows the unexecuted blocks of code. The local menus of both panes determine how and what gets displayed in each of the panes.

Now that you have seen how to use both the Microsoft and Borland profilers, let's look at some ways to optimize Windows C applications.

Optimizing Your Program after Profiling It

After you have discovered specific performance problems within an application, you need to decide how to optimize it. Sometimes obvious ways to optimize your program will appear, as we saw in Resource Monitor's OnTimer function.

Examine the data structures and algorithms you are using—can a quick sort be used rather than a shell sort? Loops provide other optimization opportunities. For example, you may be able to move code outside of a loop. There are a number of ways to optimize code, but there is a fine line between over optimization and making your code understandable. You do not want to optimize your application code to the point that you can no longer give your program to someone else to support. When your program gets to this point, optimizations are best left up to an optimizing compiler. However, there are still a number of approaches you can attempt by hand. They are:

- Reduce excessive calls and recursive function calling.
- Rewrite portions of the code in assembly language.
- Convert arrays of text to arrays of pointers to text.
- Modify data structures to align them on word boundaries.
- Use integers in place of reals or longs, if possible.
- Use near pointers in place of far pointers if possible.
- Use your local heap to cache frequently accessed data.
- Restructure code so that data is evaluated only as needed.
- Structure the order of conditional tests so that those most likely to produce failure are evaluated first. (This is what I needed to do in the OnTimer function.)

As we said previously, optimization is also accomplished with the use of an optimizing compiler. Both Microsoft and Borland C/C++ products provide a high degree of optimization. Although automated optimization generally doesn't adhere to the 80/20 rule, it does generally improve performance in every part of your program. Rather than trying to optimize the 20 percent of the program that is running 80 percent of the time, the compiler attempts to streamline every line of code.

There are a number of techniques that Microsoft and Borland both use to streamline code that you can apply to your applications, even if you don't use an optimizing compiler. Let's look at some of the more common ones.

- Algebraic optimization: replacing an expression with another that is less time-consuming. For example, you can replace the expression (3 * 2) with the expression (3 << 2)—a bitwise shift is the same as multiplying a number by 2.

- Constant folding: the process of removing unnecessary constants from arithmetical statements in your application and replacing them with the result. For example:

```
#define EXPRESSION1 10
#define EXPRESSION2 20
j = EXPRESSION1 * EXPRESSION2;
becomes,
j=200;
```

- Constant propagation: replacing variables with constants if their value never changes throughout the application. For example:

```
j=1;
k=j*1000;
becomes,
k=1*1000;
```

- Common subexpression elimination: replacing an expression with a constant if the value of the expression is always the same. For example:

```
short j,k,l,m,n,o,p;
j=(k * l * m) * n;
o=(k * l * m) * p;
becomes,
short j,k,l,m,n,o,p;
register temp;
temp=(k * l * m);
j=temp * n;
o=temp * p;
```

- Copy propagation: replacing references to variables that contain results of expressions with the expressions themselves. For example:

```
short i,j,k,l,m,n,o,p;
k=i;
j=(k * l * m) * n;
```

```
o=(k * 1 * m) * p;
becomes,
short i,j,l,m,n,o,p;
j=(i * 1 * m) * n;
o=(i * 1 * m) *p;
```

- Dead store elimination: the process of removing variables that are no longer used. For example, many API functions return values that are stored in variables but are never used, or are used once and never again.

- Invariant code motion: moving variable expressions, that never change within a loop, to the outside of the loop. For example:

```
for(i=0;i<100;++i){
m[i]= k * 1;
}
becomes,
n=k*1;
for(i=0;i<100;++i){
m[i]=n;
}
```

- Strength reduction: replacing an expression in a loop with a faster one. For example:

```
#define NULL '\0'
short i;
int j[10];
 for(i=0;i<10;++i){
 j[i]=NULL;
 }
becomes,
#define NULL '\0'
short register i;
int j[10];
int register *temp;
 for(i=0,temp=j;i<10;++i,++temp){
 *temp=NULL;
 }
```

- Loop unrolling: reproducing lines of code executed in a loop. This minimizes the number of loop iterations. For example:

```
for (i=0;i<100,++i){
j[i]='\0';
}
```

```
becomes,
for (i=0;i<100,i+=2){
j[i]='\0';
i[++i]='\0';
}
```

- Loop fusion: the process of combining two loops into one. For example:

```
for(i=0;i<100,++i){
j[i]=(k[i] * l[i] * m[i]) * n[i];
}
for(i=0;i<100,++i){
o[i]=(k[i] * l[i] * m[i]) * p[i];
}
becomes,
for(i=0;i<100,++i){
j[i]=(k[i] * l[i] * m[i]) * n[i];
o[i]=(k[i] * l[i] * m[i]) * p[i];
}
```

- Cross-jump elimination: reducing redundant code within code that produces jumps, such as a switch statement. For example:

```
switch(i){
case 1:
 j=i * 10;
 k=j * 20;
 break;
case 2:
 j=i * 100;
 k=j * 200;
 break;
case 3:
 j=i * 10;
 k=j * 20;
 break;
}
becomes,
switch(i){
case 1:
case 3:
 j=i * 10;
 k=j * 20;
 break;
case 2:
 j=i * 100;
```

```
k=j * 200;
break;
}
```

- Instruction alignment: forcing the alignment of a jump to an even address if the compiler produces code that jumps to a uneven address. Unfortunately, this is rather difficult to do by hand if you are coding in C, but if you are coding in assembler, simply insert an NOP after the uneven jump.

- Use of registers. Since it takes less time to get data from a register than from memory, storing variables that are used in more than one sequentially executed program block within registers is important.

- Tail merging: maintaining control over the exiting procedures within a function. For example, if a break command in a switch statement is going to send you to a return command, then it is more efficient to replace the break with a return command.

Most of the techniques described previously are best left up to the optimizing compiler, for the simple reason that your application code can become unbearable to read and maintain. However, when you are profiling an application, it is important for you to understand all the options you have to increase your code's performance.

Summary

After working with both Microsoft's and Borland's profilers, I feel that either one can help you to improve the performance of your Windows application. Turbo Profiler for Windows is an interactive programming tool that has the look and feel of debuggers such as Turbo Debugger for Windows and CodeView for Windows. It has more features than Microsoft's Source Profiler and is easier to use.

Microsoft's Source Profiler is also an excellent tool to use for profiling your Windows application. It's just a shame that its interactive mode that is available from Programmer's Workbench does not work for Windows applications. Maybe the next version of Microsoft C/C++ will have his feature. Overall, your choice of profilers depends on which development environment you use, Microsoft C/C++ 7.0 or Borland C++ 3.1. Both tools will do the job of profiling your application. All you need to do is try them out to see how they can help your Windows applications perform faster.

Now that we are finished learning how to use profilers to make our applications faster, it's time to learn how to use debuggers to make our programs work the way they are designed to.

PART IV

Debugging Windows Applications

Now that we have worked with Windows programming tools that help us audit how Windows programs work, we are shifting our focus to one of the most indispensable Windows programming tools you need as a Windows developer: the interactive debugger. In Part IV we'll go over the basics of debugging Windows applications, develop a debugging strategy, and then investigate the interactive debuggers and associated tools that help you isolate program problems.

In Chapter 9 we will explore the debugging tools that Microsoft includes with QuickC for Windows, Microsoft C/C++ 7.0, and the Windows 3.1 SDK. We'll start by tackling a debugging project using the QuickC debugger. Then we will look at CodeView for Windows 4.0. You will learn how to set up CodeView for both single-monitor and secondary-monitor hardware configurations. You will also find out how CodeView can be used with the debugging version of Windows and the new Windows 3.1 debugging utility DBWIN.

In Chapter 10 we'll investigate two more Windows debuggers: Turbo Debugger and MultiScope Debuggers for Windows. You will find out how Turbo Debugger for Windows works and why I consider it to be the best Windows debugger available for use with a secondary monitor setup. You will also find out how MultiScope Debuggers for Windows work within the Windows environment and how the MultiScope Crash Analyzer can be used to debug Windows applications after they have perished.

Using Microsoft Tools for Debugging Applications

■ A debugging strategy for writing Windows applications

■ Preventing bugs in a Windows application

■ Using the QuickC for Windows debugger

■ Using the CodeView for Windows debugger

■ Using and understanding Dr. Watson

■ Using the debugging version of Windows with DBWIN

9

In this chapter we will look at the process of debugging a Windows application and at how to use the tools included with Microsoft's QuickC for Windows, C/C++ 7.0, and the Windows 3.1 SDK to debug a program. These tools are

- the QuickC for Windows Debugger,

- CodeView for Windows Version 3.07,

- CodeView for Windows 4.0,

- Dr. Watson,

- DBWIN, and

- the debugging version of Windows.

Before we start learning how to use the Microsoft interactive Windows debugging tools, let's review the process of debugging a Windows application and develop some debugging strategies you may find helpful. Let's look at how to avoid errors and write Windows applications that are easier to debug. All of the concepts and strategies we'll discuss will apply to using any Windows debugger; only the mechanics of running the debugger may differ.

Developing a Debugging Strategy

Debugging is a difficult process to describe. By their nature, program bugs are unexpected and irrational, so it is hard to develop a way of finding them that works in all programming situations. The best debugging tool you have is your own intuition about the places a program has problems. Along with intuition a systematic debugging process will help you isolate and fix the errors in your program. This debugging process consists of five general steps:

- Determining your program has an error

- Finding out where the error occurred

- Finding out why the error occurred

- Repairing the program

- Testing the program

Was There a Program Error?

Did your application cause a General Protection Fault (GPF) error? Did your application display erroneous data? After you determine the application has an error, you need to note exactly what the error is and to learn all you can about what was going on when it occurred. This is especially important for finding bugs in Windows applications as compared to debugging a DOS character-mode application. For instance, what were the states of Windows memory and resources when the error occurred? What other Windows applications were running? The more you know about the circumstances surrounding an error, the easier it will be to find.

Where Did the Error Occur?

The second step is usually the most difficult—isolating where the error occurred. Your best approach is the "divide and conquer" strategy. If your program is designed using small modular components that each do a limited number of tasks, you will find it much easier to isolate program errors. If your program is a mishmash of spaghetti code in large functions, good luck! The rule to remember is "Proper prior preparation avoids poor programming problems."

Why Did the Error Occur?

After you have found out where the bug is, you need to know why it occurred. Did your program get a GPF error because you used an uninitialized pointer? Did a variable declared inside a function's scope not contain data you expected it to each time the function was called, because you forgot to make the variable static? Finding where a program error is located can be difficult. Figuring out why the error occurred can sometimes be even more frustrating.

Repair the Error

After you have located the bug and know why it happened, you need to fix it. Sometimes the error can be fixed with one line of code. In other cases it may require redesign.

Test Your Program

Testing is the step most often overlooked by programmers. Test your program after fixing it. Test for the error you fixed. Test to make sure you did not cause some new bug when you changed your program code.

Preventing Bugs

Reviewing your program listing uncovers a fair number of bugs. Looking for simple logic errors and for typos that have slipped by the compiler can solve many problems.

Programming bugs in Windows applications can be put into three categories; bugs common to any programming language and environment, bugs peculiar to the language you are working with (in this case C), and bugs that are peculiar to the Windows programming environment. Understanding these different categories and learning the types of problems that can occur will get you off to a good start writing bug-free Windows applications, and will help you find and stamp out bugs more quickly.

One of the best tools you can use to avoid making the same programming mistakes in the future, and to improve your programming practices, is a journal of your programming experiences. When you fix a bug, note what the bug was, the circumstances surrounding it, how you fixed it, and how it can be prevented in the future. You should set up categories such as General Programming, Language-Specific Problems, and Windows-Specific Problems in your journal, so you can more easily find information later.

Understanding that each programming error belongs to a category of program bugs will improve your ability to write bug-free applications. The following guidelines, organized by programming category, will start you on your way toward building your own programming journal.

General Program Bugs and Strategies

To keep your program as bug-free as possible, you should consider the following guidelines when you're developing a program in any programming language.

- Are program loop limits what they should be?

- Was all user input anticipated? A user should be able to click on any program object with the mouse and type in whatever he or she wants without causing a program error.

- Are all variables initialized correctly? Don't assume that variables were initialized in another function or in another part of the program.

- Did you create a debugging version of your program, where data validation checks can be turned on when the program is being tested, and turned off to improve program performance in the released application?

- Have you compiled the program using the highest level of warning error messages? Have you fixed all the compiler warning error problems, or at least justified them?

- Did you mentally step through the program, line by line, checking your code to see if it really does what you intended?

- Did you check your program's output? What did the program output? What should it have output? Simple formatting errors are usually found this way.

- Does the programming team conduct code reviews? External debugging via code reviews by peer programmers can uncover many software bugs. While the old adage about an ounce of prevention applies here, it is my experience that scheduling peer code reviews is usually subordinated to meeting other product deadlines.

C-Peculiar Bugs and Strategies

Now that we have thought about common programming problems, let's look at problems peculiar to the C programming language.

- Have you confused the (=) and (==) operators?

- Have you used the correct format specifiers in `sprintf` and `wsprintf` statements?

- Have you checked for a /* that may have commented out real C code?

- Have all pointers been initialized correctly?

- If you expect a variable defined inside a function's scope to retain its value every time the function is called, have you made it static?

- Have you confused operator precedence? C has many operators, and it is difficult to remember which ones have a higher precedence when an expression is evaluated.

- Have you tested the results of pointer arithmetic expressions? One of the most difficult areas of C for new programmers to understand, pointers and pointer arithmetic is also one of the areas of a C program most likely to have an error.

- Have you checked for misplaced semicolons?

- Have you tested all your program macros thoroughly? It is very easy to make a mistake writing a macro in C by not anticipating how it will be expanded in all the different ways it can be referenced.

- If you defined a function with a return value, did you make sure it returns a value?

- Have you kept source code statements to one line each? Since multiple-line source code statements do not show up well in the debugger's source code display, you can get a better feel for the relationship between source and compiled code by avoiding long, complex C statements.

Windows-Peculiar Bugs and Strategies

There are many things you can do to prevent errors and make your Windows application easier to debug. The following important tips could help you avoid problems before they start.

Prototype Every C Function

For examples of prototyping, just look at the WINDOWS.H file, where you will see declarations like the following:

```
BOOL FAR PASCAL TextOut (HDC, short, short, LPSTR, short);
```

This declaration gives the compiler some very useful information, such as the return value (Boolean), the calling convention (FAR and PASCAL), the number of parameters (5), and the type of each parameter.

If you prototype your routines, you can quickly and easily eliminate some C programming errors. For example, in the course of development it is common to add and change parameters to functions. If you forget to change every call to a function whose parameters you have altered, your program has a bug. If you are lucky, this bug will cause your application to fail immediately. Otherwise, the bug may cause unpredictable problems in your program.

Avoid Casting

Casting is redundant and may hide bugs. Let the compiler tell you about type mismatches, and in those cases respond by casting. Casting was included in the early examples of Windows programs because the C compiler did not support prototyping at that time. Microsoft QuickC for Windows, Microsoft C 6 and 7, and Borland C++ support prototyping and eliminate the need to cast in many circumstances.

Limit Variable Scope

Whenever a window procedure stores data in a global or static variable that is to be used only within a specific window, such as a GDI handle or a pointer to a function, problems can occur in multiple window applications. If two or more windows store data in the same global or static variable, one window will lose its data. You can avoid this problem by storing a window's data in a locally or globally allocated data structure whose handle (or pointer) is stored in the extra bytes of the window data structure, using the Windows functions SetWindowWord, SetWindowLong, GetWindowWord, and GetWindowLong.

Modularize Your Program Code

Modular source code simplifies debugging. This is especially true for Windows applications. One of the quickest ways to isolate a program bug is to identify the function that is malfunctioning; this is easier if the function is small and performs only one operation.

In almost all of the Windows programming books I have read, however, all the program examples have program code that processes Windows messages inline in the window procedure. In the real world of Windows programming, however, this makes large, unmanageable window procedures which are more difficult to debug. As an alternative, you should put the code to process each Windows message into a separate function called from the window procedure. One Windows message should equal one program function. If you follow this programming strategy, you will find that your C program is easier to debug and easier to convert to new programming languages such as C++ or to port to new programming environments such as Microsoft's New Technology.

Include Call-Back Functions in the .DEF File

You need to include every window procedure, dialog box procedure, callback procedure, hook function, and subclass function in the EXPORTS list of your application's module definition (.DEF) file. Failing to do this is a common error that creates unpredictable results in Windows. There are no compiler or link errors that will identify this problem for you.

Use the Debugging Version of Windows

You set up the debugging version of Windows by using special copies (from the Windows SDK) of KRNL286.EXE, KRNL386.EXE, USER.EXE, GDI.EXE, and MMSYSTEM.DLL, along with their symbol tables. The debugging version of Windows performs error-checking not available in the retail version, catching problems such as bad handles and wild pointers.

When you install the Windows 3.1 SDK, two directories, \DEBUG and \NODEBUG, are created under your \WINSDK directory. Since I have Microsoft C/C++ 7.0 installed on my system, the \WINSDK directory is named \C7. This is the way Microsoft recommends installing the Windows SDK and the Microsoft C/C++ 7.0 compiler. The \NODEBUG directory has the standard Windows executables in it. The \DEBUG directory has the debugging version of Windows in it. To copy the debugging version of Windows to your Windows directory so you can debug programs, type in N2D. To restore the standard version of Windows by copying the files from the \NODEBUG directory to your Windows directory, type in D2N.

> **TIP**
>
> When I first started working with QuickC for Windows, I set it up as a separate development system. However, now that Microsoft C/C++ 7.0 includes the full Windows 3.1 SDK in the same development directories as the compiler, I decided to integrate QuickC into the Microsoft C/C++ 7.0 development system too. I have the Microsoft C/C++ 7 development system installed in the directory D:\C7. The QuickC files that used to be in D:\QCWIN\BIN are now in D:\C7\QCW. In the process of reorganizing the files, I copied all of the files from my D:\QCWIN\BIN directory to the new D:\C7\QCW that I created and included on my PATH statement. Then I deleted all the files and directories for all the QuickC libraries, header files, and sample programs and deleted the Dialog Editor and Image Editor utilities (along with their Help files) that came with QuickC for Windows. After reorganizing my directories, I used the Directories command in the QuickC Options menu to point to the Microsoft C/C++ 7 libraries and INCLUDE file directories. I also used the Tools command in the QuickC Options menu to have Quick C use the Image Editor and Dialog Editor that come with the Microsoft 3.1 SDK.

Check Your Program's Output

I like to get feedback about the progress of my programming projects each step of the way. Using a hexadecimal file dump application lets me check output files to see if they are formatted the way I planned and if they contain the right data. You can use the DumpIT program developed for this book to help you examine files created by your application. Figure 9.1 shows DumpIT with some of its own files loaded.

I also like to check up on the progress of my programs by examining the DGROUP and global memory segments they create. For this task, I usually choose HEAP-WALK. As we discussed in Chapter 6, HEAPWALK lets me examine any chunk of memory in the Windows environment.

Embed Debugging Code in Your Program

Embedding debugging code directly in the program is an anachronism from a time when adequate debugging tools were not available. Using this debugging strategy, the programmer decides where in the code he or she wants something done, such as testing an assertion (is this pointer valid?) and conditional compilation.

FIGURE 9.1:

DumpIT displaying the contents of
its own files

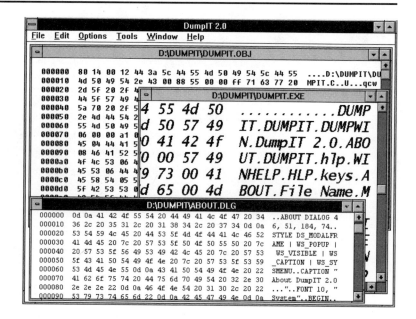

One approach is to display message boxes with program debug information. For short programs, such as the examples in this book, the simple strategy of inserting MessageBox statements at appropriate places in the code may uncover most bugs. Such diagnostic statements display values of relevant variables at particular points in the program, so that the error eventually becomes clear. Many programmers use this system exclusively, but it has its disadvantages.

One disadvantage is that each time the diagnostic MessageBox statements are changed, the program must be recompiled. This is time-consuming. MessageBox statements are a cumbersome way to follow the path a program is taking from place to place, unless you put them almost everywhere. In long loops, where trouble may not show up until after hundreds of iterations, MessageBox statements are useless.

Another way to debug a program, which I prefer, is to use the assert macro found in ASSERT.H, one of the header files included with your development system. Normally, you call assert in your program in the following fashion:

```
assert (pProgramPointer != NULL);
```

If the assertion fails, a message box is displayed identifying the source code file and line number of the `assert` statement. When you click on OK, you will get a GPF error that terminates your program. The `assert` macro is a good way to check for errors that should never happen but sometimes do anyway. It is written so the `assert` statements will be inserted in your program only if debugging is turned on.

If you would like an `assert` statement that does not cause a GPF error and allows your program to continue, use `WinAssert`, an `assert` macro written for this book. You will find it in the header file ASSERT.H in the \ATOOLS\DLL directory that was created when you installed the disk set on your hard disk.

Use an Interactive Program Debugger

It would be nice if we could step through a program line by line, at whatever speed we wanted, checking the values of variables and expressions as we went along, without having to modify the program itself. Happily, interactive debuggers such as the Microsoft QuickC for Windows Debugger, Microsoft CodeView for Windows, Borland Turbo Debugger, and the MultiScope Debuggers for Windows do just that. These interactive debuggers are so good and so versatile that every Windows programmer should learn how to use one of them.

What Does a Debugger Do?

Debuggers help you to do the first two steps of the debugging process: finding the location of the error and finding its cause. A debugger lets you slow down your program's execution so you can examine its state for each instruction as it is processed. You can look at and even change the value of program variables—while the program is executing. The following list is a superset of the functions offered by all the Windows debuggers that will be covered:

- Tracing. Executing your program one statement at a time and tracing into functions as they are called to follow the execution path through your program.

- Back-tracing. Stepping backwards through your executed code, reversing the execution as you go.

- Stepping. Executing your program one line at a time but stepping over any function calls. Stepping over functions that you don't need to debug speeds the debugging process.

- Breakpointing. Setting places (breakpoints) for your program to stop unconditionally or conditionally in your program code. This can be as simple as always having your program stop on a specific line of code. Or it can be as complicated as stopping your program when the WM_MOUSEMOVE message is received by a window procedure with the mouse coordinates inside a defined range.

- Viewing. Being able to open up windows to inspect the state of your program and of the computer from various perspectives: variables, breakpoints, the stack contents, data files, program code, memory, microprocessor registers, execution history, and program output.

- Inspecting. Investigating your program by looking inside and breaking down complicated data, such as arrays and structures. MultiScope even presents a graphic picture of data structures and arrays.

- Modifying. Replacing the current value of a variable with a value you specify.

- Watching. Isolating specific program variables to keep track of their changing values as the program runs.

- Editing. Having the debugger integrated into the development system, so that when an error is spotted you can fix it without exiting the debugger and switching to the editor.

- Building. Having the debugger integrated into the development system, so that when an error is spotted you can fix it without exiting the debugger and rebuild your application in an integrated development environment.

Now that we have discussed debuggers in general, let's look at what each of these debuggers does and how well it does it. The first Windows debugger we will look at is the QuickC for Windows Debugger.

Using the QuickC for Windows Debugger

To learn about how the QuickC Debugger can help us, we will first see what it can and cannot do, and then go through a "hands-on" debugging project using the DRAW.EXE example application included on the disk set to see how the debugger operates.

QuickC for Windows Debugger Environment

The integrated debugger that comes with QuickC is my favorite QuickC feature. As a Windows programmer I spend almost as much time using a debugger as using a program editor. The QuickC Debugger is much easier to use than any of the other Windows program debuggers. Since it is a Windows-hosted application development environment, you don't need to switch to a DOS window or hook up a debugging monitor to debug a Windows program. The QuickC Debugger can be used to debug Windows DLLs as well as applications, and it is the only Windows debugger that has the editing and building features. QuickC does not, however, have a backtracing command, and it has the most limited number of views compared to other debuggers.

Preparing a Program for Debugging

Before you can use the QuickC Debugger to debug a program, the program must be compiled and linked. The mechanics of preparing a program for QuickC are simple. The QuickC Debugger needs the source files (.C), the executable file (.EXE), and relevant dynamic link libraries (.DLL) in order to operate. You must start with an error-free compilation; the QuickC Debugger can't deal with errors of syntax in the source file—its strength is in finding logical errors in your program's operation.

You must choose Project from the Options menu to select the Debug Build mode to tell the compiler and linker to create the appropriate symbol tables. The QuickC Debugger requires a symbol table in order to operate, and the Debug option is required to generate the symbol table when your executable is built.

program execution control commands: Go, Continue To Cursor, Trace Into (function), Step Over (function call), and Restart. The Trace Into and Step Over commands are also available on the toolbar. The commands described in the following sections are available in the Run menu.

Restart   The Restart command (Shift+F5) resets execution of the program back to the first executable line. It reloads the program into memory and initializes all program variables.

Stop Debugging   The Stop Debugging (Alt+F5) command terminates the debugging session and returns to the normal editing session. I rarely use this command, because its action is done automatically for you on many occasions. For instance, if you see a problem, fix it in your code, and then choose the GO command, the QuickC Debugger will recognize that you modified the program and will prompt you to rebuild your application. When you choose Yes to the rebuild question, QuickC will terminate your application, rebuild it, and restart the debugger (if no compile errors occurred).

Go   The Go command (F5) executes code from the current statement until a breakpoint or the end of the program is reached. You cannot stop the QuickC Debugger after choosing Go unless you force a breakpoint.

> **TIP**
>
> As you will see later in the debugging project, I like to set a program breakpoint on the WM_RBUTTONUP mouse message. If you are not using the right mouse button for another purpose, this is a handy way to stop your Windows program while you are debugging it. WM_MBUTTONUP is an alternative if you have a three-button mouse and want to use the right mouse button for another function.

Continue to Cursor   The Continue to Cursor command (F7) executes your program as far as the line that the cursor is on. This is a way of setting a temporary breakpoint at the cursor location.

Trace Into The Trace Into command (F8 or toolbar button), like the Step Over command, executes one program step. The Trace Into function lets you follow the program execution path by stepping into functions when they are called. After stepping into the function, you can trace the program steps in the function and trace into other functions that are called.

Step Over The Step Over command (F10 or toolbar button) single-steps through the instructions in a function without stepping into program functions as they are called. The Step Over command is useful when you want to stay in the function you are working in without getting sidetracked into other functions.

Animate The Animate command (no shortcut available) automatically single-steps through your program for you, running at a slow speed to let you watch the program flow in your Source Code window. When you are animating your application, you can press any key to halt execution. Animation has three speed settings, Slow, Medium, and Fast.

Stopping Your Program

Often when debugging you will want to run the program full speed up to a certain point and then stop it at a particular line so you can investigate things at your leisure. For instance, you might use this strategy if your program contains a long loop. In a long loop you wouldn't want to step through every cycle of the loop—you only want to see what will happen when the loop terminates. Breakpoints accomplish this.

A breakpoint marks a line where the program will stop. You choose Go from the Run menu, or press F5, and your program executes all the statements up to the breakpoint, then stops. The QuickC Debugger provides you with a variety of ways to stop program execution using breakpoints. To set a program breakpoint, choose Breakpoints in the Debug menu and you will be presented with a variety of breakpoint options in the Breakpoints dialog box. Choosing the Breakpoints button (the hand icon) on the toolbar sets an unconditional program breakpoint.

You can set unconditional breakpoints on a program line that evaluates a set of assembly-language instructions or a window procedure entry point. You can also set breakpoints when an expression is true or is changed, and link the expression test to specific program locations or window procedures.

When you set a window procedure breakpoint, you can specify that the break occur when a certain message or class of messages is received. You can choose to break on classes of messages by setting check boxes or by selecting individual messages from a list box.

Keeping Track of Where You Have Been

Choosing Calls in the Debug menu displays a window that lists the functions that have been called up to the currently executing statement. The calls are displayed in a list box with the most recently called function first. The Calls window is convenient for finding out the path of program execution from one function to another. The Calls list is also valuable for finding your way around in an unfamiliar program created by another programmer.

Watching and Changing Variables

The easiest way to watch a variable or variable expression is to highlight it in the Source Code window and choose the QuickWatch button on the toolbar to add the variable expression to the Watch window. You can also specify variable expressions that you type in by choosing Watch Expression in the Debug menu. The QuickC Debugger also lets you modify the value of any program variable during program execution by choosing Modify Variable in the Debug menu.

The QuickC Debugger displays numeric values in both decimal and hexadecimal. You can toggle between the two views by choosing Hex Mode in the Debug menu.

Now that you have learned what the QuickC Debugger can do, let's put it to work to find some program bugs in a simple drawing program written for this book.

A QuickC for Windows Debugging Project

You will find all the files you need for this project in the \ATOOLS\DEBUG directory that was created when you installed the disk set on your hard disk. In this directory is a drawing program that should be able to create ellipses and rectangles using three different colors of brushes and pens. DRAW.EXE is the executable that contains all the bugs. It's accompanied by a source file (DRAW.C), a module definition file (DRAW.DEF), a resource script file (DRAW.RC), a header file (DRAW.H), a dialog box file (DRAW.DLG), and an icon file (DRAW.ICO). To load the project into QuickC, open the project file DRAW.MAK.

First try executing and playing with the program to see what it does and doesn't do. You also might want to load the Resource Monitor program discussed in Chapter 6 to see if the application acquires Windows resources without releasing them, as shown in Figure 9.3.

After you have had a chance to experiment with the program, the following should become apparent:

- The program does not draw any GDI objects until you choose either Rectangle or Ellipse from the Shape menu. It seems the program is not initialized properly.

- The program creates GDI resources without releasing them. As you draw different shapes, notice how the percentage of GDI resources drops, one point at a time.

- If you choose About from the Help menu, and if you are using Windows 3.1, everything should be OK. However, you may get some very unpredictable results if you are using Windows 3.0, such as Windows locking up, your PC rebooting itself, and strange characters being displayed on the screen when you open the About dialog box.

FIGURE 9.3:
DRAW.EXE running with Resource Monitor keeping track of Windows resources

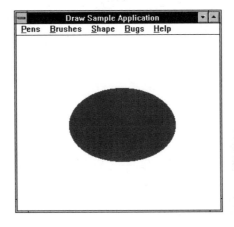

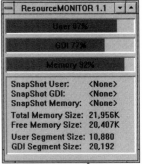

- The Bugs menu has some obvious program bugs in it. Choosing NULL Pointer will cause DRAW.EXE to get a GPF error. Choosing Bad hWnd or Bad hDC doesn't seem to cause any errors, but you can bet that choosing these menu commands is causing something to happen that shouldn't.

Now that we know what the problems are, let's start fixing them.

Hunting for Bugs

As I mentioned before, a handy way to stop a program after it has started is to put a breakpoint in an obvious place that is not being used by the program. I like to use the right mouse button. If you check in the WndProc function of DRAW.C, you will find out where the WM_RBUTTONUP message is handled, as shown in the following source code.

```
case WM_RBUTTONUP:
  // Set breakpoint on next statement for handy way to stop program
  break;
```

I even put in a comment as a reminder of where to set the breakpoint. Go ahead and set an unconditional breakpoint on the "break" statement following the comment, and then choose Go from the Run menu (or press F5) to run the program. To stop the program at the breakpoint, press the right mouse button inside the DRAW.EXE window.

Now that the program has stopped, as shown in Figure 9.4, you can try stepping and tracing through the code if you want to see how program execution flows from statement to statement.

Try restarting the program again by pressing F5 or choosing Go in the Run menu. After the program is running, press the right mouse button again to stop it at the breakpoint.

As you can see, unconditional breakpoints are simple to use. Just make sure you are setting them on a valid program statement—don't try setting breakpoints on variable declarations or comments.

FIGURE 9.4:

Program stopped after processing the WM_RBUTTONUP message

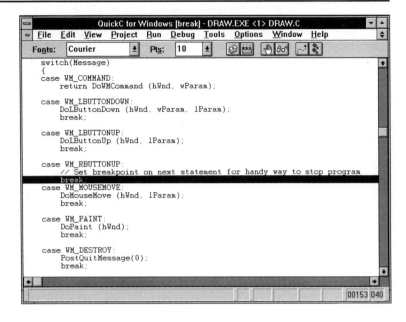

TIP

The QuickC Debugger sometimes highlights a line when you set a breakpoint as if it's really setting the breakpoint, and then complains that the breakpoint you set is not valid when you run the debugger. This occurs when you try to set a breakpoint on a program line that's not valid. For example, comment lines and the wrong line of a multiline program statement are incorrect.

Both the QuickC Debugger and CodeView for Windows require that you set breakpoints on the last line of a multiline statement. Borland's Turbo Debugger requires that you set the breakpoint on the first line of a multiline statement.

All of the other debuggers discussed in this book give you immediate feedback as to whether the breakpoint you are setting is valid. The QuickC Debugger waits until you start debugging your program to tell you if some of your breakpoints are invalid. If all of your breakpoints are invalid, you must terminate your program, correct the breakpoints, and start over.

Now let's investigate what happens to the DRAW.EXE program when a WM_PAINT message is received by the window procedure WndProc, to see if we can find out why the program is not drawing objects correctly. After the program is stopped in the debugger, set this breakpoint using the following steps:

1. Choose Breakpoints from the Debug menu.

2. When the Breakpoints dialog box is displayed, as shown in Figure 9.5, choose "at WndProc if Message is Received" from the Break combo box.

3. Choose WndProc for the name of the window procedure in the WndProc combo box.

4. Choose the Messages push button to display the Messages dialog box. Select the Single radio button for the Message Type and choose WM_PAINT from the Single Message combo box. Every possible Windows message is listed, so you will have to scroll through a number of messages to find WM_PAINT. At this point both the Breakpoints and the Messages dialog boxes are displayed, as shown in Figure 9.6.

FIGURE 9.5:

Using the Breakpoints dialog box in the QuickC Debugger

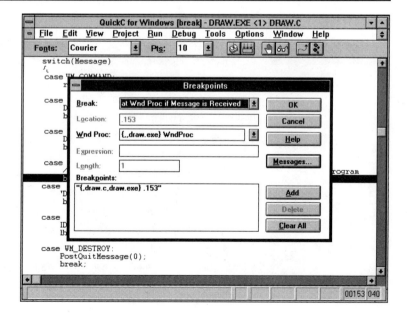

FIGURE 9.6:

Selecting the WM_PAINT message in the Messages dialog box

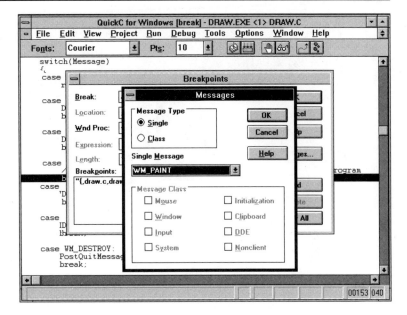

5. Choose OK in the Messages dialog box, and then choose the Add push button in the Breakpoints dialog box. The line "WndProc"/MWM_PAINT should appear in the Breakpoints list box, as shown in Figure 9.7.

6. Choose OK to close the Breakpoints dialog box.

Now that you have set a breakpoint for the WM_PAINT message, press F5 to continue program execution; the dialog box in Figure 9.8 is displayed. Choose OK and the program is stopped at line 135, the starting line of the function WndProc.

After the program is stopped, press F8 (or use the Trace Into button on the toolbar) to trace each program step, following the program path into the DoPaint function where WM_PAINT messages are processed. As you trace through the program steps in the DoPaint function, notice how the pen and the brush are created using the constant value for the menu item to specify the color for each. Unless you have changed the pen and brush color in the menus, a blue brush and pen should be created and then selected into the device context.

FIGURE 9.7:

The Breakpoints dialog box as it should appear after you have added the breakpoint for the WM_PAINT message

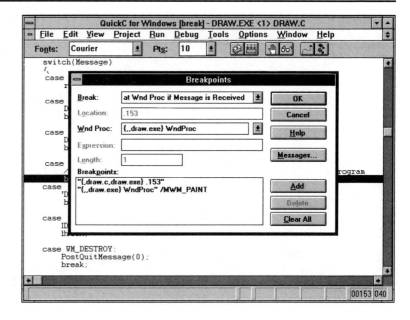

FIGURE 9.8:

The DRAW.EXE program stopped at the WM_PAINT message breakpoint

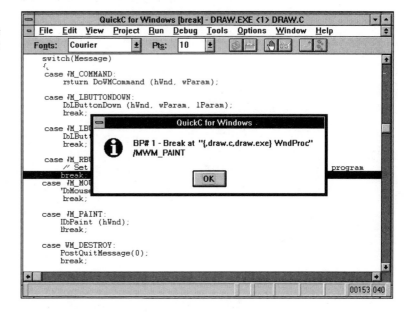

Everything should go well until the `switch` statement for deciding which object shape is processed, as shown in Figure 9.9. Neither of the two choices was valid, so neither the ellipse nor the rectangle was drawn. Why wasn't `nCurrentShape` processed correctly?

To check the value of the `nCurrentShape` variable, put the caret in it and press Shift+F9 for QuickWatch (or choose the QuickWatch button on the toolbar). You will see that `nCurrentShape` has the value zero, as shown in Figure 9.10. It wasn't initialized correctly. If you check the global variable definitions, you will find that `nCurrentPen` and `nCurrentBrush` were initialized correctly, but `nCurrentShape` wasn't. If you change the program code to initialize `nCurrentShape` to `IDM_SHAPE_RECTANGLE` and rebuild the application, you will find that the program draws shapes properly from the start.

Now that the first problem is fixed, let's try to determine the cause of the missing resources.

FIGURE 9.9:

Tracing through the `DoPaint` function

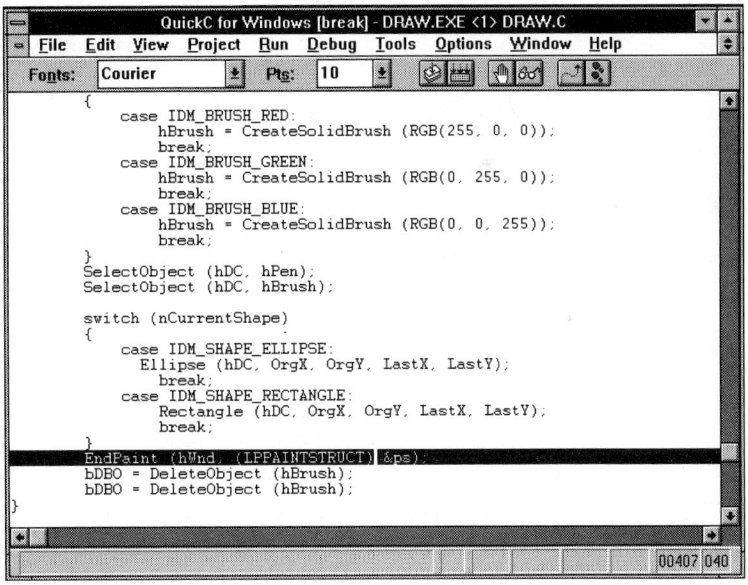

FIGURE 9.10:

Checking the value of
nCurrentShape using
QuickWatch

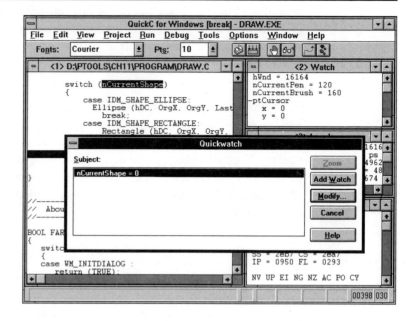

Finding Lost Resources

Lost resources is a subtle problem that is easily overlooked and difficult to find. An easy way to check for this situation is to use the Resource Monitor discussed in Chapter 6. After starting the Resource Monitor, note the percentage of free resources before starting a Windows application and after terminating it. Make sure not to start or work with any other Windows applications while you are testing an application. If the percentage of free resources drops consistently, the application likely has a Windows resource problem. For more details on how this works, you should refer back to the Resource Monitor section of Chapter 6.

After you have fixed the initialization problem for the nCurrentShape variable, rebuild the DRAW.EXE application. Make sure to clear the breakpoint for processing WM_PAINT messages, but keep the breakpoint for stopping DRAW.EXE when WM_RBUTTONUP messages are processed. If the Resource Monitor is not already loaded, start it so we can begin keeping track of Windows resources.

After you have rebuilt DRAW.EXE, run it by pressing F5 and then minimize the QuickC graphical environment so you can see the Resource Monitor icon and the DRAW.EXE program on the screen at the same time. Go ahead and draw some objects, changing pens, brushes, and shapes as you test the program. The system resources should drop one percent for approximately every ten objects you draw. After seeing the system resources drop consistently, stop the program by pressing the right mouse button.

There are two places where GDI objects are created in the DRAW.EXE program: DoMouseMove, where the dotted-line rectangle is drawn as you move the mouse, and DoPaint, where the graphic object is drawn. Set unconditional breakpoints at the start of each function and step through them, setting watch points on any questionable variable to try to identify the problem. One of these functions is working correctly, the other isn't.

Looking at the code and stepping through the functions may not make the problem apparent. In both functions graphic objects such as pens are created, selected, and deleted. In both functions each object that is created is deleted—or is it? The DeleteObject function returns a Boolean value to tell you whether the GDI object was deleted correctly. This return value is not checked in the program. Let's add some code to double-check the return value of DeleteObject.

Add a new global BOOL variable, named bDebug, to the program and modify each DeleteObject statement in the program to put the DeleteObject return value into bDebug. After changing each line where DeleteObject occurs, rebuild the application and restart the debugger, with breakpoints set at the start of the DoPaint and DoMouseMove functions.

After you have started tracing through the DRAW.EXE program, set a watch point on the variable bDebug. After each DeleteObject statement is executed, check the value of bDebug. If its return value is zero, the object was not deleted correctly.

After checking to see if all the GDI objects are deleted correctly, you will find that the DRAW.EXE program is trying to delete the brush object, identified by hBrush, twice, instead of deleting both the pen and the brush, identified by hPen and hBrush, as shown in Figure 9.11. In other words, pens get created but never deleted.

FIGURE 9.11:

Watching the value of **bDebug** to find out whether objects are deleted

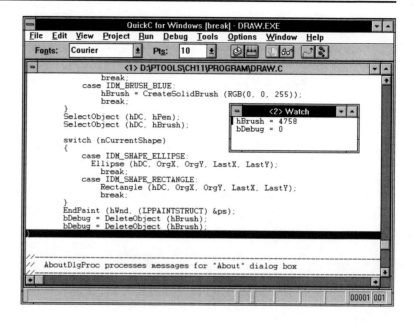

A Buggy Dialog Box

The next program bug that the DRAW.EXE program has is related to the About dialog box. If you display the About dialog box using Windows 3.0, strange things may occur. If you are using Windows 3.1 the problems disappear.

Forgetting to export a dialog box procedure in your module definition file (.DEF) is one of the easiest mistakes to make in developing Windows applications and one of the most common programming bugs. In Windows 3.0, this causes unexpected things to happen, such as UAE errors, strange characters appearing on the screen, and having the PC do a cold reboot.

A Windows application's DS and SS registers should always point at the same place—the application's DGROUP segment—for a small or medium memory model Windows application. If you forgot to export a dialog box procedure in Windows 3.0, the SS register points to Windows' DGROUP—not the application's. If you tried to put data into the program stack in a dialog box procedure, you would be writing into Windows DGROUP—not yours—with very unpredictable results.

If you still have Windows 3.0 available, you can test this problem using the QuickC Debugger, as shown in Figure 9.12.

To test the DRAW.EXE program, set a breakpoint in the AboutDlgProc function where the WM_INITDIALOG message is processed. Display the Registers window to monitor the DS and SS registers. Notice the different values. If you perform this same test with Windows 3.1, you will see that the DS and SS registers have the same value. Windows 3.1 is more robust than Windows 3.0 and catches more program errors for us automatically.

Windows 3.1 has now fixed this problem, but you should still try to remember to *export* all call-back window functions, including dialog box procedures. Relying on the system to take care of things for you when you forget is sloppy programming.

FIGURE 9.12:

Tracing through the AboutDlgProc dialog box procedure while monitoring the microprocessor registers in Windows 3.0

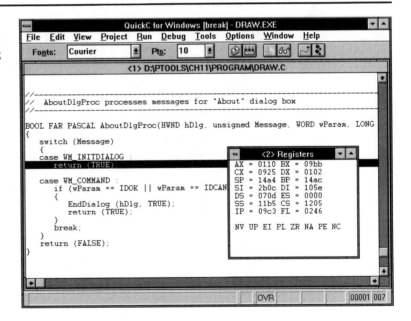

> **TIP**
>
> For C (not C++) you can optionally leave out the exported function names in your module definition file (.DEF) if you use _export in your function declaration and definition. For example, you can omit WndProc from the EXPORTS section of DRAW.DEF if you add _export to the function definition of WndProc. For C++ you must use _export in your function definitions and declarations and not use the EXPORTS section of the module definition file. In C++ all function names are "mangled" (how a function name is changed before it's written to the .OBJ file). The only way you can put function names in the EXPORTS section of the .DEF file is to know how they are mangled. Name mangling is implementation-dependent: Borland C++ does it one way and Microsoft C++ does it another.
>
> As you may know, using the EXPORTS section to export function names using ordinal numbers speeds up your application. Ordinals are faster for Windows to process and they are important for security. When you use _export, someone can use the EXEHDR utility to look up the names of the functions in your program. The problem is how to take advantage of using ordinals in a C++ program that mangles names. The easiest way is to use EXEHDR to look up the mangled function names in your program after you have compiled and linked it. You can then use these mangled names in your .DEF file along with ordinal numbers to identify these functions. If you are concerned with security, you can remove the _export from your function declaration and definition after you have added the function names to the .DEF file.

Trying Out the Bugs Menu

As we discussed previously, commands in the Bugs menu cause three different types of program errors to happen:

- Choosing Bad hWnd causes a window function to be called (ShowWindow) with an invalid handle.

- Choosing Bad hDC causes a GDI function to be called (LineTo) with an invalid handle to a device context.

- Choosing Null Pointer causes a memory reference with a NULL FAR pointer.

Go ahead and try each of these menu items while you are running DRAW.EXE using the QuickC Debugger. The first two menu items (Bad hWnd and Bad hDC) will not usually cause a fatal error. However, when I was testing this program using the QuickC Debugger, the debugger would sometimes get a GPF error message when I chose the Bad hDC menu command.

By setting breakpoints in DRAW.C for each error, as shown in Figure 9.13, you can check the return values for each function. All you need to do is watch the variable nRC.

As you can see, the only way you can tell there is something wrong is by looking at the return values from the functions ShowWindow and LineTo. If this were not a test program, the only way you could tell that these functions didn't work would be visually to see that something didn't happen that was supposed to. However, if you were to choose Null Pointer while running DRAW.EXE using the QuickC Debugger, the error would be caught and the offending line of code in DRAW.C would be highlighted.

In many cases the QuickC Debugger will catch a serious error, but in some cases it won't. When it doesn't you need to rely on using other tools. Later on in this chapter

FIGURE 9.13:

Using QuickC to debug invalid handles

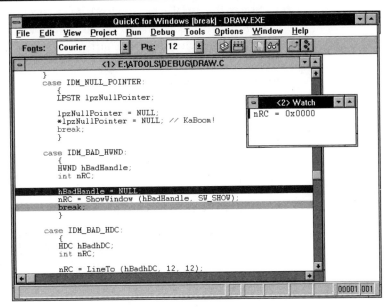

you will see how to use DBWIN and the debugging version of Windows to track down these errors in your program.

At this point you know how the QuickC Debugger works and have seen how to use it in our debugging project. The programming project we stepped through with QuickC can be used with each of the other debuggers. All of the steps we went through would be the same; only the commands may be different.

Now let's take a look at CodeView for Windows. It's more difficult to set up and to use than the QuickC Debugger, but it also has more debugging power.

Using the CodeView for Windows Debugger

The CodeView for Windows Version 3.07 (CVW) debugger is a DOS character-oriented application that has a user interface similar to Windows. CVW 3.07 employs many of the features found in Windows applications, including drop-down menus, dialog boxes, windows, and mouse support.

Although its interface is similar to that of Windows, CVW is not a Windows application in the usual sense. Instead, it is a special version of the original CodeView for DOS that has been made aware of the way in which the Windows memory manager juggles memory. What strikes you first when using CVW is that it does not share the screen with Windows. It either sends output to a secondary display monitor or swaps the screen back and forth between the DOS character-mode screen and Windows.

CVW has many features similar to those of the QuickC Debugger, and it uses the same keyboard commands. But the QuickC Debugger is easier and more convenient to use than CVW. The QuickC Debugger

- is easier to set up. You don't need to worry about installing a secondary monitor and passing command line arguments;

- makes it easier to prepare a program for debugging. With the QuickC Debugger, you only need to set the Build mode to Debug after choosing Project in the Options menu. Using CVW you have to set command line parameters on the compiler and linker command lines;

- is easier to use. The QuickC Debugger is a Windows application that does not require screen-swapping or a secondary monitor; and

- lets you edit and rebuild your program in the same integrated development environment without exiting the debugger.

So why would you want to use CVW instead of the QuickC Debugger? The primary reasons are the following:

- You are developing your application using Microsoft C—not QuickC.

- You like the convenience of using a secondary debugging monitor that lets you view both your application and the debugger without crowding them both on the same display.

- You want to take advantage of one of CVW's advanced features, such as added views, the ability to call functions in your program from the debugger, the ability to redirect input and output to DOS files, and the ability to take advantage of the debugging version of Windows.

CVW 3.07 can be used with both QuickC executables that were linked using the CV 3.X format option that's specified in the QuickC Customize Linker Options dialog box. You can also use CVW 3.07 with Microsoft C 6.0 and previous versions.

CodeView for Windows 4.0

The new CodeView for Windows 4.0 (CVW4) is included with Microsoft C/C++ 7 —not the Windows 3.1 SDK. CVW4 now runs in a graphical window, thanks to a licensing agreement between Nu-Mega Technologies, Inc. and Microsoft. The CVW4 debugger incorporates Nu-Mega's CV/1 technology to run in a graphical window. I had used CV/1 with the CVW debugger that came with Windows 3.0. This solution provided similar capabilities, but it had a few quirks, such as sometimes not restoring the screen correctly. Now that Microsoft and Nu-Mega are working together to incorporate both technologies, the implementation is almost flawless.

Besides working in a graphical window, the new CVW4 debugger includes many new features, such as overlapping windows, remote debugging using either a LAN or serial connection, and a revamped user interface. CVW4 now has a File Open dialog box that prompts you for the application you want to debug, instead of giving you a blank command line to type in the the program's full path and file name.

CVW4 debugs both C and C++ programs created with Microsoft C/C++ 7.0. If you are using QuickC or Microsoft C 6.0, you will need to make your program using Microsoft C/C++ 7.0 to debug it with CVW4. In Figure 9.14, CVW4 is shown debugging the DRAW.EXE program inside the Windows environment.

Using CVW4 you can easily display and hide the debugging window by pressing F4. CVW4 lets you trace and step through your program without the annoying screen flash that occurs with the older version of CodeView for Windows. You can also shrink the CVW4 display window down to a few lines of code and a control bar. This is called Small Window mode. Small Window mode lets you step through your program seeing both the current source lines and most of your program's window.

FIGURE 9.14:

Using CVW4 to debug the DRAW.EXE program used in the QuickC debugging project

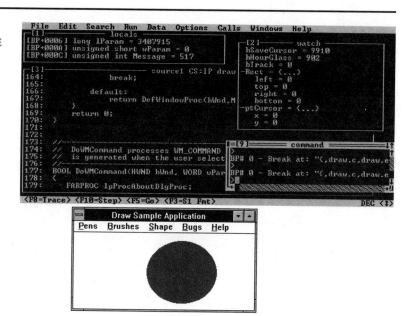

Setting Up CVW4

Since CVW4 is a character-mode debugger that coexists with Windows, we have to consider the alternatives for setting up our system. For systems with one video adapter, CVW4 shares the display surface with Windows. Although CVW4 is much more cooperative than previous versions of CodeView for Windows, you can't move its window on the screen. Every time you trace a statement, CVW4 switches the display to program output and back again. Although CVW4 works much better on one display than either CVW 3.07 or Turbo Debugger, it's still preferable to use CVW4 with two monitors.

You can also use a serial connection or a NETBIOS-compatible LAN to run CVW4 and Windows on two PCs during a debugging session. Although this method may sound nice, it's really quite cumbersome to set up. You must have the application you want to debug installed on both PCs in the same directory setup. You must also have CVW4 installed on both systems. The only time you should consider this setup is when other setups don't work. This usually occurs when you are having memory problems and can't reliably run both your application and CVW4 on the same system.

How to Set Up a Secondary CVW4 Monitor

Using a secondary monitor is preferable to a single-monitor setup (if you have the hardware to support it) because you can use the CVW4 debugger on one monitor and see the output of your program on another monitor at the same time. The procedure described here on how to set up a secondary monitor for CVW4 also works for Borland's Turbo Profiler for Windows and Turbo Debugger for Windows. After you have your secondary monitor installed and working, you can easily use any of these programs with it.

To run CVW4 on a secondary monitor, you will need a graphics adapter card and a graphics display monitor for your Windows display. You will also need an additional monochrome adapter card and monochrome display monitor.

The following steps will guide you through setting up CVW4 to work with a secondary monitor. Each step is listed succinctly here and then explained in more detail in the following sections.

1. Make sure your graphics card can coexist with a monochrome display adapter (MDA) card.

2. Install a monochrome display adapter and connect it to a monochrome display.

3. Test the setup.

Is Your Video Graphics Card Compatible with an MDA Card?   Not all video graphics cards (adapters) can coexist with a monochrome adapter (MDA). You must check the documentation for the video graphics card you are using with Windows to see if the card is compatible. One important factor is the address range the video graphics card uses for its video memory. Both enhanced graphics adapters (EGAs) and most VGAs can coexist with an MDA card.

The normal address ranges for various video cards are as follows:

- MDA occupies from B000H to B800H

- EGA occupies from A000H to C000H, with room for MDA at B000H to B800H

- VGA occupies from A000H to C800H, with room for MDA at B000H to B800H

- VGA on the motherboard occupies from A000H to C000H

If your system is an IBM PS/2, it must be configured with an 8514/a monitor as the primary monitor and a VGA as the secondary monitor. To use this configuration, specify the /8 (8514/a) option when you choose the Run command from the CVW4 File menu. If your VGA monitor is monochrome you must also use the /B (black and white) option. The 8514/a serves as the Windows screen and the VGA as the debugging screen.

Do not attempt to run non-Windows applications or the DOS shell while running CVW4 with the /8 option. By default the debugging screen operates in 50-line mode in this configuration. If you specify the /8 option you can optionally specify the /25 or /43 option for 25- or 43-line mode, respectively, on the VGA debugging screen. With the secondary monitor connected to your system, you can view CVW4 output and Windows output simultaneously. To use CVW4 with a secondary monitor you must execute it using the /2 command line option.

Install an MDA Card and Connect to a Monochrome Display   Installation of a mono-chrome monitor as the second screen requires that the monochrome display adapter be plugged into an empty expansion slot. Once this is done you must connect the display adapter card to the monochrome display via cable. Set the secondary display adapter switches to the appropriate settings. Follow the display adapter and computer manufacturer's recommendations.

Testing the Setup

From DOS type in MODE MONO. DOS should now direct all output to your secondary MDA monitor. Try typing in DIR to see how it works. You can type in MODE COLOR to get back to your other display adapter.

Now that we have discussed how to set up CVW4 with two monitors, let's see how to prepare a program for debugging using CVW4.

Preparing a Program for CVW4

Before you can use CVW4 to debug a program, the program must be compiled and linked using Microsoft C/C++ 7.0. The mechanics of preparing a program for CVW4 are simple. CVW4 needs the source files (.C), the executable file (.EXE), and relevant dynamic link libraries (.DLL) in order to operate. You must start with an error-free compilation; CVW4 can't deal with errors of syntax in the source file. Its strength is in finding logical errors in your program's operation.

You must use several command-line options when using the compiler and linker. CVW4 requires a symbol table in order to operate, and the following options are required to generate the symbol table;

- The first compile option is /Zi. This creates an object file with a symbol table and line numbers.

- The second compile option is /Od. This disables optimization, which might rearrange the order in which statements are executed.

- The link option is the /CO (CVW4) switch. The /CO switch directs LINK to include the debugging information from each .OBJ file in the .EXE file, together with directory paths of the .OBJ files. CVW4 uses these directory paths to search for the C source code file.

- You will want to help CVW4 out by keeping source code and object files in the same directory.

Starting CVW4

Once you've used the appropriate options to compile and link a version of your program that is acceptable to CVW4, you can start CVW4 and your program at the same time by typing CVW followed by the program's name, after choosing Run from Program Manager's File menu. After CVW4 loads your program, the CVW4 screen shown in Figure 9.14 appears.

As the figure shows, the program listing appears in a window in the middle of the screen, called the *source window*. The window at the bottom of the screen is called the *command window*. It's here that you type instructions to CVW4. The line at the top of the screen, with the words "File," "Search," and so on, is the menu bar. The *local window* is for keeping track of local variables, and the *watch window* is for keeping track of local variables, global variables, and variable expressions you want to "watch."

Using CVW4

CVW4 displays information in a series of overlapped windows that you view as you debug your program. Each window is a discrete section of the display that operates independently of the other windows, and each has a distinct function. Regardless of whether you use CVW4 on a secondary monitor, on one monitor, or on a PC attached via a serial cable or NETBIOS-compatible LAN, the display will be the same. The name of each window is shown on its caption bar. CVW4 uses the following different windows to help you debug your program:

- The Source window, to display your program source code. You can also open a second Source window to view an include file, another source file, or the same source file at a different location. In the QuickC Debugger you can open up to 16 windows, but you can view only one source file in one window—not two.

- The Command window, to type in debugging commands.

- The Watch window, to display the current values of selected variables.

- The Locals window, to list the values of all variables local to the current function or block.

- The Memory window, to show the contents of memory. You can open a second memory window to view a different section of memory. (QuickC does not have a memory viewer function; you would have to run HEAP-WALK with the QuickC Debugger to get the same functionality.)

- The Register window, to display the contents of the microprocessor registers, as well as the processor flags.

- The 8087 window, to display the registers of the numeric coprocessor or its software emulator.

CVW4 starts with three windows displayed: the Locals window appears at the top, the Source window fills the middle of the screen, and the Command window is at the bottom. You can activate a window by clicking on it with the mouse. You can also choose or activate a window in the View menu.

Working with CVW4 Windows

CVW4 display windows often contain more information than they can display on the screen. You can manipulate a selected window using the mouse, as follows:

- To scroll a window vertically or horizontally, use the vertical or horizontal scroll bar.

- To move a window, grab the top side of the window (similar to the Windows caption bar) using the mouse and drag it to its new position.

- To maximize a window so that it fills the screen, click the Up arrow at the right-hand end of the window's top border. To restore the window to its previous size and position, click the Double arrow at the right-hand end of the top border when the window is maximized.

- To minimize a window, click on the Down arrow at the right-hand end of the window's top border. To restore it, double-click on the small square that represents its icon equivalent.

- To change the size of a window:

  1. Position the cursor in the lower-right corner of the window.

  2. Press and hold down the left mouse button.

  3. Drag the mouse to enlarge or reduce the window.

- To remove a window, click the small dotted box at the left-hand end of the top border. The adjacent windows automatically expand to recover the empty space.

Alternatively, you can use the following keyboard commands:

Keyboard Command	Description
PAGE UP or PAGE DOWN	Scrolls through the text vertically
Ctrl+F10	Maximizes a selected display window
Ctrl+F8	Changes the size of a selected display window
Ctrl+F4	Removes a selected display window

In addition, you can choose the Maximize, Size, and Close commands from the Windows menu to manipulate a selected display window.

Running the Debugger

Running CVW4 is very similar to running the QuickC Debugger. Since both were developed by Microsoft, the user interface across both of them is consistent. You can use the keyboard instead of menus for many functions. Instead of choosing functions by selecting them in dialog boxes, you type commands into the command window. Using CVW4 you can perform the following operations:

- Restart the program. Choose Restart in the Run menu or type in L followed by any command line arguments in the Command window to restart the program.

- Go. To execute the program from the current statement until a breakpoint or the end of the program is reached, press F5 or type in G in the command window. You can also click the mouse on the F5=Go button on the status bar. To execute the program to a specific address, type G followed by the address in the command window. You can also stop the program while it is running in CVW4 by pressing Ctrl+Alt+SysRq. However, because this doesn't always work reliably, I recommend setting a breakpoint on the WM_RBUTTONUP mouse message (or any unused function key message) to stop your program, as I discussed in the QuickC Debugger section.

- Continue to Cursor. To execute your program to the line the cursor is on, press F7 or click the right mouse button at the cursor's location in the Source window.

- Trace Into. To step through your program one statement at a time and trace into functions, press F8 or click the mouse on the F8=Trace button on the status bar.

- Step Over. To step through your program one statement at a time and step over function calls, press F10 or click the mouse on the F10=Step button on the status bar.

- Animate. To animate your program, choose Animate in the Run menu.

- Breakpoints. To set an unconditional breakpoint at the line where the cursor is located, press F9 or double-click on the line with the mouse. You can set conditional breakpoints in the Set Breakpoint dialog box, displayed by choosing Set Breakpoint in the Watch menu.

Working with Breakpoints

Both the QuickC Debugger and CVW4 give you a great deal of control in setting breakpoints. As we just saw, F9 toggles on and off an unconditional breakpoint on the line where the cursor is located, and you can set conditional breakpoints using the Set Breakpoints dialog box.

As you learned in the QuickC Debugger section, you can also set a breakpoint on a Windows message or an entire class of Windows messages. This feature lets you track your application's response to user input and window-management messages.

You can trace the occurrence of a Windows message or an entire class of Windows messages by using the Breakpoint Set (BP) command. You can stop at each message, or you can execute continuously and display the messages in the Command window as they are received. For example, to set a breakpoint at the window procedure WndProc when a WM_CREATE message is received, you type in:

```
BP WndProc /MWM_CREATE
```

To break at WndProc when a mouse message is received, you type in:

BP WndProc /Mm

The WndProc parameter is the symbol name or address of an application's window function. The msgname parameter is the name of a Windows message, such as WM_PAINT. The msgclasses parameter is a string of characters that identify one or more classes of messages. The classes are consistent with those defined in the Windows Spy application; they are:

Message Class	Type of Windows Message
m	mouse
w	window management
n	input
s	system
i	initialization
c	Clipboard
d	DDE
z	nonclient

Keeping Track of Where You Have Been

Choosing the Calls menu displays a list of the functions that have been called up to the currently executing statement. The most recently called function appears first in the list.

Watching and Changing Variables

The easiest way to watch a variable using CVW4 is to put the cursor on the variable name and press Shift+F9 or Ctrl+W. This displays the QuickWatch dialog box. The variable at the current cursor position in the Source, Locals, or Watch window will appear in the QuickWatch dialog box. To add a variable to the Watch window, choose the Add button in the QuickWatch dialog box. You can also specify variable expressions that you type in by choosing Add Watch in the Watch menu.

CVW4 also lets you modify the value of any program variable during program execution by positioning the cursor at the value you want to change in the Local, Register, Memory, 8087, or Watch window and typing in the new value. If you change your mind, press Alt+Backspace to undo the last change you made.

Now that you have learned what the CVW4 debugger does in comparison to the QuickC Debugger, let's take a look at the advanced features in CVW4 that set it apart from the QuickC Debugger.

Advanced CVW4 Features

After you have learned how to control a program's execution as well as how to display and modify program variables, you might want to experiment with CVW4's advanced features in the following ways:

- Use multiple Source windows.
- Call functions.
- View and manipulate memory.
- Debug multiple applications.
- Check for undefined pointers.

Using Multiple Source Windows

You can have two CVW4 Source windows open at the same time. The windows can display two different sections of source code for the same program. They can both track CS:IP addresses. One can display a high-level listing and one can display an assembly-language listing. You can move freely between the Source windows, executing a single line of source code or a single assembly instruction at a time.

Calling Functions

You can call any C function in your program from the Command window. The format for calling C functions is

```
?funcname (varlist)
```

CVW4 evaluates the function and displays its returned value in the Command window.

> **WARNING** Directly calling a Windows application procedure or dialog box function might have unpredictable results.

View and Manipulate Memory

CVW4 lets you view and manipulate memory easily. Choosing the Memory command from the View menu opens a Memory window. CVW4 allows you to have two Memory windows open at one time.

By default, memory is displayed as hexadecimal byte values, with 16 bytes per line. At the end of each line is a second display of the same memory in ASCII form. Values that correspond to printable ASCII characters (decimal 32 through 127) are displayed in that form. Values outside this range are shown as periods (.).

Byte values are not always the most convenient way to view memory. If the area of memory you are examining contains character strings or floating-point values, you might prefer to view them in a directly readable form. The Memory Window command on the Options menu displays a dialog box with a variety of display options, which you can select individually or cycle through by pressing Shift+F3:

- ASCII characters
- Byte, word, or double-word binary values
- Signed or unsigned integer decimal values
- Short (32-bit), long (64-bit), or 10-byte (80-bit) floating-point values

Using CVW4 you can search through your program's memory to locate specific values using the S command. CVW4 also lets you move the memory within your program from one location to another using the M command.

Debug Multiple Applications

You can debug two or more applications at the same time, such as a DDE Client and Server. However, global symbols shared by both applications (such as the symbol name "WinMain") are not distinguished. CVW4 always resolves symbol references to the first application named when you started CVW4.

Display Local and Global Memory Objects

CVW4 lets you display global and local memory objects in their respective Windows heaps. You can display the heap of global memory objects with the wdg (Display Global Heap) command, and the heap of local memory objects with the wdl (Display Local Heap) command. Both of these commands display the entire heap of their respective memory objects in the Command window.

Check for Undefined Pointers

Until a pointer has been explicitly assigned a value, its value is undefined. The value can be completely random, or it can be some consistent value that does not point to a useful data address.

Accessing a memory object using an uninitialized pointer address is a program bug, because the data is not being read from or written to the intended location.

At present, all Microsoft C static or global near pointers have an uninitialized value of zero. That is, they point to the base address of the data segment. (There is no guarantee, however, that future versions of the Microsoft C Compiler will be the same; C language specifications do not define the value of an uninitialized pointer.)

You can take advantage of this consistency. If you specify DS:0 as a breakpoint expression, CVW4 automatically halts execution if your program attempts to write a non-zero value to a null pointer address. This is an easy way to see whether or not you have initialized all of your pointers.

You cannot take advantage of this in QuickC, because the QuickC Debugger does not set breakpoints when you try to modify a location in memory.

A CVW4 Debugging Project

If you would like to take CVW4 out for a test drive, I suggest using the DRAW.EXE program and going through the same steps we used in the QuickC debugging project. To use DRAW.EXE with CVW4, you need to rebuild it using Microsoft C/C++ 7.0.

More Debugging Tools

There are several other debugging tools that come with Windows 3.1 and the Windows 3.1 SDK that need to be discussed before looking at Borland's Turbo Debugger for Windows and MultiScope for Windows. These tools are Dr. Watson, DBWIN, and the debugging version of Windows.

Dr. Watson

Dr. Watson, a diagnostic tool for the Microsoft Windows operating environment, comes with the retail version of Windows 3.1. It detects system and application failures caused by Windows applications, and it can store information in a disk file that can help you find and fix problems. Dr. Watson uses the dynamic link library TOOLHELP.DLL. It cannot trap faults in a Windows MS-DOS session, and only a single instance of Dr. Watson can be run at a time.

To see how Dr. Watson works you should execute it from your Windows directory if it's not already running on your system. Its executable name is DRWATSON.EXE. It's a good idea to add Dr. Watson to your Program Manager StartUp group, so it's always there to collect information when a Windows application has a fatal error. To make sure you have a clean log file, delete the file DRWATSON.LOG from your \WINDOWS directory.

Next run the bug-infested DRAW.EXE program and choose Null Pointer in its Bugs menu. Boom! You should get a GPF error. Choose Close Application and the Windows Error dialog box and let Dr. Watson produce his report in his .LOG file. If you want to, go ahead and add a few notes about what happened in Dr. Watson's Clues dialog box. Following is a listing of the report Dr. Watson wrote to his .LOG file, annotated with comments preceded by # to help you figure out its contents:

```
Stop Dr. Watson 0.80 - Thu Jul 9 09:53:16 1992

Start Dr. Watson 0.80 - Thu Jul 9 09:53:43 1992
*********************************************************************************
# The date and time of the reported event.
Dr. Watson 0.80 Failure Report - Thu Jul 9 09:53:48 1992
# The next line reports that the application DRAW.EXE had a Null Selector
# write fault.
DRAW had a 'Null Selector (Write)' fault at DRAW 1:03c2
# The following line repeats the previous information formatted for
```

```
# automatic parsing code. It also includes the instruction that caused
# the fault (a mov instruction in this case).
$tag$DRAW$Null Selector (Write)$DRAW 1:03c2$mov
byte ptr es:[bx], 00$Thu Jul 9 09:53:48 1992

# The following lines report the contents of the CPU registers:
CPU Registers (regs)
# The 16-bit registers are listed first. This information can be
# useful to determine what address an instruction modified when the
# fault occurred.
CPU Registers (regs)
ax=00d2 bx=0000 cx=344f dx=0111 si=164e di=1a20
# The next items are the instruction pointer (otherwise known as the
# program counter), stack pointer, and base pointer. This line also
# lists the state of the flag bits. In this example, the program stopped
# at address 0x03c2. You will find this same address in the stack trace
# as well.
ip=03c2 sp=1608 bp=1616 O- D- I+ S- Z+ A- P+ C-
# The code segment selector is 0x33ff
cs = 33ff 807af2a0:0fbf Code Ex/R
# The following line provides information about the stack segment selector.
ss = 344f 80dcaea0:1a9f Data R/W
# The following line provides information about the data segment selector.
ds = 344f 80dcaea0:1a9f Data R/W
es = 0000    0:0000 Null Ptr

# The next lines provide information about the 32-bit registers.
CPU 32 bit Registers (32bit)
eax = 000000d2 ebx = 00000000 ecx = 0000344f edx = 00000111
esi = 0000164e edi = 00001a20 ebp = 00001616 esp = 800115f8
fs = 0000    0:0000 Null Ptr
gs = 0000    0:0000 Null Ptr
eflag = 00000202

# The next lines provide information about the Windows installation.
System Info (info)
Windows version 3.10
Retail build
Windows Build 3.1
Username Arthur English
Organization
System Free Space 17949120
Stack base 792, top 5762, lowest 4170, size 4970
# System resource statistics that tell you if the application
# faulted when resources were low.
```

513

```
System resources: USER: 68% free, seg 07bf GDI: 50% free, seg 0617
LargestFree 44146688, MaxPagesAvail 10778, MaxPagesLockable 2929
TotalLinear 12860, TotalUnlockedPages 2936, FreePages 1269
TotalPages 3390, FreeLinearSpace 10831, SwapFilePages 2099
Page Size 4096
# How many tasks were executing.
12 tasks executing.
WinFlags -
 Math coprocessor
 80486
 Enhanced mode
 Protect mode


# The following records the contents of the stack to determine what
# code called the routine that failed:

Stack Dump (stack)
# Stack frame 0 indicates that the failure occurred in DRAW at
# address 0x03b2.
Stack Frame 0 is DRAW 1:03c2     ss:bp 344f:1616
# The offending instruction is disassembled in context, as follows:
33ff:03b2 e9 00a7           jmp near 045c
33ff:03b5 c7 46 f6 0000     mov word ptr [bp+f6], 0000
33ff:03ba c7 46 f8 0000     mov word ptr [bp+f8], 0000
33ff:03bf c4 5e f6          les bx, [bp+f6]
(DRAW:1:03c2)
33ff:03c2 26 c6 07 00       mov byte ptr es:[bx], 00
33ff:03c6 e9 0093           jmp near 045c
33ff:03c9 c7 46 f6 0000     mov word ptr [bp+f6], 0000
33ff:03ce ff 76 f6          push word ptr [bp+f6]


Stack Frame 1 is DRAW 1:01a8     ss:bp 344f:1626
33ff:019c e9 007c           jmp near 021b
33ff:019f ff 76 0a          push word ptr [bp+0a]
33ff:01a2 ff 76 0e          push word ptr [bp+0e]
33ff:01a5 e8 00be          call near 0266
(DRAW:1:01a8)
33ff:01a8 83 c4 04          add sp, 04
33ff:01ab 99                cwd
33ff:01ac e9 00b0          jmp near 025f
33ff:01af ff 76 08          push word ptr [bp+08]


Stack Frame 2 is USER GLOBALGETATOMNAME+054c ss:bp 344f:1640
Stack Frame 3 is DRAW 1:0082     ss:bp 344f:1662
Stack Frame 4 is DRAW 1:0930     ss:bp 344f:1670
```

```
Stack Frame 5 is DRAW 1:08fd    ss:bp 344f:1680
System Tasks (tasks)
Task WINOLDAP, Handle 0ae7, Flags 0002, Info 49248 03-10-92 3:10
 FileName D:\WIN\SYSTEM\WINOA386.MOD
Task WINOLDAP, Handle 3057, Flags 0002, Info 49248 03-10-92 3:10
 FileName D:\WIN\SYSTEM\WINOA386.MOD
Task NHOOKEXE, Handle 243f, Flags 0001, Info 6144 03-20-92 2:00
 FileName D:\NDW\NHOOKEXE.EXE
Task  NDW, Handle 064f, Flags 0001, Info 8096 03-20-92 2:00
 FileName D:\WIN\NDW.EXE
Task DBWINEXE, Handle 22ff, Flags 0001, Info 16384 03-23-92 3:10
 FileName D:\C7\BIN\DBWIN.EXE
Task DESKEDIT, Handle 1587, Flags 0001, Info 221919 03-20-92 2:00
 FileName D:\NDW\DESKEDIT.EXE
Task WINHELP, Handle 44c7, Flags 0001, Info 256192 03-10-92 3:10
 FileName D:\WIN\WINHELP.EXE
Task MSWORD, Handle 367f, Flags 0001, Info 1273024 02-11-92 2:00
 FileName D:\WORD\WINWORD.EXE
Task DRWATSON, Handle 2a0f, Flags 0001, Info 26864 03-10-92 3:10
 FileName D:\WIN\DRWATSON.EXE
Task NDWMAIN, Handle 157f, Flags 0001, Info 12192 03-20-92 2:00
 FileName D:\NDW\NDWMAIN.EXE
Task CLOCK, Handle 2587, Flags 0001, Info 16416 03-10-92 3:10
 FileName D:\WIN\CLOCK.EXE
Task  DRAW, Handle 0c77, Flags 0001, Info 38924 07-09-92 8:39
 FileName E:\ATOOLS\DEBUG\DRAW.EXE

1> A bug was found in the bug-infested
2> DRAW.EXE program.
```

The Dr. Watson log provides you with the following useful information:

- When your application faulted.

- The register contents.

- The state of system resources.

- How many other tasks were executing, as well as their names.

- A stack trace to help you identify where your program stopped.

In this example, DRAW.EXE's error was in its own code, and the stack trace points to where the error occurred. If an error occurs in Windows you should try to follow the stack backward to find the point in your program where you called Windows, in order to isolate the line of code where the error occurred. If the stack trace doesn't go far enough, you can enlarge it using Dr. Watson's WIN.INI settings, or use another tool to debug your program to find out where the error occurred. The best tools to use are CVW4, DBWIN, and the debugging version of Windows—all working together.

To find the function that caused this error to occur, we need a MAP listing that's produced by the linker. If you use QuickC, choose the option Map File in the Customize Linker Options dialog box. If you use Microsoft C/C++ 7.0, specify a MAP file in your make file and use the compiler option /Fm.

The MAP file lists all the variables and functions in your program, along with their addresses. The following listing shows the function inside DRAW.EXE in address order:

```
Address    Publics by Value

0000:0000 Abs __wiobused
0000:0000 Imp CREATEPEN    (GDI.61)
  .
  .
  .
001:0010   WINMAIN
0001:0092  _InitApplication
0001:0114  _InitInstance
0001:018E  WndProc
0001:0266  _DoWMCommand
0001:0466  _DoLButtonDown
0001:04C8  _DoLButtonUp
0001:050A  _DoMouseMove
0001:06AC  _DoPaint
0001:080A  ABOUTDLGPROC
```

The address of the instruction that caused the error is 0x03b2. This information comes from the stack trace in the Dr. Watson .LOG file. If you look at the .MAP file you will find that this address is in the function DoWmCommand (it's between 0x0266 and 0x0466). If this is enough information for you to figure out where the error occurred, fine. If you want to isolate the instruction that caused the error, you need an object file listing.

QuickC cannot produce an object file listing, but Microsoft C/C++ 7.0 can. To produce this listing you use the /Fl option to produce only an object file listing or /Fc to produce a combined listing that includes both source and object file listings. After you make your application, this listing is put into a file with the extension

.COD. Following is the segment of the DRAW.EXE object listing where the offending instruction was located. For brevity's sake, I used the object listing instead of the combined listing.

```
; Line 243
; Line 244
      *** 00037f  ff 36 00 00            push  WORD PTR _hInst
      *** 000383  b8 66 00        mov    ax,OFFSET L03396
      *** 000386  8c da          mov    dx,ds
      *** 000388  52          push  dx
      *** 000389  50          push  ax
      *** 00038a  9a 00 00 00 00        call  FAR PTR LoadCursor
      *** 00038f  a3 00 00      mov    WORD PTR _hSaveCursor,ax
                                 L03395:
; Line 245
      *** 000392  ff 36 00 00            push  WORD PTR _hSave-
Cursor
      *** 000396  9a 00 00 00 00        call  FAR PTR SetCursor
; Line 246
      *** 00039b  6a 01            push  OFFSET 1
      *** 00039d  9a 00 00 00 00        call  FAR PTR ShowCursor
; Line 247
      *** 0003a2  e9 00 00          jmp   L03382
; Line 248
; Line 249

                                 L03397:
; Line 250
; lpzNullPointer = fff6
; Line 251
; Line 253
      *** 0003a5  c7 46 f6 00 00        mov   WORD PTR -
10[bp],OFFSET 0
      *** 0003aa  c7 46 f8 00 00        mov   WORD PTR -
8[bp],OFFSET 0
; Line 254
      *** 0003af  c4 5e f6        les   bx,WORD PTR -10[bp]
      *** 0003b2  26 c6 07 00          mov   BYTE PTR
es:[bx],OFFSET 0
; Line 255
      *** 0003b6  e9 00 00          jmp   L03382
; Line 256
; Line 258
                                 L03399:
; Line 259
; nRC = fff8
```

```
; hBadHandle = fff6
; Line 260
; Line 261
; Line 263
    *** 0003b9  c7 46 f6 00 00           mov    WORD PTR -
10[bp],OFFSET 0
; Line 264
    *** 0003be  ff 76 f6          push   WORD PTR -10[bp]
    *** 0003c1  6a 05             push   OFFSET 5
    *** 0003c3  9a 00 00 00 00    call   FAR PTR ShowWindow
    *** 0003c8  89 46 f8          mov    WORD PTR -8[bp],ax
; Line 265
    *** 0003cb  e9 00 00          jmp    L03382
; Line 266
; Line 268
                          L03402:
; Line 269
; nRC = fff8
; hBadhDC = fff6
; Line 270
; Line 271
; Line 273
    *** 0003ce  ff 76 f6          push   WORD PTR -10[bp]
    *** 0003d1  6a 0c             push   OFFSET 12
    *** 0003d3  6a 0c             push   OFFSET 12
    *** 0003d5  9a 00 00 00 00    call   FAR PTR LineTo
    *** 0003da  89 46 f8          mov    WORD PTR -8[bp],ax
; Line 274
    *** 0003dd  e9 00 00          jmp    L03382
; Line 275
; Line 277
                          L03405:
; Line 278
    *** 0003e0  b8 00 00          mov    ax,OFFSET 0
    *** 0003e3  e9 00 00          jmp    L03379
; Line 279
; Line 279
```

The address 0x03b2 points to line 254 in the DRAW.EXE program. The following listing shows the contents of DRAW.C with line numbers:

```
249:   case IDM_NULL_POINTER:
250:   {
251:   LPSTR lpzNullPointer;
252:
```

```
253:    lpzNullPointer = NULL;
254:    *lpzNullPointer = NULL; // KaBoom!
255:    break;
256:    }
```

As you can see, the C instruction this address points to is where DRAW.EXE tries to use a null pointer. As the comment says: KaBoom!

DBWIN

DBWIN can be used with both the retail and the debugging versions of Windows. Since Windows 3.1 is a lot more robust than Windows 3.0, it catches more errors when its API is called. When it catches an error, it writes it to the debugging terminal using `OutputDebugString`. If the debugging terminal doesn't exist, then the error message is lost. DBWIN catches these errors and displays them. If you use the retail version of Windows, you will catch some errors. If you use the debugging version of Windows, you will catch a lot of errors.

First you need to configure debug output in SYSTEM.INI, if you haven't already done so. Add this section to your SYSTEM.INI file if it doesn't exist already:

```
[Debug]
outputto=NUL
```

This directs the debug output to NUL so DBWIN can intercept it and display it. DBWIN is located in the \WINDEV\BIN directory. If you have your Windows 3.1 SDK and Microsoft C/C++ 7.0 in a combined directory called C7, this directory would be \C7\BIN. You will also find the source code for DBWIN in the \WINDEV\SAMPLES\DBWIN directory that was created when you installed the Windows 3.1 SDK. If you don't have the Windows 3.1 SDK, DBWIN is available on Microsoft's Software Library Forum on CompuServe.

As of the writing of this book, DBWIN has been updated to provide a few more features and to work better with a secondary-monitor setup. This updated version can be found in the Microsoft Developer Forum on CompuServe.

Compuserve's Microsoft Developer Forum is the best way available to keep up with what's going on in the international community of Windows developers. It has been referred to as the "back fence" where Windows developers of all backgrounds gather to discuss technical issues and gossip. I highly recommend you drop by. You will find the latest in shareware Windows development tools as well as programming examples in the Forum libraries. You will also find a lot of useful information in the message area of the Forum.

After you start DBWIN with the retail version of Windows 3.1, the DBWIN window that shows debug messages from Windows will be displayed. Try executing the DRAW.EXE program and choosing both Bad hWnd and Bad hDC from its Bugs menu. Figure 9.15 shows the messages that appear in DBWIN's window.

FIGURE 9.15:

Using DBWIN with the retail version of Windows 3.1

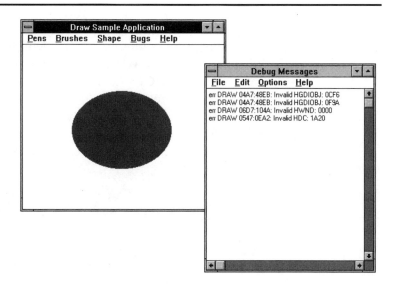

As you see, DBWIN logs two errors that neither CVW4 nor the QuickC Debugger recognized. If you want to debug your Windows applications fully, you need to test them using DBWIN with both the retail and the debugging versions of Windows. So let's look now at how DBWIN can be used with Windows' debugging version.

Using the Debugging Version of Windows

To test and debug your Windows application fully, you need to test it with DBWIN and the debugging version of Windows. You should consider this step to be mandatory in all your Windows application development projects.

Testing your application with the debugging version of Windows used to require a debugging terminal or a second PC. The Windows 3.0 debugging version provided limited information on the invalid use of resources such as User and GDI objects. The Windows 3.1 debugging version is much more robust and easier to use. Using the OUTPUTTO parameter in the DEBUG section of your SYSTEM.INI file, you can direct the output of the debugging version of Windows to any output device or even to a DOS file. If you set the OUTPUTTO parameter to NUL and use the DBWIN application as mentioned earlier, your debugging output is directed to the DBWIN window on your Windows desktop.

Since DBWIN has so many capabilities, it is the preferred way to work with the debugging version of Windows. Besides just displaying the debugging messages generated by the debugging version of Windows, DBWIN allows you to control the output of various kinds of messages—whether they're displayed or whether you break to the CodeView for Windows debugger. Furthermore, you can save your DBWIN settings in WIN.INI so that they'll remain in effect the next time you use it to test your Windows application.

Using the Tools Together

Before you can debug DRAW.EXE, you must build it using Microsoft C/C++. In the \DEBUG directory that was created when you installed the disk set on your PC you will find all the files you need to rebuild and debug DRAW.EXE, including a make file. I have already turned all the debug options on, so all you need to do is type in NMAKE to rebuild DRAW.EXE. To see how these tools work together, let's go through the following steps:

1. Exit Windows if it's running and type in N2D to load the debugging version of Windows that comes with the 3.1 SDK.

2. Start Windows as you would normally. If the debugging version of Windows is loaded correctly, you should see the message "Enhanced Mode Debug Windows 3.1" in the lower-right corner of your display to let you know that it is running.

3. Start DBWIN. Open the DBWIN Options menu to choose where you want the debugging output to go: the DBWIN window, COM1, COM2, or a secondary debugging monitor. I set my output to go to the DBWIN window.

4. Choose Setting in the DBWIN Options menu to display the System Debug Options. As you can see in Figure 9.16, I have DBWIN set to break on INT 3 and to validate the heap, to check free blocks, and to fill buffers. After you have finished with this dialog box, click on OK.

5. Start CVW4 and load DRAW.EXE.

FIGURE 9.16:

Setting DBWIN's options

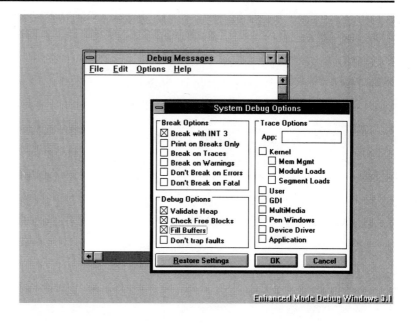

6. Get rid of any breakpoints that may have been set previously. The DRAW.EXE program should be in the same shape it was in when you installed the disk set. If you have changed DRAW.EXE, you should reload and rebuild it using Microsoft C/C++ 7.0.

7. Run DRAW.EXE using CVW4 by pressing F5.

As soon as DRAW.EXE executes, you should see an error appear in the DBWIN window. Press B to break on the error and control will be returned to the CVW4 debugger. Now you will see assembly-language code displayed in the Source window. Use F10 to step through this code slowly one step at a time until you are returned to the source code in DRAW.C. Bingo!— the instruction that caused the error was `DeleteObject (hBrush)`.

As you saw in the previous QuickC debugging project, I had two `DeleteObject` function calls to delete `hBrush`. The first one is fine; the next one tries to delete an object that doesn't exist. While none of the other debugging setups could isolate this problem, this set of tools working together can.

Now let's exit CVW4 and fix this error. After you exit, notice the messages that appear in DBWIN's window, seen in Figure 9.17, that tell you about all the GDI objects that didn't get deleted.

The following C source code shows you how the code in DRAW.C should look to fix the lost resources problem:

```
EndPaint (hWnd, (LPPAINTSTRUCT) &ps);
bRC = DeleteObject (hBrush);
bRC = DeleteObject (hPen);
```

You can also fix the other problem DRAW.C has with the uninitialized variable. The source code that causes this problem is near the start of the source code module:

```
unsigned nCurrentShape = IDM_SHAPE_ELLIPSE; // current object shape
```

Now that you have fixed these problems, rebuild DRAW.EXE using Microsoft C/C++ 7.0. Then start CVW4 again, using the same setup as before, with DBWIN running as well. Press F5 to run DRAW.EXE and try all of its functions except the ones in the Bugs menu. After working with DRAW.EXE, go ahead and exit the program but don't exit CVW4.

FIGURE 9.17:

DBWIN displays error messages from the debugging version of Windows about the GDI objects that DRAW.EXE forgot to delete

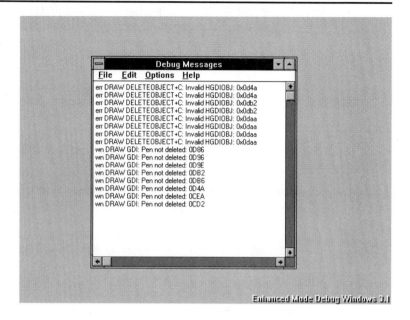

Notice that all the system resource problems are now fixed. Unless you played with the commands in DRAW.EXE's Bugs menu, no messages should have been displayed in DBWIN's window.

Now restart DRAW.EXE in CVW4 by choosing Restart in CVW4's Run menu. Go ahead and choose Bad hWnd in DRAW.EXE's Bugs menu. The following message should appear in DBWIN's window, and control should be passed to CVW4:

```
err DRAW SHOWWINDOW+C: Invalid HWND: 0x0000
```

If DRAW.EXE is locked up at this point and CVW4 doesn't have control, put the focus on the DBWIN window and press B for Break. Control should then be passed to CVW4. After CVW4 has control, assembly-language code will be displayed in the Source window. Slowly step through this code—as you did before—until you return to your program's C source code. You should arrive back in DRAW.C with the following line of code highlighted:

```
nRC = ShowWindow (hBadHandle, SW_SHOW);
```

Using this setup with CVW4, you are easily able to determine the C command that caused the error. No other setup using the Microsoft tools gives you this much power and flexibility in debugging your program. Go ahead and press F5, and your program will begin to execute again. If you choose Bad hDC in the Bugs menu and use the steps described previously, you can use CVW4 to go right to the instruction that caused the error.

Summary

As you can see, there are many ways you can debug a program using Microsoft tools. It can be as easy as using the QuickC Debugger. Or it can be as complex and powerful as using CVW4, DBWIN, and the debugging version of Windows all working together.

Now that we know how to use the Microsoft tools, let's take a look at Borland's Turbo Debugger and the MultiScope Debuggers for Windows. Learning about Turbo Debugger will help you understand some the differences in an important component of the Microsoft and Borland Windows development environments. Learning about MultiScope will introduce you to a powerful debugger that works as a Windows-hosted debugger like QuickC.

CHAPTER
TEN

Using Turbo Debugger for Windows and MultiScope for Windows

- What's included with Turbo Debugger for Windows

- Setting up Turbo Debugger

- A debugging project using Turbo Debugger

- Using the MultiScope Debuggers for Windows

- Using the MultiScope Crash Analyser

10

After covering in the last chapter the fundamentals of debugging a Windows application and learning to use the Microsoft debugging programs, let's look now at two other Windows debuggers—Borland's Turbo Debugger for Windows (TDW) and MultiScope for Windows. Each of these programs is very powerful and has features that are not included in the Microsoft debuggers. In fact, many of the new features in CodeView for Windows Version 4 (CVW4), such as overlapping windows, were included to match existing features in Borland's TDW. First let's find out how Turbo Debugger for Windows can be used to trap bugs in a Windows application, and then we will take MultiScope for a test drive.

Turbo Debugger for Windows

Borland's Turbo Debugger for Windows is a powerful source-level debugger that supports all of the Borland-language products. TDW has a commanding lead as the most full-featured debugger bundled with a Windows development system. It has more features and is easier to use than CVW4.

TDW was the first Windows debugger that did not require you to use a second monitor. It still provides many features that the competition has not put into their debuggers, including functionality such as back-tracing and logging execution history.

TDW is a full-screen, DOS character-mode Windows application. It looks the same as its counterpart, Turbo Debugger for DOS, but it is a Windows application and doesn't run from DOS. Turbo Debugger for Windows operates in the same way as Turbo Debugger for DOS, paging the display out and its text-mode interface in as you step and trace through your program.

TDW's strongest points are its powerful logging facility, its back-tracing features, its class hierarchy displays, its variable inspection, and its global or local heap data displays. TDW makes debugging dynamic link libraries easy. If you are tracing through a program that calls a DLL, the DLL's source code and symbols are loaded automatically.

What's Included with TDW

TDW includes a number of useful utilities. These utilities can convert a program compiled for debugging into a release version of your program with all the debugging information removed; add debug information to a program that was compiled without debugging turned on; and display useful information about device drivers and memory. The utilities bundled with TDW include the following:

TDSTRIP

The symbol table stripping utility, TDSTRIP.EXE, lets you strip the symbol table (debugging information) from your program without relinking. You can use this utility to convert a program linked for debugging into a release version. For large programs this can save you a considerable amount of time.

> **TIP**
>
> For help on how to use any of these utilities, including their command-line options, type the program name without the extension and then press Enter.

TDMAP

TDMAP appends debugging information from the corresponding .MAP file. This feature allows you to debug an executable program that is not compiled or linked with a Borland product.

> **NOTE**
>
> The version of TDMAP included with Borland C++ 3.1 will work only with Microsoft C 6.1 and earlier. It will not work with QuickC for Windows or Microsoft C/C++ 7.0. Incidentally, TDMAP can only give you source file/line number information and global variables. In other words, you'll be able to statement-step, and all your globals will be displayed as an `int`, but you won't have any local variables, nor will the debugger know anything about structures, pointers, etc. That information just isn't in the .MAP file.

TDUMP

TDUMP lists the contents of an object module or executable program. If TDUMP recognizes the file extension, either .EXE, .OBJ, or .LIB, it displays the file's components according to the type. If TDUMP doesn't recognize an extension, it produces a hexadecimal dump of the file.

TDDEV

TDDEV displays information about all the device drivers currently installed on your system, as well as how much memory each uses and what interrupt vectors are taken over. The following listing shows the report that TDDEV displays:

```
TDDEV Version 1.0 Copyright (c) 1990 Borland International

Address   Bytes  Name        Hooked vectors
---------  ------ ------------------------------
0070:0023    -    CON
0070:0035    -    AUX
0070:0047    -    PRN
0070:0059    -    CLOCK$
0070:006B    -    3 Block Units
0070:007B    -    COM1
0070:008D    -    LPT1
0070:009F    -    LPT2
0070:00B8    -    LPT3
0070:00CA    -    COM2
0070:00DC    -    COM3
0070:00EE    -    COM4
0000:11A8   7760  NUL         1B 29
0255:0000   416   SETVERXX
026F:0000   41776 1 Block Unit  20 21 25 26 27
0CA2:0000   1088  XMSXXXX0
0CE6:0000   6832  $MMXXXX0
Detected device drivers patched in after CONFIG.SYS
```

TDMEM

TDMEM displays a report that shows how the memory is currently being used on your PC system. This report displays information about memory availability and about expanded and extended memory. The following listing shows the report that TDMEM displays:

```
TDMEM Version 1.0 Copyright (c) 1991 Borland International

 PSP blks bytes owner  command line    hooked vectors
----------------------------------------------------------------
0008  2  57296 command
```

```
1053  2   2624 N/A                  2E
110C  1   6192 N/A
1290  3   1648 @                    2F
12F6  2  12672 WIN386   N/A              08 10 15 1C 4B 67
1610  3   2848 N/A                  22
16C5  2 562096 free


block  bytes  (Expanded Memory)
-----  ------
   0  393216
 free 1048576
total 1048576
```

Setting Up TDW

TDW runs in Standard or 386 Enhanced mode and requires at least an 80286 with 1MB of memory. If you plan to use TDW as a hardware debugger, an 80386 PC is necessary because of the way TDW uses the 386 debug registers.

TDW can run on either a dual-monitor system or in a full-screen DOS window in a Windows environment. If you use TDW with a single monitor, the screen swaps back and forth between TDW running in DOS character mode and your application running under Windows. Using a dual-monitor system allows you to view the TDW screens on one monitor and your Windows application on another.

You can also use a serial connection or a NETBIOS-compatible LAN to run TDW and Windows on two PCs during a debugging session. Although this method may sound nice, it's really quite cumbersome to set up. You must have the application you want to debug installed on both PCs. You must also have TDW installed on both systems. The only time you should consider this setup is when other setups don't work. This usually occurs when you are having memory problems and can't reliably run both your application and TDW on the same system.

Using TDW with One Monitor

Single-monitor debugging is the default way to run TDW. If you are using the standard Windows VGA graphic mode, everything should run perfectly. But if you are using a high-resolution video adapter, you may have problems. For example,

TDW did not initially support video adapters that used the S3 chipset in a high-resolution mode such as 1024 by 768 with 256 colors. A TDW video DLL that supports video adapters that use the S3 chipset is now available on the Borland CompuServe Forum for you to download.

The best way to find out whether or not your video system works with TDW is to try it. If you encounter problems you should check the README file that comes with the Borland C/C++ development system to see if there is a Turbo Debugger video DLL that works with your video adapter. The following video DLLs are available for Borland C/C++ 3.1:

- ATI VGA Wonder and XL cards in certain video modes.

- ATI 8514 Graphics Ultra and Vantage cards (8514/Ultra, 8514/Vantage, Graphics/Ultra, and Graphics/Vantage) and 8514-based cards configured for a single monitor (including most IBM 8514/a cards). If you use this DLL with an IBM 8514/a card, set "ATI=no" in the [VideoOptions] section of TDW.INI.

- TSENG ET-3000/ET-4000–based cards in certain video modes.

- TDVESA.DLL supports any video card that does VESA emulation. This includes the Video Seven VRAM II and Weitek Power Windows video adapters.

- STB.DLL supports the STB MVP2 series of multiscreen video cards.

- Video adapters that use the S3 chipset (as of this writing, this video DLL is available on CompuServe and from Borland technical support).

If the version of TDW that you purchased does not work with your video adapter in high-resolution modes, you should investigate the Borland forum on CompuServe to see if an updated video DLL exists. You can also contact Borland technical support.

If there is not a TDW video DLL available for your video adapter that works in a high-resolution video mode, you must choose another video mode to work in. For example, the 800 by 600 SuperVGA driver included with Windows and TDW works just fine. You can also use the standard VGA driver that comes with Windows to work with TDW on a single monitor.

Setting Up a Dual-Monitor System

Using a secondary monitor is preferable to using a single-monitor setup, if you have the hardware to support it. This is because you can use TDW on one monitor and see the output of your program on another monitor at the same time. The procedure for setting up the hardware for a secondary monitor for TDW is the same as that for CodeView for Windows. Instructions are found in the section "How to Set Up a Secondary CVW4 Monitor" in Chapter 9. After you have your secondary monitor installed and working, you can easily use either of these debuggers with it. To start TDW using the secondary monitor, use the –do command-line option.

TIP

You might want to consider setting up a Program Manager icon for each application you are debugging with TDW. To do this, copy the Program Manager icon for TDW by dragging it with the mouse while holding down the Ctrl key. After you have made a copy of the icon, choose Properties in the File menu. After the Program Item Properties dialog box is displayed, type the following in the Command Line edit box: TDW.EXE -DO [program name]. You put the name of your program in the specified field. This command is also set up for using a dual-monitor system. Now that all your options are set up and your program name is specified, all you need to do to start debugging your application is double-click on the icon.

To debug your application from the Borland C++ for Windows Integrated Development Environment (IDE) using a secondary monitor, all you need to do is choose Debugger Arguments in the IDE Run menu, then type in –do. The IDE will save the debug specification as part of your project setup. You can specify a unique debugger argument for each application you work on with the Borland IDE. If the application you are debugging requires command-line arguments, you need to type in the TDW options, followed by the program name, followed by the arguments. For example, to pass the command-line argument XYZ to DRAW.EXE you would type in –do DRAW.EXE XYZ.

Setting Up a Remote Debugging System

Besides single-monitor and dual-monitor debugging, you can also set up TDW for remote debugging using a NETBIOS-compatible LAN or a null modem cable and another computer. To debug a Windows application remotely, you must run Windows, WREMOTE, and the application on one PC and Turbo Debugger on the other. In this discussion, the PC running Windows, WREMOTE, and the application is referred to as the remote system. The PC running Turbo Debugger is referred to as the local system. To set up and run TDW on two PCs connected by a serial cable, you need to do the following:

1. Set up your application directories on both systems. Your best bet is to make sure all files match each other. I use LapLink Pro for this task, since I already have the two PCs cabled together using a serial connection. LapLink also verifies that the serial connection is set up correctly. I have found that Lap-Link Pro and LapLink Pro for Windows are easy to use to move files back and forth between my notebook computer and my PC for remote debugging and other purposes.

2. At a minimum, you need the following installed on your remote and your local system (since I already have Borland C/C++ installed on both my desktop system and my notebook computer, I don't need to worry about putting files on both systems):

    - On the remote system, you need to have Windows, your application, WREMOTE.EXE, and WRSETUP.EXE installed.

    - On the local system, you need to have Turbo Debugger (TD.EXE) installed—not TDW.EXE.

3. Run WRSETUP on your remote system to set up the environment for either a serial or a LAN configuration. WRSETUP will save all of the settings in the file WREMOTE.INI and put the file in the Windows directory.

4. Start WREMOTE from Windows; the mouse cursor becomes an hourglass. You are now ready to start Turbo Debugger on the local system.

5. Start Turbo Debugger (TD.EXE), not TDW, on your local system from the directory your application is in. For example, type in the following to use a serial connection attached to COM1 at 19.2KB:

```
TD -rp1 -rs2 -w DRAW.EXE
```

The expression -rp1 tells Turbo Debugger to use the COM1 port; -rs2 tells it to use 19.2KB for the communication speed; and -w tells it that it's debugging a Windows application remotely. All of these options can be found in the Turbo Debugger User Guide. Turbo Debugger should now appear on your local system for you to start debugging the program that's running on the remote system.

When you first use WRSETUP you should start by configuring your system for the slowest speed (9600 baud). After you have your remote debugging system working, you can try the higher speeds to find out which one works best. If things don't work at a higher speed, you can back up to the previous level.

Using TDW with Hardware Debuggers

TDW also has a hardware debugger interface. It supports hardware debugging through the use of the device driver TDH386.SYS or with hardware debugging boards such as Periscope, Atron, or Purart Trapper. If your application requires you constantly to watch areas of memory for variable changes, I would suggest purchasing a debugging board such a Periscope, because you can greatly speed up this type of breakpoint. TDW has a general interface for accessing these boards. Borland provides a recipe for designing a device driver that TDW can communicate with in order to make use of the capabilities of a particular hardware debugger. This "how- to" recipe is located in the README files DBGBOARD.TD and HDWDEBUG.TD.

Using TDW

TDW is a source-level debugger that is made up of multiple overlapping sizable windows, pop-up menus, and dialog boxes. The dialog boxes within TDW are similar to the modal dialog boxes in a graphical Microsoft Windows application. They contain buttons, check boxes, radio buttons, input boxes, and list boxes. When you are in one of these dialog boxes, the global menus and windows of TDW are not accessible. The menu bar works in a way similar to that of a Windows application, listing the available menus. The Borland terminology refers to menu bar menus as global menus. As in most Windows applications, the TDW menu bar contains a File menu and a Help menu. Figure 10.1 shows the Turbo Debugger for Windows enviroment.

Whenever you work with TDW, you'll have a number of different windows open on the desktop. You can move, size, and close these windows at random, with either a mouse or the keyboard, in a manner similar to moving and sizing a window in Windows.

Nevertheless, there are some differences between Windows and the text-based TDW application. For example, TDW must be run full-screen. When you size a window it must be grabbed in the lower-right corner—you can't size it using any other corner or side.

Using Local Menus

In addition to the menu bar menus (global menus), TDW has a convenient feature that reduces program complexity by reducing the number of menus. TDW keeps track of which window you have open and which part of the window the mouse pointer is in. In other words, TDW is always aware of what object you are working with, and its local menus are tailored to that particular object. You display a local menu by clicking the right mouse button or pressing Alt+F10. Figure 10.2 shows the TDW local menu for the Module window.

Using TDW Windows

All of TDW's features are accessed by its menus, either global or local, in contrast to many of CVW4's features, which you must access by typing commands in its Command window. To get Help on any command, press Shift+F1.

FIGURE 10.1:

The Turbo Debugger for Windows environment

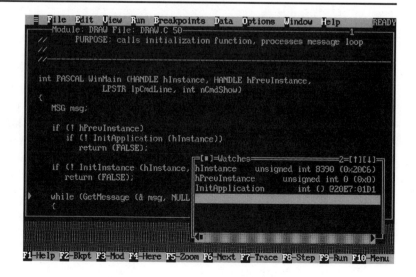

FIGURE 10.2:

The TDW local menu for the Module window

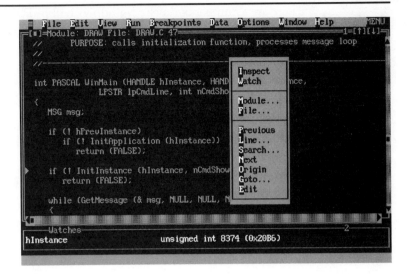

The power of a Windows debugger lies within the information displayed in each of its windows. You display all but one of TDW's windows, except Inspector, using the View menu. The Inspector window is opened by choosing the Data command from the Inspect menu. TDW windows can also be displayed using local menus, depending upon the TDW object that is selected.

Using TDW you can have as many windows as you can keep track of open at the same time while you are debugging a program. By overlapping windows and using the mouse to activate the window with the data you want to view, you can easily switch among each of the TDW windows. The active window is the topmost one and is framed by a double border. You can also open up more than one Module, Dump, or File window by choosing the View command from the Another menu. This is a nice feature if you want to view more than one section of memory.

TDW also has some helpful features, such as retrieving a window after it's been closed. If you close a window by accident, simply choose the Undo command from the Window menu. You can also save a window configuration to a file using the Save Options command from the Options menu. The file can then be restored using the Restore Options command. Both of these features have saved me considerable time.

There are a number of types of windows within TDW. Some windows display messages and others display variables. A window's type depends on the information it displays. TDW offers you 17 windows to display information in. In comparison, CVW4 has 7. TDW provides the following windows for you to work with:

- Module
- Watches
- Variables
- Windows Messages
- Inspector
- Breakpoint
- Log
- Stack
- Registers
- Dump
- CPU
- File
- Hierarchy
- Numeric Processor
- Execution History
- Clipboard
- Another

Since much of TDW's debugging power is derived from the information it can display about your program and the Windows environment, let's take a look into each of TDW's windows.

Module   The Module window displays the contents of the source file you are debugging. You use the Module window to step visually through your program's code as it's executing and to set breakpoints to stop your program at specific points. This window is the same as CVW4's Source window. Although you can display your program from this window, you cannot edit it from here, or from anywhere within TDW, as you can with the QuickC for Windows Debugger.

The dialog box that appears when you choose the Module command from the View menu shows you a list of source modules and a list of DLLs and executables already loaded by Windows. The source file is loaded for the module that is selected. The notations *opt* or *modified* may appear after the filename in the title of the module window. *Opt* means the program is optimized. *Modified* means that the program has changed since you last compiled and linked it.

> **NOTE**　At the bottom of TDW's screen are ten buttons for invoking TDW commands. You can choose them by using a function key or by clicking on them with the mouse. You use these buttons to step and trace through program code and to set breakpoints. (I just wish I could configure which command is linked to which function key, so I would not have to remember the differences between CVW4 and TDW. For example, to run a program, TDW uses F9 and CVW4 uses F5.)

Watches　The Watches window displays expressions and variables you select as they change during your program's execution. To watch a variable, click on it with the mouse to put the caret in it, and choose Watch from the TDW Module window local menu. You can also Add Watch from the TDW Data menu. The easiest way to watch a variable is to press Ctrl+W. Within the Watches window, you can display both simple and complex data objects, as well as create expressions that do not refer directly to a specific memory location. Be careful you do not mistype a variable name within the Watches window, because it is not noticed by the debugger. The only warning to you that a variable does not exist is the ???? after the variable's name. This is a mistake I often make. The Watches window with its local menu displayed is shown in Figure 10.3.

The local menu that corresponds to the Watches window allows you to add, edit, remove, inspect, or change values within the window.

Variables　To display the Variables window, choose the Variables command from the View menu. This window shows all the variables and their associated values that are accessible from your current location in the program. This window has two panes: the top pane shows the global symbols in your program, and the bottom pane shows the variables that are local to your program. You can change the contents of a local variable or a global variable at any time by using either pane's local menus. The Variables window is shown in Figure 10.4.

FIGURE 10.3:

The TDW Watches window with its local menu displayed

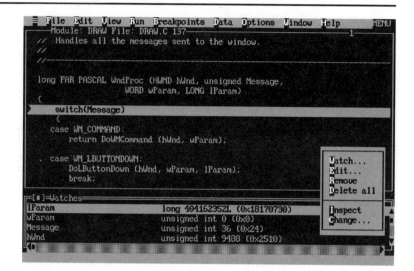

FIGURE 10.4:

The TDW Variables window

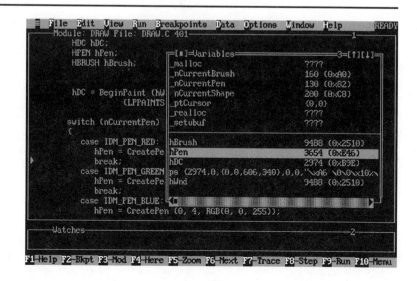

As in CVW4, if you have a lot of local variables in the function you are debugging and you need to monitor only some of them, you will find the Watches window more useful than the Variables window.

Windows Messages This is a very important window. It displays all messages passed between your application and Microsoft Windows. The upper-left pane allows you to specify a Windows procedure or handle to track messages to. The lower pane shows the messages being tracked as well as the wParam and lParam values for each message. This window can hold up to 200 messages. If you want to save all messages to a file, you can display the Windows Messages window local menu and specify a file name. The upper-right pane shows the class of messages that you are tracking. If you are logging more than one Windows procedure or handle, do not log "all" messages because of the large number of messages being sent and received. This may hang up the system and require you to reboot. Figure 10.5 shows the Windows Messages window.

To specify the window whose messages you want to track, click with the mouse in the upper-left window pane to activate it and then choose Add from its local menu. To specify the message class (or specific message type) to keep track of, click with the mouse in the upper-right window pane to activate it and choose Add from its local menu to display the Set Message Filter dialog box, shown in Figure 10.6.

FIGURE 10.5:

The TDW Windows Messages window

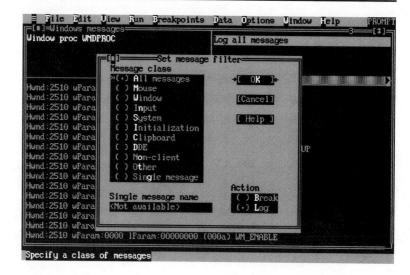

Inspector   The Inspector window displays a list of the items contained in a data object. It is not displayed from the View menu but is opened by choosing either Inspect from a local menu or the Inspect command from the Data menu. Inspector windows are different for each separate data object. If the object being displayed is a scalar, the address and value of the object is displayed. If the object is a pointer, the address of the variable and the value of the item being pointed to are displayed. A structure or union Inspector window shows you the value of each member of the object as well as the data type of the highlighted member. Array Inspector windows display the value of each array item. Function Inspector windows show you the value of each parameter within the function as well as the return value.

The local menu for the Inspector window provides you with increased functionality. It allows you to display a range of values, change a value, inspect to another level, or even typecast the selected item with a new data type. Figure 10.7 shows the Inspector window displaying the contents of rectClient from the Do-MouseMove function in DRAW.EXE. This RECT structure is used to keep track of the client area boundaries after the mouse has been captured when the user is drawing a graphic shape.

FIGURE 10.7:

The Inspector window in DRAW.EXE displays the values for the `rectClient` structure before its values are initialized

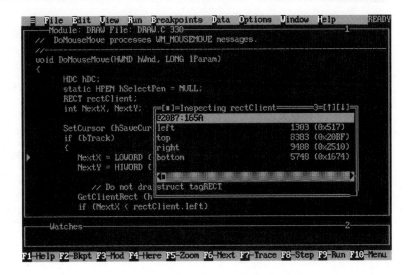

Breakpoint   As we discussed in the last chapter, CVW4 can be used to set program breakpoints for a large variety of situations using the CVW4 command language. TDW, on the other hand, gives you a more extensive facility for setting program breakpoints that is much easier to use. With the mouse, just click in either of the two leftmost columns of the line where you want to set or remove an unconditional breakpoint. If you are in the correct column, an asterisk appears in place of the cursor. You can also press F2 or click on the Bkpt button at the bottom of the TDW display to toggle breakpoints. To display the breakpoints you have set and to edit their conditions, you use the Breakpoints window.

The Breakpoints window is displayed by choosing Breakpoints in the View menu. It has two panes. On the left is the Breakpoint List, showing all the addresses at which breakpoints are set. The Breakpoint Detail pane on the right shows the details of the breakpoint that is highlighted in the left-hand pane. Although a breakpoint may have multiple sets of actions and conditions associated with it, only the first set of details is displayed in the Breakpoints Detail pane. The Breakpoints window is shown in Figure 10.8.

FIGURE 10.8:

TDW's Breakpoints window

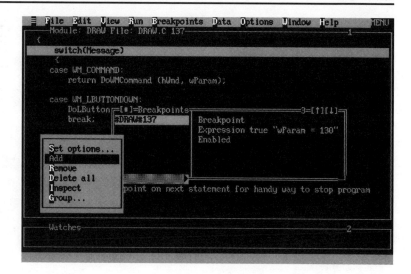

The Breakpoints List pane has a local menu that you can use to add new break-points, delete existing ones, and change the behavior of an existing breakpoint. You can execute the following tasks from this menu:

- *Set Options* displays the Breakpoint Options dialog box, so you can modify the properties of a breakpoint you have already set.

- *Add* displays the Breakpoint Options dialog box so you can add a new breakpoint.

- *Remove* deletes a breakpoint.

- *Delete All* deletes all the breakpoints you have set.

- *Inspect* displays the source code line (or assembler instruction) where the breakpoint is set.

- *Group* displays the Edit Breakpoint Groups dialog box, so you can work with breakpoint groups.

Using CVW4 you can set conditional breakpoints that stop your program at a specific address when an expression evaluates to being true. You can also disable and enable breakpoints without having to remove them. This lets you turn breakpoints on and off at will without having CVW4 forget where they were placed and the condition associated with them.

In comparison, using TDW you can set breakpoints with multiple conditions. You can also specify actions that occur when a breakpoint is encountered. For example, you could set a breakpoint that would write the wParam and lParam values of a WM_PAINT message to a log file whenever the message is received by a window procedure.

You can put breakpoints into groups. A breakpoint group is identified by a positive integer that's either generated automatically by TDW or assigned by you using the Breakpoint Options dialog box. TDW assigns a group number to each breakpoint as it is created, choosing the lowest group number that's not already in use. For example, if the numbers 1, 2, 3, and 5 are already in use, the next breakpoint set would be assigned the group number 4. You can organize your breakpoints into groups using the Breakpoint Options dialog box by changing the group ID for the breakpoint. Grouping breakpoints together lets you enable, disable, or remove a collection of breakpoints with a single action using the Edit Breakpoint Groups dialog box.

You can even set a hardware breakpoint that uses hardware debugging support through either a hardware debugging board or the debugging registers of the Intel 80386 (or higher) processor.

In most cases you will find that all you need to debug a program is a set of unconditional breakpoints placed in your program to isolate the problem area. You will not need to use TDW's extensive breakpoint features often, but when you do you will appreciate their power and flexibility.

NOTE

As good as TDW's breakpoint facility is, it does have one flaw that CVW4 doesn't: there is no way to save where and how you set breakpoints in your program from one debugging session to another. There is one way around this problem, however—record a macro while you are setting your breakpoints and play it back when you start a new debugging session. This method works, but it's not a perfect solution.

TDW's macro recorder is a simple keystroke recorder. You cannot edit your macro after it's recorded. To use macros with TDW and have them work, you need to record them carefully. If you need to alter your breakpoints after recording a macro, you have only two choices: if the changes to your breakpoint setup are minor, you can keep the old macro and revise your breakpoint setting after playing the macro; if the changes are major, you need to record a new macro.

Log   The Log window lets you review a list of significant events that have taken place during the debugging session. As we discussed in the previous section, you can set up TDW to write specific information to the Log window when a breakpoint occurs. Log windows display a scrollable list of the lines output to the window. If more than 50 lines are written to the log, the oldest lines are lost from the top of the list. If you want to change the number of lines allowed, use the TDINST customization program. Here is a list of events that cause output to be written to the Log window:

- Your program stops because of a breakpoint or error, as shown in Figure 10.9.

- You add a comment to the log using the Log window's local menu.

- A breakpoint is encountered that writes information to the log.

- You choose Dump Pane to Log in the Edit menu to record the current contents of a window in the log.

- You choose Display Windows Information in the Log window's local menu to write global heap information, local heap information, or the module list to the log.

- You toggle Send to Log so all messages will go to the Log window, if you are keeping track of window messages in the Window Messages window.

FIGURE 10.9:

TDW's Log window

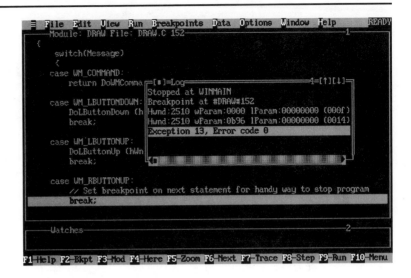

Using the Log window's local menu, you can open a file in which to save all your log messages by choosing Open Log File. To close the file and save the information written to it, choose Close Log File. Using the Log window along with carefully designed breakpoints and writing the output to a file can be a powerful tool for solving even the most pesky debugging problems.

Stack The Stack window is similar to CVW4's Calls window because it lists all active functions in your program—but that is where the comparison ends. The TDW Stack window lists not only all the functions that have been called, with the most recently called routine first; it also lists the values of the parameters that were passed to each function when it was called.

The Stack window local menu has two commands, Inspect and Locals. Choosing Locals displays a two-pane window that lists all your global variables in one pane and your local variables in the other. If a function calls itself recursively, there are multiple instances of the function in the Stack window. By positioning the highlight bar on one instance of a function, you can use the Locals command to look at the local variables for that instance.

The Inspect command is also very useful. If you highlight the function that called the function you are in and choose Inspect, the cursor is positioned on the line in the function that will be executed after the called function returns.

Registers   The Registers window displays a quick look at the state of the CPU's flags and registers. This window is a combination of the Registers and the Flags panes of the CPU window. The local menu of the Registers window allows you to modify all values. On an 80386 or later processor you can also toggle between displaying the CPU registers as 16-bit or 32-bit values.

Dump   The Dump window displays areas of memory. You can display a memory dump a number of ways, for example, byte, word, long, comp, float, real, double, or extended. The local menu of the Dump window lets you search for data and select the display format.

Typically, you use this window to verify that your program is operating on data the way it was designed. You could also use HEAPWALK for this task, but while you are debugging a program, the Dump window is closer at hand.

File   The File window displays the contents of a disk file in ASCII or in hex. This can be useful if your application uses external disk files. If the file you want to view is in ASCII, you can call a text editor by using the local menu of the File window. To configure the text editor of your choice to use with TDW, you must run the TDINST program that comes with the debugger.

Numeric Processor   The Numeric Processor window shows the current state of the math coprocessor. This window displays the control flags, status flags, and floating-point registers.

Execution History   Execution History is one of the unique features of TDW that's not part of either the Microsoft debuggers or MultiScope. This window lets you back-trace through the code. However, you need to be aware of its limitations, which are the following:

- Only instructions that have been executed using the Trace Into command are logged into the Execution History window.

- You cannot undo reads or writes by using back-trace.

- If you step over a function call, you cannot trace back beyond the instruction following the return. (This makes back-tracing within an application such as DRAW.C difficult).

The Execution History window displays the code for your program up to the last line executed (provided you are tracing the code). To use this functionality, Full History must be turned on in the local menu of the Execution History window. (The default has Full History turned off.) The local menu also contains the commands Inspect and Reverse Execute. The Inspect command takes you to the command currently highlighted within the window. If the line is source code, you are taken to the Module window; otherwise the CPU window opens. The Reverse Execute command reverses your program to the location highlighted in the window.

NOTE   Back-tracing has limited use in debugging Windows programs, because you cannot back-trace through calls to the Windows API. You can use back-tracing with TDW only if you are executing through your own code.

CPU   The CPU window is intended for programmers who are familiar with programming the Intel 8086 family of microprocessors in assembler language. TDW is a debugger for all of Borland's languages, including Turbo Assembler. If you are an assembler programmer or a C programmer who knows assembler language, you will be impressed with the information available in the CPU window for you to work with. If you are a C programmer who understands the PC architecture but doesn't understand assembler, you can still benefit from using this window.

Whereas in CVW4 you can view your program code in the Source window in C, mixed C and assembler, or assembler language, TDW's Module window shows only the source language your program was written in: C, Pascal, or assembler. To view the assembler instructions generated by the compiler, you use the CPU window, where you can view your program as assembler instructions only, or as both C (or Pascal) and the assembler instructions for each line of source code.

When you are debugging a program, you can usually determine the cause of most problems by working at the source level; you view your program as it executes through your source code and refer to the variables you created in your program by their symbolic names. Sometimes, however, you can gain insight into a problem by looking at the exact instructions that the compiler generated, the contents of the CPU registers, and the contents of the stack. To do this you use TDW's CPU window.

> **TIP**
>
> Although TDW's CPU window is primarily intended as a debugging tool, it is also an excellent learning tool. If you want to gain insight into how the CPU works or how to program in assembler, I highly recommend you use TDW's CPU window as one of your learning tools. As you will soon see, the CPU window displays your C program and its generated assembler code along with all the CPU registers and flags. You can step through your program one instruction at a time using the CPU window and see exactly how your program is executing, including the use of 32-bit registers and selector registers.

The CPU window shows you the entire state of the CPU. You can examine and change the bits and bytes that make up your program's instructions and data. You can use the built-in assembler in the Code pane to patch your program's code temporarily by entering instructions exactly as you would type in assembler source statements.

The CPU window has six panes. The top left pane (*Code pane*) shows your program source code mixed with the assembler code that gets generated. The pane to its right is the *Register pane,* which shows the contents of the CPU's registers. The *Flags pane* is in the top right-hand corner. It shows the state of the eight CPU flags. On the left, underneath the Code pane, is the *Selector pane,* which shows all the selector registers along with their contents. The bottom left pane is the *Data pane.* It shows a raw hex dump of any area of memory that you choose. The bottom right pane is the *Stacks pane.* It shows the contents of the stack. The CPU window is shown fully maximized in Figure 10.10.

The two CPU window panes you as a C programmer will work with the most are the Code pane and the Dump pane. The Code pane, like the Module window, shows your program instructions. You can step through your program in the CPU window using the same commands you use in the Module window. In the Code pane, your program steps one assembler instruction at a time instead of one C instruction at a time.

The left part of each line of assembler code shows the address of the instruction. The address is displayed either as a hex segment and an offset, or with the segment value replaced with the CS register name if the segment value is the same as the

FIGURE 10.10:

TDW's CPU window

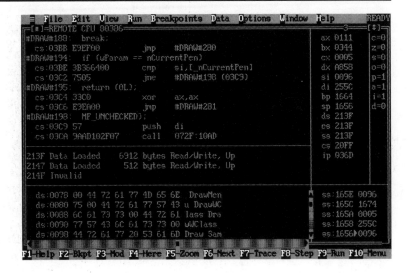

current CS register. The left part of each line of source code shows the module name bounded by pound-sign (#) characters, followed by the line number and C language instruction.

The local menu for the Code pane contains commands by which you navigate through your program code and follow addresses. For example, the Follow command will position you at the destination address of the currently highlighted instruction. For conditional jumps, the address will be shown as if the jump had actually occurred. The Caller command will position you at the instruction that called the current subroutine. The other commands let you go to a specific address and search through the code using a text string.

The Data pane shows a raw display of an area of memory you've selected. The left part of each line shows the address of the data displayed in that line. Using the local menu of the Data pane, you can display the contents of memory as byte, word, long, float, real, double, and extended floating point. The Data pane local menu also gives you access to other powerful commands for

- clearing a block of memory to zeros,

- moving blocks of memory from one address to another,

- setting a block of memory to a specific byte value,

- reading and writing to memory from a DOS file,

- following a memory address through either local or global memory, and

- changing the bytes at the cursor location.

Hierarchy   The Hierarchy window lists and displays a hierarchy tree for C++ programs of all object or class types used by the current module. The window has two panes: one for the object type or class list, the other for the object type or classes in a class hierarchy tree. This window shows you the relationship of the object types or classes used by the current module. By using this window's local menu commands, you can examine any object type's or class's data fields or members and its methods or member functions.

Clipboard   TDW has a Clipboard window that you can use in a way similar to the Windows Clipboard. While the Windows Clipboard is a simple facility for cutting, copying, and pasting data within one program or between programs, the TDW Clipboard window has many features that can help you in a number of ways to debug a program.

Using the TDW Clipboard, you can copy and paste between TDW windows and dialog boxes. The items you copy into the Clipboard are dynamic. If an item has an associated value (such as a variable copied from the Watches window), the Clipboard keeps that value current as it changes in your program.

To copy an item to the Clipboard, simply highlight it with the mouse or the Insert key and press Shift+F3. To paste an item into a dialog box or window, put the cursor in the desired location and press Shift+F4. You can also use the Clip push button that appears in most dialog boxes. This brings up a dialog box that shows a scrolling list of items within the Clipboard. Choose the item you want to paste and select the Paste push button. Choosing Clipboard in the TDW View window lets you see the contents of the Clipboard window, which lists all clipped items.

The leftmost field of this window describes the type of entry, followed by a colon and the clipped item. If the clipped item is an expression from the Watches window, a variable from the Inspector window, or a register or flag from the CPU window, the item is followed by its value. When you clip an item from a window, TDW assigns it a type to help you identify its source. The TDW Clipboard supports the following types:

- String, such as a text string from a Module of the File window.

- Module context, which keeps track of your source code position.

- File context, which keeps track of your position in a file.

- CPU code, an address and byte list of data in memory from the Data pane of the CPU window.

- CPU data, an address and byte list of data in memory from the Data pane of the CPU window or from the Dump window.

- CPU stack, the source position and stack frame from the Stack pane of the CPU window.

- CPU Register, the register name and value from the Registers pane of the CPU window or from the Registers window.

- CPU flag, the value from the Flags pane of the CPU window.

- Inspector, the variable name or constant value from the Inspector or Watches window.

- Address.

- Expression from the Watches window.

The Clipboard local menu helps you to manage the Clipboard's contents. *Copying* an item to the Clipboard only appends the item—it does not overwrite the Clipboard's contents. Choosing the *Inspect* command from the Clipboard local menu positions the cursor in the window the clipped item came from. *Remove* and *Delete All* let you get rid of Clipboard items that are no longer needed. *Freeze* stops a Clipboard item from being dynamically updated. This is very helpful for comparing variable values as they change.

As you can see, the TDW Clipboard gives you a very flexible facility for storing and keeping track of you progress while debugging a Windows application. Here are a few tips on how you can use the TDW Clipboard to help you debug a Windows program:

- TDW does not have a bookmark feature, as does QuickC for Windows, where you can use Toggle Tag to mark positions within your program, but you can use the Clipboard to do the same thing. To set a bookmark, copy a line of code from the Module window into the Clipboard. To go to the marked code, open the Clipboard window and choose Inspect from the Clipboard's local menu.

- Paste strings into the Log window so you can keep track of what you did during a debugging session.

- Paste expressions into conditions and actions of breakpoints. This saves you some typing and referring back to information in other windows.

- To keep track of the previous contents of a variable at different points during the execution of your program, copy the variable to the Clipboard and freeze its value, as shown in Figure 10.11. This figure shows four variables that have been frozen. Notice the new values for these variables in the Watches window.

Another   By choosing the Another command from the View menu, you can duplicate a Dump, File, or Module window. Occasionally, under certain circumstances, TDW will open one of these windows on its own. I use this command when I want to look at two different functions in the same source code module at the same time.

FIGURE 10.11:

TDW's Clipboard window

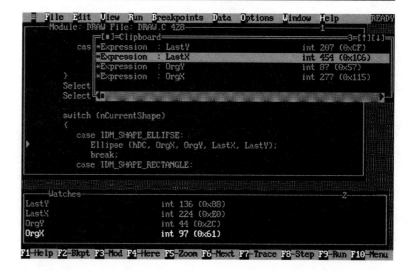

Debugging DRAW.EXE Using TDW

To allow you to become familiar with TDW and at the same time introduce you to a few things you *cannot* do with CVW4, let's use TDW to do the following projects with the DRAW.EXE program that we used in the QuickC for Windows and CVW4 debugging projects:

- Finding out why DRAW.EXE doesn't draw a shape until you choose one from its menu.

- Trapping a NULL pointer.

- Finding lost resources.

- Trapping bad parameters on calls to the Windows API.

Each of these projects was covered in Chapter 9 on Microsoft debuggers. If you skipped that chapter, you may want to go back and read it before proceeding. If you are new to using a debugger or to Windows programming, Chapter 9 provides a thorough introduction to debugging Windows applications and the basics of using an interactive Windows debugger.

Preparing DRAW.EXE for Debugging

Before you can debug DRAW.EXE, you must build it using the Borland C++ (BC++) Windows IDE. In the \DEBUG directory that was created when you installed the disk set on your PC you will find all the files you need to rebuild and debug DRAW.EXE, including a project file (DRAW.PRJ). I have already turned all the debug options on, so all you need to do is choose Build All in the BC++ IDE Compile menu to build a debugging version of DRAW.EXE.

Unlike CVW4, BC++ 3.1 includes debugging information in your executable by default. To toggle debug information on or off before you build your program using BC++, you use the Include Debug Information switch in the Linker Settings dialog box. This dialog box is displayed by choosing Settings in the Linker submenu in the Options menu.

Running TDW

The easiest way to start TDW is to choose Debugger from the BC++ Windows IDE. If you are using a secondary monitor, remember to set up the -do option by choosing Debugger Arguments in the Run menu.

> **TIP**
>
> TDW needs to have the latest version of your C source files on disk in order to display the correct information about your C source code in the Module window. Since the BC++ IDE does not save files for you automatically every time you make changes to your program and compile it, you must save all your C source code files before running TDW from the BC++ IDE. However, if you're like me, you can easily forget to save your files before starting TDW because you're concentrating on the project at hand, not the mechanics of using the BC++ IDE.
>
> There is a solution. To have the BC++ IDE save your files for you automatically before you run the TDW, choose the Preferences command in the Environment submenu of the Options menu to display the Preferences dialog box. Then, select Editor Files in the Auto Save options. (I have all of the Auto Save options turned on in my own development system.)

Why Doesn't DRAW.EXE Draw?

To start, let's step through this first project in the same way we did using QuickC for Windows in Chapter 9, to give you a feel for using TDW. After executing and trying out DRAW.EXE, you will notice that it does not draw any objects on the screen until you choose either Rectangle or Ellipse from the Shape menu. You will also find the other following problems with DRAW.EXE:

- The program creates GDI resources without releasing them. As you draw different shapes, notice how the percentage of GDI resources drops, one point at a time.

- The Bugs menu has some obvious program bugs in it. Choosing NULL Pointer will cause DRAW.EXE to get a GPF error. Choosing Bad hWnd or Bad hDC doesn't seem to cause any errors, but you can bet choosing these menu commands is causing something to happen that shouldn't.

After executing TDW and displaying the DRAW.C source code in the Module window, let's set a breakpoint in the function WndProc where the WM_RBUTTONUP message is handled. This lets you experiment with the program and stop it in the debugger at any time you want. To set an unconditional breakpoint, find the "break" statement that follows the case statement for processing the WM_RBUT-TONUP message. Click in either of the two leftmost columns of the line on which the break statement appears. TDW will underline the break statement to indicate that a breakpoint has been set.

After setting the breakpoint, press F9 or click on the Run button at the bottom of the screen to run the program. Experiment with its functions, and whenever you want to stop the program at the breakpoint you set, click the right mouse button in the DRAW.EXE window.

After stopping the program, try stepping through the program code to see how execution flows from statement to statement. Restart the program again by pressing F9. After the program is running, press the right mouse button again to stop it.

TIP

You may also want to open the CPU window at this point, to see how you can step through assembler code in the same way you can step through C source code. Notice how your C source code and the generated assembler code are mixed. Also note the state of the registers and how they change as you execute your program one line at a time.

Now that you have seen how to set an unconditional breakpoint and step through program code using TDW, let's see how to set a breakpoint when the WM_PAINT message is received by WndProc, so we can investigate why the screen is not being redrawn correctly by DRAW.EXE.

NOTE

If you have already selected Ellipse or Rectangle from the DRAW.EXE Shapes menu, you should restart the program so it will be in its initial state. To restart a program at any point in the debugging process, choose Program Reset in the TDW Run menu.

To set all other conditional breakpoint types using TDW, you use the breakpoints menu. For Windows messages, you use the Windows Messages window to set a message breakpoint. To set a program breakpoint on the WM_PAINT message, do the following:

1. Choose Windows Messages from the TDW View menu.

2. Click the right mouse button inside the upper-left pane of the Windows Messages window to display its local menu, and choose Add to display the Add Window or Handle to Watch dialog box.

3. Type in WndProc as the Window Identifier and select Identify by Window Procedure.

4. Click on OK and you will return to the Windows Messages window. You will see the name of the window procedure (WndProc) listed in the upper-left pane and Log All Messages listed in the upper-right pane. At this point TDW is set up to log all window messages sent to WndProc in the bottom pane of the Windows Messages window. Let's set it up to track only the WM_PAINT message and to break into TDW when the message appears.

5. Click the right mouse button inside the upper-right pane of the Windows Messages window and choose Add to Display in the Set Message Filter dialog box.

6. In the Set Message Filter dialog box, type in WM_PAINT for the Single Message Name and select Break as the action.

7. Choose OK, and the Windows Messages window should appear as it does in Figure 10.12.

Now that you have set a breakpoint for the WM_PAINT message, press F9 to continue program execution. The program will immediately stop, and you will see the message in the bottom pane of the Windows Messages window. The Module window will appear in the background with the program stopped at the beginning of the WndProc function, as shown in Figure 10.13.

After the program is stopped, press F7 (or use the Trace button at the bottom of the screen) to trace each program step, following the program path into the DoPaint function where WM_PAINT messages are processed. As you trace through the program in the DoPaint function, notice how the pen and brush are created using the

FIGURE 10.12:

TDW's Windows Messages window with a breakpoint set on the WM_PAINT message

FIGURE 10.13:

The DRAW.EXE program stopped at the WM_PAINT message breakpoint

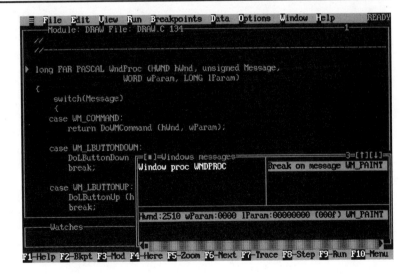

constant value for the menu item to specify the color for each. Unless you have changed the pen and brush color, a blue brush and pen should be created and then selected into the device context.

Everything goes well until the switch statement for deciding which object shape is processed. Neither of the two choices was valid, so neither the ellipse nor the rectangle was drawn. To check the value of the nCurrentShape variable, set a watch point on it. Put the cursor on nCurrentShape in the Module window and choose Watch from the local menu to watch the variable. You can also press Ctrl+W or choose Add Watch in the TDW Data menu to set a watch point.

You will see that nCurrentShape has the value zero. It wasn't initialized correctly. If you check the global variable definitions for nCurrentPen, nCurrentBrush, and nCurrentShape, you will find that nCurrentPen and nCurrentBrush were initialized correctly, but nCurrentShape wasn't. If you change the program code to initialize nCurrentShape to IDM_SHAPE_RECTANGLE and rebuild the application, you will find that the program draws shapes properly from the start.

Now that the first problem is fixed, let's see how good TDW is at trapping a NULL pointer.

Trapping a NULL Pointer

After starting TDW, press F9 to run the DRAW.EXE program. When the application window is displayed, choose NULL Pointer in the Bugs menu. The program will immediately stop and control will be returned to TDW. TDW displays the CPU window when it traps the NULL pointer error, as shown in Figure 10.14.

It's easy to trap simple errors such as NULL pointers using TDW. If you try the other commands in the DRAW.EXE Bugs menu, however, you will find that TDW does not trap these errors. You will also find that TDW doesn't trap an attempt to delete a GDI object (an HBRUSH) either. Each of these bugs in DRAW.EXE requires you to realize that a problem exists and then use TDW to investigate its cause.

In tracking down these bugs, TDW's power is no greater or less than the power in CVW4 or MultiScope. The easiest way to track down these bugs is to use TDW (or one of the other debuggers) along with the debugging version of Windows. Now let's look at this combination, using TDW to trap the remaining bugs in DRAW.EXE.

Finding Lost Resources

To do the remaining projects, you need both TDW and the debugging version of Windows. The debugging version of Windows is not included with BC++ 3.1. You can only get it directly from Microsoft by purchasing it separately or as part of one of their development systems, such as the Windows 3.1 SDK.

FIGURE 10.14:

TDW trapping a NULL pointer error in DRAW.EXE

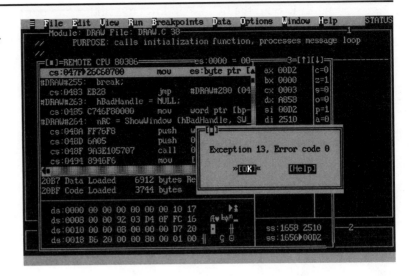

As I discussed in the last chapter, to test and debug your Windows application fully, you need to use the debugging version of Windows. You should consider this step to be mandatory in all your Windows application development projects. To see how to use TDW and the debugging version of Windows together, let's go through the following steps:

1. Make sure to configure debug output in SYSTEM.INI, if you haven't already done so. Add this section to your SYSTEM.INI file if it doesn't exist already:

```
[Debug]
outputto=NUL
```

This directs the debug output to NUL. Directing your debug output to NUL gets rid of error messages coming from the debugging version of Windows because it cannot write to the Aux device.

2. Exit Windows if it's running and type in N2D to load the debugging version of Windows that comes with the 3.1 SDK.

3. Start Windows as you would normally. If the debugging version of Windows is loaded correctly, you should see the message "Enhanced Mode Debug Windows 3.1" in the lower-right corner of your display to let you know that the debugging version of Windows is running.

4. Start the BC++ Windows IDE and open your DRAW.EXE project.

5. Start TDW by choosing Debugger in the BC++ IDE Run menu. As soon as TDW has started, you will notice that the Log window appears, because the debugging version of Windows has already sent it a message using `Output-DebugString`.

6. Press F9 to run the DRAW.EXE program.

As soon as DRAW.EXE executes, you should see an error appear in TDW's Log window. Press B to break on the error, and control is given to the TDW debugger. With TDW in control, you will see assembler code displayed in TDW's CPU window. Use F8 to step through this code slowly, one step at a time, until you see the mixed C source and assembler code displayed in the CPU window. If you scroll back in the CPU window, you will see that the instruction that caused the error was `Delete-Object (hBrush)`, as shown in Figure 10.15.

As you saw in the debugging projects in Chapter 9, I have two `DeleteObject` function calls to delete `hBrush`. The first one is fine; the next one tries to delete an object that doesn't exist. While a debugger by itself could not isolate this problem, a debugger in combination with the debugging version of Windows can. Now let's

FIGURE 10.15:

Finding a resource program bug using TDW and the debugging version of Windows

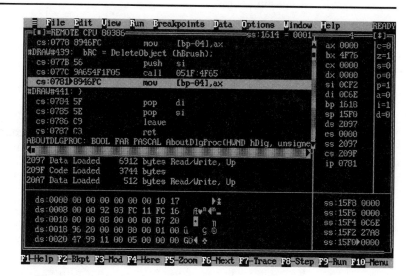

exit TDW and fix this error. You can fix the GDI problem in DRAW.EXE by changing the code in the function `DoPaint` in DRAW.C to match the following code:

```
EndPaint (hWnd, (LPPAINTSTRUCT) &ps);
bRC = DeleteObject (hBrush);
bRC = DeleteObject (hPen);
```

Trapping Bad Parameters on Calls to the Windows API

Now that you have fixed these problems, rebuild DRAW.EXE using BC++ 3.1, then start TDW again. You will see the Log window appear, as it did in the previous project, when the debugging version of Windows sends a message to TDW. Press F9 to run DRAW.EXE and try all of its functions except the ones in the Bugs menu. Notice that all the system resource problems are now fixed. Unless you played with the commands in DRAW.EXE's Bugs menu, no messages should appear in TDW's Log window other than the first message you encountered when TDW was started.

Now go ahead and choose Bad hWnd in DRAW.EXE's Bugs menu. The following message should appear in TDW's Log window, and control should be passed to TDW:

```
err DRAW SHOWWINDOW+C: Invalid HWND: 0x0000
FatalExit code = 0x6040
Abort, Break, Exit, or Ignore?
```

Press B to break the program and give control to TDW. After TDW has control, the CPU window appears and assembler code is displayed in it. Slowly step through this code, as you did before, until the mixed C source and assembler code appears. Then scroll backwards in the CPU window to find the following C source statement that caused the error:

```
nRC = ShowWindow (hBadHandle, SW_SHOW);
```

Using TDW along with the debugging version of Windows, you are easily able to identify the C command that caused the error. Go ahead and press F9, and your program will begin to execute again. If you choose Bad hDC in the Bugs menu and go through the steps described previously, you can use TDW to go right to the instruction that caused the error.

As you can see from these projects, TDW offers the same capabilities as CVW4, but it gives you much more information to help you debug your program. Before we go on to look at MultiScope for Windows, let's look at some tips for using TDW that were contributed by Amrik Dhillon, the technical editor for this book and a support engineer for Borland. We'll also do two more projects—logging messages and producing a global memory list—that show off some of TDW's unique features.

Tips for Using TDW

Using a debugger to control a program's execution is an important software innovation that we sometimes take for granted. Because of the unique environment the debugger must create, things don't always happen as you may assume. Here are a few tips on using TDW that resolve frequent questions from TDW users.

Using TDW to Track Mouse Events   Sometimes things might not always work the way you think they should when you're debugging mouse events such as mouse movement and button clicks. You need to monitor mouse messages with care, since the debugger traps the mouse messages for itself and throws away those that don't apply. For example, if you set a breakpoint on WM_LBUTTONDOWN for a scroll bar window, run your program, and click the mouse button on the scroll bar, TDW catches the breakpoint and switches to the TDW screen. When you release the mouse button that you pressed (which activated TDW) the WM_LBUTTONUP message goes to TDW—not to your program—and the message is thrown away by TDW. When you continue running your program, your program thinks that the mouse button is still pressed since it never received the WM_LBUTTONUP message, and the scroll bar continuously scrolls. The remedy is to press the mouse button in TDW before continuing the program's execution, so you can release the mouse button with Windows—not TDW—in control.

TDW.INI Ins and Outs   TDW uses a TDW.INI file to keep track of TDW's configuration. If you set up TDW to come up in 43/50-line mode and it stays in 25-line mode, put ROWS=50 in your TDW.INI file in the [VideoOptions] section. If you are using an EGA card, you should use the SVGA.DLL (Version 3.2.1 or later) and set ROWS=43.

The BC++ installation process incorrectly puts a TDW.INI in both the \BOR-LANDC\BIN directory and the \WINDOWS directory. If you are having TDW configuration problems, try deleting the TDW.INI in \BORLANDC\BIN and making modifications to the TDW.INI file only in the \WINDOWS directory.

Using TDW 3.1 with Windows 3.0 and Vice Versa   Any time you use software versions that don't match up exactly with each other, problems can (and usually do) occur. The best fix is to use versions that do match. In this case you should use

BC++ 3.1 with Windows 3.1. If you have to disregard this guideline, there are work-arounds to the problems that might occur. Your best remedy is to contact Borland technical support through CompuServe to find out about these work-arounds. I have contacted Borland technical support on CompuServe to get questions answered many times during the course of writing this book and have been impressed with the results. I am also very pleased with the support I have received from Microsoft on their CompuServe forums. If you don't have access to CompuServe, you can also call Borland technical support directly to get answers to your questions, but you may find that you will have to play a game of telephone tag before you get your questions answered.

Logging Messages

There may be a time when you want to analyze all messages that get sent to a particular window within your application. If the window procedure is not behaving as you expected, a possible cause may be that your function is not receiving a particular message you intended it to receive. To find out what is happening, let's log all messages sent to the WndProc function by doing the following:

1. Open the Window Message window by choosing Window Messages from the TDW View menu.

2. Add WndProc to the first pane by choosing Add on the local menu, as you did in the first TDW project in this chapter.

3. In the top right pane, you'll see "Log all messages." If this message doesn't appear, then use the local menu to display the Set Message Filter dialog box and select All Messages as the Message Class.

4. Go to the bottom pane and display its local menu. Choose the Send To Log Window command. If it is set to No, toggle it to Yes.

5. Open the Log window by choosing Log from the View menu.

6. Using the local menu, choose the Open Log File command. You can name the file WNDPROC.LOG.

Now you are ready to run the application by pressing the F9 key. When the application window executes, draw a rectangle on the screen and suspend the application by pressing the Ctrl+Alt+SysRq key sequence to break the program and return to

TDW. After returning to TDW, display the Log window. The Log window now contains all of the WndProc messages. You can examine the window messages in the Log window to find out which messages were sent to the window and which were not. You can save the WndProc message log by choosing Close Log File on the local menu of the Log window.

Producing a Global Memory List

Have you ever written an application that seems to slow down the longer it is in use? Maybe your program is not freeing up the global memory it is using once it is through with it. One way to check on global memory usage is to write the entire contents of global memory to a file at two points within the application. To produce these two lists do the following:

1. Restart Windows to clear the current contents of global memory.

2. Set a breakpoint on the WM_RBUTTONDOWN message by using the local menu in the upper-right pane of the Windows Messages window.

3. Move to the bottom pane of the Windows Messages window and invoke the local menu. Choose the Send To Log Window command. If it is set to No, toggle it to Yes by pressing Return.

4. Press F9 to run the application.

5. Draw a rectangle or two, and then press the right mouse button. This will trigger a WM_RBUTTONDOWN message and break back into TDW.

6. Open the Log window.

7. Using the local menu, choose the Open Log File command. You can name the file DRAW_G01.LOG.

8. Display the Log window local menu again, and this time choose Display Windows Info. Choose the Global Heap command from the dialog box and choose OK. The Log window is filled with the contents of the global memory.

9. Use the local menu to Close the log file, and press F9 to continue the application.

10. After using the application for a while, repeat steps 5 through 9 and save the new Log file with a new name, such as DRAW_GO2.LOG. You can now compare the files to determine whether you are freeing up global memory or not.

After you have tried these scenarios on the DRAW.EXE application, go ahead and test-drive some of the other features of TDW that we have discussed. I think you will find that TDW is not only powerful but very easy to use. TDW is a tool you need to study and experiment with to grasp all its features. You may not use many of its features in your day-to-day debugging, but you can count on them to be there when you get involved in a difficult debugging project.

MultiScope Debuggers for Windows

MultiScope Debuggers for Windows is a Windows-hosted debugger that runs within the Windows environment, like the QuickC for Windows Debugger. While the QuickC Debugger offers basic debugging capabilities, MultiScope provides advanced debugging power that surpasses CVW4 and matches the features in TDW. MultiScope is a stand-alone debugger that is not integrated into a Windows development system. You cannot edit your program's source code or run a compiler and linker to rebuild your program using MultiScope, as you can with the QuickC Debugger.

MultiScope is not just one debugger—it's a full system of debugging tools. MultiScope includes debuggers for Windows and for DOS (separate versions exist for running on DOS applications from Windows and for running entirely in DOS). MultiScope offers runtime debuggers (RTD) and post-mortem-dump (PMD) debuggers for each operating mode.

One of the most interesting tools included with MultiScope is its PMD debugger. Program-dump analyzers date back to the days of mainframes, when they were often the only tool available to tell what had gone wrong. The first widely distributed software tool that I developed was a PMD tool called the ASCII COBOL Debugging Program (ACDP). ACDP analyzed the contents of an ASCII COBOL program dump for Sperry Univac 1100/2200 mainframe systems.

When a program crashed, the Sperry mainframe system would spit out a foot-high stack of paper covered with octal digits for the developer to trace the program's operation through—machine code by tedious machine code—to find where things went wrong. Instead, ACDP formatted the program dump to make it more readable for locating the cause of the error and examining the contents of the program's data areas.

MultiScope's Crash Analyzer is a vast improvement over ACDP, but it's based on the same concept: Windows discovers a fatal error, such as an Exception 13, and special PMD error-handling code linked into your program does a complete RAM and register dump to a disk file. After creating the program dump, you use MultiScope's Crash Analyzer to examine the program internals at the point the program perished.

The MultiScope Crash Analyzer has the same look and feel as the MultiScope interactive Windows debugger. It shows source code and lets you trace through the operation right up to the point of the crash and examine all the program's variables. The only thing you cannot do is modify memory.

Language Support

MultiScope Debuggers for Windows 3.1 supports any programming language that can generate CVW4- and TDW-compatible debug symbol tables, including all Microsoft- and Borland-language products. MultiScope can also support languages such as Zortech C++, because they produce CVW4-compatible debug tables. Recently, Symantec (the software publisher of the Norton Utilities and the Norton Desktop for Windows) purchased both Zortech (the software publisher of Zortech C++) and MultiScope, Inc. (the software publisher of MultiScope Debuggers for Windows). At this point, both Zortech C++ and MultiScope are separate products. However, their future can only be speculated about. My prediction is that Symantec will integrate these two products into a comprehensive Windows development system that will compete head-to-head with the Microsoft and Borland windows development systems.

Unique Features

MultiScope offers the usual commands, such as Until Function Return, Animate, and Restart, but the command interface is not as broad as its competition's. For example, it doesn't have a Back Trace command as TDW does. The MultiScope command names are not consistent with those used by CVW4 and TDW. For example, TDW and CVW4 use Step for executing across a function call and Trace to execute into one. MultiScope uses Flat for executing across a function call and Step to execute into one.

MultiScope has features that match and sometimes exceed those found in other debuggers. For example, a Log window lets you track the commands executed during a debugging session and post this information to a disk file, and a Spy window lets you track messages sent to an application's windows. MultiScope and TDW include these two features, but CVW4 does not. However, MultiScope goes beyond TDW's capabilities to identify some of the undocumented Windows messages by name. Moreover, you can automatically treat each message's lParam as a memory address to be viewed, and manually post messages to other windows.

MultiScope's Crash Analyzer lets you analyze the state of a program after it crashes. To use it with a Windows program, you only need to link in a special library and run an execution monitor system named MED. When a Windows application errs, MED captures the state of the program to a disk file. Analysis of this file using the Crash Analyzer shows you the state of memory, the CPU registers, and the contents of your program's variables at the moment the error occurred. The MultiScope Crash Analyzer also includes options for saving the Windows kernel and capturing the contents of the global heap.

Using MultiScope

MultiScope is a Multiple Document Interface (MDI) Windows application. Each MultiScope window is a window into a particular debugging task, such as inspecting source code or viewing data structures. The MDI frame window contains a menu bar for global commands. Each MDI child window has a menu bar for local commands. The global menu has commands that are common to all the child windows, such as starting or quitting a program, and its commands never change. Figure 10.16 shows the MultiScope window with all its default windows open just after it has been started.

FIGURE 10.16:

MultiScope for Windows

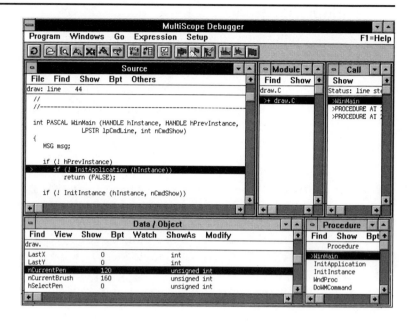

The figure shows what MultiScope looks like on a VGA monitor. Personally, I prefer to run MultiScope on an 8514 or a SuperVGA display that has 1024 by 768 resolution. MultiScope is much easier to use when you have ample screen real estate to work with.

MultiScope has many windows that display detailed information. Its power lies in the information displayed in each of its windows. You can have as many windows open as you can keep track of while you are debugging a program. If you want to work with only one window and see all its detail, you can easily maximize the window you are using.

There are a number of windows within MultiScope. Some windows display messages and others display variables. Each of these windows is opened by choosing a command from the Windows menu. MultiScope has 16 windows for you to work with, including its Help window. In comparison, CVW4 has 7 windows and TDW has 17. Each of the following sections looks inside one of the MultiScope windows.

The Assembly Window

MultiScope has a window, shown in Figure 10.17, that's dedicated to viewing disassembled assembly instructions. Using MultiScope you don't have to switch between source code and assembly-language views in the same window, as you do with CVW4. MultiScope gives you both a Source window and an Assembly window, as TDW does. Using the Assembly window you can set and clear breakpoints and browse through assembly code. By choosing display options in MultiScope's View menu, you can specify whether you see high-level language source interspersed in the assembly language and whether the disassembly uses mnemonics or shows the bytes that make up the opcodes.

The Breakpoint Window

The Breakpoint window, shown in Figure 10.18, displays the breakpoints that are currently set in your program. It displays the location of each breakpoint both as an assembly-language address and in the form `module.function:line#`. Breakpoints can have a pass count, which means the debugger does not stop at this breakpoint until it has encountered the breakpoint a specified number of times. The Breakpoint window shows both the current pass count and the limit. You can also

FIGURE 10.17:

The MultiScope Assembly window

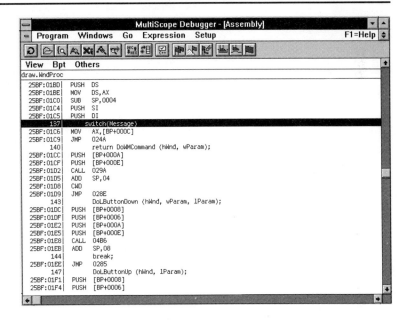

specify an expression with a breakpoint. Each time the debugger encounters the breakpoint, it evaluates the expression and stops if it evaluates to TRUE. Multi-Scope also has a Watchpoint window that shows all of the watchpoints you have set at any given time. A watchpoint is like a breakpoint, except it stops program flow when specific data is accessed.

> **NOTE** MultiScope will save all of your breakpoint settings from debugging session to debugging session. You don't have to reset all your program breakpoints each time, as you do with TDW.

The Call Window

Figure 10.19 shows MultiScope's default set of windows when DRAW.EXE is stopped at a breakpoint set in DRAW.C right after processing the WM_RBUTTONUP message. The Call window, which provides a stack traceback, is one of the windows shown in the figure.

FIGURE 10.18:

The MultiScope Breakpoint window

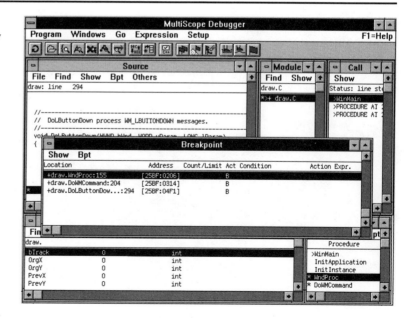

FIGURE 10.19:

MultiScope's default set of windows

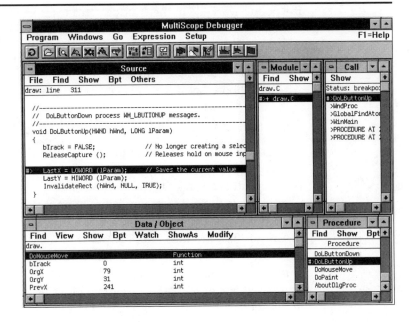

The Call window shows each function that is currently active, with the most recently called function at the top. Besides the function name, the window displays the name of the module it is from. Leaving this window displayed lets you see at a glance the state of your program when you hit a breakpoint. Besides providing a stack traceback, the Call window provides an easy way to switch the view of other debugging windows. If you double-click on a function in the Call window, the Data, Source, and Assembly windows will switch to display the source and data for the function you selected.

The Data Window

The Data window lets you view the contents of local and global variables in your program. Each line in the window displays a different variable or element of a variable. The expression or set of variables currently displayed appears at the top of the window. You can also set watchpoints on data from this window.

Tracing through linked data structures, such as trees and linked lists, is easy using your mouse with this window. To display what a pointer points to, double-click on the pointer variable in the window. To back up a pointer chain you are following, double-click the right mouse button on the expression at the top of the window.

The Data window displays either local or global data, but not both at the same time, the way TDW does. To switch the view between local and global variables, press Alt+X or choose Local/Global Data in the MultiScope Show menu.

The Graphic Data Window

The Graphic Data window is the flashiest MultiScope window. To display data structures graphically, first select a data structure in the Data window, then press Alt+G. MultiScope tries to follow the pointers in the data to construct a graph. The Graphic Data window lets you zoom in on the data displayed by double-clicking the left mouse button, or zoom out by double-clicking the right mouse button. Figure 10.20 shows the Graphic Data window displaying the contents of the data structure used to keep track of the data variables associated with a window in the DumpIT 3.1 program. I chose this data structure because it is more complex than those used in the DRAW.EXE program example we have been using. (The DumpIT application is covered in Chapter 3. DumpIT 3.1 is an enhanced version of DumpIT that is discussed further in Chapter 12.)

FIGURE 10.20:

MultiScope's Graphic Data window

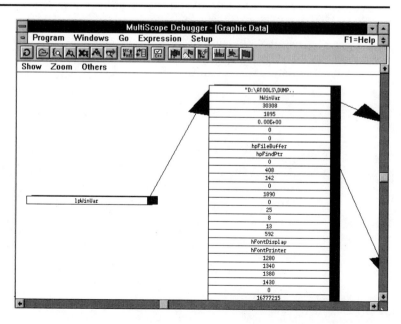

The Log Window

The Log window keeps track of all the events that occur during your debugging session. This feature is useful for reconstructing the debugging steps that led to a particular state of the program. The window displays the last 100 entries. You can also save all the log entries to a file.

The MultiScope Log window is useful, but it does not have the power that the TDW Log window has. You cannot customize or even control what is written to the MultiScope Log window, and you cannot keep track of Windows messages, as you can with TDW.

The Memory Window

When you want to examine the memory in a Windows application, you use the Memory window. If you select a data item in the Data window and then press Alt+E, the Memory window will display a dump of the data. You can view data in a variety of formats: character, text, byte, word, unsigned, integer, long integer, short real, long real, extended real, or address. You can also set data watchpoints from the Memory window and modify memory locations directly.

One interesting feature of the Memory window is the "live memory expression." You can enter an expression that evaluates to a memory address and associate the expression with the Memory window. Then, each time the debugger stops at a breakpoint, it evaluates the expression and changes the Memory window dump to that address. This can save a lot of thumbing through memory, if you can come up with the right expression for what you are doing.

The Module Window

The Module window lists the names of the object modules that make up your program. To the left of each module name is status information. For each module that contains a breakpoint, the first column contains an asterisk (*). If you are currently stopped at a breakpoint in that module, a pound sign (#) appears instead. A greater-than sign (>) in column two indicates that some procedure in the module is in the current function stack listed in the Call window. If the module has not been loaded, a "v" will appear. Column three also contains a + for each module with Trace enabled. To turn Trace on and off for a module, choose either Enable or Disable in the Trace local menu that appears when the Module window is selected.

> **TIP**
>
> One of my favorite ways to use the Module window is to go from one module to another by double-clicking on the module name. If you are working on a very large Windows application, you will find this to be a real time-saver. You can also use this technique in the Procedure window. If you want to display the source code for a specific function, double-click on its name in the MultiScope Procedure window. The source code module will be loaded automatically, and the function you clicked on will be displayed.

The Procedure Window

The Procedure window provides a more detailed view of the information in the Module window. Here each function appears on a separate line along with the module in which it appears, its address, and whether it is a near or far procedure. As we just discussed, you can automatically load the C source module a function is in and display it in the Source window by double-clicking on the function name.

The Registers Window

You can view the current state of the CPU registers in the Registers window. You can display the registers in either decimal or hex formats, and you can alter a register by selecting it with the mouse and pressing Alt+M. Since the Registers window displays the current values of the CPU and arithmetic coprocessor registers, it is an ideal companion to the Assembly window.

The Source Window

The Source window is the center of most debugging. You use it to step visually through your program's code as it's executing and to set breakpoints. You can also update the assembly window from here to display the same routine that's in the Source window in assembly language.

One of the most common debugging tasks is executing to a certain spot in the program. With the Source window you just double-click on a source line and MultiScope sets a breakpoint there, then executes to that point. This is convenient when you are doing exploratory debugging.

NOTE It is worth noting that all of MultiScope's windows scroll dynamically. That is, the window's contents move up and down in the window as you thumb the scroll bar. In many Windows applications, the windows are not updated until you release the scroll bar, making it difficult to browse to the spot you want.

The Spy Window

The Spy window gives you a superset of the capabilities of the Microsoft Windows SDK Spy utility. The Spy window in MultiScope logs any Windows messages that you want to monitor. You select classes of messages, such as mouse or window messages, by choosing Specify Messages in the Commands local menu for the Spy window. You can select the window or windows to spy on from the dialog box that appears when you choose Specify Windows in the same menu.

You can also manually post messages to a particular window by choosing Post Message in the Commands menu. This feature can be very useful for debugging Windows applications that communicate using DDE.

You can set breakpoints on messages that the Spy window is spying on. You just select the window and the message that you are interested in, using commands in the Bpt local menu. MultiScope then sets a breakpoint at the entry point of the correct window procedure that stops the program only when the specified message arrives.

The Watchpoint Window

MultiScope has a Watchpoint window that shows all of the watchpoints you have set at any given time. A watchpoint is like a breakpoint except it stops program flow when specific data is accessed. For example, if a bug causes a certain variable to be set to zero incorrectly, you can set a watchpoint on that variable that will stop the debugger when the variable is accessed. You can specify whether to stop on read accesses, write accesses, or both—a flexibility missing in most debuggers. MultiScope takes advantage of the debugging facilities of the 80386, so watchpoints do not slow down program execution.

> **NOTE**
>
> MultiScope's Watchpoint window is not like CVW4's Watch window and TDW's Watches window, and you should not confuse them. The best way to view data using MultiScope is the Data window, where you can switch between displaying local and global variables. This is not as convenient as the Watch window in the other debuggers, where you can specify the exact variables you want to watch, but it's the best that MultiScope provides.

The Remote Control Window

The MultiScope Remote Control window is very handy for running your program with the main MultiScope window minimized, so you can see what your program is doing while it's executing. The Remote Control window is set up like the controls on a video recorder. You get to see which line of your C source code is executing, and there are buttons for controlling your program's execution. You display the window by choosing Remote Control in the MultiScope Debugger Go menu or by pressing F12. The Remote Control window is shown in Figure 10.21.

FIGURE 10.21:

The MultiScope Remote Control window

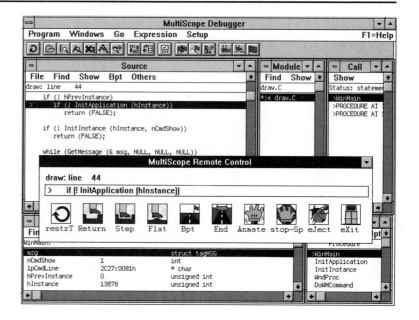

The Remote Control window is very useful, but it keeps dropping behind any window you click on while you are debugging a Windows application. To solve this problem I use the Topper utility included on the disk set to lock the Remote Control window on top of all the other windows on the Windows desktop.

Post-Mortem Debugging

Now that we have discussed what MultiScope does, let's see how it can be used in a debugging project. Instead of covering the same ground we already have with the other debuggers, let's try out a unique feature of MultiScope that the other debuggers don't have—post-mortem dump (PMD) debugging. In this project we will use the DRAW.EXE program and the MultiScope Crash Analyzer to track down where DRAW.EXE stops when you choose Bad hWnd in DRAW.EXE's Bugs menu. To track down this error we will use MultiScope along with the debugging version of Windows.

Preparing DRAW.EXE

In preparation for debugging, DRAW.EXE needs to be rebuilt using any compiler that is compatible with MultiScope. These compilers are Microsoft C/C++ 7.0, Microsoft QuickC for Windows, Borland C++ 3.1, and Zortech C++, among others.

Make sure to take out the errors that delete the handle to the brush twice and that do not initialize the variable nCurrentShape. For this project, only the bugs that are in the DRAW.EXE Bugs menu should be left in the program. Otherwise, the debugging version of Windows will trip over these errors, and MultiScope's monitoring utility, MED, will pop up before we want it to.

To take full advantage of all of multiscope's post-mortem debugger facilities, DRAW.EXE should be modified and linked with MultiScope's MED library, using the following steps:

1. Include the MED header file in DRAW.C:

```
#include <medw.h>
```

2. Add a program call to the MED initialization function as one of the first (if not the first) things done in DRAW.C:

```
MEDInit ();
```

The `MEDInit` function creates the link between the C Windows application and the MED system. The default operation of the MED system for Windows will catch all runtime exceptions provided by the C compiler.

In addition, you can add a forced dump capability to your application with MED. The MED system provides two functions to produce a PMD: `MEDDump` and `MEDQueryDump`. The `MEDDump` function takes one argument, a status value that's typed as an `unsigned int` (`UINT`). This status value is to be used for your own reference.

`MEDQueryDump` uses two arguments, a message pointer typed as an `LPSTR` and a status value. Using `MEDQueryDump` you can display a message box before the dump is taken. The string you specify will be displayed in the message box. When called, the message box offers three choices:

- Yes, take the dump.
- No, don't take the dump.
- Cancel, forget about it. Don't take the dump and continue execution.

3. Set up your compile and link options for full debug information. For information on how to do this with Microsoft's QuickC for Windows and C/C++ 7.0, refer to Chapter 9. To find out how to set up debug information for Borland C/C++, check out the first part of this chapter.

4. Use the MED library when you link your program. MultiScope includes libraries for linking with CVW4- and TDW-compatible languages. For example, use LMEDCW.LIB for linking with medium and large memory model Microsoft C Windows applications.

NOTE   The MultiScope header and library files are installed by the MultiScope installation program in the \MSCOPE\MED directory. You will need to copy these files into the respective header and library files that your compiler uses before you can debug your program using Crash Analyzer.

Using MED to Trap a Bug

Now that we have prepared DRAW.EXE, it's time to run it and let MED produce a PMD when we force DRAW.EXE to cause an API error with the debugging version of Windows. As always, we must first set up and run the debugging version of Windows. To install it, we must run the .BAT file N2D. You must use the debugging version of Windows in order to trap API errors, such as using a bad handle to a window. To trap simpler program errors, such as null pointers, you can use the standard retail version of Windows.

After the debugging version of Windows is installed and running, you need to execute MEDWP.EXE, the MultiScope MED system Protected mode monitoring program. To use MEDWP, simply execute it from Windows, and the MED icon appears on the Windows desktop. After it's running, MED monitors all Windows applications that are executed. Make sure that the Enabled option in the MED System menu is selected with a check mark. When an error occurs, such as a GPF, MEDWP will create a post-mortem dump file (.PMD) that contains the entire state of the application when it crashed. The .PMD file can then be examined using the Multi-Scope Crash Analyzer.

After executing MED, the next step is to execute DRAW.EXE and choose Bad hWnD from DRAW.EXE's Bugs menu. When the error is encountered by the debugging version of Windows, it will be passed to MED, which will trap the bug and display a dialog box. After the MED dialog box appears, choose OK to have MED create a PMD of DRAW.EXE named DRAW.PMD. At this point MED has created a dump that we can analyze using the MultiScope Crash Analyzer. But before we look at the dump MED created, let's take a closer look at MED itself.

The MultiScope MED Utility

The MED System menu has the following commands that let you specify how MED will work:

- *MED Enabled* is used to enable and disable MED. This menu option must be checked in order for MED to take a PMD.

- *Set Options* displays the MED Options dialog box. You use this dialog box to make sure MED is enabled every time it's started and to specify what kinds of information you want included in the PMD.

- *Specify Libraries/Modules* displays a dialog box that lets you specify which DLLs and program executables should be captured in the dump file along with the crashing application.

Examining the Dump with the Crash Analyzer

The MultiScope Crash Analyzer has the same user interface as the MultiScope interactive debugger. To examine and analyze the dump created by MED, all I needed to do was execute the Crash Analyzer, WPMD.EXE, and load the DRAW.PMD dump file. After the Crash Analyzer loaded the PMD, it showed that the error occurred in the Windows function ShowWindow. Since ShowWindow is a Windows function, there is no C source code associated with it. To see the Windows API call in DRAW.EXE that caused the error, I clicked with my mouse on the preceding function (DoWmCommand) in the Crash Analyzer Procedure window, and the instruction that caused the error in DRAW.EXE was displayed, as shown in Figure 10.22.

As you can see in the figure, the Crash Analyzer displays in the Source window exactly where the program stopped. The Data window displays the contents of all the DRAW.EXE local and global variables at the time DRAW.EXE crashed. The Calls window displays all the functions that were called, up to ShowWindow and DoWmCommand.

FIGURE 10.22:

Analyzing the DRAW.PMD file using the MultiScope Crash Analyzer

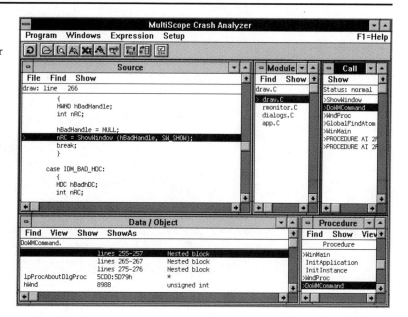

Wrapping Up Windows Debugging

MultiScope Debuggers for Windows is a powerful system that offers you debugging power inside a Windows application with an attractive user interface. Compared to CVW4, MultiScope has more features and is easier to use. By now I am sure you have thought about what each of the debuggers offers and have started drawing your own conclusions about which one you think is best.

The QuickC Debugger is easy to use and is integrated into the QuickC for Windows development environment. You can use it to find a bug, fix it, and rebuild your program without ever leaving the window your program source code is displayed in. Overall, the QuickC Debugger is elegantly simple and will serve you well for most of your debugging projects.

The CodeView for Windows Debugger Version 4.0 is an improvement over previous CodeView debuggers, but it is still the most difficult to use of all the debuggers we have looked at. CVW4 has an improved user interface and uses Nu-Mega's CV/1 technology to make one-monitor debugging as painless as possible.

TDW is the most powerful debugger that we have examined, but why can't it save what you have done from one debugging session to another? TDW offers many options to customize breakpoints and other aspects of your debugging environment, but you must set up whatever you do over and over in each debugging session. TDW does not have the elegant solution CVW4 has for one-monitor debugging. If you use a secondary monitor setup for your Windows debugging, you will find that TDW is the best debugger available for Windows applications.

MultiScope offers an elegant Windows interface, but it cannot match TDW in all its features. MultiScope can only be used as a Windows-hosted debugger or with a remote system hooked up using a serial connection or LAN. It doesn't support a secondary monitor, as do CVW4 and TDW. Overall, MultiScope has a pretty face, but I prefer using TDW. TDW has more features, and if you use a two-monitor setup for debugging Windows applications, it's the best debugger that you will find.

Now that you have learned how to debug a Windows application and what each of the Windows debuggers offers, it's time to move on to the last part of the book, "New Windows 3.1 Development Tools." In this part, you will learn about how to use new tools to build Windows Dynamic Data Exchange (DDE) into your applications and how to build more robust Windows applications using the new Windows 3.1 header files and the STRESS.EXE stress-testing program.

PART V

New Windows 3.1 Development Tools

In this last part of the book, we are going to focus on some new tools that just became available with Windows 3.1. In Chapter 11 you will learn about tools that make implementing Windows Dynamic Data Exchange (DDE) much easier in your Windows applications: the Windows Dynamic Data Exchange Management Library and DDE Spy. In Chapter 12 you will learn about new Windows 3.1 programming tools that help you to build more robust Windows applications: the new Windows header files (WINDOWS.H and WINDOWSX.H) and the new stress-testing application STRESS.EXE. WINDOWS.H provides a new stricter type-checking that helps you to trap more bugs at compile time instead of having to wait until your program executes to find them. WINDOWSX.H includes an entirely new macro API that makes it easier to code Windows programs.

Using DDEML

- Understanding DDE

- Using DDEML

- Using DDEML Spy

- Adding DDE-server functionality to Resource Monitor

11

DDE has always been regarded as one of the most challenging areas of Windows programming. Using the Windows messaging system, DDE provides a basic level of interprocess communication between Windows applications. Even though DDE is a powerful feature you can implement to exchange data with other Windows applications, many programmers have avoided it because of its difficulty. Windows 3.1 provides a new way to do Dynamic Data Exchange, the Dynamic Data Exchange Management Library (DDEML). DDEML is a function-based API layer built on top of the DDE messaging system. DDEML makes putting DDE functionality into your Windows application easier and safer.

Microsoft Windows provides three ways for Windows applications to transfer data: Clipboard data transfer, Dynamic Link Libraries (DLLs), and Dynamic Data Exchange (DDE). DDE is the best way that an application can pass global memory handles to another application because:

- The Clipboard cannot pass global memory handles and the communication through the Clipboard is not private, meaning that other applications can overwrite the Clipboard before the application that needs to read it has had a chance to.

- Sharing memory through a DLL requires that both of the communicating applications possess the library file in order to create the executable.

- There is no standard for sharing the memory through a DLL.

- DDE is a standard protocol that Windows and other Windows applications support.

- There is no need to create a memory manager to handle the global memory that is being passed from one application to another.

- DDE is a compatible way for Windows applications to communicate. It is a standard developed and supported by Microsoft that's been around since Windows 2.0.

DDE was developed as a standard for applications to transfer data or remote commands from one application to another. This data transfer must be done with the full understanding that both applications have to support and cooperate with the DDE standard.

This cooperation to support the DDE standard could be called a relationship. Such a relationship between two applications is known as a client-server relationship. An application that requests data or services from another application is called a client application. A server application is an application that responds to a client application's request.

What Is DDE Used For?

DDE gives you the ability to integrate Windows applications. Using DDE, applications that each do a specific task can work together to produce a result that is much better than what any single application can do. For example, by integrating applications using DDE, you can do the following:

- Link the PackRat or Act! personal information system to Word for Windows or Ami Professional. When you type a name into a letter, you can have your personal information system find and insert the associated address from your personal phone book file. Figure 11.1 shows the dialog box displayed in Word for Windows for finding a name and address in the PackRat personal information system and inserting them into a Word for Windows document. This dialog box and the DDE API calls to communicate with PackRat are in a WordBASIC macro. The WordBASIC program to communicate with PackRat and insert the information into a document is just over 400 lines long.

- Link numbers and charts from Microsoft Excel into a word processor, such as Word for Windows or Ami Professional. When you change numbers in the spreadsheet, the numeric tables and charts in your word processed report change too.

- Query real-time data servers, such as stock market information, inventory control, electronic instrument drivers, or process control equipment drivers.

As was stated earlier, DDE is one of the best methods for transferring data between two applications. This is because it is automatic and requires little user intervention. DDE does not require user interaction, as the Clipboard transfer does. DDE only requires the user to initiate the DDE conversation. This conversation can then be continued until the user terminates the application or the client application automatically terminates the conversation. DDE is able to transfer text string

FIGURE 11.1:

Communicating with the PackRat personal information system from Word for Windows using DDE

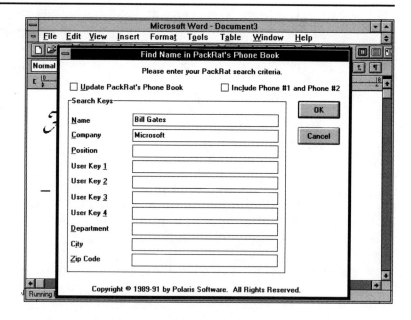

objects between applications using atoms and global data handles. An atom is a global Windows text object that can be created and maintained using the Windows atom management API. DDE is also able to transfer commands that would be executed by the server application. The DDE conversation is initiated by the client application, and after the conversation is established, the client sends data requests or command requests to the server application. Once this link is in place, the user does not have to be further involved in the data exchange done by the two applications.

You do not have to be a C Windows programmer to do DDE programming. You can take advantage of DDE in Microsoft Visual Basic, Microsoft Excel, Word for Windows, and Ami Professional (as well as other Windows applications). Both Word for Windows and Ami Professional have programming languages built into them that allow you to create custom functionality. Using the Word for Windows BASIC language, you can write functions that take advantage of DDE as well as other Windows APIs. For example, you could use the following WordBASIC function to start Microsoft Excel and load a spreadsheet named EXPENSES.XLS:

```
Sub MAIN
  channel1 = DDEInitiate("EXCEL", "EXP.XLS")
End Sub
```

Object Linking and Embedding

Object linking and embedding (OLE) is a powerful Windows feature that you can take advantage of in many different ways, both as a user and as a Windows programmer. Although its details are beyond the scope of this book, let's take a quick look at what the new Windows 3.1 OLE feature does, because it is built on top of both DDE and the new DDEML library.

OLE lets you embed and access application objects across applications. Using OLE you can embed a drawing inside a Word for Windows document. When you double-click on the drawing, OLE starts the server application that is responsible for the drawing so you can edit it. Using OLE and the new multimedia features of Windows 3.1, you can attach voice annotations to documents. You can use the new Sound Recorder accessory to record and play back sounds created using a sound board such as Creative Lab's SoundBlaster. After creating a recording you can add it to your document by dragging the sound file with the .WAV extension from File Manager and dropping it in your Word for Windows document. To play the recording, all you need to do is double-click on it.

As you can see, OLE is a significant new feature in Windows 3.1. OLE is built on top of DDE and involves 66 new function calls. It is the largest and most complex single enhancement to Windows 3.1.

Prior to Windows 3.1 the only ways applications could share data were the Clipboard and DDE. The Clipboard let applications pass data from one application to another in either a standard or custom format. Usually data was passed as ASCII text, a bitmap, or a metafile. DDE let applications establish conversations and share data using the same types of formats used by the Clipboard. In addition, using DDE the client application could maintain a link to the server application, to get an updated version of the data when it changed.

Now, using OLE with Windows 3.1, client applications manage compound documents that contain objects connected to server applications. OLE objects use two formats for the client and server applications to work with the data. For example, when you use OLE to add a chart created in Excel to a Word for Windows document, Word for Windows is passed two formats. One format is understood only by the program that created the chart—in this case Excel. The other format is one that Word for Windows uses for displaying the document on the screen. When you select the chart in the Word for Windows document, Excel is started, and Word for

Windows passes Excel the chart data in the format only Excel understands so you can use Excel to update the chart.

Adding OLE support to your Windows application is a complicated process. OLE is a powerful new technology that is easy for a user to work with in an OLE application, but it's also a significant project for a programmer to implement. While DDE can be discussed in one chapter of a book, OLE really requires a book dedicated to the entire subject.

Now that you know what OLE can do, let's take a look backward in time to see how DDE worked prior to Windows 3.1. This will give you a better understanding of how DDE works and of the advantages you gain by using DDEML instead of working directly with DDE messages.

History of DDE

Dynamic Data Exchange began as a set of rules and guidelines published by Microsoft about how applications should communicate using messages to share data objects and manage interprocess communication. These rules and guidelines became the standards of DDE. Microsoft began utilizing these standards in their own applications, such as Excel, to enable these applications to communicate with other Microsoft applications. Now many other vendors also incorporate the standards in their applications. The communication between the Windows applications is performed by sending messages, global atoms, and global memory handles.

Microsoft formally published these sets of rules and guidelines in the *Programming Tools, Application Style Guide, and Microsoft Windows Extensions* manual of the Windows Software Development Kit. Thus, the "DDE protocol" was born.

The protocol used a predefined set of Windows messages that was communicated by using the `SendMessage` and `PostMessage` functions. Since the Windows messaging system allows only two parameters, `wParam` and `lParam`, to be passed between applications, nine different messages were utilized to transfer data and commands from a client application to a server application. The same method was used by the server application to transfer data or acknowledgments of commands back to the client application.

This method required that applications support the exact specifications of the DDE protocol. It also brought on a sense of complexity to the protocol, which led Microsoft to create an easier way for an application to support DDE. This easier way is to use a set of API functions bundled in a DLL called the Dynamic Data Exchange Management Library, or DDEML. An application can call these API functions instead of having to handle messages.

DDE Messages

To understand how DDE works and how DDEML improves on the older method of using DDE messages, let's take a look at the nine DDE message types and overview the types of DDE conversations that client and server applications can have. Table 11.1 briefly describes the nine types of DDE messages.

TABLE 11.1: DDE Message Types

Message Type	Description
WM_DDE_ACK	Notifies an application of the receipt and processing of a WM_DDE_INITIATE, WM_DDE_EXECUTE, WM_DDE_DATA, WM_DDE_ADVISE, WM_DDE_UNADVISE, or WM_DDE_POKE message, and in some cases of a WM_DDE_REQUEST message.
WM_DDE_ADVISE	A client application posts the WM_DDE_ADVISE message to a DDE server to request the server to supply an update for a data item whenever it changes.
WM_DDE_DATA	A server posts a WM_DDE_DATA message to a client to pass a data item to the client or to notify the client of the availability of a data item.
WM_DDE_EXECUTE	A client posts a WM_DDE_EXECUTE message to a DDE server application to send a string to the server to be processed as a series of commands. The server is expected to post a WM_DDE_ACK message in response.
WM_DDE_INITIATE	A client application sends a WM_DDE_INITIATE message to initiate a conversation with a server for the specified application and topic names. After receiving this message, all server applications with matching names and topics are expected to acknowledge it (see the WM_DDE_ACK message).

TABLE 11.1: DDE Message Types (continued)

Message Type	Description
WM_DDE_POKE	A client posts a WM_DDE_POKE message to a server. A client uses this message to request the server to accept an unsolicited data item. The server is expected to reply with a WM_DDE_ACK message indicating whether it accepted the data item.
WM_DDE_REQUEST	A client posts a WM_DDE_REQUEST message to a server to request the value of a data item.
WM_DDE_TERMINATE	A client or server posts a WM_DDE_TERMINATE message to terminate a conversation.
WM_DDE_UNADVISE	A client application posts a WM_DDE_UNADVISE message to inform a server application that the specified item or a particular Clipboard format for the item should no longer be updated. This terminates the warm or hot link for the specified item.

Types of Conversations

The previous table describes each of the DDE message types and gives you an idea of how each message type is used for servers and clients to communicate. To understand completely how this process works, you need to know how a client initiates a conversation with a server, what happens after the conversation starts, and how it terminates. Further, you need to understand the three basic types of DDE conversations: cold link, hot link, and warm link. The simplest type of conversation is the cold link.

A Cold Link Conversation

A cold link conversation begins when a client broadcasts a WM_DDE_INITIATE message identifying the application and the topic it requires. The application and topic may be set to NULL to begin a conversation with any server application or any data topic. A server application that supports the specified topic responds to the client with a WM_DDE_ACK message.

After establishing the conversation, the client then requests a particular data item by posting a WM_DDE_REQUEST message. If the server can supply this data item, it responds by posting a WM_DDE_DATA message to the client. If the client posts a WM_DDE_REQUEST message to the server and the server cannot supply the requested data item, then the server posts a WM_DDE_ACK message to the client.

The DDE conversation continues with the client posting WM_DDE_REQUEST messages to the server, for the same data item or different data items, and the server responding with WM_DDE_DATA or WM_DDE_ACK messages. The conversation is terminated when either the client or the server posts the other a WM_DDE_TERMINATE message.

A Hot Link Conversation

Using the cold link the client does not know when the data changes. The hot link solves this problem. Again, the DDE conversation begins with a WM_DDE_INITIATE message and a WM_DDE_ACK message. The client indicates the data item it requires by posting a WM_DDE_ADVISE message to the server. The server responds by posting a WM_DDE_ACK message indicating whether it has access to this item. A positive response indicates the server can supply the data; a negative response indicates that it cannot.

At this point the server must notify the client whenever the value of the data item changes. This notification uses a WM_DDE_DATA message, to which the client (on the basis of a flag set in the WM_DDE_DATA message) may or may not respond with a WM_DDE_ACK message. When the client no longer wishes to be advised of updates to the data item, it posts a WM_DDE_UNADVISE message to the server, and the server acknowledges. The conversation is terminated with the posting of a WM_DDE_TER-MINATE message.

A Warm Link Conversation

The warm link combines the functionality of both the cold link and the hot link. The conversation begins with the hot link: the client posts a WM_DDE_ADVISE message to the server, and the server acknowledges either positively or negatively. A flag is passed with the WM_DDE_ADVISE message indicating that the client wishes only to be informed of changes in data without immediately receiving the new data item. So the server posts WM_DDE_DATA messages with NULL data. Now the client knows that a particular data item has changed. To obtain this item the client uses a WM_DDE_REQUEST message, just as in the cold link.

As in the hot link, a client can stop being advised of changes in data items by posting a WM_DDE_UNADVISE message to the server. The conversation is terminated with a WM_DDE_TERMINATE message.

These three types of conversations use all the DDE messages except the following two:

- WM_DDE_POKE, where a client gives a server unsolicited data.

- WM_DDE_EXECUTE, where a client sends a command string to a server.

These messages are rarely used in DDE conversations between a client and a server. The following example shows how a client application was written to handle all the DDE messages that would be sent by a server;

```
ClientWndProc(HWND hWnd, UINT uMsg, WPARAM wParam, LPARAM lParam)
{
switch (uMsg) {
     case WM_COMMAND:
            switch (wParam) {
                  case IDM_DDE_START:
                        InitializeDDEConverstation(...);
                  break;
            }
            break;
     case WM_DDE_ACK:
            AcknowledgeDDEConversation(...);
            break;
     case WM_DDE_DATA:
            ProcessDDEData(...);
            break;
     case WM_DDE_TERMINATE:
            AcknowledgeTerminateDDE(...);
            break;
     .
     .
     .

}
```

The server application would be written like the following example to handle all the DDE messages that would be sent by a client;

```
ServerWndProc(HWND hWnd, UINT uMsg, WPARAM wParam, LPARAM lParam)
{
switch (uMsg) {
     case WM_DDE_INITIATE:
```

```
                ProcessDDEConversation(...);
                break;
        case WM_DDE_ACK:            // Acknowledgement from client
                                    // of Data sent OK
                AcknowledgeDDEDataSent(...);
                break;
        case WM_DDE_REQUEST:        // Received DDE Request Msg
                ProcessDDERequest(...);
                break;
        case WM_DDE_POKE:           // Received DDE Poke Msg
                ProcessDDEPoke(...);
                break;
        case WM_DDE_EXECUTE:        // Received Execute Command Msg
                ProcessDDEExecute(...);
                break;
        case WM_DDE_ADVISE:         // Establish Permanent Link
                ProcessDDELink(...);
                break;
        case WM_DDE_UNADVISE:       // Terminate Permanent Link
                TerminateDDELink(...);
                break;
        case WM_DDE_TERMINATE:
                TerminateDDE(...);
                break;
        .
        .
        .
}
```

How to Use DDE in Windows 3.1

DDE is still used to transfer data and to invoke remote commands between applications. But the usage and implementation of DDE in an application has become easier with the introduction of the DDEML in Windows 3.1. An application can now call the DDEML API functions instead of having to handle the DDE messages, as in previous Windows releases.

DDEML helps you work with DDE messages in an easier, more consistent way. It also includes functions for working with global string objects and global memory objects shared by Windows applications that communicate using DDE. As you will see, DDEML is a comprehensive solution to using DDE. It is well designed and encapsulates almost all the functionality required for two Windows applications to communicate and share data.

Dynamic Data Exchange Management Library

DDEML contains 27 API functions that are used for connecting two Windows applications and managing their conversation. Instead of sending, posting, and processing DDE messages directly, you use the functions provided by DDEML to manage DDE conversations. DDEML also provides a facility for managing the strings and data that are passed between DDE applications. Applications that communicate using DDEML create and exchange string handles and data handles instead of atoms and pointers to shared memory objects.

Much of the DDEML terminology is the same as that for message-based DDE. DDE takes place between a client and a server application. The client initiates the exchange by establishing a conversation with the server so it can send a request for data or services. DDE conversations are based on an application name, a topic name, and an item name. With DDEML the terms have been changed to a service name, a topic name, and an item name.

DDEML implements six new data management functions in addition to the Windows global memory functions: DdeAddData, DdeCreateDataHandle, DdeFreeDataHandle, DdeAccessData, DdeUnaccessData, and DdeGetData. You use DdeCreateDataHandle to allocate a global memory block, copy data in, and return a data handle for the block. When this handle is given to a callback function, it can copy the data into local memory using DdeGetData. The receiving program accesses the data—without copying it—using calls to DdeAccessData and DdeUnaccessData. When the program that created the data block is done, it calls DdeFreeDataHandle to free the global memory.

The DDEML code for string and memory management functions is simpler to implement than the code required for message-based DDE. A client application initiates a DDE conversation by calling DdeConnect with its instance handle and string handles for the desired service and topic names or setting the handles to NULL. The server callback function then receives a transaction type of XTYP_CONNECT or XTYP_WILDCONNECT if one or both string handles are NULL. The server can return TRUE if it supports the topic or FALSE if it doesn't. If it returns TRUE, then the client's DdeConnect call returns a conversation handle.

After a conversation has been established, the client uses `DdeClientTransaction` to request data from the server by specifying either a transaction type for a one-time request (`XTYP_REQUEST`) or an advise link (`XTYP_ADVSTART`). The server's callback function receives this transaction. If the transaction was an advise, the server calls `DdePostAdvise` to let the client know when the server has modified its data. Table 11.2 lists the DDEML functions with a short description of each.

TABLE 11.2:   DDEML Functions

Function	Description
DdeAbandonTransaction	Abandons an asynchronous transaction
DdeAccessData	Accesses a DDE global memory object
DdeAddData	Adds data to a DDE global memory object
DdeClientTransaction	Begins a DDE data transaction
DdeCmpStringHandles	Compares two DDE string handles
DdeConnect	Establishes a conversation with a server application
DdeConnectList	Establishes multiple DDE conversations
DdeCreateDataHandle	Creates a DDE data handle
DdeCreateStringHandle	Creates a DDE string handle
DdeDisconnect	Terminates a DDE conversation
DdeDisconnectList	Destroys a DDE conversation list
DdeEnableCallback	Enables or disables one or more DDE conversations
DdeFreeDataHandle	Frees a global memory object
DdeFreeStringHandle	Frees a DDE string handle
DdeGetData	Copies data from a global memory object to a buffer
DdeGetLastError	Returns an error value set by a DDEML function
DdeInitialize	Registers an application with the DDEML
DdeKeepStringHandle	Increments the usage count for a string handle
DdeNameService	Registers or unregisters a service name
DdePostAdvise	Prompts a server to send advise data to a client
DdeQueryConvInfo	Retrieves information about a DDE conversation
DdeQueryNextServer	Obtains the next handle in a DDE conversation list
DdeQueryString	Copies string-handle text into a buffer

TABLE 11.2:   DDEML Functions (continued)

Function	Description
DdeReconnect	Reestablishes a DDE conversation
DdeSetUserHandle	Associates a user-defined handle with a transaction
DdeUnaccessData	Frees a DDE global memory object
DdeUninitialize	Frees DDEML resources associated with an application

To use the new DDEML library, you need to include DDEML.H in your program's source code. The following excerpt from the DDE.H header file shows the function prototypes for all of the new DDEML functions, grouped by category:

```
/* DLL registration functions */
DdeInitialize(DWORD FAR* pidInst,
PFNCALLBACK pfnCallback, DWORD afCmd, DWORD ulRes);
DdeUninitialize(DWORD idInst);

/* conversation enumeration functions */
DdeConnectList(DWORD idInst, HSZ hszService,
HSZ hszTopic, HCONVLIST hConvList, CONVCONTEXT FAR* pCC);
DdeQueryNextServer(HCONVLIST hConvList,
HCONV hConvPrev);
DdeDisconnectList(HCONVLIST hConvList);

/* conversation control functions */
DdeConnect(DWORD idInst, HSZ hszService, HSZ hszTopic, CONVCONTEXT FAR* pCC);
DdeDisconnect(HCONV hConv);
DdeReconnect(HCONV hConv);
DdeQueryConvInfo(HCONV hConv, DWORD idTransaction, CONVINFO FAR* pConvInfo);
DdeSetUserHandle(HCONV hConv, DWORD id, DWORD hUser);
DdeAbandonTransaction(DWORD idInst, HCONV hConv,
DWORD idTransaction);

/* app server interface functions */
DdePostAdvise(DWORD idInst, HSZ hszTopic, HSZ hszItem);
DdeEnableCallback(DWORD idInst, HCONV hConv,
UINT wCmd);
DdeNameService(DWORD idInst, HSZ hsz1, HSZ hsz2,
UINT afCmd);

/* app client interface functions */
```

```
DdeClientTransaction(void FAR* pData, DWORD cbData, HCONV hConv, HSZ hszItem,
UINT wFmt, UINT wType, DWORD dwTimeout,
DWORD FAR* pdwResult);

/* data transfer functions */
DdeCreateDataHandle(DWORD idInst, void FAR* pSrc, DWORD cb, DWORD cbOff, HSZ
hszItem, UINT wFmt, UINT afCmd);
DdeAddData(HDDEDATA hData, void FAR* pSrc, DWORD cb, DWORD cbOff);
DdeGetData(HDDEDATA hData, void FAR* pDst, DWORD cbMax, DWORD cbOff);
DdeAccessData(HDDEDATA hData, DWORD FAR* pcbDataSize);
DdeUnaccessData(HDDEDATA hData);
DdeFreeDataHandle(HDDEDATA hData);
DdeGetLastError(DWORD idInst);
DdeCreateStringHandle(DWORD idInst, LPCSTR psz, int iCodePage);
DdeQueryString(DWORD idInst, HSZ hsz, LPSTR psz, DWORD cchMax, int iCodePage);
DdeFreeStringHandle(DWORD idInst, HSZ hsz);
DdeKeepStringHandle(DWORD idInst, HSZ hsz);
DdeCmpStringHandles(HSZ hsz1, HSZ hsz2);
```

Requirements of DDEML

DDEML requires that both client and server applications are executed under Windows 3.0 or later. It will run only in the Protected mode of Windows and not in the Real mode, but it is compatible with existing applications that still support the DDE messaging protocol. To utilize the DDEML's API functions, you include the DDEML.H header file and link with the DDEML.LIB library. Both these files are included in the Windows 3.1 SDK and Borland C++ 3.1. Also, the DDEML.DLL must reside in your system's path. This file is included in both Windows 3.1 and the Windows 3.1 SDK.

> **NOTE**
>
> Since DDEML needs to run in Protected mode, an application should call the GetWinFlags function and check the return value for the WF_PMODE flag before calling any of the DDEML functions. This will ensure that Windows is currently running in Protected mode and is able to support the DDEML.

DDEML Concepts

To understand how to use DDEML, let's examine the concepts behind DDE and DDEML. DDE conversations always involve a client and a server interaction or communication. The client application is the one that initiates the DDE conversation; it is also the one requesting or sending transactions to the server application. In turn, the server application responds by providing the requested data or performing the requested transaction or service for the client.

A client may interact with multiple servers. A server may have conversations with many clients. An application can also act as a client and a server at the same time. As the DDE protocol states, the client application has control of initiating and terminating the DDE conversation. DDEML provides the tools necessary for an application to become a client and/or a server.

As we saw in the previous example, an older application that supported DDE would have to handle all the DDE messages that are relevant to the conversation. DDEML notifies the application of DDE events, instead of DDE messages, by sending transactions to the client's DDE callback function. This transaction is similar to the DDE message in that it includes a transaction type and information about the transaction. In turn, the application's callback function acts upon the transaction and returns the appropriate response back to DDEML. In the next section we will go into further detail about how the callback function works.

A DDE conversation consists of data transmission between one client application and one server application. This data transmission is divided into three different data identification keys, enabling each side of the conversation to uniquely identify the data object that has been transmitted. The three data identification keys are called *service name* or *application name, topic name*, and *item name.*

Service Name   A service name identifies the application or server that should respond to the DDE conversation. A server application can support many service names, but generally it will support only one. This service name is specified by the client during the connection request phase of the DDE conversation.

Topic Name   The topic name is a string that specifies the service type that the client is requesting. It can also specify a file name for servers that operate on files. The topic is specified by the client during the connection request phase of the DDE conversation.

Item Name   An item name identifies the actual data item, a string, an integer, a data handle, or a graphic data item, such as a bitmap or metafile. The item name is passed from the server application by a DDE transaction to the client's callback function during the DDE conversation.

Supporting the System Topic   In addition to these three data types, a server application should support the System topic. The System topic provides information that any DDE client may want to find out about the server. The System topic name is defined as SZDDESYS_TOPIC in the DDEML.H file.

For example, a client application may want to find out which server applications are currently present and what kind of information or services they can provide. In order to query this, a client can perform a DDE conversation on the System topic with the service name set to NULL. This will initialize a conversation with all DDE servers and will allow each server to respond to the query.

This type of conversation is called a *wildcard conversation*. It should not be used frequently, because it degrades system performance. Most of the time a client would perform this type of conversation only once at startup. Table 11.3 lists item names within the System topic that a server should support. All of these item names are defined in the DDEML.H header file, which you must include in your source code modules in order to use DDEML.

TABLE 11.3:   Item Names in the System Topic

Item	Description
SZDDE_ITEM_ITEMLIST	A list of items that are supported under a non-System topic.
SZDDESYS_ITEM_FORMAT	A list of the Clipboard format numbers that are supported by the server. This list will be sorted to contain the most descriptive formats first.
SZDDESYS_ITEM_HEL	Help information supported by the server.
SZDDESYS_ITEM_RTNMS	A detailed list of information for the most recently used WM_DDE_ACK message. This enables the server to return more than 8 bits of return data to the client.
SZDDESYS_ITEM_STATU	Current status of the server, indicating whether the server is Ready or Busy.
SZDDESYS_ITEM_SYSITEM	List of items supported under the System topic by the server.
SZDDESYS_ITEM_TOPIC	List of topics supported by the server at the current time.

Initializing DDEML

Before any application can call any of the DDEML's functions, the application needs to call the DdeInitialize function. This function is used to identify the instance handle of the application and to register the application's callback function with DDEML. It also specifies the transaction filter flags that the application does not want to get from DDEML.

DDEML supports applications that allow multiple instances of DDEML. It uses the instance handle to differentiate between the instances. It is also recommended that an application assign a different DDE callback function to each instance. This enables an application to identify the different instances from the callback function. The reason for the multiple instances support is to support DLLs using DDEML.

The transaction filter optimizes the system performance by trapping DDEML's unwanted transactions, which would otherwise be passed to an application's callback function. This filter is passed to DDEML by way of the DdeInitialize function and can be changed by subsequently calling the same function.

The following is an example of an initialization routine:

```
DWORD idInst = OL;
HANDLE hInst;
FARPROC lpDdeProc;
lpDdeProc = MakeProcInstance ((FARPROC) MyDdeCallback, hInst);
if (DdeInitialize(&idInst,          // instance handle from DDEML
      (PFNCALLBACK) lpDdeProc,      // address of callback func-
tion
      CBF_FAIL_EXECUTES |           // filter XTYP_EXECUTE trans-
actions
      CBF_FAIL_POKES, OL);          // filter XTYP_POKE transac-
tions
  return FALSE;
```

This example obtains the procedure-instance address for the application's callback function, named MyDdeCallback, and then passes this address to DDEML. The initialization also informs DDEML not to pass the XTYP_EXECUTE and XTYP_POKE transactions to MyDdeCallback function.

An application should call the DdeUninitialize function once DDEML is no longer needed. This will terminate all conversations that this application currently has open and will also release any DDEML resources that the system has allocated for this application. The DdeUninitialize function should be called after the application's message loop has been terminated. This prevents any problems that may occur if the other application fails to terminate the conversation, thus causing the client application to enter a modal loop to wait for the conversation to terminate. If the client gets into this situation, the loop will continue until the specified timeout period is reached. At that point a message box will be displayed so the user can decide whether to retry and wait for another timeout period, ignore and wait indefinitely, or abort the modal loop.

DDEML's Callback Functions

As stated before, the client's callback function address is passed to the server during the DDE initialization process. This callback function will receive the transactions that are passed from the DDEML. It should also be able to support all the DDEML's transactions, except those that have been specified to be filtered by the DDEML.

The following is an example of a typical callback function that the client application would contain:

```
HDDEDATA CALLBACK MyDdeCallback (
                UINT uType,        // transaction type
                UINT uFmt,         // clipboard data format
                HCONV hConv,       // handle of conversation
                HSZ hString1,      // handle of string
                HSZ hString2,      // handle of string
                HDDEDATA hData,    // handle of global memory object
                DWORD dwData1,     // transaction specific data
                DWORD dwData2)     // transaction specific data
{
switch (uType) {
case XTYP_REGISTER:
case XTYP_UNREGISTER:
    .
    .
    .
    return (HDDEDATA) NULL;
case XTYP_ADVDATA:
    .
    .
    .
    return (HDDEDATA) DDE_FACK;
case XTYP_XACT_COMPLETE:
    .
```

```
        .
        .
        .
        return (HDDEDATA) NULL;
case XTYP_DISCONNECT:
        .
        .
        .
        return (HDDEDATA) NULL;
default:
        return (HDDEDATA) NULL
}
}
```

The uType parameter specifies the transaction type that is sent from DDEML. The other parameters are used by the different transaction types. We'll examine these different transaction types in the following sections of this chapter.

DDEML's Management Schemes

DDEML makes writing DDE applications easier because of the management schemes it provides. These management schemes relieve you of a lot of the programming work you used to have to do when writing applications using raw DDE. The following sections describe how these management schemes work and how they make it easier to use DDE.

Client-Server Conversation Management

The DDE conversation between a client application and a server application is always initiated by the client application. This conversation is a request from the client to connect to a server. When the server accepts the connect request, a conversation is established and each application will receive a handle that identifies the conversation. The applications in turn use this handle to call other DDEML functions, to send transactions, and to perform management services of the DDE conversation.

The client is not limited to establishing a conversation with just a single server but can request conversations with multiple servers. Let's examine these two types of conversations that clients and servers can have.

Single Conversations   A client application calls the DdeConnect function to request a single conversation with a server. The client supplies the string handle specifying the service name of the server and the topic name the client desires. The DDEML in turn sends the XTYP_CONNECT transaction to the DDE callback functions of each server application that has registered a service name that matches the one supplied by the DdeConnect function. A server that has turned off service-name filtering by calling the DdeNameService function will also be notified by DDEML. A server should then return a TRUE response if it supports the service and topic that has been requested or a FALSE response if it does not.

If no server is available for conversation, DDEML returns a NULL from the Dde-Connect function. If a server returns a TRUE response to XTYP_CONNECT, a conversation is established, and DDEML returns a conversation handle to the client. DDEML will also notify the server with an XTYP_CONNECT_CONFIRM transaction and the same conversation handle.

The following example shows a DdeConnect call from a client application:

```
HCONV   hConv;
HSZ     hszServerName;
HSZ     hszSysTopic;
hConv = DdeConnect (idInst,             // instance identifier
                    hszServerName,      // service name string handle
                    hszSysTopic,        // System-topic string handle
                    (PCONVCONTEXT) NULL);  // reserved NULL only
if (!hConv) {
MessageBox(hWnd, "A Server is unavailable.", (LPSTR)NULL,
MB_OK);
return FALSE;
}
```

The idInst parameter in the example specifies the instance identifier that is returned from the DdeInitialize function.

The DdeConnect function shown in the example will cause DDEML to notify the server application's callback function with an XTYP_CONNECT transaction. The following is an example of the server's callback function and how it responds to the XTYP_CONNECT transaction:

```
#define CTOPICS 3
HSZ     hzString1;              // string handle passed by DDEML
HSZ     ahszTopics[CTOPICS];    // array of supported topics
int i;
```

```
case XTYP_CONNECT:
for (i=0; i< CTOPICS; i++) {
if (hzString1 == ahszTopics[i])
return TRUE;        // conversation established
}
return FALSE;       // topic not supported, no conversation
```

The server will return a TRUE response to the XTYP_CONNECT transaction if it supports the topic, and in turn DDEML will send an XTYP_CONNECT_CONFIRM transaction to the server's DDE callback function. This transaction contains the handle of the conversation that was established.

A client can also establish a wildcard conversation by specifying NULL for the service name string handle, the topic name string handle, or both in the DdeConnect function. DDEML will send the XTYP_WILDCONNECT transaction to the callback functions of all DDE applications that do not have that transaction filtered. Each server should respond to this transaction by returning a data handle that identifies a null-terminated array of HSZPAIR structures. This array contains one structure for each service/topic name pair that matches the pair specified by the client. DDEML will then select one of the pairs to establish a conversation and return the client a handle that identifies that conversation. The DDEML also sends the XTYP_CON-NECT_CONFIRM transaction to the server with the same conversation handle.

The following is an example of the server application's callback function and its response to the XTYP_WILDCONNECT transaction:

```
#define CTOPICS 3
HSZ    hszServ, hszTopic;       // string handle passed by DDEML
HSZPAIR ahp[CTOPICS + 1];
HSZ    ahszTopics[CTOPICS];     // array of supported topics
int i, j;
        .
. // switch to examine transaction types
case XTYP_WILDCONNECT:
// scan topic list and create array of HSZPAIR structures
for (i=0, j=0; i< CTOPICS; i++) {
if (hszTopic == (HSZ) NULL ||
     hszTopic == ahszTopics[i]) {
ahp[j].hszSvc = hszServ;
ahp[j++].hszTopic = ahszTopics[i];
}
}
// end the list of HSZPAIR structure with a NULL string handles
```

```
ahp[j].hszSvc = NULL;
ahp[j].hszTopic = NULL;
// return a handle to a global memory handle containing the
// HSZPAIR structures
return DdeCreateDataHandle(
idInst,             // instance of identifier
&ahp,               // pointer to HSZPAIR array
sizeof(HSZ) * j,    // length of array
0,                  // pointer to start at beginning
NULL,               // no item-name string
fmt,                // return the same format
0);                 // let the system own memory handle

}
return TRUE;        // conversation established
}
return FALSE;       // topic not supported, no conversation
. // process other transaction types
.
```

A DDE conversation can be terminated by either the client or the server by calling the DdeDisconnect function. DDEML will notify the callback function of the other party with an XTYP_DISCONNECT transaction.

Multiple Conversations   A client can perform multiple conversations with multiple servers by calling the DdeConnectList function to determine whether any servers in the system are needed. The client specifies a service name and topic name with the DdeConnectList call. This will cause DDEML to broadcast an XTYP_WILDCON-NECT transaction to all servers that match the service name. DDEML will return a handle to a list of the valid conversations. The client can then call DdeQueryNext-Server to get the conversation handle to each server and transmit transactions to the server the client wants to initiate a conversation with. The client can also call the DdeQueryConvInfo function to obtain the server's service name string handle and other information about the conversation. A client can call the Dde-Disconnect function to terminate conversations to an individual server that is not applicable, or it can call the DdeDisconnectList to terminate all conversations.

String Management

We have seen that almost all of the DDEML functions utilize string handles to pass data among one another. To create and manage these string handles, DDEML provides the following essential functions:

Function	Description
DdeCreateStringHandle	Creates the string handle.
DdeFreeStringHandle	Frees the DDE string handle. The string handle is kept in a string table with a usage count. If an application calls the DdeCreateStringHandle function and the string already exists in the string table, DDEML increments the usage count instead of adding another string entry to the table. When the usage count of the string equals zero, the string is removed from the string table.
DdeCmpStringHandles	Compares two DDE string handles.
DdeKeepStringHandle	Increments the usage count of the string handle.
DdeQueryString	Copies the string from a string handle to a specified buffer and returns the length of the string copied.

The following example shows an application creating a string handle for the service name string and a topic name string of the application and then querying the string handle of the service name:

```
HSZ hszServName;
HSZ hszSysTopic;
DWORD count;
PSTR pszServName;
hszServname = DdeCreateStringHandle(
idInst,          // instance indentifier
"MyServer",      // service name to register
CP_WINANSI);     // code page
hszSysTopic = DdeCreateStringHandle(
```

```
idInst,            // instance indentifier
SZDDESYS_TOPIC,    // system topic to register
CP_WINANSI);       // code page
cb = DdeQueryString(idInst, hszServName, (LPSTR) NULL,
                    0l, CP_WINANSI) + 1;
pszServName = (PSTR) LocalAlloc(LPTR, (WORD) cb);
DdeQueryString(idInst, hszServName, pszServName, cb, CP_WINANSI);
```

A string handle that is passed to an application's callback function becomes invalid when the callback function returns, unless the application saves the string handle for use after the callback function returns by using the DdeKeepStringHandle function. The string built by an application using the DdeCreateStringHandle function will add the specified string to a systemwide string table, and the system will maintain the usage count for each string in the string table.

Since this string table contains unique strings and usage counts, and since more than one application can obtain the handle to a particular string, an application should not free a string handle more times than it has created or kept the handle. This will prevent the string from being removed from the table prematurely and from causing other applications to be unable to obtain the string handle. DDEML's string management uses the Windows atom manager and has the same restrictions in size as atoms—256 bytes.

Data Management

Since passing string handles is limited to 256 bytes, an application may need another way of passing large memory objects. DDEML provides a set of functions to create and manage the large global memory objects that are passed from one application to another. The DdeCreateDataHandle function enables DDEML to return a data handle to a local buffer that is passed from the application to DDEML. This data handle can then be shared between applications by passing this data handle to DDEML, which in turn passes the data handle to the other application's callback function.

The following example shows how a callback function creates a global memory object and obtains a data handle to the object. This data handle is then returned to DDEML, which returns the data handle to the client application.

```
char szBuf[50];
switch (uType) {
case XTYP_ADVREQ:
// create the current Dow Jones Industrial Average
```

```
wsprintf(szBuf, "DJIA: %4.3f, Vol: %4.3f Million", fDJIA,
fVolume);
return (DdeCreateDataHandle(
idInst,             // instance identifier
(LPBYTE) szBuf,     // string buffer
strlen(szBuf) +1,   // size of string
OL,                 // offset from beginning
hszDJIA,            // item-name string handle
CF_TEXT,            // format type
0));                // no creation flags
```

The client application can obtain a pointer to the data object by calling the Dde-AccessData function. This data pointer is provided with read-only access. After the application has finished processing the data, you call the DdeUnaccessData to invalidate the pointer. The client can also copy the data to a local buffer by calling the DdeGetData function. The following example shows a client application's callback function receiving an advise data notification and the way the function would process the data object:

```
HDDEDATA hData;
LPBYTE lpszAdviseData;
DWORD cbLen, i;
char szData[32];

case XTYP_ADVDATA:
lpszAdviseData = DdeAccessData(hData, &cbLen);
DdeGetData(hData, &szData, 32, 0); DdeUnaccessdata(hdata);
return (HDDEDATA) TRUE;
```

When a data handle is passed from the application that created it, DDEML makes the data handle invalid to that application. This can be prevented by specifying the HDATA_APPOWNED flag when the application calls the DdeCreateDataHandle function. With this flag set, the application becomes the owner of the data object, and DDEML will not invalidate the data handle until the owner of the data object calls the DdeFreeDataHandle function. The application that creates a data handle can add to the data object or overwrite data in the object by calling the DdeAddData function. This can be done only before the application passes the data handle to DDEML. Once DDEML receives the data handle, the data handle cannot be changed; it can only be freed.

Transaction Management

DDEML uses transactions to notify and pass data between the client application and the server application. Transaction management is one of DDEML's most important features. Prior to DDEML, "raw DDE" based on `PostMessage` and `SendMessage` had to be used for client and server Windows applications to communicate with each other. These messages were usually directed to an invisible window that was created only to process DDE conversations.

DDEML makes transaction management much easier for both the client and the server application. Instead of posting and sending messages to another Windows application, you call a DDEML function. DDEML in turn sends a message for you to the Windows application you are communicating with. This message is directed to the application's DDEML callback procedure. DDEML provides four different transaction types that the client can request or send to the server. These are a *request transaction*, a *poke transaction*, an *advise transaction*, and an *execute transaction*.

Using the Request Transaction A request transaction is a one-time request by the client for a data item that the server application owns. The client calls the `DdeClientTransaction` function with `XTYP_REQUEST` as the transaction type and with the data item the application is requesting. DDEML in turn passes the `XTYP_REQUEST` transaction to the server's callback function. Within the `XTYP_REQUEST` transaction, the topic, item, and data format requested are also passed. The server will then return the data item that is requested, or a NULL if it does not support the requested topic, item, or format.

Using the Poke Transaction A poke transaction is used by the client to send data to a server. The client will call the `DdeClientTransaction` function with the `XTYP_POKE` transaction type. The data that is sent to the server is a data handle that has been created by the client by calling the `DdeCreateDataHandle` function. DDEML will pass the `XTYP_POKE` transaction to the server's callback function. The server will either accept the data item and return a `DDE_FACK` acknowledgment or reject the data item and return a `DDE_FNOTPROCESSED` acknowledgment.

Using the Advise Transaction An advise transaction is used by the client to establish a link to a server and to enable the server periodically to send updates about the linked object to the client. This link remains active until the client ends the conversation. The advise transaction is further defined by either a hot or a warm link. In a hot advise link, the server will immediately send a data handle that identifies

613

the updated data. In a warm advise link, the server will send only a notification flag that the data has been updated and will wait until the client requests the data before it actually sends the data. A client sets up a hot link by sending the XTYP_ADVSTART transaction type when calling the DdeClientTransaction function. A warm link is set up by adding the XTYP_NODATA flag to the XTYP_ADVSTART transaction type when calling the DdeClientTransaction function.

DDEML will notify a client application of a DDE advise by sending an XTYP_ADVDATA transaction to the client's callback function. A server can send updates to a data item faster than a client could process them. If the client must perform long processing operations on the data, in order not to be overrun by XTYP_ADVDATA transactions from the server the client should specify the XTYPF_ACKREQ flag when it calls the DdeClientTransaction function. A client ends the advise link by sending the XTYP_ADVSTOP transaction type by calling the DdeClientTransaction function.

Using the Execute Transaction   An execute transaction is used by the client to pass a command that should be executed by the server. The client specifies the execute transaction by passing the XTYP_EXECUTE transaction type to the server's callback function. The client creates the command by way of a data handle and passes this command to the server application. The server should then return DDE_FACK if it has executed the command, DDE_FNOTPROCESSED if it does not support the command or cannot complete the transaction, or DDE_FBUSY if it is too busy to complete the transaction.

Transaction Types   A client can send either synchronous or asynchronous transactions. In a synchronous transaction, the client waits for the server to perform the data or command request. The client essentially goes into a modal loop until the server returns the result of the transaction. The client can still process other messages, such as user input, but it cannot send another synchronous transaction to the server until the DdeClientTransaction returns from the server with the result of the transaction.

In an asynchronous transaction, the client specifies a timeout value by using the TIMEOUT_ASYNC flag in the DdeClientTransaction function. The function will then return after it is called, and DDEML will pass a transaction identifier to the client. When the server has completed processing the transaction, DDEML will send an XTYP_XACT_COMPLETE transaction to the client's callback function. This transaction will contain the transaction identifier so the client can distinguish it from other transactions it may have started.

An asynchronous transaction will allow any client application to proceed in performing other processing, such as calculations of data received. This type of transaction will also allow multiple transactions to be performed simultaneously with the same server.

If necessary, an application can suspend sending transactions to its callback function by returning CBR_BLOCK from the callback function. This will enable the application to process a long transaction or to perform other processing that needs to be done without the interruptions that are received from the DDE callback function.

When the application is ready to continue with the DDE conversation, it calls the DdeEnableCallback function to notify DDEML that it is ready to receive transactions to its callback function. By calling the DdeEnableCallback function with the EC_DISABLE flag, an application can suspend all transactions associated with a specific conversation. The application specifies the conversation handle in the call. It could also pass a NULL handle, which would suspend all transactions for all conversations. To reenable the transactions, the DdeEnableCallback function needs either EC_ENABLEALL to enable all transactions or EC_ENABLEONE to enable just one transaction at a time.

Transaction Classes   DDEML has defined four different classes of transactions. The class type is defined in the DDEML.H, and it always begins with the XCLASS_ prefix. This class type constant is passed along with the transaction type constant to the DDE callback function of the receiving application. The class specification determines the type of return value that the callback function is to receive. Table 11.4 shows the class types and their expected return values.

Transactions   Table 11.5 shows each DDE transaction message type, the receiver of each type, and a description of the activity that causes the DDEML to generate each type of message.

Server-Name Service

A server application can register the service names that it supports by calling the DdeNameService function. This will make DDEML send the XTYP_REGISTER transaction

TABLE 11.4:   DDEML Class Types

Class	Return Value	Transaction
XCLASS_BOOL	TRUE or FALSE	XTYP_ADVSTART XTYP_CONNECT
XCLASS_DATA	Data handle	XTYP_ADVREQ XTYP_REQUEST XTYP_WILDCONNECT
XCLASS_FLAGS	Transaction flag	XTYP_ADVDATA XTYP_EXECUTE DDE_FACK DDEFBUSY XTYP_POKE DDE_FNOTPROCESSED
XCLASS_NOTIFICATION	none	XTYP_ADVSTOP XTYP_CONNECT_CONFIRM XTYP_DISCONNECT XTYP_ERROR XTYP_REGISTER XTYP_UNREGISTER XTYP_XACT_COMPLETE

to the callback function of each DDEML application that is currently running. The server application could also unregister the service name by calling the DdeName-Service function.

DDE Spy

Microsoft includes an application called DDESPY.EXE with the Windows SDK to help you develop DDE applications. DDE Spy lets you see the DDE conversations that are going on in your system.

DDE Spy is a typical DDE monitoring application. Because DDE is a cooperative activity, DDE monitoring applications must follow certain guidelines for your Windows system to operate properly while they are in use. In particular, DDE monitoring applications should not perform DDE server or client communications because problems may arise when the monitoring application intercepts its own communications.

TABLE 11.5: DDE Transaction Message Types

Transaction Type	Receiver	Cause
XTYP_ADVDATA	Client	A server responded to an XTYP_ADVREQ transaction by returning a data handle.
XTYP_ADVREQ	Server	A server called the DdePostAdvise function to indicate that the value of a data item has changed.
XTYP_ADVSTART	Server	A client started an advise link in the DdeClientTransaction function call.
XTYP_ADVSTOP	Server	A client stopped an advise link in the DdeClientTransaction function call.
XTYP_CONNECT	Server	A client called the DdeConnect function with a service name and a topic name included.
XTYP_CONNECT_CONFIRM	Server	The server returned TRUE in response to the XTYP_CONNECT or the XTYP_WILDCONNECT transaction.
XTYP_DISCONNECT	Client/Server	A conversation disconnected; both applications will receive the message.
XTYP_ERROR	Client/Server	A critical error has occurred.
XTYP_EXECUTE	Server	A client needs a command to be executed by the server.
XTYP_MONITOR	DDE Monitor App	A DDE event occurred in the system.
XTYP_POKE	Server	A client poked data to the server.
XTYP_REGISTER	Client/Server	A server application registered a service name.
XTYP_REQUEST	Server	A client requested data from the server.
XTYP_UNREGISTER	Client/Server	A server application unregistered a service name.
XTYP_WILDCONNECT	Server	A client requested a connect with a NULL service name.
XTYP_XACT_COMPLETE	Client	An asynchronous transaction has been completed.

DDE Spy lets you monitor the DDE messages that are passed from the client and server applications. It shows which application is the client and which is the server. It also shows the elements of the DDE messages, the server name, the topic, and the item.

DDE Spy also gives you information about all the DDE servers that are currently running on the system. It can track the topics that those DDE servers support. DDE Spy can even track all the string handles that have been defined by all of the applications that are utilizing DDE string handles. All of this information is shown in different child windows displayed by DDE Spy. To see how DDE Spy works, let's use it in a project—building a DDE server.

Building a DDE Server

To illustrate how DDEML works and how you can use DDE Spy to monitor DDE messages, let's look at how to build a DDE server application. For this project we will take the Resource Monitor application that was introduced in Chapter 6 and make it a DDE server. As a DDE server, Resource Monitor has one topic, named Resources. The Resource topic has three items: User, to report on free User system resources; GDI, to report on free GDI system resources; and Memory, to report on free global memory resources. You will find the DDE server version of Resource Monitor in the \DDE\RMONITOR directory that was created when you installed the disk set. You will also find the following two other directories under the \DDE directory on the disk set:

- \CLOCK contains a Windows clock application that's a DDE server which reports on the current time. As you will soon see, we will use the C source code in the Clock application to help us make Resource Monitor into a DDE server.

- \CLIENT contains a DDE client program named SBIDDU1.EXE. This client DDE utility is a freeware application developed by SoftBlox Inc. in Huntington, New York. SBIDDU1 has a nice graphical look and feel and even includes a Windows Help file to explain how it works. It's a very useful utility for testing DDE servers, and we will use it later to show how the DDE version of Resource Monitor works.

Using Resource Monitor as a DDE Server

Before we look at the source code that shows how I made Resource Monitor into a DDE server, let's learn how the DDE version of Resource Monitor works and how it can be monitored using DDE Spy. All of the information displayed in DDE Spy's windows is written once when an event happens. If you activate DDE Spy after an event happens, the event will not be noted in DDE Spy's windows. For example, if you execute Resource Monitor and then execute DDE Spy, you will not find Resource Monitor listed in the DDE Spy Registered Servers window. However, if you start DDE Spy before Resource Monitor, Resource Monitor will be displayed as a registered server.

Whenever you use DDE Spy to monitor DDE conversations, you should start DDE Spy first so you can keep track of everything that occurs while you are recording DDE conversations. You can save the information collected by DDE Spy by choosing the File option in the DDE Spy Output menu. You can select the types of information DDE Spy collects by choosing options in the DDE Spy Monitor menu. You can select the DDE Spy windows that you want displayed by choosing Options in the DDE Spy Track menu. Figure 11.2 shows the main DDE Spy window. This window records all the DDEML events that occur. These events can be messages sent between clients and servers. They can also be the acquisition and release of DDE resources such as string handles and global memory objects.

FIGURE 11.2:

Keeping track of Resource Monitor using DDE Spy

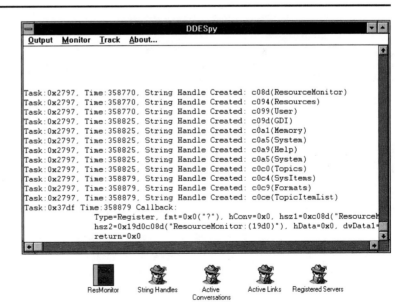

Figure 11.2 shows DDE Spy keeping track of Resource Monitor's DDE activities. As you can see in the figure, Resource Monitor has just started. It first acquired some string handle resources and registered itself as a DDE server. Below the DDE Spy window, you can see the Resource Monitor icon and the icons for the other DDE Spy overlayable windows. Besides tracking DDE events in its main window, DDE Spy keeps track of the following information in other windows:

- String handles
- Active DDE conversations
- Active DDE links
- Registered DDE servers

You use the Track menu to specify which DDE activity DDE Spy is to track. When you choose a command from the Track menu, DDE Spy creates a separate window for the display of information in conjunction with the DDE functions. DDE Spy updates the information displayed in each window as DDE activity occurs. However, as we noted previously, events that occurred prior to creation of the tracking window are not displayed.

> **TIP**
>
> DDE Spy can sort the displayed information in the tracking window. If you select the heading for a particular column in the tracking window, DDE Spy will sort the displayed information on the basis of the column you selected. This can be useful if you are searching for a particular event or handle.

Tracking String Handles

Windows maintains a systemwide string table containing the string handles applications used in DDE transactions. To display the system string table so that the string, the string handle, and the string usage count are shown, choose the String Handles command from the Track menu.

Tracking Active Conversations

To see a display of all active DDE conversations in your Windows system, choose the Active Conversations command from the Track menu. The Active Conversations window shows the server name, the current topic, and the server and client handles for each active conversation.

Tracking Active Links

To see a display of all active DDE advise loops, choose the Active Links command from the Track menu. The Active Links window shows the server name, topic, item format, transaction type, client handle, and server handle for every active advise loop in your Windows system.

Tracking Registered Servers

Server applications use the DdeNameService function to register with the DDEML. When the DDEML receives the DdeNameService function call, it adds the server name and an instance-specific name to a list of registered servers. Figure 11.3 shows the DDE Spy Registered Servers window. At this point I have started both Resource Monitor and the DDEML Clock so you can see what's displayed in the Registered Servers window when more than one DDE server is active.

FIGURE 11.3:
Checking on which Windows applications are DDE servers using DDE Spy

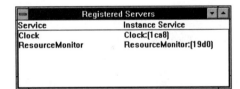
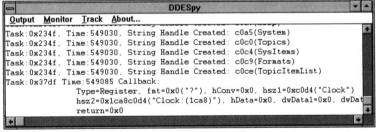

Communicating with Resource Monitor Using SBIDDU1

Now that you have seen how Spy operates, let's start up a DDE client and initiate a hot link conversation with the Resource Monitor DDE server. We will keep DDE Spy active while all of this is going on to see how DDE Spy can monitor the project activities.

To start, I executed the SBIDDU1 client DDE utility from SoftBlox that is included on the disk set. After the main window of SBIDDU1 was displayed, I clicked on the SBIDDU1 Initiate push button. SBIDDU1 tried to initiate a conversation with all active DDE servers using the XTYP_WILDCONNECT transaction type. DDE servers that wanted to respond to this transaction returned TRUE in their DDEML callback function. Then the client's DdeConnect call returned a conversation handle. Figure 11.4 shows the SBIDDU1 Select DDE Conversation dialog box. This dialog box lists all the DDE servers that responded to the XTYP_WILDCONNECT transaction. To establish a conversation, all you need to do is select the DDE server and topic in the list box and click on OK.

FIGURE 11.4:

Selecting a DDE server to communicate with using the SBIDDU1 client DDE utility

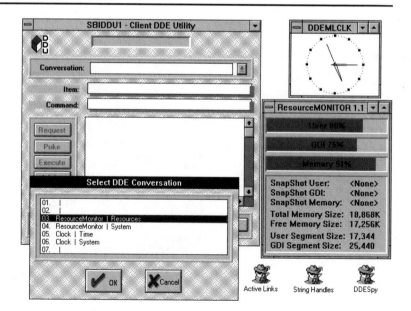

After a conversation is established for a specific server and topic, information can be obtained from the DDE server by requesting an item. Resource Monitor has one topic, Resources. The Resources topic has three items:

- *User* reports on free User heap space.
- *GDI* reports on free GDI heap space.
- *Memory* reports on free global memory.

All of the system resource information that Resource Monitor keeps track of is stored in global variables. The source code for the DDE version of Resource Monitor is included on the disk set, so you can add to or modify the kinds of information that Resource Monitor reports on. Figure 11.5 shows the result of having SBIDDU1 ask about the Memory item. To get this information back from Resource Monitor, I typed in Memory in the Item edit box and clicked on Advise.

I could have clicked on either Request or Advise to get the information. You click on the Request push button for a one-time request and on the Advise push button to establish a hot link conversation. After setting up a hot link conversation, Resource Monitor will let the clients it's communicating with know when an item's

FIGURE 11.5:

Using the SBIDDU1 client DDE utility to communicate with Resource Monitor

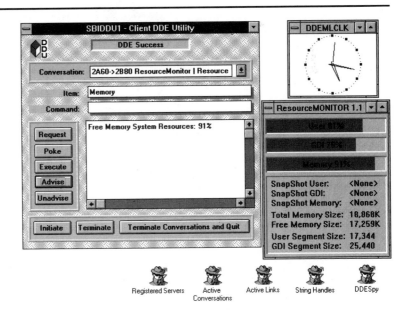

value has changed. In this specific example, the value displayed in SBIDDU1's window will change as system resources change.

After establishing a DDE conversation with Resource Monitor using SBIDDU1, I started one with the DDEML Clock application as well. Using SBIDDU1 you can establish as many DDE conversations with as many DDE servers as you want. Figure 11.6 shows the DDE Spy Active Conversations window keeping track of all the DDE conversations.

After I had finished experimenting with SBIDDU1, I used the Terminate Conversations and Quit push button to exit. SBIDDU1 is a handy application to test the DDE server applications you are building.

Now that you have seen how to use the DDE server version of Resource Monitor with SBIDDU1 and how to monitor the conversation with DDE Spy, let's learn how to use Microsoft Excel as a DDE client to gather information from Resource Monitor.

FIGURE 11.6:

Keeping track of the active DDE conversations using DDE Spy

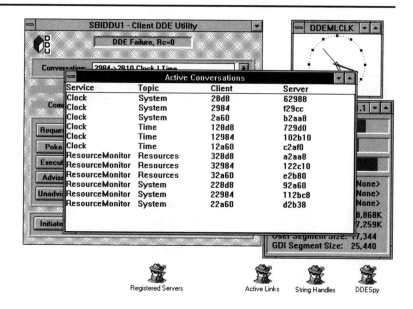

Using Resource Monitor with Excel

You can use Excel to do many wonderful things with DDE. For example, you could use Excel to keep track of events, such as changes in the price of Microsoft stock over time, using a DDE server application that can connect with telecommunication services such as Dow-Jones. In the example here we will keep things simple to show what can be done using Excel. If you learn the Excel macro language, you can build on this example to create more elaborate DDE applications.

To start a hot link DDE conversation, all you need to type in for your spreadsheet formula is

```
=SERVER|TOPIC!ITEM
```

You start with an equal sign (=), followed by the DDE server name, followed by the bar (|), followed by the DDE topic name, followed by an exclamation point (!), followed finally by the DDE item name. For example, to find out about the User heap system resources from Resource Monitor, you would type in

```
=ResourceMonitor|Resources!User
```

The Excel spreadsheet RMONITOR.XLS in the \DDE\RMONITOR directory is an example of how to do this. First you need to start the DDE version of Resource Monitor and then start Excel. After Excel has started, open the file RMONITOR.XLS as shown in Figure 11.7. Make sure to choose Yes when Excel asks you if you want to Re-establish Remote Links.

Figure 11.7 shows RMONITOR.XLS with its accompanying chart deleted, so we can concentrate on what's going on in Excel's formulas. Figure 11.8 shows the Excel spreadsheet with both the data and a 3-D column chart created from the data. The Excel spreadsheet uses three formulas to gather information from Resource Monitor on User heap space, GDI heap space, and global memory. Since these formulas set up a hot link conversation, Excel's information is updated as Resource Monitor reports on the change. The information displayed in the cells labeled Used and Free is derived from the information gathered from Resource Monitor that appears in cells A4 through A6.

As shown in Figures 11.8 and 11.9, you can also graph the information that's obtained from Resource Monitor. Figure 11.8 shows the column chart as part of the Excel spreadsheet. Figure 11.9 shows the same chart in a maximized window where it can be edited. This chart was created by highlighting the information in cells B3 through D6 and using Excel's ChartWizard to help create a 3-D column chart.

FIGURE 11.7:

Using Excel to get information from Resource Monitor using DDE

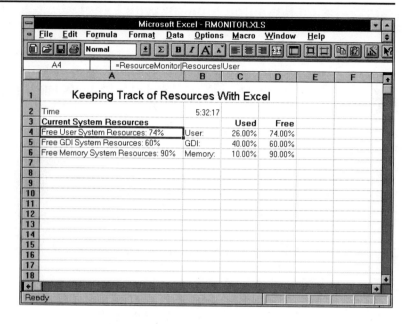

FIGURE 11.8:

Creating an Excel chart to display the current status of system resources

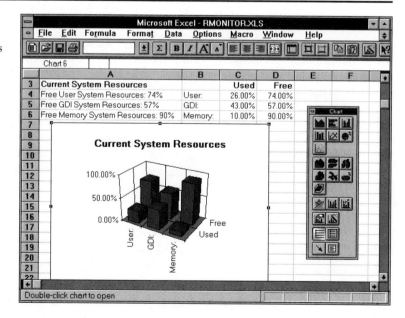

FIGURE 11.9:

The Current System Resources Excel chart

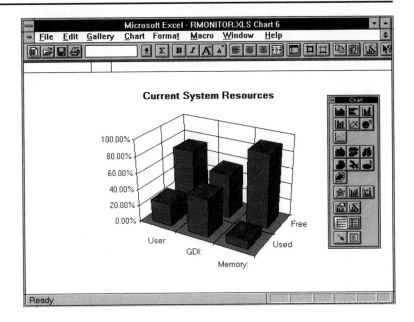

Now that you have seen how to get information from the Resource Monitor DDE server using SBIDDU1 and Excel, let's look at what's going on inside Resource Monitor. You will be surprised at how easy it is to build DDE server functionality into Resource Monitor using the WRAPPER.C and WRAPPER.H source files that are included with the DDEML Clock application.

Building DDEML Functionality into Resource Monitor

All of the functionality in the Clock DDE server application (DDEMLCLK.EXE) is encapsulated in the source code file WRAPPER.C. Since this was so well implemented, I reused the code in WRAPPER.C in Resource Monitor to make it a DDE server application. The code in WRAPPER.C is table-driven. You do not need to change a line of code in WRAPPER.C to use it to implement a basic DDE server application. All you need to do is the following:

1. Include WRAPPER.C and the .OBJ file it generates as part of the make file process when you build a Windows application.

2. Include WRAPPER.H in the C source code files that need to call the DDE functions in WRAPPER.C.

3. Copy the table definitions from DDEMLCLK.C and modify them to use in your program.

4. Call the WRAPPER.C function `InitializeDDE` to initialize your program as a DDE server.

5. Call the DDEML function `DdePostAdvise` for hot and warm link conversations to let client applications know that the data the DDE item identifies has changed.

6. Identify the function in your program that needs to be called when a client asks for data. This function is defined in the tables UserFormats, GDIFormats, and MemoryFormats.

7. Unregister the program as a DDE server before it terminates using the WRAPPER.C function `UninitializeDDE`.

It's All in the Tables

Steps 1 and 2 are pretty basic, so I won't bother to explain them. Step 3 is the most involved and is the key to getting everything to work correctly. If you look inside WRAPPER.H, you will find the type definitions for four tables that identify to the functions in WRAPPER.C the service name, topic names, and item names that your DDE server suplies:

- `DDESERVICETBL` identifies the service name of your DDE application and the data objects associated with it. The `LPDDETOPICTBL` pointer in this structure points to the `DDETOPICTBL`.

- `DDETOPICTBL` identifies the topic names your DDE application supports and the data objects associated with each topic. The `LPDDEITEMTBL` pointer in each occurrence of a table record points to `DDEITEMTBL`.

- `DDEITEMTBL` identifies the item names your DDE application supports for each topic and the data objects associated with it. The `LPDDEFORMATTBL` pointer in each occurrence of an item table record points to `DDEFORMATTBL`.

- `DDEFORMATTBL` identifies the format types your DDE application supports for each item and the data objects associated with it.

The following listing shows how the structures for each of these tables are defined in WRAPPER.H. Notice the similarity in the structures of the last three tables listed, `DDEITEMTBL`, `DDETOPICTBL`, and `DDESERVICETBL`.

```
typedef struct _DDEFORMATTBL {
  LPSTR       pszFormat;    // Format name.
  WORD        wFmt;         // Clipboard format supported such as CF_TEXT
  WORD        wFmtFlags;    // Optional flags parameter for you to customize.
  CBFNIN      lpfnPoke;     // Function pointer for function to call to
                            // handle a XTYP_POKE transaction.
  CBFNOUT     lpfnRequest;  // Function pointer for function to call to
                            // handle a XTYP_REQUEST transaction.
} DDEFORMATTBL;
typedef DDEFORMATTBL *PDDEFORMATTBL;
typedef DDEFORMATTBL FAR *LPDDEFORMATTBL;

typedef struct _DDEITEMTBL {
  LPSTR       pszItem;      // Item name.
  HSZ         hszItem;      // DDE string handle for item.
  CBFNIN      lpfnExecute;  // Function pointer to execute function for
                            // XTYP_EXECUTE transaction.
  WORD        cFormats;     // Number of CF_ formats supported by item
  WORD        wItemFlags;   // Optional flags parameter for you to customize.
  LPDDEFORMATTBL fmt;       // Pointer to format table structure.
} DDEITEMTBL;
typedef DDEITEMTBL *PDDEITEMTBL;
typedef DDEITEMTBL FAR *LPDDEITEMTBL;


typedef struct _DDETOPICTBL {
  LPSTR       pszTopic;     // Topic name.
  HSZ         hszTopic;     // DDE string handle for topic.
  WORD        cItems;       // Number of items for this topic.
  WORD        wTopicFlags;  // Optional flags parameter for you to customize.
  LPDDEITEMTBL  item;       // Pointer to item table structure.
} DDETOPICTBL;
typedef DDETOPICTBL *PDDETOPICTBL;
typedef DDETOPICTBL FAR *LPDDETOPICTBL;

typedef struct _DDESERVICETBL {
  LPSTR       pszService;   // Service name.
  HSZ         hszService;   // DDE string handle for service.
  WORD        cTopics;      // Number of topics for this service.
  WORD        wServiceFlags; // Optional flags parameter for you to customize.
  LPDDETOPICTBL  topic;     // Pointer to topic table structure.
```

```
} DDESERVICETBL;
typedef DDESERVICETBL *PDDESERVICETBL;
typedef DDESERVICETBL FAR *LPDDESERVICETBL;
```

All of the last three structures have the same organization. Each has five elements that you must provide information for. As an example, let's look at the DDESER-VICETBL structure.

- pszService is a string pointer that points to a string that your program supplies for the service name. The function InitHszs in WRAPPER.C calls the DDEML DdeCreateStringHandle to create a string handle for the service name, hsz-Service, that's stored in this structure. Resource Monitor's service name is "ResourceMonitor."

- hszService is the string handle for the service name that was created by calling DdeCreateStringHandle. Among other things, this string handle is used in InitializeDDE in WRAPPER.C when the DDEML DdeNameService function is called to register Resource Monitor as a DDE server.

- cTopics is the number of topics that the DDE server application supports. Resource Monitor has one topic, Resources.

- wTopicFlags is an option field (it's not referenced anywhere in WRAPPER.C or in the DDEML Clock source code), so you don't need to worry about providing a value. You can delete it from the structure or use it however you want.

- topic is a pointer to the DDETOPICTBL structure.

Each of these structures contains a string that identifies either the service name, the topic, or the item. Following this is a string handle that's obtained from DDEML by a function call in WRAPPER.C. The next element is the number of topics or items in the next table that the pointer (either topics or items) in the structure points to.

The original version of WRAPPER.H included with the Windows 3.1 SDK has only a few comments to guide you in using WRAPPER.C and WRAPPER.H for building a DDE server application. The versions of WRAPPER.C and WRAPPER.H included on the book's disk set contain additional comments to help you use this source code for implementing DDE server functionality in your Windows application. None of the functional C statements have been changed. For example, the original C source code for the structures we have just discussed did not contain any comments to identify what each structure element was used for. The comments you see in the previous header file listing were added to show you how to create the table structures and to identify how each element is to be used.

To create these table structures I started with the DDESERVICETBL to identify the service name and then created the DDETOPICTBL to identify the topic that Resource Monitor supports. After finishing the DDETOPICTBL, I created the three rows in the DDEITEMTBL for the three DDE items that Resource Monitor supports. Each row in the DDEITEMTBL points to a DDEFORMATTBL structure that describes the Clipboard formats each item supports. For Resource Monitor the only format supported is CF_TEXT. After creating the table structures, I added function calls to use the functions in WRAPPER.C and added some functions in RMONITOR.C to respond to information requests from DDE client applications.

Calling WRAPPER.C Functions

Before DDE server functionality was added to it, Resource Monitor had three source code files. APP.C is responsible for program initialization and termination. It also includes the WinMain function. DIALOGS.C is responsible for managing the program's dialog boxes, and RMONITOR.C includes the program's window procedure and most of the functional code. When I added DDE server functionality to Resource Monitor, the only source code file that I changed was RMONITOR.C. The table structures we just discussed and all of the Resource Monitor DDE server functionality is encapsulated in RMONITOR.C.

> To help you easily find the C code that was added to RMONITOR.C to make it a
> DDE server, I prefixed any new code with a comment that starts with "//DDE."
> This will help you to find all the code in RMONITOR.C that is associated with this
> project.

The first function call that I added to RMONITOR.C was InitializeDDE in the On-
Create function. InitializeDDE is a function in WRAPPER.C that registers your
application with DDEML as a DDE server and creates all the string handles needed
by the application.

The only other function call I needed to add to a function in WRAPPER.C was a call
to UninitializeDDE to notify DDEML that Resource Monitor was terminating.
The code in WRAPPER.C manages all of the DDE conversations for your application, from the time your program is initialized as a DDE server with a call to
InitializeDDE until it terminates with a function call to UninitializeDDE.
WRAPPER.C contains all the code necessary for working with DDEML based on
the information that's provided to it in the table structures we discussed earlier.

Responding to Information Requests

The table structures contain function pointers to functions that respond to information requests from DDE client applications. These function pointers are members of
the DDEFORMATTBL structure. Resource Monitor has three functions that I set up to
respond to information requests about the three items that Resource Monitor supports as a DDE server. All of the source code for Resource Monitor functions that
were created to add DDE server functionality are included at the end of
RMONITOR.C. The following functions are responsible for handling information
requests for Resource Monitor:

```
//---------------------------------------------------------------------------
//
// The following functions were added to Resource Monitor to provide DDE
// server functionality. These functions are identified in the table
// structures at the front of this source and they are subsequently called
// from functionS in the source code file WRAPPER.C.
//


//---------------------------------------------------------------------------
```

```
//
// RequestHelp function - responds to a DDE request for information on the
// topics and itmes that Resource Monitor supports.
//
HDDEDATA PASCAL RequestHelp(HDDEDATA hDataOut)
{
   static char szHelp[] = "DDE Help for Resource Monitor.\r\r\n\t"
    "Request or advise on 'Resources!User' for User system resources.\n";
    "Request or advise on 'Resources!GDI' for GDI system resources.\n";
    "Request or advise on 'Resources!Memory' for Memory system resources.\n";

   return(DdeAddData(hDataOut, szHelp, sizeof(szHelp), 0));
}


//-------------------------------------------------------------------------
//
// RequestUser function - responds to a DDE request for information on the
// free User heap space DDE item.
//
HDDEDATA PASCAL RequestUser(HDDEDATA hDataOut)
{
   char szBuf[40];

        wsprintf ((LPSTR) szBuf, (LPSTR) "Free User System Resources: %d%%",
             wPctFreeUser);
   return(DdeAddData(hDataOut, (LPBYTE)szBuf, strlen(szBuf) + 1, OL));
}


//-------------------------------------------------------------------------
//
// RequestGDI function - responds to a DDE request for information on the
// free GDI heap space DDE item.
//
HDDEDATA PASCAL RequestGDI(HDDEDATA hDataOut)
{
   char szBuf[40];

        wsprintf ((LPSTR) szBuf, (LPSTR) "Free GDI System Resources: %d%%",
             wPctFreeGDI);
   return(DdeAddData(hDataOut, (LPBYTE)szBuf, strlen(szBuf) + 1, OL));
```

```
}
```

```
//-------------------------------------------------------------
//
// RequestMemory function - responds to a DDE request for informa-
tion on the
// free global memory DDE item.
//
HDDEDATA PASCAL RequestMemory(HDDEDATA hDataOut)
{
  char szBuf[40];

      wPctFreeMem = (UINT) (((float) dwGmemFree / dwTotMemSize)
* 100);
      wsprintf ((LPSTR) szBuf, (LPSTR) "Free Memory System
Resources: %d%%",
            wPctFreeMem);
  return(DdeAddData(hDataOut, (LPBYTE)szBuf, strlen(szBuf) + 1,
OL));
}
```

```
//-------------------------------------------------------------
//
// PokeRM function - Since Resource Monitor does not support DDE
Poke requests,
// it returns FALSE to this request.
//
BOOL PASCAL PokeRM(HDDEDATA hData)
{
  return(FALSE);
}
```

The three functions that respond to information requests from a DDE client are
RequestUser, RequestGDI, and RequestMemory. Each of these functions checks
the corresponding global variables for the type of information requested and builds
a message string to respond to the request. After the string is constructed it is added
to the global memory object created in WRAPPER.C using the DdeAddData function. The handle returned from DdeAddData is returned to the calling function in
WRAPPER.C.

Since Resource Monitor does not support a DDE poke request, FALSE is returned if a DDE client calls `DdeClientTransaction` with a transaction type of `XTYP_POKE`.

Responding to Hot and Warm Link Conversations Resource Monitor supports both hot and warm link conversations. The following code to handle this is included in the `OnTimer` function in RMONITOR.C:

```
for (nIx = 0; nIx < 3; nIx++)
   {
   DdePostAdvise(idInst, MyServiceInfo->topic[0].hszTopic,
      MyServiceInfo->topic[0].item[nIx].hszItem);
   }
```

If Resource Monitor detects a change in system resources, it calls the DDEML function `DdePostAdvise`. This results in an `XTYP_ADVREQ` transaction being sent to the Resource Monitor callback function in WRAPPER.C. The function `DoCallback` in WRAPPER.C responds to this transaction by processing it the same way as it would an `XTYP_REQUEST` transaction. `DdeCreateDataHandle` is called to create a global memory object, and then the respective function (`RequestUser`, `RequestGDI`, or `RequestMemory`) is called in RMONITOR.C to supply the information requested.

The function in RMONITOR.C calls `DdeAddData` to put the data requested into the global memory object and then returns to the `DoCallback` function in WRAPPER.C. `DoCallback` in WRAPPER.C returns a data handle to the DDEML that identifies the global memory buffer. The DDEML then notifies the client that the specified data item has changed by sending the `XTYP_ADVDATA` transaction to the client's callback function.

If the client requested a hot advise, the DDEML passes the data handle for the changed item to the client during the `XTYP_ADVDATA` transaction. Otherwise, the client can send an `XTYP_REQUEST` transaction to obtain the data handle. In the old way of doing DDE, it was up to the server to manage whether the conversation was a hot or warm link. As you can see, this burden has been removed by DDEML. The server responds the same way for both hot and warm link conversations. It's up to DDEML to respond to the client appropriately for the type of conversation being managed.

NOTE

It's possible for a server to send updates faster than a client can process them. This can be a problem for a client that must perform long processing operations on the data. In this case, the client should specify the XTYPF_ACKREQ flag when it requests an advise loop. This causes the DDEML to wait for the client to acknowledge that it has received and processed a data item before the DDEML sends the next data item.

Summary

DDEML makes building DDE applications easier than the old method of working with DDE messages directly. The WRAPPER.C and WRAPPER.H files included with the DDEML Clock application that's provided by Microsoft make implementing DDE even easier. The C source code files from the DDEML Clock application are some of the most useful source code files provided with the Windows 3.1 SDK, and they should be considered an additional tool to help you implement DDE server functionality in your Windows applications. Don't forget to use the versions of WRAPPER.C and WRAPPER.H that are included on the disk set, instead of the version that comes with the Windows 3.1 SDK. The disk set version contains additional comments to help you use the source code.

Now that we have finished looking at Windows 3.1 DDE tools, it's time to look at some other new tools that were introduced by Microsoft for Windows 3.1. These tools will help you to build more bug-free Windows applications that can be more easily ported to the new Win32 API for the Microsoft New Technology operating system.

Creating Robust Windows Applications

- Using the new Windows 3.1 STRICT type-checking to improve your application's robustness

- Using PC-Lint to remove program bugs

- Understanding the new Windows 3.1 macro APIs

- Using message crackers and forwarders

- Taking advantage of memory, window, and control window macro APIs

- Using STRESS to test how well your application works when Windows resources are low

12

Wouldn't it be nice if your C compiler could catch every conceivable program bug at compilation time—instead of your having to track them down with a debugger at execution time? Wouldn't it also be nice if you could build Windows applications that would work with the new Win32 API and the New Technology (NT) operating system—without making major changes to your C code?

Both the Windows 3.1 SDK and Borland C/C++ 3.1 come with a new WINDOWS.H header file that helps you eliminate more program bugs at compile time when you turn on the new STRICT option. STRICT does not eliminate program bugs altogether, but it does isolate more program errors than before the new Windows 3.1 WINDOWS.H header file was available.

To make Windows applications more portable, the new Windows 3.1 header files provide the new STRICT programming style. It is enforced by turning the STRICT option on when you include WINDOWS.H and a new set of portable macro APIs in WINDOWSX.H for handling messages and working with global memory, GDI, and Windows control messages. Windows 3.1 is a significant improvement for Windows users today, but the future of Windows is Win32 and the NT operating system. Win32 and NT will give users the reliability and robustness they need with a full protected-mode operating system. Win32 will make building Windows applications easier because of its flat 32-bit address space. It will also be much easier to develop and test Windows applications in an operating environment that is resilient, where an application cannot crash the system.

In this chapter I am going to show you how to take advantage of new Windows 3.1 features, such as the STRICT coding style and the macro APIs in WINDOWSX.H, to make your Windows application more robust. To illustrate how to use the new STRICT coding style and implement the new macro APIs, we will use Resource Monitor, first introduced in Chapter 6, for our example application. Besides being a useful tool for keeping track of your system's resources, Resource Monitor is a STRICT C Windows application that takes full advantage of the macro APIs found in WINDOWSX.H.

To follow along with the examples in this chapter, you can use the Resource Monitor application found in either the \ATOOLS\RMONITOR or the \ATOOLS\DDE\RMONITOR directory, both of which were created when you installed the disk set. If you haven't done so already, you should print out the source code for the Resource Monitor application. This will also help you follow along with our discussions of how STRICT and message crackers work inside a Windows application.

You will also learn in this chapter how to use the Windows development tool STRESS. STRESS helps you test your Windows application to see how well it performs when any of the following Windows resources are in short supply: User heap space, GDI heap space, global memory, file handles, or disk space. We will use Resource Monitor again to show how STRESS works.

Implementing STRICT

The best way to understand the new features included in the Windows 3.1 SDK is to see how they are put to use in a "real-world" example. I will use Resource Monitor to show you how to implement the new Windows 3.1 STRICT coding style because it's a one-window application that uses dialog boxes. You will find that the following other Windows applications developed for this book, which were not built using a code generator, also use the STRICT coding style and take advantage of the WINDOWSX.H macro APIs:

- DumpIT 3.1 is a descendant of DumpIT 2.0, introduced in Chapter 3. DumpIT 3.1 is a good example of how to develop a Multiple Document Interface (MDI) Windows application using STRICT and the new macro API.

- Topper 1.0 and Topper 2.0, introduced in Chapter 7, both use the STRICT coding style and the Windows 3.1 macro API.

All of the Windows applications that were developed for this book using the STRICT coding style were debugged using the debugging version of Windows, DBWIN, and CodeView Version 4 to make sure that they work as advertised and don't leak resources. (Having made this claim, I bet someone will still find a program bug!)

Using WINDOWS.H

The new WINDOWS.H header file is completely reorganized so that related functions, types, structures, and constants are all grouped together. Prior to Windows 3.1,

WINDOWS.H was one of the last reference tools I would choose for answering technical questions about Windows development. I have found, however, that the new version of WINDOWS.H included with Windows 3.1 is much easier to read and use as a reference tool, so I refer to it much more often.

You can now compile your Windows application with the highest degree of compiler warning turned on without WINDOWS.H generating warning messages, as it did in older versions of WINDOWS.H. WINDOWS.H is also fully compatible with C++ and ANSI.

To make WINDOWS.H compatible with C++, Microsoft added some preprocessor directives to the WINDOWS.H header file. Inside WINDOWS.H you will find the following preprocessor directives that enclose almost all of the code in WINDOWS.H:

```
#ifdef __cplusplus
extern "C" {        /* Assume C declarations for C++ */
#endif        /* __cplusplus */
 .

 .

header file statements

 .

 .
#ifdef __cplusplus
}               /* End of extern "C" { */
#endif        /* __cplusplus */

#endif /* _INC_WINDOWS */
```

The extern "C" directive specifies that the C code is to be used in a C++ program. If this directive were not specified and you used WINDOWS.H (or any other header file) when you compiled a C++ program, the compiler would mangle the function names declared in the header file, and they would not match the function names in the corresponding libraries (.LIB) or Dynamic Link Libraries (.DLL) that would be eventually referred to.

For example, using Microsoft C/C++ 7.0 in a C++ program, if you compile a function defined as int MyFunction(int), Microsoft C/C++ 7.0 will generate the following function name: ?MyFunction@@YAHH@Z. This would not match the corresponding function name that would be generated by compiling the same function in a C program.

The C++ compiler encodes the data types and number of arguments passed to a function into the function name. Name mangling is implementation-dependent. A C++ compiler vendor must support name mangling, but the vendor can do it any way it pleases. Consequently, you will not be able to mix object modules produced by different C++ compilers. All of the Windows header files use the `extern "C"` convention, so you can access the header file from either or a C or a C++ program without difficulty.

Using STRICT

The new STRICT option is an important feature for Windows developers because it provides you with stricter type-checking to help you find more bugs at compilation time. To take advantage of the new STRICT type-checking, you define STRICT before including WINDOWS.H to turn on the STRICT option to enforce STRICT type-checking in your program. For example, without STRICT defined, it's possible to pass a handle to a window (`HWND`) to a function that requires a handle to a device context (`HDC`) without any kind of compiler warning. When STRICT is defined, defining an `HWND` where an `HDC` is required results in a compiler error.

WINDOWS.H also includes a number of new type definitions for you to use when you call a Windows function. If you don't use STRICT, your program will compile adequately without referencing any of these new data types. However, if you compile a Windows program with STRICT turned on, you must use these new data types to avoid compiler errors. A list of the new WINDOWS.H handle types appears in Table 12.1.

You can avoid using these new type definitions only if you write C Windows applications that don't have the STRICT `#include` directive. The new data types are required for both C++ and C Windows applications that use the STRICT directive.

To complement the new STRICT type-checking in C++ and C programs, many new typedefs and constants have also been added to WINDOWS.H. All of the new typedefs and constants are backward-compatible to Windows 3.0, except one—HDRVR, a handle to a driver. For example, you should use `LPCSTR` instead of `LPSTR` for read-only string pointers, because this limits how the pointer can be used. `LPCSTR` is defined as a `const char FAR *`. A list of the new typedefs, constants, and helper macros appears in Table 12.2.

TABLE 12.1:   New Windows 3.1 Handle Types

Handle	Description
HINSTANCE	Instance handle type
HMODULE	Module handle type
HLOCAL	Local handle type
HGLOBAL	Global handle type
HTASK	Task handle type
HFILE	File handle type
HRSRC	Resource handle type
HGDIOBJ	Generic GDI object handle type (except HMETAFILE)
HMETAFILE	Metafile handle type
HDWP	DeferWindowPos handle
HACCEL	Accelerator table handle
HDRVR	Driver handle (3.1 only—not backward-compatible to 3.0)

TABLE 12.2:   New Windows 3.1 Typedefs, Constants, and Helper Macros

Typedef, Constant, or Macro	Description
WINAPI	Used in place of FAR PASCAL in API declarations. If you are writing a DLL with exported API entry points, you can use this for your own APIs.
CALLBACK	Used in place of FAR PASCAL in application callback routines such as window procedures and dialog procedures.
LPCSTR	Same as LPSTR, except used for read-only string pointers. Defined as a const char FAR*.
UINT	Portable unsigned integer type whose size is determined by host environment (16 bits for Windows 3.1). Synonym for unsigned int. Used in place of WORD except in the rare cases where a 16-bit unsigned quantity is desired even on 32-bit platforms.
LRESULT	Type used for declaration of all 32-bit polymorphic return values.
LPARAM	Type used for declaration of all 32-bit polymorphic parameters.
WPARAM	Type used for declaration of all 16-bit polymorphic parameters.
MAKELPARAM(low, high)	Macro used for combining two 16-bit quantities into an LPARAM.

TABLE 12.2:   New Windows 3.1 Typedefs, Constants, and Helper Macros (continued)

Typedef, Constant, or Macro	Description
MAKELRESULT(low, high)	Macro used for combining two 16-bit quantities into an LRESULT.
MAKELP(sel, off)	Macro used for combining a selector and an offset into a FAR VOID* pointer.
SELECTOROF(lp)	Macro used to extract the selector part of a far pointer. Returns UINT.
OFFSETOF(lp)	Macro used to extract the offset part of a far pointer. Returns a UINT.
FIELDOFFSET(type, field)	Macro used for calculating the offset of a field in a data structure. The type parameter is the type of structure, and field is the name of the field whose offset is desired.

The C language has always been known for being flexible—sometimes too flexible. If you call a function in C and use an int instead of a long that's defined in the function declaration and definition, the C compiler will automatically convert the argument for you and not even warn you about the implicit conversion. In earlier versions of Windows all handles were derived from an unsigned integer. In Windows 3.1 all handles are still derived from an unsigned integer if you don't define STRICT. Let's look at an example to explore the consequences of using STRICT. In this example we will use a handle to a device context (HDC) when a function argument calls for a handle to a window (HWND) and see what happens with STRICT turned off and then on. For this example we will use the C source code module RMONITOR.C. To start, I commented out the #define STRICT preprocessor directive at the beginning of the C source code module. Then I introduced a program bug in the function PaintIcon. PaintIcon is responsible for painting the resource gauge on the Resource Monitor icon. For the PaintIcon function to draw the resource gauge on its icon, it must call the Windows function BeginPaint. The following source code shows the PaintIcon function up to the point where it calls the BeginPaint function.

```
//-----------------------------------------------------------
//
// PaintIcon - Paints the window when it's iconized
//
void PaintIcon (HWND hWnd)
{
```

```
char szBuffer[4], szAnotherBuffer[5];
int x, xText, yText, yTextNextLine;
DWORD dwExtent;
HDC hDC;
PAINTSTRUCT ps;
RECT rect, rectTmp;

SetWindowText (hWnd, szIconCaption);
hDC = BeginPaint (hWnd, & ps);
```

The last line in the listing shows the call to `BeginPaint`. Now let's swap `hDC` and `hWnd` so the last line looks like the following:

```
hWnd = BeginPaint (hDC, & ps);
```

After making these changes, I compiled Resource Monitor and did not get any compiler warnings or errors about the program bug that I introduced. If this were a real program bug, the only way you would find out about it would be to execute the program. If you executed Resource Monitor with this error, you would get the following results:

- The Resource Monitor icon would not get painted.

- The icon caption would be continuously redrawn.

- The cursor would become an hour glass.

- Windows would be locked up and would not respond to either the mouse or the keyboard.

The only way you could get out of Resource Monitor would be to do the "three-finger salute" (Ctrl+Alt+Delete). Windows 3.1 would then take charge and let you terminate Resource Monitor. These are some pretty devastating results for accidentally swapping two different variables. Now let's see what happens with STRICT turned on.

To find out what STRICT can do for you, all you need to do is remove the comment characters that we put in earlier to comment out the `#define STRICT` preprocessor directive. After removing the comment, recompile Resource Monitor and see what happens. If you are using Borland C++ you will get the following error messages that indicate that something is wrong:

```
Compiling RMONITOR.C:
Warning RMONITOR.C 609: Suspicious pointer conversion
Warning RMONITOR.C 609: Suspicious pointer conversion
```

```
Linking RMONITOR.EXE:
Binding RMONITOR.EXE:
```

As the error messages indicate, the C compiler finds more bugs in your program related to using the wrong function argument types when STRICT is turned on. In some cases the C compiler will give you warnings. In other cases it will give you an error. So what is happening in WINDOWS.H when STRICT is turned on to produce these errors?

As we discussed earlier, the C compiler is very flexible when it comes to automatically converting variable types that are derived from unsigned integers. To implement STRICT, all handle types are defined as pointers in WINDOWS.H when STRICT is turned on. To understand what's going on, let's look at the following code from WINDOWS.H:

```
#ifdef STRICT
typedef const void NEAR*    HANDLE;
#define DECLARE_HANDLE(name)  struct name##__ { int unused; }; \
                typedef const struct name##__ NEAR* name
#define DECLARE_HANDLE32(name) struct name##__ { int unused; }; \
                typedef const struct name##__ FAR* name
#else  /* STRICT */
typedef UINT            HANDLE;
#define DECLARE_HANDLE(name)  typedef UINT name
#define DECLARE_HANDLE32(name) typedef DWORD name
#endif /* !STRICT */
```

Notice that if STRICT is defined, HANDLE is defined as a void near pointer. If STRICT is not defined, HANDLE is defined as an unsigned integer. This is done because C compilers don't do careful type-checking for all derived types, but only for types derived from pointers. For example, both HPEN and HBRUSH are derived from the HANDLE data type. If STRICT is not defined and you use an HPEN variable in place of an HBRUSH, the C compiler doesn't care, because both variables are derived from an unsigned integer. If STRICT is defined, the C compiler will generate a level 1 warning, because you are trying to use one type of pointer in place of another.

> **NOTE**
> You should remember that HANDLE can still be used instead of all the other handle types such as HWND, HDC, and others—even if STRICT is turned on. You can do this because these types are directly derived from HANDLE. If you are going to use STRICT you should completely eliminate the use of the HANDLE data type, because it defeats the use of STRICT type-checking.

Using STRICT with C++

Using STRICT type-checking is just as important for writing C++ programs as it is for writing C programs, even though C++ offers stricter type-checking than C. In C++ you are permitted to have many functions with the same name as long as these functions have different formal parameter lists. In order to have unique link symbols, the C++ compiler will mangle these names, as we discussed earlier, using an algorithm that encodes information about a function, such as the name, the number and type of formal parameters, and the calling convention.

This newly generated name is used as the external link symbol for the function. This is known as *typesafe linkage* and is a big benefit of C++. This name mangling does not apply to functions within an `extern "C"` block, and it is why all APIs in WINDOWS.H are in such a block. If WINDOWS.H were converted to C++ instead of C, we would not need STRICT type-checking. Since WINDOWS.H is now used by several compilers, such as Microsoft C/C++ 7.0, Borland C++ 3.1, and Zortech C++, it must be left in a C format that's enclosed using the `extern "C"` block, because each of these different compilers uses a different coding scheme when it comes to name mangling.

STRICT type-checking is not needed in a C++ program if you are only calling functions (or methods) defined in a C++ class library, such as the Microsoft C++ MFC. If your C++ program calls functions that are defined directly in WINDOWS.H, the STRICT option offers stricter type-checking that is not available otherwise.

Using Strict with the Borland C++ OWL

If you are using Borland C++ 3.1, you can use STRICT with both C and C++ Windows applications. Borland strongly endorses the idea of using the STRICT coding style, and their Object Window Library (OWL) is fully compatible with STRICT.

The Borland OWL was built with the STRICT option turned on, and Borland recommends that you use the STRICT option in the C++ Windows applications that you develop using Borland C++ 3.1. You can define STRICT using the Borland C++ compiler in a number of different ways:

- If you use the Borland C++ command-line compiler, add -DWIN31;STRICT to the beginning of your command line. For example, you might compile a module like this:

  ```
  BCC -WE -DWIN31;STRICT myprog.cpp owlws.lib tclasss.lib
  ```

- If you use the Borland Windows-hosted IDE, add WIN31;STRICT to the Defines dialog box. To display the Defines dialog box, choose the Code Generation command in the Compilers submenu in the Options menu.

- You can also add #define WIN31 and #define STRICT in your source code before you include OWL.H in the same way you see it defined in the Resource Monitor C source code files.

Using STRICT with the Microsoft MFC Library

If you examine all the "readme" files and technical notes that are included with the MFC libraries, you will recognize that Microsoft seems confused about whether or not you should use STRICT in a C++ Windows application. For example, if you read the README.TXT file that gets installed in the \MFC directory that's below the directory you installed the Microsoft C/C++ compiler in, you will find the following statement: "To improve robustness, the Microsoft Foundation Class Library fully supports the STRICT data types defined in the Windows 3.1 interface file, WINDOWS.H."

If you go on to read the technical notes (TN012.TXT, to be exact) for the Microsoft MFC libraries, you will find that MFC was not compiled using STRICT and doesn't support it. The MFC libraries rely on the strict type-checking of C++, and STRICT is disabled by default. If you use the MFC library header files in your application, STRICT is turned off for your application using an #undef directive.

If you use Microsoft C/C++ 7.0 and are developing a C Windows application, you should seriously consider using the STRICT coding style. If you are going to use C functions called from C++, you should make sure to use the C++ conventions for your exported header file, such as putting extern "C" {} around your C APIs. If you are going to use C++ and plan to call only methods that are defined in the MFC library, you don't need to worry about using STRICT. If you want to use the Windows API directly and want to define STRICT so you can take advantage of the stricter type-checking it offers, you will need to recompile the MFC libraries with the STRICT option turned on. You must do this because of typesafe linkage. The external link symbols are different for STRICT and non-STRICT.

Recompiling the MFC Libraries   If you would like to use STRICT and the Microsoft MFC libraries, you will need to rebuild them using the following procedure:

1. Define the STRICT option at the start of the header file AFXWIN.H. You will find AFXWIN.H in the Microsoft C/C++ 7.0 directory \C700\MFC\IN-CLUDE. All you need to do is add the #define STRICT statement at the start of AFXWIN.H:

```
#ifndef __AFXWIN_H__
#define __AFXWIN_H__
#define STRICT
```

2. Comment out the #undef for STRICT that is in the same header file, AFXWIN.H, as shown below:

```
#ifdef STRICT
// The default for MFC is not STRICT, since C++ and MFC
// provide all of the same benefits (see TN012.TXT). If
// you wish to use STRICT typechecking, then you must rebuild
// the library after removing the following #undef.
// #undef STRICT // This is the line I commented out.
#endif
```

3. Rebuild the MFC libraries. In the directory \C700\MFC\SRC, you will find a make file named MAKEFILE. If you read it you will find comments at the beginning that explain how to rebuild the MFC libraries. For example, to rebuild the no-debug and the debug versions of the MFC libraries for the medium memory model, type in

```
NMAKE TARGET=W MODEL=M DEBUG=0
NMAKE TARGET=W MODEL=M DEBUG=1
```

Once you have rebuilt the MFC libraries using these steps, you no longer have to worry about defining STRICT when you build a C++ application. Since STRICT is already defined in AFXWIN.H, it is automatically turned on every time you compile a C++ source code module that uses MFC and the AFXWIN.H header file.

Using STRICT with C++: An All-or-Nothing Proposition

For C Windows applications, you can implement STRICT one source code module at a time to implement your conversion one step at a time. If you are developing a C++ application, you don't have the option of applying STRICT to only some of your source code modules. Because of the way C++ type safe linking works, you will get linking errors if you mix and match STRICT and non-STRICT source code modules.

Implementing STRICT

As we have discussed, you should seriously consider converting existing Windows applications to the new STRICT coding style and using it in all your new Windows development. STRICT is most valuable with newly developed code or code that is being changed on a regular basis. If you have stable C or C++ source code modules that have already been written and tested, you may decide that it's not worth the effort to convert to STRICT.

If you decide to implement STRICT in your Windows applications, it's wise to approach using STRICT with a systematic process—especially for converting an older Windows application to using STRICT. You should not try to turn STRICT on in an existing Windows application and expect to start fixing compiler warning and error messages. In a large Windows application you can expect to receive hundreds of warning and error messages when STRICT is turned on. To implement STRICT you should try using the steps outlined in the following sections. You will find that implementing STRICT in a step-by-step process will go much more smoothly than jumping into it both feet first.

Eliminate as Many Compiler Warning Messages as Possible

You should start by compiling your program with a high level of warning messages turned on. Even though you can ignore many of the informational type warnings, such as doing an assignment inside of an `if` statement, you should try to eliminate as many warning messages as possible. Microsoft C/C++ 7.0 groups warning messages into four levels, the highest being level W4. Borland C++ 3.1 for Windows groups warning messages according to category: ANSI violations, frequent errors, less-frequent errors, portability, and C++ warnings. Within each category you can turn a warning message on or off. The default warning messages for Borland C++ 3.1 for Windows are quite comprehensive.

Convert to the New Windows 3.1 Data Types

After eliminating as many compiler errors as possible, change your code to use the new STRICT types defined in WINDOWS.H. These new data types are listed in Tables 12.1 and 12.2. HANDLE should be changed to the exact type of handle to be used. For example, you should convert the HANDLE type to HINSTANCE, HMODULE, HGLOBAL, HLOCAL, HFONT, HBRUSH, etc., as appropriate. WORD should be converted to UINT (except where you really want a 16-bit value) or WPARAM, depending on its use. Instead of using LONG as the type for the lParam of a message, you use LPARAM.

For a particular function call, how do you find out the correct variable types to use? Your best bet is to check the online SDK documentation to see which types the Windows API you are using expects. If you really want to make sure about the correct variable type, look in WINDOWS.H to see how the function API is declared.

For window procedures and dialog box functions, you should use CALLBACK instead of FAR PASCAL in the function declaration and definition. All of your callback functions should use this function type.

You should declare function pointers with the proper function type. For example, a dialog box function pointer should be declared DLGPROC—not FARPROC. You'll need to cast function pointers to and from the proper function type when using MakeProcInstance, FreeProcInstance, and other functions that take or return a FARPROC, as the following code from RMONITOR.C shows:

```
//-------------------------------------------------------------
//
// OnSysCommand - Handle WM_SYSCOMMAND message
//
void OnSysCommand(HWND hWnd, UINT cmd, int x, int y)
{
  switch (cmd)
  {
  case IDM_ABOUT :
    {
    DLGPROC lpProcAboutDlgProc;

    lpProcAboutDlgProc = (DLGPROC) MakeProcInstance ((FARPROC) About, hInst);
    DialogBox (hInst, "About", hWnd, lpProcAboutDlgProc);
    FreeProcInstance ((FARPROC) lpProcAboutDlgProc);
    break;
    }
```

As you can see in this sample code, I used typecasts only when there was no way to avoid them. When you implement STRICT, you have to decide when you should change the type of the variable being used or typecast the variable when it's used in a function call. You are defeating the purpose of STRICT if all you are going to do is use typecasts to implement it. If all you do is use typecasts to patch up function calls to Windows, there is still a chance the variable will be used incorrectly elsewhere in your program because you did not use the correct type when it was defined.

After converting your code to using the new WINDOWS 3.1 types, recompile without STRICT, and test your application to make sure it still works the way it is supposed to. You should also try to eliminate as many compiler warning messages as possible.

Turn STRICT Type-Checking On

After you have carefully redefined all the types in your program to be compliant with the new STRICT coding style, add the `#define STRICT` directive to the start of the C source code module you are working on. If you are programming in C++, you define STRICT for all your C++ source code modules before relinking your Windows application. If you have been careful you might get by without any compiler errors or warnings. If you are like me and are prone to making at least a few mistakes, you will get some compiler error and warning messages, such as the following for the Microsoft C/C++ 7.0 compiler:

```
dialogs.c(351) : warning C4047: '=' different levels of indirection
dialogs.c(372) : warning C4047: 'argument' different levels of indirection
```

These warnings indicate that you are trying to assign or pass a nonpointer type when a pointer is required. With STRICT defined, all handle types are internally defined as pointer types. If you use `int`, `WORD`, or `LONG` as a handle, you will get the following error:

```
dialogs.c(225) : warning C4049: 'argument' : indirection to different types
```

This is the type of message you will encounter when you pass the wrong type of handle to a function. Since STRICT defines all handle types as pointers to unique structures, this warning is telling you that you are using the wrong type of handle.

After you have turned STRICT on and cleaned up your errors, you can turn STRICT off if you want to, since it's needed only when you are adding to or changing your source code. Now that I'm used to using STRICT, I leave it on for all the applications

I have converted to STRICT. If you look in the C source code files for the Resource Monitor application, you will see that I have STRICT defined in all of the C source code modules before any of the #include statements.

Finding Out More about STRICT

If you try to look for more information about STRICT in the Microsoft and Borland documentation, you will find that it's barely mentioned. STRICT is a concept that matured during the Windows 3.1 SDK BETA process. It is a new feature for the Windows 3.1 SDK that just made it into the Microsoft and Borland development systems, but it was not documented thoroughly. As you can see from the Microsoft documentation, Microsoft can't seem to decide if it wants to support STRICT or not.

In summary, STRICT is a good idea that will help you to find more bugs at compile time, instead of having them lurk around when you test your program using a debugger and the debugging version of Windows. Documentation (besides this book) that covers STRICT is scarce, but it can be found in the following sources that are included with the Microsoft Windows 3.1 SDK and Borland C++ 3.1:

- Microsoft Windows 3.1 SDK *Getting Started* manual.
- WINDOWS.TXT file in the \C700 directory.
- WIN31.DOC and OWL31.DOC files for the Borland C++ 3.1 Windows development system. These files are installed on your hard disk along with your compiler.
- WINDOWS.H—the ultimate reference as to how STRICT is implemented.

You can also examine the Resource Monitor program listings to see how I implemented STRICT in this sample application. DumpIT 3.1 shows how to implement STRICT in a Windows MDI application.

Getting the Fluff Out of Your Windows Application with PC-Lint

As convenient as STRICT is for getting your compiler to spot more program bugs at compile time instead of execution time, I would not be helping you fully if I didn't mention PC-Lint. C compilers can spot many types of program errors, and the Borland C++ 3.1 compiler is particularly adept at this. But C/C++ compilers are not too hot on reporting the more subtle programming mistakes. Compilers are usually quite happy to accept a reference to an uninitialized variable or an assignment of an over large constant; and if a switch case is allowed to flow into the next one, fine.

This is reasonable behavior for a compiler. It has enough trouble looking for real errors without checking programming logic. Hence the existence of lint programs. Lint programs for C have been around almost as long as the C language has. A lint program picks up all the fluff from your source code, leaving a nice, clean program. It gives a much more in-depth analysis than a compiler ever could. It proceeds through one or more source files, in one pass, and tells you what is wrong with the code.

There are several lint programs available for the PC, but Gimpel Software's PC-Lint V5.0 is considered to be the best—especially when it comes to analyzing Windows application C code. PC-Lint Version 5 assumes your C source code is written to K&R and ANSI standards; where there is conflict, ANSI overrides K&R.

PC-Lint comes with a 300-page manual that is reasonably well laid out and easy to use. It includes sections on installation and configuration, special features and language extensions, and preprocessor handling. A major section is devoted to strong types, a new feature introduced in Version 5. The largest section is devoted to the messages; I estimate there are about 400, of which 80 are new with Version 5. There are four types of messages (errors, warnings, information, and elective notes) and two varieties of runtime errors. Messages are explained in full, usually with an indication of what to do about them.

When I installed PC-Lint I selected the Microsoft compiler, causing the installation program to install the compiler definitions file CO-MSC.LNT. Lint Version 5 comes with 28 preset compiler definitions, from the common to the obscure. PC-Lint has configuration files for all the popular Windows development systems, including the ones from Microsoft, Borland, and Zortech.

PC-Lint is normally run from a batch file to simplify control of command line switches. Output is directed to a file. (This, believe me, is necessary; there can be an awful lot of messages.) PC-Lint's command line comprises a mix of option switches and file names. Anything without a switch prefix character (+,-) is assumed to be a file name. If the name has no extension, PC-Lint looks for a matching file with an extension of .LNT, .C, or .H before giving up. Wildcards are acceptable: LIN *.C goes through all the .C files in the current directory.

When you install PC-Lint and specify a compiler, the installation program creates a single control file, STD.LNT. This contains a reference to OPTIONS.LNT and to the compiler definition file (CO-MSC.LNT). OPTIONS.LNT contains parameters which you use to customize the way PC-Lint evaluates your programs.

Using Lint

To test how PC-Lint works I used the Resource Monitor application. To run PC-Lint I typed in `LIN -elib *.C` from the Resource Monitor working directory. After PC-Lint was finished, I had a text file, LINT.TMP, that contained 1402 lines of messages. PC-Lint generated quite a few informational messages. Many of them can be omitted by adding their exclusions to the .LNT file you use for linting your program. For example, adding `-e7??` will get rid of all information messages.

Before running PC-Lint I made sure Resource Monitor had the same error that we discussed previously in the example of what defining STRICT can do: swapping the hWnd and hDC variables in a call to `BeginPaint` in RMONITOR.C. PC-Lint easily spotted the error, even without STRICT undefined. PC-Lint also spotted every time that I didn't use a function return value and every time I used PSTR instead of LPSTR or LPCSTR.

The bad thing about PC-Lint is that it spots a lot of errors in your program's C source code. You have to wade through the listing it generates carefully to take advantage of its capabilities. A serious error, such as swapping the hDC and HWND in a Windows function call, can get lost in all the other error messages that PC-Lint generates.

The good thing about PC-Lint is the same thing that is bad about it: it spots a lot of errors in your program's C source code. PC-Lint complains about many different types of errors that can be spotted only by examining your C code with all its subtle associations and pointing out where you may be going wrong. PC-Lint is not a tool you want to use in your day-to-day Windows application development. Instead, you should use it before significant milestones during development to help you eliminate as many errors as you can.

Taking Advantage of New Macro APIs

After you have changed your Windows application to use all of the new Windows 3.1 type definitions, used the STRICT option to ensure that you are calling Windows functions using the correct argument types, and scrubbed your application to eliminate errors using a tool like PC-Lint, it's time to consider whether or not to use the new macro APIs included in WINDOWSX.H. Using STRICT is a valuable debugging tool for any Windows application that is being developed or undergoing change. Using the new Windows 3.1 macro APIs will help you to build a single set of source code files that will be compatible with both Windows 3.1 and Win32.

If you have a large Windows application that you don't intend to convert to Win32, you may not want to invest the effort to convert your application to use the new macro APIs. If you do want to convert your stable Windows application to Win32, you may want to use the new Win32 development system to do so. But if you are developing a new Windows 3.1 application and you want it to be as compatible as possible with Win32, you should consider using the new macro APIs in WINDOWSX.H.

If you are building a C++ Windows application that uses either the Microsoft MFC or Borland OWL libraries, you will find that all of the macro APIs in WIN-DOWSX.H are useful, with the exception of message crackers. Both Microsoft C++ and Borland C++ provide a better way for handling Windows messages than using message crackers. Using C++ you treat a window as an object and associate a method (C++ function) with each message type. In some ways using message crackers in C is similar to handling messages using C++. In both cases you need to associate a function (C++ method) with each message type.

In the first Windows 3.1 SDK BETA, the contents of both WINDOWS.H and WIN-DOWSX.H were included in WINDOWS.H. Later, Microsoft decided it was best to put the macros used for defining the new macro API in a separate file, WIN-DOWSX.H. Splitting the contents of WINDOWS.H makes sense from both an organizational and a performance standpoint. WINDOWS.H is already very large (5373 lines). Adding WINDOWSX.H (1109 lines) just made it bigger and increased compile time for programs that don't use the new macro API. WINDOWSX.H contains many new Windows APIs implemented as macros that call other APIs. These new macros call the function APIs that were available in Windows 3.0. Since the APIs implemented in WINDOWSX.H are all macros and use the existing Windows 3.0 function API, they are backward-compatible with Windows 3.0.

Macro APIs Will Make Your Program Prettier

You will find that using the new macro APIs defined in WINDOWSX.H will make your C and C++ code easier to read and write. The macro APIs for working with control windows are especially easy to read and write. For example, let's look at the following code fragment from the Resource Monitor C source file DIALOGS.C to see what some of these new macro APIs look like:

```
Button_SetCheck (hSizeGDI, Setup.bSizeGDI);
Button_SetCheck (hSizeUser, Setup.bSizeUser);
Button_SetCheck (hSizeFreeMem, Setup.bSizeFreeMem);

if (Setup.nAlarmGDI >= 0)
  {
  itoa (Setup.nAlarmGDI, szarWorkBuf, 10);
  Edit_SetText (hAlarmGDI, (LPSTR) szarWorkBuf);
  }
```

Each control message macro API is prefixed by the type of control that the command is to be used for. As you can see from the example, `Button_` is used for a button control and `Edit_` is used for an edit control. Some of the control message macro APIs generate a Windows function call to `SendMessage`. Others use other functions that work with control windows. For example, the `Button_SetCheck` macro takes a macro call such as

```
Button_SetCheck (hSizeGDI, Setup.bSizeGDI);
```

and generates

```
SendMessage(hSizeGDI, BM_SETCHECK, Setup.bSizeGDI, 0L);
```

Besides being easier to code and read, the `Button_SetCheck` macro requires only two arguments instead of four. To illustrate how the `Edit_SetText` macro is expanded, let's look at the following two lines of code. The first line is the macro API call and the following line is the Windows function call it generates.

```
Edit_SetText (hAlarmGDI, (LPSTR) szarWorkBuf);
SetWindowText(hAlarmGDI, (LPSTR) szarWorkBuf);
```

In this example the Windows function call is almost as meaningful as the macro API that was used. Both require only two arguments. The advantages of using the `Edit_SetText` macro API are consistency and ease of use. All of the macro APIs for working with edit control windows use `Edit_` as a prefix. Using the WINDOWSX.TXT file included with the Windows 3.1 SDK or the section on control message APIs you will find later on in this chapter, it's very easy to identify the macro API you need to use and to figure out the arguments that it requires.

Macro APIs Will Make Your Program Portable to Win32

In Win32 the wParam of a Windows message is expanded to a single 32-bit word, and some of the Windows messages, including WM_COMMAND, have been reorganized accordingly. The reason for this message reorganization is to retrieve a widened return value, such as the new 32-bit Window handles. The list below shows the Windows messages that are affected by this reorganization:

EM_GETSEL

EM_LINESCROLL

EM_SETSEL

WM_ACTIVATE

WM_CHANGECBCHAIN

WM_CHARTOITEM

WM_COMMAND

WM_CTLCOLOR

WM_DDE_ACK

WM_DDE_ADVISE

WM_DDE_DATA

WM_DDE_EXECUTE

WM_DDE_POKE

WM_HSCROLL

WM_MDIACTIVATE

WM_MDISETMENU

WM_MENUCHAR

WM_MENUSELECT

```
WM_PARENTNOTIFY

WM_VKEYTOITEM

WM_VSCROLL
```

Many of these message types you have probably never used. As you read in the last chapter, the best way to avoid the reorganization of the DDE messages is to use DDEML. It's easier to use DDEML than to work with raw DDE, and it isolates you from the change from Windows 3.1 to Win32. To understand the changes going on in this message reorganization, let's look more closely at how WM_COMMAND is being reorganized.

The format of the WM_COMMAND message for Windows 3.1 stores the control ID of the command in wParam, the notification code in the HIWORD of lParam, and the hWnd for a message from a control in a dialog box in the LOWORD of lParam. In Win32, the format of the WM_COMMAND message has been reorganized so that the notification code is in the HIWORD of wParam, the command control ID is in the LOWORD of wParam, and the hWnd of the control is in the lParam.

Using STRICT and the new Windows 3.1 macro API may not isolate you completely from the change from Windows 3.1 to Win32, but it can save you a considerable amount of the work. By using the new type definitions that go hand-in-hand with STRICT, you will be using the same type definitions used in the Win32 WINDOWS.H header file. By using the new Windows 3.1 macro APIs, such as message crackers, you isolate your program code from the changes being made to message formats in Win32.

Using Message Crackers

An important subset of the new macro API is called message crackers. Message crackers provide a concise way to handle messages in a window procedure that is source code compatible with Win32. To understand how this works, let's take a close look at how the message cracker for WM_COMMAND works to make your application more portable to Win32.

To use message crackers, you need to rebuild your Windows application into a modular set of functions where each window message is handled by one window function. For example, the following code would be used for handling the WM_COM-MAND message:

```
case WM_COMMAND:
        OnCommand (hWnd, wParam, lParam);
        break;
```

Converting to message crackers can be a considerable amount of work for you if your program uses large window procedures instead of using modular functions that are called from your window procedure. The majority of the work you will do to convert your Windows application to using the message crackers is encapsulating the code for handling window messages into functions called from a window procedure.

To illustrate how to build a message cracker, let's see what needs to be done to convert the previous code fragment into a message cracker macro. The following code shows what the message cracker macro that replaces the function call to OnCommand looks like:

```
case WM_COMMAND:
        HANDLE_WM_COMMAND (hWnd, wParam, lParam, OnCommand);
        break;
```

When the HANDLE_WM_COMMAND message cracker macro is called, the first three parameters are the same parameters used in the previous function call. The last parameter is the name of the function in our program to handle the WM_COMMAND message. In Resource Monitor, message crackers are used for the main program window and the Setup dialog box. To see what the HANDLE_WM_COMMAND looks like in a Windows application, let's look at the Setup dialog box function in the Resource Monitor DIALOGS.C source code file:

```
//-----------------------------------------------------------
//
// SetupMsgProc - Setup dialog procedure
//
BOOL CALLBACK _export SetupDlgProc (HWND hDlg,
                UINT msg,
                WPARAM wParam,
                LPARAM lParam)
{
  switch (msg)
   {
   case WM_INITDIALOG:
      return (BOOL) HANDLE_WM_INITDIALOG (hDlg, wParam, lParam,
```

```
                              Setup_OnInitDialog);

    case WM_COMMAND:
        HANDLE_WM_COMMAND (hDlg, wParam, lParam, Setup_OnCommand);
        return TRUE;

    case WM_CLOSE:
        HANDLE_WM_CLOSE (hDlg, wParam, lParam, Setup_OnClose);
        return TRUE;

    default:
        return FALSE;
    }
}
```

As you can see, this dialog box function is simple and concise. It does not contain any local variables. It only contains one case statement with three message crackers in it. The three message crackers are responsible for processing the WM_INITDIALOG, WM_COMMAND, and WM_CLOSE window messages. The three functions that are called to process these messages are Setup_OnInitDialog, Setup_OnCommand, and Setup_OnClose. I prefixed each command with Setup_ to identify the window or dialog box function that the function was called from. Now let's take a closer look at the definition for the Setup_OnCommand function. The following code shows what it looks like:

```
void Setup_OnCommand(HWND hDlg, int id, HWND hwndCtl,
                     UINT codeNotify)
```

The function takes the values that have been extracted from wParam and lParam by the message cracker macro and have been put into variables that reflect the exact type and use of the data. To make this message cracker macro portable, the Windows 3.1 version puts wParam into id, the LOWORD of lParam into hWndCtl, and the HIWORD of lParam into codeNotify. The Win32 message cracker macro for WM_COMMAND puts the LOWORD of wParam into id, the lParam into hWndCtl, and the HIWORD of wParam into codeNotify. The code for the WM_COMMAND message cracker macro in the Windows 3.1 version of WINDOWSX.H is implemented as follows:

```
/* void Cls_OnCommand(HWND hwnd, int id, HWND hwndCtl, UINT codeNotify);
*/

#define HANDLE_WM_COMMAND(hwnd, wParam, lParam, fn) \
  ((fn)((hwnd), (int)(wParam), (HWND)LOWORD(lParam), (UINT)HIWORD
  (lParam)), 0L)
#define FORWARD_WM_COMMAND(hwnd, id, hwndCtl, codeNotify, fn) \
```

```
        (void)(fn)((hwnd), WM_COMMAND, (WPARAM)(int)(id),      MAKEL-
PARAM((UINT)(hwndCtl), (codeNotify)))
```

At first message crackers may look mysterious to read. After you have written a few of them, you will find that they are much easier to use than they seem. To illustrate, let's review the steps I went through to create the message cracker for WM_COMMAND.

All message crackers use a standard format, as shown below for the WM_COMMAND message cracker:

```
    case WM_COMMAND:
        HANDLE_WM_COMMAND (hDlg, wParam, lParam, Setup_OnCommand);
```

The message cracker replaces the code used to call a function (or do other processing) to process a window message. Each message cracker is prefixed by HANDLE_ and then the message type. The arguments to the message cracker macro are the window (or dialog box window) handle, the message WPARAM, the message LPARAM, and the function that is to be called to handle the message.

After you have decided which message you need a message cracker for, look it up in WINDOWSX.H. For example, the macro for the WM_COMMAND message in WINDOWSX.H is

```
/* void Cls_OnCommand(HWND hwnd, int id, HWND hwndCtl, UINT codeNotify);*/
#define HANDLE_WM_COMMAND(hwnd, wParam, lParam, fn) \
 ((fn)((hwnd), (int)(wParam), (HWND)LOWORD(lParam), (UINT)HIWORD
 (lParam)), 0L)
#define FORWARD_WM_COMMAND(hwnd, id, hwndCtl, codeNotify, fn) \
    (void)(fn)((hwnd), WM_COMMAND, (WPARAM)(int)(id),      MAKEL-
PARAM((UINT)(hwndCtl), (codeNotify)))
```

If you don't know how to read C macros, I recommend you take the time to learn how they are coded. Knowing how C macros work will solve any problems you have in implementing message crackers and other macro APIs. Notice the comment at the start of the message cracker macro for WM_COMMAND. This comment tells you what the format of the function definition (and declaration) should be for the function in your program that gets called as a result of processing the message cracker macro. You can copy and paste this comment directly into your program to use as a template for coding your function's definition and declaration. The number of the arguments used and their respective types cannot be changed unless you want to change the macro that generates the function call. In all cases the function called receives every parameter it needs to process the Windows message.

Now that you know the basics of setting up message crackers, let's take a look at the message crackers that are used in the main window procedure for Resource Monitor in RMONITOR.C and see how they differ from the ones used in the Setup dialog box function.

```
//-------------------------------------------------------------
//
// WndProc - Resource Monitor window procedure
//
LRESULT CALLBACK _export WndProc (HWND hWnd, UINT msg, WPARAM w-
Param, LPARAM lParam)
{
  switch (msg)
  {
  HANDLE_MSG (hWnd, WM_CREATE,         OnCreate);
  HANDLE_MSG (hWnd, WM_SYSCOMMAND,     OnSysCommand);
  HANDLE_MSG (hWnd, WM_TIMER,          OnTimer);
  HANDLE_MSG (hWnd, WM_PAINT,          OnPaint);
  HANDLE_MSG (hWnd, WM_MOVE,           OnMove);
  HANDLE_MSG (hWnd, WM_SIZE,           OnSize);
  HANDLE_MSG (hWnd, WM_DESTROY,        OnDestroy);
  HANDLE_MSG (hWnd, WM_QUERYENDSESSION, OnQueryEndSession);

  default:
   return DefWindowProc (hWnd, msg, wParam, lParam) ;
  }
}
```

When you examine the Resource Monitor window procedure, you will see that I used another form of message cracker that eliminates the need for using a case statement inside a window procedure. The HANDLE_MSG macro can be used to reduce the complexity of your window procedure and save you some typing. So instead of

```
case WM_COMMAND:
  HANDLE_WM_COMMAND (hWnd, wParam, lParam, MyCls_OnCommand);
  break;
```

you can code

```
HANDLE_MSG (hWnd, WM_COMMAND, MyCls_OnCommand);
```

HANDLE_MSG is optional. Some programmers will prefer to delineate what's going on in a window procedure, and others will prefer the convenience and brevity of the `HANDLE_MSG` macro. `HANDLE_MSG` makes your program easier to read and comprehend because of its simplicity. Because it's easier to code, you will find that the `HANDLE_MSG` macro helps reduce syntax errors as well.

Message Forwarders

If you look inside WINDOWSX.H, you will see that for each window message, there are two macros: a cracker and a forwarder. Message forwarder macros let you forward a message to `DefWindowProc`. This macro does the work of packing explicitly typed arguments into the `WPARAM` and `LPARAM` message fields of the message that is sent to `DefWindowProc`. With both message crackers and message forwarders, you don't have to worry about what parameters go where and the kind of casting you need to do. The message cracker and forwarder take care of this for you.

Since there are message forwarders defined for every message type, do you use message forwarders all the time? Are they optional? When should message forwarders be used?

Message forwarders are used in the function called by a message cracker as a method for forwarding a message on to `DefWindowProc`. You need to worry about using message forwarders only when you know you need to pass messages along to `DefWindowProc` for the same reasons you pass window messages along to `DefWindowProc` in a switch case statement.

If you look at the function `WndProc` in RMONITOR.C, you will see that all the messages that have not been handled by a message cracker are forwarded to `DefWindowProc`. If you examine the functions called by each message cracker, you will find that only one has a message forwarder—`OnSysCommand`.

Instead of using a normal menu, Resource Monitor appends its menu commands to the System menu to conserve space. The `HANDLE_MSG` macro for `WM_SYSCOMMAND` passes the message along to `OnSysCommand` to handle the menu command that Resource Monitor has appended to the System menu. A Windows application's System menu is a very important data pipe inside a Windows application. Although you can process `WM_SYSCOMMAND` messages, you must make sure that any message you don't process is sent to `DefWindowProc`. If you forget to send `WM_SYSCOMMAND` messages to `DefWindowProc`, your application window will become locked on the screen. You will not be able to move, size, maximize, or minimize it.

You will not even be able to close the application by choosing Close from its System menu. To exit your application you can use the End Task command in the Windows Task Manager to terminate it.

As you can see, message forwarders are an important aspect of using message crackers. You do not need to use message forwarders in every function called by a message cracker, but only when you need to return a message to DefWindowProc.

Using Message Crackers in a Dialog Box Function

Dialog box functions are different from window procedures in that they return a BOOL indicating whether the message, rather than an LRESULT, was processed. For this reason you cannot use the HANDLE_MSG macro. You must use the explicit message cracker associated with the window message. The following C source code shows the Setup dialog box function for Resource Monitor to show you how its message crackers are set up:

```
//-------------------------------------------------------------
//
// SetupMsgProc - Setup dialog procedure
//
BOOL CALLBACK _export SetupDlgProc (HWND hDlg,
                    UINT msg,
                    WPARAM wParam,
                        LPARAM lParam)
{
  switch (msg)
   {
   case WM_INITDIALOG:
        return HANDLE_WM_INITDIALOG (hDlg, wParam, lParam,
                                Setup_OnInitDialog);

   case WM_COMMAND:
        HANDLE_WM_COMMAND (hDlg, wParam, lParam, Setup_OnCommand);
        return TRUE;

   case WM_CLOSE:
        HANDLE_WM_CLOSE (hDlg, wParam, lParam, Setup_OnClose);
        return TRUE;

   default:
```

```
        return FALSE;
    }
}
```

Since the `Setup_OnInitDialog` function returns a BOOL value, all I needed to do was return what's returned by the function. Both `Setup_OnCommand` and `Setup_OnClose` are void functions, so I explicitly returned TRUE to indicate that the message was processed. The default for the case statement returns FALSE to indicate that the message has not been processed by the dialog box function.

While message crackers can require a lot of work to implement, the rest of the macros included in WINDOWSX.H are easy to implement and understand. WINDOWSX.H includes macros for working with global memory, GDI objects, windows, and control windows. You will find that these macro APIs are easy to write and will make your program code more readable.

Using Macro APIs for Working with GDI, Memory, and Windows

Besides the message cracker and forwarder macros, you will find macros for working with global memory and GDI and for managing Windows. These macro APIs wrap window functions inside them to guarantee the portability to Win32 of the macros you use. In most cases you will find these macros more intuitive to write and easier to understand than the Windows functions they are wrapped around.

Using Memory Macro APIs

For example, instead of using `GlobalAlloc` and `GlobalLock`, try using `GlobalAllocPtr`. `GlobalAllocPtr` works the same as `GlobalAlloc`, except that it returns a far pointer directly. Since Windows 3.1 no longer supports Real mode, you no longer have to worry about unlocking global memory segments, and this new macro will make your program easier to code and to read. The following list shows the new Windows 3.1 macro APIs for working with Windows global memory:

Macro	Description

`void FAR* WINAPI`
`GlobalAllocPtr (WORD`
`flags, DWORD cb)`
	Same as `GlobalAlloc`, except that it returns a far pointer directly.

Macro	Description
void FAR* WINAPI GlobalReAllocPtr (void FAR* lp, DWORD cbNew, WORD flags)	Same as GlobalReAlloc, except that it takes and returns a far pointer.
BOOL WINAPI GlobalFreePtr (void FAR* lp)	Same as GlobalFree, except it uses a far pointer.
BOOL WINAPI GlobalLockPtr (void FAR* lp)	Same as GlobalLock, except used with far pointer.
BOOL WINAPI GlobalUnlockPtr (void FAR* lp)	Same as GlobalUnlock, except used with far pointer.
HMODULE WINAPI GetInstanceModule (HINSTANCE hInstance);	Maps an instance handle to a module handle.
HGLOBAL GlobalPtrHandle (void FAR* lp)	Returns the global handle for the far pointer.

Using GDI Macro APIs

Using the new GDI macro APIs, you can use SelectPen(HDC hDC, HPEN hPen) instead of using SelectObject to select a pen into a device context. The parameters are the same, but the macro API is more readable. The new Windows 3.1 GDI macro API provides macros for working with GDI objects such as pens, brushes, fonts, and bitmaps. There are also GDI macro APIs for working with RECT structures and regions, as shown in the following list of the GDI macro APIs:

Macro	Description
BOOL WINAPI DeletePen (HPEN hpen)	Deletes a pen (with proper typecasting).
HPEN WINAPI GetStockPen (int i);	Returns one of the stock pens indicated by i (properly cast to HPEN).

Macro	Description
`HPEN WINAPI SelectPen (HDC hdc, HPEN hpenSelect)`	Selects a pen and returns previously selected pen (with proper typecasting).
`BOOL WINAPI DeleteBrush (HBRUSH hbr)`	Deletes a brush (with proper typecasting).
`HBRUSH WINAPI GetStockBrush (int i)`	Returns one of the stock brushes indicated by `i` (properly cast to `HBRUSH`).
`HBRUSH WINAPI SelectBrush (HDC hdc, HBRUSH hbrSelect)`	Selects a brush and returns previously selected brush (with proper typecasting).
`BOOL WINAPI DeleteFont (HFONT hfont)`	Deletes a font (with proper typecasting).
`HFONT WINAPI GetStockFont (int i);`	Returns one of the stock fonts indicated by `i` (properly cast to `HFONT`).
`HFONT WINAPI SelectFont (HDC hdc, HFONT hfontSelect)`	Selects a font and returns previously selected font (with proper typecasting).
`BOOL WINAPI DeleteBitmap (HBITMAP hbm)`	Deletes a bitmap (with proper typecasting).
`HBITMAP WINAPI SelectBitmap (HDC hdc, HBITMAP hbmSelect)`	Selects a bitmap and returns previously selected bitmap (with proper typecasting).
`BOOL WINAPI DeleteRgn (HRGN hrgn)`	Deletes a region (with proper typecasting).
`int WINAPI CopyRgn (HRGN hrgnDst, HRGN hrgnSrc)`	Copies `hrgnSrc` to `hrgnDst`.
`int WINAPI IntersectRgn (HRGN hrgnResult, HRGN hrgnA, HRGN hrgnB)`	Intersects `hrgnA` with `hrgnB`, setting `hrgnResult` to the result.

Macro	Description
`int WINAPI SubtractRgn (HRGN hrgnResult, HRGN hrgnA, HRGN hrgnB)`	Subtracts `hrgnB` from `hrgnA`, setting `hrgnResult` to the result.
`int WINAPI UnionRgn (HRGN hrgnResult, HRGN hrgnA, HRGN hrgnB)`	Computes the union of `hrgnA` and `hrgnB`, setting `hrgnResult` to the result.
`int WINAPI XorRgn (HRGN hrgnResult, HRGN hrgnA, HRGN hrgnB)`	XORs `hrgnA` with `hrgnB`, setting `hrgnResult` to the result.
`void WINAPI InsetRect (RECT FAR* lprc, int dx, int dy)`	Insets the edges of a rectangle by `dx` and `dy`.
`void DeletePalette (HPALETTE hPal)`	Deletes a palette with proper typecasting.

Using Windows Management Macro APIs

The set of macro APIs included in WINDOWSX.H for managing windows will help you to determine if a window is maximized or minimized. There are three macro APIs for determining which of three mouse buttons is being held down. The Windows management macros don't cover all of the Windows management functionality, but they do offer you a convenient way to work with windows for the functions that they cover. I am especially fond of the `SubClassWindow` macro that provides a much more elegant way to subclass a window. The Windows management macro APIs are detailed in the following list:

Macro	Description
`HINSTANCE WINAPI GetWindowInstance (HWND hwnd)`	Returns the instance handle associated with a window.
`DWORD WINAPI GetWindowStyle (HWND hwnd)`	Returns the window style of a window.
`DWORD WINAPI GetWindowExStyle (HWND hwnd)`	Returns the extended window style of a window.

Macro	Description
`int WINAPI GetWindowID (HWND hwnd)`	Returns the window ID of a window.
`HWND WINAPI GetWindowOwner (HWND)`	Returns the window handle of the window's owner.
`HWND WINAPI GetFirstChild (HWND)`	Returns the window handle of the first child window.
`HWND WINAPI GetFirstSibling (HWND)`	Returns the window handle of the first sibling window.
`HWND WINAPI GetLastSibling (HWND)`	Returns the window handle of the last sibling window.
`HWND WINAPI GetNextSibling (HWND)`	Returns the window handle of the next sibling window.
`HWND WINAPI GetPrevSibling (HWND)`	Returns the window handle of the previous sibling window.
`void WINAPI SetWindowRedraw (HWND hwnd, BOOL fRedraw)`	Disables or enables drawing in a window, without hiding the window.
`WNDPROC WINAPI SubclassWindow (HWND hwnd, WNDPROC lpfnWndProc)`	Subclasses a window by storing a new window procedure address. Returns previous window procedure address.
`BOOL WINAPI IsMinimized (HWND hwnd)`	Returns TRUE if hwnd is minimized.
`BOOL WINAPI IsMaximized (HWND hwnd)`	Returns TRUE if hwnd is maximized.
`BOOL WINAPI IsRestored (HWND hwnd)`	Returns TRUE if hwnd is restored.
`BOOL WINAPI IsLButtonDown (void)`	Returns TRUE if the left mouse button is down.
`BOOL WINAPI IsRButtonDown (void)`	Returns TRUE if the right mouse button is down.

Macro	Description
BOOL WINAPI IsMButtonDown (void)	Returns TRUE if the middle mouse button is down.
LRESULT SetWindowFont (HWND hWnd, HFONT hFont, (WPARAM) BOOL fRedraw)	Uses the FORWARD_WM_SETFONT message cracker to send a message to a window to set its font.
LRESULT (HFONT) GetWindowFont (HWND hWnd)	Uses the FORWARD_WM_GETFONT message cracker to send a message to a window to get its font.
DLGPROC SubclassDialog (HWND hwndDlg, DLGPROC lpfn)	Subclasses a dialog box procedure.
void WINAPI MapWindowPoints (HWND hwndFrom, HWND hwndTo, POINT FAR* lppt, WORD cpt);	Maps cpt points at *lppt from the coordinate system of hwndFrom to that of hwndTo. This macro can only be used with Windows 3.1.
void WINAPI MapWindowRect (HWND hwndFrom, HWND hwndTo, RECT FAR* lprc)	Maps a rectangle from the coordinate system of hwndFrom to that of hwndTo. This macro can only be used with Windows 3.1.

Using Control Message Macro APIs

New macro APIs have been added for working with control windows. These APIs are implemented as macros that call SendMessage or use other Windows functions such as SetWindowText that work with control windows. These macro APIs take care of packing the various parameters into wParam and lParam and casting the return value as needed. Which would you rather use in your Windows program: ListBox_GetText (hwndCtl, index, lpszBuffer) or SendMessage (hwnd-Ctl, LB_GETTEXT, index, lpszBuffer)? Each of the new macro APIs for control windows is prefixed by the control window class it works with, followed by an underscore and a meaningful API that reflects what it is used for. Following is a complete list of all the new Windows 3.1 control message macro APIs:

```
Static_Enable (hwnd, fEnable)

Static_GetText (hwnd, lpch, cchMax)

Static_GetTextLength (hwnd)

Static_SetText (hwnd, lpsz)

Static_SetIcon (hwnd, hIcon)

Static_GetIcon (hwnd, hIcon)

Button_Enable (hwnd, fEnable)

Button_GetText (hwnd, lpch, cchMax

Button_GetTextLength (hwnd)

Button_SetText (hwnd, lpsz)

Button_GetCheck (hwnd)

Button_SetCheck (hwnd, check)

Button_GetState (hwnd)

Button_SetState (hwnd, state)

Button_SetStyle (hwnd, style, fRedraw)

Edit_Enable (hwnd, fEnable)

Edit_GetText (hwnd, lpch, cchMax)

Edit_GetTextLength (hwnd)

Edit_SetText (hwnd, lpsz)

Edit_LimitText (hwnd, cchMax)

Edit_GetLineCount (hwnd)

Edit_GetLine (hwnd, line, lpch, cchMax)

Edit_GetRect (hwnd, lprc)

Edit_SetRect (hwnd, lprc)

Edit_SetRectNoPaint (hwnd, lprc)
```

```
Edit_GetSel (hwnd)

Edit_SetSel (hwnd, ichStart, ichEnd)

Edit_ReplaceSel (hwnd, lpszReplace)

Edit_GetModify (hwnd)

Edit_SetModify (hwnd, fModified)

Edit_LineFromChar (hwnd, ich)

Edit_LineIndex (hwnd, line)

Edit_LineLength (hwnd, line)

Edit_Scroll (hwnd, dv, dh)

Edit_CanUndo (hwnd)

Edit_Undo (hwnd)

Edit_EmptyUndoBuffer (hwnd)

Edit_SetPasswordChar (hwnd, ch)

Edit_SetTabStops (hwnd, cTabs, lpTabs)

Edit_SetWordBreak (hwnd, lpfnWordBreak)

Edit_FmtLines (hwnd, fAddEOL)

Edit_GetHandle (hwnd)

Edit_SetHandle (hwnd, h)

Edit_GetFirstVisible (hwnd)

ScrollBar_Enable (hwnd, flags)

ScrollBar_Show (hwnd, fShow)

ScrollBar_SetPos (hwnd, pos, fRedraw)

ScrollBar_GetPos (hwnd)

ScrollBar_SetRange (hwnd, posMin, posMax, fRedraw)

ScrollBar_GetRange (hwnd, lpposMin, lpposMax)

ListBox_Enable (hwnd, fEnable)

ListBox_GetCount (hwnd)
```

```
ListBox_ResetContent (hwnd)

ListBox_AddString (hwnd, lpsz)

ListBox_InsertString (hwnd, lpsz, index)

ListBox_AddItemData (hwnd, data)

ListBox_InsertItemData (hwnd, lpsz, index)

ListBox_DeleteString (hwnd, index)

ListBox_GetTextLen (hwnd, index)

ListBox_GetText (hwnd, index, lpszBuffer)

ListBox_GetItemData (hwnd, index)

ListBox_SetItemData (hwnd, index, data)

ListBox_FindString (hwnd, indexStart, lpszFind)

ListBox_FindItemData (hwnd, indexStart, data)

ListBox_SetSel (hwnd, fSelect, index)

ListBox_SelItemRange (hwnd, fSelect, first, last)

ListBox_GetCurSel (hwnd)

ListBox_SetCurSel (hwnd, index)

ListBox_SelectString (hwnd, indexStart, lpszFind)

ListBox_SelectItemData (hwnd, indexStart, data)

ListBox_GetSel (hwnd, index)

ListBox_GetSelCount (hwnd)

ListBox_GetTopIndex (hwnd)

ListBox_GetSelItems (hwnd, cItems, lpIndices)

ListBox_SetTopIndex (hwnd, indexTop)

ListBox_SetColumnWidth (hwnd, cxColumn)

ListBox_GetHorizontalExtent (hwnd)

ListBox_SetHorizontalExtent (hwnd, cxExtent)

ListBox_SetTabStops (hwnd, cTabs, lpTabs)
```

```
ListBox_GetItemRect (hwnd, index, lprc)

ListBox_SetCaretIndex (hwnd, index)

ListBox_GetCaretIndex (hwnd)

ListBox_SetAnchorIndex (hwnd, index)

ListBox_GetAnchorIndex (hwnd)

ListBox_Dir (hwnd, attrs, lpszFileSpec)

ListBox_AddFile (hwnd, lpszFilename)

ListBox_SetItemHeight (hwnd, index, cy) (3.1 only)

ListBox_GetItemHeight (hwnd, index)   (3.1 only)

ComboBox_Enable (hwnd, fEnable)

ComboBox_GetText (hwnd, lpch, cchMax)

ComboBox_GetTextLength (hwnd)

ComboBox_SetText (hwnd, lpsz)

ComboBox_LimitText (hwnd, cchLimit)

ComboBox_GetEditSel (hwnd)

ComboBox_SetEditSel (hwnd, ichStart, ichEnd)

ComboBox_GetCount (hwnd)

ComboBox_ResetContent (hwnd)

ComboBox_AddString (hwnd, lpsz)

ComboBox_InsertString (hwnd, index, lpsz)

ComboBox_AddItemData (hwnd, data)

ComboBox_InsertItemData (hwnd, index, data)

ComboBox_DeleteString (hwnd, index)

ComboBox_GetLBTextLen (hwnd, index)

ComboBox_GetLBText (hwnd, index, lpszBuffer)

ComboBox_GetItemData (hwnd, index)

ComboBox_SetItemData (hwnd, index, data)
```

```
ComboBox_FindString (hwnd, indexStart, lpszFind)

ComboBox_FindItemData (hwnd, indexStart, data)

ComboBox_GetCurSel (hwnd)

ComboBox_SetCurSel (hwnd, index)

ComboBox_SelectString (hwnd, indexStart, lpszSelect)

ComboBox_SelectItemData (hwnd, indexStart, data)

ComboBox_Dir (hwnd, attrs, lpszFileSpec)

ComboBox_ShowDropdown (hwnd, fShow)

ComboBox_GetDroppedState (hwnd)        (3.1 only)

ComboBox_GetDroppedControlRect (hwnd, lprc) (3.1 only)

ComboBox_GetItemHeight (hwnd)          (3.1 only)

ComboBox_SetItemHeight (hwnd, cyItem)  (3.1 only)

ComboBox_GetExtendedUI (hwnd)          (3.1 only)

ComboBox_SetExtendedUI (hwnd, flags)   (3.1 only)
```

You can examine the Resource Monitor, DumpIT 3.1, and Topper program listings to see how I implemented macro APIs in my sample applications. In Resource Monitor I used message crackers in both the window procedure and the dialog box function. In DumpIT 3.1 I used message crackers in both of its window procedures—the MDI frame window procedure in FRAME.C and the MDI child window procedure in CHILD.C. I also used the macro APIs for global memory allocation, for working with GDI objects, and for working with control windows.

For more examples of how to implement the new WINDOWSX.H macro APIs, you should look at the MAKEAPP sample application included with the Windows 3.1 SDK. Using MAKEAPP.BAT you can create an application template for a one-window program, fully STRICT, that uses the new macro APIs. You might also want to check out MAKEMDI. It is similar to MAKEAPP and is available on the Microsoft WINSDK Forum on CompuServe. MAKEMDI.BAT lets you create an MDI application template that is fully STRICT and uses the Windows 3.1 SDK macro APIs. You will also find documentation included with the Microsoft Windows 3.1 SDK on using the macro APIs in the file WINDOWSX.TXT.

I have been able to use the new macro APIs in many different Windows applications without problems. There were some bugs reported for the macro APIs on the CompuServe Beta Test Forum, and all but one, the message cracker for WM_DRAWITEM, got fixed in the final release. You can correct it by making the following change in WINDOWSX.H:

```
/* void Cls_OnDrawItem(HWND hwnd, const DRAWITEMSTRUCT FAR* lpDrawItem); */
#define HANDLE_WM_DRAWITEM(hwnd, wParam, lParam, fn) \
  ((fn)((hwnd), (const DRAWITEMSTRUCT FAR*)(lParam)), 0L)
#define FORWARD_WM_DRAWITEM(hwnd, lpDrawItem, fn) \
  (BOOL)(fn)((hwnd), WM_DRAWITEM, 0, (LPARAM)(const DRAWITEMSTRUCT FAR*)
  (lpDrawItem))
```

The change is indicated in bold type. You should replace void with BOOL. One nice thing about the macro APIs is that they can be corrected and extended easily.

Now that we have finished with learning about how WINDOWS.H and WINDOWSX.H can help you to build more robust Windows applications, let's take a look at one more Windows development tool new to Windows 3.1 that helps you improve the reliability for your Windows applications—STRESS.

Stressing Your Windows Application

The Microsoft Stress Tester (STRESS) is a new tool added to the Windows 3.1 development toolkit. It utilizes the dynamic link Stress Library (STRESS.DLL) that artificially consumes system resources. Using the STRESS program you can test your Windows application to detect how it behaves in unusual resource situations.

STRESS provides fixed, random, and message-dependent allocations of these resources. In addition, it provides several logging options to help locate and reproduce bugs. All of the options are saved in the file STRESS.INI. Figure 12.1 shows the main window of STRESS.

As you can see in the figure, STRESS is capable of allocating and monitoring global memory, User heap space, GDI heap space, disk space, and file handles. The main window monitors the state of Windows system resources while STRESS is executing.

FIGURE 12.1:

The STRESS main window

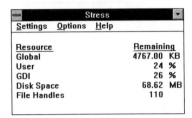

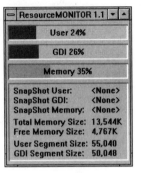

The figure also shows how STRESS can consume Windows system resources. When this screen was created, I was doing a random-time stress-test using the STRESS executer feature. The stress level setting was level 3. You can also see Resource Monitor running in the background keeping track of Windows resources while STRESS is running.

STRESS.DLL

STRESS uses the STRESS.DLL to do its work. The STRESS dynamic link library makes scarce-resource testing easier and more realistic. You can use STRESS either to test your Windows program or to access the functions in STRESS.DLL from inside your Windows program. You could also use the STRESS.DLL to build your own Windows stress-testing tool. Table 12.3 shows a list of the functions available in STRESS.DLL and the resource that it correlates with.

`AllocMem`, `AllocGDIMem`, and `AllocUserMem` are responsible for allocating and releasing Windows memory resources. The `AllocDiskSpace` function actually creates a file on the disk partition to consume space, while `AllocFileHandles` creates up to 256 file handles and frees them using the `UnAllocFileHandles` function.

TABLE 12.3:   New Windows 3.1 Stress API

Resource	Memory Allocation Function	Memory UnAllocate Function
Global memory	`AllocMem`	`FreeAllMem`
GDI heap memory	`AllocGDIMem`	`FreeAllGDIMem`
User heap memory	`AllocUserMem`	`FreeAllUserMem`
Disk space	`AllocDiskSpace`	`UnAllocDiskSpace`
File handles	`AllocFileHandles`	`UnAllocFileHandles`

Fixed Allocations

STRESS allows specific allocation values to be selected for any of the resources. To access the Fixed Settings dialog box, select the Fixed Settings command from the Settings menu. This dialog box contains five edit fields which specify the amount of the resource to leave available. A value of 0 consumes an entire resource, while a value of -1 frees any STRESS allocations for that resource. Pressing the Set button performs the specified allocations. You can set all of the fields to -1 by pressing the Free All button. Once the fields are changed, a Set is done to free all STRESS allocations. Figure 12.2 shows the Fixed Settings dialog box.

The Executer

The Executer allows applications to be tested while STRESS dynamically allocates and unallocates resources in the background. One or more of the five resources can be requested to be allocated in the background. The two modes that the Executer runs in are random and message-dependent. Random allocation performs resource allocation depending on the time interval set (from 1 to 120 seconds) in the Time Interval edit box. One aspect you need to be aware of is that randomness makes reproducibility difficult. Message-dependent allocation, on the other hand, occurs when Windows sends specific messages to an application. STRESS intercepts the message, sends it on to its original destination, and then performs a resource allocation. This type of allocation can be reproduced more easily, because allocations are done on a specific message basis rather than a time basis.

FIGURE 12.2:

The Fixed Settings dialog box

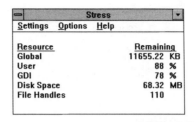

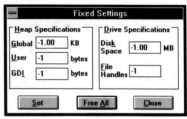

ResMonitor,
U:88%, G:78%

To display the Executer dialog box, choose the Executer command from the Settings menu. As you can see in Figure 12.3, you can identify the types of Windows resources you want to stress, select between random and message-dependent allocations, choose the messages to use for message-dependent allocations, and choose the stress level you want to use.

Stress Level

You have four different stress levels to choose from. Each has its own set of global, GDI heap, User heap, disk space, and file handle values assigned to it. To adjust the amounts that correspond to each stress level, choose the Advanced push button in the Executer Options dialog box to display the Stress Level Ranges dialog box. This dialog box lets you specifically configure the ranges to any test situation.

Seed

The Seed (starting point for the STRESS random number generator) determines the set of random or message-dependent allocations chosen. If the same Seed is used and the state of Windows is the same each time you test, then the same dynamic allocation occurs. Since the value of the Seed can range from 0 to 65,535, there are many execution paths that can be traveled.

FIGURE 12.3:

The Executer dialog box

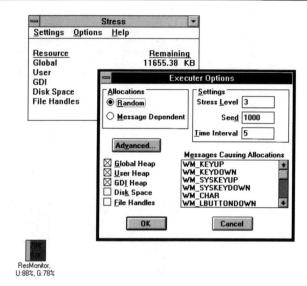

Logging Options

STRESS provides several logging options to help reproduce bugs. You can send logging information to a file and/or a COM port. Several different logging levels may be selected. To set up logging, choose the Log Options command from the Settings menu to display the dialog box shown in Figure 12.4.

There are five different logging levels to choose from, ranging from 1 through 5. Level 1 logs nothing. Level 2 logs only the most recent command sent to STRESS. Level 3 logs all commands sent to STRESS. Level 4 logs the state of Windows resources every four to six seconds. Finally, level 5 logs all the past STRESS commands and the status of Windows resources every five to six seconds.

You can choose the file name to log to by pressing the Change Log File button. If the log file already exists, the original will be renamed as *.001 and then *.002, etc. This makes sure that all of your old log files are retained.

The log file is a very useful tool for keeping track of how your Windows application allocates and frees system resources over a period of time. The Resource Monitor application included with this book shows you the state of Windows resources, but it does not record this information as the stress-tester does. Even if you don't use STRESS for allocating and freeing system resources, you can use it to keep a log of

FIGURE 12.4:

The Logging Options dialog box

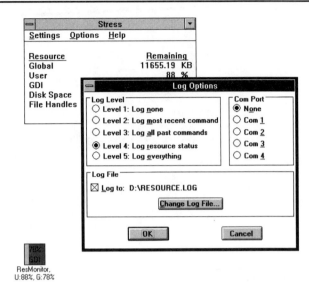

the state of Windows resources while you are testing your application. The following abbreviated listing shows the types of information that STRESS writes to the log file:

```
*********************** Stress Log: Begin Header ****************
Date: 08/01/92  Time: 07:37:06

Initial State of Resources
---------------------------
Global Memory    : 10056.56 KB
User Heap    :    74 %
GDI Heap    :    57 %
Disk Space    :    67.46 MB
File Handles    :    103


*********************** Stress Log: End Header ******************
TIME    LOCATION    TYPE OF ACTION SPECIFIC DESCRIPTION

07:37:16 Global : 10056.56 KB User  :    74 %  GDI  :    59 %
        Handles:    103    Disk  :    67.46 MB
07:37:21 Global : 10056.56 KB User  :    74 %  GDI  :    59 %
        Handles:    103    Disk  :    67.46 MB
07:37:27 Global : 10056.56 KB User  :    74 %  GDI  :    59 %
```

```
       Handles:    103    Disk  :   67.46 MB
07:37:32 Global : 10056.56 KB User  :    74 %  GDI  :    59 %
       Handles:    103    Disk  :   67.46 MB

*********************** Stress Log: Begin Footer *****************
Date: 08/01/92  Time: 07:38:32

Final State of Resources
--------------------------
Global Memory    : 10050.91 KB
User Heap    :    74 %
GDI Heap     :    57 %
Disk Space   :    67.46 MB
File Handles :     106

*********************** Stress Log: End Footer *******************
```

Using STRESS

The best way to learn what STRESS can do to help you test your Windows application is to use it to create low resource conditions under Windows. I found STRESS very easy to operate and have used it to test all my Windows applications, as well as Windows applications from other vendors. I have usually found that most Windows applications will operate normally up to stress level 3 set by the STRESS executer. When you move the stress meter up to level 4, things really begin to happen—or I should say not happen. Your program may not be able to display a dialog box window, or all the controls in the dialog box may not appear.

Using Windows system resources wisely has been a theme that has been replayed over and over again throughout this book. It is a topic that is extremely important for Windows developers to know and be aware of. Tools such as STRESS, HEAP-WALK, and Resource Monitor can provide the help you need to make sure that your Windows application uses Windows system resources effectively.

APPENDIX

Windows Development Tools Directory

A

This appendix lists the Windows development tools that were available when this book was published. Some of the tools are discussed in much more depth within the body of the book. I have included references when this is the case, so you will know where to look to find out more about a particular tool. If I have used one of the tools listed here but did not write about it in the book, I have included a personal comment about the tool.

Some of the tools listed in this directory are information resources for Windows developers—not programs for developing Windows applications. In short, I have tried to list any type of resource that might help make your Windows software development easier.

The tools are listed in alphabetical order by the name of the company that produces them. I have included the companies' names and addresses as well as their technical support telephone numbers. Many of these companies also have forums on CompuServe where they provide technical support. It is worthwhile to visit these forums to find out what other programmers think about a particular development tool. Larger companies such as Microsoft, Borland, and Symantec have their own forums on CompuServe. Other companies are part of the Microsoft vendor forums. They can be found in the WINAPA, WINAPB, and WINAPC forums. As long as you are on CompuServe, you should also visit Microsoft's WINSDK Forum. This forum is the primary meeting place for Windows developers on CompuServe.

Since I have not had the chance to use all the tools in this directory (I wish I had), please don't consider it a personal recommendation if a tool is listed here. Before purchasing any of these development tools, you should investigate it further. If I reference the tool in this book, you should read the material in the book to find out more about it. Otherwise, you can contact the company that produces the tool to obtain more information. One of my favorite ways to find out about a development tool is to ask other Windows developers about it on the WINSDK Forum on CompuServe.

Development Tool Descriptions

The directory is organized alphabetically, first by the names of the companies that produce the tools, then within each company by the names of the development tools themselves.

Applegate Software

4317 264th Ave., NE
Redmond, WA 98053-8730
Phone: 206-868-8512
Tech support: Use main number

OptiMem for Windows

Windows DLL that provides optimum memory management. Lets you use standard C and C++ memory allocation APIs while improving memory utilization and performance. OptiMem for Windows addresses several problems with the Windows memory API, including overhead, granularity, handles, fragmentation, and limited selectors. The library provides enhanced versions of C's `malloc/free` and C++'s `new/delete`.

OptiMem for Windows detects a number of memory errors, including double `free`-ing, invalid parameters, memory overwrites, failure to free memory, wild pointers, and running out of memory. In addition, the library provides a centralized error handler for memory problems, similar to the `new_handler` of C++. Besides standard heap memory management the product also offers a fixed-size allocator with no per-allocation space overhead. This can significantly speed up memory management for fixed-size objects.

Black Ice Software, Inc.

Crane Rd.
Somers, NY 10589
Phone: 914-277-7006
FAX: 914-276-8418

PCX SDK for Windows

Tools for developing PCX file formats for applications without ever having to learn PCX file formats. Provides complete set of documentation and sample program to demonstrate how to use PCX SDK and Image SDK for Windows. Allows user to zoom in/out of, rotate, and invert PCX images.

TIFF SDK for Windows

Library of functions that can be used to add the ability to read or write TIFF files in all common TIFF formats—including the file format specification which supports 24-bit color—to a Windows application. Enables developers to include image manipulation features that size, crop, rotate, flip, and invert TIFF images.

Blaise Computing, Inc.

819 Bancroft Way
Berkeley, CA 94710
Phone: 800-333-8087; 510-540-5441
FAX: 510-540-1938
Tech support: Use main number

WIN++

Class library for Borland C++ Windows applications. Win++ adds more than 30 classes and supports the dynamic data exchange management library, including clients, servers, advise loops, and multiple simultaneous conversations.

Windows Control Palette

Set of custom control DLLs for producing Windows interfaces. Creates 3-D Canvases group and separate controls, creates toolbars, provides default bitmaps and customizable buttons. Includes C, C++, Turbo Pascal, and Visual Basic support. I had the chance to work with the Blaise Windows Control Palette on a project after finishing the book. It is an excellent product. When I get around to writing another book on Windows development tools, the Windows Control Palette will definitely be in it.

Blue Sky Software Corp.

7486 La Jolla Blvd., Suite 3
La Jolla, CA 92037
Phone: 800-677-4946; 619-459-6365
FAX: 619-459-6366
Tech support: Use main number

Magic Fields Version 1.0

Object-oriented data field validation for Windows 3.0. Provides predefined objects, including numeric, text, alphanumeric, date, currency, phone number, social security number, and others. Offers support for international date and currency formats. Eliminates coding data entry fields. To learn more about what Magic Fields does and how it works, you should read Chapter 5.

RoboHELP Version 1.0

Windows Help authoring system that works with Word for Windows. Generates source code for indexes, topics, keywords, categories, defined terms, pop-up definitions, bitmaps, cross references, hypertext links, and context-sensitive help. Generates required .RTF, .HPJ, and .H files. RoboHELP is fun and easy to use. After learning how to use RoboHELP, I have never written another README.TXT file for my Windows applications—only README.HLP. To find out how good RoboHELP is, you should read Chapter 5.

WindowsMAKER Professional Version 4.0

Automates construction of Windows applications for C/C++ Windows programmers. WindowsMAKER Professional lets you create Windows user interfaces by clicking on menu selections with a mouse. Automatically retrieves/compiles C/C++ modules to generate user interface features. Lets you prototype, animate, and test Windows applications in complete WYSIWYG environment. Very customizable. WindowsMAKER Professional is my favorite Windows application generator. (CASE:W Corporate Edition comes in a close second.) To find out why, you should read Chapter 4.

Borland International, Inc.

P.O. Box 660001, 1800 Green Hills Rd.
Scotts Valley, CA 95066-0001
Phone: 800-331-0877
FAX: 408-439-9262
Tech support: 408-438-5300

Borland C++ & Application Frameworks Version 3.1

High-end Windows C/C++ development system. Includes optimizing C/C++ compiler with a Windows-hosted Integrated Development Environment (IDE). Borland C++ contains every conceivable Windows development tool that Borland offers for C/C++ Windows developers. If you are serious about Windows software development, this is the best development system you can buy. Includes Object-Windows that provides functioning Windows class library to save you time and code and Turbo Vision that enables you to produce DOS applications with character-based window user interfaces. The only features that Borland C++ lacks are Microsoft's excellent MFC C++ class library and the debugging version of Windows. See Chapter 1 for more information about the tools included with the Borland C++ & Application Frameworks development system.

Borland C++ for Windows Version 3.1

Optimizing C/C++ compiler that lets you build object-oriented Windows applications. Includes all the tools in the Borland C++ Application Frameworks Version 3.1 system except ObjectWindows and Turbo Vision. See Chapter 1 for more information about the tools included with the Borland C++ development system.

Resource Workshop for Windows

Visual programming tool for building Windows resources. Features palette of tools for creating interface components and editors for each resource, including text, font, dialog box, bitmap, icon, cursor, menu, and string table. Provides dynamic message dispatching, allowing user to treat resources as callable objects. Included with all of the Borland C/C++ and Pascal Windows development systems. May also be purchased separately. See Chapter 2 to get an in-depth view of what Borland Resource Workshop can do and how it works.

Turbo C++ for Windows Version 3.1

Windows-based C++ compiler. Contains ObjectBrowser graphical source browser, Turbo Debugger for Windows, Resource Workshop tool used for building Windows GUI, and EasyWin library for porting DOS applications to Windows. Includes ObjectWindows Library, which is a set of C++ classes used for developing Windows applications. Turbo C++ for Windows is limited because it cannot do program optimization. Otherwise, it's a "best buy" among Windows development systems. If you are on a budget and want to get into Windows software development, this is the best system you can buy. Turbo C++ for Windows also includes the ObjectWindows C++ class library, while the more expensive Borland C++ doesn't. See Chapter 1 for more information about the tools included with the Turbo C++ for Windows development system.

Turbo Pascal for Windows Version 1.5

Pascal compiler that develops Windows applications without having to switch to C. Performs standard Windows programming using Windows API, ports DOS programs to run in 80-column by 25-line window, or uses Borland's Object-Windows. Includes the same set of tools for developing Windows applications that is included with Borland C++ for Windows and Turbo C++ for Windows.

CASEWORKS, Inc.

1 Dunwoody Park, Suite 130
Atlanta, GA 30338
Phone: 800-635-1577; 404-399-6236
FAX: 404-399-9516
Tech support: Use toll-free number

CASE:W Corporate Edition Version 4.0

Automates construction of Windows applications for C/C++ Windows programmers. CASE:W uses one code generation tool for Windows and offers separate knowledge bases for generating ANSI C, Microsoft C++ 7.0 Foundation Class Library (MFC), and Borland C++ ObjectWindow Library (OWL). CASE:W Corporate Edition is an excellent Windows application generator. To learn how CASE:W works and how you can build Windows applications using it, you should read Chapter 3.

Computer Associates International, Inc.

One Computer Associates Plaza
Islandia, NY 11788-7000
Phone: 800-CALL-CAI; 516-DIAL-CAI
FAX: 516-DIAL-FAX

Realizer Version 1.0

BASIC language application development environment for Windows. Allows user to import files from Lotus 1-2-3 and Excel, access programs written in C, and exchange data through DDE. Includes BASIC, optimized array processing, math, string and date-time functions, integrated debugger, and tools, including charts, spreadsheets, forms, scheduler, and animation. Runtime version available.

CompuThink, Inc.

15127 NE 24th, Suite 344
Redmond, WA 98052-5530
Phone: 206-881-7354
FAX: 206-883-1452

WindowsWatcher

Expensive ($295 per year) but informative industry newsletter that focuses on the Microsoft Windows development community. *WindowsWatcher* received the Best Computer Newsletter award from the Computer Press Association in 1992. If you want to find out the latest news (or the latest gossip) inside the Windows development community, *WindowsWatcher* is the place to look. When I am not writing books or Windows programs, I write articles for *WindowsWatcher* as a contributing editor.

Data Techniques, Inc.

1000 Business Center Dr., Suite 120
Savannah, GA 31405
Phone: 800-868-8003; 912-651-8003
FAX: 912-651-8021

ImageMan Version 1.04

Object-oriented Windows library. Allows developers to add advanced image display and print capabilities to Windows applications. Allows applications to access all types of images with the same set of standard function calls. Supports TIFF, PCX, EPS, Windows Metafile, and bitmap formats. Customizable.

EMS

4505 Buckhurst Ct.
Olney, MD 20832-1830
Phone: 301-924-3594
FAX: 301-963-2708

Windows Pro

Comprehensive collection of Windows utilities, both shareware and freeware. Takes up about 50MB on your hard disk. Some of the utilities include source code. You have your choice of diskettes or a CD-ROM.

FarPoint Technologies, Inc.

P.O. Box 309, 75 Walnut Street
Richmond, OH 43944
Phone: 614-765-4333
FAX: 614-765-4939
Tech support: Use main number

Drover's Professional Toolbox for Windows

Collection of tools for writing Windows applications. Features more than 300 ANSI C functions in DLL, including low-level disk access, background sound and music, window printing, and file manipulation. Controls include formatted edit classes, animated picture control, superbutton displaying text and graphics, graphical directory tree listings, and spreadsheet control. The spreadsheet control is especially full-featured. You can optionally purchase the source code to all of the Drover's Professional Toolbox for Windows functions.

Genus Microprogramming

2900 Wilcrest, Suite 145
Houston, TX 77042-3355
Phone: 800-227-0918; 713-870-0737
FAX: 713-870-0288
Tech support: 713-977-0680

PCX Programmer's Toolkit for Windows

Lets you display any number of images, of any size, at any point on the screen. You can scroll images within windows, scale them to any size, capture and convert screens from other programs, print black-and-white images, scale images, inspect image headers, translate text screens into PCX images, fix older PCX files, and more. PCX Programmer's Toolkit for Windows includes new color conversion and image resolution functions and VESA support. In addition to conventional, expanded, and disk-based memory, PCX Toolkit v5.0 now supports XMS extended memory.

Gimpel Software

3207 Hogarth Lane
Collegeville, PA 19426
Phone: 215-584-4261
FAX: 215-584-4266
Tech support: Use main number

PC-Lint Version 5.0

C/C++ source code analyzer. Reports on bugs, glitches, and inconsistencies. Supports K&R C and ANSI. Turns off any message globally or locally. Checks for inconsistencies between modules. Includes strong type-checking facility and control-flow based analysis of variable initialization. PC-Lint is discussed in Chapter 12.

Inmark Development Corp.

2065 Landings Dr.
Mountain View, CA 94043
Phone: 800-346-6275; 415-691-9000
FAX: 415-691-9099
Tech support: Use main number

zAPP for Windows Version 1.1

C++ class library designed to simplify Windows development by encapsulating Windows 3.0 API within C++ classes. Provides memory manager and avoids depleting pool of global memory handles. Contains built-in support for selecting and configuring printers. Implements dynamic message handling facility that can dispatch messages or ranges of messages to individual C++ member functions.

IntelligenceWare, Inc.

5933 W. Century Blvd., Suite 900
Los Angeles, CA 90045
Phone: 800-888-2996; 310-216-6177
FAX: 310-417-8897
Tech support: Use main number

WindowsTeach for Windows Version 1.0

Interactive system that teaches Windows programming through graphic tutorials, hypertext, and stepwise code annotations and explanations. The program presents key Windows concepts graphically and supplies source code explanations along with hypertext clarifications within a multiwindowed environment.

WindowsTeach has three components: the Concepts Track, the Programs Track, and the Hints and Suggestions section. The Concepts Track graphically explains the structure of Windows. The Programs Track has 21 programs, each illustrating a feature of Windows, showing the top level first and allowing the user to zoom in to more details and then get to the source code with hypertext. The Hints and Suggestions section provides tips to save programming time.

Magma Software Systems

15 Bodwell Terrace
Millburn, NJ 07041
Phone: 201 912-0192
FAX: 201-912-0103
Tech support: Use main number

MEWEL 4.0

Cross-platform code library. Character-oriented windowing system that uses a subset of the Microsoft Windows application programming interface (API) to approximate the Windows look and feel under DOS. Uses Windows' message-passing and event-driven operation and has very few incompatibilities. MEWEL handles colors differently from Windows and has no counterpart to Windows' memory-management system. The C compiler has enough conditional compilation facilities to handle some of these differences, but others require minor manual modification of code. A Windows porting layer provides a set of macros and functions that map Windows functions into MEWEL functions. You can also buy the source code to MEWEL as an option.

Magna Carta Software, Inc.

P.O. Box 475594
Garland, TX 75047
Phone: 214-226-6909
FAX: 214-226-0386

C Windows Toolkit

Creates pop-up windows, pull-down menus, spreadsheet menus, and context-sensitive help screens. Stores windows. Includes font editor. Includes data entry and validation functions. Includes tutorial.

Communications Toolkit/Windows

Adds professional serial communications to Windows C/C++ applications. Provides ASCII, Xmodem, Kermit, Ymodem, and Zmodem protocol support.

MicroQuill, Inc.

4900 25th Ave., NE, Suite 206
Seattle, WA 98105
Phone: 800-441-7822; 206-525-8218
FAX: 206-525-8309

DeMystifiers

Set of programming utilities. Includes Colonel, Voyeur, Ecologist, and Mechanic modules. Captures information on memory management, message processing, window class and instance management, GDI display and device capabilities, and systemwide environment settings. DeMystifiers is discussed in Chapter 7.

Performance Tracer for Windows

Performance Tracer uses a proprietary check stack to capture the entry point, exit point, and timing data information for every one of an application's functions exercised in a given session. Application-wide performance data is provided in a single pass, including complete call trees, exact function frequencies, execution times for every instance of each function, and all functions called by or calling a given function.

The data captured using Performance Tracer is summarized in a series of reports and is available in ASCII format for further manipulation by the developer. When Performance Tracer is used to trace Windows applications, the program may spawn a window that dynamically reflects the call stack history of the host application as it is being exercised.

Segmentor for Windows

Optimizes application's segmentation map to minimize number of intersegment calls and to create segments of equal size.

Win-Profiler

Profiles entire application simultaneously, including call counts, function timing, call trees, and object sizes. Picks up indirect calls made from function pointers and messages.

Microsoft Corp.

One Microsoft Way
Redmond, WA 98052-6399
Phone: 800-426-9400; 206-882-8080
FAX: 206-883-8101
Tech support: 206-454-2030; 206-637-7098 (Windows)

Developer's Network CD

The Microsoft Developer's Network CD contains hundreds of articles, tips, techniques, and application source code for Windows applications. Technical articles are written by Microsoft Development Network engineers. These articles provide in-depth explanations of specific programming topics and address known areas of complexity. The CD includes articles on TrueType, using device-independent bitmaps (DIBs), implementing metafiles, and many other topics. The Developer's Network CD contains complete documentation with full text-retrieval indexing for the Windows 3.1 SDK, Microsoft C/C++ 7.0, and the Win32 documentation. The Developer's CD also includes all issues of the Microsoft Systems Journal and selected Microsoft books. The Developer's Network CD replaces the Microsoft Programmer's Library CD. If you have a CD-ROM drive, you should subscribe to the Developer's Network CD. If you don't have a CD-ROM drive, you should buy one just so you can access this information.

Visual Basic Version 2.0
Visual Basic with Professional Toolkit Version 2.0

Graphical application development system that combines visual design tools with the BASIC programming language. Visually creates full set of Windows interface components, including command buttons, text fields, list boxes, pictures, dropdown menus, and file system controls, without your writing any code. Supports DDE and DLL. Includes icon library of 400 designs and icon editor.

The Professional Toolkit includes custom controls and programming tools to enhance Visual Basic applications with technologies including OLE, pen-based computing, multimedia, graphing, grids, and multiple document interfaces. Features Windows Help compiler, Windows API on line reference, setup kit, and custom control development kit.

Microsoft C/C++ Version 7.0

Windows C/C++ development system from the developer of Microsoft Windows. Includes optimizing C/C++ compiler with a DOS-hosted Programmer's Workbench (PWB) environment. Microsoft C/C++ contains every conceivable Windows development tool that Microsoft offers. If you are serious about Windows software development and committed to using Microsoft tools, this is the system to buy. Many of the tools included with this development system, such as Spy and CodeView, do not have all the features that Borland's tools come with. While the DOS-based PWB works much better than previous versions and integrates well with Windows using the WX Server, it cannot compare to Borland's Windows-hosted IDE.

For Windows C++ developers, the most important tool that Microsoft includes with Microsoft C/C++ 7.0 is the Microsoft C++ Foundation Class Library (MFC). MFC does not include the programming power that you find in Borland's OWL, but it does have some very important points in its favor. MFC covers the entire Windows API—OWL covers only a portion of the Windows API. The way MFC is written, if you already know the Windows API, it's much easier to learn how to use MFC than ObjectWindows. MFC source code is portable to the Win32 API used in Windows NT. To find out more about Microsoft C/C++ 7.0 and how it compares with Borland C/C++, you can start at Chapter 1 to see them summarized. The rest of the book goes into much more detail about how these development systems stack up against each other.

QuickC for Windows Version 1.0

"One-box" Windows application development system that doesn't require the use of the Windows SDK. The QuickC for Windows IDE uses MDI windows for working on source code files. As the first Windows-hosted integrated development environment based on the C language, QuickC for Windows lets you experience the benefits of working within Windows while you are developing a Windows application. The editor, compiler, and debugger are all integrated and all Windows-based; there's no need to switch to a DOS window to use the compiler or debugger, as you need to do with Microsoft C and the Windows SDK.

The QuickC for Windows development environment contains all the development tools required for developing Windows applications, but not all the tools you really need. While QuickC contains a compiler, the required libraries and DLL for building Windows applications, Image Editor, and Dialog Editor, it's missing tools such as the debugging version of Windows, HEAPWALK, and others. These tools can be purchased separately from Microsoft as an upgrade package.

Microsoft's QuickC for Windows also comes with a version of CASEWORKS' CASE:W called QuickCase:W. QuickCase:W lets you interactively design your program's windows and menus, and it generates skeleton Windows code that you can edit and enhance. QuickC Version 1.0 is compatible with Windows 3.0. To develop Windows 3.1 applications, QuickC must be used with the Microsoft Windows 3.1 SDK. To learn more about working with QuickC for Windows and Quick-Case:W, you should read Chapter 3.

Test for Windows

Automated testing package that lets you test Windows 3.0 and 3.1 applications. Creates test scripts for applications and reduces task of manually having to run test procedures. Simulates keyboard and mouse movements and intercepts unrecoverable application errors and traces them back to source. Consists of five components, including Test Driver, FastTest, Test Dialogs, Test Screen, and group of DLLs.

Windows Software Development Kit (SDK) Version 3.1

Mother of all Windows development systems. Since Windows 1.0, it has been the primary source of Windows development tools for Windows programmers. The Windows 3.1 SDK is now included with Microsoft C/C++ 7.0. Major portions of it are also included with Borland C++ and Zortech C++. The Windows 3.1 SDK is also sold separately for Windows developers who don't have a C/C++ development system that includes the SDK tools required to develop Windows applications. To learn more about the Windows 3.1 SDK and its components, read Chapter 1.

Nu-Mega Technologies, Inc.

P.O. Box 7780
Nashua, NH 03060-7780
Phone: 603-888-2386
FAX: 603-888-2465
Tech support: Use main number

Soft-ICE/W Version 1.0

Debugger that uses Protected mode of 80386 processor to provide hardware-level debugging capabilities typically found only in hardware-assisted debuggers and in-circuit emulators. Provides real-time breakpoints. Includes back-trace history and source-level debugging. Compatible with other popular software debugging tools. Includes soft-boot function that allows debugging with non-DOS operating systems and self-booting programs. If you are building Windows device drivers, this is a debugger that you should look into.

Pioneer Software, Inc.

5540 Centerview Dr., Suite 324
Raleigh, NC 27606
Phone: 800-876-3101; 919-859-2220
FAX: 919-859-9334
Tech support: 919-851-1152

Q+E Database Library for Windows Version 1.1

Collection of DLLs providing developers with a common call level interface for Windows applications to access dBASE, Oracle, SQL Server, DB2, Sybase, Database Manager, NetWare SQL, XDB, Gupta SQLBase, and Btrieve. Allows user to call from macro, script, or any programming language of Windows. Enables products including spreadsheets and word processors to retrieve and manipulate database information directly.

Premia Corp.

1075 N.W. Murray Blvd., Suite 268
Portland, OR 97229
Phone: 800-547-9902; 503-647-9902
FAX: 503-647-5423
Tech support: Use main number

Codewright Version 2.0

Configurable, extensible editor created for Windows programmers. Provides standard programmer's editor features, such as unlimited file size, unlimited undo and redo of changes, automatic indenting, and multiple file and multiple window editing. Codewright is extensible by means of an API of over 500 functions that can be called from user-written procedures.

Beyond the normal editing features, Codewright also offers selective text display and a programmatic method for displaying only certain parts of the file you are editing. Two built-in examples of this capability are analysis of conditional code and location of lines containing a user-specified pattern. Codewright also offers ChromaCode, the ability to automatically render designated parts of a file in user-specified colors.

The latest version of Codewright is compatible with Windows 3.1 and exploits new Windows features such as drag and drop, TrueType (fixed pitch), and vertical tiling of windows. Other features include search and replace across multiple files, user-specified menu modification, and merging. Merging helps you combine independent sets of changes made to the same file. Codewright is the best Windows program editor available. I now use it for all of my Microsoft C/C++ and Borland C++ Windows development.

ProtoView Development Corp.

353 Georges Rd.
Dayton, NJ 08810
Phone: 908-329-8588
FAX: 908-329-8624

ProtoGen Version 3.0

Application generator for Windows. Integrates with ProtoView Screen Management Facility for Windows. Allows user to design application menu with separators, menu breaks, grayed items, and accelerators; attach dialog boxes to menu items or dialog boxes to other dialog boxes; and generate C or C++ source code. ProtoGen can't compare with CASE:W Corporate Edition or WindowsMAKER Professional, but it is less expensive. It is even included free with Borland C++ & Application Frameworks Version 3.1.

ProtoGen is easy to use and is much more powerful than QuickCase:W for Windows that's included with QuickC for Windows. Code regeneration is easy, as long as you put your program code between comment lines that ProtoGen puts in the

C/C++ source code it generates. ProtoGen can generate both C and C++ source code. I just wish it would not generate a separate C source code file for every dialog box in a Windows application.

Raima Corp.

3245 146th Place, SE, Suite 230
Bellevue, WA 98007
Phone: 800-327-2462; 206-747-5570
FAX: 206-747-1991
Tech support: 206-562-2622

Raima Data Manager for Windows Version 3.21

Database management system that includes Data Manager, db Query SQL-based query system, and db Revise database restructure program. Includes relational B-tree indexing, network database model, multiple database access, built-in reference integrity, record and file locking functions, automatic recovery, and relational query and report writer. Supports most C compilers.

Raima Object Manager for Windows Version 1.1

Object-oriented DBMS for C++ applications that includes source code. Provides object persistence and object relationship management. Encapsulates object storage and database navigation into C++ class definitions. Includes automatic management of currency, multitasking, and incremental opening and closing of database. Compatible with all existing Raima databases. Supports network, relational, and direct-object access.

Rogue Wave Software, Inc.

P.O. Box 2328
Corvallis, OR 97339
Phone: 800-487-3217; 503-754-3010
FAX: 503-757-6650
Tech support: 503-794-2311

Tools.h++ Version 5.0

C++ foundation class library. Includes over 60 classes to handle strings, dates, times, files, B-tree, collections, link lists, queues, stacks, and more. Provides DDE and Clipboard stream buffer classes for data exchange with other applications while using stream I/O. Offers regular expression and tokenize class, expanded virtual I/O streams, and error checking.

Softbridge, Inc.

125 Cambridge Park Dr.
Cambridge, MA 02140
Phone: 800-955-9190; 617-576-2257
FAX: 617-864-7747
Tech support: Use main number

ATF for Windows (Automated Test Facility)

Automates testing of client/server or stand-alone Windows applications. Provides executive-related and controller-related features.

Bridge ToolKit for Windows

Bridge is a versatile, easy-to-use batch language for creating customized workstation applications under Windows. Provides linkage between DOS and Windows. Helps user integrate DOS and Windows applications. Executes DOS application; sends keystrokes to DOS application; reads characters from DOS screen; responds to messages, screen text, and keyboard input; sends messages to/from DOS application; and automates copying/pasting from Windows Clipboard.

Software Blacksmiths, Inc.

6064 St. Ives Way
Mississauga, Ontario
Canada L5N 4M1
Phone: 416-858-4466
FAX: 416-858-4466

C-DOC Professional

C/C++ source code formatter that contains many other tools to help you document your programs. C-CALL creates tree diagrams showing function hierarchies. C-CMT generates and inserts function comment blocks in your program source code. C-LIST generates diagrams that show the logic/control flow within your programs. C-METRIC calculates function complexity. I have tried many C code formatting and documentation tools, but I always return to using the first one I started with—C-DOC. C-DOC Professional is simply the best C/C++ formatting and documentation toolkit I have found. The latest version even includes a Windows user interface.

The Software Organization, Inc.

56 Kirkland St., Suite 3
Cambridge, MA 02138
Phone: 617-354-2012
FAX: 617-354-0667

DialogCoder Version 2.0

Source code generator for Microsoft's Windows 3.1 dialog box functions. Generates C and C++ source code for use in any existing or future Windows applications. Allows user to establish relationships among controls and specify initialization state of each control. Prompts user to fix ambiguities or omissions if specifications are incomplete. Supports list box initialization from ASCII files, resources bound to application, and directory lists. Provides validation code for edit fields. To learn what DialogCoder can do, read Chapter 5.

The Stirling Group

172 Old Mill Dr.
Schaumburg, IL 60193
Phone: 800-3SHIELD; 708-307-9197
FAX: 708-307-9340

DbxSHIELD for Windows

Programming system for creating dialog boxes. Includes libraries of prewritten C code and inference engine that generates appropriate dialog box code based on set of user-specified rules. DbxSHIELD supports formatted/validated edit fields using picture masks. It also lets you expand and contract dialog boxes, as well as hide and show controls within a dialog box.

DemoSHIELD for Windows

Demo and tutorial builder. Accessible from within application or used in stand-alone mode. Includes scripting language, which controls sequencing of events. Features built-in VCR-like controls, which allow user to navigate through presentation. Supports standard graphics formats, including bitmaps, metafiles, icons, and PCX. Includes built-in demo tools such as explain lines and pointers. Allows you to import slides and images created by PowerPoint, PC-Paint, and CorelDRAW presentation packages.

InstallSHIELD for Windows

Installation program builder. Includes built-in feedback controls, data compression, and Help and instruction windows. Automatically builds program groups, items, and icons. Bases installation logic on hardware configuration and memory. Allows editing of .INI files, AUTOEXEC.BAT, and CONFIG.SYS.

LogSHIELD for Windows

Flexible-session recording and playback library that can be embedded and called from within application. Records all keystrokes, mouse movements, and mouse clicks to individual log files for later playback. Used for macro recording, automated regression testing, error recovery, and remote diagnostics. Compatible with Stirling Group's DemoShield.

MemSHIELD for Windows

Memory manager library that eliminates memory management problems, including overhead, limited sectors, locking, and fragmentation. Allows control over allocation and suballocation of heaps. Reporting functions allow user to monitor memory usage. Includes debugging mode, which tracks memory problems.

TbxShield for Windows

Library of software objects that let you add toolboxes to applications. Creates toolboxes of any size, shape, or style and advanced toolboxes, such as 3D ToolCubes. Accommodates toolbox selectors, including bitmaps, metafiles, animation, icons, and user-specified forms.

Symantec Corp.

10201 Torre Ave.
Cupertino, CA 95014-2132
Phone: 800-441-7234; 408-253-9600
FAX: 408-554-4403
Tech support: 408-252-5700

MultiScope Debuggers for Windows Version 2.0

Debugs CodeView- and Turbo Debugger-compatible Windows applications. Includes Windows and character-mode user interfaces. Supports single- and dual-monitor debugging, remote debugging, data browsing, 386/486 watches, DLL debugging, expression evaluation, and spy capabilities. Includes Crash Analyzer. To learn what you can do with MultiScope Debuggers for Windows, you should read Chapter 10.

Norton Desktop for Windows

User's and developer's Windows desktop enhancement that you should not do without. Provides built-in file viewer, directory tree, copy/delete, unerase, file find, directory sort, file attribute, text search, memory viewer, and screen saver. Provides schedule tools to run unattended to download at user-specified times. Allows password protection to certain applications, speed disk, user-customizable icons, and batch builder. As a programmer, I use the NDW SuperFind file find text search utility almost every day. NDW also includes a very good text/program editor. While the NDW program editor is no WinEdit or Codewright, it's handy to have around for quick editing tasks such as working on .INI files, AUTOEXEC.BAT, and CONFIG.SYS.

Zortech C++ Compiler Version 3.0

Implementation of C++ language. Conforms to definition of Bjarne Stroustrup. Superset of ANSI C standard. Provides integrated environment, allowing developer to edit, compile, link, and debug. Supports Windows 3.1 software development. Although I did not discuss Zortech C++ in this book, it is an excellent C++ compiler for developing Windows applications. With the Symantec acquisition of Multi-Scope and Whitewater development tools, I expect a very formidable Windows development system from them in the future.

Walnut Creek CDROM

1547 Palos Verdes Mall, Suite 260
Walnut Creek, CA 94596
Phone: 800-786-9907
FAX: 510-947-1644

MS Windows CDROM

Inexpensive ($24.95) CD-ROM that's published quarterly. The CD-ROM contains hundreds of freeware and shareware utilities. It also includes many Windows programs with their source code. This CD-ROM is a comprehensive collection of Windows programs that have been gathered from many other sources and included on one CD-ROM.

WexTech Systems, Inc.

310 Madison Ave., Suite 905
New York, NY 10017
Phone: 212-949-9595

Doc-To-Help

Word for Windows utility that helps you produce product documentation and then convert your documentation into Windows online Help automatically. Creates keyword lists, cross-references, browse sequences, and pop-up definitions. I have used Doc-To-Help and it makes creating Help files much easier, but I prefer using RoboHELP from Blue Sky Software instead of Doc-To-Help.

Wilson WindowWare, Inc.

2701 California Ave., SW, Suite 212
Seattle, WA 98116
Phone: 800-762-8383; 206-938-1740
FAX: 206-935-7129
Tech support: 206-937-9335

Command Post Version 7.0

Provides customizable menu system allowing user complete control over Windows
environment and initiation of other applications via creation of drop-down menus.
Includes file viewing utility, screen blanker, and time and date clock.

WinEdit

Programmer's editor designed for creating and maintaining program source code.
Includes ASCII file format, ability to edit files of almost unlimited size, and word
processing features such as word wrap, headers, and footers. Features multiple
document interface, compiler output monitoring, and on line help. If you want an
inexpensive Windows-hosted program editor (WinEdit is shareware), WinEdit is
the best you will find.

WUGNET

1295 N. Providence Road
Suite C107
Media, PA 19063
Phone: 215-565-1861
FAX: 215-565-7106

WUGNET

WUGNET (Windows User Group Network) is an organization formed to assist
Windows users and programmers. This group is the largest independent resource
on Windows programming information. WUGNET offers a forum on CompuServe
(in WINAPA), a monthly technical journal, and regular issues of a group disk that
contains programs, tools, and utilities. Both individual and corporate memberships
are available.

Xian Corp.

625 N. Monroe St.
Ridgewood, NJ 07450
Phone: 201-447-3270
FAX: 201-447-2547

Winpro/3

Windows application code generator for C applications.

Zinc Software, Inc.

405 South 100 East, Suite 201
Pleasant Grove, UT 84062
Phone: 800-638-8665; 801-785-8900
FAX: 801-785-8996
Tech support: 801-785-8998

Zinc Interface Library for DOS & Windows Version 3.0

One of the finest C++ class libraries available for interface design. The Zinc Interface Library (ZIL), Version 2.0, was a significant upgrade of Version 1.01. With this release Zinc Software adds support for Windows application development to its support for DOS character and graphics modes. It features Zinc Designer, a screen designer for visually and interactively creating user interfaces.

The ZIL class libraries shield you from many of the intricate details of GUI programming. For example, Zinc manages details such as which video adapter (VGA and so on) and which target video mode (DOS graphics or text modes, or Windows) is being used. It does this by using a display class (an abstract class) called UI_DISPLAY to define the general features needed for screen output. Four classes are derived from UI_DISPLAY, and each class handles one of four modes: Borland graphics, Zortech graphics, Microsoft Windows, or text. So instead of writing code to handle the low-level details of the video interface, programmers can focus on high-level issues such as user interface design. If you want to use a C++ class library to develop common C++ code applications for both DOS and Windows, you should seriously consider looking at the ZIL class library.

INDEX

Boldfaced page numbers indicate topics discussed in the primary subsections of each chapter. *Italic* page numbers indicate figures.

E

T

X

Z

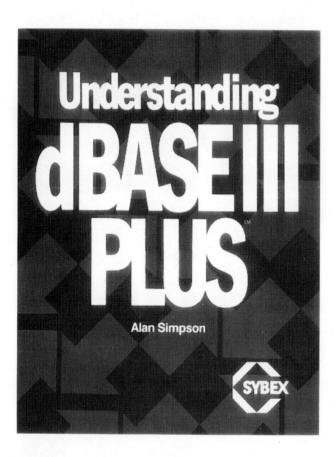

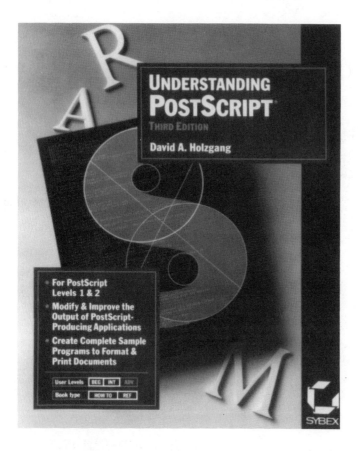

Help Yourself with
Another Quality Sybex Book

Supercharging Windows
Judd Robbins

Here's a gold mine of answers to common questions, with details on undocumented features, optimization, and advanced capabilities. This book's wide-ranging topics include Windows for laptops, programming language interfacing, memory-resident software, and networking—just to name a few. Includes two disks full of productivity tools, utilities, games, and accessories.

1011pp; 71/2" x9"
ISBN: 0-89588-862-9

Available
at Better
Bookstores
Everywhere

Sybex. Help Yourself.

SYBEX

FREE BROCHURE!

Complete this form today, and we'll send you a full-color brochure of Sybex bestsellers.

Please supply the name of the Sybex book purchased.

_____

How would you rate it?

_____ Excellent   _____ Very Good   _____ Average   _____ Poor

Why did you select this particular book?

_____ Recommended to me by a friend

_____ Recommended to me by store personnel

_____ Saw an advertisement in _____

_____ Author's reputation

_____ Saw in Sybex catalog

_____ Required textbook

_____ Sybex reputation

_____ Read book review in _____

_____ In-store display

_____ Other _____

Where did you buy it?

_____ Bookstore

_____ Computer Store or Software Store

_____ Catalog (name: _____)

_____ Direct from Sybex

_____ Other: _____

Did you buy this book with your personal funds?

_____ Yes   _____ No

About how many computer books do you buy each year?

_____ 1-3   _____ 3-5   _____ 5-7   _____ 7-9   _____ 10+

About how many Sybex books do you own?

_____ 1-3   _____ 3-5   _____ 5-7   _____ 7-9   _____ 10+

Please indicate your level of experience with the software covered in this book:

_____ Beginner   _____ Intermediate   _____ Advanced

Which types of software packages do you use regularly?

_____ Accounting	_____ Databases	_____ Networks
_____ Amiga	_____ Desktop Publishing	_____ Operating Systems
_____ Apple/Mac	_____ File Utilities	_____ Spreadsheets
_____ CAD	_____ Money Management	_____ Word Processing
_____ Communications	_____ Languages	_____ Other _____

(please specify)

Which of the following best describes your job title?

_____ Administrative/Secretarial   _____ President/CEO

_____ Director   _____ Manager/Supervisor

_____ Engineer/Technician   _____ Other _____

(please specify)

Comments on the weaknesses/strengths of this book: _____

_____

_____

_____

_____

Name _____

Street _____

City/State/Zip _____

Phone _____

PLEASE FOLD, SEAL, AND MAIL TO SYBEX

SYBEX, INC.

Department M

2021 CHALLENGER DR.

ALAMEDA, CALIFORNIA USA

94501

SYBEX

SEAL

Advanced Tools for Windows Developers

Installation of Disk

Place disk #1 in a floppy disk drive, choose Run from the Windows 3.1 Program Manager File menu, and type in Drive:Setup (for example, if the disk is in drive A, type `A:Setup` to start the installation process). To install the disk set, follow the instructions that appear on your screen.

Disk Contents

Inside the envelope are two high density 5¼-inch disks, containing approximately 6.5MB of useful applications, utilities, and tools, as well as the sample programs developed for this book.

Everything contained on these disks is freeware, written either by the author or included by permission of another author. You'll find tools to help you generate MDI Windows Applications, build a DDEML server, monitor Windows system resources, debug windows applications, and more. Other utilities on these disks will demonstrate how to build dialog box procedures and application resources, enable you to switch betweeen different video drivers, and help you learn how window classes and instances work.

Copy Protection

None of the programs on the disks are copy-protected. However, in all cases, reselling these programs without authorization is expressly forbidden.

If you need 3½-inch disks...

To receive 3½-inch disks, please return the original 5¼-inch disks with a written request to:

Customer Service Department
2021 Challenger Drive
Alameda, CA 94501
(800) 227-2346
Fax: (510) 523-2373

Be sure to include your name, complete mailing address, and the following reference number: 1029-0. Otherwise, your request cannot be processed. Allow six weeks for delivery.

If your disk is defective...

To obtain a replacement disk, please refer to the instructions outlined on the warranty page at the front of the book.